Functional Magnetic Resonance Imaging

FUNCTIONAL
Magnetic Resonance Imaging

Scott A. Huettel
Brain Imaging and Analysis Center, Duke University

Allen W. Song
Brain Imaging and Analysis Center, Duke University

Gregory McCarthy
Brain Imaging and Analysis Center, Duke University and
Department of Veterans Affairs Medical Center, Durham, N.C.

Sinauer Associates, Inc • *Publishers*
Sunderland, Massachusetts U.S.A.

FUNCTIONAL MAGNETIC RESONANCE IMAGING

Copyright © 2004 by Sinauer Associates, Inc. All rights reserved. This book may not be reproduced in whole or in part for any purpose. For information address Sinauer Associates, Inc., 23 Plumtree Road, Sunderland, MA. 01375 U.S.A.

Fax: 413-549-1118
Email: publish@sinauer.com
www.sinauer.com

Library of Congress Cataloging-in-Publication Data

Huettel, Scott A., 1973-
　　Functional magnetic resonance imaging / Scott A. Huettel,
　　Allen W. Song, Gregory McCarthy.—1st ed.
　　　　p. ; cm.
　　Includes bibliographical references.
　　ISBN 0-87893-288-7 (hardcover : alk. paper)
　　　1. Brain—Magnetic resonance imaging. 2. Cognitive neuroscience.
　　[DNLM: 1. Magnetic Resonance Imaging. 2. Brain Mapping—methods.　WN 185 H888f 2004] I. Song, Allen W., 1971- II. McCarthy,
Gregory,　　　　　　　1952- III. Title.
　　RC386.6.M34H84 2004
　　616.8'047548—dc22　　　　　　　　　　　　　　　　　2004000500

Printed in U.S.A.

We dedicate this book to our families,
especially Lisa, Jan-Ru, and Paula,
for their patience and support during its development.

Brief Contents

Contents

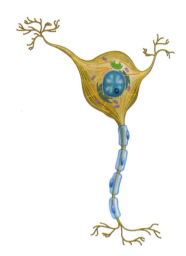

8 Spatial and Temporal Properties of fMRI 185

9 Signal and Noise in fMRI 217

10 Preprocessing of fMRI Data 253

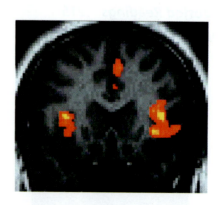

Preface

By any measure, the growth of functional magnetic resonance imaging has been extraordinary. A decade ago, fMRI was the province of a handful of institutions and only a few papers had been published. Now, hundreds of laboratories publish thousands of studies annually. While much of this growth has occurred within the core discipline of cognitive neuroscience, fMRI has become an important research technique in many other fields, from psychiatry and neurobiology to radiology and biomedical engineering. Yet, the very success of fMRI has created challenges for its instruction. How does one teach courses on a technique that is rapidly evolving, highly interdisciplinary, and attracts students from more than a dozen disciplines?

Like many of our colleagues, we have struggled with this question. When we offered our first fMRI courses at Duke University, we expected that the courses would attract primarily undergraduate and graduate students with a psychological background and that those students' interests would be largely limited to psychological applications of fMRI. We soon recognized that these expectations were misguided. The course participants came from many programs; psychology was prevalent, to be sure, but there were also aspiring engineers, medical and pre-medical students, biologists, neurobiologists, and physicists. Nor were the students interested merely in fMRI applications—they wanted to understand how MR scanners worked, what physiological processes led to fMRI data, and how to actually conduct fMRI research. Yet, no textbook existed that introduced these topics at a level appropriate for students (or faculty!) who are new to the field. We have therefore designed this textbook to be a true introduction to fMRI, one that covers this technique in a systematic, accurate, and easy-to-understand fashion.

Because of the highly interdisciplinary nature of fMRI, a systematic review must necessarily encompass many fields. We begin the textbook by establishing strong foundations in the physics and biology of fMRI. Although these are complex topics, we believe that they can be described without unnecessary complication. We introduce physical concepts using both intuitive analogies and step-by-step explanations of theories, referring frequently to fMRI applications. We adopt a similarly functional approach to concepts in biology, progressing from the metabolic consequences of neuronal activity, through the supply of energy via the vascular system, to the changes in blood oxygenation that form the basis for fMRI. As examples of the diversity of topics advance, students will learn about proton spin, ions moving through membrane channels, neurovascular organization, the general linear model, signal processing, experimental design, and human consciousness. Any student, regardless of background, will find much new material throughout the text.

Nevertheless, we have not sacrificed accuracy to gain this breadth of coverage. Without accurate, careful discussion of key concepts, any text (especially one on such a youthful field) risks mystifying its readers. The beginning student of fMRI faces a bewildering array of terms, often only operationally defined. Many of the most tantalizing ideas await empirical support and have not yet crystallized into guiding theory. Therefore, we have worked to introduce key concepts in a logical, straightforward manner, with clear definitions of research jargon. Throughout the book, we illustrate ideas by describing the primary research studies that support (or disconfirm) them. We present abstract ideas in the context of their consequences for real-world fMRI studies, so that students can make informed decisions about research questions.

Finally, we have worked to ensure that this book can be easily understood by beginning researchers, whether undergraduate students, graduate students, postdoctoral fellows, or research faculty. We recognized from the outset that many aspects of fMRI are considered to be very technical by those new to the field. It is easy to become daunted when faced with the physics of MR image formation, or the biological principles underlying neuroenergetics, or the statistical procedures of the general linear model. Yet these concepts are important and cannot be omitted simply to reduce the complexity of the book. Rather than simplifying the topical coverage, we instead have focused on simplifying the explanations of these topics. We have organized the textbook in a logical form that progresses across disciplines, so that each chapter builds on its predecessor. And, we have included a CD-ROM with fMRI data, a searchable glossary, and self-assessment questions, to provide students with additional instructional resources to complement the primary text.

We have included in the textbook a number of pedagogical tools for student instruction. Although these features were designed for undergraduate and graduate courses, we anticipate that they will be appreciated by anyone learning fMRI for the first time. We recognize that many instructors may not have direct experience with MRI, and thus we have included features to facilitate their development of new courses. Several of these features, especially the comprehensive glossary and reading lists, will also be of interest to practicing scientists in the field.

Key instructional features include:

- Course-oriented organization. The textbook contains 15 chapters, each covering a discrete topic, with a clear progression across topics.

- Boxes illustrating important examples or key topics. Throughout the book, a large number of exciting concepts are set aside in boxes for special emphasis. These boxes make ideal stepping-off points for instructors to delve more deeply into the literature.

- Copious use of color figures. More than 300 figures are included, many of fMRI data. The numerous figures within the chapters on physics and physiology complement the detailed discussions of those often-challenging topics.

- A marginal glossary. In addition to the standard glossary at the end of the book, key terms are defined in the margins at their first occurrence in a chapter.

- Thought problems in-line with the text. Within each chapter, several thought problems are included to challenge the reader's understanding. The thought problems are intended to reinforce key ideas and promote critical evaluation of the material.

- Self-assessment questions. Included on the CD-ROM are self-assessment questions that allow students to evaluate their comprehension of the topics from each chapter. After reading each chapter, students can use the self-assessment questions to gauge which topics are mastered and which require future study.

- Comprehensive reference lists within each chapter. Two types of references are included: *Suggested Readings* and *Chapter References*. The *Suggested Readings*, typically 6-8 per chapter, are selected for their comprehensiveness and accessibility. Annotations guide students to suggested readings of interest. All other primary source material are cited with full bibliographic information in the *Chapter References* section.

- Clear summaries of equations. When equations are introduced, their terms are systematically described and all variables are labeled explicitly. These annotations allow students with less mathematical background to work through the conceptual bases of the equations. Where a particular set of equations is not essential to the main text, those equations are indicated by a colored box.

- Discussion of the historical progression of ideas. Within the textbook are descriptions of the physical and physiological discoveries that led to the development of fMRI. Students learn about the earliest fMRI studies and how those studies sparked future research. Conversely, we include chapters that discuss the latest findings from cognitive neuroscience and MR physics, including many studies from 2003 and 2004.

- A focus on primary source material. We discuss the research of a large number of laboratories, many of which have graciously allowed use of images from their work.

- Included MR data and suggested exercises. To provide students with an opportunity to analyze real fMRI data, we have supplied sample data sets on the included CD-ROM. These data sets are stored in a form that can be read by many freely available analysis packages, and suggested laboratory exercises are included.

We would like to thank the numerous colleagues, collaborators, and students who have contributed to this project. The many students in our fMRI courses have provided inestimable inspiration, criticism, and guidance, and our thinking has been greatly honed by their feedback. Thanks go to our fellow faculty at the Duke-UNC Brain Imaging and Analysis Center: Ayse Belger, Guven Guzeldere, Edith Kaan, Martin McKeown, Kevin Pelphrey, and Jim Voyvodic. Special thanks go to Jim and Martin for writing the boxes on Real-Time Analysis and Data-Driven Analyses, respectively. In addition, we thank our other collaborators at Duke University, including Liz Brannon, Roberto Cabeza, Al Johnson, Kevin LaBar, Greg Lockhead, James MacFall, Dave Madden, Mike Platt, and Marty Woldorff. Many discussions with these talented individuals have shaped our thinking. We appreciate the institutional support of Ranga Krishnan and Carl Ravin, as well as the support and assistance from Dale Purves, Mark Williams, and the other faculty authors of *Neuroscience*.

We have been fortunate in this project to have received guidance from an extraordinarily conscientious group of external reviewers. Greg Berns,

Amishi Jha, Noah Sandstrom, and several anonymous reviewers provided helpful comments on early drafts of sample chapters and helped us shape the direction of the manuscript. We greatly appreciate the comments of our chapter reviewers, including Kalina Christoff, Mark D'Esposito, Darren Gitelman, Fahmeed Hyder, Ravi Menon, Mary Meyerand, Kia Nobre (and her students), and Ken Paller. Special thanks go to reviewers of multiple chapters, including Peter Bandettini and Doug Noll, as well as Vince Clark for his comments on the entire book.

We also want to thank a number of individuals for their discussions about issues raised in the text, including Steve Baumann, Sarah Blakemore, Michael Chee, Michele Diaz, Guido Gerig, Katy Harris, Joe Hopfinger, Jim Hyde, Andre Jesmanowicz, Dae-Shik Kim, Tom Liu, Susumu Mori, John Mosher, Mary Beth Nebel, Seiji Ogawa, and Charles C. Wood. We also want to single out Charles Michelich for particular thanks. Chuck has been an invaluable resource, both technical and theoretical, for shaping our thinking on many of the issues covered in the book. We appreciate the many scientists who contributed figures from their work, and we thank them individually with their provided figure(s).

Production and technical assistance was provided by many of our students and colleagues at BIAC, including Dave Bernstein, Josh Bizzell, Elise Dagenbach, Evan Gordon, Todd Harshbarger, Kari Karcher, Tianlu Li, Richard Sheu, Melissa Slavin, Hiromi Terawaki, and Michael Wu. Assistance in construction of many of the physics figures was provided by Hua Guo. We thank Sean Fannon, Harlan Fichtenholtz, and Wayne Khoe for their efforts as teaching assistants for our undergraduate classes. Francis Favorini, Susan Music, Carolyn Ross, and Ershela Sims provided technical guidance and support. Finally, we greatly appreciate the tireless efforts of Jon Smith throughout the entire process, from editing to production.

A number of funding agencies have supported our teaching efforts, our research programs, and many of the studies discussed in this book. They include NIDA, NINDS, NCRR, NIMH, NSF, and the Department of Veterans Affairs. We thank the Howard Hughes Medical Institute for support of the teaching laboratory used in our courses.

Finally, we would like to thank our friends at Sinauer Associates for their guidance throughout this process. We thank Andy Sinauer for his support of this project since its inception, Sydney Carroll for walking us through production, Jason Dirks for developing the CD-ROM, and Marie Scavotto for marketing the finished product. Under the guidance of Christopher Small, the production team at Sinauer Associates did excellent work, particularly Joan Gemme whose skill in design and layout are evident in this book. We also wish to thank Mark Via for his copyediting expertise, Joni Fraser for creating the index, and the talented artists at Imagineering Media Services, Inc., in Ontario, Canada for creating most of the figures in this text.

Special thanks go to our editor, Graig Donini, for leading us from concept to reality.

Scott A. Huettel
Allen W. Song
Gregory McCarthy

Supplements to Accompany

Functional Magnetic Resonance Imaging

For the Student

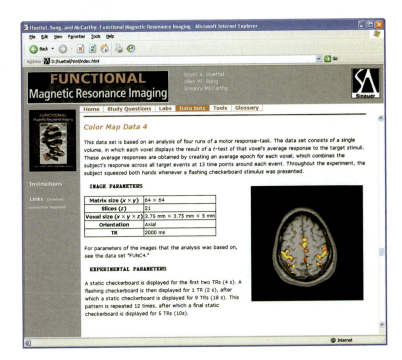

Student CD (ISBN 0-87893-289-5)

Included with each copy of *Functional Magnetic Resonance Imaging*, the Student CD provides a wealth of study material, lab exercises, and data sets. Contents include:

- Study questions for each chapter of the textbook, both in HTML and Microsoft® Word® formats. These short-answer style questions are designed to test students' understanding of the material presented in each chapter. They can be used for student self-assessment or can be printed and submitted to the instructor as an assignment.

- 14 Suggested lab exercises. These lab exercises are adapted from exercises used at Duke University. They can be completed using a variety of data analysis software packages and used to explore the data sets provided on the CD.
- 13 fMRI data sets, including both functional and anatomical data. These data sets can be loaded into readily available software packages for fMRI data analysis. They can be used in conjunction with the suggested lab exercises provided on the CD or with custom lab exercises.
- A Tools section with information on obtaining suggested freely available software packages for fMRI data analysis.
- A complete glossary
- A Links webpage listing online fMRI resources

For the Instructor

Instructor's Resource CD (ISBN 0-87893-293-3)

The Instructor's Resource CD includes electronic versions of all of the figures from the textbook. Both line art and photographic images are included in high-resolution JPEG format, and all have been formatted and optimized for excellent legibility and projection quality. In addition, a ready-to-use PowerPoint® presentation of all figures is provided for each chapter of the textbook. Also included are the study questions, lab exercises, and data sets from the Student CD.

1

An Introduction to fMRI

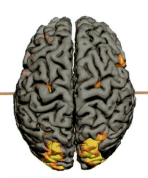

Few scientific developments have been more striking than the ability to image the functioning human brain. Why do images of the brain evoke such wonder? To many, the human brain represents a barely explored new world, with each image providing a glimpse of hidden structure. Like the maps used by early explorers, our current understanding of brain function is riddled with errors, inconsistencies, and puzzles deserving of solution. Yet the difficulty in understanding the brain has only added to the excitement of the quest.

The first popular mapping of brain function was proposed by the **phrenologists** in the early nineteenth century. The phrenologists believed that the amount of brain tissue devoted to a cognitive function determined its influence on behavior. Although they were unable to measure cortical volume directly, they assumed that increases in brain size would translate into measurable bumps on the skull. So, a devoted mother should have a protrusion over the brain area supporting "love for one's offspring," whereas a common thief should have a flattening of the skull above the area supporting "honesty" (Figure 1.1). The most prominent advocates, notably Franz Joseph Gall and Johann Spurzheim, lectured widely on the new maps of brain function they had developed. Popular books used phrenology to explain differences among individuals, to provide self-improvement advice, and to advise employers on qualities desired for workers.

But, as the initial novelty of the phrenologists' maps wore off, other scientists began to dispute their validity. To create their maps of the brain, the phrenologists used correlational methods, relying largely on anecdotal descriptions of individuals with an extreme characteristic. Notably absent were experimentation and statistical validation of their maps. The phrenologists were unable to document the mechanism by which cortex growth would lead to behavioral change, nor could they replicate their maps across individuals. Faced with criticism, the phrenologists changed their maps, adding more and more areas to already complex systems of bumps and valleys. In the most extreme cases, phrenological systems contained more than 150 distinct areas and used obscure terms such as "comicality" and "velocity" to describe brain organs. By the late 1830s, the idea of mapping the brain through bumps on the skull had collapsed on scientific grounds.

phrenologists Adherents to the belief that bumps and indentations on the skull provided information about the magnitude of some trait supported by the underlying brain region.

localization of function The idea that the brain may have distinct regions that support particular mental processes.

functional magnetic resonance imaging (fMRI) A neuroimaging technique that uses standard MRI scanners to investigate changes in brain function over time.

static magnetic field The strong magnetic field at the center of the MRI scanner whose strength does not change over time. The strength of the static magnetic field is expressed in Tesla (T).

pulse sequence A series of changing magnetic field gradients and oscillating electromagnetic fields that allows the MRI scanner to create images sensitive to a particular physical property.

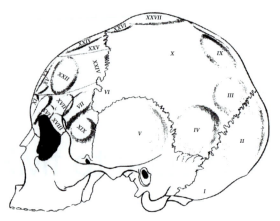

Figure 1.1 The phrenological mapping system created by Franz Joseph Gall. The phrenologists believed that people with an extreme trait (e.g., very wise, prone to thievery) would have an abundance of cortex devoted to that function. To find out what brain area was associated with the trait, researchers would examine the skulls of such people for bumps or protrusions. Each numbered region in this figure represents a different trait, from "reproductive instinct" (I) to "firmness of purpose" (XXVII).

While phrenology failed as a description of brain organization, it introduced the idea of **localization of function;** different aspects of the human mind may be represented in different brain regions. In the succeeding decades, scientists abandoned the approach of examining bumps on the skull and began looking at changes in brain physiology, whether caused by lesions or recorded as electrical pulses. These measures, usually obtained in animals, could be related directly to brain function and could be validated across many cases. Yet the invasive nature of these measures prevented the systematic study of the human brain, and thus much of cognition remained inaccessible. Nearly 200 years later, a new group of modern-day explorers are mapping the human brain. These scientists use **functional magnetic resonance imaging (fMRI)** to take pictures of the active brain in both clinical and research settings. In little more than a decade, fMRI has grown to become the dominant technique in cognitive neuroscience.

What Is fMRI?

As its name implies, magnetic resonance imaging (MRI) uses strong magnetic fields to create images of biological tissue (Figure 1.2). The **static magnetic field** created by an MRI scanner is expressed in units of Tesla (one Tesla is equal to 10,000 Gauss). Scanners used for fMRI are typically within the range of 1.5 to 4.0 Tesla, with even stronger fields of 7.0 Tesla now becoming available. For comparison, the earth's magnetic field is approximately 0.00005 Tesla. To create images, the scanner uses a series of changing magnetic gradients and oscillating electromagnetic fields, known as a **pulse sequence.** Depending on their frequency, energy from the electromagnetic fields may be absorbed by atomic nuclei. For MRI, scanners are tuned to the frequency of hydrogen nuclei, which are the most common in the human body due to their prevalence in water molecules. After it is absorbed, the electromagnetic energy is later emitted by the nuclei, and the amount of emitted energy depends on the number and type of nuclei present.

Depending on the pulse sequence used, the MRI scanner can detect different tissue properties to distinguish between tissue types. For example, an

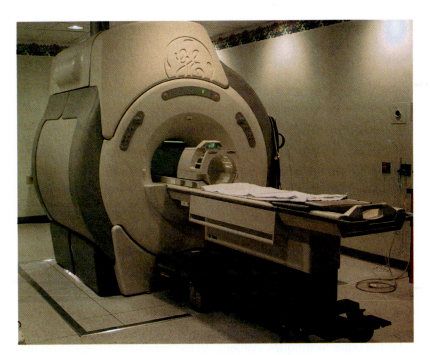

functional neuroimaging A class of research techniques that create images of the functional organization of the brain. Common functional neuroimaging techniques include fMRI, PET, SPECT (single-photon emission computerized tomography), and optical imaging.

positron emission tomography (PET) A functional neuroimaging technique that creates images based upon the movement of injected radioactive material.

Figure 1.2   A modern MRI scanner. The main magnetic field of the scanner shown is 1.5 Tesla, or about 30,000 times the strength of the earth's magnetic field. The subject lies down on the table at the front of the scanner, placing his or her head inside the volume coil at the center of the image. The table then moves back into the bore of the scanner until the head is positioned at the very center.

MRI of the knee can reveal whether ligaments are intact or torn, and an MRI of the brain can detect the difference between gray and white matter.

Different pulse sequences can be constructed that create images sensitive to tumors, abnormalities in blood vessels, bone damage, and many other conditions. The ability to examine multiple biologically interesting properties of tissue makes MRI an extraordinarily flexible and powerful clinical tool.

While much knowledge about the brain has come from the study of its structure, notably by relating neurological disorders to the patterns of brain injury that cause them, structural studies are limited in that they cannot reveal short-term physiological changes associated with the active function of the brain. To understand the workings of the normal human brain, **functional neuroimaging** studies are necessary. Functional neuroimaging attempts to localize different mental processes to different parts of the brain, in effect creating a map of which areas are responsible for which processes. However, unlike the phrenologists, who believed that very complex traits were associated with discrete brain regions, modern researchers recognize that many functions rely upon distributed networks and that a single brain region may participate in more than one function.

Functional neuroimaging did not begin with fMRI, which has only reached prominence within the past decade. Before that time, the most commonly used functional neuroimaging technique was **positron emission tomography (PET),** which relies on the injection of radioactive tracers to measure changes in the brain, including blood flow and/or glucose metabolism. Using PET, researchers could identify parts of the brain that are metabolically associated with a given perceptual, motor, or cognitive function, like seeing faces, moving the right hand, or mentally reciting sentences. However, PET imaging suffers from several disadvantages, including the invasiveness of the radioactive injections, the expense of generating radioactive isotopes, and the slow speed at which images are acquired. As we will discuss in Chapter 7, these limitations have slowed the growth of PET, although it still has important uses.

The development of fMRI has catalyzed an explosion of interest in functional neuroimaging. Most fMRI studies measure changes in blood oxygenation over time. Because blood oxygenation levels change rapidly following activity of neurons in a brain region, fMRI allows researchers to localize brain activity on a second-by-second basis and within millimeters of its origin. And, because changes in blood oxygenation occur intrinsically (endogenously) as part of normal brain physiology, fMRI is a noninvasive technique that can be repeated as many times as needed in the same individual. Because of these advantages, fMRI has been rapidly adopted as a primary investigative tool by thousands of researchers at hundreds of institutions.

Why Image Brain Function?

When evaluating the importance of functional neuroimaging, it is important to consider the other techniques available to the neuroscientist for studying brain function. Three major classes of non-imaging techniques are commonly used: lesion studies, drug manipulations, and recordings of electrical activity. Each provides important information about the brain, and all are central to modern neuroscience. By using neuroimaging in conjunction with these other approaches, scientists can address complex issues that may be beyond the scope of a single technique.

The most venerable approach is to evaluate the effects of damage to the brain upon behavior. A landmark result was reported by the French physician Paul Broca regarding his examination of a single patient named Leborgne. This patient was effectively unable to speak, being only able to repeat the word "tan" in response to prompting. At Leborgne's autopsy in 1861, Broca demonstrated that the patient had damage to the brain that was largely restricted to the inferior frontal lobe in the left hemisphere. This demonstration provided conclusive evidence that language-production abilities are localized, at least in part, to the area of the brain that now bears Broca's name. During the following decades, many other nineteenth-century researchers created lesions in animals to test whether a brain region must be intact for expression of a behavior.

Although lesion studies have unquestionable value for elucidating brain function and they remain an important part of the neuroscientist's arsenal, they are limited in their applicability. A well-appreciated problem results from the network structure of the brain: The fact that damage to area X impairs behavior Y indicates that X is *necessary* for Y, but not that X is *sufficient* for Y. In an oft-cited analogy, damage to any one of the many parts of a radio, such as the speakers, the tuner, or even the power switch, will result in its inability to play music, but one should not claim that one of these parts independently is the "music-playing" area of the radio. As an interconnected part of a complex system, a given brain region may support more than one function, and each function may be supported by multiple brain regions. Furthermore, the effects of a lesion often change over time. As the brain heals, an injured region may once again be able to support processing; or, other regions may change their processing to compensate for the damage. It is therefore critical, in lesion studies, to evaluate the effects of many different lesion locations and to track the effects of those lesions over time.

A related problem for human lesion studies comes from the difficulty in finding patients with isolated damage. Many patients have diffuse damage resulting from head trauma or stroke, and as such their lesions may encompass multiple functional brain regions. Given the infrequency of many kinds of brain damage, human lesion studies are often most interpretable when considered in the context of other techniques, including functional imaging. One way of overcoming this problem is to create lesions in a particular region, so that the researcher can control the spatial extent of the damage. The introduction of permanent lesions is limited to animal models, for obvious reasons, and thus it is not possible to address many aspects of human cognition, such as language or higher reasoning abilities. However, temporary interruption of function within a brain region is possible using **transcranial magnetic stimulation (TMS)**, which can be used in human subjects to complement imaging methods like fMRI.

A second method for studying functional systems in the brain comes from drug manipulations in both animals and humans. Neurons throughout the brain have receptors that are sensitive to particular neurotransmitters, such as acetylcholine or serotonin. Drugs that influence the action of these neurotransmitters may cause widespread changes across a number of brain regions. Drug studies are powerful, in that they allow investigation of large-scale brain systems that often are not associated with simple lesions; and they are clinically relevant, in that many drugs have well-understood effects upon brain disorders (e.g., Parkinson's disease and drugs that manipulate the availability of the neurotransmitter dopamine). A central disadvantage, however, is the difficulty in identifying functions of specific brain regions following systemic application of a drug. If the motor skills of a patient with Parkinson's disease improve after administration of a drug that supplies dopamine to the brain, that improvement could be due to better function in the midbrain, the basal ganglia, the prefrontal cortex, or any number of regions responsive to that drug. In addition, many drug manipulations have relatively slow time courses, with functional changes that can take place over weeks, so inferences about short-term cognitive processes become challenging.

Measurement of electrical changes is a third major technique used for assessing brain function. Recordings of electrical potentials from electrodes that are inserted near or into single neurons provide the most direct measure of neuronal activity. For example, if a monkey is trained to remember a picture over a delay of a few seconds, individual neurons in its lateral frontal lobes exhibit increased activity during the delay interval. One cannot implant electrodes into healthy human subjects, although this is sometimes done in patients with severe epilepsy to help localize the source of their seizures. However, the electrical and magnetic activity generated inside the brain can be measured outside the skull using techniques known as **electroencephalography (EEG)** and **magnetoencephalography (MEG)**. Using these electromagnetic recording methods, very rapid changes in electrical potentials and magnetic flux can be measured, so these techniques are valuable for studying the timing of brain processes.

Electrophysiological methods suffer from a trade-off between localization accuracy and invasiveness. Single-unit studies allow very precise localization of activity to a specific cell in a specific brain region, but require the insertion of electrodes directly into the brain and are thus restricted to animal studies. While extracranial EEG and MEG studies do not damage the

transcranial magnetic stimulation (TMS) A technique for temporarily stimulating a brain region to disrupt its function. TMS uses an electromagnetic coil placed close to the scalp; when current passes through the coil, it generates a magnetic field in the nearby brain tissue, producing localized electric currents.

electroencephalography (EEG) The measurement of the electrical potential of the brain, usually through electrodes placed on the surface of the scalp.

magnetoencephalography (MEG) A noninvasive functional neuroimaging technique that measures very small changes in magnetic fields caused by the electrical activity of neurons, with potentially high spatial and temporal resolution.

inverse problem The mathematical impossibility of determining the distribution of electrical sources within an object based upon the measurement of electrical or magnetic fields at the surface of the object.

brain, it is mathematically impossible to uniquely identify the locations of the neural sources that cause a given pattern of activity on the skull. This **inverse problem** has limited the value of EEG and MEG in creating maps of brain function.

In conclusion, functional neuroimaging is one tool among many available to neuroscientists. Lesion studies provide clear evidence that a brain region is necessary for a behavior but do not specify the timing of that region's activity or the specific function it serves. Drug studies indicate the effects of distributed transmitter systems but are not appropriate for all experimental questions. Electrophysiological methods provide good information about the timing of activity but, in human subjects, do not specify the precise locations of electrical sources. Although each of these techniques can be improved by using animal, rather than human, subjects, many aspects of human cognition are impossible to study using animal models. Functional neuroimaging, and fMRI in particular, complements these studies by measuring activity throughout the brain in healthy human subjects. However, this complementarity is not absolute, as will be discussed in the following section. We will return to the discussion of these techniques and their relations to fMRI in Chapter 15.

Key Concepts

Any imaging technique, from X-rays to fMRI, can be evaluated by simple criteria: What quantity does it measure, how sensitively can it measure that quantity, how precisely in space does it measure that quantity, and how often can it make the measurement? Consider the simple imaging system formed by the sun, you, and a wall (Figure 1.3). If you stand between the bright sun and the wall, your shadow will appear. For opaque objects, like people, the shadow will be very dark compared to the wall around it. However, if the sun's rays pass through something insubstantial, like a cloud or

Figure 1.3   Images and contrast. In the very simple imaging system formed by the sun, an object, and a wall, the opacity of the object can be estimated by the darkness of the shadow that is cast. This imaging system shows contrast based on opacity to visible light.

a sheer curtain, the shadow will be much lighter. In this imaging system, the quantity being measured is the number of photons of sunlight that strike the wall and, by inference, the degree to which the intervening object absorbs photons. By comparing the shadows cast by different objects, like you or a cloud, one could estimate the optical opacity of the objects. Here, the difference between dark and light on the wall indexes the opacity (i.e., light transmittance) of the object being imaged, with dark areas indicating opaque objects and bright areas indicating transparency. In fact, this simple system captures the essence of the familiar X-ray technique.

The difference between the lightest and darkest shadows is a measure of the **contrast** available in our system for creating images of optical opacity. If the imaging technique is sensitive to small gradations in the quantity being measured, the resulting image will have good contrast and will enable us to make fine discriminations in our measurements of different objects. Contrast, however, is not an absolute quantity. Because no imaging method is perfect, there will always be some amount of variation in the measured signal. For example, a plane passing overhead can momentarily block the sun and change the intensity of your shadow on the wall. It is typical, then, to express contrast with respect to variation in contrast due to noise and to discuss results in terms of the **contrast-to-noise ratio (CNR).** We will explore this topic in more detail later.

Depending on the pulse sequence used by the scanner, images can be created that differentiate low versus high proton density, gray matter versus white matter, or fluid versus tissue. Thus, the quantity being measured is different for each of these image types. In this context, contrast has another special meaning that may be initially confusing. Shown in Figure 1.4 are images that have contrast based upon the intrinsic tissue properties T_1 and T_2. We will describe these tissue properties and how these different types of images are created in Chapters 3 to 5. On T_1-weighted images, the difference, or contrast, between light and dark is a measure of the relative difference in T_1 of the tissues. Thus, we also refer to these images as T_1-contrast

contrast The intensity difference between different quantities being measured by an imaging system. It also can refer to the physical quantity being measured (e.g., T_1 contrast).

contrast-to-noise ratio (CNR) The magnitude of the intensity difference between different quantities divided by the variability in their measurements.

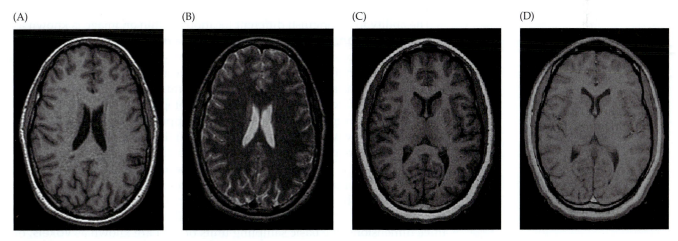

(A) (B) (C) (D)

Figure 1.4 Contrast and contrast-to-noise in MR images. Shown in (A) and (B) are images sensitive to two different contrast types. (A) An image sensitive to T_1 contrast, while (B) is an image sensitive to T_2 contrast. Note that although much of the same brain structure is present in both images, the relative intensities of different tissue types are very different. Shown in (C) and (D) are two images with the same contrast type but different contrast-to-noise ratios. (C) An image with very high contrast-to-noise, and significant detail can be seen in the image. (D) An image with lower contrast-to-noise, and some distinctions such as the boundary between gray and white matter are more difficult to identify.

Figure 1.5 A functional map of the brain. This image shows a reconstruction of the right hemisphere of the brain with areas of statistically significant activity indicated in color. The experimental task involved visual search, and thus areas in the occipital and parietal lobes (at right) are highly active. A high-resolution anatomical image was used to create the reconstructed cortical surface, and a series of functional analyses were conducted to identify which parts of the brain were active.

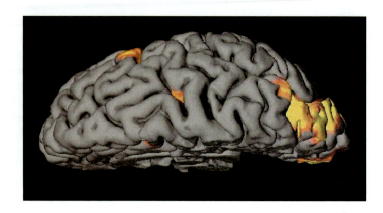

functional contrast A type of contrast that provides information about a physiological correlate of brain function, such as changes in blood oxygenation.

spatial resolution The ability to distinguish changes in an image (or map) across different spatial locations.

pixel A two-dimensional picture element.

voxel A three-dimensional volume element.

images. On T_1-contrast images, fluid appears as black, gray matter appears as dark gray, and white matter appears as light gray. On T_2-contrast images, the contrast between light and dark now measures a different tissue property called T_2, and now gray matter is light, white matter is dark, and fluid is very bright.

To map brain function, researchers must create images that distinguish between active and non-active areas of the brain (Figure 1.5). These images rely on **functional contrast.** In PET studies, functional contrast is based on the number of emitted radioactive decay particles. For researchers to say that one area of the brain is more active than another, there must be a statistically significant difference in the number of emitted particles between those regions. In fMRI studies, functional contrast is usually based on the total amount of deoxygenated hemoglobin in the blood, as will be discussed in detail in Chapter 7, and whether a region is classified as active or inactive depends on the magnitude of the change in deoxygenated hemoglobin. We emphasize that contrast-to-noise, whether anatomical or functional, depends on both the *amount of signal change* and the *variability of signal change.* An image may have high contrast-to-noise despite small absolute intensity differences if there is very little variability within each property being measured.

The ability to distinguish different locations within an image is known as **spatial resolution.** Imagine looking down at a digital satellite photograph of a college campus and the surrounding countryside. If that photograph is of low resolution and covers many miles of terrain, then even the largest structures, such as an enormous athletic stadium, might be represented as a single dot. But if you zoom in so that the photograph only covers a single street block, then much more detail can be appreciated; now you can see buildings, walkways, and automobiles. In a digital photograph of a scene, the smallest elements that can be resolved are known as **pixels,** or picture elements. So, in a satellite photograph of the countryside the pixel size might be several hundred yards, while in a photograph of a street block the pixel size might be a few feet. Similarly, MR images may be able to resolve relatively coarse or fine elements. Since all MR images sample the brain in three dimensions, the basic sampling units of MRI are known as **voxels,** or volume elements. As the voxel size decreases, the ability to identify fine structure in a brain image improves (Figure 1.6). In principle, the voxel size in MRI can be made arbitrarily small; high-spatial-resolution images of rodent brains (see Figure 14.1) may have voxels less than 0.05 mm on a side. But, as you will learn in Chapter 8, the total signal recovered from a voxel is

(A)

(B)

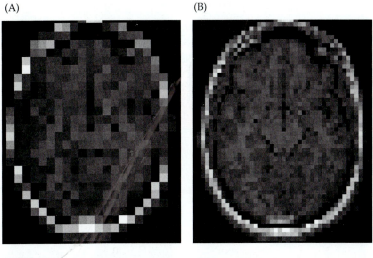

Figure 1.6   The human brain at different spatial resolutions. Spatial resolution refers to the ability to resolve small differences in an image. In general, we can define spatial resolution based upon the size of the elements used to construct the image. The images shown here present the same brain sampled at five different element sizes: (A) 8 mm, (B) 4 mm, (C) 2 mm, (D) 1.5 mm, and (E) 1 mm. Note that the gray–white structure is well represented in the latter three images, which all sample at more than twice the resolution of the typical gray-matter thickness of 5 mm.

(C)

(D)

(E)

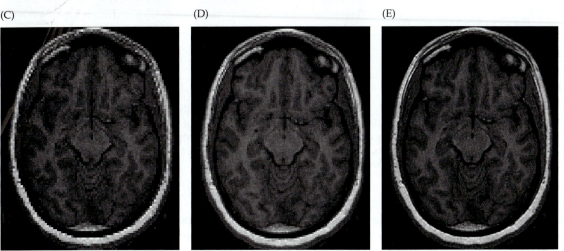

proportional to its size, and voxels that are too small may have insufficient signal to create high-quality images. In structural MRI of the human brain, voxels are often about 1 to 2 mm in each dimension, while in functional MRI, voxels are typically about 3 to 5 mm on a side.

Although structural MR images are considered to be static representations of the brain, functional MRI is inherently dynamic, in that it measures changes in brain activity over time. The rate at which a technique acquires images, or its **sampling rate,** determines its **temporal resolution.** Across fMRI studies, the sampling rate typically varies from a few hundred milliseconds to a few seconds, which is much faster than earlier PET studies that integrated brain activity over intervals of about a minute or even longer. The fundamental rule for temporal resolution is that a signal must be sampled twice as frequently as the fastest change present in the signal. This limit, known as the Nyquist frequency, will be described further in Chapter 10. However, the theoretical Nyquist frequency is not the only limit on temporal resolution. Our ability to determine the timing of functional activity in the brain is also limited by the sluggishness of the physiological changes that we seek to measure. Most fMRI studies measure changes in blood oxygenation, which resolve over a period of a few seconds to a few tens of seconds. Even if

sampling rate   The frequency in time with which a measurement is made.

temporal resolution   The ability to distinguish changes in an image (or map) across time.

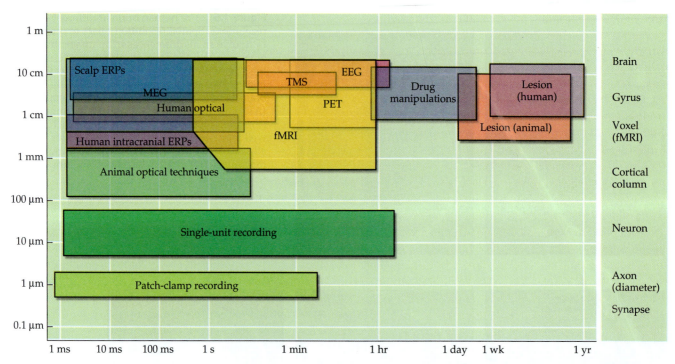

Figure 1.7   Neuroscience techniques differ in their spatial and temporal resolution. Functional MRI provides a good balance of spatial and temporal resolution and thus is appropriate for a wide range of experimental questions. Other approaches, including electrophysiology, lesion studies, and drug manipulations, can provide complementary information.

functional resolution   The ability to map measured physiological variation to underlying mental processes.

we sample the brain very rapidly, the hemodynamic changes may occur too slowly for us to make inferences about more rapid neuronal activity.

Together, spatial and temporal resolution have been used to describe a "technique space" that shows how different experimental methods provide potentially complementary information about brain function (Figure 1.7). The canonical example of complementarity combines the hemodynamic measurement of fMRI and the electrophysiological measurement of EEG. Since the former technique has very good spatial resolution (millimeters) and the latter technique has very good temporal resolution (milliseconds), it is argued that combining them would apply the best aspects of each to a single research question. While seductive, this argument conceals a deeper issue that is introduced here and discussed in more detail in Chapter 15. Spatiotemporal graphs like Figure 1.7 suggest that some fundamental quantity (i.e., brain activity) is a continuous variable that can be measured at different scales of time and space. However, no such fundamental quantity exists; rather, each of the methods represented provides a different measure of brain physiology. That these measures do not always correlate among themselves or, more importantly, do not always correlate with the mental processes we study indicates that temporal and spatial resolution alone are not sufficient criteria to evaluate techniques. We suggest that the value of a technique is determined by its **functional resolution,** or ability to map physiological variation to cognitive or behavioral processing.

Although the above properties—contrast, spatial resolution, and temporal resolution—all contribute to functional resolution, other factors are also critical. The brain property being measured determines, in several ways, how well one can localize function in the brain. The changes in blood oxygenation measured by fMRI reflect the local vascular structure of the brain, with larger effects often measured around draining veins. In EEG studies using extracranial recording, the local vascular structure has little effect on activity, but the orientation and temporal synchrony of the active neurons has an enormous effect. So, while a given task might evoke significant activity using one technique, it might not evoke activity using a different technique. While fMRI is, in our view, the most promising technique for studying the intact human brain, it possesses many significant limitations on functional resolution. We will return to this theme, the limitations of fMRI, throughout this book.

> ### Thought Question
> How could a technique have very good spatial and temporal resolution but very poor functional resolution?

History of fMRI

The scientific developments leading to modern fMRI can be characterized through five main phases. Basic physics work in the 1920s to 1940s set forth the idea that atomic nuclei have magnetic properties and that these properties can be manipulated experimentally. Seminal studies reported by two laboratories in 1946 described the phenomenon of nuclear magnetic resonance (NMR) in solids and ushered in several decades of nonbiological studies. The first biological MR images were created in the 1970s and were coupled with advances in image acquisition methods. By the 1980s, MR imaging became clinically prevalent, and structural scanning of the brain was commonplace. Finally, in the early 1990s, the discovery that changes in blood oxygenation could be measured using MRI ushered in a new era of functional studies of the brain. We provide in this section a brief overview of the history of MRI, and we will discuss specific physical principles in more detail in subsequent chapters.

Early Studies of Magnetic Resonance

The beginnings of MRI can be traced to a single conjecture made by the Austrian physicist Wolfgang Pauli in 1924. At that time, very small (or hyperfine) splitting of spectral lines emitted by excited atoms posed a problem for existing quantum mechanical theories. To account for these anomalies, Pauli postulated that atomic nuclei had two properties, called spin and magnetic moment, that could only take discrete values (or quanta). As an analogy, think of atomic nuclei as continually spinning tops. Pauli's suggestion, taken roughly, was that these tops could spin only at some frequencies but not others and exert only particular magnetic forces but not others. At that time, nuclear properties were poorly understood (indeed, the discovery of the neutron by the English physicist James Chadwick did not occur until 1931), and this suggestion would not be tested for more than a decade.

An early technique for investigating whether different atomic nuclei spin at discrete frequencies was the molecular beam apparatus developed by Stern and Gerlach. A gaseous beam of a single element was passed through

BOX 1.1 What is fMRI Used For?

Over the past few years, fMRI has been applied to a vast and ever growing set of research questions. To illustrate this point, we selected a recent issue of the journal *NeuroImage* and identified all of the studies using fMRI. Within that single issue, there were research articles describing object processing, speech, language plasticity in bilingual individuals, how spatial extent of visual cortex activation changes under different conditions, visual attention, effects of neuronal interactions on blood flow, and connectivity between brain regions, as well as other studies describing the use of fMRI in conjunction with other techniques. And that was just one issue! Each year, many hundreds of fMRI studies are published within dozens of academic journals by researchers from the fields of psychology, neurobiology, neurology, radiology, electrical engi-

neering, biomedical engineering, and many others. In this box, we provide examples of some creative ways in which researchers have used fMRI.

Many fMRI studies attempt to discover patterns of brain activity that are associated with phenomena of interest. These patterns of activity are often called **neural correlates,** to emphasize that changes in the brain vary along with changes in some external phenomenon. As an example, consider the curious and remarkable fact that people cannot tickle themselves. If you are very ticklish, even a very slight touch from someone else might elicit peals of laughter, but you cannot tickle yourself no matter how hard you try. At one level, this may seem like an interesting but unimportant phenomenon, something more suited for light conversation than serious science. However, its simplicity cloaks an interesting question. Specifi-

neural correlates Patterns of brain activity that covary with another phenomenon, such as a mental state or behavior.

cally, why does the same physical stimulus (e.g., a motion across your palm) evoke very different experiences depending on its source? One possible explanation is that the brain discounts or cancels somatosensory cortex activity associated with self-generated, and therefore predictable, sensory stimuli. Blakemore and colleagues hypothesized that this cancellation signal was associated with the cerebellum, a part of the brain involved with organizing motor movements. Note that even though the authors scanned their subjects using fMRI of the entire brain, they were particularly interested in certain areas.

(A)

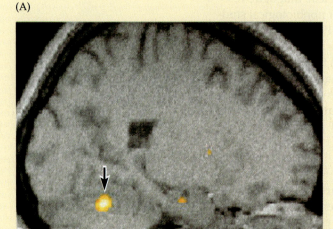

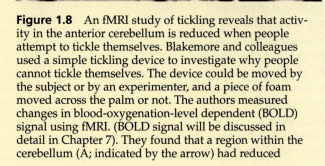

(B)

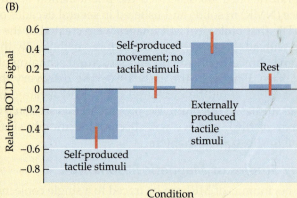

Figure 1.8 An fMRI study of tickling reveals that activity in the anterior cerebellum is reduced when people attempt to tickle themselves. Blakemore and colleagues used a simple tickling device to investigate why people cannot tickle themselves. The device could be moved by the subject or by an experimenter, and a piece of foam moved across the palm or not. The authors measured changes in blood-oxygenation-level dependent (BOLD) signal using fMRI. (BOLD signal will be discussed in detail in Chapter 7). They found that a region within the cerebellum (A; indicated by the arrow) had reduced

BOLD signal compared to baseline when subjects moved the device and the foam moved across their hand (B; self-produced tactile stimulation). However, when an experimenter moved the device and the foam moved across their hand (B; externally-produced tactile stimulation), there was increased BOLD signal. When no sensory stimulus was felt (other conditions) there was no change in BOLD signal. This study provided evidence that the cerebellum initiates an inhibitory signal that reduces the sensory experience of self-generated movements. (A from Blakemore et al., 1998; B after Blakemore et al., 1998.)

BOX 1.1 *(continued)*

They designed a simple tickling device consisting of a piece of foam attached to a long lever. The lever moved the foam up and down, and a pulley could retract or extend it to touch or not touch the palm. Their subjects lay down inside the fMRI scanner with the tickling device adjacent to their left hand. The device could be moved either by the experimenter or by the subject and would either touch (when extended) or not touch the subject when moved. The authors used fMRI to test two predictions: (1) that activity in sensory cortex would be increased when the experimenter moved the device compared to when the subjects moved it themselves, consistent with the tickling sensation in the former but not the latter case; and (2) that activity in the cerebellum would actually be *decreased* by the sensory feedback when subjects moved their hands compared to when no sensations were felt.

Their fMRI results supported their experimental hypotheses. As expected, activity in sensory cortex was evoked when the moving device touched the subjects but was greater when the experimenter moved the device than when the subject did. The authors suggest that this activity may underlie the sensation of tickling. However, a different pattern of results was found in a small region of the right cerebellum (Figure 1.8), which is involved with movements of the right side of the body. There brain activity, in response to self-generated movements with tactile stimulation, was less than that measured in response to similar movements without stimulation and was even less than activity found in rest conditions without movement or stimulation. The cerebellar activity, the authors speculate, represents a neural correlate of somatosensory predictions associated with self-generated movements.

While the Blakemore study used fMRI to study the relation between motor behavior and sensory experience, others use fMRI to investigate the relation between

emotion, affect, and perception. Even though emotion seems abstract and ephemeral, it has become a topic of great interest in cognitive neuroscience, and fMRI studies have played a large part in its resurgence. One brain region that is commonly associated with emotional processing is the amygdala, an almond-shaped region of cortex in the medial temporal lobe. It is well known that patients with amygdala damage show abnormal responses to emotional stimuli, but it is less clear what aspects of emotional processing are impaired. In a recent study,

Anderson and colleagues used fMRI to dissociate two aspects of emotion: valence and intensity. Valence refers to whether an emotion is positive or negative, and intensity refers to whether it is strong or weak. For most types of stimuli, these dimensions are interrelated, such that increasing intensity makes valence more extreme as well. An annoying sound, for example, becomes even more annoying when it is very loud. However, these factors can be dissociated for odor stimuli (Figure 1.9). The authors presented pleasant and unpleasant smells in low and high concen-

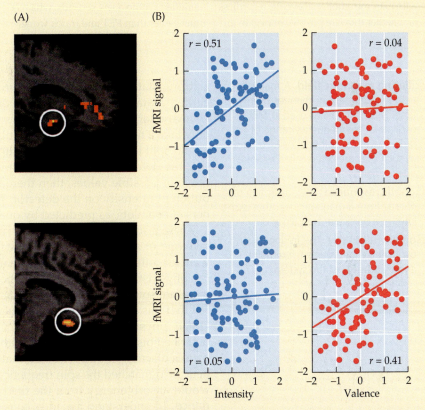

Figure 1.9 Different parts of the brain are associated with the intensity and the pleasantness of smells. Anderson and colleagues presented odors of different intensity and valence (i.e., pleasantness or unpleasantness) while measuring fMRI activity in brain systems that support emotional processing. Within the amygdala, circled at top in (A), the fMRI signal increased with the perceived intensity of the odor but was unaffected by the valence of the odor (B, upper graphs). However, within the orbitofrontal cortex, circled at bottom in (A), the fMRI signal did not depend upon the intensity of the odor but was greater for pleasant odors than for unpleasant odors (B, lower graphs). This result suggests that different components of an emotion may be processed in different brain regions. (From Anderson et al., 2003.)

BOX 1.1 *(continued)*

trations and then examined which brain regions exhibited signal changes as a function of valence but not intensity, or vice versa. Activity in the amygdala increased with increasing stimulus intensity but did not change as a function of valence. In contrast, the orbitofrontal cortex was more active for pleasant stimuli than for unpleasant stimuli but was not influenced by the intensity of those stimuli. For these basic stimuli, at least, different parts of the brain seem to code different aspects of emotional responses. The authors speculate that the amygdala may be associated with extreme emotional events, regardless of whether they are positive or negative.

While fMRI can be used to study such diverse topics as laughter and emotion, or sensation and smell, it is not an answer for all experimental questions. The scanning environment makes some research topics challenging to study, since subjects must remain confined for an hour or two within a small, restrictive, and noisy space. Areas of activity can be localized within a few millimeters, which allows identification of the gross brain regions that are active but may not be suitable for creation of functional maps within those brain regions. The timing of neural activity can be identified within a few seconds, which is much better than PET and much worse

than electrophysiological methods. And there are many difficult decisions that researchers must make as they design and implement even simple studies. Nevertheless, fMRI has become the dominant technique in modern cognitive neuroscience because of its combination of strengths. It is very flexible and powerful, can be conducted with standard (albeit expensive) equipment, and has functional resolution sufficient for most current research questions. A number of extraordinary fMRI studies have been conducted already, and we hope to introduce the reader to many of them throughout this book.

oscillating magnetic field A magnetic field whose intensity changes over time. Most such fields used in MRI oscillate at the frequency range of radio waves (megahertz, or MHz) and as such they are often called radiofrequency fields.

magnetic resonance The absorption of energy from a magnetic field that oscillates at a particular frequency.

resonant frequency The frequency of oscillation that provides maximum energy transfer to the system.

a strong static magnetic field before hitting a detector plate. As described earlier, a static magnetic field is one whose intensity (ideally) does not change over space or time. If the spin frequencies of atomic nuclei could only take a number of discrete quantum states, then the static magnetic field would split the beam into some finite number of smaller beamlets before hitting the detector; whereas if the spin frequencies could take a continuous range of possible values, then there would be a similarly continuous distribution of intensity on the detector. The beams did split into different numbers of beamlets, as predicted by quantum theory.

These results proved that atomic nuclei have spin frequencies that can only take one of a number of discrete values. However, what these frequencies were for different atomic nuclei remained to be measured. In 1933, the American physicist Isidor Rabi modified the Stern–Gerlach technique to measure the quantum spins of hydrogen nuclei as well as nuclei of alkali metals. But Rabi felt that this beam technique was inelegant and sought a better method. The Dutch physicist Cornelis Gorter visited Rabi's laboratory in 1937 and described his recent experiments with **oscillating magnetic fields.** Stimulated by this discussion, Rabi realized that if the frequency of the oscillating magnetic field matched the spin frequency of the atomic nucleus, then the nucleus would absorb energy from the field. This concept is called **magnetic resonance.** To understand this idea, consider the analogy of a swing set, to which we will return in Chapter 3. If your friend is sitting on the swing set, you can help her swing back and forth by pushing her. A single hard push will have only a limited effect. But by pushing her gently and at the right times, at each cycle she will swing a little higher. The frequency of pushing that has the most effect is known as the **resonant frequency.** Energy can be given to atomic nuclei in the same way, by a large number of small "pushes" from a magnetic field that oscillates at the resonant frequency of the nucleus.

This idea catalyzed work in Rabi's lab, which had published a paper earlier that year that predicted such a result, and scant days after Gorter's visit the classic beam technique was modified to include an oscillating magnetic field. Rabi recognized that the resonant frequency needed for the oscillating

(A)

(B)

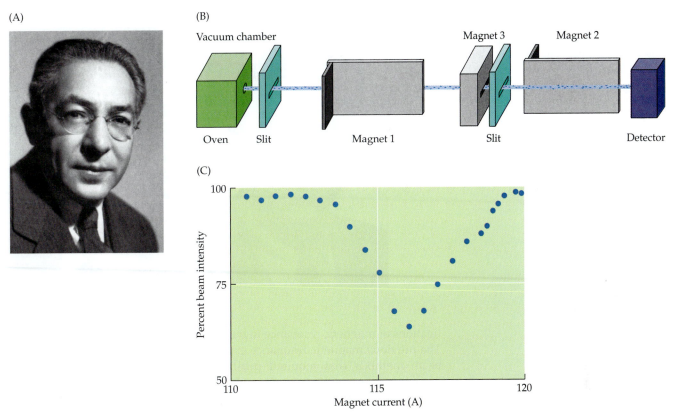

Vacuum chamber

Magnet 3

Magnet 2

Oven   Slit

Magnet 1

Slit

Detector

(C)

Figure 1.10   The determination of the magnetic moment of the lithium nucleus by Isidor Rabi (A). The beam technique devised by Rabi involved passing a beam of gaseous nuclei through several magnetic fields (B). The key innovation introduced by Rabi was an oscillating electromagnetic field (Magnet 3). If the oscillation rate was equal to the resonant frequency of an atomic nucleus (at the current strength of the static magnetic field), the spin of the atomic nuclei would change and then the subsequent magnetic field (Magnet 2) would deflect the nuclei away from the detector. Shown in (C) are data from Rabi's experiment, in which he kept the oscillation rate fixed and changed the current in the static field magnet to modify its magnetic field strength. He found a sharp reduction in beam intensity at about 116 amperes, allowing him to calculate the spin properties of the lithium nucleus. (A ©The Nobel Foundation.)

field would depend upon the strength of the static magnetic field, just like the speed at which someone swings depends upon the strength of the gravitational field. So, he held the frequency of the oscillating field constant and changed the strength of the static field by adjusting the current in the magnet. (Note that this approach is the opposite of that used by modern MR scanners, as will be discussed in the next chapter. Modern scanners keep the static field constant and vary the oscillating field to examine different atomic nuclei.) As the strength of the main field approached the resonant frequency of the sodium atoms in the beam, the atoms in the beam were deflected away from the detector (Figure 1.10A–C). This experiment represented the first demonstration of nuclear magnetic resonance effects, for which Rabi received the Nobel Prize in Physics in 1944.

NMR in Bulk Matter: Bloch and Purcell

During the early 1940s, much basic research in physics stopped as top physicists worked on military applications, such as the development of the atomic bomb and the improvement of radar and counter-radar measures. As the war ended in 1945, two physicists, Felix Bloch at Stanford (Figure 1.11A) and Edward Purcell at MIT/Harvard (Figure 1.11B), resumed independent inves-

Figure 1.11 Nobel laureates Felix Bloch (A) and Edward Purcell (B) shared the 1952 Nobel Prize in Physics for their simultaneous but separate discoveries of magnetic resonance in bulk matter. (©The Nobel Foundation.)

(A)

(B)

tigations of magnetic resonance in bulk matter (i.e., normal solid substances). The previous magnetic resonance experiments by Rabi and others had used beam methods that required purified gases; for magnetic resonance to become practical as a measurement technique, it would need to be applicable to normal substances, not just laboratory creations like beams of atoms.

On December 13, 1945, Purcell and his colleagues began their first experiment in which they attempted to demonstrate magnetic resonance in bulk matter. Borrowing a strong magnet that had originally been used for astronomical research, they placed paraffin wax into the center of the magnetic field. They reasoned that if they matched the resonance frequency of the wax to the oscillating magnetic field, the wax would absorb energy. This, in turn, would change the wax's electrical conductance, which could be detected by a simple circuit. Like Rabi, they recognized that the resonant frequency of the wax would depend on the static magnetic field strength, so they changed the current flowing through the coils of their electromagnet to change its field strength. Despite their careful planning, when they adjusted the current in the magnetic field no resonance was found!

At first, Purcell and colleagues suspected that they had not left their wax sample in the magnetic field for a long enough time before initiating their experiment. Scientists had previously theorized that it took some time before atomic nuclei became aligned with an external magnetic field, a concept known as relaxation time (discussed in detail in Chapter 3). However, Purcell and his colleagues did not know the relaxation time for the atomic nuclei in their sample—it could be as short as a few seconds or as long as a few years. On the chance that relaxation was a very slow process, they placed the wax in the magnetic field for several hours before repeating their experiment two days later. Even with this presaturation, the second experiment likewise failed; at the predicted current level of the magnet, there was no resonance effect. Finally, before ending the experiment, the researchers decided to test all possible magnetic field strengths, so they increased the magnet current to the maximum level and then slowly decreased it. To their surprise, they found a clear resonance effect at a near maximum value that was much higher than they had predicted; subsequent investigation revealed that they had simply miscalculated how much current was necessary to generate the appropriate magnetic field. Their discovery was reported in *Physical Review* in January 1946.

Nearly simultaneously at Stanford, Bloch and his colleagues were also attempting to measure resonance effects in bulk matter, although they were using a very different apparatus. They placed a sample of water in a brass box between the poles of a strong magnet, whose field strength they could manipulate. An adjacent **transmitter coil** sent electromagnetic energy into the sample, while a second **detector coil** was used to measure changes in the energy absorbed by the water (as emitted back to the environment). As in the MIT/Harvard experiment, the sample was presaturated for 24 hours in the magnetic field to ensure that relaxation would take place. These long presaturation periods turned out to be overly conservative; for bulk substances like paraffin and water, relaxation times are only a few seconds, three to four orders of magnitude less than the time allotted.

In a striking parallel to Purcell's experiment, Bloch's group also detected magnetic resonance effects in their water sample. They labeled this phenomenon **nuclear induction,** and reported their findings in *Physical Review* two weeks after Purcell's report. Nuclear induction, or **nuclear magnetic resonance (NMR),** forms the basis of all modern MR imaging techniques, and all MR scanners share the basic design principles of Bloch's simple apparatus: a strong static magnetic field, a transmitter coil that sends electromagnetic energy to the sample, and a detector coil that measures energy emitted back from the sample. For their independent contributions to the discovery of nuclear magnetic resonance, Purcell and Bloch were awarded a joint Nobel Prize in Physics in 1952.

While the discoveries that enabled NMR were made by physicists, the first applications of the new technique came from chemistry. By the early 1950s, the Varian Associates company had patented, with Felix Bloch's assistance, the basic ideas for using NMR to do chemical analysis of samples. NMR soon proved to be a very useful technique for understanding the chemical composition of a homogeneous substance, sharing both theory and methodology with modern MRI spectroscopy. Despite (or perhaps because of) the considerable commercial success of NMR, at least in fields like geology and organic chemistry, the primary uses of the new technique would remain chemical, rather than biological, for more than two decades.

The First MR images

By the late 1960s, NMR measurements had revealed differences between water molecules depending on whether or not they were within biological tissue. Specifically, the atomic nuclei composing water in biological tissue were shown to be constrained in their diffusion and orientation, and these differences could be identified using NMR. The American physician Raymond Damadian hypothesized that similar differences might be observed between cancerous and noncancerous cells; if so, NMR could become an extremely useful method for identifying cancerous tissue. Damadian tested this hypothesis in tissue samples taken from rats, and found that relaxation times were much longer in the cancerous tissue than in healthy tissue; this result was published in *Science* in 1971. Damadian's results were enormously influential in that, for the first time, research suggested a clear biological application for NMR. Yet it is important to also recognize that this application, assessing the properties of a tissue sample, still predated the advance that led to the explosion of interest in magnetic resonance: the ability to form spatial images.

transmitter coil   An electromagnetic coil that generates an oscillating magnetic field at the resonant frequency of atomic nuclei within a sample.

detector coil   An electromagnetic coil that measures energy emitted back to the environment after its initial absorption by the sample.

nuclear induction   The initial term for nuclear magnetic resonance effects, as labeled by Bloch and colleagues.

nuclear magnetic resonance (NMR)   The measurable changes in magnetic properties of atomic nuclei induced by the application of an oscillating magnetic field at the resonant frequency of the nuclei.

image A visual description of how one or more quantities vary over space.

spatial gradients (G) A magnetic field whose strength varies systematically over space. Note that since a given spatial location only experiences one magnetic field, which represents the sum of all fields present, spatial gradients in MRI act to change the effective strength of the main magnetic field over space.

In a formal sense, an **image** provides information about how one or more quantities vary over space. As examples, standard photographs are images of the intensity (and frequency) of visible light and X-ray films are images indicating the density of intervening matter. The first NMR studies did not create images, because they measured the total energy absorbed and emitted by the entire sample. In fact, in order to improve the interpretation of their results, early NMR researchers strove to remove spatial information from their samples to ensure homogeneity. Without image formation, NMR remained a relatively obscure curiosity.

Having seen the results of NMR experiments like those conducted by Damadian, the American physicist Paul Lauterbur recognized that NMR had considerable potential for biological and physical applications, if a method for image formation could be developed. In 1972 Lauterbur had a novel idea: If the strength of the magnetic field varied over space, the resonant frequencies of protons at different field locations would also vary. By measuring how much energy was emitted at different frequencies, one could identify how much of that object was present at each spatial location. This idea, of inducing **spatial gradients (G)** in the magnetic field, proved to be the fundamental insight that led to the creation of MR images. Lauterbur also realized that a single gradient could only provide information about one spatial dimension; to recover two-dimensional structure, it would be necessary to use a series of gradients at different orientations. By acquiring data using four gradients in succession, each turned 45° from its predecessor, Lauterbur created an image of a pair of water-filled test tubes (Figure 1.12A and B). This picture, which was reported in *Nature* in 1973, was the very first MR image.

Lauterbur's method, though revolutionary, was inefficient, since it essentially acquired a succession of one-dimensional projections through the object and then combined them into a two-dimensional image. Not only was

(A)

(B)

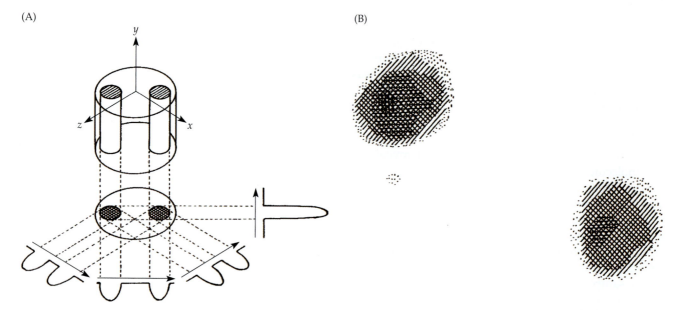

Figure 1.12   The first MR image. The physicist Paul Lauterbur used a series of spatial gradients to take a succession of measurements of a beaker containing two water-filled test tubes (A). Data collected under each gradient provided different information about the object. By combining this data using projection methods, Lauterbur was able to reconstruct the spatial organization of the object (B). The resulting picture was the first magnetic resonance image. The use of spatial variation in the magnetic field set the stage for modern MR imaging. (From Lauterbur, 1973.)

(A)    (B)

Figure 1.13 Nobel laureates Paul Lauterbur (A) and Peter Mansfield (B). Lauterbur and Mansfield shared the 2003 Nobel Prize in Medicine for contributions to the development of MRI. Lauterbur was cited for his introduction of magnetic field gradients, which changed the spin frequency of atomic nuclei over space and thus allowed recovery of spatial information. Mansfield was recognized for his development of echo-planar imaging methods, which allowed rapid collection of images. (A ©The Nobel Foundation; B courtesy of Lisa Gilligan, University of Nottingham.)

there considerable redundancy in the data that were collected, but the approach was quite time-consuming due to the need for many separate acquisitions. A much superior technique, known eventually as **echo-planar imaging (EPI),** was proposed by the British physicist Peter Mansfield in 1976. Echo-planar imaging collected data from an entire image slice at one time, by sending one electromagnetic pulse from a transmitter coil and then introducing rapidly changing magnetic field gradients while recording the MR signal. The resulting complex MR signal could be reconstructed into an image using Fourier analysis techniques, as will be discussed in Chapter 4. Echo-planar imaging reduced the time needed to collect a single image from minutes down to fractions of a second, which greatly improved the feasibility of clinical imaging. Concepts derived from echo-planar imaging underlie the most important approaches to MRI even today, and they have been particularly important for fMRI studies, due to the need for fast imaging to measure changes in brain function. For their contributions to the development of image formation using magnetic resonance, Lauterbur (Figure 1.13A) and Mansfield (Figure 1.13B) were jointly awarded the 2003 Nobel Prize in Physiology or Medicine.

While the theoretical underpinnings of MRI were largely in place, significant engineering challenges were yet to be solved. In 1977, the first human NMR scanner was created by Damadian's FONAR Corporation and was christened "Indomitable" (Figure 1.14A). At that time it was difficult to create a strong, homogeneous magnetic field in a scanner large enough to fit an adult human. Therefore, the magnetic field in Damadian's scanner was weak (0.05 T) and only homogeneous within a small volume at its center. Data could only be acquired from a single small part of the body at one time, whereupon the subject would have to be moved so that another part of the body could be located at the scanner center. Note that this approach did not take advantage of the gradient methods developed by Lauterbur and Mansfield, and instead is more analogous to collection of each voxel as an independent NMR volume.

The first attempt to collect a NMR image using Indomitable failed, perhaps due to problems with adjusting the transmitter/receiver coil system to

echo-planar imaging (EPI) A technique that allows collection of an entire two-dimensional image by changing spatial gradients rapidly following a single electromagnetic pulse from a transmitter coil.

(A)

(B)

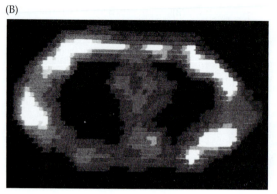

Figure 1.14 The first MR image of the human body. Raymond Damadian and colleagues constructed an early large-bore MRI scanner, which was called "Indomitable." Larry Minkoff, a postdoctoral fellow in the laboratory, was the first subject from whom data were recorded (A). The resulting image of his chest (B), while primitive by modern standards, shows the heart, lungs, and surrounding musculature. (A from FONAR corporation; B from Damadian et al., 1977.)

fit the large subject, Damadian himself (see Mattson and Simon for a complete narrative). After several months of additional adjustment and preparation, they were ready for another attempt. On the morning of July 3, 1977, one of the postdoctoral fellows in Damadian's laboratory, Larry Minkoff, entered the scanner. They slowly collected data from one voxel at a time, changing Minkoff's position slightly after each acquisition. Each voxel in the image took more than 2 minutes to acquire, and the complete image of 106 voxels took nearly 4 hours. At the end of the marathon session, the researchers' patience was rewarded with the first full-body MR image, a single slice through Minkoff's torso (Figure 1.14B). Within 2 years, Damadian's group and other laboratories had created multiple images of the abdomen, upper torso, and head. In addition, researchers acquired the first coronal and sagittal cross-sections of the brain, which were previously difficult to acquire using X-ray-based scanning.

With image formation using NMR a reality, many medical applications became evident. In the late 1970s, computerized tomography (or CT) imaging was commonly used to generate high-resolution images of the human body. CT uses a beam of X-rays that rotates around the body part of interest; the X-ray absorption at each angle is measured, and the resulting projections are combined to form a single picture representing one plane through the tissue. While CT is still commonly used even today, it does require concentrated X-ray exposure. Because NMR images could provide similar information to CT scans without X-ray exposure, there was substantial interest in NMR as a potential diagnostic tool. Around the same time period, the term *nuclear magnetic resonance* fell into disfavor. As usually explained, the term *NMR* was abandoned in large part due to the negative health connotations of the word *nuclear*, which was justified because NMR does not use ionizing radiation. The change in terminology also can be attributed to the desire of hospital officials to separate MR scanning from nuclear medicine departments. As a result of these factors, by the early 1980s, NMR became MRI: magnetic resonance imaging.

> ### Thought Question
> What do you think about the awarding of the 2003 Nobel Prize in Medicine to Paul Lauterbur and Peter Mansfield, but not to other pioneers like Raymond Damadian? What was the likely reasoning of the Nobel Committee, and do you agree with its decision?

Growth of MRI

As noted previously, MRI had three primary advantages over other imaging techniques. It had the potential of very high spatial resolution for both bones and soft tissue. It did not require ionizing radiation, as did X-rays or CT scans. And it could obtain images in any plane through the body. Nevertheless, the capital costs involved in setting up an MRI center were rather large, especially for hospitals facing the budgetary constraints of the recessionary economy of the early 1980s. A typical MRI scanner could cost up to one million dollars to purchase, with maintenance, personnel, and supply contracts adding hundreds of thousands of dollars annually. Many hospitals had just invested heavily in expensive CT scanners and were loathe to commit to an unproven technique. In addition, since MRI was only approved for research purposes by the U.S. Food and Drug Administration (FDA), insurance companies would not reimburse hospitals for the procedure. Nevertheless, there was enough appreciation of the potential of MRI that a number of companies, including FONAR, General Electric (GE), Philips, Siemens, and Varian, began developing MRI scanners for clinical use.

One consequence of the research and development investment in MRI was a substantial increase in scanner power. The use of superconducting magnets overcame limitations on field strength and homogeneity obtainable using standard resistive magnets, although expensive cooling agents were necessary to maintain superconductivity. GE created the first commercial human-body 1.5-T scanner in 1982, and began shipping them to hospitals shortly thereafter. While other companies focused on low- to medium-field scanners (0.1 to 1.0 T), GE's emphasis on high-field MRI resulted in considerable market success. As MRI grew, the 1.5-T scanner would be the standard workhorse for clinical imaging for more than two decades.

In 1985, the FDA approved MRI scanners for clinical use, opening the door for MRI scans to be prescribed by physicians and billed to insurance companies and Medicare. Rather than having to subsidize the enormous cost of a scanner that was used for research purposes, hospitals now saw scanners as a source of profit, both by billing for the scans and by attracting new patients. Over the following decade, thousands of MRI scanners were installed in North America alone, making structural MRI one of the most common diagnostic imaging procedures (Figure 1.15). This prevalence of MRI scanners was a necessary precondition for the subsequent explosion of interest in functional MRI. Without the clinical need for MRI and the abundant resources provided by the installation of many new scanners, the

Figure 1.15 An example of an early-model scanner. (Courtesy of General Electric Medical Systems, Waukesha, Wisconsin.)

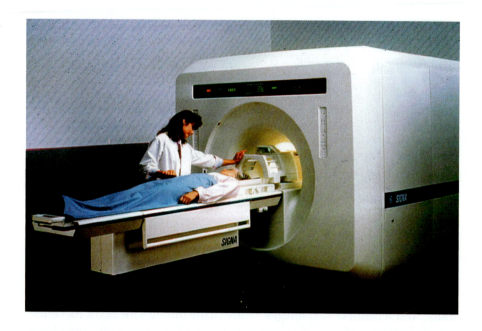

growth of functional MRI would have been greatly slowed. We will return to this history in Chapter 7 by describing how the clinical MRI scanning of the 1980s led to the functional MRI scanning of the 1990s.

Organization of the Textbook

The history of fMRI outlined above suggests an incremental progression, beginning with basic physics (and biological principles), through improvements in image collection and hardware design, to the relatively recent onset of fMRI as a neuroscientific tool. The chapters in this textbook recapitulate this progression, by first establishing a foundation in the physical and biological properties of fMRI and then describing how modern researchers use fMRI to study brain function.

We continue our introduction in Chapter 2, which describes how MRI scanners work. It is important to note that even the most modern MRI scanner has the same basic components found in the experiments described above: a strong static magnetic field to reorient atomic nuclei, weaker but directionally oriented gradient magnetic fields to introduce spatial variation in nuclear magnetic properties, and oscillating radiofrequency fields to induce changes in energy states of the nuclei. While these three components are integral parts of all MRI scanners, their generators are not the only hardware needed for fMRI. In addition, researchers need equipment for ensuring the homogeneity of the magnetic field, for measuring physiological changes like heart rate and respiration, and for presenting experimental stimuli. While MRI presents no dangers to research subjects if conducted correctly, the strong and rapidly changing magnetic fields used in scanning present a set of safety challenges. As safety should be the primary concern for all fMRI experimenters, we discuss these challenges in detail.

Physical Bases of fMRI

From this introduction, we turn to the physics of nuclear magnetic resonance. Chapter 3 introduces the basic principles of magnetic resonance using a combination of intuitive and mathematical descriptions. We describe how atomic nuclei behave in magnetic fields, and how the energy states of those nuclei can be changed by applying oscillating magnetic fields at a particular frequency. This discussion leads to the concept of relaxation processes, or the recovery and decay of magnetization over time, which provide the contrast we measure in MR imaging.

For "nuclear magnetic resonance" to become "magnetic resonance imaging," spatial information must be recovered from the raw MR signal. In Chapter 4, we discuss how the introduction of magnetic gradients allows measurement of signal changes across space. This process is known as image formation. As discussed earlier in this chapter, image formation sparked the explosive growth in the use of magnetic resonance for clinical purposes. We introduce the concept of *k*-space, which provides a useful metric for understanding the relation between scanning hardware and the measured data.

Our final chapter in this section, Chapter 5, links biology and physics by describing the different approaches used by researchers to measure brain structure and function. The extraordinary power of MRI for biological imaging comes from its flexibility; by changing the properties of the gradient and oscillating magnetic fields of the scanner over time, images sensitive to many different types of contrast can be obtained. We discuss two major classes of contrasts, and the pulse sequences used to acquire them. Static contrasts provide information about the characteristics of the atomic nuclei at a spatial location, such as their density or tissue type. Motion contrasts provide information about how atomic nuclei change position over time, through diffusion through space or perfusion within the local blood vessels. We focus on how images can be made sensitive to changes in brain function, which will set the stage for the discoveries outlined in the following section.

Principles of BOLD fMRI

Next, we introduce the biological underpinnings of fMRI. For neuroimaging to be possible, there must be physiological markers of brain activity that can be measured. In general, there are two types of markers that are of interest to physiologists. On the one hand, researchers can measure direct consequences of neuronal activity, such as changes in electrical potentials or in chemical gradients. Or, researchers can measure metabolic correlates of neuronal activity (but not activity itself). Functional MRI relies upon the latter approach, in that it measures blood oxygenation level, which changes based upon the metabolic demands of active neurons. In Chapter 6, we describe the metabolic demands of the brain and how those demands are met by its vascular function. We also provide a primer for gross brain anatomy, as background for subsequent discussions of fMRI research.

Even if the metabolic consequences of neuronal activity are understood, there remains the challenge of measuring how they change using MRI. The technique that forms the basis for nearly all fMRI studies is blood-oxygenation-level dependent (BOLD) contrast. Chapter 7 begins with a history of the developments that led to the discovery of BOLD contrast in the 1990s; this history both parallels that described earlier in this chapter, and picks up where it left off in the early 1990s. We discuss the early fMRI studies that first demonstrated the feasibility of this technique, and how those studies extended previous neuroimaging work with PET. We also introduce a number of important concepts that will recur throughout the remainder of the book.

To demonstrate why fMRI has been such a successful imaging technique, Chapter 8 discusses the spatial and temporal properties of fMRI, with an emphasis on its limitations. We focus on three issues. First, we discuss the spatial resolution of fMRI, which is often claimed to be extremely good, such that images can be collected with millimeter or better resolution. We discuss challenges to spatial mapping, notably that introduced by the transformation between neuronal activity of interest and the measurable changes in the vascular system. Second, we discuss the temporal resolution of fMRI, which is often claimed to be rather poor. We describe approaches to improving temporal resolution and discuss studies in which fMRI has been used to identify subsecond changes in activity. Third, we describe fMRI refractory effects, which are introduced when stimuli are presented in rapid succession, as is common in many experiments. Throughout the chapter we emphasize how the design choices made by researchers influence these properties.

We next describe, in Chapter 9, issues related to signal and noise in fMRI data. The central problem in fMRI research is that the signal we measure is very small compared to other sources of variability in the data. We provide definitions of experimental signal and noise and show how different signal-to-noise ratios influence the spatial and temporal patterns of activity measured by fMRI. We also discuss methods for improving the detectability of fMRI signals, including improving experimental power through signal averaging and the elimination of extraneous physiological variability.

Design and Analysis of fMRI Experiments

While fMRI can be an extraordinarily useful tool for understanding the workings of the human brain, even the most powerful tool can be rendered ineffective if used improperly. The next section of the book describes how to transform fMRI data from a raw time series of images into a statistically valid map of brain function. In Chapter 10, we begin with a discussion of procedures for preprocessing, which have the goal of reducing variability in the data unrelated to the experimental task. The main topics include correction for head motion, time of slice acquisition, and coregistration and normalization of images to match shape, size, and orientation of the brain throughout a data set.

Next, in Chapter 11, we discuss the key concepts of experimental design, or the means by which researchers set up tests of their hypotheses. Most fMRI studies use either blocked or event-related designs. In a blocked design, subjects perform tasks for extended periods of time (e.g., 30 seconds), and activity while performing one task is compared to activity while performing another. Event-related designs, in contrast, examine activity associated with discrete events that could occur at any time point in the experiment. We describe the advantages and disadvantages of each design type for addressing different experimental questions. Furthermore, we consider advanced design types that combine features of both designs.

Going hand in hand with design is analysis, which describes the ways in which tests of hypotheses are evaluated statistically. We begin Chapter 12 by describing the major statistical tests used for fMRI studies, such as t-tests, correlation tests, and Fourier analyses. From these common tests we move to the general linear model, which subsumes them and allows more-complex analyses. While these approaches are similar to those used in other domains of science, their use in fMRI raises additional challenges. Chief among these is the problem of multiple comparisons, in that when tens of thousands of voxels are tested for statistical significance, many may appear to be significant merely by chance. We discuss the different approaches to compensating for the multiple comparisons problem, including thresholding, smoothing, cluster analyses, and region-of-interest analyses. While the bulk of the chapter focuses on traditional hypothesis-driven analyses, we also introduce data-driven analyses, which are useful for discovering hidden structure in data sets.

Applications and Future Directions

We close this book by looking to the future of fMRI. In Chapter 13, we examine some of the research areas where fMRI has made the greatest contributions. Because of the phenomenal success of fMRI, any such survey must be incomplete. Thus, we divide our review into two sections. First, we identify several themes that underlie many fMRI studies and have contributed to its growth as a technique. Though these themes are discussed in the context of particular studies, they can be extended more generally throughout the field. Second, we focus on a small set of topic areas where fMRI has been particularly successful, including attention, memory, and executive function. We discuss why fMRI has been profitably applied to these topic areas, and we describe notable studies within each.

While this textbook necessarily focuses on current state of the art experimental methods, in Chapter 14 we describe a number of methodological advances that promise to change the way fMRI experiments are conducted. Many laboratories are investigating ways to improve spatial resolution, temporal resolution, or signal-to-noise ratio, all of which will have significant benefits for many types of studies. Some researchers have even proposed alternative forms of contrast that could complement or replace the current BOLD imaging methods. We hope that the reader will share our optimism that the pace of technological development will continue to accelerate, facilitating new studies and discoveries.

Finally, Chapter 15 will consider fMRI in the context of other neuroscientific techniques. We end with this chapter to emphasize that fMRI is one of many techniques available to the neuroscientist. Although in our view it is one of the most flexible and powerful, it nevertheless has many limitations that can be addressed by converging studies using other methods. We discuss the theoretical basis for combined studies, and we speculate on the future directions of fMRI research.

Summary

Functional magnetic resonance imaging, or fMRI, is one of the most important techniques for understanding the human brain in action. Although fMRI is a relatively new technique, the developments that led to its current stage span nearly a century. Many of the advances that made fMRI possible resulted from basic physics research, and the experimental apparatuses used in these early studies laid the groundwork for modern MRI equipment. Unlike most structural MRI, which measures differences between tissues, most functional MRI studies measure changes in the blood oxygenation of the brain over time. From these changes, researchers make inferences about the underlying neuronal activity and how different brain regions may support different perceptual, motor, or cognitive processes. The strengths of fMRI include its noninvasiveness, its high spatial and temporal resolution, and its adaptability to many types of experimental paradigms. While fMRI cannot address every experimental question, it provides important information about the brain beyond that obtained from lesion, electrophysiological, or drug studies.

Suggested Readings

*Bloch, F., Hansen, W. W., and Packard, M. (1946). Nuclear induction. *Phys. Rev.*, 69: 127. This very short note describes the discovery of nuclear magnetic resonance in solid matter, for which Felix Bloch would share the 1952 Nobel Prize in Physics with Edward Purcell.

Cabeza, R., and Nyberg, L. (2000). Imaging cognition II: An empirical review of 275 PET and fMRI studies. *J. Cogn. Neurosci.*, 12: 1–47. A review article that provides a good perspective of the breadth of research questions that can be addressed with functional neuroimaging studies.

Finger, S. (2000). *Minds behind the Brain.* Oxford University Press, New York. This very accessible set of short biographies of neuroscience pioneers contains a description of the life and works of Franz Joseph Gall, who founded the discipline of phrenology.

*Lauterbur, P. C. (1973). Image formation by induced local interactions: Examples employing nuclear magnetic resonance. *Nature*, 242: 190–191. This seminal article describes the first use of magnetic field gradients for the formation of images using magnetic resonance.

*Mattson, J., and Simon, M. (1996). *The Pioneers of NMR and Magnetic Resonance in Medicine: The Story of MRI.* Dean Books, Jericho, NY. This encyclopedic text describes in detail the histories of major twentieth-century figures in the discovery of MRI, providing both personal and scientific context for their work.

*Purcell, E. M., Torrey, H. C., and Pound, R. V. (1945). Resonance absorption by nuclear magnetic moments in a solid. *Phys. Rev.*, 69: 37–38. Published scant weeks before Bloch's similar report, this article describes the procedures and results from the very first study of nuclear magnetic resonance.

Indicates a reference that is a suggested reading in the field and is also cited in this chapter.

Chapter References

Anderson, A. K., Christoff, K., Stappen, I., Panitz, D., Ghahremani, D. G., Glover, G., Gabrieli, J. D., and Sobel, N. (2003). Dissociated neural representations of intensity and valence in human olfaction. *Nat. Neurosci.*, 6: 196–202.

Blakemore, S. J., Wolpert, D. M., and Frith, C. D. (1998). Central cancellation of self-produced tickle sensation. *Nat. Neurosci.*, 1: 635–640.

Churchland, P. S., and Sejnowski, T. J. (1988). Perspectives on cognitive neuroscience. *Science*, 242: 741–745.

Damadian, R., Goldsmith, M., and Minkoff, L. (1977). NMR in cancer: XVI. FONAR image of the live human body. *Physiol. Chem. Phys.*, 9: 97–108.

Damadian, R. V. (1971). Tumor detection by nuclear magnetic resonance. *Science*, 171: 1151–1153.

Rabi, I. I., Zacharias, J. R., Millman, S., and Kusch, P. (1938). A new method of measuring nuclear magnetic moment. *Phys. Rev.*, 53: 318.

2

MRI Scanners

Since the beginning of MRI, technological advances have resulted in continual improvements in the speed at which data can be acquired, in the ability to localize signal in space, and in the types of contrast that can be measured. Consequently, the practice of MRI today differs drastically from that of the early pioneers, and modern MRI scanners (Figure 2.1A–C) do not resemble the devices first used to detect nuclear magnetic resonance. However, the fundamental principles of MRI are unchanged. Just as Rabi used a strong magnetic field to measure spin properties of nuclei, today's MRI scanners use a strong magnetic field to induce changes in proton spin. Just as Bloch detected nuclear induction using transmitter and receiver coils, scanners now use similar coil systems to obtain MR signal. And just as Lauterbur manipulated magnetic field strength using changing gradient fields to create an image, every current MRI study relies on magnetic gradients for image acquisition. In this chapter, we identify the major components of MRI scanners, describe their use in practice, and discuss their safety implications.

How MRI Scanners Work

The three main components of an MRI scanner, as alluded to above, are the static magnetic field, radiofrequency coils, and gradient coils, which together allow collection of images. Yet these are not the only components important for fMRI. Also necessary are shimming coils, which ensure the homogeneity of the static magnetic field; specialized computer systems for controlling the scanner and the experimental task; and physiological monitoring equipment. This section introduces these components and their implementation on modern MRI scanners (Figure 2.2). We will return to a detailed discussion of how they are used to change the magnetic properties of atomic nuclei in Chapters 3 to 5.

Static Magnetic Field

The static magnetic field is an absolute necessity for MRI, providing the *magnetic* in magnetic resonance imaging. Magnetic fields were discovered in naturally occurring rocks, known as lodestones, by ancient Chinese almost 2000 years ago. By the eleventh century, the Chinese had recognized that the

(A)

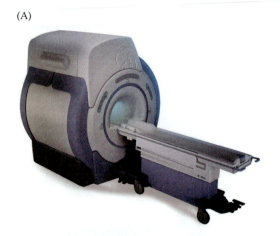

(B)

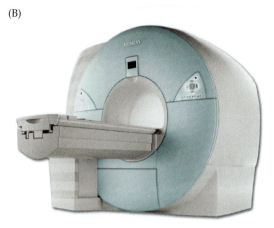

(C)

Figure 2.1 Examples of MRI scanners. Most MRI scanners use a closed-bore design, in which the patient/subject lies down on a table at the front of the scanner and then is moved back into the middle of the bore (i.e., central tube). Shown in (A) is a Signa series scanner from General Electric, and in (B) is a MAGNETOM Avanto scanner from Siemens. A small fraction of scanners use a more open design, such as FONAR's 360 Open Sky scanner, shown in (C). In an open scanner, the subject does not have to go into a tube, so the chance of a claustrophobic reaction is reduced. However, it is more difficult to maintain a strong homogeneous static magnetic field in an open scanner, and thus most scanners used for fMRI employ traditional closed-bore designs. (A courtesy of GE Medical Systems, Waukesha, Wisconsin; B courtesy of Siemens AG, Berlin, Germany; C courtesy of Fonar Corporation, Melville, New York.)

earth itself has a magnetic field, so that a magnet suspended in water will orient itself along the earth's magnetic field lines (i.e., from north to south). The eventual rediscovery of magnetism centuries later by European scientists proved invaluable for subsequent nautical exploration, as ships adopted magnetic compasses for directional guidance. MRI scanners use strong static magnetic fields to align certain nuclei within the human body (most commonly, hydrogen within water molecules) to allow mapping of tissue properties.

Some early MRI scanners used permanent magnets to generate the static magnetic fields used for imaging. Permanent magnets typically generate weak magnetic fields that are fixed by their material composition, and it is difficult to ensure that their magnetic fields are not distorted over space. Another way of generating a magnetic field was discovered by the Danish physicist Hans Oersted in 1820, when he demonstrated that a current-carrying wire influenced the direction of a compass needle below the wire, redirecting it perpendicularly to the direction of current. This relation was quantified later that year by the French physicists Jean-Baptiste Biot and Félix Savart, who discovered that magnetic field strength is in fact proportional to current strength, so that by adjusting the current in a wire (or sets of wires), one could precisely control field intensity. These findings led to the development of electromagnets, which generate their fields by passing current through tight coils of wire. Nearly all MRI scanners today create their static magnetic field through electromagnetism.

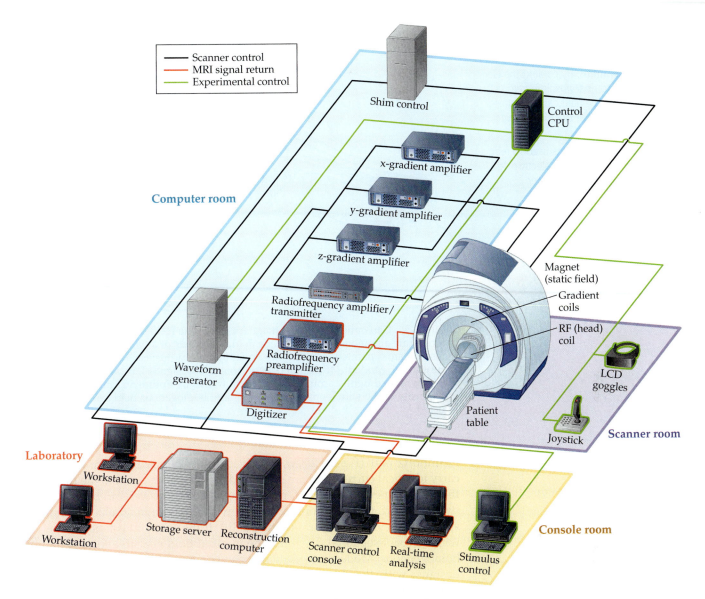

Figure 2.2 Schematic organization of the MRI scanner and computer control systems. Two systems are important for fMRI studies. The first is the hardware used for image acquisition, which in addition to the scanner itself consists of a series of amplifiers and transmitters responsible for creating gradients and pulse sequences (shown in black), as well as recorders of MR signal from the head coil (shown in red). The second system is responsible for controlling the experiment in which the subject participates and for recording behavioral and physiological data (shown in green).

There are, in general, two criteria for a suitable magnetic field in MRI. The first is uniformity (or **homogeneity**), and the second is strength. Uniformity is necessary in that we want to create images of the body that do not depend on which MRI scanner we are using or how the body is positioned in the field. If the magnetic field were inhomogeneous, the signal measured from a given part of the body would depend upon where it was located in the magnetic field. (In fact, MRI takes advantage of this effect by introducing controlled changes in magnetic field strength by adding magnetic field gradients.) A simple design for generating a homogeneous magnetic field is the

homogeneity Uniformity over space and time. In the context of MRI, a homogeneous magnetic field is one that has the same strength throughout a wide region near the center of the scanner bore.

superconducting electromagnets A set of wires made of metal alloys that have no resistance to electricity at very low temperatures. By cooling the electromagnet to near absolute zero, a strong magnetic field can be generated with minimal electrical power requirements.

cryogens Cooling agents used to reduce the temperature of the electromagnetic coils in an MRI scanner.

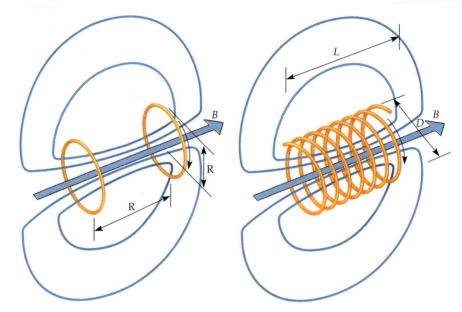

Figure 2.3 Generation of a static magnetic field. The Helmholtz pair design (A) can generate a homogeneous magnetic field. It consists of a pair of circular current loops that are separated by a distance equal to their radius; each loop carries the same current. Modern MR scanners use a solenoid design (B), in which a coil of wire is wrapped tightly around a cylindrical frame. By optimizing the locations and density of the wire loops, a very strong and homogenous field can be constructed.

Helmholtz pair (Figure 2.3A), which is a pair of circular wire loops that carry identical current and are separated by a distance equal to the radius of the loops. An even more uniform magnetic field, however, can be generated by a solenoid, which is constructed by winding wire in a helix around the surface of a cylindrical form (Figure 2.3B). If the solenoid is long compared with its cross-sectional diameter, the internal field near its center is highly homogeneous. Modern magnets are based on a combination of these classic designs, with the density of wires, and therefore the electrical current, numerically optimized to achieve a homogeneous magnetic field of the desired strength.

Field strength, in contrast to uniformity, requires force rather than finesse. To generate an extremely large magnetic field, one can inject a huge electric current into the loops of wire. For example, the very large electromagnets used to lift cars in junkyards have magnetic fields on the order of 1 T, similar to that in the center of some MRI scanners. To generate this field, they require enormous electrical power, and thus enormous expense. Modern MRI scanners use **superconducting electromagnets** whose wires are cooled by **cryogens** (e.g., liquid helium) to reduce their temperature to near absolute zero. Coil windings are typically made of metal alloys such as niobium–titanium, which when immersed in liquid helium reach temperatures of less than 12 K (–261°C). At this extremely low temperature, the resistance in the wires disappears, thereby enabling a strong and lasting electric current to be generated with no power requirements and minimal cost.

Combining the precision derived from numerical optimization of the magnetic coil design and the strength afforded by superconductivity, modern MRI scanners can have homogeneous and stable field strengths in the range of 1 to 9 T for human use and up to 20 T for animal use. Since maintaining a field using superconductive wiring requires little electricity, the static fields used in MRI are always active, even when no images are being collected. For this reason, the static field presents significant safety challenges, as will be discussed later in this chapter.

Radiofrequency Coils

While a strong static magnetic field is needed for MRI, the static field itself does not produce any MR signal. MR signal is actually produced by the clever use of two types of electromagnetic coils, known as transmitter and receiver coils, that generate and receive electromagnetic fields at the resonant frequency of the atomic nuclei within the static magnetic field. This process gives the name *resonance* to magnetic resonance imaging. Because most atomic nuclei of interest for MRI studies have their resonant frequencies in the radiofrequency portion of the electromagnetic spectrum (at typical field strengths for MRI), these coils are also called **radiofrequency coils.** Unlike the static magnetic field, the radiofrequency fields are turned on and off during small portions of the image acquisition process and remain off for any other period. Radiofrequency coils are evaluated on the same criteria as the static field: uniformity and sensitivity.

An equilibrium state exists when the human body is placed in any magnetic field, such that the net magnetization of atomic nuclei (e.g., hydrogen) within the body becomes aligned with the magnetic field. The radiofrequency coils send electromagnetic waves that resonate at a particular frequency, as determined by the strength of the magnetic field, into the body, perturbing this equilibrium state. This process is known as **excitation.** When atomic nuclei are excited, they absorb the energy of the radiofrequency pulse. But, when the radiofrequency pulse ends, the hydrogen nuclei return to the equilibrium state and release the energy that was absorbed during excitation. The resulting release of energy can be detected by the radiofrequency coils, in a process known as **reception.** This detected electromagnetic pulse defines the raw **MR signal.**

One can think of the measurement of MR signal through excitation and reception as analogous to the weighing of an object by lifting and releasing it in a gravitational field. If an object sits motionless on a supporting surface, so that it is in an equilibrium state with respect to gravitational force, we have no information about its weight. To weigh it, we first lift the object to give it potential energy and then release it so that it transfers that energy back into the environment. The amount of energy it releases, whether through impact against a surface or compression of a device like a spring (e.g., in a scale), provides an index of its weight. In the same way, we can perturb the magnetic properties of atomic nuclei (excitation) and then measure the amount of energy returned (reception) during their recovery to an equilibrium state.

The amount of energy that can be transmitted or received by a radiofrequency coil depends upon its distance from the sample being measured. In the case of fMRI, the radiofrequency coils are typically placed immediately around the head, either in a **surface coil** or **volume coil** arrangement (Figure 2.4). Surface coils are placed directly on the imaged sample, that is, adjacent to the surface of the scalp for functional imaging. The design of surface coils is based upon a single-loop inductor–capacitor (LC) circuit (Figure 2.4A). Within this circuit, the rapid charge and discharge of electricity between the inductor and capacitor generates an oscillating current that can be tuned to the frequency of interest. Because of their close spatial proximity to the brain, surface coils usually provide high imaging sensitivity and are often

radiofrequency coils Electromagnetic coils used to generate and receive energy at the sample's resonant frequency, which for field strengths typical to MRI is in the radiofrequency range.

excitation The application of an electromagnetic pulse to a spin system to cause some of the spins to change from a low-energy state to a high-energy state.

reception The process of receiving electromagnetic energy emitted by a sample at its resonant frequency (also called detection). As spins return to a low-energy state following the cessation of the excitation pulse, they emit energy that can be measured by a receiver coil.

MR signal The current measured in a detector coil following excitation and reception.

surface coil A radiofrequency coil that is placed on the surface of the head, very near to the location of interest. Surface coils have excellent sensitivity to signal from nearby regions but poor sensitivity to distant regions.

volume coil A radiofrequency coil that surrounds the entire sample, with roughly similar sensitivity throughout.

(A)

R = Resistor
C = Capacitor
L = Inductor
⚡ = Adjustable capacitor

(B)

(C)

(D)

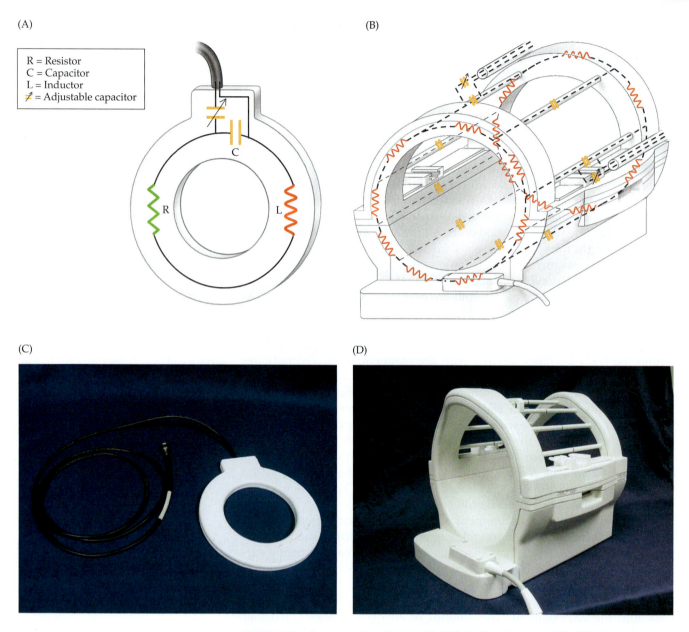

Figure 2.4 Surface and volume coils. (A) Surface coils consist of a simple inductor (L) –capacitor (C) circuit, with additional resistance (R) also present. The rapid charging and discharging of energy between the inductor and resistor generates an oscillating magnetic field. The signal from the surface coil is modulated by a variable capacitor (shown with the arrow). (B) Volume coils repeat the same LC circuit around the surface of a cylinder. This results in better spatial coverage than is provided by a surface coil, at the expense of reduced local sensitivity. (C) A typical surface coil, and (D) volume coil.

used for fMRI studies that are targeted toward one specific brain region, such as the visual cortex. The trade-off with high local sensitivity is poor global coverage. Since the amount of signal recovered from a given part of the brain depends on its distance from the surface coil, areas very near the coil provide a great deal of signal but areas far away provide very little (Figure 2.5A). Thus, the signal recovered by a surface coil is spatially inhomoge-

(A)   (B)

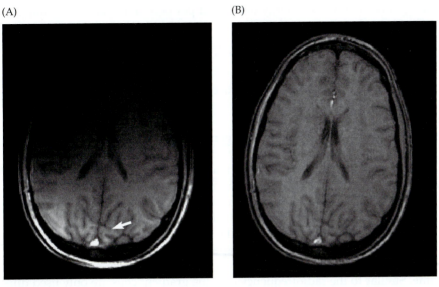

phased array A method for arranging multiple surface detector coils to improve spatial coverage while maintaining high sensitivity.

Figure 2.5 Signal recorded from surface and volume radiofrequency coils. The use of a receiver coil adjacent to the surface of the skull can increase signal-to-noise in nearby brain regions (visible here as reduced graininess, e.g., at arrowed location), but the recorded signal will drop off in intensity as the distance from the coil increases (A). Thus, the use of a single surface coil is more appropriate for fMRI studies that are targeted toward a single brain region. Volume coils have relatively similar signal sensitivity throughout the brain (B), so they are more appropriate for fMRI studies that need coverage of multiple brain regions.

neous, which makes a single surface coil inappropriate when whole-volume imaging is desired.

A second class of MR coil is the volume coil (Figure 2.4B), which provides uniform spatial coverage throughout a large volume. The basic element of the volume coil is the same LC circuit (described in the previous paragraph) for the surface coil. The LC circuit is replicated around a cylindrical surface to achieve uniform distribution of energy within the enclosed volume (Figure 2.5B). The arrangement resembles a birdcage, and thus a volume coil is sometimes referred to as a birdcage coil. Because the volume coil is farther from the head than a surface coil, it has less sensitivity to the MR signal but more even coverage across the brain.

A compromise approach that combines the best features of both coil types is to use a volume coil for exciting the imaging volume and a set of surface coils for receiving the MR signal. If multiple receiver coils are arranged in an overlapping pattern known as a **phased array,** the spatial coverage of a single coil can be increased considerably while the high sensitivity of the coils is maintained. Though sensitivity does change somewhat across the image, the use of multiple receiver coils is an increasingly important technique in fMRI.

The sensitivity of a radiofrequency coil is proportional to the strength of the magnetic field generated within the coil by a unit current. Thus, a coil that generates a strong magnetic field is also a sensitive receiver coil—an example of the principle of reciprocity. A stronger magnetic field can be generated by adding more wire loops to produce higher current density. Assuming that the coil resistance is not zero, because radiofrequency coils are not typically superconducting, some energy will be lost in the heat generation, which will hamper the coil sensitivity. To obtain a quantitative measure of the coil sensitivity, a quality factor is defined as the ratio of the maximum

gradient coils Electromagnetic coils that create controlled spatial variation in the strength of the magnetic field.

energy stored and total energy dissipated per period. For an LC circuit, that quantity can be represented as:

$$Q = \frac{1}{R}\sqrt{\frac{L}{C}}$$

Minimizing resistance (R) thus boosts coil sensitivity.

Gradient Coils

The ultimate goal of MRI is image generation. The combination of a static magnetic field and a radiofrequency coil allows detection of MR signal, but MR signal alone cannot be used to create an image. The fundamental measurement in MRI is merely the amount of current through a coil, which in itself has no spatial information. By introducing magnetic gradients superimposed upon the strong static magnetic field, **gradient coils** provide the final component necessary for imaging. The purpose of a gradient coil is to cause the MR signal to become spatially dependent in a controlled fashion, so that different locations in space contribute differently to the measured signal over time. Similar to the radiofrequency coil, the gradient coils are only used during image acquisition, as they are typically turned on briefly after the excitation process to provide spatial encoding needed to resolve an image.

To make the recovery of spatial information as simple as possible, gradient coils are used to generate a magnetic field that increases in strength along one spatial direction. The spatial directions used are relative to the main magnetic field, with z going parallel to the main field and x and y going perpendicularly to the main field. Like the previously discussed components of the scanner, gradient coils are evaluated on two criteria: linearity (comparable to the uniformity measure for the main magnet and the radiofrequency coils) and field strength.

The simplest example of a linear gradient coil is a pair of loops with opposite currents, known as a Maxwell pair (Figure 2.6A). A Maxwell pair

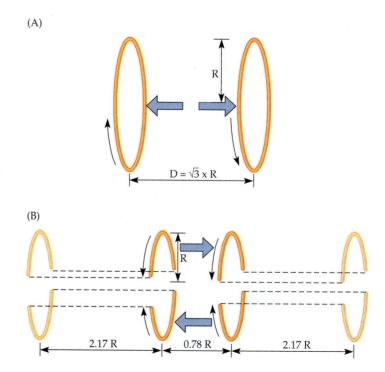

(A)

(B)

Figure 2.6 Coil arrangements for generating magnetic gradients. (A) Shows a Maxwell pair, two loops with opposing currents, which generates magnetic field gradients along the direction of the main magnetic fields. The configuration in (B) is known as a Golay pair. It allows generation of magnetic field gradients perpendicular to the main magnetic field.

generates opposing magnetic fields within two parallel loops, effectively producing a magnetic field gradient along the line between the two loops. This design, in fact, is the basis for generating the z-gradient used today. Of course, the z-gradient coils have a more complicated geometry than a simple pair, but the same concept underlies their design.

The x- and y-gradients, also known as transverse gradients, are both created in the same fashion, since the coils that wrap around the scanner are circular and thus symmetrical across those directions. It is important to understand that the transverse gradients change the intensity of the main magnetic field across space (i.e., along z); they do not introduce smaller magnetic fields along x and y, as one might suppose. That is, the introduction of an x-gradient, for example, makes the main magnetic field slightly weaker at negative values along x and slightly stronger at positive values along x. Therefore, to generate a transverse gradient, one cannot simply place the Maxwell pair along the x or y axis (which would generate a magnetic field pointing perpendicular to the main field). Instead, scanners use a configuration similar to that shown in Figure 2.6B to generate these gradients. This slightly more complicated double-saddle geometry is known as a Golay pair. The final geometry that actually produces the x- or y-gradient field is numerically optimized and contains many more windings than the simple saddle coil shown here. Figure 2.7 illustrates the different patterns of coil windings used for the magnetic gradients and the static magnetic field.

The strength of the gradient coil is a function of both the current density and the physical size of the coil. Increasing the current density by increasing the electrical power supplied to the coil produces a stronger gradient field. Reducing the size of the coil, so that a given current travels through a smaller area, also produces a stronger gradient field. The trade-off between field strength, size, and power is not linear. In fact, as the bore size increases, the power required for generating a gradient of the same strength increases with the 5th power of the bore size. The implications of this fact can be appreciated in a simple example. Consider that a physicist wants to increase the bore size of a scanner by a factor of 2, while maintaining the same gradient strength. Although the bore size is only doubled, the power requirements increase by a factor of 2^5, or 32. This constraint imposes a practical limitation on the bore size of an MRI scanner.

> ### Thought Question
> Some manufacturers have begun developing "head-only" MRI scanners for clinical and functional studies of the brain. Based upon what you know so far, what would be the advantages of such scanners?

Shimming Coils

In an ideal MR scanner, the main magnet would be perfectly homogeneous and the gradient coils would be perfectly linear. This is hardly the case in reality, as the authors (and everyone who has ever conducted fMRI studies!) can attest. MRI scanners must correct for inhomogeneities in the static magnetic field; in some locations the field may be too strong, in others too weak. This process is analogous to what we do when a table is rocking—we simply put a wedge under one of the uneven legs to make it stable. This wedge is called a shim. In the scanner, additional coils generate high-order compensatory magnetic fields (like the analogous wedges) that correct for the inho-

(A)

(B)

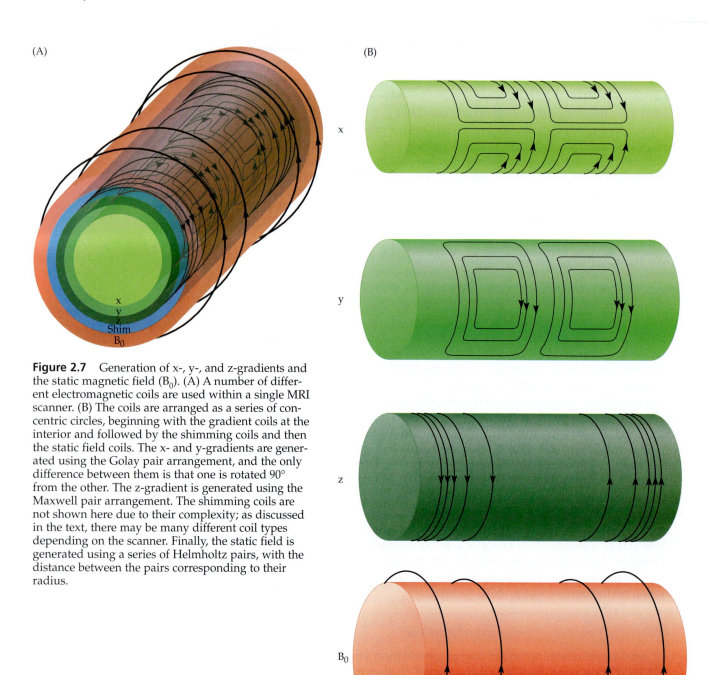

Figure 2.7 Generation of x-, y-, and z-gradients and the static magnetic field (B_0). (A) A number of different electromagnetic coils are used within a single MRI scanner. (B) The coils are arranged as a series of concentric circles, beginning with the gradient coils at the interior and followed by the shimming coils and then the static field coils. The x- and y-gradients are generated using the Golay pair arrangement, and the only difference between them is that one is rotated 90° from the other. The z-gradient is generated using the Maxwell pair arrangement. The shimming coils are not shown here due to their complexity; as discussed in the text, there may be many different coil types depending on the scanner. Finally, the static field is generated using a series of Helmholtz pairs, with the distance between the pairs corresponding to their radius.

shimming coils Electromagnetic coils that compensate for inhomogeneities in the static magnetic field.

mogeneity of the magnetic field. These coils, intuitively, are named **shimming coils.**

Typically, shimming coils can produce first-, second-, or even third-order magnetic fields. For example, an x-shimming coil would generate a magnetic field that depends on position along the *x*-axis (first-order), while an x^3-shimming coil could generate a magnetic field that depends upon the cube of the *x* position (third-order). Combinations of these high-order magnetic fields can usually correct for the inhomogeneity of a typical magnet so that the magnetic field is uniform to roughly 0.1 part per million (ppm) over a spherical volume of 20-cm diameter. For a 1.5-T magnet, this represents a deviation of only 0.00000015 Tesla.

Unlike the other magnetic fields, the shim fields are adjusted for each subject. For fMRI studies, each person's head distorts the magnetic field slightly differently. Shimming procedures used in fMRI thus account for the size and shape of the subject's head so that the uniformity of the magnetic field can be optimized over the brain. Also unlike the radiofrequency and gradient coils, which are turned on and off throughout the imaging session, the shimming coils are usually adjusted once and then left on for the duration of the session.

Computer Hardware and Software

Digitizing, decoding, and displaying MR images require a considerable amount of computer processing power. All MRI scanners are equipped with at least one central computer to coordinate all hardware components (e.g., gradient coils, radiofrequency coils, digitizers), and often multiple computers are used to control separate hardware clusters. The computer type, processor, and operating system vary greatly across scanner manufacturers. In addition to the hardware requirements, two types of specialized software are needed for fMRI. The first type of software sends a series of instructions to the scanner hardware so that images can be acquired. These programs, often called **pulse sequences,** coordinate a series of commands to turn on or off certain hardware at certain times. The type of pulse sequence used determines which kind of images are acquired. Usually the selection of parameters for a pulse sequence is done via a graphic user interface (Figure 2.8). The second type of software is the reconstruction and analysis package to create, display, and analyze the images. Creation of many images, especially anatomical, is done online at the scanner, but often images are sent to other more powerful computers for reconstruction and/or analysis. We will discuss the principles of image formation and pulse sequence generation in Chapters 4 and 5.

Experimental Control System

To induce changes in brain function in response to task manipulations, an experimental control system is necessary. Although the particular hardware and software used will differ across laboratories, there are three basic components. First, the control system must generate the experimental stimuli, which may include pictures or words that subjects see, sounds that subjects hear, or even taps on the skin that subjects feel. Since normal computer monitors cannot go into the strong magnetic field of the scanner, visual stimuli are often shown to the subject by custom virtual-reality goggles that are MR compatible or by projecting an image onto a screen in the bore of the scanner. Second, the control system must record behavioral responses made by the subject, such as pressing a button or moving a joystick. Usually, both the timing and the accuracy of the response are measured. Third, the presentation of stimuli and recording of responses must be synchronized to the timing of image acquisition, so that the experimental paradigm can be matched to the fMRI data. This may be done through direct electrical connection of the scanner hardware and experimental control system, so that starting the scanner sends an electrical pulse to the control system that triggers the start of the experiment as well. Specialized software packages are often used for the experimental control system in conjunction with standard personal computers. The

pulse sequence A series of changing magnetic field gradients and oscillating electromagnetic fields that allows the MRI scanner to create images sensitive to a particular physical property.

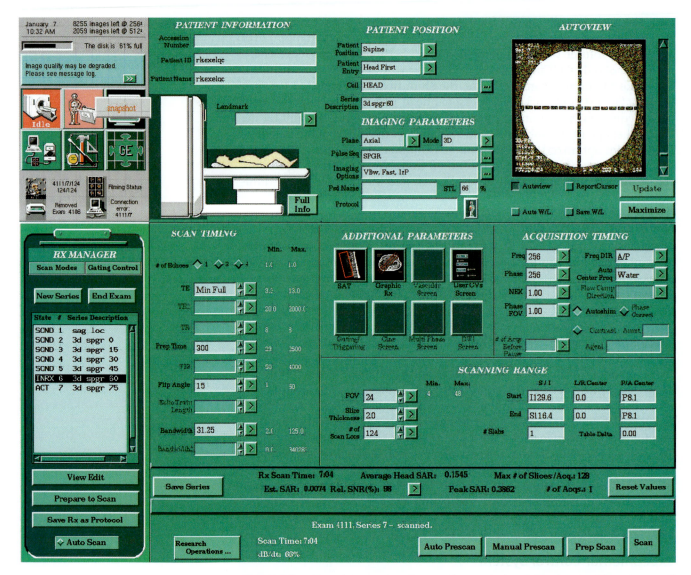

Figure 2.8   A graphic user interface used to control an MRI scanner. The operator of an MRI scanner will use an interface similar to this one to select the pulse sequence parameters for a given study. (Courtesy of General Electric Medical Systems, Waukesha, Wisconsin.)

key challenge for any experimental setup is to ensure that the equipment used in the scanner room, such as display devices or joysticks, is not attracted by the strong magnetic fields and does not interfere with imaging.

Physiological Monitoring Equipment

Many MRI scanners have equipment dedicated to recording physiological measures like heart rate, respiratory rate, exhaled CO_2, and skin conductance. In clinical studies, such equipment allows attending physicians to monitor patients' vital signs. If a patient has trouble breathing or has heart problems during the scanning session, a doctor may choose to remove the individual from the scanner. Physiological monitoring is especially important for patients who may be uncomfortable within the MRI environment, including the elderly, the severely ill, or young children. In functional MRI experiments, research subjects are often healthy young adults, and as such they have little risk of clinical problems. Physiological monitoring in fMRI studies, therefore, often has a different goal: to identify changes over time that may contaminate the quality of the functional images. Each time the heart beats or the lungs inhale, for example, the brain moves slightly. Also, changes in the air volume of the lungs can affect the stability of the magnetic field across the brain. By recording the pattern of physiological changes over time, researchers can later compensate, at least partially, for some of the variability in fMRI data (see Chapter 10).

A second reason to record physiological data during fMRI sessions lies in the relation between physiology and cognition. Many physiological measures can be used as indices for particular cognitive processes. For example, the diameter of the pupil can be used as an index of arousal, in terms of both alertness and amount of cognitive processing. If the size of the pupils increases more in response to one photograph than to another, a researcher may conclude that the former picture is more arousing than the latter. Skin electrical conductance provides another indicator of arousal. Additionally, the position of the eyes can be used as an obvious indicator of the focus of a subject's attention. By examining the sequence of a subject's eye movements across a visual scene, a researcher may discover which objects are most important, due to the increased visual dwell time on them, and which are least important or ignored. Physiological monitoring thus has two primary purposes for fMRI studies: to improve the quality of the images and to provide additional information about subjects' mental states.

MRI Safety

Since the inception of clinical MRI testing in the early 1980s, more than 200 million MRI scans have been performed, with an additional 50,000 scans performed each day. The vast majority of these scans are performed without incident, confirming the safety of MRI as an imaging technique. However, the very serious exceptions to this generalization should give pause. The static magnetic field of an MRI scanner is strong enough to pick up even heavy ferromagnetic objects, like oxygen canisters, and pull them toward the scanner bore at great speed. Implanted metal objects, like aneurysm clips or pacemakers, may move or malfunction within the magnetic field. Only through constant vigilance and strict adherence to safety procedures can serious accidents be avoided.

Effects of Static Magnetic Fields upon Human Physiology

The overriding risks for any MRI study result from the use of extremely strong static magnetic fields. The magnetic field generated by an MRI scanner is sufficiently strong to pick up heavy objects and pull them toward the scanner at very high velocity. This motion of objects is known as a **projectile effect.** Given the dramatic influence of the MRI static field on metal objects, it is not surprising that many people assume that magnetic fields themselves have substantial biological effects. However, this is a misconception. Static magnetic fields, even the extremely strong fields used in MRI, have no known long-term deleterious effects on biological tissue.

projectile effect The movement of an untethered ferromagnetic object through the air toward the bore of the MRI scanner.

BOX 2.1 Outline of an fMRI Experiment

A biology major at college, Emily has always been interested in the brain. One day, while walking back from class, she saw a flyer advertising a "Functional Neuroimaging Study" that used MRI to study the brain. The flyer said that the study would last about two hours, she would be compensated for her time, and she would be able to see pictures of her own brain. The study sounded intriguing, and she called the laboratory to get more information.

Before the Experiment

When she called the laboratory, Emily was nervous. She didn't know very much about MRI, and she wanted to learn more about the technique. The researcher on the phone told her about what would happen in the study. The primary goal of this research, he said, was to investigate which parts of the brain were responsible for working memory, the ability to actively maintain information over time. During the experiment, she would lie in the MRI scanner and watch a series of shapes presented one after another. Whenever she saw a particular shape, she would press a button on a joystick. The MRI scanner would then measure the changes in her brain that occurred each time she pressed the button. The experiment sounded interesting to Emily, and she told the researcher that she wanted to participate.

The researcher then told Emily that he would need to ask her a set of questions to determine whether she was eligible to participate in the study. He asked her whether she had any metal in her body, like a pacemaker or aneurysm clip; whether she had any nonremovable body piercings; and whether she was claustrophobic. Emily did not have any medical condition that prevented her from participating, so she passed this screening test. The

researcher then scheduled Emily for an fMRI session the following week.

Setting Up the Subject

On the day of the fMRI session, Emily was only slightly apprehensive. She was prepared for the scanning when she arrived at the hospital MRI center, having left her wallet, jewelry, and

book bag in her dorm room. She had also worn clothing without any metal, as she had been instructed. She was greeted at the entrance by a graduate student, who escorted her to the MR console room. There she met an MR technologist, whose job it was to run the MR scanner. The console room was large and contained several computers.

Brain Imaging and Analysis Center

Part I: For all individuals entering the scanner room

Name _____ Birth Date_____
　　　　　　Last name　　　　　First name　　　　M.I.
Address_____ City_____
State_____ Zip Code_____ Phone (H)(____)_____ (W)(____)_____

1. Have you had any previous MRI studies or been in a MR scanner?　　　❏ No ❏ Yes
　 If yes, please list (most recent first):
　　Body part _____ Date _____ Facility Location _____

2. Have you ever worked with metal (grinding, fabricating, etc.) or ever had an injury　❏ No ❏ Yes
　 to the eye involving a metallic object (e.g., metallic slivers, shavings, foreign body)?
　 If yes, please describe:_____

3. Have you ever had surgery or other invasive medical procedure?　　　❏ No ❏ Yes

---

Some of the following items may be hazardous to your safety or may interfere with the MRI examination. Do you have any of the following:

❏ Yes ❏ No　Cardiac pacemaker or defibrillator　　　❏ Yes ❏ No　Artificial limb or prosthesis?
❏ Yes ❏ No　Insulin or infusion pump　　　　　　　❏ Yes ❏ No　Bone/joint pin, screw, nail, wire, plate
❏ Yes ❏ No　Cochlear, otologic, or ear implant　　　❏ Yes ❏ No　Wire sutures or surgical staples
❏ Yes ❏ No　Hearing aid　　　　　　　　　　　　　❏ Yes ❏ No　Any implant held in place by a magnet
❏ Yes ❏ No　Any implanted metal (e.g., clamps,　　　　　　　　　　　　 (e.g., dental)
　　　　　　　 valves, clips, shunts, catheters?)　❏ Yes ❏ No　Transdermal delivery system (Nitro)
❏ Yes ❏ No　Body piercing(s)　　　　　　　　　　　❏ Yes ❏ No　Tissue Expanders (plastic surgery)
❏ Yes ❏ No　Tattoos or permanent makeup　　　　　❏ Yes ❏ No　Colored contact lenses
　　　　　　　 (e.g., eyeliner, lips)　　　　　　　❏ Yes ❏ No　Any metal fragments (e.g., shrapnel)

Other, please explain: _____

Before you may enter the scanner room you must remove all metallic objects.

❏ All contents of pockets, including back pockets　　❏ Shoes that contain any metal (e.g., steel-tipped)
❏ Wrist watch; any bracelets　　　　　　　　　　　❏ Hearing aids or other electonic devices
❏ Hair pins, clips, weaves, fasteners　　　　　　　❏ Pagers, cell phones, PDAs
❏ Pins or badges on shirt　　　　　　　　　　　　　❏ Dentures or removable retainer
❏ Belt with metal (e.g., buckle)　　　　　　　　　　❏ Necklaces, chains

Note: You are required to wear earplugs or earphones during the MRI examination.

_____　　　　　　　　_____/_____/_____
　　Signature of Person Completing Form　　　　　　　　　　　　 Date

Figure 2.9 A sample screening form used for functional MRI studies. This form would be filled out by a prospective subject before a research study. The experimenter would then examine the form to make sure that the subject has no condition (e.g., ferrous metal in the body) that would preclude participation in the study.

BOX 2.1 *(continued)*

Through a window, she saw the MR scanner, which was behind a locked door. The graduate student gave her several pieces of paperwork to fill out, including a consent form that described the study and a screening form that asked her questions about metal, medical conditions, and medications (Figure 2.9). The graduate student explained that Emily was participating in this experiment as a research volunteer, so she could quit the study at any time for any reason. Emily was also told that the experimenters would talk with her throughout the experiment to make sure that she was not having any problems. After Emily read and signed the consent and screening forms, she was ready to begin the study.

The technologist looked over Emily's forms to verify that she could participate and then asked her whether she had anything in her pockets or in her hair. At first, Emily thought that this was a strange question, but the technologist quickly explained that they wanted to make sure that people did not bring any metal with them into the scanner room. When Emily checked, she realized that she had left her keys in her pocket, and she placed them on a table. Once Emily made sure that she had no metal on her, the technologist unlocked the scanner room and escorted her inside. Emily sat down on the table at the front of the scanner, and the technologist handed her some earplugs. As Emily put the earplugs in, the technologist explained that the scanner would be loud and that the earplugs would reduce the noise to a comfortable level. Emily then lay down on the table. The technologist handed her a joystick and placed a pair of goggles over her eyes. The goggles had tiny computer screens inside! The technologist also gave her a squeeze ball that was connected to an alarm in the console room. If Emily became uncomfortable or needed help immedi-

ately, she could squeeze the ball to summon the technologist.

Although she couldn't see the scanner room anymore, due to the goggles, she could feel a pillow being wrapped around the sides of her head. The technologist told her that this was a vacuum pack that would support her head and help keep her from moving during the experiment; after a few seconds, Emily heard a hissing sound and the pillow hardened to form a solid cushion. A plastic cylinder called a volume coil then slid around her head (Figure 2.10). The technologist then told her that she was about to go into the scanner, and Emily found herself slowly moving back into the bore.

Structural and Functional Scanning

The technologist returned to the control room and then asked Emily over an

intercom how she was feeling. Emily said that she was doing fine; her nervousness had worn off, and she was pretty comfortable in the scanner. The technologist then told her that she would hear some knocking noises while the scanner took pictures, called structural images, of her brain anatomy. The first knocking noise startled her, because she had expected the scanner to be quiet, like an X-ray machine. After the initial shock wore off, she ignored the noise and just thought about the scanner session. She looked forward to seeing pictures of her brain and wondered whether it was normal. The structural images took about 10 minutes, and then the technologist told her that it was time for the experiment to begin. The graduate student had previously explained that she was supposed to watch for circles to be presented on the screen. Whenever she saw a circle,

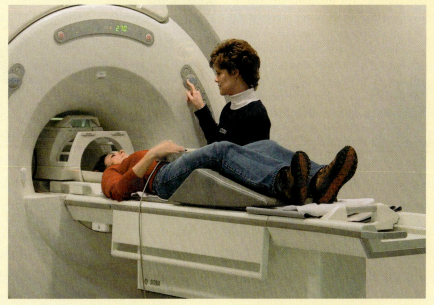

Figure 2.10   Setting up a subject in the scanner. The experimental subject is being positioned in the scanner before a research study. She is holding a joystick in her right hand that will be used for recording behavioral responses. The technologist standing next to the scanner is moving the table so that the subject's head is in a particular position. Once the subject is positioned properly, the technologist will move the volume radiofrequency coil forward so that it fits around the subject's head and then send her into the bore of the scanner.

BOX 2.1 *(continued)*

she was supposed to press a button on the joystick. Emily told the technologist that she was ready to begin.

The experiment was broken into a series of 6-minute runs. In each run, Emily saw a large number of different shapes. Each time she saw a circle she pressed the button. Once or twice, she was trying so hard to look for the circles that she pressed the button for another shape. Overall, though, she made very few mistakes. Between the runs, the technologist talked to her to see how she was doing. After about 10 runs, the experiment was finished and the technologist came into the room to bring her out of the scanner. Emily was a little tired from concentrating for an hour, but she had still enjoyed the experiment and she wanted to see the pictures of her brain.

After the Experiment

Emily sat down in a chair next to the MR console. The graduate student explained that they were investigating changes in the brain associated with how people remember and use rules for behavior. Each time a shape was presented, her brain had to identify the correct shape and to remember what rule to follow when that shape was presented. Emily asked which areas of her brain were active during

the experiment, and the graduate student told her that her data would have to be analyzed by computer programs back in the laboratory before they could answer that. They could, however, show her the structural images they had collected. The graduate student loaded the structural images onto the scanner console (Figure 2.11). They had collected two sets of structural images: a set of sagit-

tal images that showed a side view of her brain and a set of axial images that showed a bottom-up view of her brain. After Emily was finished asking questions, she picked up her keys from the table, and the graduate student walked her back to the entrance to the scanner. Emily said she would be happy to participate in another session in the future, and then she went back to her dorm to rest.

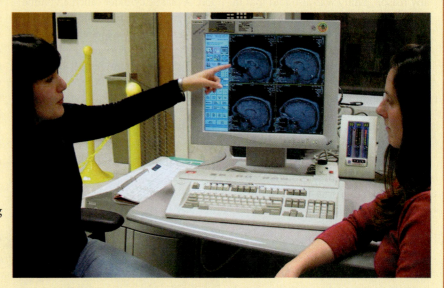

Figure 2.11   Reviewing the anatomical MR images after the experiment. The graduate student who ran the experiment explains the nature and purpose of the experiment. She shows the subject pictures of her brain and discusses the goals of the research.

Thought Question

Why do you think that belief in the biological effects of magnetic fields has persisted, in the absence of strong evidence in support of such effects?

The study of the health effects of magnetic fields long predates MRI. In the 1920s, the prevalence of large industrial magnets in the factories of the day prompted the physiologists Drinker and Thompson to study the effects of magnetic fields upon both cells and animals. No health effects were found. Yet by the 1980s and 1990s, the possible health consequences of magnetic fields reemerged into public awareness, as people worried about exposure to power lines, cellular telephones, and MRI scanners. While a full discussion of the history of magnetic field safety is beyond the scope of this book, the outcome of a century of research can be stated succinctly: No replicable experimental protocol has ever been developed that demonstrates a long-term negative effect of magnetic fields upon human or animal tissue. Where plausible mechanisms for biological effects of magnetic fields have been postulated, they involve very high magnetic field strengths that are greater than those typically used in MRI—and orders of magnitude greater than those generated by power lines, cellular telephones, or other common sources. We refer the interested student to the comprehensive reviews cited in the references for fuller treatments of this issue.

There have been anecdotal reports of minor and short-lived effects associated with static field strengths greater than 2 T. These include reports of visual disturbances known as phosphenes, metallic taste sensations, sensations in teeth fillings, vertigo, nausea, and headaches. These sensations happen infrequently, but appear to occur when the subject's head is moved quickly within the static field. It is believed that some of these effects—particularly vertigo, nausea, and phosphenes—may be related to magnetohydrodynamic phenomena. When an electrically conductive fluid, such as blood, flows within a magnetic field, an electric current is produced, as is a force opposing the flow. In the case of blood flow, magnetohydrodynamic forces are resisted by an increase in blood pressure. However, this effect is negligible, requiring a field strength of 18 T to generate a change of 1 mm Hg in blood pressure. These resistive forces could, however, impose torque upon the hair cells in the semicircular canals of the inner ear, causing vertigo and nausea, or upon the rods or cones in the retina, causing the sensation of phosphenes. We emphasize that these latter effects are likely to occur only during quick movements of the head within the field. Moving the subject slowly in and out of the scanner and restricting head movement should eliminate these sensations.

Given the paucity of evidence in support of magnetism-induced health risks, as well as the absence of any plausible mechanism for such effects, why have magnetic fields engendered such concern? We speculate that the issue of magnetic field safety is symptomatic of two larger problems in public understanding and evaluation of scientific findings. First, magnetic fields and electric currents are mysterious to most nonphysicists, acting invisibly and over large distances. Surely a force powerful enough to lift a car or pull an oxygen canister across the room must have some effect upon the human body! The mysterious nature of magnetic fields makes any consequence of exposure plausible, from the threat of cancer by prolonged exposure to power lines to the circulatory improvements of magnetic bracelets, even if those consequences are themselves contradictory. Indeed, some data suggest that the experiences related to magnetic field exposure may partially result from psychological suggestion. A group of researchers at the University of Minnesota put subjects into the bore of a 4-T scanner and found that 45% reported unusual sensations. The researchers noted that this high rate of self-reported effects was interesting, given that the magnet had been powered down for repair and there was no magnetic field present at the time of the study.

Second, people, even many scientists, tend to select evidence in support of a preconceived viewpoint and reject evidence that refutes their ideas. While the vast majority of studies (and all replicated studies) show absolutely no health risks for magnetic fields less than 2 T, there remain a few studies that have claimed specific consequences of exposure. Even

translation The movement of an object along an axis in space (in the absence of rotation).

though these results have failed under replication, they plant a seed of doubt that grows in the minds of believers. In closing, we note that the efforts to demonstrate health consequences, either positive or negative, from magnetic fields fall perilously close to what has been called "pathological" or "voodoo" science: a conjecture for which, despite more and more studies, the evidence never gets any stronger.

Translation and Torsion

The primary risk of the static field used in MRI results not from the field itself but instead from the field's effects on metal objects. Objects that are constructed in part or whole with ferromagnetic materials (iron, nickel, cobalt, and the rare earth elements chromium, gadolinium, and dysprosium) are strongly influenced by magnetic fields. Steel objects are highly ferromagnetic, and even some medical grades of stainless steel are ferromagnetic. Metals such as aluminum, tin, titanium, and lead are not ferromagnetic, but objects are rarely made of a single metal. For example, ferromagnetic steel screws may secure titanium frames for glasses.

The most dramatic risks with a strong magnetic field are projectile effects that result in the **translation,** or movement, and subsequent acceleration of a ferromagnetic object toward the scanner bore. The magnetic pull on an object can increase dramatically as it nears the scanner. A movement of just a few inches toward the bore of the magnet can exponentially increase the force experienced by the object, making it impossible for a person to hold on to a ferromagnetic object such as a wrench or screwdriver. Similarly, a pager may stay clipped to a belt at the doorway to the magnet room, but become propelled into the magnet bore at 20 to 40 mph when the wearer takes a few steps forward. Projectile injuries have resulted from a number of metal objects, including scissors, IV-drip poles, and oxygen canisters (Figure 2.12).

(A)

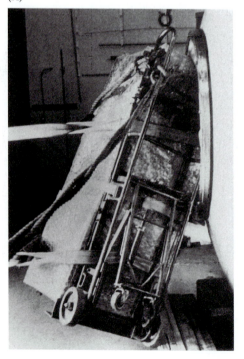

(B)

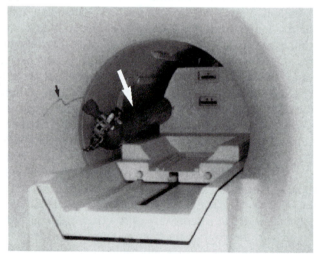

Figure 2.12 Ferromagnetic objects near MR scanners become projectiles. The primary safety risk in MRI scanning comes from the static magnetic field. External ferromagnetic objects, such as RF power supply, brought within the magnetic field (A) will become attracted to the scanner, accelerating toward the center of the bore. Shown in (B) is an oxygen canister (white arrow) lodged in the bore of an MRI scanner. The black arrow indicates damage to the scanner casing. Projectiles present a severe risk to subjects within the bore. (A from Schenck, 2000; B from Chaljub et al., 2001.)

In a tragic example of the danger of projectile effects, a 6-year-old boy was killed in 2001 when a ferromagnetic oxygen canister was brought into the MRI scanner room to compensate for a defective oxygen supply system.

Even if unable to translate toward the scanner center, ferromagnetic devices and debris will attempt to align parallel with the static magnetic field. This alignment process is known as **torsion.** Torsion poses an enormous risk for individuals with implanted metal in their bodies. In 1992 a patient with an implanted aneurysm clip died when the clip rotated in the magnetic field, resulting in severe internal bleeding. Another potential problem is metal within the eyes, as may be present in someone who suffered an injury while working with metal shavings. If lodged in the vitreous portion of the eye, the metal may have no ill effects upon vision. Yet exposure to a strong magnetic field may dislodge such fragments, blinding the patient. Torsion effects have also been used to explain the swelling and/or irritation that have been reported for subjects with tattoos and wearing certain makeup—particularly mascara and eyeliner. The pigments in tattoos and makeup may contain iron oxide particles in irregular shapes that attempt to align with the magnetic field, producing local tissue irritation.

The cardinal rule of MRI safety is that no ferromagnetic metal should enter the scanner room. All participants and medical personnel should remove any ferromagnetic objects, such as pagers, PDAs, cell phones, stethoscopes, pens, watches, paper clips, and hairpins, prior to entering the scanner room. Once the scanner is ramped to its full field strength, the magnetic field is always present, even if no one is in the scanner and no images are being acquired. For this reason, it is the responsibility of all MRI researchers and technicians to be ever vigilant for metal entering the scanner room.

Gradient Magnetic Field Effects

The main safety risk from the gradient magnetic fields is the generation of electric currents within the body. Because the gradient magnetic fields are much weaker than the static magnetic field, typically changing the overall magnetic field by a few thousandths of a Tesla (mT) per meter, they do not cause translation or torsion. However, they change rapidly over time. The effect of a gradient is calculated by dividing the change in magnetic field strength (ΔB, or dB) by the time required for that change (Δt, or dt), resulting in the quantity **dB/dt.** Since the human body is a conductor, gradient switching can generate small currents that have the potential to stimulate nerves and muscles as well as to alter the function of implanted medical devices.

Currents induced in the body by dB/dt can cause peripheral nerve or muscle stimulation. This stimulation may result in a slight tingling sensation or a brief muscle twitch that may startle the subject, but it is not recognized as a significant health risk. Threshold sensations such as these should not be ignored, however, because this sensation may become unpleasant or painful at higher levels of dB/dt. Current operating guidelines in the United States are based upon the threshold for sensation, rather than a specific numerical value for dB/dt. To prevent peripheral nerve stimulation, subjects should be instructed not to clasp their hands or cross their legs during scanning; these actions create conductive loops that may potentiate dB/dt effects. Subjects should also be instructed to report any tingling, muscle twitching, or painful sensations that occur during scanning.

Gradient field changes can also induce currents in medical devices or in implanted control wires that remain after device removal. If a patient with a pacemaker were to be scanned, gradient field effects might induce voltages in the pacemaker that in turn could cause rapid myocardial contraction. This

torsion A rotation (twisting) of an object. Even if the motion of objects is restricted so that they cannot translate, a strong magnetic field will still exert a torque that may cause them to rotate so that they become aligned with the magnetic field.

dB/dt The change in magnetic field strength (dB) over time (dt).

specific absorption rate (SAR) A quantity that describes how much electromagnetic energy is absorbed by the body over time.

uncontrolled contraction due to electrical malfunction, not the translation or torsion of the pacemaker, appears to be the primary cause of pacemaker-related fatalities in the MRI setting. At least six individuals with pacemakers have died as a result of MRI sessions, and clinical or research centers do not allow patients with pacemakers to enter MRI scanners. Other implanted devices, such as cochlear implants, also pose risks for MRI participation, and patients with those devices should be excluded from research studies. To minimize the risks of gradient field effects, researchers should carefully screen potential subjects and exclude any subject who has an implanted medical device.

Radiofrequency Field Effects

Electromagnetic energy from the radiofrequency coils is absorbed by protons in the brain and then re-emitted for measurement. While this emitted energy forms the basis for MRI, not all of the energy is re-emitted. Excess energy becomes absorbed by the body's tissues and is dissipated in the form of heat—through convection, conduction, radiation, or evaporation. Thus, a potential concern in MRI is the heating of the body during image acquisition. The **specific absorption rate (SAR)** determines how much electromagnetic energy is absorbed by the body, and is typically expressed in units of watts per kilogram, or W/kg. SAR depends upon the pulse sequence and the size, geometry, and conductivity of the absorbing object. Because the resonant frequency of atomic nuclei increases with increasing field strength, and higher frequencies are more energetic than lower frequencies, there is a greater potential for heating at higher static field strengths. As will be discussed in Chapter 5, larger-flip-angle pulses (180°) deposit more energy than smaller-flip-angle pulses (90°), and SAR is greater for pulse sequences that employ many pulses per unit time (such as fast spin echo) than those that employ fewer (such as gradient-echo echo-planar imaging).

To ensure participant safety, SAR is limited in MRI studies to minimize body temperature increases. Accurately determining SAR is difficult; it depends upon heat conduction and body geometry as well as upon the weight of the subject. Subjects regulate heat dissipation through perspiration and blood flow changes, so researchers should attend to patient comfort throughout a session. Thermoregulation is impaired in patients with fevers, cardiocirculatory problems, cerebral vascular disease, or diabetes, and thus SAR thresholds should also be lowered for these individuals.

Metal devices and wires also absorb radiofrequency energy and may become hotter than the surrounding tissue. The most common source of heating results from looped wires, such as electroencephalogram or electrocardiogram leads, that act as antennae and focus energy to a small locus. Metal necklaces can also focus radiofrequency energy and cause irritation or burning. Thus, the most significant safety risk caused by the radiofrequency fields used in MRI is local burning. Note that induced currents in conductors and loops due to time-varying magnetic fields associated with gradient coils can also result in heating, through a different mechanism (described in the previous section).

To prevent radiofrequency heating, researchers should (1) screen subjects to exclude those who have metal devices or wires implanted within their bodies; (2) ensure that subjects remove all metal prior to entering the scanner—including nonferromagnetic jewelry such as necklaces, piercings, and earrings; and (3) make certain that any wire leads are not looped and that wires are not run over bare skin.

Claustrophobia

The most common risk from participation in an fMRI study is claustrophobia. Most participants find the physical confinement of the MRI bore only somewhat uncomfortable, and any concern passes within a few moments. For some subjects, however, confinement results in persistent anxiety and, in the extreme, panic. Roughly 10% of all patients experience claustrophobia during clinical MRI scans. This percentage is much lower for research studies, in our experience about 1 to 3%, as research subjects are generally younger and healthier than their clinical counterparts, and people who know that they are claustrophobic are unlikely to volunteer for research studies.

There is no simple solution to the problem of claustrophobia. Subjects who state that they are claustrophobic during a pre-experiment screening should be excluded from study. Anxiety in the scanner can be reduced by talking with subjects frequently throughout the scan, particularly at its onset; by directing air flow through the bore to reduce heat and eliminate any fear of suffocation; and by providing the subject with an emergency panic device. If subjects know that assistance is immediately available, and that they can quit the study at any time, they will feel in control of the session. For first-time subjects, an experimenter should explain that the sounds they will hear are a normal part of scanning. Subjects should also be told that mild apprehension in enclosed spaces is a normal reaction, but if they feel increasingly anxious, they can ask to stop the scan. An experimenter must listen for telltale signs of growing anxiety or discomfort, such as the subject repeatedly asking how much longer the scan will last. Taking a few minutes to enter the scanner room and reassure a subject may help avoid an escalation of anxiety. However, if a subject appears to be more than mildly anxious or declares himself or herself to be anxious, then the experimenter must remove the subject from the scanner immediately.

> ### Thought Question
>
> Under some conditions, clinical patients may have MRI scans even if they have some contraindication (e.g., an implanted device, claustrophobia) that would preclude their participation in a research study. Why should there be different standards for clinical patients and research subjects?

Acoustic Noise

The rapid changes of current in the gradient coils induce Lorentz forces, physical displacement of wires due to electric current, which in turn cause vibrations in the coils or their mountings. To the subject, the vibrations sound like knocking or tapping noises. The parameters of the noise depend on the particular pulse sequence used, but during functional scanning sequences, which make up the bulk of any fMRI session, the noises are often very loud (>95 dB) and of high frequency (1000 to 4000 Hz). In general, fast sequences, such as echo-planar imaging, and sequences that tax the gradient coils, like diffusion-weighted imaging, are louder than conventional sequences. Without some protection, temporary hearing loss could result from the extended 1- to 2-hour exposure of a typical fMRI study. To reduce acoustic noise, fMRI participants should always wear ear protection in the form of earplugs and/or headphones. Researchers should check the fit of the protective devices to ensure their effectiveness.

Summary

The basic parts of most MRI scanners include a superconducting magnet to generate the static field, radiofrequency coils (transmitter and receiver) to collect MR signal, gradient coils to provide spatial information in the MR signal, and shimming coils to ensure the uniformity of the magnetic field. Additional computer systems control the hardware and software of the scanner, present experimental stimuli and record behavioral responses, and monitor physiological changes.

Although fMRI is a noninvasive imaging technique, these hardware components do have associated safety concerns. Most important are issues related to the very strong static field, which can cause translation or torsion effects in ferromagnetic objects near the scanner. The changing gradients and radiofrequency pulses can also cause problems if researchers do not follow standard safety precautions. Some subjects report brief claustrophobic reactions upon entering the scanner, although for most people these feelings fade within a few minutes. Since these risks can be minimized for most subjects, fMRI has become an extraordinarily important research technique for modern cognitive neuroscience.

Suggested Readings

Kanal, E., Borgstede, J. P., Barkovich, A. J., Bell, C., Bradley, W. G., Felmlee, J. P., Froelich, J. W., Kaminski, E. M., Keeler, E. K., Lester, J. W., Scoumis, E. A., Zaremba, L. A., and Zinninger, M. D. (2002). American College of Radiology White Paper on MR safety. *Am. J. Radiol.*, 178: 1333–1347. A report from leading experts on MR safety about recommended procedures in the MRI environment.

Schenck, J. F. (2000). Safety of strong, static magnetic fields. *J. Magn. Reson. Imaging*, 12: 2–19. This journal article provides a scholarly and comprehensive introduction to the effects of magnetic fields on biological tissue.

Shellock, F. G., and Crues, J. V. (2002). Commentary: MR safety and the American College of Radiology White Paper. *Am. J. Radiol.*, 178: 1349–1352. This short commentary provides additional interpretation, and in some cases rebuttal, of the report authored by Kanal and colleagues.

Chapter References

Chaljub, G., Kramer, L. A., Johnson, R. F., Johnson, R. F., Singh, H., and Crow, W. N. (2001). Projectile cylinder accidents resulting from the presence of ferromagnetic nitrous oxide or oxygen tanks in the MR suite. *Am. J. Roentgenol.*, 177: 27–30.

Drinker, C. K., and Thomson, R. M. (1921). Does the magnetic field constitute an industrial hazard? *J. Ind. Hyg.*, 3: 117–129.

Guidance for Industry and FDA Staff: Criteria for Significant Risk Investigations of Magnetic Resonance Diagnostic Devices. (2003). U.S. Food and Drug Administration. http://www.fda.gov/cdrh/ode/guidance/793.pdf

Reilly, J. P. (1998). Maximum pulsed electromagnetic field limits based on peripheral nerve stimulation. *IEEE Trans. Biomed. Eng.*, 45: 137–141.

3

Basic Principles of MR Signal Generation

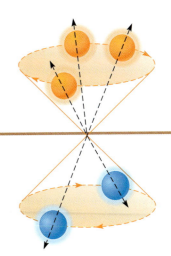

All magnetic resonance imaging, including fMRI, relies on a core set of physical principles. These principles were discovered by Rabi, Bloch, Purcell, and other pioneers during the first half of the twentieth century, and they form the basis for the detection of signal based on magnetic properties of atomic nuclei. In this chapter, we will describe how MR signal is generated. For the mathematically inclined, we have included equations that compactly describe these basic principles. For those less comfortable with mathematical notation, we have included textual descriptions and analogies that reinforce these same concepts.

Overview of Key Concepts

While the mathematical bases for concepts like spin and precession are often difficult for nonphysicists to grasp, we nevertheless believe that an understanding of these concepts is necessary for anyone who wants to be an informed user of fMRI. Therefore, we begin this chapter with an overview of the signal-generation process.

Nuclear Spins

All matter is composed of atoms, which contain three types of particles: protons, neutrons, and electrons. The protons and neutrons within an atom are bound together in the atomic nucleus. Different atoms have different nuclear composition; hydrogen nuclei, by far the most abundant in the human body, consist of single protons. Because of its abundance, hydrogen is the most commonly imaged nucleus in MRI, and we will focus on the properties of single protons throughout this discussion.

Consider a single proton of hydrogen. Under normal conditions, thermal energy causes the proton to spin about itself (Figure 3.1A). The spin motion of a proton has two effects. First, because the proton carries a positive charge, its spin generates an electrical current, just as a moving electrical charge in a looped wire generates current. This loop current induces a torque when it is placed within a magnetic field; this torque is called the **magnetic moment**, or μ. Second, because the proton has an odd-numbered atomic mass (i.e., 1), its spin results in an **angular momentum**, or **J**. Both μ and **J** are vectors pointing in the same direction, as given by the **right-hand**

magnetic moment (μ) The torque (i.e., turning force) exerted on a magnet, moving electrical charge, or current-carrying coil when it is placed in a magnetic field.

angular momentum (J) A quantity given by multiplying the mass of a spinning body by its angular velocity.

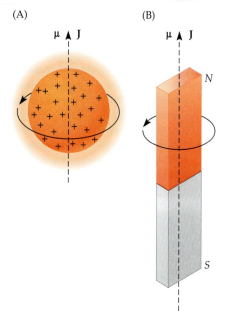

(A)   (B)

μ ↑ J   μ ↑ J

Figure 3.1 Similarity between a spinning proton (A) and a spinning bar magnet (B). Both have angular momentums (J) and magnetic moments (μ). The angular momentums are generated by the spinning masses. The magnetic moment for the spinning proton is generated by the electric current induced by the rotating charge, while the magnetic moment for the bar magnet comes from its internal magnetic field.

right-hand rule A heuristic that can be used to determine the direction of a magnetic moment generated by a moving charge or electrical current. If the fingers of the right hand are curled around the direction of spin, then the magnetic moment will be in the direction indicated by the thumb.

spins Atomic nuclei that possess the NMR property; that is, they have both a magnetic moment and angular momentum.

net magnetization (M) The sum of the magnetic moments of all spins within a spin system.

rule, along the spin axis. To remember the difference between the magnetic moment and angular momentum, think of the proton as a spinning bar magnet. As the magnet spins, its moving magnetic field generates a magnetic moment and its moving mass generates angular momentum (Figure 3.1B). For a nucleus to be useful for MRI, it must have both a magnetic moment and angular momentum. If both are present, the nucleus is said to possess the nuclear magnetic resonance (NMR) property. But if a nucleus does not have both characteristics (i.e., if it has an even-numbered atomic mass), it cannot be studied using magnetic resonance. A few commonly used nuclei for NMR include ^{13}C, ^{19}F, ^{23}Na, and ^{31}P. All these NMR-property nuclei can be generally referred to as **spins.**

An average person who weighs 150 lbs. contains approximately 5×10^{27} hydrogen protons and a comparably very small amount of other NMR-property nuclei. Each individual proton possesses a magnetic moment and angular momentum and is thus a potential contributor to the MR signal. However, in the absence of any strong magnetic field, the spins of the hydrogen protons are oriented randomly (Figure 3.2) and tend to cancel each other out. Thus, the sum of all magnetic moments from spins of different orientations, or the **net magnetization (M),** is infinitesimally small under normal conditions. To increase the net magnetization of the protons, a strong magnetic field must be applied.

Spins within Magnetic Fields

A classic demonstration of magnetism can be created by sprinkling some iron filings around a standard bar magnet. The filings clump most densely around the poles of the magnet but also form a series of arcs between the poles (Figure 3.3A). These arcs run along the field lines of the magnet and result from the tendency of individual iron filings to align with the external field. Figure 3.3B presents a schematic illustration of this alignment, which is driven by the principle of energy minimization. Just as massive objects in a gravitational field tend to lower their energy by falling rather than remaining suspended in midair, magnetically susceptible objects in a magnetic field will orient along the field lines rather than across them. For macroscopic objects, like oxygen canisters or iron filings, the alignment process is known as torsion and presents safety issues, as discussed in Chapter 2. Note that the magnetic field is still present between the field lines. The pattern of field lines is a mathematical description of the contours of the magnetic field, with the density of lines in a location indicating the local strength, or **flux,** of

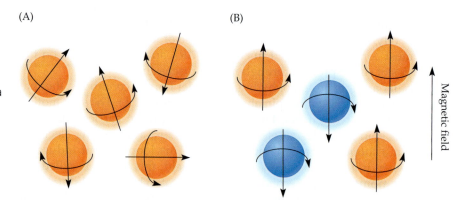

(A)   (B)

Magnetic field

Figure 3.2 Protons in free space with random orientations.

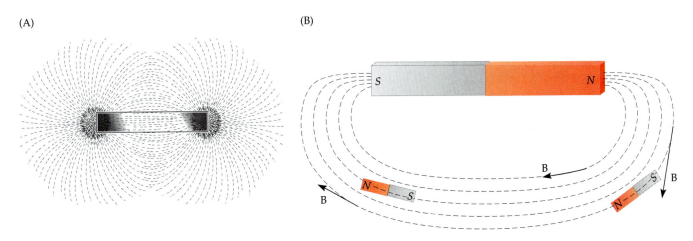

Figure 3.3 Lines of flux in a magnetic field. (A) The alignment of iron shavings in the magnetic field surrounding a bar magnet. (B) A schematic illustration of alignment along the flux lines near a bar magnet.

the magnetic field. In magnetic resonance imaging, the main magnetic field of the scanner is often indicated with the symbol B_0.

Protons, like iron filings, change their orientation when placed within an external magnetic field. However, instead of turning to align with the magnetic field, the spinning protons initiate a gyroscopic motion known as **precession** (Figure 3.4A). To understand precession, imagine a spinning top on a desk (Figure 3.4B). The top does not spin perfectly upright; instead its axis of rotation traces a circle perpendicular to the earth's gravitational field. At any moment in time the top is tilted from the vertical, but it does not fall. Why does the top spin at an angle? Spinning objects respond to applied forces by moving their axes in a direction perpendicular to the applied force. A bicycle, for example, is very stable at high speeds, due to the gyroscopic

flux A measure of the strength of a magnetic field over an area of space.

B_0 The strong static magnetic field generated by an MRI scanner.

precession The gyroscopic motion of a spinning object, in which the axis of spin itself rotates around a central axis, like a spinning top.

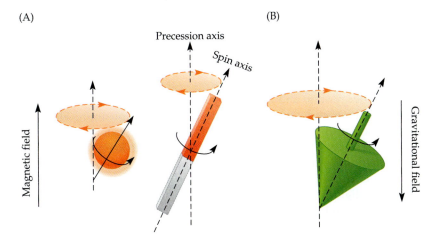

Figure 3.4 Precession. The movement of a rotating proton or magnet within a magnetic field (A) is similar to the movement of a top in the earth's gravitational field (B). In addition to their spinning motion, their axis of spin itself wobbles around a vertical axis; this motion is known as precession.

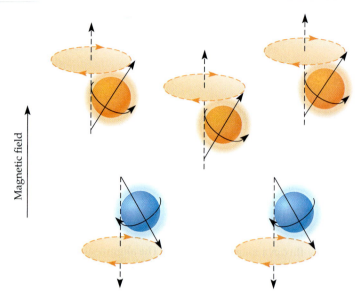

Figure 3.5 High- and low-energy states. Protons in an external magnetic field assume one of two possible states: the parallel state (in orange), which has a lower energy level, and the antiparallel state (in blue), which has a higher energy level. Note that there always will be more protons in the parallel state than in the antiparallel state.

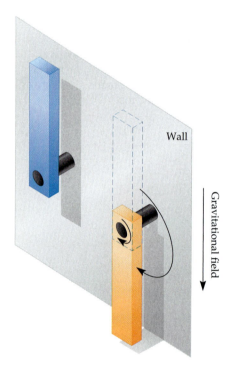

Figure 3.6 High- and low-stability states. Just like a proton in a magnetic field, a bar within the earth's gravitational field can also assume two states: the antiparallel state against gravity (blue), which has higher energy but is less stable, and the parallel state with gravity, which has a lower energy level but is more stable (orange). Energy must be applied to keep the bar in a high-energy state.

effects of its spinning wheels, and resists falling over. In fact, if a rider leans to one side, the moving bicycle will not fall but will instead turn in that direction. Similarly, a spinning top turns its axis of rotation at an angle perpendicular to the force exerted by gravity, so that the top precesses in a circle around a vertical axis.

Protons in a magnetic field behave analogously to spinning tops in a gravitational field. Specifically, protons precess about an axis determined by the magnetic field, with the angle of that axis relative to vertical determined by their angular momentum. There are two states for precessing protons: one parallel to the magnetic field and the other antiparallel (Figure 3.5). Protons in the parallel state have a lower energy level, while protons in the antiparallel state have a higher energy level. The idea of two energy states can be understood by imagining a bar that can rotate around one end (Figure 3.6). There are two vertical positions for the bar: one balanced above the pivot point and one hanging down from the pivot point. The balanced position is a high-energy state and is not very stable; even a small perturbation may tip the bar over and cause it to fall to the hanging position. The only way to keep the bar in a balanced position is to apply an external force that can counteract gravity. That is, energy must be applied to keep the bar in the high-energy state. The hanging position is much more stable, since it is at the minimum energy level for this system. For protons, the parallel (low-energy) state is slightly more stable, so there will always be more protons in the parallel state than in the antiparallel state, with the relative proportion of the two states dependent upon temperature and the strength of the magnetic field. At room temperature in the earth's magnetic field, roughly equal numbers of protons are in the two energy states, with slightly more in the parallel state. If the temperature increases, some protons will acquire more energy and jump to the antiparallel state, diminishing but never reversing the already small difference between the two levels. Conversely, if the temperature decreases, spins will possess less energy and even more will stay at the lower energy level.

Magnetization of a Spin System

It is important to emphasize that MR techniques do not measure single nuclei, but instead measure the net magnetization of all spins in a volume. We can think of the net magnetization as a vector with two components: a **longitudinal** component that is either parallel or antiparallel to the magnetic field and a **transverse** component that is perpendicular to the magnetic field. Because of the enormous number of spins within even the smallest volume, their transverse components will tend to cancel out, and there will be no net magnetization perpendicular to the main magnetic field. The amount of net magnetization, known as **M,** will be proportional to the difference in the number of the spins in the parallel and antiparallel states. The more spins at the parallel state, the bigger the **M** (Figure 3.7).

In the previous section it was established that the number of parallel spins increases with decreasing temperature, so one way to increase the net magnetization would be to reduce the temperature. While theoretically possible, this approach is rarely practical, as temperature changes of many degrees Celsius are required for noticeable increases in net magnetization. A more feasible approach is to increase the strength of the external field, based on the Zeeman effect (Figure 3.8). Just as it would be more difficult to lift an object in a stronger gravitational field than in a weaker gravitational field, it takes more energy to shift from a low-energy state to a high-energy state when the external magnetic field is stronger. Therefore, the number of parallel spins will increase as field strength increases. To increase the net magnetization of protons, therefore, one can place those protons in a very strong magnetic field. Scanners used for fMRI in humans usually have magnetic fields of about 1.5 to 4 T, with some having even stronger fields.

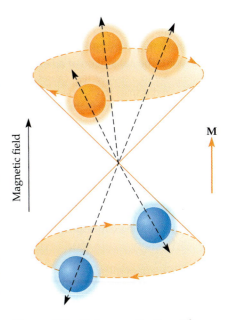

Figure 3.7 Net magnetization. The net magnetization (**M**) is determined by the difference between the number of spins in the parallel state and the number of spins in the antiparallel state. The net magnetization is also called the bulk magnetization.

longitudinal Parallel to the main magnetic field, or *z*-direction, of the scanner (i.e., into the bore).

transverse Perpendicular to the main magnetic field of the scanner, in the *x–y* plane.

> #### Thought Question
> What would happen to the proportion of parallel and antiparallel spins in the spin system if we reduced its temperature to near absolute zero?

The net magnetization of spins within a volume provides the basis for MR signal generation, but net magnetization itself cannot be measured directly under equilibrium conditions. To understand this principle, recall the analogy of an object whose weight you are trying to estimate. You cannot know its weight just by looking at it; instead, you have to lift it. By lifting the object, you perturb its equilibrium state in the gravitational field, and the reaction to that perturbation allows you to estimate its weight. Measuring net magnetization of spins in a magnetic field is no different; you must perturb the equilibrium state of the spins and then observe how they react to the perturbation. Just as lifting enables measurement of the weight of an object, excitation enables measurement of the net magnetization of a spin system.

Spin Excitation and Signal Reception

Remember that all spins can take either a high-energy state or a low-energy state within a magnetic field (Figure 3.9A). When a spin in the high-energy state falls to the low-energy state, it emits a photon with energy equal to the

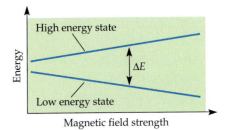

Figure 3.8 The Zeeman effect. The energy difference (ΔE) between the parallel and antiparallel states increases linearly with the strength of the static magnetic field. As the energy difference between the states increases, spins are more likely to remain in the lower-energy state.

excitation The process of sending electromagnetic energy to a sample at its resonant frequency (also called transmission). The application of an excitation pulse to a spin system causes some of the spins to change from a low-energy state to a high-energy state.

reception The process of receiving electromagnetic energy emitted by a sample at its resonant frequency (also called detection). As spins return to a low-energy state following the cessation of the excitation pulse, they emit energy that can be measured by a receiver coil.

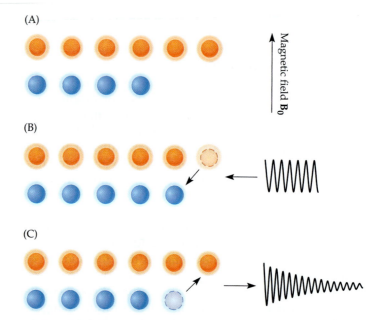

Figure 3.9 Change between states due to absorption or transmission of energy. When spins are placed in an external magnetic field (A), more will be at the low-energy state (orange) than at the high-energy state (blue). If an excitation pulse with the right amount of energy is applied, some spins will absorb that energy and jump to the high-energy state (B). But after the excitation pulse is turned off, some of the spins in the high-energy state will return to the low-energy state, releasing the absorbed energy (C).

energy difference between the two states. Conversely, a spin in the low-energy state can jump to the high-energy state by absorbing a photon with energy matching the energy difference between the two states. To spark this state transition, radiofrequency coils within MRI scanners bombard spins in the magnetic field with photons, which are actually electromagnetic fields that oscillate at the resonant frequency of the nucleus of interest (e.g., hydrogen) Some spins in the low-energy state absorb this energy and change to the high-energy state, in a process known as **excitation** (Figure 3.9B). Since excitation disrupts the thermal equilibrium, immediately after this irradiation the excess spins at the higher energy level return to the lower level, in order to reestablish the equilibrium proportions of energy states (Figure 3.9C). During this **reception** period, the spins emit electromagnetic energy that can be detected by a radiofrequency coil. Since the frequencies of excitation and reception are both determined by the energy difference between the two states, oftentimes the same radiofrequency coil is used for both processes. The receiver detects a decaying signal that depends on the molecular environment of the spins. By analyzing this time-varying signal from the receiver coil, we can learn the properties of the spins and their surrounding environment.

In its essence, MR signal generation can be understood in very simple terms. Because of thermal energy, atomic nuclei with the NMR property spin around themselves. Within a strong magnetic field, the nuclei will precess around an axis that is either parallel to the magnetic field (low-energy) or antiparallel to the magnetic field (high-energy). If energy is applied to the nuclei at a particular frequency, known as the resonant frequency, some low-energy spins will absorb that energy and change to the high-energy state. And, after the energy source is removed, some spins will return to the low-energy state by giving off that energy. Measurement of this emitted energy, or MR signal, provides the data that go into our images.

Principles of MR Signal Generation

Keeping this intuitive perspective in mind, we now move to a more mathematically rigorous description of the excitation–reception process. This description will both clarify the key concepts and provide a quantitative description of the amount of MR signal measured under different conditions. Most of the descriptions below will rely on simple algebra, and where calculus is needed for the equations we have included additional verbal description. We will use the following terms and notation.

A **scalar** is a quantity representing the magnitude of some property. Properties like mass, charge, length, and area are represented by scalars. Scalars may have units; the mass of a person may be 70 kg, for example. Scalars are indicated in italicized type. (*M*: The amount of **M**, scalar.) A **vector** is a quantity or phenomenon in which both magnitude and direction are stated. Examples of vectors in nature include force, velocity, momentum, and electromagnetic fields. Vectors are denoted by boldface type. (**M**: The net magnetization, vector.) Because vectors are directional, the rules for manipulation of vectors are different than those for adding and multiplying scalar numbers.

The **dot product,** also called the scalar product, of two vectors is a scalar quantity obtained by summing the products of corresponding components. Consider the two-dimensional vectors **A** and **B,** which can each be represented as the sum of vectors along the *x*- and *y*-dimensions. The dot product of **A** and **B** is given by **A•B** = |**A**| |**B**| cos θ, where |**A**| and |**B**| are the magnitudes of **A** and **B** and θ is the angle between the two vectors when they are placed tail to tail. The dot product may only be performed for pairs of vectors having the same number of dimensions.

The **cross product**, or vector product, of two vectors produces a third vector that is perpendicular to the plane in which the first two lie. The cross product of vectors **A** and **B** may be defined by **A** × **B** = |**A**| |**B**| sin θ, where |**A**| and |**B**| are the magnitudes of **A** and **B** and θ is the angle between the two vectors. The orientation of the cross product may be determined using the right-hand rule. As one's fingers curl through an angle θ from **A** to **B**, the cross product, or the thumb, points toward the vector perpendicular to the plane defined by **A** and **B**. The magnitude of the cross product is equal to the area of the parallelogram defined by the two vectors. If the components of vectors **A** and **B** are known, then the components of their cross product, **C** = **A** × **B,** may be expressed as:

$$C_x = A_y B_z - A_z B_y$$
$$C_y = A_z B_x - A_x B_z$$
$$C_z = A_x B_y - A_y B_x$$

A **matrix** is a set of numbers arranged in a rectangular grid of rows and columns. Matrices are a compact way to represent numbers, and matrix addition and multiplication can be easily computed.

Spins: Magnetic Moment

As described earlier in the chapter, a nuclear spin can be visualized as a small sphere of distributed positive charge that rotates at a high speed

scalar A quantity that has magnitude but not direction. Scalars are italicized in this text.

vector A quantity with both magnitude and direction. Vectors are boldface in this text.

dot product The scalar product of two vectors, it is created by summing the products along each dimension.

cross product The vector product of two vectors, its direction is perpendicular to the plane defined by those vectors and its magnitude is given by multiplying their product times the sine of the angle between them.

matrix A set of numbers arranged in a grid of rows and columns.

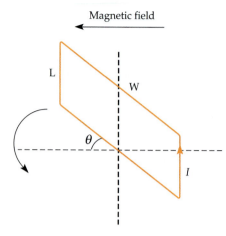

Magnetic field

L

W

θ

I

Figure 3.10   Torque on a current loop. A rectangular current loop ($W \times L$) with electric current (I) would experience a torque if placed within a magnetic field **B** at an angle θ.

torque   A force that induces rotational motion.

about its axis. Because of this rotation, it produces a current that in turn generates a small magnetic field, known as the magnetic moment and denoted as **μ**. Any moving magnet, current-carrying coil, or moving charge has a magnetic moment, which is defined as the ratio between (1) the maximum torque on that magnet, coil, or charge exerted by an external magnetic field and (2) the strength of that field (B). Magnetic moments are measured in Amperes × meters squared, or Am^2. To provide a visual representation, we consider a simple rectangular current loop [length (L), width (W), and current level (I)] within a magnetic field (Figure 3.10). Note that a moving spin will trace a circular loop through the magnetic field, so the rectangular loop is just a convenient simplification. The force (F) exerted on the segment of wire with length (L) that is perpendicular to the magnetic field is defined by Equation 3.1:

$$F = IBL \tag{3.1}$$

Put simply, force is proportional to the strength of the magnetic field (B) and the strength of the current (I). If the magnetic field increases, the force will also increase. The effect of this force upon objects in the field is to cause them to rotate; this rotational force is known as **torque**. Torque can cause rotation, and thus can also be thought of as the change in rotational momentum over time. The maximum torque (τ_{max}) exerted by the magnetic field is given by multiplying the force exerted on the current element by its width. The length and width can be replaced in the equation by the area (A) of the loop:

$$\tau_{max} = IBLW = IBA \tag{3.2}$$

Since the magnetic moment **μ** is defined as the maximum torque divided by the magnetic field, its magnitude μ can now be represented as the product of the current and the area of the current loop:

$$\mu = \frac{\tau_{max}}{B} = IA \tag{3.3}$$

Note that the direction of the magnetic moment vector is defined by the right-hand rule based on the flow direction of the current.

Spins: Angular Momentum

Because the proton also has mass, its rotation produces an angular momentum, often denoted as **J**. Angular momentum is a vector that defines the direction and amount of angular motion of an object. Angular momentum is initiated by external torques and conserved in the absence of external torques. Quantitatively, the angular momentum is defined as the product of the mass (m), velocity (**v**), and rotation radius (r), that is:

$$\mathbf{J} = m\mathbf{v}r \tag{3.4}$$

Since angular momentum is also a vector, its direction is defined by the right-hand rule based on the rotation direction. Since the vectors defining the current flow and rotation are parallel to each other, there should exist a scalar factor between the magnetic moment and angular momentum. This scalar factor is denoted as γ, such that:

$$\mathbf{\mu} = \gamma\mathbf{J} \tag{3.5}$$

It is important to recognize that Equation 3.5 merely states that the magnetic moment (from the rotating charge of the proton) and the angular momentum (from the rotating mass of the proton) are in the same direction, with one larger than the other by an unknown factor γ.

To understand what γ represents, let's consider the simplest atomic nucleus, a single proton. First we must make some assumptions, namely that the charge (q) of the proton is an infinitely small point source, the proton rotates about a radius (r), and its rotation has a period (T). From Equation 3.3, we know that the amount of magnetic moment of a moving charge is given by multiplying two properties, the size of the current and the area of the loop it traverses. The former is just the charge of the proton divided by the time it takes to move around the loop, while the latter is just the area of the circle given by radius r, or πr^2:

$$\mu = IA = \frac{q}{T}\pi r^2 \qquad [3.6]$$

We also know that the velocity of the proton is equal to the circumference of a circle ($2\pi r$) divided by the time it takes to go around the circle (T). Substituting these values into Equation 3.4, we get the equation for the amount of **J**:

$$J = mvr = m\frac{2\pi r^2}{T} \qquad [3.7]$$

Substituting Equations 3.6 and 3.7 into Equation 3.5, it can be derived that:

$$\gamma = \frac{\mu}{J} = \frac{\frac{q}{T}\pi r^2}{m\frac{2\pi r^2}{T}} = \frac{q\pi r^2}{2m\pi r^2} = \frac{q}{2m} \qquad [3.8]$$

Equation 3.8 demonstrates that the scaling factor (γ) depends only on the charge (q) and mass (m) of the proton and not on any other quantity. Since the charge and mass of the proton (or any other atomic nucleus) never change, the scaling factor (γ) is a constant for a given nucleus, regardless of the magnetic field strength, temperature, or any other factor. The constant (γ) is known as the **gyromagnetic ratio,** and is critical for MRI.

In reality, the magnetic moment and angular momentum of a proton cannot be modeled by assuming a simple point charge engaged in circular motion. A proton has a mass of about 1.67×10^{-27} kg and a charge of about 1.60×10^{-19} C, so the estimated value of γ is 4.79×10^7 radian/T. However, recent research has experimentally determined the real value of γ as 2.67×10^8 radian/T. Nevertheless, while Equation 3.8 provides only a very rough estimate of the gyromagnetic ratio, it does demonstrate that γ is a unique quantity for a given nucleus. The gyromagnetic ratio has also been measured for other common nuclei: for ^{13}C it is 6.73×10^7; for ^{19}F it is 2.52×10^8; for ^{23}N it is 7.08×10^7; and for ^{31}P it is 1.08×10^8 (all units in radians per Tesla).

Spins within Magnetic Fields

If a uniform magnetic field is applied to an isolated proton spin (Figure 3.5), the proton will assume one of the two equilibrium positions: the **parallel state** (aligned with the magnetic field) or the **antiparallel state** (opposite of the magnetic field). In MRI, the convention is to refer to the direction along the main magnetic field **B₀** as the parallel state. Both states are at equilibrium, although the energy at the parallel state is lower than that of the antiparallel state and hence the spin is more stable at the parallel state.

gyromagnetic ratio (γ) The ratio between the charge and mass of a spin. The gyromagnetic ratio is a constant for a given type of nucleus.

parallel state The low-energy state in which an atomic spin precesses around an axis that is parallel to that of the main magnetic field.

antiparallel state The high-energy state in which an atomic spin precesses around an axis that is antiparallel (i.e., opposite) to that of the main magnetic field.

The energy difference between the two states is a key concept in understanding spin excitation and signal reception. As indicated in Equation 3.3, a moving charge experiences maximum torque (τ_{max}) when its motion is perpendicular to the main magnetic field:

$$\tau_{max} = \mu B$$

However, if the moving charge is not perpendicular to the main magnetic field, but at some angle θ, then the amount of torque on that charge will be lessened. Specifically, only the component of the magnetic moment vector that is perpendicular to the static field contributes to the torque. Examination of Figure 3.10 reveals that the perpendicular component of the magnetic moment vector $\boldsymbol{\mu}$ is just $\mu \sin\theta$, since the sine of a given angle represents the opposite (perpendicular component) divided by the hypotenuse (vector):

$$\tau = \mu B \sin\theta \qquad [3.9a]$$

or, in vector form:

$$\boldsymbol{\tau} = \boldsymbol{\mu} \times \mathbf{B} \qquad [3.9b]$$

To change a spin from a low-energy (parallel) state to a high-energy (antiparallel) state, we must apply energy. This amount of energy, or work, can be calculated by integrating the torque over the rotation angle:

$$W = -\int_0^\pi \tau d\theta = -\int_0^\pi \mu B \sin\theta d\theta = -\mu B \cos\theta \,|_0^\pi = 2\mu B \qquad [3.10]$$

where d is a mathematical symbol indicating the changes, i.e., $d\theta$ indicating the change of θ. Referring back to our analogy of a bar that could rotate around a pivot point, to rotate the bar from the hanging position to the balanced position we must exert a force (torque) for the entire rotation angle. Likewise, to change the spin state of a proton, we must apply enough torque to complete the total amount of work W. Note that W depends only on the magnetic moment μ and the magnetic field B. For example, if field strength increases, more work will be required to change a spin from one state to another.

We can think of W as equivalent to the energy difference between the states (ΔE). Remember from the quantum mechanics point of view just described that when a spin changes states it will either emit or absorb energy in the form of an electromagnetic pulse. The frequency v of this electromagnetic pulse is determined by the energy difference between the states, as given by the Bohr relation:

$$\Delta E = hv \qquad [3.11]$$

where h is called Planck's constant. Combining Equations 3.10 and 3.11, we obtain:

$$v = \frac{\Delta E}{h} = \frac{2\mu}{h} B_0 \qquad [3.12]$$

It was measured experimentally by physicists that the longitudinal component (i.e., along the magnetic field) of the angular momentum $\mathbf{J}$ of a proton is $\hbar/2$ ($\hbar = h/2\pi$); thus the longitudinal magnetic moment can be calculated using Equation 3.5 to be:

$$\mu = \gamma \frac{\hbar}{2} = \gamma \frac{h}{4\pi} \qquad [3.13]$$

Substituting the result of Equation 3.13 into Equation 3.12, we find that the frequency v is equal to the gyromagnetic ratio divided by 2π and multiplied by the magnetic field strength:

$$v = \frac{2\mu}{h}B_0 = \mu\frac{2B_0}{h} = \gamma\frac{h}{4\pi}\frac{2B_0}{h} = \frac{\gamma}{2\pi}B_0 \qquad [3.14]$$

Following this series of equations, let us stop for a moment to catch our breath and review what we know so far! First, all nuclear spins can be characterized by their magnetic moment and angular momentum, both expressed as vectors with the same direction. The magnetic moment is larger than the angular momentum vector by a factor γ, which is known as the gyromagnetic ratio. Second, spins in a magnetic field can take one of two possible states, either a low-energy state parallel to the magnetic field or a high-energy state antiparallel to the magnetic field. To change from the low-energy state to the high-energy state, a spin must absorb electromagnetic energy. Conversely, when changing from a high- to a low-energy state, a spin emits electromagnetic energy. Third, Equation 3.14 demonstrates that the frequency of the absorbed or emitted electromagnetic energy depends only on the gyromagnetic ratio of that spin and the magnetic field strength. So, for a given atomic nucleus and MR scanner, we can calculate the frequency of electromagnetic radiation that is needed to make spins change from one state to another! This frequency v is known as the **Larmor frequency.**

Recognize that $\gamma/2\pi$ in Equation 3.14 is a constant for a given nucleus, expressed in units of frequency divided by field strength. For hydrogen, its numerical value is given as 42.58 MHz/Tesla. So, for common MR scanners with field strengths of 1.5 T, the Larmor frequency for hydrogen is approximately 63.87 MHz. This frequency is within the radiofrequency band of the electromagnetic spectrum. If we place a human brain into a 1.5-T MR scanner and apply electromagnetic energy at 63.87 MHz, some of the hydrogen nuclei within water molecules within that brain will change from a low-energy state to a high-energy state. This idea, that energy at a particular frequency is needed for changing nuclei from one state to another, represents the cardinal principle of magnetic resonance.

Spin Precession

Now let us consider the effects of the external magnetic field on the motion of atomic nuclei. If we place a stationary magnetic bar into a static magnetic field at an angle θ, it will oscillate back and forth symmetrically to the main field (Figure 3.11A). However, if the magnetic bar is not stationary, but is instead spinning about its axis, it will rotate around this field instead of oscillating back and forth. This is what happens for atomic nuclei. Because an atomic nucleus has intrinsic spin, its axis of rotation rotates around the direction of the external magnetic field (Figure 3.11B). This motion is known as precession, and is conceptually described earlier in this chapter. Naturally, it would be useful to determine the frequency of such precession. In this section, we will derive this frequency for hydrogen nuclei in a magnetic field.

Earlier in the chapter we learned that the cross product of two vectors is derived by multiplying their magnitudes times the sine of the angle between them. We can therefore rewrite Equation 3.9 in the following form, which means that the torque on the magnetic moment is given by the cross product of the magnetic moment and the main field:

$$\tau = \mu \times \mathbf{B_0} \qquad [3.15]$$

Larmor frequency The resonant frequency of a spin within a magnetic field of a given strength. It defines the frequency of electromagnetic radiation needed during excitation to make spins change to a high-energy state, as well as the frequency emitted by spins when they return to the low-energy state.

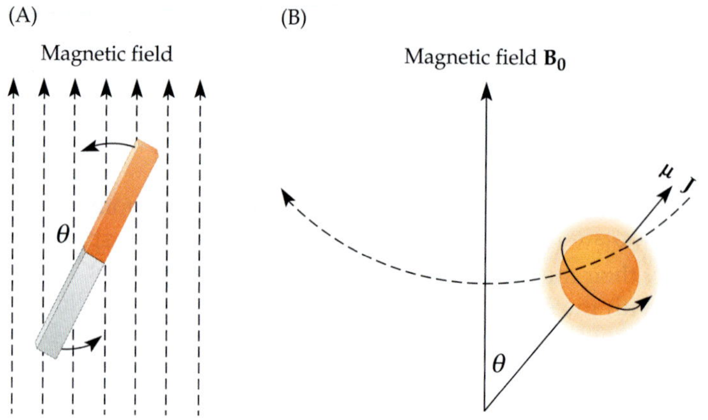

Figure 3.11   Movement within a magnetic field. If a magnetic bar is placed in an external magnetic field, it will oscillate back and forth across the main axis of the field (A). A spin within a magnetic field (B) has angular momentum and thus will precess around the magnetic field (**B$_0$**). The cross product of **μ** and **B$_0$** determines the precession direction.

Recall also that since torque indicates the change in angular momentum over time, it can be defined as the derivative of angular momentum over the derivative of time:

$$\boldsymbol{\tau} = \frac{d\mathbf{J}}{dt} \qquad [3.16]$$

Replacing τ in Equation 3.15 with that in Equation 3.16, we have the following equality:

$$\frac{d\mathbf{J}}{dt} = \boldsymbol{\mu} \times \mathbf{B_0} \qquad [3.17]$$

From Equation 3.5 we learned that angular momentum **J** is equivalent to $\boldsymbol{\mu} / \gamma$. By substitution, we get a generalized expression of the magnetic moment under the main magnetic field, **B$_0$**:

$$\frac{d\boldsymbol{\mu}}{dt} = \gamma(\boldsymbol{\mu} \times \mathbf{B}_0) \qquad [3.18]$$

Equations 3.17 and 3.18 can be read as saying that the torque ($\boldsymbol{\mu} \times \mathbf{B_0}$) on a spin induces changes in the angular momentum and magnetic moment of that spin over time.

> ## Thought Question
>
> Why does the torque on a spin cause precession? More generally, why does a spinning object precess around a central axis?

To solve for the precession frequency, we need to simplify the vector structure of Equation 3.18. We can do this by breaking down the magnetic moment **μ**, which is a vector, into scalar components along different dimensions. After defining the components along three directions as μ_x, μ_y, and μ_z, the magnetic moment is simply the sum of the three components. Here, **x, y,** and **z** are unit vectors along the three cardinal dimensions:

$$\boldsymbol{\mu} = \mu_x \mathbf{x} + \mu_y \mathbf{y} + \mu_z \mathbf{z} \qquad [3.19]$$

So, we can transform Equation 3.18 into three separate scalar equations, representing three different dimensions:

$$\frac{d\mu_x}{dt} = \gamma \mu_y B_0 \qquad [3.20a]$$

$$\frac{d\mu_y}{dt} = -\gamma \mu_x B_0 \qquad [3.20b]$$

$$\frac{d\mu_z}{dt} = 0 \qquad [3.20c]$$

We do not go through the entire derivation here, but the result can be simply summarized as follows. The change in the x-component of the magnetic moment at any point in time depends on the current y-component value; at extreme y-values, x changes quickly. The change in the y-component over time depends on the x-component in a similar way. The z-component of the magnetic moment never changes. While this set of equations may seem complex, it merely specifies that the magnetic moment will trace a circular path around the z-axis. As we have already learned, this circular path is known as precession.

Solving the set of differential equations (3.20) is beyond the scope of this introduction and is left as an exercise for the interested student. The solution, given the initial conditions at time zero (i.e., μ_x, μ_y, μ_z), is given by the following equation:

$$\boldsymbol{\mu(t)} = (\mu_x \cos \omega t + \mu_y \sin \omega t)\mathbf{x} + (\mu_y \cos \omega t - \mu_x \sin \omega t)\mathbf{y} + \mu_z \mathbf{z} \qquad [3.21]$$

where **x, y,** and **z** are unit vectors along three spatial dimensions. This indicates that magnetic moment precesses at angular velocity ω. Importantly, the angular velocity ω is given by γB_0, which is the same as the frequency of an emitted or absorbed electromagnetic pulse during spin state changes, $v = (\gamma/2\pi)B_0$ (see Equation 3.14). Note that though the quantities ω and v are identical, they are expressed in different units: ω is measured in radians per second, while v is measured in Hertz (Hz), or cycles per second.

The correspondence between ω and v means that a single quantity, the Larmor frequency, governs two aspects of a spin within a magnetic field: the energy that spin emits or absorbs when changing energy states and the frequency at which it precesses around the axis of the external magnetic field. This correspondence has deep and important consequences for understanding MR signal generation. The change in energy state is a concept from quantum mechanics, in that spins can only take discrete energy levels with a fixed energy difference between them. The frequency of precession is a concept from classical mechanics, in that it describes the motion of a particle (e.g., proton) through space. Yet, because ω and v represent the same quantity, these two perspectives, quantum and classical mechanics, are unified in describing MR phenomena. This unification allows us to visualize the quantum behavior of spins using classical mechanics modeling to derive basic equations for MR signal generation.

Magnetization of Spins in Bulk Matter

We now have completed analysis of the spin properties of a single atomic nucleus in an external magnetic field. We know characteristics of its magnetic moment and angular momentum, how to change it from a high-energy state to a low-energy state, and how it precesses through the field. While properties of individual nuclei were of interest to Rabi and other early MR physicists, we are not interested in the behavior of single atomic nuclei. Instead, we are interested in characteristics of bulk matter like the human brain, which consists of many protons with potentially different properties. Since the most abundant nuclei in the human body are hydrogen nuclei, principally within water molecules, we will focus the subsequent discussion on hydrogen.

In the absence of a magnetic field, the spin axes of all nuclei in bulk matter are oriented in random directions, so that the net magnetization (i.e., the sum of all individual magnetic moments) is zero. Once the bulk matter is moved into the magnetic field, each individual magnetic moment must align itself in either the parallel or antiparallel state. If we refer to the parallel state as p and the antiparallel state as a, and we denote the probability for a given nucleus to be found in the parallel state as P_p and that to be found in the antiparallel state as P_a, each spin must be in one state or the other, with the sum of the probabilities being 1. That is,

$$P_p + P_a = 1 \qquad [3.22]$$

If the spins are evenly distributed between these two states, such that there are as many parallel spins as antiparallel spins, there will be no net magnetization. Fortunately for MRI, there must always be more parallel spins (in the more stable low-energy state) than antiparallel spins (high-energy state), and thus there will always be a net magnetization. The relative proportion of the two spin states depends upon their energy difference (ΔE) and the temperature (T). This proportion can be determined using Boltzmann's constant, k_B (1.3806×10^{-23} J/K^{-1}), which governs the probabilities of spin distribution under thermal equilibrium.

$$\frac{P_p}{P_a} = e^{\frac{\Delta E}{k_B T}} \qquad [3.23]$$

Note that given the very small value of Boltzmann's constant, $\Delta E / k_B T$ will be much less than 1 under normal conditions. For very small exponents x, the exponential e^x can be approximated by $1 + x$. Thus, Equation 3.23 can be replaced by:

$$\frac{P_p}{P_a} \approx 1 + \frac{\Delta E}{k_B T} \qquad [3.24]$$

Equation 3.24 is called the high-temperature approximation. By algebraically solving Equations 3.22 and 3.24, we obtain:

$$P_p - P_a = \frac{1 + \dfrac{\Delta E}{k_B T}}{2 + \dfrac{\Delta E}{k_B T}} - \frac{1}{2 + \dfrac{\Delta E}{k_B T}} = \frac{\dfrac{\Delta E}{k_B T}}{2 + \dfrac{\Delta E}{k_B T}} \approx \frac{\Delta E}{2 k_B T} \qquad [3.25]$$

The quantity $P_p - P_a$ indicates how many more spins are parallel to the magnetic field than are antiparallel. Each of these spins contributes a magnetic moment with magnitude μ along the z-direction. Thus, the total magnetic moment, which is called the bulk magnetization or net magnetization, is simply this proportion multiplied by the number of protons per unit volume (n) times the magnetic moment of each spin in the z-direction. The net magnetization is represented by the symbol **M**. (Here **z** is a unit vector in the z-direction.)

$$\mathbf{M} = (P_p - P_a)n\mu\mathbf{z} = \frac{\Delta E}{2k_B T}n\mu\mathbf{z} \qquad [3.26]$$

At room temperature, the proportional difference between the numbers of spins in the parallel and antiparallel states is 0.003% per Tesla, which is a very small amount. Note that the net magnetization is parallel to the main field (i.e., the z-direction) and that as long as the temperature remains unchanged it will not vary in amplitude. If the temperature increases, the net magnetization will decrease. Also, and more importantly, since the difference between the energy states, ΔE, increases proportionally to the strength of the main field, the net magnetization is also proportional to the main field strength. This is why using a strong magnetic field increases the amount of MR signal recorded.

While the net magnetization initially points along the main magnetic field, its precession angle is 0° at equilibrium. When tipped away from this starting position by an excitation pulse, the net magnetization will precess around the main axis of the field, just like a single magnetic moment. We can describe the motion of the net magnetization, following an excitation pulse at time point $t = 0$, in three scalar equations as follows:

$$\frac{dM_x}{dt} = \gamma M_y B_0 \qquad [3.27a]$$

$$\frac{dM_y}{dt} = -\gamma M_x B_0 \qquad [3.27b]$$

$$\frac{dM_z}{dt} = 0 \qquad [3.27c]$$

This equation group is nearly identical to Equation group 3.20, with the only difference being that here the amount of net magnetization of a spin system (M) replaces the amount of the magnetic moment of a single spin (μ). The solution to this equation group is similar to that given in Equation 3.21:

$$\mathbf{M}(t) = (M_{x0}\cos\omega t + M_{y0}\sin\omega t)\mathbf{x} + (M_{y0}\cos\omega t - M_{x0}\sin\omega t)\mathbf{y} + M_{z0}\mathbf{z} \quad [3.28]$$

Here, M_{x0}, M_{y0}, and M_{z0} are initial conditions for the net magnetization. In summary, the net magnetization of bulk matter behaves similarly to the magnetic moment of a single spin, in that it precesses clockwise at the Larmor frequency around the axis of the main field. This suggests that we may be able to affect the motion of the net magnetization vector in the same way that we can affect the energy state of a single spin, by application of electromagnetic energy at the Larmor frequency. We demonstrate this in the next section.

Spin Excitation

By measuring the precession of the net magnetization of a spin system, we can discover some of its properties. For example, based on Equation 3.26 above, we can estimate the number of protons within a unit volume (i.e., proton density) based on the quantity n. But we cannot measure the net magnetization of a spin system directly. Therefore, we need to find an indi-

B₁ The magnetic field caused by the application of an electromagnetic pulse during excitation.

laboratory frame The normal reference frame that is aligned with the magnetic field of the scanner.

rotating frame A reference frame that rotates at the Larmor frequency of the spin of interest. The rotating frame is adopted to simplify mathematical descriptions of the effects of excitation.

rect approach that perturbs the spin system away from equilibrium and then measures the response of the system to that perturbation, just like the earlier analogy of lifting an unknown object to estimate its weight. This process is called spin **excitation.**

In a typical MRI experiment, the object sample to be imaged is placed within a strong, uniform magnetic field at the center of the scanner. We now know that the net magnetization of the sample precesses at the Larmor frequency. For hydrogen, the net magnetization oscillates around the main field vector about 64 million times per second if the magnetic field of the scanner is 1.5 T. Because the magnetization rotates so rapidly, it is extremely difficult to change the magnetization with a single pulse of electromagnetic energy. Instead, energy is applied at a given frequency for an extended period of time. To understand the effects of frequency upon an oscillating system, consider again our example of the backyard swing set. If you apply energy at the swing's natural frequency by pushing each time the person is in the same place, even very small pushes will help increase the velocity of the swing and thereby increase the energy in the system. This phenomenon, where small applications of energy at a particular frequency can induce large changes in a system, is known as resonance. For similar reasons, MRI scanners use specialized radiofrequency coils to transmit an electromagnetic excitation pulse (**B₁**) at the same frequency as the spin precession (i.e., the Larmor frequency), exerting torque on the spins to perturb them (Figure 3.12).

$$\mathbf{B_1} = B_1\mathbf{x} \cos \omega t - B_1\mathbf{y} \sin \omega t \qquad [3.29]$$

We are now ready to examine the effect of this electromagnetic pulse upon the sample. Because both the spins and excitation pulse are rotating at the Larmor frequency, we can adopt a reference coordinate system that is also rotating at that frequency. For clarity, we will refer to the normal frame of reference that is aligned with the magnetic field of the scanner as the **laboratory frame** (Figure 3.13A) and the frame of reference rotating at the Larmor frequency as the **rotating frame** (Figure 3.13B). Imagine that you are watching your young siblings ride a carousel at the amusement park. The laboratory frame is analogous to the situation when you are standing on the

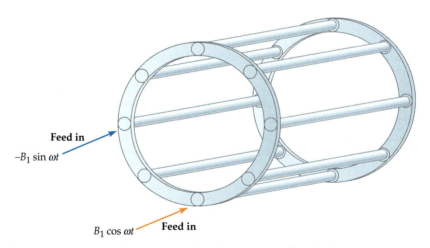

Feed in
$-B_1 \sin \omega t$

$B_1 \cos \omega t$ Feed in

Figure 3.12   Generation of a circularly polarized magnetic field. By driving the birdcage coil using orthogonal currents, the MR scanner generates a circularly polarized electromagnetic field that allows more-efficient radiofrequency excitation.

(A)   (B)

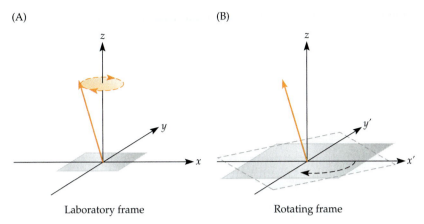

Laboratory frame   Rotating frame

Figure 3.13   Laboratory and rotating reference frames. In the laboratory frame, the magnetization rotates at a given frequency about the main axis (A). But if a rotating frame (x'–y') is adopted that spins the transverse plane (x–y plane) at that frequency, the magnetization would appear stationary (B).

ground outside the carousel watching them ride around. The rotating frame corresponds to when you get on the carousel with them and watch them as you both spin around. In the latter case, they will appear stationary, since you are both rotating at the same speed. The unit vectors in the transverse plane within the rotating frame are represented by **x'** and **y'** and correspond to the following unit vectors in the laboratory frame:

$$\mathbf{x'} = \mathbf{x} \cos \omega t - \mathbf{y} \sin \omega t \qquad [3.30]$$

$$\mathbf{y'} = \mathbf{x} \sin \omega t + \mathbf{y} \cos \omega t \qquad [3.31]$$

Within the rotating frame, both the spins and the excitation pulse become stationary, making subsequent formulas much simpler. The net magnetization (**M**) becomes a stationary quantity along the z-direction, while the excitation pulse (**B$_1$**) can now be thought of as a stationary vector along the new x'-direction. We therefore would have:

$$\mathbf{M} = M_0\mathbf{z} \qquad [3.32a]$$

$$\mathbf{B}_1 = B_1\mathbf{x'} \qquad [3.32b]$$

To assess combined magnetization, Equation 3.18 can be rewritten as Equation 3.33, which states that the change in net magnetization over time is the vector product of the net magnetization and the excitation pulse. As for Equation 3.18, this can be read as saying that applying a torque (**M** × **B**) to the net magnetization will rotate its direction over time:

$$\frac{d\mathbf{M}}{dt} = \gamma \mathbf{M} \times \mathbf{B} \qquad [3.33]$$

Note that here the torque on the net magnetization depends upon the total magnetic field **B** experienced by the spin system. However, this field is itself the sum of two magnetic fields, the static magnetic field **B$_0$** and the excitation pulse **B$_1$**. The effect of the excitation pulse, when it is presented at the resonant frequency of the sample, or **on-resonance,** is a simple rotation of

on-resonance excitation The presentation of an excitation pulse at the resonant frequency of the sample, resulting in maximal efficiency.

off-resonance excitation The presentation of an excitation pulse at a frequency other than the resonant frequency of the sample, resulting in reduced efficiency.

the net magnetization vector from the z-direction toward the transverse ($x-y$) plane. But if the pulse is presented at a slightly different frequency, so that it is **off-resonance,** its efficiency greatly decreases. While this loss of efficiency makes intuitive sense, its mathematical derivation is complex. The effective magnetic field experienced by the spin system is not just $\mathbf{B_1}$ itself but is instead a new field called $\mathbf{B_{1eff}}$ that is influenced by both $\mathbf{B_1}$ and $\mathbf{B_0}$. We have included the derivation of $\mathbf{B_{1eff}}$ within the following box for interested students, and its conclusion is given in Equation 3.37.

Expanding Equation 3.33 in the rotating frame results in the following, which illustrates how the magnetization vector changes over time in each direction:

$$\frac{d\mathbf{M}}{dt} = \frac{(\mathbf{x'}M_{x'} + \mathbf{y'}M_{y'} + \mathbf{z'}M_{z'})}{dt}$$

$$= M_{x'}\frac{d\mathbf{x'}}{dt} + M_{y'}\frac{d\mathbf{y'}}{dt} + \mathbf{x'}\frac{dM_{x'}}{dt} + \mathbf{y'}\frac{dM_{y'}}{dt} + \mathbf{z'}\frac{dM_{z'}}{dt} \qquad [3.34]$$

Since it can be derived that::

$$\frac{d}{dt}\begin{pmatrix}\mathbf{x'}\\\mathbf{y'}\end{pmatrix} = \begin{pmatrix}\omega\cdot(-\mathbf{x}\sin\omega t - \mathbf{y}\cos\omega t)\\\omega\cdot(\mathbf{x}\cos\omega t - \mathbf{y}\sin\omega t)\end{pmatrix} = \begin{pmatrix}\omega\cdot(-\mathbf{y'})\\\omega\cdot(\mathbf{x'})\end{pmatrix} = -\omega\mathbf{z}\times\begin{pmatrix}\mathbf{x'}\\\mathbf{y'}\end{pmatrix} \qquad [3.35]$$

where $\omega\mathbf{z}$ indicates ω as a vector pointing along the z-direction. And if we define the changing magnetization in the rotating frame as $\delta\mathbf{M}/\delta t$, in addition to the changing magnetization in the laboratory frame, $d\mathbf{M}/dt$, Equation 3.33 can be rewritten in the following form (Equation 3.35). It states that the net magnetization (in the laboratory frame) can be considered to have two independent components, precession around the z-direction with frequency ω and a rotation from the longitudinal to transverse planes (within the rotating frame):

$$\frac{d\mathbf{M}}{dt} = -\omega\mathbf{z}\times\mathbf{M} + \frac{\delta\mathbf{M}}{\delta t} \qquad [3.36]$$

By reorganizing Equation 3.36 and substituting Equation 3.33, we can describe a new quantity, $\mathbf{B_{1eff}}$, which depends on the frequency and amplitude of the applied $\mathbf{B_1}$ field. This quantity is the applied magnetic field that the spin system actually experiences, and it governs the behavior of the net magnetization within the rotating frame of reference:

$$\frac{\delta\mathbf{M}}{\delta t} = \frac{d\mathbf{M}}{dt} + \omega\mathbf{z}\times\mathbf{M} = \gamma\mathbf{M}\times\mathbf{B} + \omega\mathbf{z}\times\mathbf{M}$$

$$= \gamma\mathbf{M}\times(\mathbf{B} - \frac{\omega\mathbf{z}}{\gamma}) = \gamma\mathbf{M}\times\mathbf{B_{1eff}} \qquad [3.37]$$

In conclusion, the change in the magnetization in the rotating frame over time ($\delta M/\delta t$) is determined by a new quantity, $\mathbf{B_{1eff}}$, not by $\mathbf{B_1}$ itself. The net magnetization rotates around the vector $\mathbf{B_{1eff}}$ during excitation:

$$\frac{\delta\mathbf{M}}{\delta t} = \gamma\mathbf{M}\times\mathbf{B_{1eff}} \qquad [3.38]$$

The value of the effective excitation pulse experienced by a spin system, $\mathbf{B_{1eff}}$, is given by the following equation (derived from Equation 3.37), such that it has both longitudinal ($\mathbf{z}$) and transverse ($\mathbf{x'}$) components:

$$\mathbf{B_{1eff}} = (B_0 - \frac{\omega}{\gamma})\mathbf{z} + B_1\mathbf{x'} \qquad [3.39]$$

(A)   (B)

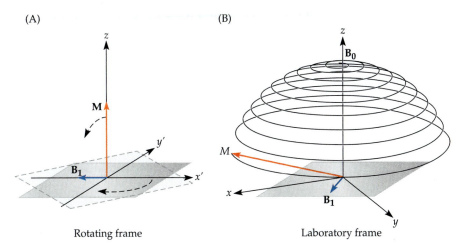

Rotating frame   Laboratory frame

Figure 3.14 Spin nutation. Tipping the longitudinal magnetization into the transverse plane by a simple rotation in the rotating reference frame (A) results in a wobbling motion known as nutation in the laboratory frame (B).

If the excitation pulse (**B$_1$**) is at the resonance frequency of the spin system, so that $\omega = \gamma B_0$, the term $(B_0 - \omega/\gamma)$ will be equal to zero. This means that if the excitation pulse is on-resonance, the net magnetization vector (in the rotating frame) will simply rotate around the **x′**-component (Figure 3.14A) with an angular velocity ω_{rot} (Equation 3.40). Note that this equation nicely illustrates why γ is known as the gyromagnetic ratio, in that γ determines the rate at which an introduced magnetic field, in this case **B$_1$**, causes a gyroscopic rotation of the net magnetization:

$$\omega_{\mathrm{rot}} = \gamma B_{1\mathrm{eff}} = \gamma B_1 \qquad [3.40]$$

At this point, we want to again stop for a moment to emphasize the critical importance of Equation 3.40. What this equation tells us is that the application of an electromagnetic field at the Larmor frequency will induce a rotation within the rotating reference frame. This sounds complicated, but it is actually very simple (see Figure 3.14A). We can think of the rotation within the rotating frame as tipping the net magnetization vector downward from the longitudinal or z-direction to the transverse or $x′-y′$ plane. Within the laboratory frame, the net magnetization vector will follow a spiral path that combines the tipping motion from the rotating frame with precession at the Larmor frequency. This spiral motion in the laboratory frame is known as **nutation** (Figure 3.14B). The angle θ around which the net magnetization rotates following excitation is determined by the duration T of the applied electromagnetic pulse:

$$\theta = \gamma B_1 T \qquad [3.41]$$

This simple equation determines how long we must apply an electromagnetic field to change the net magnetization vector by an angle θ, called the **flip angle.** To change the net magnetization by 90°, from along the main field to perpendicular to the main field, the excitation pulse should be presented for a brief period, on the order of milliseconds. Now why would we want to tip the net magnetization from the longitudinal direction into the transverse plane? Note that when the net magnetization is entirely in the longitudinal direction, it is stable and does not change over time. Therefore,

B$_{1eff}$ The effective magnetic field experienced by a spin system during excitation.

its amplitude is impossible to measure. But if we tip the magnetization into the transverse plane with an excitation pulse, there will be very large changes in the direction of magnetization over time as it rotates. This changing magnetic field can be detected by external receiver coils. In short, by tipping the net magnetization we can create measurable MR signal.

> ## Thought Question
>
> What are the relative proportions of low-energy spins and high-energy spins following application of a 90° excitation pulse?

The concept of the **B$_{1eff}$** (see Equation 3.39) is also very important in understanding off-resonance excitation due to application of an inhomogeneous field, such that the actual rotation frequency does not match the Larmor frequency for a spin system. As such, the difference between B$_0$ and ω/γ is not zero, which means that the excitation pulse would have a longitudinal component. Because the spins always rotate about the axis of **B$_{1eff}$**, the effectiveness of the excitation pulse will be compromised. To understand the effects of off-resonance excitation, think of an extreme condition in which the excitation pulse has a **z**-component approaching the size of the main field, **B$_0$**. As a result, the **B$_{1eff}$** would be pointing along the z-direction. Because the **B$_{1eff}$** has the same direction as the spins themselves, it would exert no torque on the spins, and their angle of rotation would not change. (Mathematically speaking, the cross product between two vectors with the same direction is equal to zero). Consequently, an excitation pulse along the same direction as **B$_0$** would have absolutely no effect. In practice, if due to hardware problems the **z**-component of **B$_{1eff}$** is sufficiently large, then full excitation may be impossible to achieve.

But what if **B$_{1eff}$** is only slightly off-resonance? The rotational trajectories of a perfectly on-resonance pulse and a slightly off-resonance pulse are illustrated in Figure 3.15. Although the on-resonance pulse has a more efficient rotation trajectory, which reduces the duration of the pulse needed to tip the

(A)   (B)

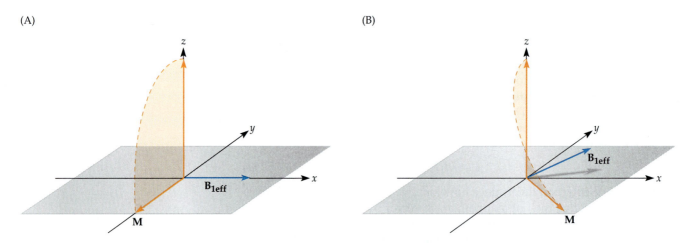

Figure 3.15 On-resonance and off-resonance excitation. Application of an on-resonance excitation pulse (A) will efficiently tip the longitudinal magnetization into the transverse plane (orange trajectory). But application of an off-resonance excitation pulse (B) will result in an inefficient trajectory (blue) that takes longer to completely tip the magnetization. The goal of excitation is to achieve full rotation of the magnetization from the longitudinal axis to the transverse plane.

magnetization into the transverse plane, it is still possible to achieve full excitation using the off-resonance pulse. However, this full excitation comes at the cost of additional time (required to traverse the longer path to the transverse plane), and if the duration of the pulse is held constant there will only be incomplete excitation.

electromotive force A difference in electrical potential that can be used to drive a current through a circuit. The MR signal is the electromotive force caused by the changing magnetic field across the detector coil.

Thought Question

If the excitation pulse is only slightly off-resonance, it is still possible to reach full excitation, but if the pulse is considerably off-resonance, then full excitation cannot be reached. Based on what you have learned (and Figure 3.15), what is the threshold angle of B_{1eff} beyond which full excitation cannot be achieved?

Signal Reception

So far, we have shown that an electromagnetic excitation pulse applied by a transmitter coil can change the net magnetization of a spin system. To measure this change, we need another receiver coil (or detector coil). Receiver coils acquire signal through the mechanism of electromagnetic coupling, as governed by Faraday's law of induction. After the magnetization of the sample is tipped to the transverse plane, its precession at the Larmor frequency sweeps across the receiver coil, causing the magnetic flux (Φ) experienced by the receiver coil to change over time (Figure 3.16). This change of flux, $d\Phi/dt$, in turn induces an **electromotive force (emf)** in the coil. By definition,

$$\mathrm{emf} = -\frac{d\Phi}{dt} \qquad [3.42]$$

where the magnetic flux penetrating the coil area is given by $\Phi = \int_s B(dS)$. The measurement of electromotive force in a receiver coil is known as reception.

(A)   (B)

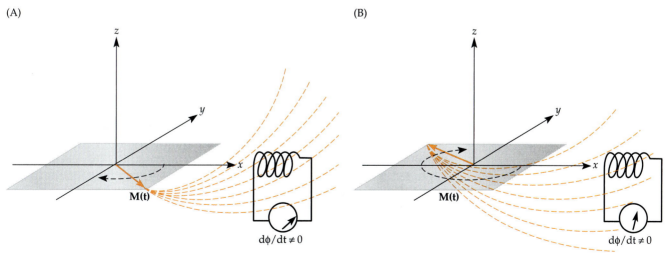

Figure 3.16 MR signal reception. As the net magnetization rotates through the transverse plane, the amount of magnetic flux experienced by the receiver coil changes over time (A and B). The changing flux generates an electromotive force, which provides the basis for the MR signal.

principle of reciprocity The rule stating that the quality of an electromagnetic coil for transmission is equivalent to its quality for reception (i.e., if it can generate a homogeneous magnetic field at excitation, it can also receive signals uniformly).

relaxation A change in net magnetization over time.

The excitation–reception process simulates the scenario of mutual coupling of two coils. Just as a current change in one coil induces a similar current change in another nearby coil through mutual inductance, magnetic field changes in a sample (i.e., the brain) induce magnetic field changes in the receiver coil. The magnetic flux generated by the sample and penetrating through the receiver coil can be represented as:

$$\Phi(t) = \int_v \overline{B}_1(M(t)dv) \qquad [3.43]$$

where $\overline{B}_1$ is the magnetic field per unit current of the receiver coil and $M(t)$ is the magnetization created by the sample.

This relation shows that the magnetic flux through the receiver coil actually depends on the magnetic field that could be produced by the coil. That is, the stronger the magnetic field that can be generated by a coil, the better its reception. Likewise, if a radiofrequency coil can generate a homogeneous magnetic field within a sample for transmission, it can also receive signals uniformly within the sample. These relations are consistent with the **principle of reciprocity.**

Substituting Equation 3.43 into Equation 3.42, we get:

$$emf = -i\omega_o \int_v \overline{B}_1(M(t)dv) \qquad [3.44]$$

The additional scaling factor ω_0 comes from taking the time derivative of $M(t)$, which contains the term $\omega_0 t$ (consult Equation 3.28).

Note that the electromotive force (emf) oscillates at the Larmor frequency like the excitation pulses themselves, so that the receiver coil must be tuned to the resonant frequency to best measure the changes in MR signal. Since both M and ω_0 are proportional to the main field strength B_0, the measured emf is proportional to B_0^2. Simply stated, the amount of MR signal received by the detector coil increases with the square of the magnetic field strength. Unfortunately for high-field MRI, the amplitude of noise in the MR signal is also proportional to the strength of the magnetic field, so the signal-to-noise ratio increases only linearly with B_0. The effects of field strength on signal and noise will be discussed in detail in Chapter 9.

Equation 3.44 also confirms that before the excitation pulse tips the net magnetization into the transverse plane, there is no detectable emf and thus no MR signal. This is because when the net magnetization is in its original longitudinal direction, its amplitude and direction do not change, so there is no signal to be measured by the receiver coil (Figure 3.17A and B). We emphasize that only changes in the transverse plane contribute to the MR signal.

Spin Relaxation

The MR signal created following an excitation pulse does not last indefinitely; it decays over time, generally within a few seconds. This phenomenon is called spin **relaxation.** Two primary mechanisms contribute to the loss of the MR signal: longitudinal relaxation (Figure 3.18A) and transverse relaxation (Figure 3.18B). For a given substance (e.g., water, fat, or bone) in a magnetic field of a given strength, the rates of longitudinal and transverse relaxation are given as time constants, which we introduce in this section. (We provide the mathematical derivation of these equations in the next chapter.)

When the excitation pulse is taken away, the spin system gradually loses the energy absorbed during the excitation. The simplest way to think about this energy loss is by using the quantum mechanics perspective. As they lose

(A)

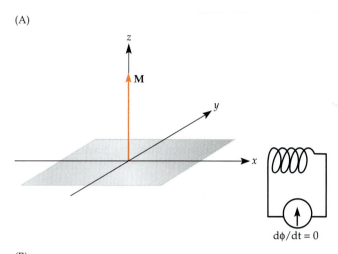

Figure 3.17   Effects of net magnetization orientation upon recorded MR signal. When the net magnetization is along the longitudinal axis (A), there is no detectable change in the magnetic field and thus no electromotive force in the detector coil. After the net magnetization has been tipped into the longitudinal axis (B), its motion causes changes in the measured current within the detector coil. Magnetization must be in the transverse plane for detection using MR.

(B)

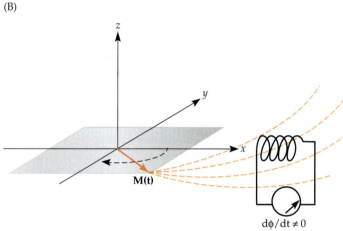

energy, excited spins in the high-energy (antiparallel) state go back to their original low-energy (parallel) state. This phenomenon is known as **longitudinal relaxation,** or **spin–lattice relaxation,** because the individual spins are losing energy to the surrounding environment, or lattice of nuclei. As

longitudinal relaxation (or spin–lattice relaxation)   The recovery of the net magnetization along the longitudinal direction as spins return to the parallel state.

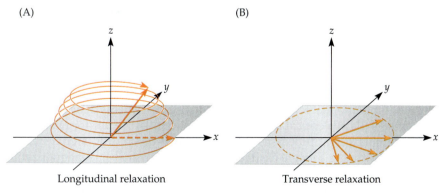

Figure 3.18 T_1 and T_2 relaxation. Schematic illustration of longitudinal relaxation, or T_1 recovery (A), and of transverse relaxation, or T_2 decay (B). The time constant T_1 governs the rate at which longitudinal magnetization recovers, while the time constant T_2 governs the rate at which longitudinal magnetization decays. Note that T_2^* relaxation is similar to T_2 relaxation, except that the decay of transverse magnetization results from both spin–spin interactions (as in T_2) and local field inhomogeneities.

T$_1$ (recovery) The time constant that describes the recovery of the longitudinal component of net magnetization over time.

transverse relaxation The loss of net magnetization within the transverse plane due to the loss of phase coherence of spins.

T$_2$ (decay) The time constant that describes the decay of the transverse component of net magnetization due to accumulated phase differences caused by spin–spin interactions.

T$_2^*$ (decay) The time constant that describes the decay of the transverse component of net magnetization due to both accumulated phase differences and local magnetic field inhomogeneities. T$_2^*$ is always shorter than T$_2$. BOLD-contrast fMRI relies on T$_2^*$ contrast.

more and more individual spins return to their low-energy state, the net magnetization likewise returns to be parallel to the main field. From a classical mechanics point of view, the transverse magnetization is gradually going back to the longitudinal direction, as it was before the excitation pulse. Because the total magnetization is constant, the growth of the longitudinal magnetization naturally results in a smaller transverse magnetization and hence also a smaller MR signal. The time constant associated with this longitudinal relaxation process is called **T$_1$**, and the relaxation process is called **T$_1$ recovery**. The amount of longitudinal magnetization, M_z, present at time t following an excitation point is given by Equation 3.45, where M_0 is the original magnetization.

$$M_z = M_0(1 - e^{-t/T_1})$$ [3.45]

After the net magnetization is tipped into the transverse plane by an excitation pulse, it is initially coherent, in that all of the spins in the sample are precessing around the main field vector at about the same phase. That is, they begin their precession within the transverse plane at the same starting point. Over time, the coherence between the spins is gradually lost and they become out of phase. This phenomenon is known as **transverse relaxation.** In general, there are two causes for transverse relaxation, one intrinsic and the other extrinsic. The intrinsic cause is from spin–spin interaction: When many spins are excited at once, there is loss of coherence due to their effects on one another. As an analogy, consider a single race car driving rapidly around a track; the driver can adopt a high and constant speed because no other cars are present. But in a pack of many cars, the movement of one car influences the speed of the others, making it impossible for all the cars to maintain a constant high speed. Likewise, interactions among spins cause some to precess faster, and some slower, causing the relative phases of the precessing spins to gradually fan out over time. The signal loss by this intrinsic mechanism is called **T$_2$ decay** (Equation 3.46) and is characterized by a time constant known as **T$_2$.**

$$M_{xy} = M_0 e^{-t/T_2}$$ [3.46]

An additional, extrinsic source of differential spin effects is the external magnetic field. More often than not, the external field is inhomogeneous. Because each spin precesses at a frequency proportional to its local field strength, variations in field from location to location cause spins at different spatial locations to precess at different frequencies, also leading to the loss of coherence. The combined effects of spin–spin interaction and field inhomogeneity lead to signal loss known as **T$_2^*$ decay,** characterized by the time constant **T$_2^*$.** Note that T$_2^*$ decay is always faster than T$_2$ decay alone, since it includes an additional factor of field inhomogeneity, and thus for any substance the time constant T$_2^*$ is always smaller than T$_2$. The equation for T$_2^*$ decay is similar to that for T$_2$ decay. We will discuss T$_2^*$ decay again in Chapter 5 because it plays a critical role in the BOLD contrast we use for fMRI.

These relaxation processes constrain how much MR signal can be acquired following a single excitation pulse. Since transverse magnetization decays over a short period of time, there is a limited window within which MRI data can be collected. To acquire an entire image, a pulse sequence often must excite the sample many times to allow collection of all data points. The trade-offs between MR signal and acquisition time are discussed further in Chapter 5. It is important to realize that relaxation processes are not a problem for MRI, but instead they provide the capability for measuring different properties of bulk matter. The versatility of MRI as an imaging tool results from its sensitivity to different relaxation properties of tissues.

The Bloch Equation

The physical principles introduced in this chapter provide an overview of MR signal generation, including establishment of net magnetization of a spin system within a magnetic field, excitation of those spins using electromagnetic pulses, reception of MR signal in detector coils, and relaxation of magnetization over time. Because these components are related, we can describe MR phenomena in a single equation, which modifies Equation 3.33 by adding T_1 and T_2 effects:

$$\frac{d\mathbf{M}}{dt} = \gamma \mathbf{M} \times \mathbf{B} + \frac{1}{T_1}(\mathbf{M}_0 - \mathbf{M}_z) - \frac{1}{T_2}(\mathbf{M}_x + \mathbf{M}_y) \qquad [3.47]$$

Stated generally, the net magnetization vector of a spin system precesses around the main magnetic field axis at the Larmor frequency, with its change in the longitudinal or z-direction governed by T_1 and its change in the transverse plane governed by T_2. This equation is called the **Bloch equation,** after the physicist Felix Bloch, and it describes the behavior of magnetization in the presence of a time-varying magnetic field. As we will learn in the following chapters, solving this equation leads to mathematical representations of the evolution of magnetization at steady state, during excitation, and during relaxation. It provides the theoretical foundation for all MRI experiments.

Bloch equation An equation that describes how the net magnetization of a spin system changes over time in the presence of a time-varying magnetic field.

Summary

A set of physical principles underlies the generation of MR signal. The primary concept is that of nuclear spin. Atomic nuclei with a magnetic moment and angular momentum are known as spins and exhibit rapid gyroscopic precession in an external magnetic field. The axis around which they precess is known as the longitudinal direction, and the plane in which they precess is known as the transverse plane. Each spin adopts either a low- or high-energy state, parallel or antiparallel to the magnetic field, respectively. Under normal conditions, the net magnetization across all spins is a vector parallel to the static magnetic field. By applying an electromagnetic pulse that oscillates at the resonant (Larmor) frequency of the spins, a process known as excitation, one can tip the net magnetization vector from the longitudinal direction into the transverse plane. This causes the net magnetization to change over time in the transverse plane, generating MR signal that can be measured in an external detector coil. A single formula known as the Bloch equation forms the basis for the quantitative description of magnetic resonance phenomena.

Suggested Readings

Haacke, E. M., Brown, R. W., Thompson, M. R., and Venkatesan, R. (1999). *Magnetic Resonance Imaging: Physical Principles and Sequence Design.* John Wiley & Sons, New York. A comprehensive encyclopedia of the theoretical principles of MRI.

Jin, J. (1999). *Electromagnetic Analysis and Design in Magnetic Resonance Imaging.* CRC Press, Boca Raton, FL. This book describes the basic theory and design underlying the structure of MRI scanners.

Slichter, C. P. (1990). *Principles of Magnetic Resonance* (3rd ed.). Springer-Verlag, New York. Provides a detailed mathematical treatment of the physics of MRI.

4

Basic Principles of
MR Image Formation

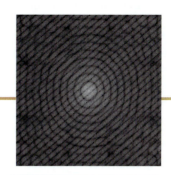

Introduction

As its name implies, the goal of magnetic resonance imaging is the formation of an image. It is important to recognize, however, that in the context of MRI, an **image** is not a photograph of the object being scanned, but rather it is a map that depicts the spatial distribution of some property related to the spins within the sample. Those properties might reflect the density of the spins, their mobility, or the T_1 or T_2 relaxation times for the tissues in which the spins reside. For example, T_1-weighted images depict the spatial distribution of T_1 values, so that voxels with short T_1 values are bright and voxels with long T_1 values are dark. Similarly, T_2^* images, as used in BOLD-contrast fMRI, are brighter where T_2^* values are long and darker where T_2^* values are short. Images can also be constructed that depict the spatial distribution of statistical properties, such as the difference between two experimental conditions. We will return to the construction of this type of image in Chapter 12.

While creating an image from MR signal may seem to be trivial or commonplace, remember from Chapter 1 that more than 25 years passed between the first NMR experiment (1945) and the first MR image (1972). Indeed, during that period, researchers actively strove to make their samples as homogeneous as possible so that no spatial variability could corrupt the data. Remember also that the 2003 Nobel Prize in Physiology or Medicine was awarded not for the discovery of medical applications of magnetic resonance, but instead for the development of techniques for image formation. In this chapter, we describe the fundamental concepts of image formation by illustrating how spatial information is encoded and decoded by MRI scanners. Specific topics include slice excitation, frequency encoding, phase encoding, and the representation of MRI data in *k*-space.

The fundamental concept underlying image formation in MRI is that of the magnetic gradient, or spatially varying magnetic field. In the first MRI experiments conducted by Purcell, Bloch, and other early researchers, the magnetic fields used were uniform, so that all spins in the entire sample experienced the same magnetic field. But as Lauterbur later demonstrated, superimposition of a second magnetic field that varies linearly across space will cause spins at different locations to precess at different frequencies in a controlled fashion. By measuring changes in magnetization as a function of

image A visual description of how one or more quantities vary over space.

Larmor frequency The resonant frequency of a spin within a magnetic field of a given strength. It defines the frequency of electromagnetic radiation needed during excitation to make spins change to a high-energy state, as well as the frequency emitted by spins when they return to the low-energy state.

B The sum of all magnetic fields experienced by a spin.

Bloch equation An equation that describes how the net magnetization of a spin system changes over time in the presence of a time-varying magnetic field.

spatial gradient (G) A magnetic field whose strength varies systematically over space. Note that since a given spatial location only experiences one magnetic field, which represents the sum of all fields present, spatial gradients in MRI act to change the effective strength of the main magnetic field over space.

precession frequency, the total MR signal can be parsed into components associated with different frequencies. We will thus begin this chapter by analyzing MR signal using the Bloch equation and by discussing the influence of magnetic gradients upon the MR signal.

Analysis of MR Signal

Recall that the precession frequency of a spin within a magnetic field (i.e., the **Larmor frequency**) is determined by two factors: the gyromagnetic ratio, which is a constant for a given atomic nucleus, and the magnetic field strength (see Equation 3.14). Likewise, the net magnetization of a spin system precesses around the main field axis at the Larmor frequency when tipped toward the transverse plane (see Equation 3.28). Since the Larmor frequency depends upon the strength of the magnetic field, changes in the strength of the magnetic field will also change the Larmor frequency. Keep in mind that during MR imaging, a spin experiences only one magnetic field, **B**, which represents the sum of all magnetic fields at its location.

In the previous chapter, we described two types of magnetic fields that are important for the generation of MR signal: the static (or main) field, **B$_0$**, and the electromagnetic (or radiofrequency) field, **B$_1$**. The static magnetic field aligns the precession axes of the nuclei and generates the net magnetization, **M**, and the electromagnetic field excites the net magnetization so that it can be measured in detector coils. The combined effects of these fields upon the net magnetization of a spin system were described by the **Bloch equation** (see Equation 3.47). We now introduce a third kind of magnetic field, the **spatial gradient, G**, which alters the precession frequencies of spins dependent upon their spatial location. With the addition of gradient fields as a component of **B**, we will solve the Bloch equation to account for all external magnetic fields, including gradient fields that vary over space. This will allow us to understand the strategies used for image formation. We repeat the Bloch equation here as Equation 4.1 for ease of reference:

$$\frac{d\mathbf{M}}{dt} = \underbrace{\gamma \mathbf{M} \times \mathbf{B}}_{\substack{\text{Precession} \\ \text{term}}} + \underbrace{\frac{1}{T_1}(\mathbf{M}_o - \mathbf{M}_z)}_{T_1 \text{ term}} - \underbrace{\frac{1}{T_2}(\mathbf{M}_x + \mathbf{M}_y)}_{T_2 \text{ term}} \qquad [4.1]$$

$$\underbrace{\phantom{\frac{d\mathbf{M}}{dt}}}_{\substack{\text{Change in} \\ \text{magnetization} \\ \text{over time}}}$$

The Bloch equation describes the change in net magnetization as the sum of three terms. As given by the precession term, the MR signal precesses around the main axis of the magnetic field at a rate given by the gyromagnetic ratio and the field strength (see Figure 3.11). The T$_1$ term indicates that the longitudinal component of the net magnetization recovers at a rate given by T$_1$ (see Figure 3.18A), and the T$_2$ term indicates that the transverse component of the net magnetization decays at a rate given by T$_2$ (see Figure 3.18B). Remember that in MR, the term *longitudinal* refers to the axis parallel to the main magnetic field and the term *transverse* refers to the plane perpendicular to the main magnetic field.

We will next attempt to solve the Bloch equation to determine the MR signal at each point in time, *M(t)*. First we break down the Bloch equation, which describes the MR signal in a three-dimensional vector format, into a simplified scalar form along each axis. Figure 4.1 illustrates that the net magnetization vector can be thought of either as a single vector in three dimen-

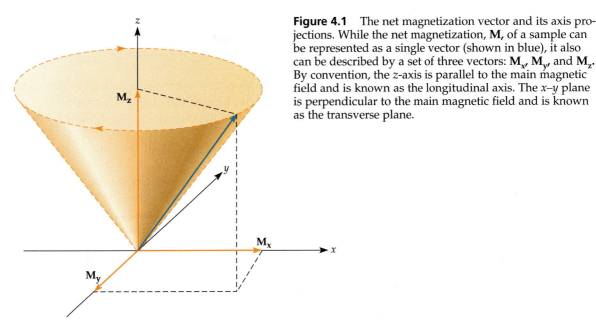

Figure 4.1 The net magnetization vector and its axis projections. While the net magnetization, **M,** of a sample can be represented as a single vector (shown in blue), it also can be described by a set of three vectors: $\mathbf{M_x}$, $\mathbf{M_y}$, and $\mathbf{M_z}$. By convention, the z-axis is parallel to the main magnetic field and is known as the longitudinal axis. The x–y plane is perpendicular to the main magnetic field and is known as the transverse plane.

sions or as a set of three vectors along each of the three cardinal axes. To represent the Bloch equation in scalar form, we need to isolate changes along each axis. Note that the behavior of the net magnetization in the x- and y-axes depends on both the precession term and the T_2 term. In contrast, the change in magnetization in the z-axis depends only on the T_1 term. Considering the axes separately, we can rearrange Equation 4.1:

$$\frac{dM_x}{dt} = \gamma M_y B - \frac{M_x}{T_2} \qquad [4.2a]$$

$$\frac{dM_y}{dt} = -\gamma M_x B - \frac{M_y}{T_2} \qquad [4.2b]$$

$$\frac{dM_z}{dt} = -\gamma \frac{(M_z - M_0)}{T_1} \qquad [4.2c]$$

So, Equations 4.2a and 4.2b describe the changes in the x- and y-directions of the magnetization over time, as the spin precesses about the main axis. The time constant T_2 specifies the rate of decay of magnetization in the transverse plane defined by the x- and y-axes, but it has no effect upon the longitudinal magnetization along the z-axis. Equation 4.2c describes the change in the longitudinal magnetization over time, as it recovers at a rate specified by T_1.

Longitudinal Magnetization (M_z)

The longitudinal magnetization depends only on a single equation (4.2c), which is a first-order ordinary differential equation. Thus, its solution is an exponential recovery function that describes the return of the main magnetization to the original state. Equation 4.3 replaces dM_z/dt with a mathematical equivalent, $d(M_z - M_0)/dt$, that represents the change in longitudinal magnetization from the fully relaxed state, M_0:

$$\frac{d(M_z - M_0)}{dt} = -\frac{M_z - M_0}{T_1} \qquad [4.3]$$

Swapping sides for dt and $M_z - M_0$, we get:

$$\frac{d(M_z - M_0)}{M_z - M_0} = -\frac{dt}{T_1}$$ [4.4]

By integrating both sides of this equation, we obtain Equation 4.5. This equation states that the natural log of the change in longitudinal magnetization over time (0 to t') is equal to the change in time divided by the constant T_1:

$$ln[M_z(t) - M_0]\Big|_0^{t'} = -\frac{t}{T_1}\Big|_0^{t'}$$ [4.5]

If we assume that the initial magnetization at time zero is given by M_{z0}, the solution for M_z at a later time point (t) is given by Equation 4.6. This equation states that the longitudinal magnetization (M_z) is equal to the fully relaxed magnetization, plus the difference between the initial and fully relaxed magnetization states, multiplied by an exponential time constant. Note that since M_{z0} is always less than M_0, the exponential term describes how much longitudinal magnetization is lost at a given point in time. As t increases, more longitudinal magnetization is recovered and the signal M_z approaches the fully relaxed signal M_0:

$$M_z = M_0 + (M_{z0} - M_0)e^{-t/T_1}$$ [4.6]

To illustrate T_1 recovery, let us consider some extreme values for the initial magnetization, M_{z0}. Consider when the net magnetization is fully relaxed (Figure 4.2A). Here, M_{z0} is equal to M_0, and the term ($M_{z0} - M_0$) will therefore be zero. Once the net magnetization is fully relaxed, it does not change over time, as indicated by the horizontal line segment. However, after an excitation pulse is applied (Figure 4.2B), the net magnetization is tipped entirely into the transverse plane and the net longitudinal magnetization is zero. The subsequent recovery of longitudinal magnetization is given by:

$$M_z = M_0(1 - e^{-t/T_1})$$ [4.7]

as shown in Figure 4.2C. This equation is important for determining the imaging parameters for T_1-contrast images. For example, by choosing when to acquire an image, we can make that image more or less sensitive to T_1 dif-

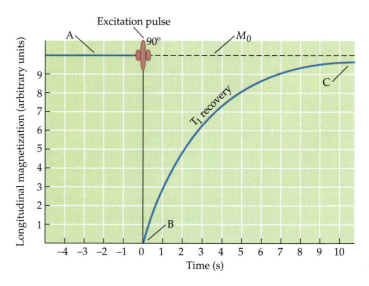

Figure 4.2 The change in longitudinal magnetization over time is known as T_1 recovery. When fully recovered (A), the longitudinal magnetization is at its maximum value, as shown by the dotted line, and does not change over time. However, following an excitation pulse that tips the net magnetization into the transverse plane, there will be zero longitudinal magnetization (B). As time passes following excitation, the longitudinal magnetization recovers toward its maximum value (C). The time constant T_1 governs this recovery process.

ferences between tissues. The details of pulse sequences used for T_1 contrast generation are further discussed in Chapter 5.

Solution for Transverse Magnetization (M_{xy})

The solution for the transverse magnetization is complicated by the fact that we must now consider the plane defined by two axes, x and y. Equations 4.2a and 4.2b reorganize the Bloch equation, treating the precession term as one-dimensional projections along the x- and y-axes of an object undergoing circular motion and the T_2 term as a decay factor (Figure 4.3). Solving for M_x and M_y, given an initial magnetization of $(-M_0, 0)$, we get the following equation pair:

$$M_x = (-M_0 \cos \omega t)e^{-t/T_2} \qquad \text{[4.8a]}$$

$$M_y = (M_0 \sin \omega t)e^{-t/T_2} \qquad \text{[4.8b]}$$

Though these equations appear complex, each describes two components that are illustrated in Figure 4.3. The parenthetical term (e.g., $M_0 \cos \omega t$) describes a one-dimensional projection of circular motion with constant velocity. The exponential term (i.e., e^{-t/T_2}) describes the decay of the circle over time. Together, they form an inward spiral pattern. As time (t) increases, the transverse magnetization will spiral farther inward and more and more transverse signal will be lost. The constant T_2 determines the rate at which the

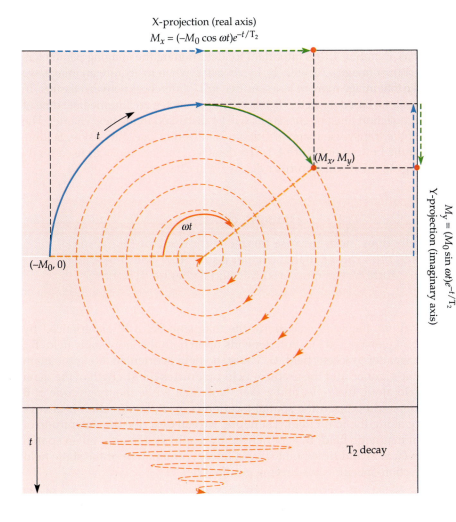

Figure 4.3 The change in transverse magnetization over time (t). The magnetism in the transverse plane is a vector defined by its angle and magnitude. As time passes, its angle follows a circular motion with constant angular velocity ω, while its magnitude decays with time constant T_2. These two components combine to form the inward spiral path shown (dashed lines). Shown at the top and right sides of the spiral path are its projections onto the x- and y-axes, respectively. Within each axis, the projection of the transverse magnetization is a one-dimensional oscillation, as illustrated by the blue and green lines. This oscillation is shown over time at the bottom of the figure, which illustrates the decaying MR signal.

phase Accumulated change in angle.

spiral shrinks. The quantity ωt is the angle of the net magnetization within the transverse plane and thus determines how fast the spiral turns.

We can combine the x- and y-components of the net magnetization into a more generalized single quantity, M_{xy}, which represents the transverse magnetization. The quantity M_{xy} is traditionally represented as a complex number, with one dimension represented using a real component and another represented using an imaginary component (Equation 4.9). The distinction between real and imaginary components will be very useful for the discussion of image formation later in this chapter.

$$M_{xy} = M_x + iM_y = -M_0(\cos \omega t - i \sin \omega t)\, e^{-t/T_2} \qquad [4.9]$$

This equation depends on a specific initial condition for (M_x, M_y) at $(-M_0, 0)$. For an arbitrary initial magnitude of the transverse magnetization $M_{xy0} = M_{x0} + iM_{y0}$, the transverse magnetization can be represented as:

$$M_{xy} = M_{xy0}\, e^{-t/T_2} e^{-i\omega t} \qquad [4.10]$$

Here we use the term, $e^{-i\omega t}$, which is identical to the term, $(\cos \omega t - i \sin \omega t)$, from Equation 4.9, to simplify the later derivation of the MR signal equation. The solution shown in Equation 4.10 states that the transverse magnetization depends upon three factors: the initial magnitude of the transverse magnetization (M_{xy0}), a loss of transverse magnetization over time due to T_2 effects (e^{-t/T_2}), and the accumulated **phase** ($e^{-i\omega t}$). Note that at $t = 0$, the exponential terms e^{-t/T_2} and $e^{-i\omega t}$ both reduce to $e^0 = 1$, so that the transverse magnetization is given by M_{xy0}. But after a long period of time (i.e., $t = \infty$), the term e^{-t/T_2} will become exceedingly small, and thus the transverse MR signal will be zero. Thus, Equation 4.10 is important for determining the imaging parameters for T_2-contrast images. As with T_1, by choosing when to acquire an image, we can make that image more or less sensitive to T_2 differences between tissues. To obtain contrast based upon the T_2 relaxation parameter, an intermediate time of image acquisition must be chosen, as will be discussed in the next chapter. The decay of the transverse magnetization, visualized in one dimension, is illustrated at the bottom of Figure 4.3. The details of pulse sequences used for T_2 contrast generation will be further discussed in Chapter 5.

Thought Question

Why does the transverse magnetization vector take a spiraling path rather than a circular path? How does the amplitude of the measured MR signal change over time?

Now (after the spin excitation), the magnetic field, **B**, experienced by spins at a given spatial location depends upon both the large static field, **B$_0$**, and the smaller gradient field, **G**. The static field is oriented along the main axis of the scanner, and the gradient field modulates the strength of the main static field along the x-, y-, and z-axes. Note that while the magnitude of **B** varies depending upon the spatial location (x, y, z), its direction is always pointing along the main field. Therefore, we can describe the magnitude of the total magnetic field, **B**, experienced by a spin system at a given spatial location (x, y, z) and time point (t) as a linear combination of the static field and direction-specific time-varying gradient fields:

$$B(t) = B_0 + G_x(t)x + G_y(t)y + G_z(t)z \qquad [4.11]$$

Knowing that $\omega = \gamma B$, we can substitute the ω term in Equation 4.10 using the magnitude of the total magnetic field described in Equation 4.11 and get the following rather intimidating equation. Here we have split the exponential $e^{-i\omega t}$ into separate terms that describe the accumulated phase caused by the strength of the static magnetic field (B_0) and by the time-varying gradient fields ($G_x(t)$, $G_y(t)$, $G_z(t)$):

MR signal The current measured in a detector coil following excitation and reception.

$$M_{xy}(x,y,z,t) = M_{xy0}(x,y,z)e^{-t/T_2}e^{-i\gamma B_0 t}e^{-i\gamma \int_0^t (G_x(t)x + G_y(t)y + G_z(t)z)dt} \qquad [4.12]$$

Again, although this equation has many components and seems complex, it can be broken down into simpler and more understandable parts. It states that the transverse magnetization for a given spatial location and time point, $M_{xy}(x, y, z, t)$, is governed by four factors: (1) the original magnetization at that spatial location, $M_{xy0}(x, y, z)$; (2) the signal loss due to T_2 effects, e^{-t/T_2}; (3) the accumulated phase due to the main magnetic field, $e^{-i\gamma B_0 t}$; and (4) the accumulated phase due to the gradient fields:

$$e^{-i\gamma \int_0^t (G_x(t)x + G_y(t)y + G_z(t)z)dt}$$

Note that this last factor is indicated as an integral over time because gradients may change over time in some forms of MRI. If a constant gradient along one direction were used (e.g., G along the x-direction), the accumulated phase it causes could be more simply described as $\gamma G_x t$.

Let us pause for a moment to review what we have learned so far. We know that the net magnetization of a sample within a magnetic field can be thought of as a vector with magnitude and direction. The net magnetization vector can be broken down into longitudinal (along the static magnetic field) and transverse (perpendicular to the static magnetic field) components. After the net magnetization is tipped toward the transverse plane by an excitation pulse, it precesses around the longitudinal axis at the Larmor frequency. The precession of the net magnetization in the transverse plane allows measurement of MR signal. We also have just learned that the introduction of a spatial magnetic gradient alters the transverse magnetization over time because the frequency of precession depends upon the local magnetic field strength. This last point suggests that spatial gradients may allow encoding of spatial information within the MR signal. We explore this possibility in the next section.

The MR Signal Equation

MRI does not use separate receiving antennae for individual voxels. Indeed, such a setup would be impossible given that there may be 100,000 or more voxels within a single imaging volume. We use instead a single antenna (e.g., a volume coil) that covers a large region. The **MR signal** measured by the antenna reflects the sum of the transverse magnetizations of all voxels within the excited sample. We emphasize this important point because it underlies all of the principles of image formation discussed later in this chapter: The total signal measured in MRI combines the changes in net magnetization generated at every excited voxel. This can be restated in the formal mathematical terms of Equation 4.13, which expresses the MR signal at a given point in time, $S(t)$, as the spatial summation of the MR signal from every voxel:

$$S(t) = \int_x \int_y \int_z M_{xy}(x, y, z, t)dx\, dy\, dz \qquad [4.13]$$

MR signal equation A single equation that describes the obtained MR signal as a function of the properties of the object being imaged under a spatially varying magnetic field.

slice A single slab of an imaging volume. A slice has thickness defined by the strength of the gradient and the bandwidth of the electromagnetic pulse used to select it.

Combining Equations 4.12 and 4.13 results in Equation 4.14:

$$S(t)=\int_x \int_y \int_z M_{xy0}(x,y,z)e^{-t/T_2}e^{-iw_0 t}e^{-i\gamma\int_0^t (G_x(t)x+G_y(t)y+G_z(t)z)dt}dx\,dy\,dz \quad [4.14]$$

Equation 4.14 can be read as stating that the total MR signal measured at any point in time reflects the sum across all voxels of the net magnetization at time point zero, multiplied by a decay factor based upon T_2, with accumulated phase given by the strength of the static magnetic field and of the gradient field at that point in space. This vastly important equation is known as the **MR signal equation,** because it reveals the relationship between the acquired signal, $S(t)$, and the properties of the object being imaged, $M(x,y,z)$. It is important to recognize that this equation is sufficiently general to describe the MR signal in virtually all imaging methods.

In practice, the term $e^{-i\omega_0 t}$ is not necessary for calculation of MR signal, because modern MRI scanners demodulate the detected signal with the resonance frequency ω_0. That is, they synchronize data acquisition to the resonance frequency. This demodulation process is analogous to the idea of transformation from laboratory to rotating reference frames, as introduced in Chapter 3. Imagine that you were watching the precession of the transverse magnetization from the laboratory (i.e., normal) reference frame. You would see the transverse magnetization spinning around the longitudinal axis at the Larmor frequency. Now imagine that you were rotating around the longitudinal axis at the same speed as the precessing magnetization. The magnetization vector would now appear to be still.

The T_2 decay term, e^{-t/T_2}, affects the magnitude of the signal but not its spatial location. Because it does not contain any spatial information, we can ignore it for the moment. By removing these two terms, we arrive at a simpler version of the MR signal equation:

$$S(t)=\int_x \int_y \int_z M_{xy0}(x,y,z)e^{-i\gamma\int_0^t (G_x(t)x+G_y(t)y+G_z(t)z)dt}dx\,dy\,dz \quad [4.15]$$

This equation illustrates the profound importance of the gradient fields for encoding spatial information within an MR image. In principle, we can collect a single MR image of an entire volume by systematically turning on gradient fields along x, y, and z. However, because three-dimensional (3-D) imaging sequences present additional technical challenges and are less tolerant of hardware imperfection, most forms of imaging relevant to fMRI studies use two-dimensional (2-D) imaging sequences. For the sake of simplicity, we will next discuss the principles underlying common 2-D imaging techniques. We will return to the less common 3-D imaging techniques at the end of this chapter.

Slice Selection, Spatial Encoding, and Image Reconstruction

Note that the simplified MR signal equation (see Equation 4.15) is still in 3-D form, in that the signal contribution from each spatial location depends upon all three spatial gradients. In order to reduce this signal equation to two dimensions, there must be some way to eliminate variation over one spatial dimension. This can be accomplished by separating the signal-acquisition process into two steps. First we select a particular **slice** within the total imaging volume using a one-dimensional excitation pulse. Then we use a two-dimensional encoding scheme within the slice to resolve the spatial distribution of the spin magnetizations. This two-step process forms the basis for most pulse sequences used in MRI, including those used for acquisition of fMRI BOLD images. We will discuss the theoretical bases for these steps in this section, and describe their practical implementation in the following sections.

The basic concept of **slice selection** is the application of an electromagnetic pulse that excites spins within one slice but has no effect on spins outside the slice. The slice chosen by the selection process is defined by its location, orientation, and thickness. For example, let us assume that we want to create an image of a plane centered at $z = z_0$. For a given location (x, y) within that slice, the total magnetization summed along the z-direction, $M(x,y)$, for a thickness Δz is given by Equation 4.16. This equation describes the bulk magnetization of an individual voxel, or x–y coordinate pair, within the slice.

$$M(x,y) = \int_{z_0 - \frac{\Delta z}{2}}^{z_0 + \frac{\Delta z}{2}} M_{xy0}(x,y,z)dz \qquad [4.16]$$

Note that since we are integrating all signals along the z-direction, the magnetization, M, is dependent only on x and y, but not on z. Thus, by first selecting an imaging slice, the simplified MR signal equation (see Equation 4.15) can be further reduced into a 2-D form, as follows:

$$S(t) = \int_x \int_y M(x,y)e^{-i\gamma \int_0^t (Gx(\tau)x + Gy(\tau)y)d\tau} \, dx \, dy \qquad [4.17]$$

Equation 4.17 states that the total signal recorded from a slice depends upon the net magnetization at every (x, y) location within that slice, with the phase of individual voxels dependent upon the strength of the gradient fields at that location. Although the parts of Equation 4.17 are individually understandable, this equation is difficult to visualize and solve in its present form. To facilitate a better understanding of the relation between the MR signal, $S(t)$, and the object to be imaged, $M(x,y)$, MR researchers have adopted a different notation scheme known as **k-space.** Recognize that k-space differs in an important way from normal image space, in which the object resides. Consider the terms k_x and k_y in Equation 4.18. Each equation represents the time integral of the appropriate gradient multiplied by the gyromagnetic ratio:

$$k_x(t) = \frac{\gamma}{2\pi} \int_0^t G_x(\tau)d\tau \qquad [4.18a]$$

$$k_y(t) = \frac{\gamma}{2\pi} \int_0^t G_y(\tau)d\tau \qquad [4.18b]$$

These equations state that changes in k-space over time, or **k-space trajectories,** are given by the time integrals of the gradient waveforms. In other words, the k-space trajectories are simply the areas under the gradient waveforms, as illustrated in Figure 4.4 for a uniform gradient change over a time interval (t). By substituting these terms into Equation 4.17, we can restate the MR signal equation using k-space coordinates:

$$S(t) = \int_x \int_y M(x,y)e^{-i2\pi k_x(t)x} \, e^{-i2\pi k_y(t)y}dx \, dy \qquad [4.19]$$

Equation 4.19 is remarkable, because it indicates that k-space and image space have a straightforward relation: they are 2-D Fourier transforms of each other. Any signal that changes over time or space, no matter how complex, can be constructed from a series of simpler components in the frequency or spatial-frequency domain, respectively (Figure 4.5A–C). The

slice selection The combined use of a spatial magnetic field gradient and an electromagnetic pulse to excite spins within a slice.

k-space A notation scheme used to describe MRI data. The use of k-space provides mathematical and conceptual advantages for describing the acquired MR signal in image form.

k-space trajectory A path through k-space. Different pulse sequences adopt different k-space trajectories.

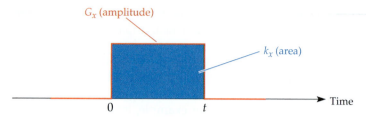

Figure 4.4 The relation between the gradient waveform and k-space. The effect of a gradient, G_x, upon a given voxel is expressed as the amplitude of the gradient signal over time. The change in k-space over time is given by the area under the square.

Fourier transform is one mathematical tool for this construction process. The mathematics of the Fourier transform are well established, so we can take advantage of those mathematics to decode the k-space representation of the MR signal, $S(t)$, into the magnetization at each spatial location, $M(x,y)$, creating a spatially informative image. Equation 4.19 suggests that an inverse Fourier transform can convert k-space data into an image, a process known

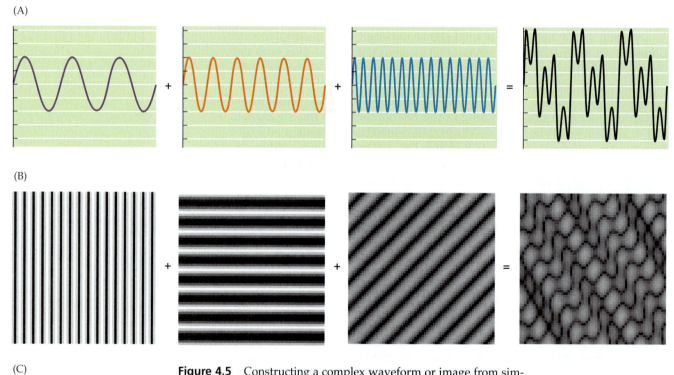

Figure 4.5 Constructing a complex waveform or image from simpler components. Any data, no matter how complex, can be constructed from simpler components. Shown in (A) are three sine waves, each with a different frequency. When combined, they form the waveform at right. By combining more and more sine waves of different frequencies and phases, very complex waveforms can be created, such as that of music. The same principle holds for two-dimensional data (B), except that here the components are gratings of particular spatial frequencies (i.e., how closely spaced are the bars), phases, and angles. By combining a very large number of these gratings, complex images can be created, such as those used in MRI. Shown in (C) is the k-space plot of the summed image; the individual gratings are associated with the three bright pixels.

Figure 4.6 Images and their Fourier transforms. (A) A single circle at the center of the image space and the representation of the circle in *k*-space. Note that the *k*-space representation follows a sinc function, with greatest intensity at the center and intensity bands of decreasing amplitude toward the edges of the *k*-space. Addition of a second circle to the image space (B) introduces a grating pattern to the *k*-space. An image of the brain (C) contains much more spatial information, and thus its representation in *k*-space is similarly more complex.

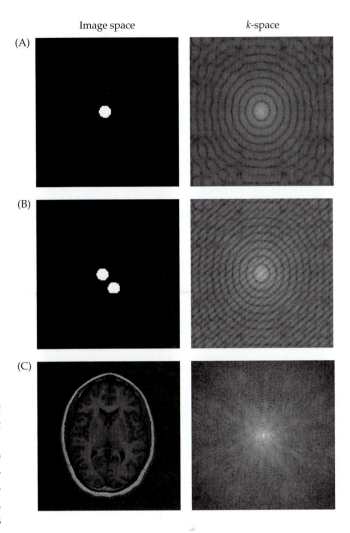

Image space   *k*-space

(A)

(B)

(C)

as **image reconstruction.** Conversely, a forward Fourier transform can convert image-space data into *k*-space data.

To illustrate the relation between image space and *k*-space, Figure 4.6 shows some sample images and the resulting Fourier transforms. Think of each pair as showing an object and the acquired MR signal in its raw form within *k*-space. An image with a single circle at its center corresponds to a pattern of alternating light and dark circles throughout *k*-space (Figure 4.6A). As an aside, this pattern is equivalent to a 2-D Bessel sinc function. Note that the center of *k*-space represents the point in time when signal from all voxels is at the same phase, so it represents the total transverse magnetization within that slice. Thus, the center of *k*-space always has the highest signal of any point.

We can add a second circle to the image to illustrate another concept, that *k*-space reflects the **spatial frequency** of the object(s) in the image space. Spatial frequency defines how often some pattern occurs in space, just like temporal frequency (e.g., musical pitch) defines how often something occurs in time. Shown in Figure 4.6B are two circles, one offset from center. If we trace a line from the top left to the bottom right of the image, it will encounter two circles separated by a distance between their centers. The *k*-space data will thus have a spatial-frequency component along that line, with frequency equal to the inverse of that distance. This is visible as a grating running from top left to bottom right in the *k*-space image, on top of the concentric pattern that results from the shape of the circles.

image reconstruction The process by which raw MR signal, as acquired in *k*-space form, is converted into spatially informative images.

spatial frequency The frequency with which some pattern occurs over space.

Thought Question

How would the *k*-space data in Figure 4.6B change if the lower circle were moved to the bottom-left quadrant of the image? How would the *k*-space data change if it were moved farther toward the bottom-right corner?

Any image, no matter how complex, can be represented as an ensemble of spatial-frequency components. The *k*-space representation of an anatomical image is shown in Figure 4.6C. The *k*-space image is brightest in the center and darkest near the edges. This illustrates that low-spatial-frequency data from near the center of *k*-space is most important for determining the signal-to-noise ratio of the image. In comparison, high-spatial-frequency data collected at the periphery of *k*-space helps to increase the spatial resolution of the image. Figure 4.7 illustrates this important distinction between the low-spatial-frequency and high-spatial-frequency regions of *k*-space. If from a normal photograph (Figure 4.7A) we take only the low-spatial-frequency region of its *k*-space data, the image would have most of the signal but would lack good spatial resolution (Figure 4.7B). But if we take only the high-spatial-frequency region of its *k*-space data, the image would have a low signal level but the spatial detail would be preserved (Figure 4.7C).

Contrary to intuition, there is *not* a one-to-one relation between points in *k*-space and voxels in image space. For an illustration of what each point in *k*-space represents, consider Figure 4.8. The center plot shows the *k*-space data (or raw MR signal). Each point in the *k*-space data is acquired at a different point in time and has contributions from all voxels within the slice. We have highlighted four sample *k*-space points, each showing the net magnetization vectors within each voxel (in image space) at the moment in time when that point in *k*-space was acquired. For the point at the center of *k*-space (Figure 4.8A), all of the magnetization vectors are at the same phase, and thus the total signal is at its maximum. At other *k*-space points (Figure 4.8B–D), the magnetization vectors differ across voxels, and the intensity of

Image space   *k*-space

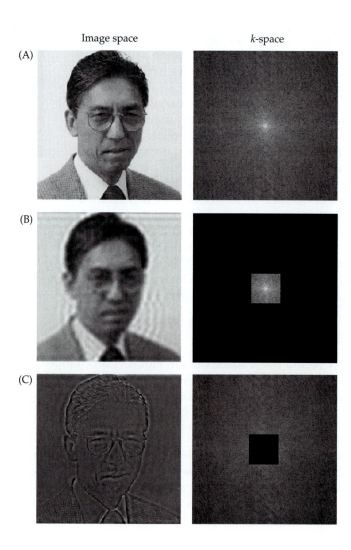

Figure 4.7 How different parts of *k*-space contribute to image space. Images such as this photograph of Dr. Seiji Ogawa can be converted using a Fourier transform into *k*-space data (A). Different parts of the *k*-space data correspond to different spatial-frequency components of the image. The center of *k*-space (B) provides low-spatial-frequency information, retaining most of the signal but not fine details. The periphery of *k*-space (C) provides high-spatial-frequency information, and thus image detail, but contributes relatively little signal to the image.

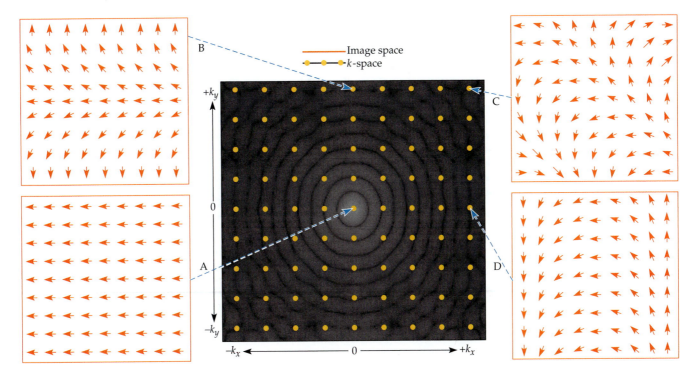

Figure 4.8 Contributions of different image locations to the raw *k*-space data. Each data point in *k*-space (shown in yellow) consists of the summation of MR signal from all voxels in image space under corresponding gradient fields. For four sample *k*-space points (A–D), the magnetization vectors across voxels in image space are illustrated. For the center of *k*-space, the phases for all voxels in the respective image space are identical (A), therefore leading to the maximum signal in *k*-space. For a data point where k_y is at the maximum and k_x is at zero (B), the phases of magnetization vectors in image space change rapidly along the *y*-direction but remain the same along the *x*-direction. For a data point where both k_x and k_y are large (C), the phases change rapidly along the combined diagonal direction. And finally, where k_y is zero and k_x is at its maximum (D), the phases change rapidly only along the *x*-direction.

the *k*-space point represents the sum of those vectors. In the section on 2-D spatial encoding, we will discuss how MR scanners adjust the spatial gradients over time to systematically sample all of these *k*-space points.

In summary, the process of 2-D image formation has the following stages shown in the flowchart below. First, the longitudinal magnetization of a single slice is tipped into the transverse plane by a process known as slice excitation. Next, the resulting transverse magnetization is encoded into two-dimensional raw data represented in *k*-space. Finally, the desired MR image is reconstructed using a two-dimensional inverse Fourier transform. We will discuss the practical implementation of these steps in the following sections.

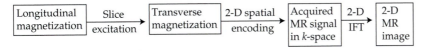

Slice Excitation

As indicated in the theoretical discussion in the previous section, the first step in an imaging sequence is slice selection. Remember that the goal of slice selection is to excite only a particular thin slab of the sample so that signal within that slab can be spatially encoded. From Chapter 3 we know that an electromagnetic field (**B₁**) at the Larmor frequency, when applied in the transverse plane, tips the longitudinal magnetization. If the duration and

(A)

(B)

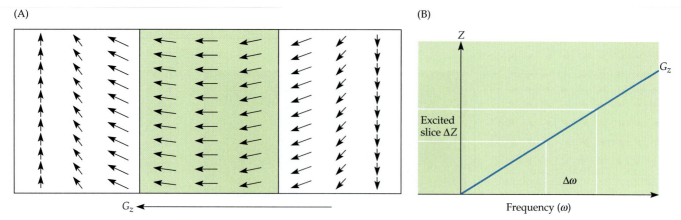

Figure 4.9 Slice selection. As shown in (A), application of a slice selection gradient (G_z) changes the Larmor frequency of spins within the sample. The gradient is chosen so that spins within the slice of interest (shading) will precess at the desired frequency. Following the application of the gradient, a subsequent excitation pulse at a given frequency (ω) and bandwidth ($\Delta\omega$) is applied. As shown in (B), the excitation frequency and frequency bandwidth determine the slice location (Z) and slice thickness (ΔZ).

interleaved slice acquisition The collection of data in an alternating order, so that data is first acquired from the odd-numbered slices and then from the even-numbered slices, to minimize the influence of excitation pulses upon adjacent slices.

strength of the electromagnetic field are appropriately calibrated, the longitudinal magnetization will rotate exactly into the transverse plane. Such a calibrated electromagnetic field is known as an excitation pulse. But if the magnetic field were uniform, the applied excitation pulse would affect all of the spins within the volume. However, by introducing a static gradient along the slice selection axis (e.g., G_z), we can tune the Larmor frequencies of all spins in the slice (and only spins in the slice) to match the frequency of the excitation pulse (Figure 4.9A and B).

Ideally, we would like to excite a perfectly rectangular slice along the z-direction; for example, we might excite all spins from z = +10 mm to z = +15 mm and no spins outside of that range. One might think that this could be achieved by a rectangular slice selection pulse, as shown in Figure 4.10A. However, a rectangular pulse actually contains a distribution of frequencies shaped like a sinc function, so it does not excite a rectangular slice. Instead, we must use a sinc-modulated electromagnetic pulse (Figure 4.10B). Since the Fourier transform of a sinc function is a rectangular function, a sinc-modulated pulse has a rectangular frequency response; thus it contains all frequencies within a band and no frequencies outside that band.

Although a perfectly rectangular slice profile would be optimal, it is difficult to achieve because of off-resonance excitation. As discussed in the previous chapter, off-resonance effects may excite spins to some intermediate stage, as they rotate about the $\mathbf{B_{1eff}}$ field. The primary consequence for fMRI is cross-slice excitation, or the bleeding of excitation from one slice to the next. If we excite adjacent slices sequentially (i.e., first, second, third, etc.), each slice will have been pre-excited by the previous excitation pulse, leading to saturation of the MR signal. To minimize this problem, most excitation schemes use **interleaved slice acquisition.** For example, if we are to excite ten contiguous slices, we will excite in order the first, third, fifth, seventh, ninth, second, fourth, sixth, eighth, and tenth slices. The use of interleaved slice acquisition effectively eliminates excitation overlap problems.

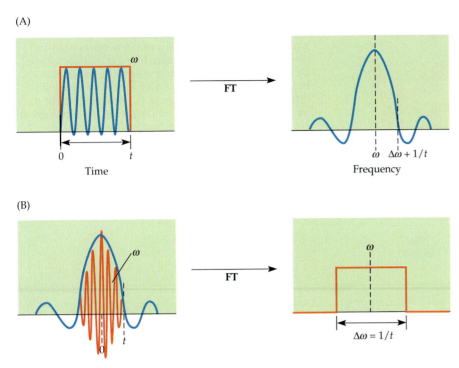

(A)

ω

FT

0   t

Time

ω   Δω + 1/t

Frequency

(B)

ω

FT

ω

0   t

Δω = 1/t

Figure 4.10 Possible slice selection pulses. (A) A rectangular slice selection pulse that consists of a constant application of a radiofrequency field at frequency ω_0 for a time t. The slice selection profile of this pulse is given by its Fourier transform (FT) and shown at right as a sinc function with fundamental frequency ω_0. This profile is not ideal for selection of a rectangular slice. However, (B) shows the use of a pulse with time amplitude given by a sinc function. This pulse gives a rectangular frequency profile and allows excitation of spins within a rectangular slice.

Slice location and thickness are determined by three factors: the center frequency of the excitation pulse (ω), the bandwidth of the excitation field ($\Delta\omega$), and the strength of the gradient field (G_z), as illustrated in Figure 4.11. Together, the center frequency and the gradient field determine the slice location, while the bandwidth and the gradient field determine the slice thickness. By sliding the center frequency up and down over successive acquisitions, MR signal from different slices can be selectively acquired. Likewise, by choosing a wide or narrow excitation bandwidth, thick or thin slices can be collected. Note that use of a stronger gradient, in principle, means that spins at nearby spatial locations will have greater differences in their Larmor frequencies, allowing more-selective excitation by a given electromagnetic pulse. Thus, stronger gradients increase spatial resolution across slices.

Thought Question

Assume that we doubled the strength of the gradient fields in our scanner. How would the frequency and bandwidth of the excitation pulse need to change to keep the same slice selection?

(A)

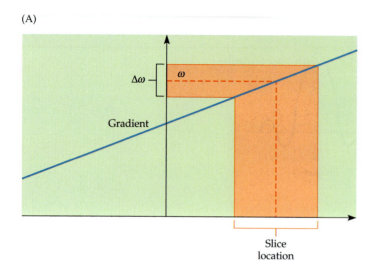

Figure 4.11 Changing slice thickness and location. (A) The combined use of a linear gradient (solid line) and a radiofrequency pulse with a center frequency (ω) and bandwidth (Δω) to select a slice location (horizontal axis). By changing the slope of the gradient (B), the same radiofrequency pulse can be used to select a slice with a different location and thickness. (C) By changing the center frequency of the excitation pulse to ω′, the same gradient can be used to select a different slice location.

(B)   (C)

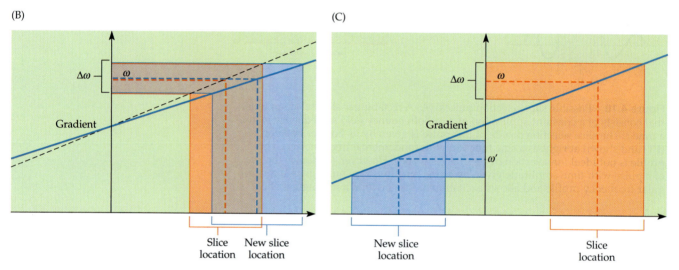

filling *k*-space The process of collecting samples from throughout *k*-space in order to collect data sufficient for image formation.

2-D Spatial Encoding

Once spins are excited within the desired slice, they can be spatially encoded so that MR signal from different parts of the image can be resolved. A unique frequency is assigned to all voxels within the slice, in a process known as frequency and phase encoding, to facilitate later reconstruction of the signal using the Fourier transform. To do this, a gradient magnetic field that differs across two dimensions (e.g., G_x, G_y) is applied to the sample. These gradients influence the individual spin phases for different voxels, as illustrated in Figure 4.12. To understand how the scanner hardware and software accomplish the encoding process, we must return to the concept of *k*-space. As we learned earlier in this chapter, if we reorganize signal $S(t)$ to $S(k_x(t), k_y(t))$ as indicated in Equation 4.19, then the MR signal can be represented by a 2-D function in a coordinate system where k_x and k_y are the two axes. This coordinate system defines *k*-space and has units in spatial frequency (1/distance). Because a complete sample of the *k*-space is usually required to construct an image, collecting the MR signal is often referred to as **filling *k*-space.**

Remember from Figure 4.4 that k_x and k_y are actually time integrals of the gradient waveform. Thus, by manipulating the gradient waveforms, we can

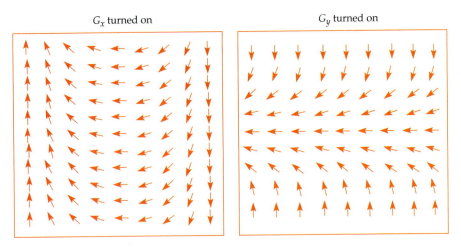

G_x turned on G_y turned on

Figure 4.12 Effects of magnetic field gradients on spin phase. Application of magnetic field gradients influences the frequency of spins over space, and thus the accumulated phase over time. Shown are examples of gradients in the x- and y-directions.

control the sampling path within k-space during MR signal acquisition. For example, by altering the strength of different gradients over time, we could first collect data from the upper-left point in k-space, and then move rightward, and then downward, and then leftward, etc., tracing a snakelike path throughout the image. While any path that covers all of k-space can be used to collect the k-space data, in practice regular paths such as straight lines are preferred.

In typical anatomical imaging sequences (Figure 4.13A), k-space is filled one line at a time, following a succession of individual excitation pulses. During each excitation the combination of the electromagnetic pulse and the G_z gradient selects the desired slice. Then the G_y gradient is turned on before the data acquisition period, so that it accumulates a certain amount of phase offset before the activation of the G_x gradient. This results in the movement

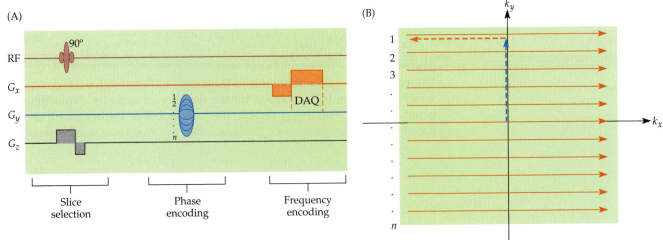

Figure 4.13 A typical two-dimensional gradient-echo pulse sequence. Shown in (A) are lines representing activity of the radiofrequency field (RF) and the three spatial gradients. The pulse sequence begins with a combined slice selection gradient (G_z) and excitation pulse. The G_y gradient is used for selecting one line of k-space following each excitation pulse, while the G_x gradient is turned on during data acquisition (DAQ). This sequence is known as a gradient-echo sequence, and it acquires each line of k-space following a separate excitation (B). Following n excitations, all of k-space is filled and image acquisition is complete.

phase-encoding gradient A gradient turned on before the data acquisition period, so that spins can accumulate differential phase offset over space.

frequency-encoding gradient A gradient turned on during the data acquisition period, so that the frequency of spin precession changes over space.

field of view (FOV) The total extent of an image along a spatial dimension.

of the effective location of data acquisition in k-space along the y-direction, as shown by the blue arrow in Figure 4.13B. In this example, G_y can be considered to be the **phase-encoding gradient.** During data acquisition, the G_x gradient is turned on, changing the frequency of the spins, so by convention G_x becomes the **frequency-encoding gradient.** Note, however, that both gradients act similarly in k-space, because k_x and k_y both reflect the time integrals of the gradient waveforms.

Recognize that k-space is sampled in a discrete fashion. Along the k_y direction, each line represents a separate amplitude of the G_y gradient (shown as 1...n steps in Figure 4.13). While the trajectory along the k_x direction is continuous, the MR signal is sampled digitally with a specific interval, so that each row consists of a number of discrete data points.

2-D Image Formation

After k-space is filled, a 2-D inverse Fourier transform is necessary for conversion of the raw data from k-space to image space, $M(x,y)$. It is important to recognize that the sampling parameters in these two spaces are inversely proportional to each other. In image space, the basic sampling unit is distance, while in k-space, the basic sampling unit is spatial frequency (1/distance). Qualitatively speaking, this means that a wider range of coverage in k-space results in higher spatial resolution in image space (i.e., smaller voxels). This concept can be appreciated by the photographs shown in Figure 4.7, which demonstrate that the periphery of k-space contributes to fine details of the image (i.e., spatial resolution). Conversely, finer sampling in k-space results in a greater extent of coverage, or a larger field of view, in the image domain. This relationship is illustrated graphically in Figure 4.14A–C and quantitatively in Equation 4.20a,b. Here, **field of view (FOV)** is defined as the total spatial extent along a dimension of image space (i.e., how large the image is). Typical fields of view in fMRI experiments are about 20 to 24 cm.

$$\text{FOV}_x = \frac{1}{\Delta k_x} = \text{sampling rate along } k_x = \frac{1}{\frac{\gamma}{2\pi}(G_x \Delta t)} \qquad [4.20a]$$

$$\text{FOV}_y = \frac{1}{\Delta k_y} = \text{sampling rate along } k_y = \frac{1}{\frac{\gamma}{2\pi}(\Delta G_y t)} \qquad [4.20b]$$

These equations can be reorganized (Equation 4.21a,b) to give the voxel size, which is just the FOV divided by the number of samples. Note that the quantities $2k_{x\text{max}}$ and $2k_{y\text{max}}$ refer to the total extent of k-space along each of the cardinal dimensions. If k_{max} is large, then the voxel size will be small.

$$\frac{\text{FOV}_x}{M_x} = \frac{1}{M_x \Delta k_x} = \frac{1}{2k_{x\text{max}}} \qquad [4.21a]$$

$$\frac{\text{FOV}_x}{M_y} = \frac{1}{M_y \Delta k_y} = \frac{1}{2k_{y\text{max}}} \qquad [4.21b]$$

In summary, the raw MR signal, $S(t)$, is a one-dimensional string of data points through k-space that has been sampled at a very high rate. This signal can be broken into two dimensions, according to k_x and k_y, to facilitate a 2-D inverse Fourier transform. Decreasing the separation between adjacent data points in k-space increases the FOV in image space. Likewise, increasing the extent of k-space decreases the voxel size in image space. Note also that if we

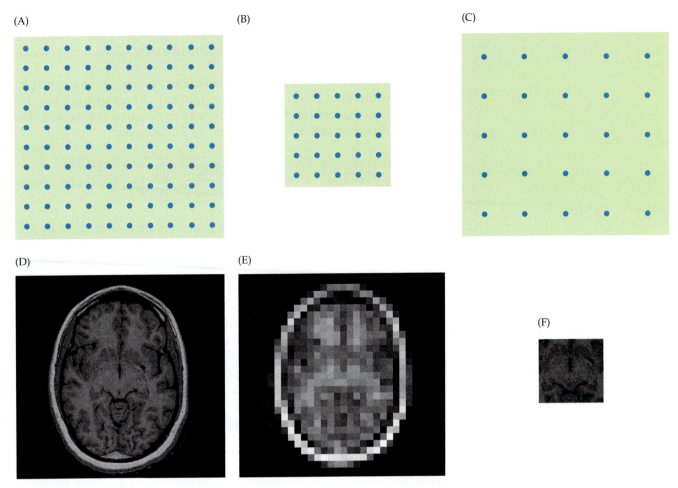

Figure 4.14 Effects of sampling in *k*-space upon the resulting images. Field of view and resolution have an inverse relation when applied to image space and *k*-space. (A) A schematic representation of densely sampled *k*-space with a wide field of view, resulting in the high-resolution image (D). (B) If only the center of *k*-space is sampled, albeit with the same sam-pling density, then the resulting image (E) has the same field of view but lower spatial resolution. (C) Conversely, if *k*-space is sampled across a wide field of view but with a limited sampling rate, the resulting image will have a small field of view but high resolution (F).

want to collect $N \times N$ voxels worth of data in our image, then we need an equal number of *k*-space data points ($N \times N$).

3-D Imaging

While 2-D imaging methods are common for most applications, not all MR imaging techniques are based on 2-D principles. Pulse sequences that collect *k*-space data in three dimensions are often used, especially for high-resolution anatomical images. Compared with 2-D imaging, 3-D sequences provide the primary advantage of a high signal-to-noise ratio, due to the fact that the 3-D volume can be larger than a single slice and therefore more excited spins can contribute to the MR signal. The principles of 3-D imaging can be easily extrapolated from those of 2-D imaging, so in theory any 2-D imaging sequence can be converted to 3-D. Since slice selection is unnecessary, the traditional slice excitation step is replaced by a volume excitation step that uses a very small *z*-gradient to select a thick slab. To resolve spatial information along the z-direction, another phase-encoding gradient is presented along that dimension during the data acquisition phase. Therefore, within a typical 3-D pulse sequence, there are two phase-encoding gradients and one frequency-encoding gradient.

The concept of k-space can be expanded to three dimensions by adding k_z, defined by the time integral of the G_z gradient. To reconstruct the 3-D images, an inverse Fourier transform in three dimensions is executed. The following flowchart summarizes the steps of 3-D imaging:

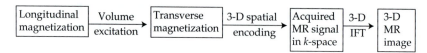

Unfortunately, the advantages of 3-D sequences are accompanied by several disadvantages. For example, the dimension of phase encoding usually is more vulnerable to field inhomogeneities and motion artifacts than the dimension of frequency encoding. Because 3-D imaging methods have two phase-encoding dimensions, they are more vulnerable to these artifacts. Also, more time is required to fill k-space when an entire volume is excited than when only a single slice is excited. Thus, movement of the head at any point within the acquisition window will cause distortions throughout the entire imaging volume. Within fMRI studies, 3-D imaging is typically restricted to anatomical scans, since the major classes of BOLD fMRI pulse sequences use 2-D methods.

Potential Problems in Image Formation

The goal of any image formation method is to achieve a true representation of the imaged object. Of course, in an ideal scanning environment with a perfectly uniform main magnetic field, exactly linear gradient fields, an absolutely square excitation profile, and optimized image acquisition software, there could be no problems! Under such perfect conditions, the acquired image will exactly match the scanned object in every way. It will be of the same size and shape, with local intensities dependent on the appropriate proton density and relaxation characteristics. Yet, as anyone with substantial MRI experience will attest, the images acquired under normal laboratory conditions are not always faithful to the original objects. We next consider some of the typical problems encountered in forming MR images.

The first problem to consider is inhomogeneity of the static magnetic field, meaning that the actual value of the field at one or more spatial locations is not the same as the theoretically desired quantity. Note that inhomogeneity of the static magnetic field across space becomes of increasing concern at higher field strengths, because it becomes more difficult to adequately shim the field to correct for local distortions. The imperfection in the static field can be mathematically represented by a difference quantity, ΔB_0, representing the increased or decreased field strength at a given location. Equation 4.22 is a modified version of the MR signal equation that contains the new term ΔB_0:

$$S(t) = \int_x \int_y m(x,y)e^{-i2\pi(k_x(t)x + k_y(t)y + \Delta B_0 t)}dxdy \qquad [4.22]$$

We usually do not know the exact nature of static field inhomogeneities, but if present they will introduce artifacts to images, following conventional

(A)   (B)
      Original image   Distorted image

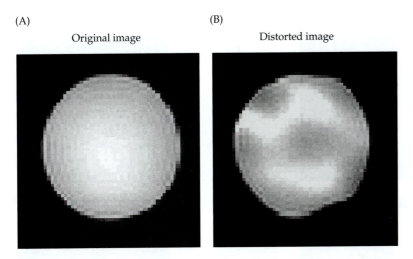

Figure 4.15 Spatial and intensity distortions due to magnetic field inhomogeneities. Under a homogeneous magnetic field, the image of a circular phantom is
itself circular and of relatively similar intensity throughout (A). Local magnetic
field inhomogeneities cause two types of distortions, geometric distortions and signal losses, both of which are visible on the distorted image (B).

inverse Fourier transformation. In practice, ΔB_0 can lead to two distinct
types of artifacts: geometric distortions and variations in signal intensity. We
can think of these artifact types, taken roughly, as macroscopic and microscopic effects.

Large-scale inhomogeneities cause geometric distortions due to spatial
shifting of voxels. Because the frequency of spins depends upon the magnetic field strength, magnetic field inhomogeneities will lead to changes in
spin frequencies. Remember from earlier in this chapter that the position of
a voxel is encoded by its spin frequency. Thus, a voxel with the incorrect
spin frequency will be displaced to an incorrect spatial location. Small-scale
inhomogeneities cause spins within a voxel to lose coherence due to T_2^*
effects. This reduces the total magnetization available within a voxel and
thus reduces its signal intensity. These two effects may be present within the
same image (Figure 4.15).

A second problem results from nonlinearities of the gradient fields.
Because the spatial gradients control the k-space trajectories, we use k-space
to evaluate their artifacts. Again, we consider a typical gradient-echo pulse
sequence. First, if the x-gradient G_x is off by a small amount, as shown in
Figure 4.16A, the resulting k-space trajectories will have an error along the
k_x direction. Second, if the y-gradient G_y is off, the k-space trajectories will be
skewed along the k_y direction (Figure 4.16B). Note that this skew affects both
the onset of each line in k-space as well as the path taken through k-space.
The magnitude of this skew depends on the time integral of the gradient
amount. Third, if the z-gradient G_z is off, the slope of the excitation gradient
will be altered. Altering the slope of the slice-selection gradient can compromise the match between the gradient-induced changes in spin frequency
and the excitation pulse. However, because the k-space trajectory in the x–y
plane would not change, the shape of the object would not be distorted.
Thus, problems with the G_z gradient can lead to changes in slice thickness
and signal intensity (Figure 4.16C).

Figure 4.16 Image distortions caused by gradient problems. Each row shows the ideal image, the problem with acquisition in *k*-space, and the resulting distorted image. (A) Problems with the *x*-gradient will affect the length of the trajectory along the *x*-dimension in *k*-space, resulting in an image that appears compressed. (B) Problems with the *y*-gradient will affect the path taken through *k*-space over time, resulting in a skewed image. (C) Problems with the *z*-gradient will affect the match of excitation pulse and slice selection gradient, here resulting in a thinner slice and reduced signal intensity.

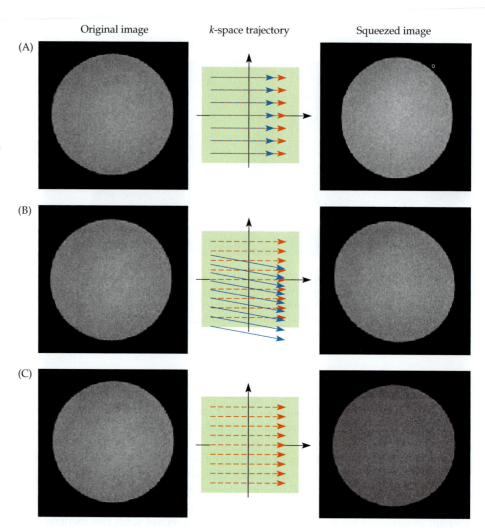

Original image   k-space trajectory   Squeezed image

(A)

(B)

(C)

Summary

The net magnetization of a spin system, as described by the Bloch equation, can be broken down into separate spatial components along the *x*-, *y*-, and *z*-axes. By convention, the longitudinal magnetization is defined as $\mathbf{M_z}$ and the transverse magnetization is defined as $\mathbf{M_{xy}}$. The recovery of the longitudinal magnetization following excitation is governed by the time constant T_1, while the decay of the transverse magnetization following excitation is governed by the time constant T_2. The total MR signal measured is the combination of the transverse magnetization from all voxels in the sample and can be described using a single equation. The use of spatial gradients is necessary for measurement of spatial properties of a sample, in essence allowing MR to become MRI. The simultaneous application of a G_z gradient and an excitation pulse allows selection of a defined slice within the imaging volume. The use of two additional gradients within the slice allows unique encoding of spatial locations. Image acquisition can be considered using the concept of *k*-space, which reflects the Fourier transform of image space. Different pulse sequences sample *k*-space differently, and the inverse relation between sampling in *k*-space and sampling in image space is important to understand. Inhomogeneities in the magnetic field experienced by spins can cause systematic artifacts in the reconstructed images, in the form of geometric distortions and signal loss.

Suggested Readings

Bracewell, R. N. (1986). *The Fourier Transform and Its Applications*, McGraw-Hill, New York. A textbook for everything you want to know (and more) about the Fourier transform.

Haacke, E. M., Brown, R. W., Thompson, M. R., and Venkatesan, R. (1999). *Magnetic Resonance Imaging: Physical Principles and Sequence Design*, John Wiley & Sons, New York. A comprehensive encyclopedia of the theoretical principles of MRI.

Twieg, D. B. (1983). The *k*-trajectory formulation of the NMR imaging process with applications in analysis and synthesis of imaging methods. *Med. Phys.*, 10(5): 610–621. An original description of the *k*-space trajectory formulation.

5

MR Contrast Mechanisms and Pulse Sequences

Compared to other methods for neuroimaging, MRI is extraordinarily versatile. Brain images can be generated to emphasize contrast due to different tissue characteristics. We now extend our previous discussion of contrast to include different contrast mechanisms. **Static contrasts** are sensitive to the type, number, and relaxation properties of atomic nuclei within a voxel. Typical static contrasts include density (e.g., proton density), relaxation time (e.g., T_1, T_2, T_2^*), content of a particular molecular type (e.g., magnetization transfer to detect large or small molecules), and general chemical content (e.g., spectroscopy). We use images based upon static contrast to determine brain anatomy in fMRI experiments. **Motion contrasts** are sensitive to the movement of atomic nuclei. Typical motion contrasts provide information about the dynamic characteristics of the proton pools in the brain, such as blood flow through MR angiography, water diffusion through diffusion-weighted imaging, or capillary irrigation through perfusion-weighted imaging. Since nearly all fMRI studies use fast imaging techniques, we will also discuss some of the most common techniques and their pulse sequences in this chapter.

A further distinction can be drawn depending on whether contrast depends on intrinsic properties of biological tissue (i.e., **endogenous contrast**) or upon the presence of foreign substances that have been introduced into the body (i.e., **exogenous contrast**). The BOLD-contrast mechanism is an example of an endogenous contrast mechanism, in that it depends upon the amount of deoxygenated hemoglobin within a brain region. An example of an exogenous contrast mechanism is the injection of gadolinium-DTPA, a rare earth compound that has extremely high magnetic susceptibility, which greatly distorts the surrounding magnetic field. The use of exogenous contrast agents is a common practice in clinical MRI, but it is less prevalent in functional studies due to the obvious safety issues associated with any injections. In the following sections, we will focus on endogenous contrast measures, especially those commonly used in structural and functional brain imaging. Potentially valuable advances in exogenous contrast agents are considered in later chapters.

static contrasts Contrast mechanisms that are sensitive to the type, number, and relaxation properties of spins (e.g., T_1, T_2, proton density).

motion contrasts Contrast mechanisms that are sensitive to the movement of spins through space (e.g., diffusion, perfusion).

endogenous contrast Contrast that depends upon an intrinsic property of biological tissue.

exogenous contrast Contrast that requires the injection of a foreign substance into the body.

repetition time (TR) The time interval between successive excitation pulses, usually expressed in seconds.

Static Contrasts and Related Pulse Sequences

Static contrast mechanisms have been widely used for MRI due to their ability to illustrate basic tissue characteristics. To understand how static contrast can be generated, we consider first the simple cases of T_1 and T_2 contrast. As derived in the previous chapters, there are two equations for magnetization after an initial excitation of a fully recovered spin system (Figure 5.1A and B). Equation 5.1 describes the longitudinal magnetization:

$$M_z(t) = M_0(1 - e^{-t/T_1})$$ [5.1]

Equation 5.2 describes the transverse magnetization:

$$M_{xy}(t) = M_0 e^{-t/T_2}$$ [5.2]

There are two important factors that govern the time at which MR images are collected. The first factor is the time interval between successive excitation pulses, which is known as **repetition time,** or **TR.** Oftentimes, consecutive excitations occur at time intervals not long enough to allow full recovery of the longitudinal magnetization. Under such short TRs, the transverse magnetization, which directly translates to detectable MR signal, should be described as

$$M_{xy}(t) = M_0(1 - e^{-TR/T_1})e^{-t/T_2}$$ [5.3]

This equation illustrates that MR signal depends not only on the original magnetization (which in turn depends upon proton density) but also on the properties of the tissue being imaged, as expressed through both T_1 and T_2 constants (Table 5.1). Shown in this table are rough values for the time con-

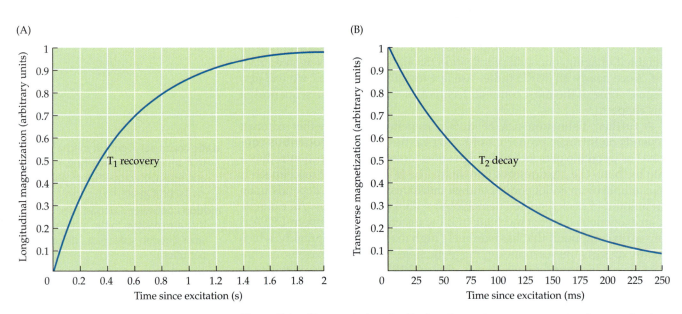

(A)

(B)

Figure 5.1 Changes in longitudinal and transverse components of magnetization. (A) The time constant T_1 is usually on the order of 1 s, so recovery of longitudinal magnetization (T_1 recovery) occurs over a period of several seconds. (B) The time constant T_2 is typically on the order of a few tens of milliseconds, so decay of transverse magnetization occurs over a period of about 100 ms. The values used for T_1 and T_2 in these plots are similar to those for gray matter at field strengths used for fMRI studies.

TABLE 5.1 Rough Values for the Time Constants T$_1$ and T$_2$ at Field Strength of 1.5 T

	Gray Matter	White Matter	Cerebrospinal Fluid
T$_1$	900 ms	600 ms	4000 ms
T$_2$	100 ms	80 ms	2000 ms

echo time (TE) The time interval between an excitation pulse and data acquisition (defined as the collection of data from the center of *k*-space), usually expressed in milliseconds.

proton-density imaging The creation of MR images that are sensitive to the number of protons present within each voxel.

stants T$_1$ and T$_2$ at a field strength of 1.5 T, which is most common for fMRI. These values are only approximate, because these constants can vary according to field homogeneity and other factors, and are intended to serve as a guideline for thinking about the contrast mechanisms discussed in this chapter. Another value of interest is the T$_2^*$ value for gray matter, which is about 40 ms at 1.5 T. This last value determines the TE used for BOLD-contrast fMRI images. In Equation 5.3, the term $(1 - e^{-TR/T_1})$ accounts for the incomplete recovery of the longitudinal magnetization. If TR is much longer than T$_1$, then this term approaches 1 (i.e., full recovery), and it can be removed from the equation.

The second factor is the time interval between excitation and data acquisition (of the center of *k*-space), which is known as **echo time,** or **TE.** Remember that the MR signal received at the center of *k*-space has the greatest amplitude, as described in the previous chapter, so at that point it resembles an echo of the initial transmission. We can replace the term *t* with TE to give the MR signal for an image with a given TE.

$$M_{xy}(t) = M_0(1 - e^{-TR/T_1})e^{-TE/T_2} \qquad [5.4]$$

Equation 5.4 provides the foundation for manipulating the signal from a particular tissue type by controlling TR and TE. However, in MRI we are interested in comparing MR signal across multiple tissue types. The signal difference between any two types of tissue is known as contrast. For tissue types A and B, the contrast between them, C_{AB}, is simply the difference between the MR signal associated with each (Equation 5.5). The terms M_{0A} and M_{0B} stand for the original magnetization for tissues A and B, the terms T$_{1A}$ and T$_{1B}$ stand for the values of A and B, and T$_{2A}$ and T$_{2B}$ stand for the T$_2$ values of A and B.

$$C_{AB} = M_{0A}(1 - e^{-TR/T_{1A}})e^{-TE/T_{2A}} - M_{0B}(1 - e^{-TR/T_{1B}})e^{-TE/T_{2B}} \qquad [5.5]$$

Proton-Density Contrast

One of the simplest forms of MR contrast is **proton-density imaging.** The net magnetization of each voxel is composed of individual spins within that voxel, typically hydrogen (i.e., protons). Proton-density images, as the name implies, provide contrast based on the sheer number of protons in a voxel, which of course differs across tissue types. To maximize proton-density contrast, researchers use pulse sequences that minimize T$_1$ and T$_2$ contrasts. To minimize T$_1$ contrast, a pulse sequence must use either a very short or very long TR, and to minimize T$_2$ contrast, a pulse sequence must use either a very short or very long TE. Logically, either long or short values for either parameter would work for proton-density weighting. In practice, however, the use of extremely short TR or long TE values results in little MR signal (see Figure 5.1). To maximize proton-density weighting while still recovering sufficient MR signal, pulse sequences are used that have very long TR

(A)

(B)

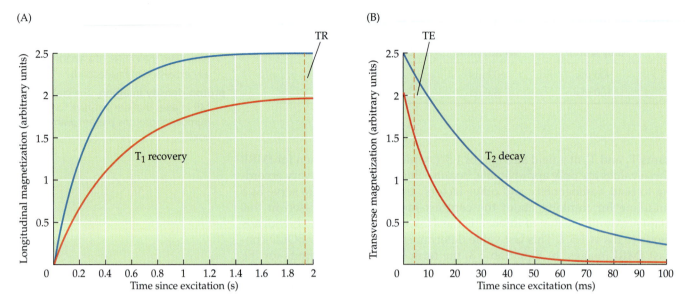

Figure 5.2 Selection of TR and TE values for proton-density contrast. The use of long TR (A) and short TE (B), (shown as vertical dashed lines in orange color) on two different tissues (red and blue), will minimize T_1 and T_2 effects, leaving only differences in overall signal intensity due to proton density.

gradient-echo (GRE) imaging One of the two primary types of pulse sequences used in MRI; it uses gradients to generate the MR signal changes that are measured at data acquisition.

(Figure 5.2A) and very short TE (Figure 5.2B). Practically, a TR greater than T_1 and a TE less than T_2 satisfy the criteria. If the TR used is much greater than the T_1 values of the tissue being imaged (e.g., 2 to 3 times as long), the protons will be nearly fully recovered after each excitation. Likewise, if the TE value is much less than the T_2 value (e.g., $1/10$ as long), there will be minimal decay before image acquisition.

> ### Thought Question
> How does the concept of proton density relate to the concept of net magnetization?

One disadvantage of using a very long TR is greatly increased imaging time. In many situations, such as when scanning patients who have difficulty tolerating lengthy MRI sessions, slow imaging sequences may not be feasible. To reduce acquisition time yet still maintain proton-density contrast, a smaller flip angle (<90°) for excitation may be used to only partially tip the longitudinal magnetization toward the transverse plane, which will in turn require less time to achieve full longitudinal recovery. The effect of using a smaller flip angle for partial excitation is illustrated in Figure 5.3, where it can be seen that a shorter TR can be used without introducing significant T_1 weighting, effectively reducing the imaging time. In summary, to generate images sensitive to proton density, we must collect those images using a pulse sequence with a long TR and short TE.

As long as there is sufficient T_1 recovery and minimal T_2 decay, any type of pulse sequence, including common **gradient-echo (GRE) imaging** and **spin-**

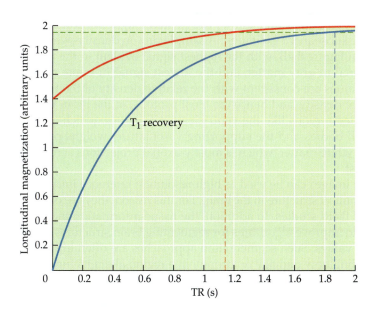

Figure 5.3   The use of a smaller flip angle in proton-density imaging. One approach for minimizing the acquisition time necessary for proton-density imaging is to reduce the flip angle of the excitation pulse. With a typical 90° excitation pulse the net magnetization (blue solid line) takes a long time to reach a near maximal level, as indicated by the blue dashed line. But if the flip angle of the excitation pulse is reduced, there is only partial excitation. In this latter case, the net magnetization (red solid line) reaches the same near maximal level much more rapidly, as indicated by the red dashed line.

echo (SE) imaging sequences, can acquire proton-density images. A gradient-echo sequence uses only gradients to generate the signal echo in the center of *k*-space. A spin-echo sequence, on the other hand, uses a second 180° electro-magnetic pulse, called a **refocusing pulse,** to generate the signal echo. We will discuss examples of these types of sequences throughout this chapter.

An example of a proton-density gradient-echo sequence, which is often used due to its very fast acquisition rate, is presented in Figure 5.4A. Here, the excitation pulse is immediately followed by the data acquisition (DAQ), so there is no significant signal decay due to transverse relaxation. In addi-

spin-echo (SE) imaging One of the two primary types of pulse sequences used in MRI; it uses a second 180° electro-magnetic pulse to generate the MR signal changes that are measured at data acquisition.

refocusing pulse A 180° electromagnetic pulse that compensates for the gradual loss of phase coherence following initial excitation.

(A)

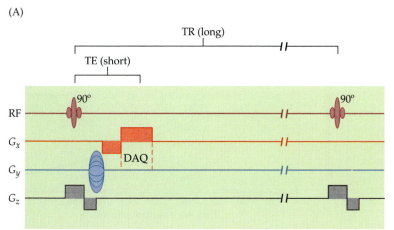

(B)

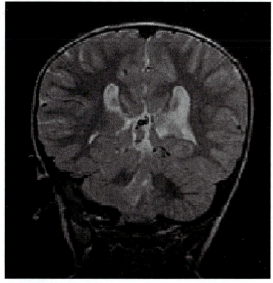

Figure 5.4   A pulse sequence used for proton-density imaging. The primary requirements for proton-density imaging are a very short TE and a very long TR, such as those used in this gradient-echo sequence (A). The resulting image (B) is brightest in voxels with high density (e.g., cerebrospinal fluid) and darkest in areas of low density (e.g., air, white matter).

T₁-weighted (T₁-dependent) Images that provide information about the relative T₁ values of tissue; also known as T₁ images.

tion, the very long repetition time allows the excited magnetization to fully recover before the subsequent excitation. A sample proton density–weighted image is shown in Figure 5.4B, with the highest signal evident in the ventricles, medium signal in gray matter, and the lowest signal in white matter. These intensity values are consistent with the relative density of the tissues. The greatest tissue density, and hence the most protons, in the brain will be found in fluid-filled regions like the ventricles. Gray matter, which is composed of both cell bodies and the supporting vasculature, weighs proportionally less, and white matter, which is mostly axonal projections across the brain, weighs least.

Proton-density images can be used as high-resolution reference images for determining anatomical structure in the brain. For this reason, they are often an important part of fMRI studies. In addition, the tissue information they provide can be used to improve algorithms for segmenting brain structures on the basis of intensity values. Such segmentation approaches are often important when understanding how damage or atrophy in a region alters its functional properties, such as in the study of disease or aging. Proton-density images are frequently acquired at the same slice locations as T₁- or T₂-weighted images so that complementary anatomical information can be acquired.

T₁ Contrast

While proton-density images have many uses, other forms of contrast emphasize different features of the brain. The most commonly used structural contrast for anatomical images of the brain is T₁ weighting. Images are called **T₁-weighted,** or **T₁-dependent,** if the relative signal intensity of voxels within the image depends upon the T₁ value of the tissue. Figure 5.5 provides

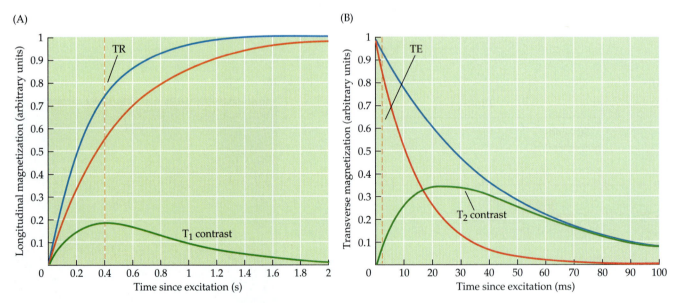

Figure 5.5 Selection of TR and TE values for T₁ contrast. The use of intermediate TR (A) and short TE (B), (shown as vertical lines in orange color) on two tissues (red and blue lines), will maximize the T₁ differences between tissues and minimize the T₂ differences between tissues. This combination provides T₁ contrast. The green lines show the MR signal based on the T₁ and T₂ differences, respectively, along time. Green lines show MR signal differences based on the T₁ and T₂ differences, respectively, along time.

an example of the TR and TE values necessary to generate T_1 contrast. At very short TRs, there is no time for longitudinal magnetization to recover and thus no MR signal is recorded for either tissue. Conversely, at very long TRs, all longitudinal magnetization recovers for both tissues. So, at short and long TR values, the amount of longitudinal magnetization will be similar between the tissues. At intermediate TRs, however, there are clear differences between them (Figure 5.5A). The tissue that has a shorter T_1 value recovers more rapidly and thus has greater MR signal. For any two tissues that differ in T_1, there is an optimal TR value that maximally differentiates between them.

To have exclusive T_1 contrast, we must also have a very short TE to minimize T_2 contrast. When TE is much less than T_2, the term e^{-TE/T_2} from Equation 5.4 becomes approximately equal to 1 (Figure 5.5B). Equation 5.5 then reduces to

$$C_{AB} = M_{0A}(1 - e^{-TR/T_{1A}}) - M_{0B}(1 - e^{-TR/T_{1B}}) \qquad [5.6]$$

which depends upon TR but not TE. It is worth noting that despite changes in TR and TE, the effect of proton density is always inherent in the contrast, as the number of spins in the imaging volume determines the original magnetization. In summary, to generate images sensitive to T_1 contrast, we must collect those images using a pulse sequence with intermediate TR and short TE.

Just as proton-density contrast can be generated with any type of pulse sequence, T_1 contrast will be evident using any pulse sequence that meets the above criteria (i.e., medium TR and short TE). In practice, both gradient-echo and spin-echo sequences are commonly used. Since a gradient-echo pulse sequence was used in the previous example, here a spin-echo pulse sequence is presented (Figure 5.6A). The hallmark of spin-echo sequences is the 180° refocusing pulse that is applied shortly after the initial 90° excitation pulse. The refocusing pulse corrects for phase dispersion due to T_2 effects, so that all spins are approximately in phase during the data acquisition period, which occurs at the time TE. This sequence elicits the most signal from white

(A)

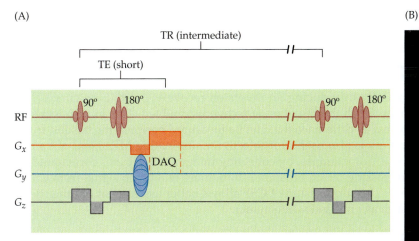

(B)

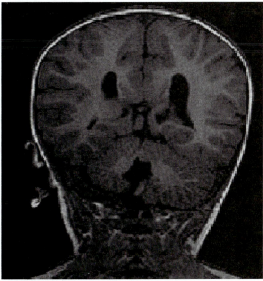

Figure 5.6   A pulse sequence used for T_1-weighted images. The primary requirements for T_1 imaging are a short TE and an intermediate TR. Either gradient-echo or spin-echo sequences can be used. Shown in (A) is a spin-echo sequence. The resulting image (B) is brightest in voxels with short T_1 values (e.g., white matter) and darkest in areas with long T_1 values (e.g., CSF).

(A)   (B)

Figure 5.7 Use of inversion recovery to increase T_1 contrast. By including a 180° inversion pulse before a typical gradient-echo or spin-echo sequence (A), the net magnetization can be flipped to the negative state. As a result, the net magnetization must recover over twice the dynamic range, and thus the relative difference in T_1 recovery between the tissues is increased. As illustrated in (B), the T_1 contrast is much greater for the same pair of tissues following an inversion pulse (blue curves) than under normal conditions (red curves). The green and purple lines indicate the differences between red curves and blue curves, respectively. Inversion recovery sequences are also used to eliminate MR signal from tissue of a particular type, by collecting images at a TR that corresponds to the zero crossing for that tissue (arrow).

inversion recovery A technique for increasing T_1 contrast by adding a 180° inversion pulse before a standard pulse sequence.

matter and bone marrow, due to their short T_1 values, and an intermediate amount of signal from gray matter. Since water has a very long T_1 value, very little signal is recovered from cerebrospinal fluid (CSF), which becomes nearly indistinguishable from air (Figure 5.6B).

To boost T_1 contrast, researchers often use a technique called **inversion recovery,** which begins the sequence with a 180° inversion pulse rather than the more common 90° pulse (Figure 5.7A). Because the inversion pulse flips the net magnetization to the negative state, it effectively doubles the dynamic range of the signal. To understand the advantage of inversion recovery, consider Figure 5.7B. Shown in red are typical effects of TR upon MR signal. By introducing an inversion recovery pulse (blue curves), the range over which the signal must recover is doubled. This in turn increases the maximal T_1 difference that can be measured between the tissues. Inversion recovery is also useful for selectively eliminating MR signal of a single tissue type. For example, by collecting images at a TR that corresponds to the zero crossing of cerebrospinal fluid, there will be no signal from CSF in any voxel. The suppression of CSF allows better assessment of other tissue types, such as gray and white matter.

T_2 Contrast

By using T_2-contrast imaging, images can be created that have maximal signal in fluid-filled regions, which is important for many clinical considerations. Many tumors, arteriovenous malformations (AVMs), and other pathological conditions show up most readily under T_2 contrast. High-resolution T_2 images are also used as anatomical references in fMRI studies, either in

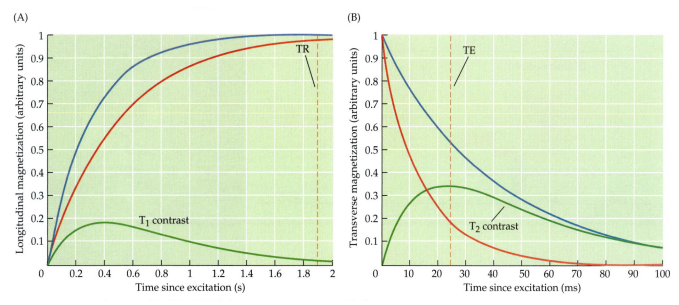

Figure 5.8   Selection of TR and TE values for T_2 contrast. The use of long TR (A) and intermediate TE (B) (shown as vertical lines in orange color) on two tissues (red and blue) will maximize the T_2 differences between tissues and minimize the T_1 differences between tissues. This combination provides T_2 contrast. The green lines show the MR signal based on the T_1 and T_2 differences, respectively, along time.

isolation or in conjunction with proton-density or T_1 images in a multi-contrast segmentation algorithm. Thus, common clinical protocols include both T_1- and T_2-weighted images.

For **T_2-weighted,** or **T_2-dependent** images, the amount of signal loss depends upon the time between excitation and data acquisition, or echo time (TE). Again, an optimal combination of TR and TE exists for any two tissues to maximize the T_2 contrast between them (Figure 5.8A). If an image is acquired immediately after excitation, such that the TE is very short, then little transverse magnetization will be lost regardless of T_2 and thus there will be no T_2 contrast. If the TE is too long, then nearly all transverse magnetization will be lost and still the image will have no T_2 contrast. But at an intermediate TE, the difference in transverse magnetization can be maximized (Figure 5.8B).

To have exclusive T_2 contrast, we must have a very long TR, so that the longitudinal recovery is almost complete and T_1 contrast is minimal. When TR is much greater than T_1, the term e^{-TR/T_1} from Equation 5.4 approaches 0 and thus can be eliminated. The resulting formula for contrast is completely T_2-weighted and depends highly on TE:

$$C_{AB} = M_{0A}e^{-TE/T_{2A}} - M_{0B}e^{-TE/T_{2B}}   [5.7]$$

In summary, to generate images sensitive to T_2 contrast, we must collect those images using a pulse sequence with long TR and intermediate TE.

Unlike proton-density or T_1-weighted images, T_2-weighted images can only be generated using spin echo–based pulse sequences. Only spin-echo sequences allow true spin–spin relaxation that does not depend on the field inhomogeneity. A typical pulse sequence is shown in Figure 5.9A. The resulting brain image will be brightest in fluid-filled regions such as the ven-

T_2-weighted (T_2-dependent) Images that provide information about the relative T_2 values of tissue; also known simply as T_2 images.

(A)

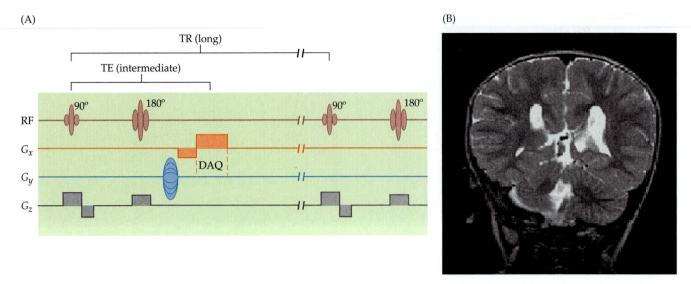

(B)

Figure 5.9 A pulse sequence used for T_2-weighted images. The primary requirements for T_2 imaging are an intermediate TE and a long TR. (A) Only spin-echo sequences can be used. The resulting image (B) is brightest in voxels with short T_2 values (e.g., CSF) and darkest in areas with long T_1 values (e.g., white matter).

susceptibility artifacts Signal losses on T_2^*-dependent images due to magnetic field inhomogeneities in regions where air and tissue are adjacent.

tricles, of medium brightness in gray matter, and darkest within white matter (Figure 5.9B). These intensity values are consistent with the relative T_2 values of the regions. Remember from the previous chapter that T_2 values depend on spin–spin interactions, and thus homogeneous tissues tend to have longer T_2. For example, CSF has the longest T_2 value due to its high water content, gray matter has intermediate T_2 from its rich blood supply, and white matter has the lowest T_2 value.

> ## Thought Question
>
> Often, proton-density and T_2-weighted images are acquired within the same pulse sequence. What aspect of their pulse sequences makes this possible?

Because the 180° pulse reverses the loss of phase coherence experienced by spins, spin-echo imaging is insensitive to static magnetic field inhomogeneities (e.g., T_2^* effects). As shown in Figure 5.10, differences in the magnetic field strength experienced by different spins cause loss of phase coherence over time, as some spins will precess faster and some slower. By introducing the 180° pulse at a time point exactly halfway between excitation and TE, the relative phase difference between the spins can be reversed. Therefore, the spins that precess faster will now be behind the spins that precess more slowly, so the faster spins will catch up at time TE. Spin-echo imaging can thus help eliminate the effects of magnetic field inhomogeneities around large blood vessels, minimizing the contaminating effects of those vessels on fMRI images. Another advantage of spin-echo imaging lies in its resistance to **susceptibility artifacts,** which are caused by mag-

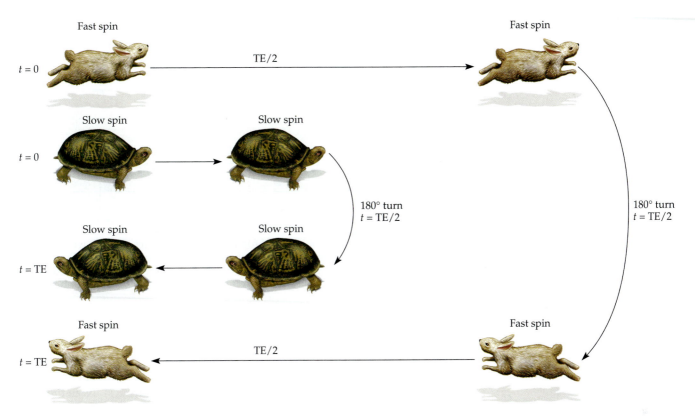

Figure 5.10 Reversing phase coherence using a 180° excitation pulse. As time progresses following excitation, magnetic field inhomogeneities will cause a loss of phase coherence over time, as some spins have fast precession frequencies and some have slow precession frequencies. If a 180° refocusing pulse is presented at time TE/2, the precession direction will be flipped. At the precise time TE, all of the spins will have their original phase (as indicated here by their returning to the original location).

netic field inhomogeneities near air–tissue interfaces in the brain, as found in the ventral frontal and temporal lobes.

T_2^* *Contrast*

Recall from Chapter 3 that there are two causes for transverse relaxation: spin–spin interaction (T_2) and changes in spin precession frequency due to inhomogeneities in the magnetic field. The combined effect of these two factors upon the decay of transverse magnetization is given by the time constant T_2^*. Though T_2 and T_2^* are related, the former constant is always greater than the latter, so T_2 decay is always slower than T_2^* decay. Quantitatively, the relationship between T_2 and T_2^* is given by $1/T_2^* = (1/T_2) + (1/T_2')$, where T_2' reflects the dephasing effect caused by field inhomogeneity. Because it forms the basis for BOLD-contrast fMRI, there has been a rapid increase in use of T_2^*-based imaging protocols since 1990. As is discussed further in Chapter 7, **T_2^*-weighted** images are sensitive to the amount of deoxygenated hemoglobin present, which changes according to the metabolic demands of active neurons.

Like T_2 contrast, T_2^* contrast is provided by pulse sequences with a long TR and medium TE. An additional requirement is that the pulse sequence

T_2^*-weighted Images that provide information about the relative T_2^* values of tissue. T_2^*-weighted images are commonly used for BOLD-contrast fMRI.

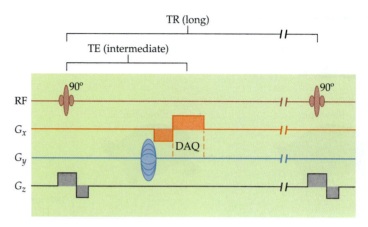

Figure 5.11 A pulse sequence used for T_2^*-weighted images. Like T_2-weighted images, T_2^*-weighted images require an intermediate TE and a long TR. Gradient-echo sequences are most commonly used, because the refocusing pulses used in spin-echo images will eliminate the field inhomogeneity effects that form the basis of the T_2^* effect.

magnetic resonance angiography (MRA) The creation of images of the vascular system using MRI.

must use magnetic field gradients to generate the signal echo, because refocusing pulses will eliminate field inhomogeneity effects. Most commonly used are gradient-echo sequences, as illustrated in Figure 5.11. Note the similarity to the proton-density sequence shown in Figure 5.4, which differs only in the echo time, TE. Here, an intermediate TE is used so that the image is sensitive to local field inhomogeneity and not just to the number of protons present. The pulse sequence shown can provide information about factors that decrease magnetic field homogeneity, such as the presence of deoxygenated hemoglobin. Because spin-echo pulse sequences have reduced T_2^* sensitivity, they are less frequently used for BOLD-contrast fMRI.

Motion-Weighted Contrasts

The human body is inherently dynamic. Within the vascular system, for example, water molecules are in constant motion, flowing on the order of 1 m/s in large arteries. Water also diffuses within and among cells, such as along axons in white matter. Pulse sequences sensitive to motion provide important information about the brain, including both structural and functional measures. Structural techniques include MR angiography and diffusion tensor imaging, which are often used for mapping the neurovascular system and white-matter tracts, respectively. Functional techniques include diffusion imaging, which maps the motion of water molecules over time, and perfusion imaging, which maps blood flow through capillaries. These techniques are collectively known as motion-weighted contrasts.

MR Angiography

Magnetic resonance angiography, or **MRA,** illustrates the structure of blood vessels using noninvasive MRI (Figure 5.12). In classic angiography, a contrast agent is injected into the bloodstream through an inserted catheter. X-ray images are then collected with and without the contrast agent present to generate a difference image (i.e., angiogram) that maps the vascular system. Although angiography provides good vascular images, it is a very

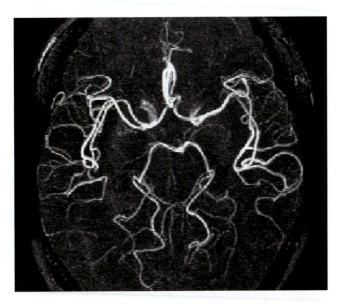

Figure 5.12   A sample magnetic resonance angiography (MRA) image.

invasive procedure, requiring both the insertion of foreign substances and exposure to ionizing radiation. Because MRA does not require ionizing radiation, it can noninvasively detect, diagnose, and aid in the treatment of many types of medical problems, including cardiac disorders, stroke, and vascular disease. MRA also complements fMRI studies by identifying major blood vessels that may confound experimental results. If identified, these vessels can be removed from analyses to improve localization of activity to the capillary bed.

MRA can use either exogenous or endogenous contrast. In some clinical settings, exogenous contrast-enhancing agents are used to increase the vessel signal. For a typical contrast-enhanced MRA, a small quantity (or **bolus**) of a gadolinium-based contrast agent is injected into the patient's bloodstream. The gadolinium itself is not visible on MR images, but it radically shortens the T_1 of nearby blood, allowing the use of specialized pulse sequences with extremely short TR (3 to 7 ms) and TE (1 to 3 ms) values. The short TR saturates signal from stationary tissues but not from the gadolinium-enhanced blood, while the short TE minimizes T_2 decay. Depending on the delay between bolus injection and image acquisition, the contrast agent may travel through different components of the vascular system, so the images can be calibrated to provide information about arterial or venous networks.

In research settings, MRA is usually obtained using noninvasive endogenous contrast. There are two primary techniques for endogenous contrast MRA. The most common is **time-of-flight (TOF) MRA,** which generates signal based upon blood displacement. The underlying principle of the TOF technique is spin saturation. By repeatedly and frequently applying excitation pulses or gradient pulses to a single imaging plane, the signal within that plane can be suppressed. Thus, tissues whose spins remain within the plane, such as gray or white matter, will produce little MR signal and will appear to be very dark on TOF images. Blood vessels, however, are constantly replenished with new spins from outside the plane. These spins have not experienced the excitation or gradient pulses, and thus they contribute

bolus A quantity of a substance that is introduced into a system and then progresses through that system over time.

time-of-flight (TOF) MRA A type of MR angiography that generates contrast by suppressing signal from spins within an imaging plane so that voxels with inflowing spins (i.e., those with blood vessels) have high signal.

Figure 5.13 Schematic illustration of the signal-generation mechanism for TOF magnetic resonance angiography. In TOF MRA, repeated excitation pulses saturate the MR signal from spins within a plane, as shown by the dark bar at left. Then there is a waiting period during which voxels with flow (e.g., blood vessels) have new spins introduced whereas voxels without flow (e.g., white matter) do not. The amount of MR signal recorded following excitation and acquisition is greatest for voxels that had the most new spins enter during the waiting period.

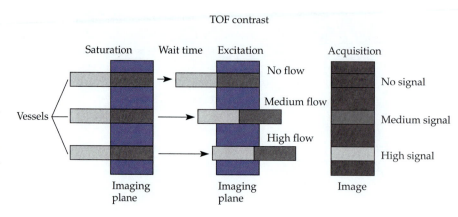

velocity-encoded phase contrast (VENC-PC) MRA A type of MR angiography that uses gradient fields to induce phase differences associated with vascular flow so that the flow velocity of vessels can be measured.

normal MR signal. TOF images are typically acquired in the axial plane and can be reformatted to other planes for ease of viewing.

The TOF signal is proportional to the amount of blood that enters the slice (Figure 5.13). If a completely new column of blood enters the slice every TR, the TOF signal will be at its maximum. But if blood flow is weak or absent, then the TOF signal will be much reduced. Consequently, TOF contrast differentiates blood vessels based upon their amount of flow; thus it is a flow-dependent contrast technique. Because of its flow sensitivity, the TR and slice thickness for TOF images must be chosen based upon the expected flow.

To acquire MRAs with TOF contrast, a specialized pulse sequence is required (Figure 5.14). As described in the preceding paragraphs, the imaging plane is presaturated by the electromagnetic excitation pulse and gradient saturation pulses. After a brief waiting period during which fresh blood can enter the plane, the MR signals are acquired by a gradient-echo acquisition technique, so that only the signal from this new blood will be present.

A second technique is **velocity-encoded phase contrast (VENC-PC) MRA,** which uses gradient fields to produce a velocity-dependent phase difference, θ, between the vasculature and surrounding tissue (Figure 5.15). The amount of phase difference accumulated depends on the velocity of the moving spins and the strength and duration of the applied gradient. By

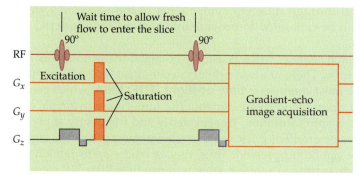

Figure 5.14 Pulse sequence used for TOF MRA. The TOF technique requires an initial saturation of a slice, followed by a wait time to allow blood to enter the slice. Then a standard gradient-echo sequence can be used to acquire the images.

acquiring phase differences in each of three orthogonal directions, a map of three-dimensional flow can be created. Typical VENC-PC protocols acquire two sets of images: one with a motion-sensitizing gradient and the other with either no gradient or a gradient in the opposite direction. The difference between these images indicates the magnitude of the phase difference at each voxel, and thus the brightness at each voxel is proportional to flow. Voxels with stationary spins will not give signal, since there are no phase differences between the images, whereas voxels with rapidly moving spins will produce bright signals due to the large phase differences. The VENC-PC technique, unlike TOF, does not depend upon TR or slice thickness, because it acts upon the blood already present in the imaging slice.

Since the VENC-PC technique relies on phase angles, it is sensitive to the strength and duration of the velocity-encoding gradients. Imagine that the gradients are set up so that a flow velocity of 20 cm/s corresponds to a phase change of 180°. Should a given vessel, such as a large artery, have a very fast flow rate of 40 cm/s, the resulting phase angle change would be 360°. As in basic geometry, an angle of 360° cannot be distinguished from one of 0°, so this fast-flowing artery would appear to have no flow whatsoever! This problem, known as velocity aliasing, demonstrates the importance of choosing appropriate velocity-encoding parameters. If the gradient is too strong, as in the above example, fast-flowing vessels may be misidentified. But if the gradient is too small, the ability to resolve differences among slow-flowing vessels is compromised. By choosing the gradient strength based upon knowledge of the expected velocities of different vessel types, selective imaging of different parts of the vascular system is possible.

To acquire MRAs with VENC-PC contrast, a different pulse sequence is necessary (Figure 5.16). Here, the velocity-encoding gradients are inserted after the excitation pulse but before the phase image acquisition. Note that they are bipolar in shape, which has no effect on static tissue. When this pulse sequence is repeated twice, once with velocity-encoding gradients and once without (or with opposite gradients), flow-dependent phase contrast will be generated.

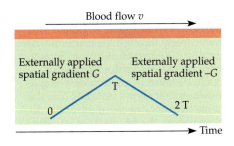

Figure 5.15 Schematic illustration of VENC-PC MRA. Two sets of images are acquired, one with a motion-sensitizing gradient, G, and one without. The phase difference between these images provides a measure of the velocity of the spins within each voxel.

Diffusion-Weighted Contrast

At all temperatures above absolute zero, thermodynamic effects cause molecules to move randomly. The motion of molecules due to thermodynamic

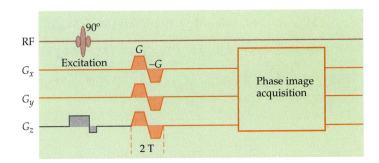

Figure 5.16 Pulse sequence used for VENC-PC MRA. This technique uses spatial gradients to induce changes in spin phase. The magnitude of the phase difference between a pair of images (e.g., one with gradients vs. one without) provides information about the velocity of spins within each voxel.

Figure 5.17 Diffusion. Over time, molecules within gases or liquids will move freely through the medium. This motion is known as diffusion. Shown here are sample random paths that could be taken by molecules within a medium that allows isotropic (i.e., the same in every direction) diffusion. As time passes, the net distance traveled by a molecule increases.

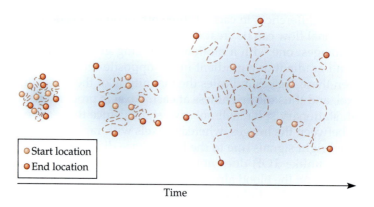

Start location
End location

Time

diffusion The random motion of molecules through a medium over time.

effects is known as **diffusion** (Figure 5.17). In gases and liquids, the molecules can move relatively freely, as when a dye spreads through a glass of water or when the smell of freshly baked bread wafts through the house. In solids, however, the motion of molecules is restricted, and thus diffusion is much slower. The abundance of water molecules in the human body makes it possible to perform diffusion-weighted imaging using MRI. And, because of the different cellular environment experienced by different water molecules, diffusion-weighted MRI can provide a new dimension of image contrast based on mobility.

The original equation proposed by Bloch (see Equation 3.47) successfully explains MR phenomena including the effects of T_1 and T_2 relaxation. However, it does not contain a term that describes the effect of diffusion. Torrey modified the Bloch equation to account for the effects of diffusion:

$$\frac{d\mathbf{M}}{dt} = \gamma \mathbf{M} \times \mathbf{B} + \frac{\mathbf{M}_0 - \mathbf{M}_z}{T_1} - \frac{\mathbf{M}_x + \mathbf{M}_y}{T_2} + \nabla \cdot D\nabla(\mathbf{M} - \mathbf{M}_0) \quad [5.8]$$

The new term $\nabla \cdot D\nabla(\mathbf{M} - \mathbf{M}_0)$ states that diffusion modulates the rate of MR signal change according to a new intrinsic tissue property, D, which describes the rate of molecular diffusion under a time-varying magnetic gradient. The symbol, ∇, is the mathematical representation of the gradient. Voxels with large D, such as those containing CSF, allow molecules to diffuse quickly and thus have a faster rate of signal decay. Voxels with small D, such as those containing lipids, have limited diffusion and thus a slower rate of signal decay. To allow easier visualization of its meaning, this equation can be further divided into three subequations that describe each of the three directional components:

$$d\mathbf{M}_x / dt = \gamma \mathbf{M}_x \times \mathbf{B} - \mathbf{M}_x / T_2 + \nabla \cdot D\nabla(\mathbf{M}_x - \mathbf{M}_{x0}) \quad [5.9a]$$

$$d\mathbf{M}_y / dt = \gamma \mathbf{M}_y \times \mathbf{B} - \mathbf{M}_y / T_2 + \nabla \cdot D\nabla(\mathbf{M}_y - \mathbf{M}_{y0}) \quad [5.9b]$$

$$d\mathbf{M}_z / dt = \gamma \mathbf{M}_z \times \mathbf{B} + (\mathbf{M}_0 - \mathbf{M}_z) / T_1 + \nabla \cdot D\nabla(\mathbf{M}_z - \mathbf{M}_{z0}) \quad [5.9c]$$

Later we will exploit the preference for water within some tissues to diffuse in one direction and not others in our discussion of diffusion tensor imaging.

If the magnetic field were perfectly homogeneous, the effect of diffusion would be hardly visible, as the water molecules would experience the same magnetic field regardless of their position over time. However, if the field were inhomogeneous, whether due to the intrinsic nonuniformity or externally applied gradients, the water molecules would experience different magnetic fields as they diffused in space over time. This would cause a loss of phase coherence, which in turn would attenuate the MRI signal. Unlike the loss of phase coherence due to static magnetic field inhomogeneity (e.g., T_2^* effects), this loss cannot be recovered even with spin-echo pulse sequences. Because diffusion is random, the path taken by each molecule cannot be reversed. Thus, the refocusing pulse of a spin-echo sequence cannot recover signal lost to phase incoherence.

Diffusion weighting is the application of controlled gradient magnetic fields to quantify the amplitude and direction of diffusion. The presence of diffusion-weighting gradients further attenuates the MR signal beyond that caused by common T_2 relaxation. Assuming equal, or **isotropic,** diffusion along all directions (Figure 5.18A), the attenuation effect (A) due to diffusion weighting is given by the exponential

$$A = e^{-\int_0^T D(\gamma G(t)t)^2 dt} \qquad [5.10]$$

In this equation, D is the **apparent diffusion coefficient, or ADC** (i.e., the measured value of the diffusion coefficient), G the strength of the external diffusion-weighting gradient, and T the duration of the diffusion-weighting gradient. We can define the degree of diffusion weighting as the **b factor**:

$$b = \int_0^T (\gamma G(t)t)^2 dt \qquad [5.11]$$

To further simplify Equation 5.10:

$$A = e^{-bD} \qquad [5.12]$$

Equation 5.12 quantifies the mean diffusivity within a voxel without providing directional information. But water molecules in the brain do not diffuse equally in all directions. Most water is contained within tissue that has considerable structure, such as the long processes of axons or the narrow

diffusion weighting The application of magnetic gradients to cause changes in the MR signal that are dependent upon the amplitude and/or direction of diffusion.

isotropic Having similar properties in all directions.

apparent diffusion coefficient (ADC) The quantification of diffusivity assuming isotropic diffusion.

b factor The degree of diffusion weighting applied within a pulse sequence.

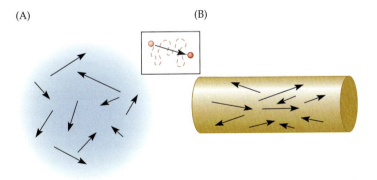

(A)   (B)

Figure 5.18 Isotropic and anisotropic diffusion. If there are no restrictions on diffusion, molecules will diffuse equally in all directions (A). This is known as isotropic diffusion. However, if there are restrictions upon diffusion, as is the case within long neuronal axons, diffusion may occur primarily along one axis (B). This is an example of anisotropic diffusion. Note that the vector representations here are simplified versions of the random-walk paths taken by molecules, as indicated in the inset figure at upper center.

anisotropic Having different properties in different directions; often referenced in the context of anisotropic diffusion, where molecules tend to diffuse along one axis but not others.

tensor A collection of vector fields governed by three principal axes.

diffusion tensor imaging (DTI) The collection of images that provide information about the magnitude and direction of molecular diffusion. It is often used to create maps of fractional anisotropy.

fractional anisotropy (FA) The preference for molecules to diffuse in an anisotropic manner. An FA value of 1 indicates that diffusion occurs along a single preferred axis, while a value of 0 indicates that diffusion is similar in all directions.

walls of blood vessels. Unequal, or **anisotropic,** diffusion (Figure 5.18B) refers to the preference in some tissues for water molecules to diffuse in one direction or another. In anisotropic diffusion, the motion of molecules over time does not resemble a sphere, in which molecules move equally in every direction, but instead resembles an ellipsoid whose long axis indicates the fastest axis of diffusion. The diffusion ellipsoid is mathematically described as a three-dimensional **tensor,** which is a collection of vector fields governed by three principal axes.

Diffusion tensor imaging (DTI) can quantify the relative diffusivity among directional components. For example, white matter, which is composed mostly of nerve fibers, shows prominent anisotropy, such that water molecules diffuse most quickly along the length of the fiber and most slowly across the width of the fiber. A scalar quantity known as **fractional anisotropy (FA)** can be computed for each voxel to express the preference of water to diffuse in an isotropic or anisotropic manner. FA values are bounded by 0 and 1 and are calculated using Equation 5.13, where Dx, Dy, and Dz represent the three principal axes of the diffusion tensor:

$$FA = \frac{\sqrt{(Dx - Dy)^2 + (Dy - Dz)^2 + (Dz - Dx)^2}}{\sqrt{2(Dx^2 + Dy^2 + Dz^2)}} \qquad [5.13]$$

FA values approaching 1 indicate that nearly all of the water molecules in the voxel are diffusing along the same preferred axis, while FA values approaching 0 indicate that the water molecules are equally likely to diffuse in any direction. Fractional anisotropy provides important information about the composition of tissue within a voxel. Notably, some neurological diseases, such as multiple sclerosis and vascular dementia, are characterized by potentially severe white-matter pathology. The resulting axonal damage can be identified as decreased FA values in affected voxels. More-complex forms of diffusion tensor imaging can track nerve fibers as they travel between functionally associated brain regions. These advanced tensor imaging techniques are discussed in more detail in Chapter 14.

To determine diffusion coefficients, we must apply controlled gradients in a pulse sequence. These gradients must be spatially balanced to preserve MR signal. In spin-echo sequences (Figure 5.19A), this balance is achieved

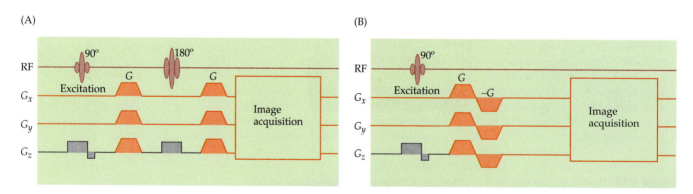

Figure 5.19 Pulse sequences used for diffusion-weighted imaging. Shown are sample pulse sequences used for diffusion-weighted spin-echo imaging (A) and diffusion-weighted gradient-echo imaging (B). Note that the spin-echo sequence has a refocusing pulse between two gradients of similar sign, while the gradient-echo sequence alternates gradients of opposite sign.

by presenting the gradients before and after the refocusing pulse. In gradient-echo sequences (Figure 5.19B), successive positive and negative gradients are applied. In an ideal isotropic medium, application of a gradient along any axis would be sufficient for measuring the ADC. However, the brain contains many tissues that constrain diffusion, and thus diffusion-weighting gradients must be applied in many directions to quantify the diffusion tensor.

> ### Thought Question
>
> Why are the gradients used in the spin-echo pulse sequence of the same sign, while the gradients used in the gradient-echo sequence are of opposite signs?

Although diffusion imaging has been primarily applied to quantify white-matter structure and pathology in the human brain, it also has great potential utility for fMRI. We discuss these applications in Chapter 14.

Perfusion-Weighted Contrast

The human brain requires oxygen for metabolism (see Chapter 6). To ensure a constant supply of oxygen, hemoglobin molecules carry oxygen through the bloodstream to all parts of the brain. The irrigation of tissue via blood delivery is known as **perfusion,** and the family of imaging procedures that measure this process are known as perfusion MRI. Perfusion is expressed as the volume of blood that travels through a tissue mass over time. In the human brain, gray-matter perfusion is approximately 60 mL/100 g/min, and white-matter perfusion is smaller, about 20 mL/100 g/min. Unlike the MRA techniques described in the section on MR angiography, (which are often used for clinical reasons to measure the properties of large blood vessels), perfusion MRI is most frequently used to image blood flow specifically in capillaries and other small vessels.

Perfusion MRI may use either exogenous or endogenous contrast. Exogenous contrast approaches use intravascular contrast agents that freely perfuse through the vascular system. The attenuation of the MR signal in each voxel is proportional to the amount of the contrast agent present. Thus, signal changes can be interpreted as a function of perfusion, and images can be created that depict different perfusion properties, such as the relative cerebral blood flow (rCBF), relative cerebral blood volume (rCBV), and mean transit time (mTT). As their names imply, relative blood flow and relative blood volume express changes in how much blood comes into a voxel and how much blood is contained within a voxel, respectively. The mean transit time measures how quickly blood passes through a particular voxel and can indicate brain regions with delayed blood flow. The use of exogenous contrast agents provides very high signal change but has limited use for research because of its invasiveness.

Endogeneous contrast perfusion imaging is noninvasive and has found use in fMRI research. Contrast is generated through the clever use of radiofrequency pulses to magnetically label, or tag, protons in blood water molecules before they reach the tissue of interest. This approach is known as **arterial spin labeling,** or **ASL,** of which there are two types: continuous and pulsed. **Continuous ASL** typically uses additional hardware, like a labeling coil, to saturate spins in upstream blood, such as in the carotid arteries of the

perfusion Blood flow through capillaries.

arterial spin labeling (ASL) A family of perfusion imaging techniques that measure blood flow by labeling spins with excitation pulses and then waiting for the labeled spins to enter the imaging plane before data acquisition.

continuous ASL A type of perfusion imaging that uses a second transmitter coil to label spins within an upstream artery while collecting images.

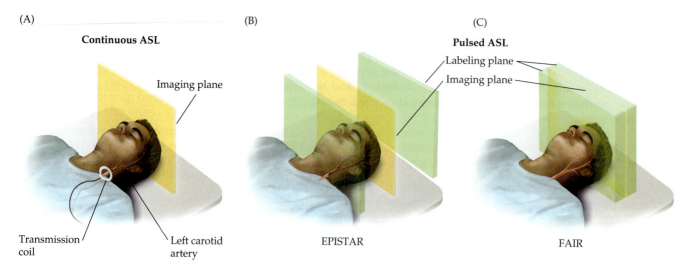

(A)

Continuous ASL

Imaging plane

Transmission coil

Left carotid artery

(B)

Pulsed ASL

EPISTAR

(C)

Labeling plane

Imaging plane

FAIR

Figure 5.20 Perfusion imaging mechanisms. (A) Continuous ASL techniques use an upstream transmission coil to saturate spins in an artery that feeds the brain. Images collected following spin saturation can be compared to images in the absence of saturation to determine flow into the imaging plane. There are two primary types of pulsed ASL techniques, EPISTAR (B) and FAIR (C). EPISTAR relies on alternating two labeling planes that are equidistant from the imaging plane, one below the plane that includes feeding arteries and one above the plane that does not include any feeding vessels (i.e., is outside the head). FAIR alternates between labeling the entire brain and just the imaging plane. For either of the pulsed ASL techniques, differences between the two sets of images can be attributed to flow into the imaging plane.

pulsed ASL A type of perfusion imaging that uses a single coil both to label spins in one plane and to record MR signal in another plane, separated by a brief delay period.

labeling plane The plane in which initial excitation pulse(s) are applied during perfusion imaging.

imaging plane The plane in which changes in MR signal are recorded during perfusion imaging.

neck (Figure 5.20A). Following this labeling process, the blood travels to the brain and enters the imaging slice. The images can then be continuously acquired in the brain in the presence of the labeled blood. After acquiring the images with the labeled blood, the labeling coil can be turned off and a second set of images are acquired without the presence of the labeled blood. The difference between the two sets of images reflects only the blood flow, as any tissue that does not contain flow will be similar in the two conditions. A drawback of the continuous ASL technique is the requirement for a second transmitter coil to label the inflowing blood.

An alternative approach, **pulsed ASL,** uses a single coil both to label blood in the **labeling plane** and to record the MR signal change in the **imaging plane** (Figure 5.20B and C). Labeling pulses are broadcast for brief periods and followed by a delay and then image acquisition. The delay period must be calibrated to account for the distance between the labeling plane and imaging plane, so the labeled bolus of blood water will enter the imaging plane during image acquisition.

Regardless of the ASL method used, labeling blood only alters the longitudinal magnetization. Thus, we can describe the endogenous perfusion signal quantitatively by modifying the T_1 term of the Bloch equation (Equation 4.1). To do so, we introduce an additional term, $f(\mathbf{M}'(t) - \mathbf{M}_0)$, that accounts for the effects of blood flow:

$$\frac{d\mathbf{M}(t)}{dt} = \frac{\mathbf{M}_0 - \mathbf{M}_z(t)}{T_{1app}} + f(\mathbf{M}'(t) - \mathbf{M}_0) \qquad [5.14]$$

In this equation, f is the blood flow in mL/g/sec and T_{1app} is the apparent T_1 value in the presence of blood flow. T_{1app} can be calculated from $1/T_{1app} = 1/T_1 + f/\lambda$, where λ is the blood–brain partition coefficient. This coefficient is defined by the ratio between blood volume and brain tissue masses that contain equal amounts of water; its typical value is about 0.9 mL/g. Because the blood is labeled with an inversion pulse, its magnetization, $\mathbf{M'}(t)$, is given by $-\mathbf{M_0}$, so that the difference between the two conditions becomes:

$$\frac{d\mathbf{M(t)}^{\text{label}}}{dt} - \frac{d\mathbf{M(t)}^{\text{control}}}{dt} = -\frac{\mathbf{M(t)}^{\text{label}} - \mathbf{M(t)}^{\text{control}}}{\mathbf{T}_{1\text{app}}} + f(-2\mathbf{M_0}) \quad [5.15]$$

and thus the signal remaining in the final perfusion image would be:

$$\mathbf{M(t)}^{\text{label}} - \mathbf{M(t)}^{\text{control}} = -2\mathbf{T}_{1\text{app}} f \mathbf{M_0} / \lambda \quad [5.16]$$

This equation defines the relation between the measured perfusion signal and blood flow in the brain.

Because the continuous ASL method uses a second transmitter coil to label blood, the images can be acquired with any standard spin- or gradient-echo pulse sequence. To achieve the maximal signal difference, the echo time (TE) must be kept as short as possible, which minimizes signal loss due to T_2^* or T_2 relaxation effects.

Pulsed ASL techniques require specialized pulse sequences to label the blood. In one type of pulsed ASL, EPISTAR (echo-planar imaging at steady state with alternating inversion recovery), alternating off-center inversion pulses are used to select labeling planes below and above the image plane (Figure 5.21A). For odd scans, the labeling plane is in the neck, below and upstream from the imaging plane. For even scans, the labeling plane is at an equal distance above the imaging plane, and can actually be outside of the brain. This is necessary to ensure that the inversion pulse has a similar effect on the spin system in both the odd and even scans.

EPISTAR is directionally specific, in that it is only sensitive to spins flowing from the labeling plane to the imaging plane. A second type of pulsed

(A)

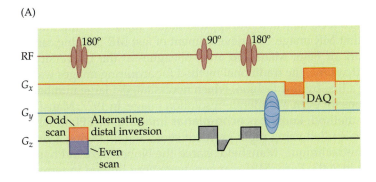

(B)

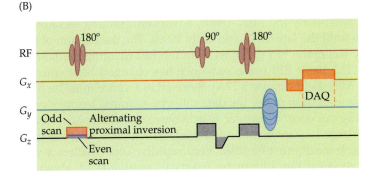

Figure 5.21 Pulse sequences for pulsed ASL imaging. Shown are typical pulse sequences used for the EPISTAR technique (A) and the FAIR technique (B). Both techniques require alternating between different labeling planes, as shown for the G_z gradient at left.

echo-planar imaging (EPI) A technique, first proposed by Peter Mansfield, that allows collection of an entire two-dimensional image by changing spatial gradients rapidly following a single electromagnetic pulse from a transmitter coil.

ASL, FAIR (flow-sensitive alternating inversion recovery), is not directionally specific (Figure 5.21B). For odd scans, the entire brain is labeled. For even scans, only the imaging plane is labeled. The difference between these two labeling conditions reflects those spins that flow into the image plane from anywhere else in the brain; thus FAIR is insensitive to the direction of flow. However, flow within the plane will be similar between the conditions and does not contribute to the image. Because the inversion pulse is present for both acquisitions, its effect within the imaging plane is identical.

Like the diffusion imaging techniques described in the previous section, perfusion imaging provides an alternative method for functional neuroimaging (see Chapter 14).

Fast Imaging Sequences for fMRI Image Acquisition

For anatomical images of the brain, contrast is more important than speed of acquisition, since structural parameters such as size and shape change little over the course of a single scanning session. However, understanding the function of the brain requires images to be acquired very rapidly, at approximately the same rate as the physiological changes of interest. Fast pulse sequences have been developed that acquire a very large number of images within a short period of time; state-of-the art sequences may acquire a volume consisting of 20 or more images within a single second. These sequences typically use variants of the gradient-echo approach described in Chapter 4 and are sensitive to T_2^* contrast. The basic principles underlying these sequences are described in the remainder of this chapter.

Echo-Planar Imaging

The first human MR images were acquired using a laborious voxel-by-voxel procedure. The image shown in Figure 1.13 took about 4 hours to acquire, as collected at the slothlike pace of about 2 minutes per voxel. To put the current ultrafast methods in perspective, a modern pulse sequence that images 20 slices per second collects data at a rate approximately 10,000,000 times faster than that of the first MR image. The development of fast MR imaging can be traced to the work of Peter Mansfield and colleagues at the University of Nottingham. At that time, the traditional method for acquiring images was to fill up *k*-space in a line-by-line fashion, which necessitated a large number of separate excitations for even a moderate-resolution image. In 1977, Mansfield proposed a new method, known as **echo-planar imaging,** or **EPI,** in which the entire *k*-space is filled using rapid gradient switching following a single excitation. For this technique, Mansfield shared the Nobel Prize in Physiology or Medicine in 2003. Early MRI scanners were very limited in terms of the strength of the gradients that they could produce and the slew rate with which they could change the gradients. While high-static-magnetic field scanners were available by the early 1980s, advanced gradient technology was not common until the late 1980s and early 1990s. The maturation of gradient technology has made EPI the most common fast imaging method for functional MRI. The basic EPI pulse sequence has changed little since its development by Mansfield (Figure 5.22A). Since all of *k*-space must be filled following a single excitation pulse, the data must be acquired before significant T_2^* or T_2 decay can occur. However, to achieve reasonable spatial resolution, a relatively large *k*-space must be sampled, which takes time. To meet these constraints, *k*-space must be filled very rapidly. This requires a very strong gradient system. For EPI to be practical, gradients of about 2.5

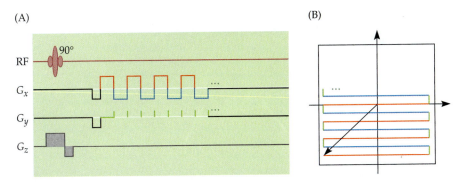

Figure 5.22   An EPI pulse sequence (A) and its *k*-space trajectory (B). Note that the directions of the gradients are changed rapidly over time to allow the back-and-forth trajectory through *k*-space.

Gauss/cm are sufficient, but stronger whole-body systems now exist that can produce gradients of up to 5 Gauss/cm. The use of very strong gradients can shorten the scan time required for one image to less than 20 ms.

To fill *k*-space, EPI uses an unconventional pattern in which alternating lines are scanned in opposite directions. This switchback approach heavily taxes the gradient hardware, since different sets of gradients must be cycled on to enable the 90° turns in the *k*-space pattern. This pattern is also inefficient in that data collected while transitioning from one line of *k*-space to another (i.e., the vertical lines on Figure 5.22B) are not used in the image-creation process. Furthermore, the raw data obtained from the EPI acquisition must be sorted and realigned to remove the influence of the zigzag trajectory before being reconstructed using a Fourier transform. Without such realignment, serious artifacts can arise (Figure 5.23A and B).

The most common EPI artifacts result from imperfections in the magnetic fields, either static or gradient, used to collect the images. Small- and large-scale static field inhomogeneities can result in signal losses and geometric

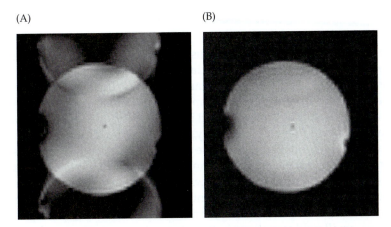

Figure 5.23   Artifacts due to misalignment of EPI images. If the raw *k*-space data from an EPI acquisition are not realigned to remove the influence of the back-and-forth trajectory, significant image distortions can arise (A). (B) The corrected image of a phantom.

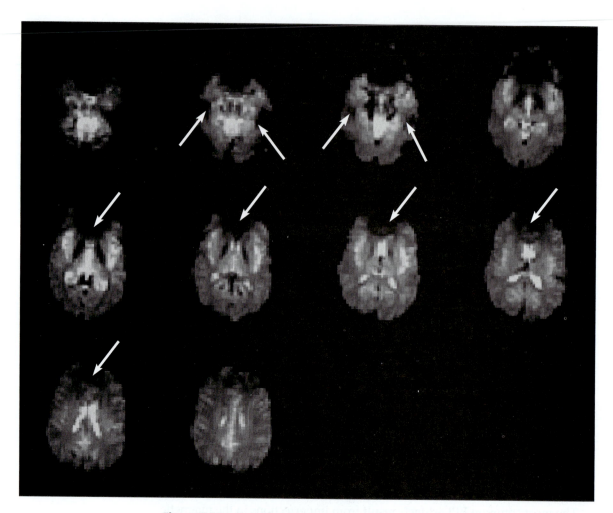

Figure 5.24   Signal loss due to susceptibility artifacts in EPI images. Shown here are a series of slices within an EPI image volume collected at a 4-T scanner (TE: 40 ms). In areas of the brain near interfaces between air and tissue, such as near the sinuses and auditory canals, there is significant signal loss due to magnetic field inhomogeneities.

distortions, respectively, and are discussed in Chapter 4. Figure 5.24 shows a set of typical EPI images, oriented axially with the lowest slice in the upper left of the figure. Visible are significant losses of MR signal in the ventral frontal lobes and inferior medial temporal lobes, due to magnetic suscepti-bility artifacts resulting from the field inhomogeneity present at the bound-ary between brain tissue and a nearby, air-filled sinus. The signal loss in the ventral frontal region results from the nasal and oral cavities, which sit just under the frontal lobe, and the loss in the inferior medial temporal region results from the auditory canals below.

Geometric distortion is also present in EPI images, due to the long read-out time for each excitation. In anatomical images, which have short readout windows, small field variations in the image plane may cause only subpixel distortions. But in EPI images with long readout periods, there can be noticeable distortions of up to several pixels. A long readout time makes the system more prone to geometric distortions due both to the reduced sam-

(A)

(B)

(C)

(D)

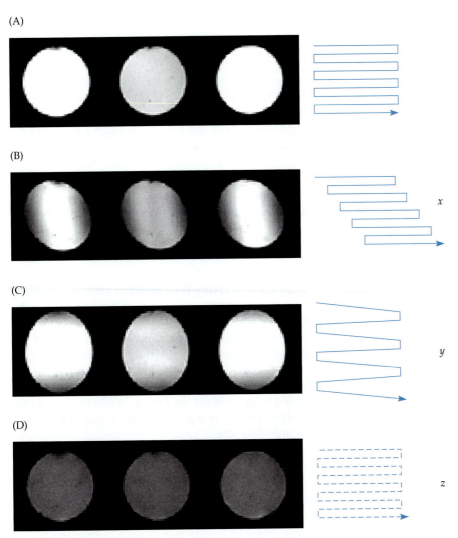

x

y

z

Figure 5.25   Effects of small field variation upon EPI images. A normal EPI image (A) will be distorted by small variations in magnetic field strength along a single direction. If the variation is along x (B) or y (C), the image is systematically stretched or sheared. If the variation is along the slice selection axis z (D), the excitation is off-resonance and MR signal intensity is reduced.

pling frequency and the reduced readout gradient strength. Variation in the magnetic field along a single in-plane direction (e.g., x or y) causes stretching and shearing of the otherwise circular phantom image (Figure 5.25A–C). Rarely, however, will geometric distortion be in a single direction; instead, gradient variation usually changes across the image in a complex fashion, resulting in more-complex patterns of distortion. A further problem results from small field variations along the z (i.e., slice-selective, or through-plane) direction, which cause off-resonance excitation and thus severe signal losses (Figure 5.25D).

Spiral Imaging

While EPI enables fast image acquisition, its speed is constrained by the physical limitations of the MR scanner gradient hardware. A new family of fast imaging sequences called **spiral imaging** utilizes a very different trajectory in k-space from that of EPI. Spiral imaging sequences use sinusoidal changes in the gradients (Figure 5.26A) to trace a corkscrew path through k-space that typically begins at the center and winds its way to the perimeter

spiral imaging   A technique for fast image acquisition that uses sinusoidally changing gradients to trace a corkscrew trajectory through k-space.

(A) (B)

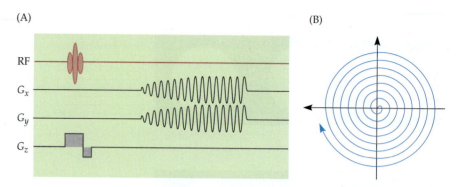

Figure 5.26 Spiral imaging. As illustrated schematically here, spiral imaging pulse sequences use sinusoidally changing gradients (A) to generate a curving path through *k*-space (B).

(Figure 5.26B). This can be much less taxing on a gradient system compared to EPI sequences and can reduce the time needed to collect an image. An additional advantage is that all points sampled along the spiral trajectory are used for reconstructing the final image, improving the efficiency of the acquisition. A disadvantage of spiral imaging is that the *k*-space data do not follow a Cartesian grid. This necessitates an additional step in which the acquired data points are resampled back onto a Cartesian grid so that a Fourier transform can be used to reconstruct the image. While this consumes additional time during postprocessing, it is a small price to pay for an often considerable increase in acquisition rate.

> ### Thought Question
>
> The echo time (TE) is defined as the interval between excitation and the collection of the center of *k*-space. How do EPI and spiral sequences differ in where the TE falls within the duration of the data acquisition window?

Spiral images have the same vulnerability as EPI to signal losses in inhomogeneous regions, as shown in Figure 5.27. In addition, even though the spiral readout is more efficient than EPI in filling up *k*-space, it is still considerably longer than that used in conventional anatomical imaging methods, and thus spatial distortions are also present. The form of spatial distortion, however, is quite different compared to EPI. Because of the non-Cartesian *k*-space sampling scheme, the regular distortion pattern seen in EPI images is usually not present in spiral images (Figure 5.28A). For example, linear field variations in the *x*- or *y*-direction commonly shear and stretch entire EPI images. These same linear field variations would cause asymmetric compression in one dimension in spiral images. Due to the rotational symmetry between the *x*- and *y*-coordinates in spiral imaging, the artifact caused by the field variation along *x* (Figure 5.28B) is simply a 90°-rotated version of that caused by the field variation along *y* (Figure 5.28C). Another potential problem is that the spatial resampling necessitated by the spiral trajectory may blur the image. Like EPI, spiral imaging is also influenced by field inhomogeneity along the *z*-direction, resulting in severe signal losses (Figure 5.28D).

(A)

(B)

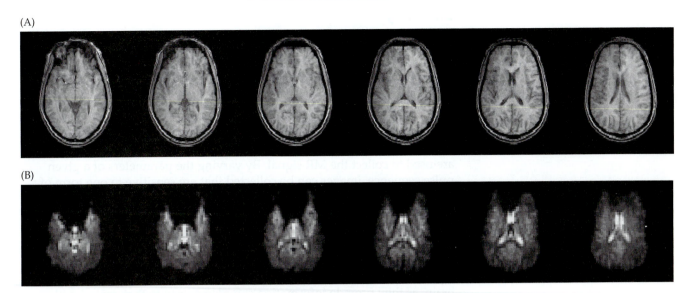

Figure 5.27   Signal losses due to susceptibility artifacts in spiral images. Compared to anatomical images (A), spiral images (B) exhibit regions of signal loss similar to those of EPI images (compare to Figure 5.24).

(A)

(B)

(C)

(D)

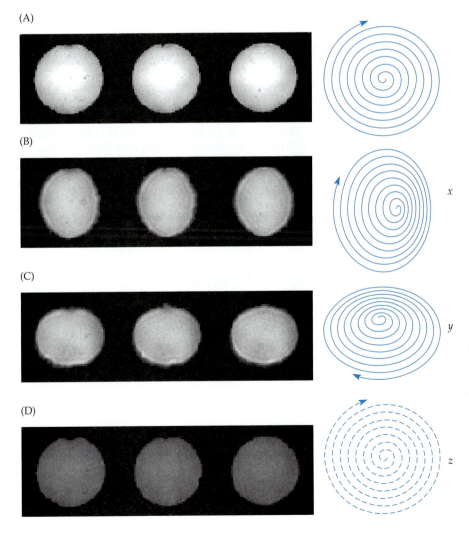

Figure 5.28   Effects of small field variation upon spiral images. A normal spiral image (A) is distorted by small variations in magnetic field strength along a single direction, although the pattern of distortion is different from that of EPI. If the variation is along x (B) or y (C), the image is systematically compressed along the y-direction or x-direction, respectively. As with EPI, however, variation along the slice selection direction (D) causes a reduction in overall MR signal intensity.

Summary

There are two general types of contrast for magnetic resonance imaging of the brain. Static contrast provides information about the number or content of atomic nuclei, while motion contrast describes how atomic nuclei move within a region of interest. Each basic type may use either endogenous mechanisms that rely on naturally occurring properties of biological tissue or exogenous mechanisms that typically involve the injection of paramagnetic compounds. Every contrast mechanism has associated pulse sequences describing the gradient changes and radiofrequency pulses that are used to collect the MR signal. By varying the parameters of a given pulse sequence, images can be collected that are sensitive to one form of contrast or another. Common static contrasts include proton-density, T_1-weighted, T_2-weighted, and T_2^*-weighted. In fMRI experiments, these static contrasts are typically used for collection of high-resolution images that provide anatomical detail. Motion contrasts include MR angiography, diffusion weighting, and perfusion imaging. Diffusion and perfusion imaging, in particular, have potential for improving localization of function in the brain, as they provide information complementary to that gained with standard fMRI approaches. Gradient-echo imaging is the most common form of fMRI pulse sequence, for which both echo-planar and spiral imaging are used. The use of T_2^*-weighted contrast provides the foundation for high-temporal-resolution study of functional changes in the human brain through fMRI.

Suggested Readings

Buxton, R. (2001). *Introduction to Functional Magnetic Resonance Imaging: Principles and Techniques.* Cambridge University Press, Cambridge, U.K. Provides an advanced overview of many facets of MRI, including a detailed discussion of perfusion imaging.

Haacke, E. M., Brown, R. W., Thompson, M. R., and Venkatesan, R. (1999). *Magnetic Resonance Imaging: Physical Principles and Sequence Design.* John Wiley & Sons, New York. A comprehensive encyclopedia of the theoretical principles of MRI.

Slichter, C. P. (1990). *Principles of Magnetic Resonance* (3rd ed.). Springer-Verlag, New York. Provides a detailed mathematical treatment of the physics of MRI.

Chapter References

Arlart, I. P., Bongartz, G. M., and Marchal, G. (eds.) (1995). *Magnetic Resonance Angiography.* Springer-Verlag, New York.

Feynman, R. P., Leighton, R. B., and Sands, M. (1964). *Lectures on Physics,* Vol. II. Addison-Wesley Publishing Company, New York.

Le Bihan, D. (ed.) (1995). *Diffusion and Perfusion Magnetic Resonance Imaging: Application to Functional MRI.* Raven Press, New York.

Moonen, C. T. W., and Bandettini, P. A. (eds.) (1999). *Functional Magnetic Resonance Imaging.* Springer-Verlag, New York.

6

From Neuronal to Hemodynamic Activity

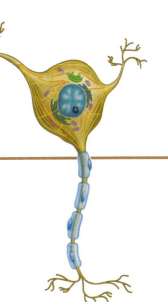

In the previous chapters, we explained how the principles of magnetic resonance can be used to create images of the brain. We have further shown that by changing how electromagnetic pulses and gradient magnetic fields are applied, we can create MR images that have contrast based upon any number of different biophysical properties, including proton density, T_1 or T_2 relaxation, diffusion, or perfusion. However, another step is necessary for MRI to become fMRI. We must identify a biophysical property that is altered by information processing within the brain, so images can be created that are sensitive to brain function.

Because information processing results from the activity of ensembles of neurons, a primary goal of functional neuroimaging is to create images sensitive to neuronal activity. Electrophysiological methods measure the ionic currents caused by the information transactions of neurons, and thus they directly measure neuronal activity. However, to make a whole-brain image of neuronal activity using electrophysiological methods, one would need to have closely spaced electrodes placed throughout the brain—a prospect that is neither practical nor ethical in humans. Electroencephalography (EEG) and magnetoencephalography (MEG) rely on sensors located outside of the brain, and thus these techniques can be used in humans, but they provide ambiguous spatial information that is insufficient for creating accurate images of function. Optical techniques measure neuronal activity using voltage-sensitive dyes that change their optical properties in response to changes in neuronal membrane potential. Optical imaging has very high spatial and temporal resolution, because changes in the optical properties of the dye occur within milliseconds of neuronal activity. However, the invasiveness of optical measurements and the toxicity of the dyes used preclude this approach for the study of the intact human brain.

How does fMRI create images of neuronal activity? The short answer is that it does not! Instead, fMRI creates images of physiological activity that is *correlated* with neuronal activity. As we describe in this chapter, the information-processing activity of neurons increases their metabolic requirements. To meet these requirements, energy must be provided. The vascular system supplies cells with two fuel sources, glucose and oxygen, the latter bound to hemoglobin molecules. We will continue this story in the following chapter, which discusses how differential magnetic properties of oxygenated and

Figure 6.1 A representation of the indirect relationship between fMRI signal and the sensory, motor, and cognitive processes that we wish to study. These processes are realized through signaling and integration within ensembles of neurons, and this neuronal activity requires energy in the form of adenosine triphosphate, or ATP. Because the brain does not store energy, it must create the ATP energy through the oxidation of glucose. Both oxygen and glucose are supplied through increased blood flow. The increase of blood flow and oxygen delivery flushes deoxyhemoglobin from the capillaries, venules, and small veins. Since deoxyhemoglobin molecules have magnetic field gradients that alter the spins of nearby diffusing hydrogen nuclei, the presence of deoxyhemoglobin reduces their MR signal intensity. By displacing deoxyhemoglobin with oxygenated hemoglobin, the increase in blood flow results in a local increase in MR signal.

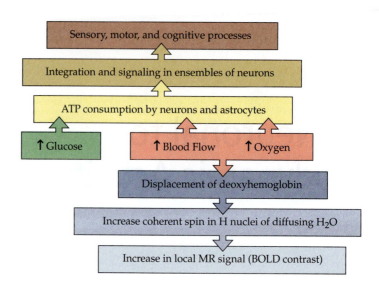

blood-oxygenation-level dependent (BOLD) contrast The difference in signal on T_2^*-weighted images as a function of the amount of deoxygenated hemoglobin.

hemodynamic Having to do with changes in blood flow or other blood properties.

neuron A cell that is the basic information-processing unit of the nervous system.

cortex (neocortex) The thin wrapping of cell bodies around the outer surface of the brain.

soma The body of the cell; it contains cytoplasm, the cell nucleus, and organelles.

dendrite A neuronal process that receives signals from other cells, performing a primarily integrative function.

axon A neuronal process that transmits an electrical impulse from the cell body to the synapse, performing a primarily signaling function.

deoxygenated hemoglobin can be used to construct images based upon **blood-oxygenation-level dependent (BOLD) contrast.** It is important to recognize that BOLD contrast is a consequence of a series of indirect effects. It results from changes in the magnetic properties of water molecules, which in turn reflect the influence of paramagnetic deoxyhemoglobin, which is a physiological correlate of oxygen consumption, which itself is a correlate of a change in neuronal activity evoked by sensory, motor, and/or cognitive processes (Figure 6.1). Through investigation of this chain of processes, a number of important questions have arisen. How direct is the link between neuronal activity and the BOLD signal? How well is the spatial distribution of neuronal activity reflected in the spatial distribution of blood flow? How well does the relative timing of vascular, or **hemodynamic,** events reflect neuronal activity in different ensembles of neurons comprising a functional network? Understanding the answers to these questions is critical for being both an informed user of fMRI methods and an informed consumer of fMRI results. We consider, in this chapter and the next, the links between neuronal activity, energy consumption, cerebral metabolism, blood flow, and MR signal.

Neuronal Activity

We begin this inquiry with the **neuron** (Figure 6.2), the basic information-processing unit of the central nervous system, focusing on the relation between information processing in the neuron and the resulting energy requirements. Modern stereological evidence has estimated that the human brain contains about 100 billion neurons. Of these, about 19 billion to 23 billion are contained within the **cortex,** or **neocortex,** a thin wrapping of cell bodies around the outer surface of the brain. Each cell body, or **soma,** of a neuron, as in other cells of the body, contains cytoplasm, organelles such as the Golgi apparatus and mitochondria, and a nucleus with DNA. In a typical neuron, the cell body gives rise to branching protoplasmic processes called **dendrites** that vary greatly in number and spatial extent. Neurons also have protoplasmic processes called **axons** that transmit information to other neurons at specialized locations on their dendrites and cell bodies.

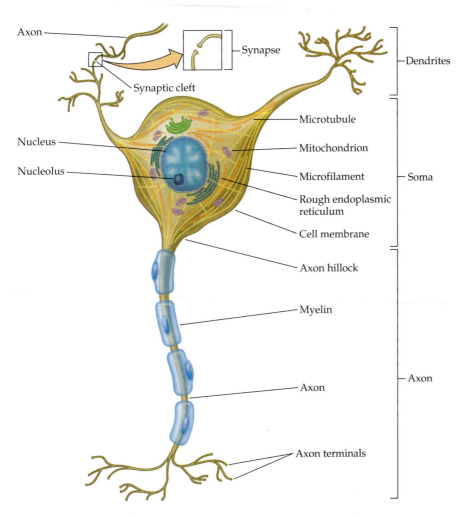

Figure 6.2 The neuron. Neurons are organized into three basic parts. Dendrites integrate signals coming from other neurons via small gaps known as synapses. The soma, or cell body, of the neuron contains a nucleus and organelles that support metabolic and structural properties of the neuron. Changes in the membrane potential of the neuron are signaled to other neurons by action potentials that travel along its axon.

Neurons come in many varieties, some with dense dendritic arbors and some without any dendrites. Some neurons have long axons that travel great distances in the nervous system, others have short axons that terminate locally, and still others have no axons at all. In addition to neurons, the human brain contains other types of supporting cells, known as **glial cells (glia),** including astrocytes, oligodendrocytes, and microglial cells. Glial cells are not thought to be directly involved in information processing within the brain, but they do participate indirectly by helping with synapse formation and regulation of the chemical environment surrounding neurons.

To a useful first approximation, neuronal activity can be characterized as either integrative or signaling. **Integrative activity** collects inputs from other neurons through connections on both dendrites and the cell body. **Signaling activity** results primarily from activity of axons, which transmit the outcome of integrative processes to one or more other neurons. The transfer of information between neurons occurs at specialized junctions called **synapses,** where the ending of an axonal process from one neuron (i.e., the presynaptic terminal) is apposed to the postsynaptic membrane of the dendrite or soma of another neuron. In most synapses, the presynaptic and postsynaptic elements are separated by a small gap, the **synaptic cleft,** in which chemicals released from the presynaptic element influence activity in the postsynaptic membrane. In a relatively small number of specialized synapses, the presynaptic and postsynaptic membranes are in physical con-

glial cells (glia) Brain cells that support the activities of neurons but are not primarily involved with information transmission.

integrative activity The collection of inputs from other neurons through dendritic or somatic connections.

signaling activity The transmission of the outcome of an integrative process from one neuron to another.

synapse A junction between neurons where the presynaptic process of an axon is apposed to the postsynaptic process of a dendrite or cell body.

synaptic cleft A gap between presynaptic and postsynaptic membranes.

concentration gradient A difference in the density of a substance across space. Substances diffuse along a concentration gradient from areas of high concentration to areas of low concentration.

ion A charged atom.

ion channel A pore in the membrane of a cell that allows passage of particular ions under certain conditions.

pump A transport system that moves ions across a cell membrane against their concentration gradient.

sodium–potassium pump A transport system that removes three sodium ions from within a cell while bringing two potassium ions into the cell.

tact and electrical signaling events cross the membranes without intervening chemical messengers. A neuron may have hundreds or even thousands of synapses on its dendrites and soma, and it has been estimated that there are 100 trillion synapses in the human brain.

Ion Channels in Neurons

Both neuronal integration and signaling depend upon the properties of neuronal membranes, which are lipid bilayers that separate the internal contents of the neuron from the external milieu. An important role of neuronal membranes is to restrict the flow of chemical substances into and out of the neurons. When substances are allowed to diffuse freely, they tend to diffuse from areas of high concentration to areas of low concentration. That is, they move along a **concentration gradient** until equilibrium is reached. However, neuronal membranes prevent free diffusion. They do, though, have embedded proteins that form pores or channels through which some **ions,** such as sodium (Na^+), chloride (Cl^-), potassium (K^+), and calcium (Ca^{2+}), can diffuse (Figure 6.3). (Note that an ion is an atom that has a negative charge from having gained one or more electrons, or a positive charge from having lost one or more electrons.) These **ion channels** are selective, such that some species of ions can pass and others cannot. Furthermore, channels have gating mechanisms that can close them or open them to ion traffic. While some gating mechanisms depend on the actions of specific molecules, others are also voltage-dependent and open when the electrical potential difference across the membrane has reached a particular threshold.

While an open channel can allow ions to diffuse passively down their concentration gradient, membranes also contain transporters, or **pumps,** that can move ions across the membrane against their concentration gradient and thereby create or maintain an unequal distribution of some ions (see Figure 6.3). One of the most important pumps is the **sodium–potassium pump.** The sodium–potassium pump uses a transporter molecule that forces three sodium ions (Na^+) out of the cell and then picks up and brings two potassium ions (K^+) into the cell on the return trip. Due to the action of the sodium–potassium pump and other transporters, as well as to the selective permeability of the membrane channels to different ions, a neuron at rest has a greater concentration of K^+ inside its membrane and a greater concentration of Na^+, Ca^{2+}, and Cl^- outside its membrane. Any transient change in the permeability of the membrane will cause an influx (movement into the cell) or an efflux (movement out of the cell) of these ions as the system attempts to eliminate the concentration gradient and establish equilibrium.

Figure 6.3 Ion channels and pumps. Ion channels allow particular ions to diffuse across membranes along concentration gradients. They may be opened by the actions of particular molecules, or they may open when the voltage difference across the membrane reaches a threshold. Pumps move ions across membranes against their concentration gradients, usually at a cost of energy supplied by ATP. A very important pump transports sodium out of the cell while bringing potassium into the cell.

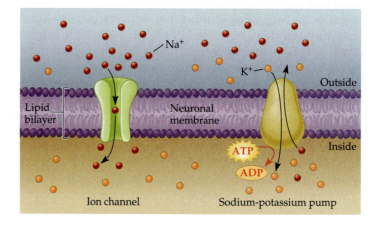

While the diffusion of substances through channels down their concentration gradients requires only sufficient kinetic energy from heat, the operation of pumps requires cellular sources of energy. For example, one turn of the sodium–potassium pump requires the energy of one molecule of adenosine triphosphate, or ATP (we will have more to say about ATP later in this chapter in the section on cerebral metabolism). Consider the analogy of a water tower where holes in the bottom of the water reservoir allow passage of the water into descending pipes below. Here the gravity gradient is analogous to the concentration gradient and the holes are analogous to open ion channels. The water will move through the holes and run through the pipes down the gravity gradient without additional energy. The situation is quite different, however, if we want to return the escaping water to the water tower. Active pumping against the gravity gradient is now required, and the pump requires energy to operate. Note that while this analogy is instructive, it is incomplete with respect to ions. Because ions have electrical charge, their unequal distribution also results in an electrical potential (about −40 to −70 mV) between the inside and outside of the membrane. Thus, the movement of ions across a membrane is governed by both chemical and electrical gradients.

Neurotransmitters and Action Potentials

The primary locus for communication between neurons is the synapse (Figure 6.4). The presynaptic process of the axon releases **neurotransmitters,** which are chemicals that diffuse across the synaptic cleft and interact with receptors on the postsynaptic membrane that gate ion channels. For example, the neurotransmitter **glutamate** opens normally blocked ion channels that allow Na^+ to move down its concentration gradient and through the postsynaptic membrane into the neuron. This influx of Na^+ ions decreases the electrical potential between the inside and outside of the membrane at the channel location. (Note that another type of glutamate receptor called the NMDA [N-methyl-D-aspartate] receptor admits Ca^{2+} through its channel when a threshold membrane potential is reached.) This local depolarization of the postsynaptic cell membrane is referred to as an **excitatory postsynaptic potential,** or **EPSP,** and thus glutamate is known as an excitatory neurotransmitter. Glutamate is the most common excitatory neurotransmitter in the brain, and it is released by about 90% of all neurons.

Other neurotransmitters, such as **γ-aminobutyric acid,** or **GABA,** interact with other receptors to open chlorine or potassium channels. Either the influx of the negatively charged Cl^- into the neuron or the efflux of the positively charged K^+ out of the neuron results in a net increase in the resting potential in the vicinity of these newly opened channels. This local hyperpolarization of the neuronal membrane is referred to as an **inhibitory postsynaptic potential,** or **IPSP,** and thus GABA is known as an inhibitory neurotransmitter.

A single EPSP or IPSP is a limited event. Afterward, the neurotransmitter will be deactivated or removed from the synaptic cleft and receptor, the channel that was opened by the neurotransmitter will close, and the pumps will restore both the unequal distribution of ions across the membrane and the resting membrane potential. However, because a neuron may have thousands of synapses, it may experience a barrage of individual EPSPs and IPSPs throughout its dendritic trees and soma. These depolarizing and hyperpolarizing membrane potentials are integrated by the neuron. Both their timing and spatial pattern influence the net polarization of a specialized region of the soma called the **axon hillock,** which is located where the axon emerges from the cell body.

neurotransmitters Chemicals released by presynaptic neurons that travel across the synaptic cleft to influence receptors on postsynaptic neurons.

glutamate One of the most important excitatory neurotransmitters.

excitatory postsynaptic potential (EPSP) A depolarization of the postsynaptic cell membrane.

γ-aminobutyric acid (GABA) One of the most important inhibitory neurotransmitters.

inhibitory postsynaptic potential (IPSP) A hyperpolarization of the postsynaptic cell membrane.

axon hillock A region of the cell body located at the emergence of the axon. Changes in its electrical potential lead to the generation of action potentials.

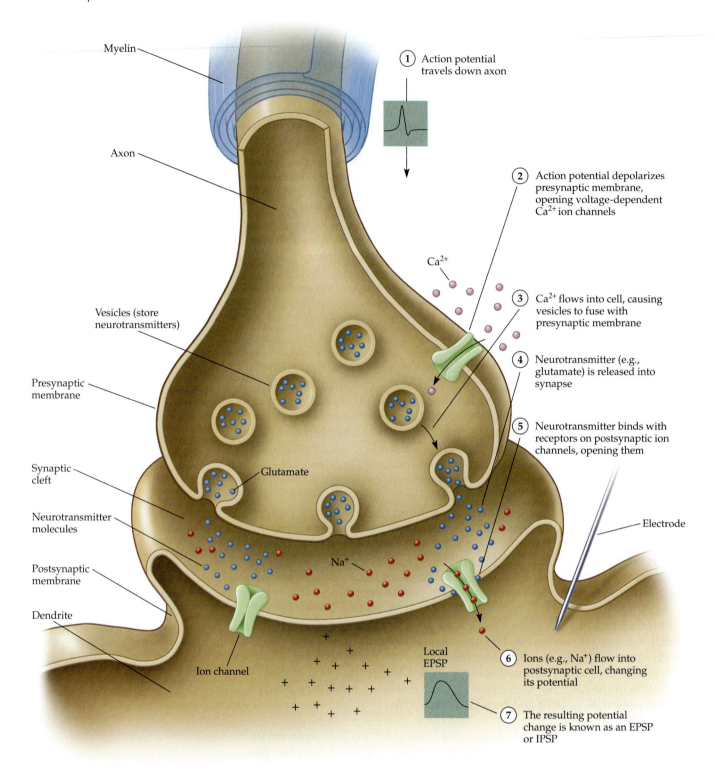

Myelin

Axon

① Action potential
travels down axon

② Action potential depolarizes
presynaptic membrane,
opening voltage-dependent
Ca^{2+} ion channels

Ca^{2+}

Vesicles (store
neurotransmitters)

③ Ca^{2+} flows into cell, causing
vesicles to fuse with
presynaptic membrane

Presynaptic
membrane

④ Neurotransmitter (e.g.,
glutamate) is released into
synapse

⑤ Neurotransmitter binds with
receptors on postsynaptic ion
channels, opening them

Glutamate

Synaptic
cleft

Electrode

Neurotransmitter
molecules

Na^+

Postsynaptic
membrane

Local
EPSP

Dendrite

⑥ Ions (e.g., Na^+) flow into
postsynaptic cell, changing
its potential

Ion channel

⑦ The resulting potential
change is known as an EPSP
or IPSP

Figure 6.4 Synapses and neurotransmitter release.

If, over a brief time interval, the net depolarization experienced at the axon
hillock (i.e., the sum of the depolarizing signals minus the sum of the hyperpolarizing signals) decreases below a threshold voltage, large numbers of
voltage-gated sodium channels will open and there will be a concomitant

large influx of Na^+ into the cell. This large depolarization spreads down the axon, opening more voltage-gated sodium channels farther and farther down the membrane. This wave of depolarization, known as a nerve impulse or **action potential,** sweeps down the axon in a self-propagating manner, independently of the EPSPs that triggered it. Eventually, the nerve impulse will reach the end of the axon, where a presynaptic terminal forms a synapse with another neuron. Here the wave of depolarization will open voltage-dependent channels in the presynaptic membrane that allow Ca^{2+} influx into the presynaptic terminal. This influx of Ca^{2+} initiates a cascade of events that causes the release of neurotransmitter into the synaptic cleft, which interacts with receptors that gate postsynaptic ion channels, and thus initiates either an IPSP or EPSP on the postsynaptic membrane of the target neuron.

One can think of information processing by neurons as the combination of their integrative and signaling roles. The spatiotemporal pattern of EPSPs and IPSPs, each generated at a synapse from another cell, determines the relative polarization of the neuron. If the axon hillock region of the neuron becomes sufficiently depolarized, an action potential occurs and the polarizations of other neurons are influenced by the action of that action potential upon their postsynaptic membranes. Note that only EPSPs can trigger action potentials. Hyperpolarizing IPSPs, in contrast, make action potentials less likely by making the membrane potential more negative. An EPSP that might have sufficient strength to depolarize the axon hillock region below threshold when this region is at its normal resting potential may not be able to do so if the axon hillock was hyperpolarized by a preceding IPSP.

The generation of an EPSP, IPSP, or action potential does not in itself require an external source of energy, because the associated movements of ions are along concentration gradients. However, these potentials cause changes in ion concentration that require energy to restore. For example, the influx of Na^+ during an action potential causes a change in the local membrane potential of the neuron, so electrical gradients now oppose the reentry of the positively charged K^+ into the cell. To restore the asymmetric distribution of Na^+ and K^+ across the cell membrane and restore the resting membrane potential, the sodium–potassium pump removes three Na^+ ions from within the cell for every two K^+ ions it brings into the cell. The energy requirements for restoration of these concentration gradients are discussed in the next section.

Cerebral Metabolism: Neuronal Energy Consumption

Although integrative and signaling properties of neurons are ultimately important for understanding brain function, our immediate interest is in their energy requirements. Why are the energy demands of neurons important for fMRI? To help answer this question, imagine that neurons have sufficient local stores of energy available to buffer moderate changes in their neuronal firing rates. Could we then construct meaningful theories of brain function based upon energy delivery by the blood supply? Or imagine that it were known that the main consumption of energy following neuronal firing was to increase the synthesis of protein, perhaps related to structural changes in the neurons initiated by learning. How would this change the interpretation of neuroimaging results? Finally, imagine that we learned (as was once thought true) that the generation of action potentials accounted for a tiny fraction, less than 3%, of the brain's energy budget. How then would one account for the enormous metabolic demands of the active brain?

action potential A wave of depolarization that travels down a neuronal axon.

adenosine triphosphate (ATP) A nucleotide containing three phosphate groups that is the primary energy source for cells in the human body.

glucose A sugar made by the human body whose stored energy is used to form ATP.

glycolysis The process of breaking down glucose into other compounds to produce ATP.

aerobic glycolysis The process, consisting of glycolysis, the TCA cycle, and the electron transport chain, that breaks down glucose in the presence of oxygen, resulting in a gain of 36 ATP.

TCA cycle The second step in aerobic glycolysis; it involves the oxidation of pyruvate.

electron transport chain The third step in aerobic glycolysis; it generates an additional 34 ATP.

anaerobic glycolysis The conversion of glucose to lactate in the absence of oxygen.

> ### Thought Question
> Assume that the brain did indeed have large local stores of energy that could support neuronal activity. Based on what you know so far, would fMRI be possible?

We now know that these hypothetical situations are not true: Local brain regions require external sources of energy to support metabolic processes, and much of this energy facilitates the restoration of concentration gradients following changes in membrane potential. Thus, functional neuroimaging methods that measure metabolic correlates of neuronal activity can be used to make inferences about brain activity. Stated another way, although our interests as neuroscientists may be in the relation between mind and brain (where in this context "brain" is usually shorthand for the activity of neurons), our measures depend upon the relation between neuronal activity and the energy needed to support that activity. Here, we delve more deeply into the energy needs of neurons and how those needs are met by the vascular system.

Adenosine Triphosphate (ATP)

The principal energy currency for cells in the human body is **adenosine triphosphate,** or **ATP.** ATP is a nucleotide that contains three phosphate groups. Free energy is released when the third phosphate group of ATP is removed by the insertion of a water molecule, in a reaction called hydrolysis. In body tissues, ATP can be produced from many substrates, including the sugar **glucose,** fatty acids, ketone bodies, and even proteins. Glucose is stored throughout the body in the form of glycogen. However, there is little glycogen in the brain, and thus, to maintain function, the brain requires that the blood provide a continuous supply of glucose and oxygen. Under normal circumstances, the brain extracts about 10% of the approximately 90 mg/dL of glucose in arterial blood. If the glucose concentration in blood falls below about 30 mg/dL, a coma may ensue.

The generation of ATP from glucose has three primary steps: glycolysis, the TCA cycle, and the electron transport chain (Figure 6.5). Glucose transporter molecules move glucose through the interstitial space from capillaries to neurons. Once in the cytoplasm of brain cells, glucose is broken down through a reaction called **glycolysis,** in which the six-carbon glucose is cleaved into two three-carbon sugars, which are then catabolized through a series of steps into a compound called pyruvate. Glycolysis consumes 2 ATP molecules but produces 4 ATP molecules, for a net gain of 2 ATP. If oxygen is present, the process is called **aerobic glycolysis** and the pyruvate product then enters a reaction called the tricarboxylic cycle, or **TCA cycle,** also known as the citric acid cycle or the Krebs cycle. The TCA cycle uses oxygen extracted from the hemoglobin in the blood to oxidize pyruvate, and a network of proteins in the cell mitochondria, known as the **electron transport chain,** passes electrons across a series of compounds to release energy, which in turn is used by an enzyme known as ATP synthase to generate an additional 34 ATP molecules. So, while glycolysis itself produces only 2 ATP molecules from each glucose molecule, the addition of oxygen allows the production of a total of 36 ATP molecules from each molecule of glucose.

If oxygen is not present, the process is called **anaerobic glycolysis** and the pyruvate is reduced to the end product lactate. During strenuous exer-

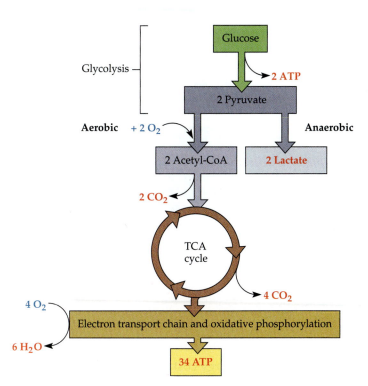

Figure 6.5 Anaerobic and aerobic glycolysis. In anaerobic glycolysis, glucose is converted to lactate via a fast process that produces 2 ATP. If oxygen is present, then the resulting aerobic glycolysis produces an additional 34 ATP.

cise with insufficient oxygen, anaerobic glycolysis occurs in muscles, and it is the buildup of lactate that can cause pain and fatigue. Lactate is removed from the muscles by the vascular system. While anaerobic glycolysis is a relatively inefficient source of ATP, it is quite fast: it can occur at a rate about 100 times faster than the further oxidation of pyruvate into ATP through the TCA cycle and electron transport chain. In addition, some cells can convert lactate back into pyruvate and use it as a fuel for the TCA cycle and the production of more ATP. (Note that the trade-off between fast but inefficient anaerobic glycolysis and slow but efficient aerobic glycolysis is important for the models of BOLD contrast, and is discussed in the next chapter.)

The energy provided by ATP supports many processes in the brain. For example, there are housekeeping functions related to the synthesis of proteins, the maintenance and turnover of membranes, and axoplasmic transport that require energy. Neurons also require energy to synthesize, package, and break down neurotransmitters and to operate the pumps that restore unequal distributions of ions following EPSPs, IPSPs, and action potentials. Noting that the gray matter of the brain consumes about 30 to 50 µmol of ATP every minute for each gram of tissue (i.e., 30 to 50 µmol/g/min of ATP), while the brain in coma consumes only about 10 µmol/g/min of ATP, Attwell and Laughlin concluded that integrative and signaling activity in neurons accounts for about 75% of the energy expenditure in gray matter while housekeeping functions account for about 25%. Because the chemical reactions associated with neuronal integration and signaling are well known, they were able to determine how the brain's energy budget was further allocated.

Attwell and Laughlin estimated that the restoration of membrane concentration gradients following the passage of an action potential consumes 47% of the energy expenditure, while restoring postsynaptic membrane concentration gradients following IPSPs and EPSPs consumes 34% (Figure 6.6). The

Figure 6.6 The energy budget of the (rodent) brain. Data from the rodent brain, shown here, indicates the vast majority of energy required to support the restoration of concentration gradients following action potentials and postsynaptic potentials. While human data are not available for these categories, the differences in brain structure in humans compared with rodents would serve to increase the budget needed for restoring gradients after postsynaptic potentials. These results indicate that the primary energy expenditure of the brain supports the integrative and signaling roles of neurons. (Data from Atwell and Laughlin, 2001.)

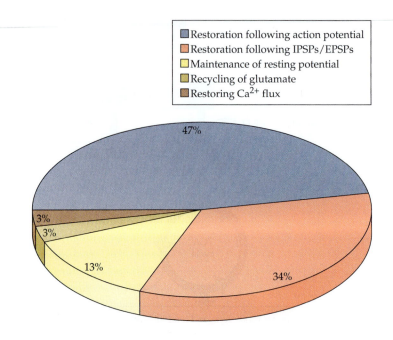

■ Restoration following action potential
■ Restoration following IPSPs/EPSPs
■ Maintenance of resting potential
■ Recycling of glutamate
■ Restoring Ca^{2+} flux

authors commented that the energy cost of IPSPs is likely less than that of EPSPs, for two reasons: Cl^- ions move down a smaller electrochemical gradient than Na^+ ions, and inhibitory synapses are outnumbered by excitatory synapses in the brain by about an order of magnitude. The maintenance of the resting potential in neurons and glia was estimated to consume 13% of the energy expenditure. Note that the consumption of energy in each of these processes principally involves the operation of the sodium–potassium pump. Furthermore, given that glutamate is by far the dominant excitatory neurotransmitter in the brain, most of the energy budget associated with signaling and integration involves this single neurotransmitter. The uptake, breakdown, and repackaging of glutamate was estimated to consume 3% of the energy budget, and restoring Ca^{2+} fluxes in presynaptic membranes accounted for the remaining 3%.

Atwell and Laughlin's calculations were based upon data from the rodent brain. In extrapolating their results to primates, they argued that the greater number of synapses per neuron in primates would cause a greater proportion of the energy budget to be spent on restoring postsynaptic concentration gradients, perhaps as high as 74%. They concluded, therefore, that the metabolic demands of integrative and signaling activity of neurons form the bulk of the energy requirements of the human brain. A continuous supply of metabolites through the vascular system is necessary for these energy demands to be met.

The Vascular System of the Brain

The idea that changes within the vascular system of the brain reflect changes in brain function is not new. The nineteenth-century British physiologists Roy and Sherrington postulated that changes in activity associated with specific brain functions might result in locally increased blood flow:

> These facts seem to us to indicate the existence of an automatic mechanism
> by which the blood supply of any part of the cerebral tissue is varied in

accordance with the activity of the chemical changes which underlie the functional action of that part. Bearing in mind that strong evidence exists of localisation of function in the brain, we are of the opinion that an automatic mechanism, of the kind just referred to, is well fitted to provide for a local variation of the blood supply in accordance with local variations of the functional activity. (1890, p.105)

A variant of this idea, that activity could cause changes in blood flow, was tested in an early experiment conducted by the Italian physiologist Angelo Mosso in the late nineteenth century. Mosso had pioneered the use of plethysmographic measurement of comparative blood volume in the brain and extremities, and he was interested in whether thinking resulted in increased blood flow to the brain. His earlier studies had revealed that blood flow to the brain decreases during sleep and increases with waking, consistent with the idea that brain activity requires a greater blood supply than inactivity. To directly test the hypothesis that active thought requires increased blood volume in the brain, Mosso constructed an ingenious apparatus (Figure 6.7), as reported by William James in his *Principles of Psychology*:

> The subject to be observed lay on a delicately balanced table which could tip downward either at the head or at the foot if the weight of either end were increased. The moment emotional or intellectual activity began in the subject, down went the balance at the head end, in consequence of the redistribution of blood in his system. (1890, p. 98)

Though its results suggest a clear relation between the vascular system and cognitive function, this experiment is unlikely to have worked as well as Mosso reported. For the table to tip downward, the total blood volume of

Figure 6.7 The crude imaging apparatus used by Angelo Mosso in the late nineteenth century. Mosso theorized that thinking drew blood to the brain, and constructed a balance device to measure changes in weight associated with this increased blood flow. The subject lay down on a large table with a fulcrum at its center, so that any change in weight would cause the table to tip.

the brain would need to increase by an appreciable amount. But blood volume is relatively constant across time, even if blood flow may change in response to metabolic demands. To use a hydraulic analogy, if pipes are filled with water, they will weigh essentially the same regardless of whether the water is flowing quickly or slowly. Nevertheless, the idea that changes in blood flow may result from local functional changes in the brain was a remarkable insight. (The discussion of this issue in James's *Principles*, especially the difference between causal and correlational roles for blood flow, is highly recommended to the interested student.) We explore this idea over the following sections, building to the idea that functional activity of neurons may evoke changes in blood flow and thus changes in the local concentration of metabolites.

Arteries, Capillaries, and Veins

From our discussion earlier in this chapter, we know that integrative and signaling activity of neurons comprises a large proportion of the brain's energy budget, and we also know that there is little energy stored in the brain. The energy needs of neurons and glia are met by the ATP created during glycolysis and during the subsequent oxidation of pyruvate. The oxygen and glucose fuel required for those reactions are delivered through the vascular system (Figure 6.8). The adult human brain consumes about 54 mL of blood for each 100 grams of tissue every minute. This adds up to about 750 mL/min for the average 1400-gram brain and represents about 15 to 20% of the blood flow in the entire human body. Thus, although the brain constitutes a mere 2 to 3% of total body weight, it consumes about 20% of blood oxygen.

The lungs are the source of the oxygen carried by the blood. Oxygen diffuses from the alveoli of the lungs, via small blood vessels, into red blood cells, where it binds to hemoglobin. Four oxygen molecules are attached to each hemoglobin molecule, and there are about 280 million hemoglobin molecules in each red blood cell. The oxygen-rich blood returns to the heart from the lungs, where it enters the left atrium, moves to the left ventricle, and is pumped from the left ventricle through the aorta. The aorta gives rise

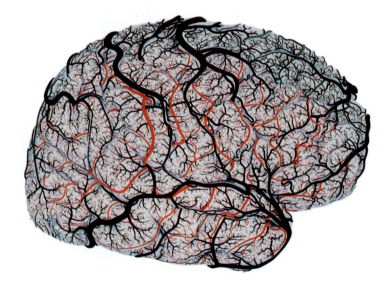

Figure 6.8 Blood supply to the human cerebrum. As illustrated here, the surface pattern of blood supply to the human cerebrum is highly complex. The red vessels are tributaries of the middle cerebral artery, the green vessels are tributaries of the anterior cerebral artery, and the blue vessels are tributaries of the posterior cerebral artery. The veins are shown in black. (From Duvernoy, Delon, and Vannson, 1981.)

to several large **arteries**—thick-walled vessels that carry blood away from the heart. Each artery branches into smaller arteries and then to even smaller **arterioles** that eventually terminate in capillaries. The change in scale as these vessels branch is remarkable. The diameter of the aorta in an adult human is about 2.5 cm (about 1 inch), typical large arteries can be 4 to 10 mm in diameter, while the diameters of arterioles are in the range of 10 to 50 µm. Thus, the largest artery has a diameter about 2500 times that of the smallest arteriole!

The extraction of oxygen and glucose from the blood and the removal of waste carbon dioxide occurs at the surfaces of the capillaries. **Capillaries** are thin-walled vessels comparable in diameter (5 to 10 µm) to the width of a red blood cell (~7.5 µm). The small size of individual capillaries is more than made up for by their number and density (Figure 6.9). It has been estimated that cells in the body are, on average, less than 50 µm from a capillary. If lined up end to end, the capillary network in the human body would stretch 60,000 miles and have a total surface area of 800 to 1000 m². Capillary density provides an indication of cellular metabolism, such that areas with high metabolism have a higher density of capillaries than those with low metabolism. For example, in the cat brain, gray matter composed of neural cell bodies has twice the capillary density as white matter composed largely of axonal processes.

arteries Blood vessels that carry oxygenated blood from the heart to the rest of the body.

arterioles Small arteries.

capillaries Small and thin-walled blood vessels. The extraction of oxygen and glucose from the blood and the removal of waste carbon dioxide occur in the capillaries.

venules Small veins.

veins Blood vessels that carry blood from the body to the heart. Blood in the veins (except for the pulmonary vein) is deoxygenated.

Thought Question

Many techniques in fMRI attempt to localize hemodynamic activity to the capillaries. Why is this desirable for studies of brain function?

After the oxygen molecules are extracted from the hemoglobin in the capillaries, the deoxygenated hemoglobin molecules, which now bind waste carbon dioxide, are carried from the capillaries to small **venules** that are comparable in size to arterioles. The venules collect into larger and larger **veins** that eventually return the oxygen-poor blood through the vena cava to the right atrium of the heart. The deoxygenated blood travels to the right ventricle, which pumps it to the lungs, where the waste carbon dioxide is released as a gas and where oxygen once again binds to the hemoglobin to start the cycle again.

Arterial and Venous Anatomy of the Human Brain

The flow of blood to the brain is supplied by two major arterial systems: the left and right internal carotid arteries and the vertebral/basilar arteries (Figure 6.10A and B). A short distance from the heart, the aortic arch gives rise to the right and left common carotid arteries, which ascend in the neck before each divides into the external and internal carotid arteries. While the external carotid arteries supply the external head and face with blood, the internal carotid arteries enter through an opening in the base of the skull called the foramen lacerum and supply blood to the brain. The aortic

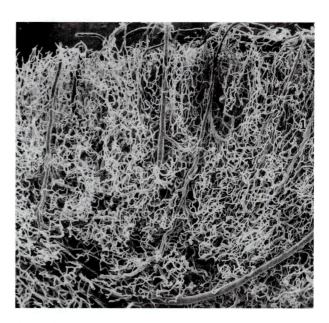

Figure 6.9 Capillary structure. This electron microscope image shows the density of capillary beds within the cortex. (From Duvernoy, Delon, and Vannson, 1981.)

(A)

(B)

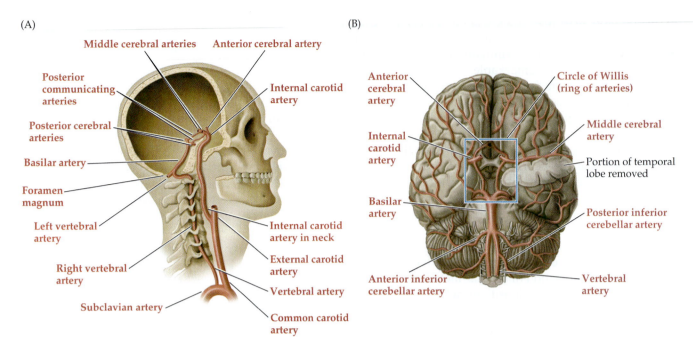

Figure 6.10 The arterial system of the human brain. The arterial distribution of blood to the human brain is shown in cross-section (A), and in a ventral view of the base of the brain (B). The box shows the anastomoses of the basilar artery and internal carotid arteries that form the circle of Willis.

circle of Willis The interconnection between the basilar artery and the carotid arteries at the base of the cranial vault.

arch also gives rise to the right and left subclavian arteries, which, in turn, give rise to the left and right vertebral arteries, which run along the anterior surface of the spinal cord and enter the brain through the foramen magnum. The vertebral arteries give rise to the descending arterial branches, which provide blood to the brain stem, medulla, and spinal cord. As the vertebral arteries ascend to the level of the pons, they fuse into the single basilar artery, which gives rise to arterial branches that perfuse the pons and cerebellum.

The basilar artery interconnects, or forms an anastomosis, with the left and right internal carotid arteries to form the **circle of Willis,** named for the celebrated English physician Thomas Willis, who first illustrated this vascular structure in 1664. The circle of Willis sits on the floor of the cranial vault, surrounding the brain stem. Supplied by blood from both arterial systems, it gives rise bilaterally to the anterior, middle, and posterior cerebral arteries (Figure 6.11A and B). Each of these major cerebral arteries provides the blood supply to distinct regions of the brain: The anterior cerebral artery primarily supplies the medial surface of the brain and the head of the caudate, branches of the middle cerebral artery supply much of the lateral and superior cerebral cortex as well as the remainder of the basal ganglia, and the posterior cerebral artery supplies the posterior temporal and occipital cortex. This specificity has important implications for neurology, in that strokes within particular arteries tend to affect particular regions of cortex and thus have functionally distinct cognitive consequences.

The venous drainage of the brain's circulation (Figure 6.11C and D) is accomplished through the left and right jugular veins, which exit the skull base through the jugular foramen, then join with the subclavian vein and eventually the superior vena cava, progressing to the right atrium and ventricle of the heart, which pumps blood to the lungs. The jugular veins themselves are fed by the sinus system of the brain. **Sinuses** are long venous channels that are formed by the meningeal covering of the brain. The superior sagittal sinus runs along the superior midline of the entire brain, where the two hemispheres meet. Large cerebral veins on the cortical surface drain into the superior sagittal sinus, and blood is transported back along the sinus to the back of the brain. The inferior sagittal sinus follows a similar midline path as the superior sagittal sinus, but deeper in the brain in the part of the dura mater called the falx, which extends down into the midline separating the cerebral hemispheres. The inferior sagittal sinus empties into the straight sinus, which runs back above the cerebellum and joins with the superior sagittal sinus at the back of the brain to form the transverse sinus.

sinuses Cavities. The term *sinus* has two primary meanings in neuroanatomy: (1) long venous channels formed by meningeal coverings that form the primary draining system for the brain, and (2) air-filled cavities in the skull.

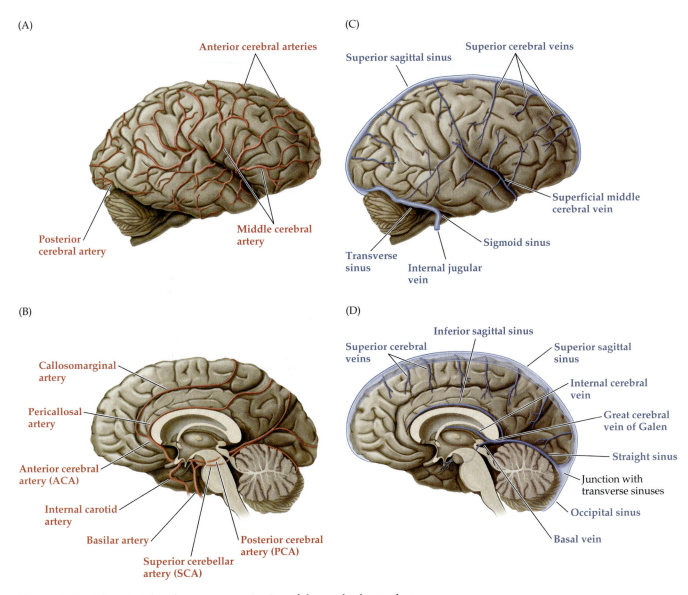

Figure 6.11 The arterial and venous organization of the cerebral vasculature. Shown are lateral (A) and medial (B) views of the major arterial systems of the human brain. Blood is drained by a system of sinuses and veins, shown here in lateral (C) and medial (D) veins.

(A)

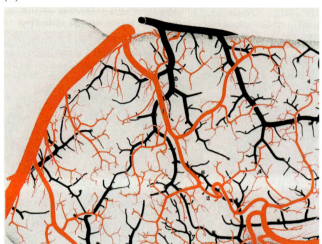

(B)

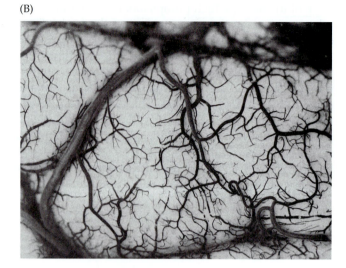

Figure 6.12   Microcirculation of the human brain. The distribution of arteries (red) and veins (black) on the medial orbital gyrus of the human brain as shown in (A). A photograph of the same region is provided in (B). (From Duvernoy, Delon, and Vannson, 1986.)

The transverse sinus wraps around to the left and right of the base of the brain, terminating in the left and right internal jugular veins.

Microcirculation

The blood supply to the cerebral and cerebellar cortices is derived from meningeal arteries that traverse the pia on the cortical surface (Figure 6.12). A distinction can be drawn between conducting and distributing arteries. Conducting arteries run for long distances along the pial surface and are about 700 µm in diameter (compared to the 4- to 5-mm diameter of the internal carotid and basilar arteries). In the cerebral cortex, many conducting arteries run along the sulci that demarcate adjacent gyri, while others run directly across the gyral surface. Many smaller distributing arteries, each about 150 to 200 µm in diameter, branch from the conducting arteries. Many researchers have noted constrictions where the distributing arteries branch from larger arteries, suggestive of the presence of muscular sphincters. The possible role of these sphincters in the control of blood flow will be discussed in more detail shortly. The distributing arteries continue to ramify on the cortical surface into yet smaller precortical arteries (or arterioles) of about 50 to 70 µm in diameter. Anastomoses between arterioles have been observed in several studies. According to Nonaka and colleagues, a distributing artery supplies a 3.5-by-2-mm area on the cortical surface, while each precortical artery supplies an approximately 1-by-1-mm area of cortical surface. Each precortical artery then ramifies into smaller arterioles of about 30- to 40 µm diameter that penetrate the cortical surface at right angles.

Duvernoy and colleagues have classified these intracortical arterioles into six categories. The first five categories appear to vascularize different cortical levels, with increasing vessel diameters noted for those that vascularize deeper layers. The density of vascularization is not uniform across cortical layers; noticeably denser vascularization is observed where the highest concentrations of neural cell bodies are located (Figure 6.13). Some intracortical vessels have been described as resembling a fountain or candelabra, with dense ramifications ascending into more superficial layers. The sixth category of intracortical arterioles consists of the largest-diameter vessels, which appear to penetrate straight though the cortex to vascularize the white matter below. The vascularization in white matter is considerably less dense than that of gray matter.

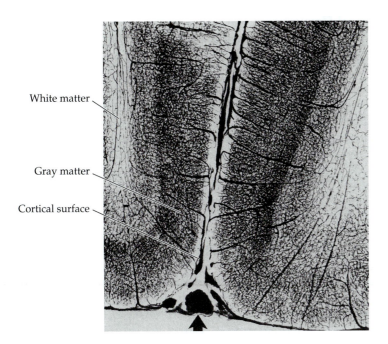

White matter

Gray matter

Cortical surface

Figure 6.13 Distribution of vascularization across cortical layers. This figure shows the distribution of the blood supply to the cortical layers in the calcarine sulcus. The penetrating arteries enter the cortical layers perpendicular to the cortical surface. The density of the vascular ramifications varies across the cortical layers and is greatest where cell density is greatest. The deep white matter beneath the cortical layers has the lowest vascular density. The arrow points to the superior sagittal sinus. (From Duvernoy, Delon, and Vannson, 1981.)

Blood Flow

Increased neuronal activity is supported by increased blood flow. Blood flow and blood flow velocity vary considerably within the vascular system and are influenced by many physical and physiological factors, including blood pressure; the diameter of the blood vessel; the density of the red blood cells; the amount of oxygen and carbon dioxide in the blood; and the age, health, and activity level of the subject. Peak flow velocity in the aorta can exceed 90 cm/s. Using a technique called transcranial Doppler, which uses the same principles as measurements of the speed of a moving ball or car, researchers have measured mean blood flow velocity in the basilar and internal carotid arteries at about 40 cm/s. Blood flow through the smaller arteries and arterioles is considerably slower, ranging from 10 to 250 mm/s, and blood flow through the capillaries can be less than 1 mm/s. As the blood collects in venules, the velocity once again increases to a range of 10 to 250 mm/s. These values are approximate, because the velocity of flow measured can vary as a function of the measurement technique.

Holding other factors constant, blood flow (volume per unit time) is proportional to the pressure difference from one end of the vessel to the other divided by the resistance of the vessel to flow. As a result, flow is proportional to vessel radius expressed to the 4th power, so very small changes in vessel diameter can produce large changes in resistance and flow. For example, doubling the size of the vessel would increase flow by a factor of 16. In large arteries, blood flow is pulsatile due to the pumping of the heart and flow velocity can vary greatly between the peak flow measures obtained during systole and the lower velocities measured during diastole.

The small arteries on the pial surface have high resistance and thus oppose flow. This high resistance to flow helps convert the pulsatile ejection of blood from the heart into a steady flow through the capillaries. Indeed, if no resistance were present and high blood pressure persisted into the capillaries, blood plasma would be pushed through the thin capillary walls, leading to a considerable loss of blood volume. These so-called **resistance vessels** are an important component in the control of blood flow through the capillary bed.

resistance vessels Arterioles that control the flow of blood through the capillary bed.

vasoactive substances Substances that change the caliber of blood vessels.

Control of Blood Flow

Changes in blood flow that accompany increases in neuronal activity are believed to be initiated when active neurons release substances that diffuse through the extracellular space and reach nearby blood vessels. These **vasoactive substances** cause the vessels to dilate, and because the increase in diameter reduces the vessels' resistance to flow, increased flow results. However, this local change is not sufficient in and of itself to regulate blood flow, because flow is controlled by the higher-resistance arterioles located on the pial surface, well upstream and distant from the locus of activation. Thus, there needs to be coordination between the local blood flow changes induced by neural activity and upstream control mechanisms.

Several candidate substances have been identified that may play a role in the local control of blood flow. These include K$^+$ ions, which enter the extracellular space as a function of synaptic activity, and adenosine, which is created during the dephosphorylation of ATP and which increases in concentration during high metabolic activity. Recent studies have focused upon nitric oxide, which is released by activation of central pathways or local neurons. Nitric oxide mediates both local and distal vasodilation, or increase in the size of blood vessels, by causing the smooth muscle cells surrounding arterioles to relax. Gap junctions between endothelial cells in arteries propagate the vasodilatory response upstream, causing increased blood flow to larger arteries. This propagated action initiated by nitric oxide along the arterioles is roughly analogous to propagated neural action potentials.

Animal studies by many investigators, including Ngai, Winn, and colleagues, and Iadecola and colleagues, have demonstrated the relationship between sensory stimulation and local blood flow changes. Winn's group applied low-intensity somatosensory stimulation to the sciatic nerve of the rat while monitoring the pial vasculature through a closed-cranial window. The time courses of vascular diameter and blood flow (using laser-Doppler) were measured in response to 20-s periods of stimulation. Vascular diameter increased rapidly with the onset of stimulation, reaching a peak 5.5 s later. The diameter of the artery increased from a mean of 33 μm at baseline to a peak of about 44 μm, an increase of about 33%. After reaching its early peak, the diameter contracted to a plateau about 10% above baseline until the stimulation ended. The Doppler blood flow measures had a very similar time course (Figure 6.14A–C).

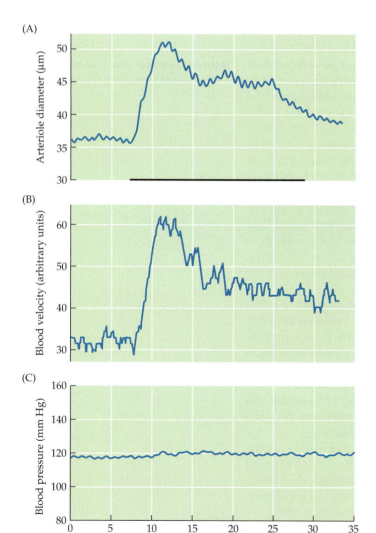

Figure 6.14 The relation between sensory stimulation and local blood flow changes. The sciatic nerve of the rat is stimulated (solid horizontal line) and the time course of arteriole dilation (A) and blood velocity are measured (LDF analysis) in somatosensory cortex (B). The neuronal stimulation caused increases in both diameter and flow. No change in mean arterial blood pressure (MABP) accompanied these functional vascular changes (C). (Data from Ngai, Morii, and Winn, 1988.)

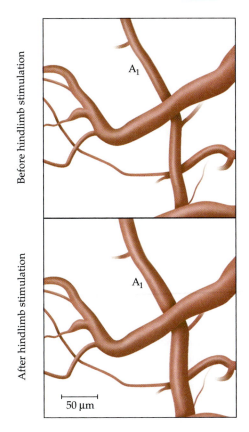
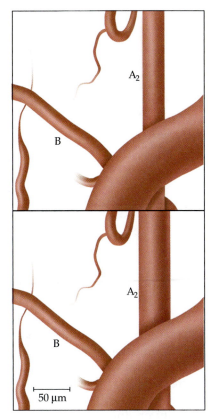
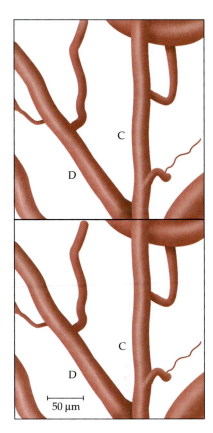

Before hindlimb stimulation

After hindlimb stimulation

50 μm

50 μm

50 μm

Figure 6.15 The change in diameter of arterioles following sciatic stimulation. Arterioles that perfuse the cortical region corresponding to the hindlimb of the rat (A_1A_2), increase in diameter. Nearby vessels (B) and those that perfuse the forepaw region (C and D) do not increase in diameter. (After Ngai, Morii, and Winn, 1988.)

Thus, in response to a sensory stimulus, the pial arteries dilate and blood flow increases. The authors also investigated the issue of the spatial extent, or coarseness, of these flow-related changes. Using an evoked field potential method to localize the neurons activated by the sciatic stimulation, the authors noted that the vasodilatory response was remarkably discrete in its anatomic distribution, and that other arterioles branching from the same distribution artery that perfused forepaw regions of the somatosensory cortex did not dilate (Figure 6.15).

Similar findings were obtained by Iadecola and colleagues. Electrical stimulation of parallel fibers in the rat's cerebellum produced focal neuronal stimulation that was exquisitely localized using evoked field potential mapping. The authors found that the arterioles supplying the activated neurons dilated by up to 26%. Larger arterioles upstream from the activated site showed a smaller diameter increase, about 8%. No field potentials were recorded in the vicinity of these larger arterioles, which were about 2 to 3 mm distant (Figure 6.16). This result demonstrated that blood flow can increase in vessels that are upstream of the local neuronal activity. In subsequent studies, these upstream responses were found to be highly attenuated in mice that were genetically deficient in an enzyme responsible for the production of nitric oxide. Thus, these data support the role of nitric oxide in triggering blood flow increases through the control of upstream resistance vessels.

Figure 6.16 Change in arteriole dilation as a function of distance from active neurons. Changes in the diameter of blood vessels on the surface of the rat's cerebellum during parallel fiber stimulation are measured. Neuronal field potential activity was recorded at the black dot. The dilation of surface vessels is indicated by the percent changes in diameter. The largest dilations occurred in the immediate vicinity of the neuronal activation. However, upstream vessels 2 to 3 mm away also showed modest dilation. (After Iadecola et al., 1997.)

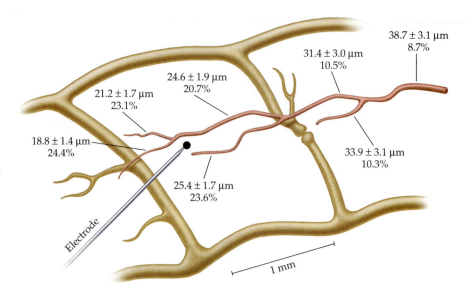

These data also put limits on the spatial specificity of blood flow changes as an indicator of neural activity. While the epicenter of the blood flow response was in the region of synaptic activity, arteriolar dilation and increased blood flow were also observed a few millimeters distant, where there was no synaptic activity. Iadecola and colleagues note that neural activity produces a hemodynamic change over an area larger than that in which neural activity is increased. This emphasizes that the distribution of hemodynamic responses measured using functional neuroimaging techniques will be ultimately constrained by the architecture of the microvascular blood supply.

Thought Question

Why do the results of Iadecola and colleagues limit the spatial resolution of neuroimaging techniques that depend upon hemodynamic changes?

Effects of Increased Blood Flow upon Capillaries

As we have reviewed, blood flow increases in arterioles as a function of neuronal activity, and such increases in flow can occur in vessels as much as several millimeters distal from the epicenter of neural activity. The result of increased blood flow in venules and veins is less well understood. In the studies of rat somatosensory cortex by Winn and colleagues discussed in the previous section, the diameters of both arterioles and venules were measured in response to sciatic nerve stimulation, and while arterioles dilated, no such effect was observed for venules. Many other studies have measured relative dilation of both arterioles and venules in response to physiological manipulations, such as hypocapnia (low levels of CO_2 in the blood) and hypercapnia (excessive CO_2 in the blood), and pharmacological manipulations in which drugs were locally injected in the vessel. In general, these studies have shown that while venules do dilate, they do so much more modestly than arterioles. For example, under hypercapnia, the diameter of

BOX 6.1 Neurogenic Control of Blood Flow

Many cortical vessels are surrounded by intertwining neuronal processes, raising the possibility that some aspects of blood flow may be controlled by direct neuronal innervation. For example, some large pial arteries receive projections from cranial nerves and sensory ganglia, and these projections surround the smooth muscles that encase the vessel. Studies have shown that the neurotransmitters released by these projections can dilate or constrict the vessel. However, the relation between neurogenic control of blood flow and local brain function remains unknown. Given that these large vessels supply extensive regions of cortex, changes in flow within these vessels would have to be constrained and shaped by local resistance vessels to direct the blood flow to the active neuronal region.

Krimer and colleagues examined the role that the neurotransmitter dopamine might play in the control of the microcirculation. Dopamine is produced centrally by a small cluster of cells in the substantia nigra, and these cells influence large regions of cortex through their widespread projections. Using histological staining techniques, light microscopy, and electron microscopy, these investigators demonstrated that dopamine terminals are found in apposition to small intracortical arterioles and capillaries. Moreover, at capillaries, the dopamine terminals are apposed to pericytes, contractile elements that can constrict or dilate the capillary and thus influence local flow patterns (Figure 6.17A–D). This pattern of apparent dopaminergic innervation of intracortical vessels was in marked contrast to the larger pial surface vessels, which were most heavily innervated by noradrenergic terminals (Figure 6.18A and B).

The direct application of dopamine onto small cortical arterioles caused a constriction of the diameter of the vessels that started about 18 to 40 s after application onset and reached a maximum constriction of 18 to 24%. Full recovery occurred over several minutes. The time course of these changes is slower than the change in MRI signal that is measured during BOLD-contrast fMRI, which can peak 4 to 5 s after the onset of a stimulus. However, these data raise the interesting possibility that central dopaminergic and noradrenergic neurons could influence blood flow *independently* of local neuronal activity, perhaps in anticipation of need based upon learned stimulus-response contingencies. Such centrally stimulated blood flow changes might be associated with long-duration changes in MRI signal that are maintained over many minutes. If true, this would require a refinement of our conceptualization that the BOLD signal is strictly related to the energy needs of active neurons.

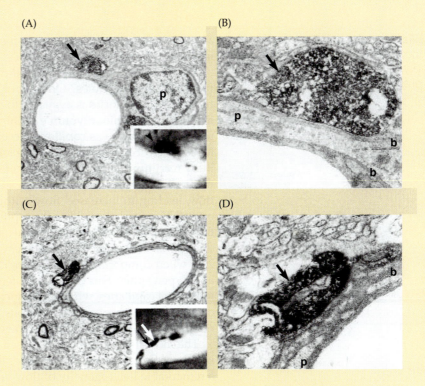

Figure 6.17 Evidence of direct innervation of capillaries by dopaminergic neurons. This figure shows the relationship between dopamine terminals and the microvasculature. (A) An electron micrograph that shows a large dopamine terminal (arrow) adjacent to a capillary. As can be seen in the light-microscopic inset, which shows a cross section of the same spatial location, this terminal is associated with this capillary over a large spatial extent. (B) An enlargement of this dopamine terminal. The terminal is separated from the basal lamina (b) of the blood vessel by only a process from an adjacent pericyte (p), a cell with contractile properties. The inset in (C) shows a light-microscopic image depicting a string of three terminals adjacent to a capillary. The electromicrograph in (C), enlarged in (D), shows that one of the terminals is directly apposed to the basal lamina of the capillary. (From Krimer et al., 1998.)

(A)

(B)

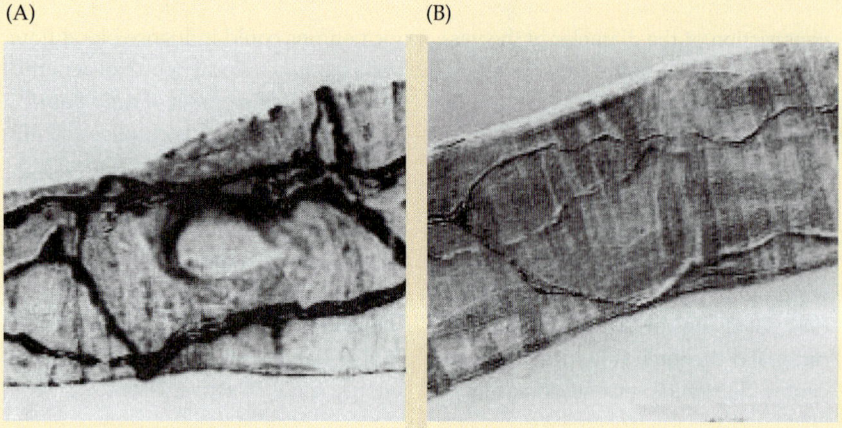

Figure 6.18 Neuronal innervation of pial surface vessels. (A) A dense plexus of noradrenergic fibers surrounds pial cortical arteries on the surface of the brain. However, these arteries show little evidence for dopaminergic influence, as shown by the lack of stain (B). (From Krimer et al., 1998.)

capillary recruitment The idea that increased blood flow through the capillary bed results in perfusion of previously unperfused capillaries.

arterioles 10 to 30 µm in diameter increased by 50%; similarly sized venules increased in diameter by only 10%.

What are the consequences in the capillary bed for this increased blood flow from the arterioles? One popular hypothesis is that a large reserve of unperfused capillaries is available to accept this increased flow, leading to an increase in total blood volume within the capillaries. This hypothetical phenomenon is known as **capillary recruitment.** In vivo studies with high-resolution microscopic techniques have failed to find evidence for significant capillary recruitment in response to increased blood flow. Another possibility is that individual capillaries distend slightly and thus decrease their resistance to flow, leading to increased flow within the capillaries and, again, increased overall blood volume within the capillary bed. Studies that have manipulated the amount of CO_2 dissolved in the blood to stimulate vessel contraction and dilation have reported that capillaries can, in fact, alter their diameters by about 20% when comparing the physiologically extreme conditions of hypocapnia and hypercapnia. This capillary distension would increase the surface area of individual capillaries, which could increase the area available for the transfer of oxygen and glucose to active neurons. The degree to which this occurs during normal physiological conditions, however, is not known.

The most likely result of increased flow into the capillaries is the regularization of flow. Studies of capillaries during baseline conditions have shown a remarkable heterogeneity of flow velocities through individual capillaries. Some capillaries have very high rates of flow, while others have very low rates. With increased flow, the distribution of flow velocities increases and becomes more uniform. This process bears similarities to capillary recruitment, as discussed in the previous paragraph. However, unlike capillary recruitment, this scenario presumes that all vessels are perfused at some baseline level. Thus, the principal response of the capillary bed to increased blood flow appears to be an increase in overall flow velocity, with an unknown contribution from capillary distension. One consequence of this increased rate of flow is that the transit time of hemoglobin molecules through the capillaries decreases, which might affect the likelihood that an individual hemoglobin molecule would have time for oxygen exchange. We resume this story in Chapter 7, where we discuss how the properties of oxygenated and deoxygenated hemoglobin can be measured by MRI.

BOX 6.2 Primer on Neuroanatomy

Throughout this book, we will be making frequent reference to neuroanatomical structures and frequent use of neuroanatomical terms. After all, our subject is functional *brain* imaging! While a detailed treatment of human neuroanatomy is beyond the scope of this book, here we present a brief overview sufficient for the discussions in this text. More information on this fascinating topic can be found in the literature listed in the Suggested Readings section at the end of this chapter.

Taken together, the brain and spinal cord form the **central nervous system,** or **CNS.** Special, sometimes confusing terms are often used to describe the relative locations of anatomical structures. Imagine that the CNS is a long cylinder that rises as a vertical column from the beginning of your spinal cord near your tailbone into your skull, and then bends 90° toward your nose. Along this axis, the term **caudal,** from the Latin term for "tail," refers to the direction of the tail or hind limbs. The term **rostral,** derived from the Latin term for "beak," refers to the direction of the nose. Again relative to this axis, **dorsal** refers to the back while **ventral** refers to the front. So your chest is ventral to your back, and your back is dorsal to your chest (cf., the dorsal fin of sharks). Once inside the brain, where the axis of the CNS bends 90°, dorsal structures are now superior and ventral structures are inferior. So the top of your brain is dorsal to the bottom of your brain, and the bottom of your brain is ventral to the top of your brain. Structures that are closer to the midline of the brain are **medial,** and structures that are closer to the edge of the brain are **lateral.**

The CNS is composed of a number of cellular elements. The principal information-processing cells of the CNS are called neurons, which have cell bodies and protoplasmic processes called dendrites and axons (see the main text for a

more complete description). Areas within the CNS composed primarily of cell bodies are sometimes called gray matter, while areas composed primarily of large axon bundles are called white matter. The white matter is so named due to the color of **myelin,** the fatty sheath that encases the axons of many neurons and speeds the propagation of action potentials. The myelin sheath is constructed by a support cell called the **oligodendrocyte.** Another type of support cell found in the CNS is the **astrocyte,** which helps regulate the extracellular environment within the CNS. The supporting oligodendrocytes and astrocytes are known collectively as glial cells, or glia (from the Greek for "glue").

Neurons come in different sizes, shapes, and typical patterns of connectivity. Two common neuron types are pyramidal cells, named for the triangular shape of their cell body, and stellate cells, which have a more spherical cell body. Pyramidal cells have long axons that can travel great distances within the brain, while stellate cells appear to play a primary role in local processing.

Three membranes, or meninges, cover the outside surface of the brain and spinal cord. The outermost covering is called the **dura,** which is quite thick and tough. The middle layer is called the **arachnoid,** its weblike appearance being the source of its name. The innermost layer is called the **pia,** which is a delicate membrane that closely adheres to the contours of the brain. The pia is highly vascularized and, as discussed in the main text, is the source of the small arteries that supply the cortex. The space between the arachnoid and pia is filled with **cerebrospinal fluid,** or **CSF,** a colorless liquid that bathes the brain and spinal cord. CSF is produced in the choroid plexus, an invagination of the pia into the **ventricles** of the brain. The ventricles are a continuous series of cavities within the brain

central nervous system (CNS) The brain and spinal cord.

caudal Toward the back of the brain.

rostral Toward the front of the brain.

dorsal Toward the top of the brain.

ventral Toward the bottom of the brain.

medial Toward the middle of the brain.

lateral Toward the edge of the brain.

myelin A fatty substance that forms sheaths surrounding axons that serve to speed the transmission of action potentials.

oligodendrocyte A type of glial cell that constructs the myelin sheaths around axons.

astrocyte A type of glial cell that regulates the extracellular environment.

dura The outermost membrane covering the brain; its name comes from its thickness and toughness.

arachnoid The middle membrane covering the brain; its name comes from its weblike appearance.

pia The innermost membrane covering the brain; it closely adheres to the brain's contours.

cerebrospinal fluid (CSF) A colorless liquid that surrounds the brain and spinal cord and fills the ventricles within the brain.

ventricles Fluid-filled cavities within the brain.

that are filled with CSF. The CSF flows down from the third ventricle of the brain into the fourth ventricle in the region of the brain stem (see the next section), and then into the cisterns, where it flows both upward to bathe the surfaces of the cerebrum and downward into the spinal cord. The CSF is eventually absorbed into the vascular system in the superior sagittal sinus, part of the venous drainage system of the brain found between layers of the dura. The CSF forms a fluid cushion that protects

BOX 6.2 (continued)

the brain, particularly from its bony encasement. It also serves to maintain a consistent external environment for the cells of the CNS and helps remove metabolic wastes.

Major Components of the CNS

Figure 6.19 shows an MRI of the head taken along the midline and thus bisecting the brain. A view of the brain in this median plane or in any parallel plane is called a **sagittal** view. The position of the brain within the head and skull can be well appreciated in this view, which also provides a convenient starting place for describing the major subdivisions of the CNS.

The most caudal aspect of the CNS visible in Figure 6.19 is the spinal cord, which can be seen entering the brain through an opening within the base of the skull called the foramen magnum (unlabeled, but located just above the line indicating the position of the spinal cord). The spinal cord contains ascending sensory fiber tracts that transmit somatosensory information to the brain from sensors throughout the body, and descending motor fiber tracts that transmit control information to the muscles

from the brain. Just rostral to the foramen magnum is a continuation of the spinal cord called the **medulla oblongata.** The medulla contains the cell bodies for several major cranial nerves, some of which are involved in the control of respiration, circulation, and vegetative functions. In many texts, the medulla is also referred to as the myelencephalon (in Greek, *enkephalos* means "in the head or brain"), one of the five major subdivisions of the brain.

The **pons** is a prominent structure just rostral to the medulla. Like the medulla, the pons is a thoroughfare that is traversed by many ascending sensory and descending motor fiber tracts. The pons contains the cell bodies that are the source of cranial nerves that innervate the face and eye muscles.

Just posterior and intimately connected through thick fiber bundles to the pons is the **cerebellum,** which is a large structure important in the coordination of walking and posture, motor learning, and other functions. The cerebellum is located within a part of the skull called the posterior fossa, which is separated from the remainder of the brain by a tough membrane called the

sagittal A side view of the brain (along the *y–z* plane in MRI).

medulla oblongata A continuation of the spinal cord at the base of the brain that is important for the control of basic physiological functions.

pons Part of the brain stem; it serves as a relay system for motor and sensory nerves.

cerebellum A large cortical structure at the caudal base of the brain that plays an important role in motor function.

midbrain A section of the brain rostral to the pons; it includes a number of important nuclei.

tentorium. Together, the pons and cerebellum comprise the metencephalon. Collectively, the metencephalon and myelencephalon are sometimes called the hindbrain.

Rostral to the pons is the **midbrain,** or mesencephalon (see Figure 6.24). The midbrain gives rise to two major cranial nerves and also contains several important cell clusters or nuclei, including the red nucleus and substantia nigra. The latter is the major source of dopamine in the brain; loss of cells in the substantia nigra can cause Parkinson's disease, a serious affliction of aging that is associated with tremor and a progressive deterioration of motor control. The superior and inferior colliculi are paired structures located on the posterior aspect of the midbrain (they appear as small bumps on the back of the midbrain in Figure 6.19). The superior colliculi are part of the visual system, while the inferior colliculi are part of the auditory system.

The midbrain, pons, and medulla contain clusters of neurons that comprise the ascending reticular formation, which is important in regulating sleep, arousal, and levels of consciousness. Many neuroanatomists refer collectively to the mid-

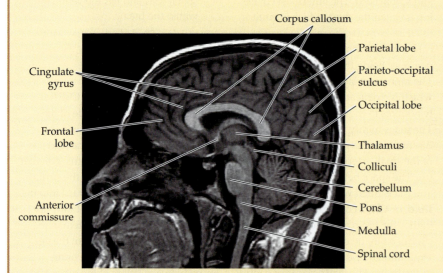

Figure 6.19   A midsagittal MRI of the human head.

Corpus callosum
Parietal lobe
Parieto-occipital sulcus
Occipital lobe
Thalamus
Colliculi
Cerebellum
Pons
Medulla
Spinal cord
Cingulate gyrus
Frontal lobe
Anterior commissure

BOX 6.2 *(continued)*

brain, pons, and medulla as the **brain stem,** as it appears to support the more rostral brain as a stem supports a flower.

Rostral to the midbrain are the **hypothalamus** and **thalamus,** which together with the epithalamus and pineal gland comprise the diencephalon. The hypothalamus is involved in autonomic functions and somatic functions, including the regulation of temperature, water intake, and hunger. The hypothalamus is also an important structure in the regulation of endocrine functions—particularly in its control of the pituitary gland.

The thalamus is a paired structure connected at the midline by the massa intermedia. The thalamus is composed of a large number of nuclei that are sometimes referred to as relay nuclei because they receive information from sensory, motor, and other regions of the brain; organize or process this information; and then project the information to specific regions of cortex. For example, the lateral geniculate is a nucleus of the thalamus that receives and processes visual information from the eyes before projecting that information to the visual cortex. Similar functions are carried out by the medial geniculate for auditory information and by the ventral posterolateral nucleus for the somatosensory system. Some thalamic nuclei are involved in relaying motor information in the brain. For example, the ventral lateral nuclei receive motor information from the cerebellum and project it to the motor cortex. Other thalamic nuclei appear to integrate information from other brain regions that are neither motor nor sensory. For example, the dorsal medial nucleus receives information from the amygdala, hypothalamus, and other thalamic nuclei and projects this information to the frontal lobes.

Rostral to the diencephalon is the telencephalon, or forebrain. The telencephalon is the largest, most complex, and most evolutionarily advanced part of the brain. It is composed of the cerebral cortical hemispheres (the cerebrum), large subcortical nuclei such as the amygdala, and complex structures such as the **basal ganglia** (composed of the caudate, putamen, and globus pallidus) and the hippocampus. Interconnecting these brain regions are extensive white-matter tracts, which can be seen in Figure 6.20.

The Cortex

The cerebral hemispheres **(cerebrum)** are composed of a continuous sheet of cerebral cortex that has been folded into an undulating pattern of **gyri** and **sulci.** Gyri are rises of cortex that are separated by infolded troughs, or sulci. If unfolded and laid out as a sheet, the cortex of the average human brain would have an area of 2500 cm^2. The most evolutionarily recent region of the cortex is called the neocortex, which is about 4 to 5 mm thick and composed of six layers, or lamina (Figure 6.21). Layer 1 is the closest to the pial surface and is composed primarily of axonal and dendritic processes with few neurons. Layers 2 and 3 are composed primarily of pyramidal cells, with layer 2 composed of pyramidal cells with smaller cell bodies. Layer 4 is relatively devoid of pyramidal cells but is densely packed with stellate cells. Layer 4 receives projections from other cortical regions and thus appears to be the primary input layer of the cortex. Layer 4 appears to project primarily to layers 1 to 3, which appear to comprise the intracortical processing layers. Layers 5 and 6 contain large pyramidal cells that project their axons to other brain regions and thus appear to represent the output layers of the neocortex. Note that although

brain stem The midbrain, pons, and medulla.

hypothalamus A brain nucleus that supports homeostatic functions, including the regulation of food and water intake.

thalamus A brain nucleus that is important for many aspects of perception and cognition; it is highly interconnected with many regions of the cerebral cortex.

basal ganglia A set of nuclei in the forebrain that includes the caudate, putamen, and globus pallidus.

cerebrum The two hemispheres forming the major part of the brain.

gyri Rises in the cortical surface.

sulci Troughs in the cortical surface.

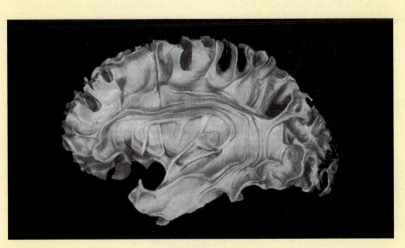

Figure 6.20 A sagittal drawing of the white-matter tracts of the human cerebral cortex. (From Ludwig and Klionger, 1956.)

BOX 6.2 *(continued)*

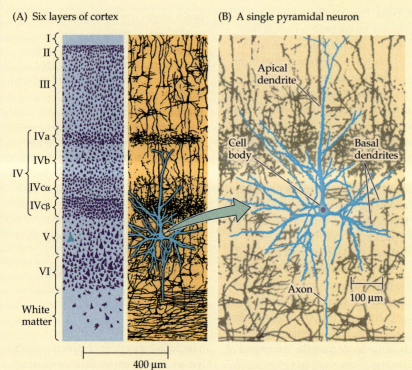

(A) Six layers of cortex

I
II
III
IV
  IVa
  IVb
  IVcα
  IVcβ
V
VI
White matter

400 μm

(B) A single pyramidal neuron

Apical dendrite

Cell body

Basal dendrites

Axon

100 μm

Figure 6.21   An illustration of the six-layer structure of the neocortex.

cytoarchitecture The organization of the brain on the basis of cell structure.

Brodmann areas Divisions of the brain based on the influential cytoarchitectonic criteria of Korbinian Brodmann.

functional brain activation measured by fMRI or by positron emission tomography (PET). Although these functional brain methods cannot measure the cytoarchitecture of the brain directly, sufficient similarities exist across individuals to permit the use of spatial transformations that warp an individual's brain into a common atlas space (such as the atlas of Talairach and Tournoux) that has been annotated with Brodmann areas.

Although the cortical sheet is continuous, the presence of several deep fissures in the typical brain has resulted in the subdivision of the brain into four major lobes: the frontal, parietal, temporal, and occipital lobes—so named for the skull bones that cover them. A fifth lobe, the insula, is hidden behind part of the anterior temporal lobe and inferior frontal lobe. Some neuroanatomists also describe a limbic lobe that is composed of midline structures including the cingulate cortex, hippocampus, and amygdala. The cerebral hemispheres and their constituent lobes and nuclei are paired structures. Although the two hemispheres appear roughly similar in

fMRI studies currently lack the spatial resolution to distinguish among these layers, given typical voxel sizes on the order of a few millimeters, other techniques like electrophysiology are able to do so.

The cortical thickness, packing density, and composition and size of constituent cells distinguish among regions of cortex. Anatomists have developed detailed maps of the cortex based upon these differences in **cytoarchitecture,** with the hope of differentiating function on the basis of structure. One popular cytoarchitectonic map published by Korbinian Brodmann in 1909 divides the cerebral cortex into 47 different regions (Figure 6.22). These regions, or **Brodmann areas,** are used today in many studies to communicate the location of a

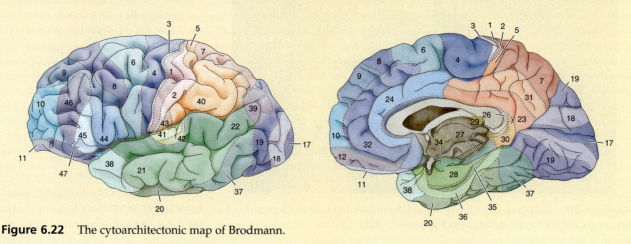

Figure 6.22   The cytoarchitectonic map of Brodmann.

BOX 6.2 *(continued)*

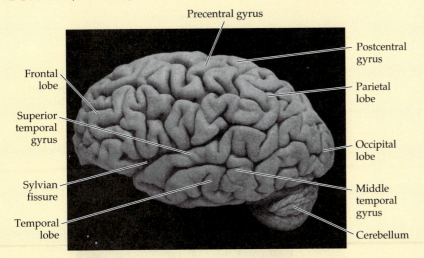

Figure 6.23 Surface view of the left hemisphere of the human brain. (Courtesy of S. Mark Williams and Dale Purves, Duke University Medical Center.)

shape, there are subtle anatomical differences between them that most likely form the basis for such lateralized functions as language and spatial skills.

The left lateral surface of the cerebral hemisphere with meninges and blood vessels removed is shown in Figure 6.23. The locations of the frontal, parietal, occipital, and temporal lobes are shown. The precentral and postcentral gyri are separated by the **central sulcus,** a deep fissure that separates the frontal and parietal lobes. The gyrus anterior to the central sulcus—the precentral gyrus—is often described as the primary motor cortex. Along its medial to lateral extent is a somatotopic representation of the body, or homunculus, with the lower extremities represented near the midline, the hands in the middle, and the mouth and tongue near its most lateral extent. Electrical stimulation of this gyrus causes involuntary movement of the represented limb. The gyrus posterior to the central sulcus—the postcentral gyrus—has a sensory representation of the body that is closely aligned to the motor representation just described. Electrical stimulation of the postcentral gyrus causes a tingling sensation in a particular body part.

The **temporal lobe** is separated from the frontal and parietal lobes by the deep

Sylvian fissure. The lateral part of the temporal lobe plays an important role in auditory and visual processing, and the temporal lobe in the left hemisphere is particularly important for language processing. The **occipital lobe** at the posterior end of the brain is the primary region of the brain for visual processing. It is separated from the parietal lobe by the parieto-occipital fissure, which is best seen in the medial view presented in Fig-

central sulcus A deep fissure that separates the frontal and parietal lobes of the brain.

temporal lobe The lobe on the ventral surface of the cerebrum; it is important for auditory and visual processing, language, memory, and many other functions.

Sylvian fissure The deep sulcus separating the temporal lobe from the frontal and parietal lobes.

occipital lobe The most posterior lobe of the brain; it is primarily associated with visual processing.

parietal lobe The lobe on the posterior and dorsal surfaces of the cerebrum; it is important for spatial processing, cognitive processing, and many other functions.

frontal lobe The most anterior lobe of the cerebrum; it is important for executive processing, motor control, memory, and many other functions.

ure 6.24. The **parietal lobe** plays an important role in spatial processing, among many other functions. The **frontal lobes** are quite large and have many functions. The dorsal lateral frontal lobe has an im-

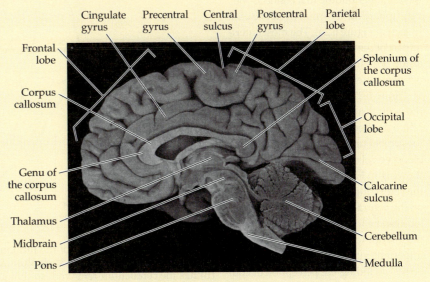

Figure 6.24 Midsagittal view of the human brain. (Courtesy of S. Mark Williams and Dale Purves, Duke University Medical Center.)

BOX 6.2 (continued)

insula The "island" cortex hidden inside the anterior part of the Sylvian fissure; it is important for emotional processing and for the chemical senses.

corpus callosum The large white-matter bundle that is the primary connection between the cerebral hemispheres. The anterior portion is known as the genu and the posterior portion is known as the splenium.

portant role in executive processing—those processes involved with stimulus-response selection when many behaviors are possible.

Within the left hemisphere in most individuals is a region supporting language production known as Broca's area. The more ventral and medial parts of the frontal lobe appear to play a role in emotional processing. The **insula,** not visible in Figure 6.23 (see Figure 6.26), is hidden deep within the anterior part of the Sylvian fissure and inferior frontal lobe. The insula is important for the chemical senses such as olfaction and gustation.

The **corpus callosum** is a large white-matter bundle that connects the hemispheres of the brain (it can be easily seen in Figure 6.24). The most anterior part of the corpus callosum is known as the genu (or knee), while the posterior enlargement is called the splenium.

Figure 6.25 presents two views of the ventral surface of the brain. The photographed brain in Figure 6.25A has the cerebellum attached, but the surface blood vessels have been removed. The drawing in Figure 6.25B has omitted the cerebellum so that the gyri and sulci on the ventral surface of the temporal lobe can be identified. Many regions in the inferior temporal lobe play an important role in higher visual processes, including the perception of complex objects. The entorhinal cortex and

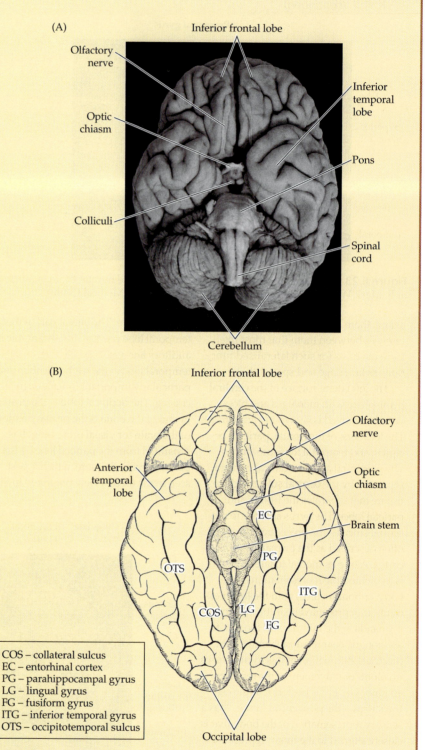

COS – collateral sulcus
EC – entorhinal cortex
PG – parahippocampal gyrus
LG – lingual gyrus
FG – fusiform gyrus
ITG – inferior temporal gyrus
OTS – occipitotemporal sulcus

Figure 6.25 Ventral view of the human brain. Shown in (A) is a photograph of the ventral surface, with the cerebellum and brain stem visible. The drawing in (B) has the cerebellum removed, so that gyri can be identified. (A courtesy of S. Mark Williams and Dale Purves, Duke University Medical Center.)

BOX 6.2 *(continued)*

axial A horizontal view of the brain (along the *x–y* plane in MRI).

coronal A frontal view of the brain (along the *x–z* plane in MRI).

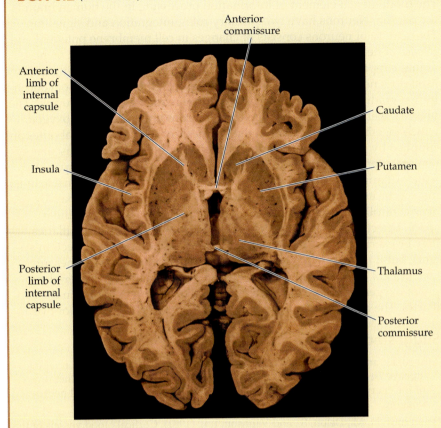

Figure 6.26 Axial view of the human brain at the level of the anterior commissure. (Courtesy of S. Mark Williams and Dale Purves, Duke University Medical Center.)

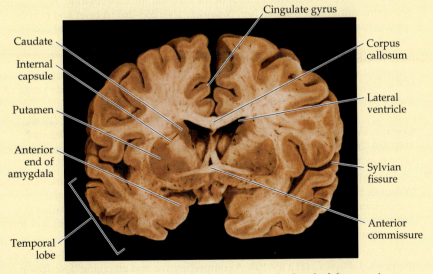

Figure 6.27 Coronal view of the human brain at the level of the anterior commissure. (Courtesy of S. Mark Williams and Dale Purves, Duke University Medical Center.)

parahippocampal gyrus, along with the adjacent hippocampus (not shown), are collectively referred to as the medial temporal lobe and support memory processes.

Figures 6.26 and 6.27 present two brain slices that have orthogonal orientations frequently used in MRI. Figure 6.26 is a **axial** view taken at one slice within the dorsal–ventral plane, in which rostral is up and caudal is down. Figure 6.27 is a **coronal** view taken at one slice within the rostral–caudal plane, in which dorsal is up and ventral is down. In both the coronal and axial views, the midline of the brain is the midline of the view. Visible is a clear distinction between the thin layer of cortical gray matter and the deep white-matter tracts; it is clear that the cortex in the deep sulci is continuous with the cortex of the gyri. The insula is visible as an island of cortex hidden behind the outer surfaces of the temporal and frontal lobes. Also visible are the basal ganglia (caudate and putamen), which are important for motor control and play key roles in many cognitive processes.

The lateral ventricles are clearly visible in Figure 6.27 near the center of the brain. Also visible is the anterior end of the amygdala, which supports emotional processing and is an important component of the limbic lobe. Notable in this coronal view are the interhemispheric white matter tracts. The corpus callosum forms by far the largest such connection, with the anterior commissure a secondary but still important source of communication between the hemispheres.

Summary

The fundamental element of information processing in the human brain is the neuron. Neurons have two primary roles, integration and signaling. The activity of neurons consists of changes in cell membrane potential and release of neurotransmitters. Movements of ions across neuronal membranes support these functions. While the integrative and signaling activity itself does not require external sources of energy, the restoration of concentration gradients following this activity does require an energy supply. The primary metabolites supplied to active neurons are glucose and oxygen, which together are important in the synthesis of ATP. These metabolites are supplied by the vascular system. The main components of the vascular system are arteries, capillaries, and veins, each present at different spatial scales. Changes within the vascular system in response to neuronal activity may occur in brain areas far from neuronal activity, initiated in part by flow-controlling substances released by neurons into the extracellular space. Direct neuronal control of pial arteries, arterioles, and capillaries may be exerted by central dopaminergic and noradrenergic projection systems, but it is unknown whether these systems influence fMRI measures. One facet of the vascular response to neuronal activity is the arterial supply of oxygenated hemoglobin, from which oxygen is extracted in the capillaries. The change in the oxygenation of hemoglobin is critical for fMRI.

Suggested Readings

Attwell, D., and Iadecola, C. (2002). The neural basis of functional brain imaging signals. *Trends Neurosci.,* 25(12): 621–625. This article provides a succinct review of the energy budget of the brain and how it may relate to functional neuro-imaging.

*Duvernoy, H. M., Delon, S., and Vannson, J. L. (1981). Cortical blood vessels of the human brain. *Brain Res. Bull.,* 7(5): 519–579. This paper provides a thorough exploration of the blood supply to the human brain with numerous and spectacularly detailed photographs.

Iadecola, C. (1998). Neurogenic control of the cerebral microcirculation: Is dopamine minding the store? *Nat. Neurosci.,* 1(4): 263–265. A brief and cogent commentary that accompanies the 1998 article written by Krimer et al., (see below).

*James, W. (1890). *The Principles of Psychology.* Dover, New York. The masterwork of a scientist who integrated brilliant introspections with a keen experimental sense, this classic compendium still provides useful insights on a wide range of topics. The chapter on brain physiology is highly recommended.

*Krimer, L. S., Muly, E. C., III, Williams, G. V., and Goldman-Rakic, P. S. (1998). Dopaminergic regulation of cerebral cortical microcirculation. *Nat. Neurosci.,* 1(4): 286–289. This paper provides strong evidence that central dopamine projections may influence blood flow within arterioles and capillaries.

Purves, D., Augustine, G., Fitzpatrick, D., Katz, L., LaMantia, A., McNamara, J., and Williams, S. (eds.) (2001). *Neuroscience* (2nd ed.). Sinauer Associates, Inc., Sunderland, MA. This wonderfully illustrated textbook provides detailed discussions of human brain anatomy, neuronal signaling and integration, and membrane channels and transporters.

*Roy, C. S., and Sherrington, C. S. (1890). On the regulation of the blood-supply of the brain. *J. Physiol.,* (11): 85–108. A comprehensive and engaging description of the vascular system in the brain, it includes speculations in its final pages about the possible functional implications of blood flow.

Indicates a reference that is a suggested reading in the field and is also cited in this chapter.

Chapter References

Attwell, D., and Laughlin, S. B. (2001). An energy budget for signaling in the grey matter of the brain. *J. Cereb. Blood Flow Metab.,* 21(10): 1133–1145.

Branston, N. M. (1995). Neurogenic control of the cerebral circulation. *Cerebrovasc. Brain Metab. Rev.,* 7(4): 338–349.

Duelli, R., and Kuschinsky, W. (1993). Changes in brain capillary diameter during hypocapnia and hypercapnia. *J. Cereb. Blood Flow Metab.,* 13(6): 1025–1028.

Friedland, R. P., and Iadecola, C. (1991). A centennial reexamination of "On the regulation of the blood-supply of the brain." *Neurology,* 41(1): 10–14.

Hudetz, A. G. (1997). Blood flow in the cerebral capillary network: A review emphasizing observations with intravital microscopy. *Microcirculation,* 4(2): 233–252.

Iadecola, C. (2002). Intrinsic signals and functional brain mapping: Caution, blood vessels at work. *Cereb. Cortex,* 12(3): 223–224.

Iadecola, C., Yang, G., Ebner, T. J., and Chen, G. (1997). Local and propagated vascular responses evoked by focal synaptic activity in cerebellar cortex. *J. Neurophysiol.,* 78(2): 651–659.

Lee, S. P., Duong, T. Q., Yang, G., Iadecola, C., and Kim, S. G. (2001). Relative changes of cerebral arterial and venous blood volumes during increased cerebral blood flow: Implications for BOLD fMRI. *Magn. Reson. Med.,* 45(5): 791–800.

Ludwig, E., and Klionger, J. (1956). *Atlas Cerebri Humani.* Little, Brown and Co., Boston, MA.

McHedlishvili, G., and Kuridze, N. (1984). The modular organization of the pial arterial system in phylogeny. *J. Cereb. Blood Flow Metab.,* 4(3): 391–396.

Menon, R. S., and Goodyear, B. G. (1999). Submillimeter functional localization in human striate cortex using BOLD contrast at 4 Tesla: Implications for the vascular point-spread function. *Magn. Reson. Med.,* 41(2): 230–235.

Ngai, A. C., Ko, K. R., Morii, S., and Winn, H. R. (1988). Effect of sciatic nerve stimulation on pial arterioles in rats. *Am. J. Physiol.,* 254(1 Pt 2): H133–H139.

Ngai, A. C., Meno, J. R., and Winn, H. R. (1995). Simultaneous measurements of pial arteriolar diameter and laser-Doppler flow during somatosensory stimulation. *J. Cereb. Blood Flow Metab.,* 15(1): 124–127.

Nonaka, H., Akima, M., Hatori, T., Nagayama, T., Zhang, Z., and Ihara, F. (2002). The microvasculature of the human cerebellar meninges. *Acta Neuropathologica,* 104(6): 608–614.

Nonaka, H., Akima, M., Nagayama, T., Hatori, T., Zhang, Z., and Ihara, F. (2003). Microvasculature of the human cerebral meninges. *Neuropathology,* 23(2): 129–135.

Raichle, M. E., and Gusnard, D. A. (2002). Appraising the brain's energy budget. *Proc. Natl. Acad. Sci. U.S.A.,* 99(16): 10237–10239.

Rodriguez-Baeza, A., Reina-De La Torre, F., Ortega-Sanchez, M., and Sahuquillo-Barris, J. (1998). Perivascular structures in corrosion casts of the human central nervous system: A confocal laser and scanning electron microscope study. *Anat. Rec.,* 252(2): 176–184.

Segebarth, C., Belle, V., Delon, C., Massarelli, R., Decety, J., Le Bas, J. F., Decorps, M., and Benabid, A. L. (1994). Functional MRI of the human brain: Predominance of signals from extracerebral veins. *NeuroReport,* 5(7): 813–816.

Sibson, N. R., Dhankhar, A., Mason, G. F., Rothman, D. L., Behar, K. L., and Shulman, R. G. (1998). Stoichiometric coupling of brain glucose metabolism and glutamatergic neuronal activity. *Proc. Natl. Acad. Sci. U.S.A.,* 95(1): 316–321.

Vafaee, M. S., and Gjedde, A. (2000). Model of blood–brain transfer of oxygen explains nonlinear flow-metabolism coupling during stimulation of visual cortex. *J. Cereb. Blood Flow Metab.,* 20(4): 747–754.

Williams, Mark S. (2000) *Sylvius 2.0: Fundamentals of Human Neural Structure,* CD-ROM. Sinauer Associates, Inc., Sunderland, MA.

Yang, G., Zhang, Y., Ross, M. E., and Iadecola, C. (2003). Attenuation of activity-induced increases in cerebellar blood flow in mice lacking neuronal nitric oxide synthase. *Am. J. Physiol. Heart Circ. Physiol.,* 285(1): H298–H304.

7

BOLD fMRI

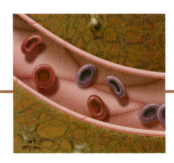

We have now established that it is the metabolic demands of active neurons and not neuronal activity per se that are measured by functional neuroimaging methods. Energy is required for the maintenance and restoration of neuronal membrane potentials necessary for integration and signaling. Even small increases in neuronal activity can result in a large increase in local energy demand. Because there are scant energy stores in the brain, energy must be continuously provided by the blood supply to the brain. The primary energy sources are glucose and oxygen, which are used to create ATP within brain cells. Oxygen is attached to hemoglobin molecules and is exchanged for waste carbon dioxide in capillaries. How is it, though, that the delivery of oxygen and glucose to active neurons results in a signal that can be measured by fMRI? In this chapter, we will consider in detail the physiological basis of blood-oxygenation-level dependent (BOLD) fMRI.

History of BOLD fMRI

In 1936, the American chemist and Nobel laureate Linus Pauling and his student Charles Coryell conducted a systematic investigation of the molecular structure of hemoglobin. In the course of these studies, they discovered a remarkable and (for our purposes) fortuitous fact of nature: The hemoglobin molecule has magnetic properties that differ depending upon whether or not it is bound to oxygen. **Oxygenated hemoglobin (Hb) is diamagnetic;** that is, it has no unpaired electrons and zero magnetic moment. In contrast, **deoxygenated hemoglobin (dHb) is paramagnetic;** it has both unpaired electrons and a significant magnetic moment. Completely deoxygenated blood has a **magnetic susceptibility** about 20% greater than fully oxygenated blood. Pauling and Coryell noted wryly that this fact had eluded previous researchers, including the great nineteenth-century physicist Michael Faraday, only because they had not separated arterial blood (which contains only oxygenated hemoglobin) and venous blood (which contains both oxygenated and deoxygenated hemoglobin).

Remember that introducing an object with magnetic susceptibility into a magnetic field causes spin dephasing, resulting in a decay of transverse magnetization that depends on the time constant T_2^*. Because blood deoxygenation affects magnetic susceptibility, MR pulse sequences sensitive to T_2^*

oxygenated hemoglobin (Hb) Hemoglobin with attached oxygen; it is diamagnetic.

diamagnetic Having the property of a weak repulsion from a magnetic field.

deoxygenated hemoglobin (dHb) Hemoglobin without attached oxygen; it is paramagnetic.

paramagnetic Having the property of being attracted to a magnetic field, though with less concentration of magnetic flux than ferromagnetic objects.

magnetic susceptibility The intensity of magnetization of a substance when placed within a magnetic field.

Figure 7.1 Effects of blood deoxygenation upon MR relaxation constants. Shown are the differential effects of blood deoxygenation upon transverse and longitudinal relaxation times, as expressed by the constants $1/T_2$ (blue circles) and $1/T_1$ (red circles). The x-axis indicates the square of the proportion of deoxygenated blood. Note that oxygenation increases from left to right. Clearly evident is the fact that $1/T_2$ decreases with increasing oxygenation; that is, the more deoxygenated hemoglobin that is present, the shorter the T_2. Note that T_1 is not affected by blood oxygenation level. (After Thulborn et al., 1982.)

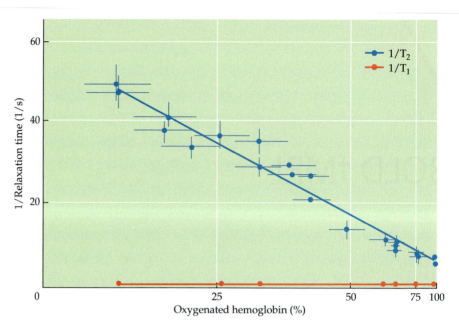

should show more MR signal where blood is highly oxygenated and less MR signal where blood is highly deoxygenated. This prediction was verified experimentally in the early 1980s by Thulborn and colleagues, who found that the decay of transverse magnetization depended on the proportion of oxygenated hemoglobin within a test tube of blood (Figure 7.1). They noted that the magnitude of this effect increased with the square of the strength of the static magnetic field. At low field strength (i.e., less than 0.5 T), there is little difference between the transverse relaxation values for oxygenated and deoxygenated blood, but in higher fields (i.e., 1.5 T or greater), their values differ significantly. So, strong static magnetic fields are necessary for MR imaging of T_2^*-based contrast in blood. These results provided a theoretical basis for measurement of blood oxygenation changes using MRI.

Discovery of BOLD Contrast

During the late 1980s, Seiji Ogawa, a research scientist at Bell Laboratories, investigated the possibility of examining brain physiology using MRI. Ogawa and his colleagues recognized that it would be challenging to use MRI to examine physiological processes directly. Since standard MRI contrasts are based on properties of hydrogen, the commonness of hydrogen in water throughout the body precludes examination of the very subtle changes in concentration associated with metabolic reactions themselves. For MRI to be useful in measuring physiology, it would need to be sensitive to some indirect measure of metabolism. One possibility was blood flow, since metabolic processes require oxygen that is supplied through hemoglobin within red blood cells. Based on the previous finding that deoxygenation decreases the T_2^* value of blood, Ogawa and colleagues (1990b) hypothesized that manipulating the proportion of blood oxygen would affect the visibility of blood vessels on T_2^*-weighted images.

They tested their hypothesis by scanning anesthetized rodents using high-field (7 T and greater) MRI. To manipulate blood oxygenation, they changed the proportion of oxygen that the animals breathed. When the rodents were breathing 100% oxygen or 100% carbon monoxide, gradient-echo images of their brains showed structural differences but few blood vessels (Figure 7.2A). But when the rodents breathed normal air (21% oxygen), the images took on a very different character. Thin dark lines became visible throughout the cerebral cortex, usually perpendicular to its surface (Figure 7.2B). If the oxygen content was further reduced to 0% (anoxic condition), the lines became even more prominent. Ogawa and colleagues concluded that these thin lines represented magnetic susceptibility effects caused by the presence of paramagnetic deoxygenated hemoglobin in blood vessels, which causes local field distortions on gradient-echo images. In the other conditions, because the hemoglobin was bound to oxygen or carbon monoxide, it was diamagnetic and had little effect on the surrounding magnetic field.

To verify this interpretation, they placed test tubes with oxygenated or deoxygenated blood into a saline-filled container. Both spin- and gradient-echo images were taken of each tube. The tubes containing oxygenated blood appeared as black circles on both types of images, since the blood had a shorter T_2^* than the surrounding saline (Figure 7.3A and B). The spin-echo image of the deoxygenated blood was likewise nearly normal, although there was a slight shape distortion resulting from the effects of induced field inhomogeneity on the resonance frequency of the surrounding water (Figure 7.3C). The largest effect by far was observed for gradient-echo images of the deoxygenated blood, which showed a very large area of signal loss that extended well beyond the test tube (Figure 7.3D). These results demonstrated that the presence of deoxygenated blood decreases the measured MR signal on T_2^* images, relative to the presence of oxygenated blood.

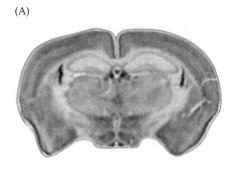

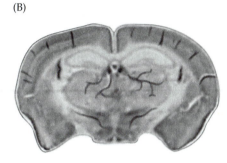

Figure 7.2 A schematic illustration of blood-oxygenation-level dependent (BOLD) contrast. Ogawa and colleagues manipulated the amount of oxygen in the blood of rats by adjusting the contents of the air breathed. When the rats breathed pure oxygen, the cortical surface had a uniform texture (A) on images sensitive to T_2^* contrast. But, when they breathed normal air, there were areas of signal loss, shown in (B) as lines corresponding to blood vessels within the cortex. These lines indicate areas with increased amounts of deoxygenated hemoglobin. This forms the basis for BOLD contrast. (After Ogawa et al., 1990.)

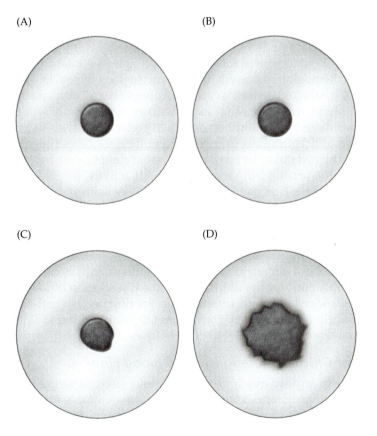

Figure 7.3 Magnetic properties of oxygenated and deoxygenated hemoglobin. To verify that the effects illustrated in Figure 7.2 resulted from changes in blood oxygen level, a series of in vitro experiments were conducted that compared images of oxygenated and deoxygenated blood using both spin- and gradient-echo imaging. The images of oxygenated blood were not distorted, regardless of whether spin-echo (A) or gradient-echo (B) images were acquired. The spin-echo image of the deoxygenated blood (C) was slightly distorted, but the distortion did not extend to the area surrounding the test tube. However, there was substantial signal loss surrounding the gradient-echo image of the deoxygenated blood (D), showing that the presence of deoxygenated hemoglobin reduces the MR signal in adjacent space. (After Ogawa et al., 1990b.)

blood-oxygenation-level dependent (BOLD) contrast The difference in signal on T_2^*-weighted images as a function of the amount of deoxygenated hemoglobin.

autoradiography An invasive imaging technique that labels molecules using radioactive isotopes and then measures the concentration of those molecules by exposing slices of tissue to photographic emulsions.

Ogawa and colleagues speculated that this finding, which would come to be called **blood-oxygenation-level dependent (BOLD) contrast,** could enable measurement of functional changes in brain activity. They hypothesized two possible nonexclusive mechanisms for BOLD contrast: changes in oxygen metabolism or changes in blood flow. Under the first mechanism, neuronal activity would cause increased metabolic demands, and thus increased oxygen consumption. This would increase the amount of deoxygenated hemoglobin, given a constant blood flow. Under the second mechanism, increased blood flow in the absence of increased metabolic demand would decrease the amount of deoxygenated hemoglobin.

In their next in vivo experiment, Ogawa and colleagues (1990a), manipulated the gases inhaled by anesthetized rats while measuring BOLD contrast at high field. To verify that the BOLD contrast resulted, at least in part, from the metabolic demand for oxygen, they compared low and high anesthesia levels. At the higher anesthesia level (3.0% halothane), there was reduced spontaneous brain activity as measured by concurrent EEG. BOLD contrast was much greater at low anesthesia levels (0.75% halothane) than at high anesthesia levels. These results indicated that the metabolic demand for oxygen was a prerequisite for BOLD contrast.

To evaluate the effect of blood flow changes upon BOLD contrast, they compared two inhalant conditions, pure (100%) oxygen and a mixture of 90% oxygen and 10% carbon dioxide. While significant BOLD contrast was observed in the pure oxygen condition, the contrast disappeared when the animals breathed the CO_2 mixture. Why did adding CO_2 have such a large effect? Carbon dioxide in the blood does not have significant paramagnetic effects in itself, but it does increase overall blood flow. Ogawa and colleagues found that the CO_2 mixture increased blood velocity within the sagittal sinus by a factor of 4. With greater blood flow in the absence of metabolic demand, the deoxygenated hemoglobin is essentially flushed from the venous system and replaced by excess oxygenated hemoglobin, causing a decrease in BOLD contrast.

In summary, BOLD contrast was found to depend upon the total amount of deoxygenated hemoglobin present in a brain region, which in turn depended upon the balance between oxygen consumption and oxygen supply. Although it seems reasonable that increased neuronal activity would result in increased oxygen consumption and thus greater decreases in MR signal, as Ogawa and colleagues originally hypothesized, experimental observations have turned out to be considerably more complicated. Indeed, when we measure the brain during increased neural activity, we find that there is an *increase* in the MR signal! How can this be? The answer requires a more complete exploration of the relations between cerebral blood flow, blood oxygenation level, and metabolism than we have thus far provided. We note in advance that a generally accepted model that relates BOLD contrast to blood flow and oxygen supply is still lacking. However, the competing models that have been offered to explain this relationship have different and profound implications for the ultimate functional resolution of BOLD-contrast fMRI. To understand these implications, we first need to consider more fully the relationship between glucose metabolism and blood flow, through the examination of data from other techniques.

The Coupling of Glucose Metabolism and Blood Flow

Autoradiography is an invasive imaging technique used in animals in which biologically active molecules labeled by radioactive isotopes are identified by exposure of brain slices to photographic emulsions. In the 1970s,

Sokoloff and colleagues used autoradiography to establish that regional brain changes in the metabolic rate of glucose metabolism were coupled to an increase in blood flow to that same region. As you now know, glucose is the major energy source for the brain, and oxygen facilitates the most efficient conversion of glucose into ATP. The overall accounting of glucose and oxygen consumption during oxidative metabolism is as follows:

$$C_6H_{12}O_6 + 6O_2 = 6CO_2 + 6H_2O \qquad [7.1]$$

We see that six oxygen molecules are consumed for each glucose molecule oxidized, and thus the ideal oxygen-to-glucose index (OGI) would be 6:1 if all of the glucose that entered the brain were oxidatively (i.e., aerobically) metabolized. Brain measurements performed under resting conditions have established an OGI of approximately 5.5:1, indicating that while the vast majority of the glucose metabolism in the brain is oxidative, a small but significant fraction of glucose may be metabolized nonoxidatively (i.e., anaerobically). The rate of oxygen and glucose consumption during focal stimulation is different, however, and this fact has engendered considerable controversy that persists today.

In an influential series of PET experiments conducted in 1988 by Fox, Raichle, and their colleagues, cerebral blood flow (CBF), cerebral metabolic rate for glucose (CMR_{glu}), and cerebral metabolic rate for oxygen ($CMRO_2$) were measured during rest and during visual stimulation. When subjects were exposed to prolonged visual stimulation, CBF in the visual cortex increased by 50% and CMR_{glu} increased by 51%, consistent with Sokoloff's autoradiographic findings in animals. However, $CMRO_2$ increased by only 5%. The authors concluded that most of the increased uptake of glucose during stimulation was not oxidized but rather was metabolized nonoxidatively through anaerobic glycolysis. Recalling our discussion from the previous chapter, anaerobic glycolysis is relatively inefficient (but fast), yielding only two ATP molecules for each glucose molecule consumed, and thus the energy produced from the increased glucose uptake would be relatively small. Corroborating evidence has come from studies by Prichard and colleagues, who demonstrated that prolonged visual stimulation results in increased lactate, which would be expected since lactate is the primary end product of anaerobic glycolysis.

A number of studies have found similar uncoupling between glucose metabolism and oxygen consumption, although the disparity has not always been quite as dramatic. But while there is general agreement on these facts, their interpretation is still controversial. This controversy has surprising relevance to BOLD fMRI, and several models have been advanced to explain this apparent uncoupling.

Glucose and Oxygen Metabolism

The observations of Fox and Raichle help explain the paradox we noted previously, namely that MR signal increases during neuronal activity even though deoxygenated hemoglobin decreases MR signal. The disparity between oxygen utilization and oxygen delivery means that more oxygen is supplied to a brain region than is consumed. Fox and Raichle note that this is consistent with the experience of neurosurgeons, who have long observed that cortex becomes more pink in color when it becomes active. As the excess oxygenated blood flows through active regions, it flushes the deoxy-

BOX 7.1   PET Imaging

Positron emission tomography, or **PET**, is a powerful functional imaging technique that has been used extensively to study the relationship between energy consumption and neuronal activity. PET uses positron-emitting radioactive tracers that are attached to molecules that enter biological pathways of interest (Figure 7.4A). For example, ^{18}F, a radioactive isotope of fluorine, can be attached to glucose, creating the molecule fluoro-2-deoxy-D-glucose, or FDG. The fluorine tracer does not prevent FDG from entering into the normal pathways for glucose metabolism. Thus, researchers can inject a bolus of FDG into an artery and then use imaging to determine where it is taken up by cells.

As the radioactive isotope decays, it emits a positron (the antimatter counterpart of an electron). When the emitted positron collides with a nearby electron, they are mutually annihilated and produce two gamma rays that take paths 180° apart and are subsequently detected by their near simultaneous impact on opposite sides of a ring of scintillation crystals that surround the subject's head (Figure 7.4B). A computer algorithm then evaluates the number and timing of impacts at all of the crystals surrounding the head and traces the paths taken by the gamma rays back to their origins. Through this method, the distribution of glucose uptake in the brain can be measured, and changes in glucose uptake in differ-

positron emission tomography (PET) A functional neuroimaging technique that creates images based upon the movement of injected radioactive material.

ent brain regions caused by sensory, motor, or cognitive activity can be determined (Figure 7.4C). PET imaging can also study oxygen metabolism or blood flow using ^{15}O, a radioactive isotope of oxygen. Certain neurotransmitters can be similarly labeled. For example, ^{18}F can be attached to dopamine to study its distribution in the human brain.

PET scanning provides a relatively direct and easily interpretable measure

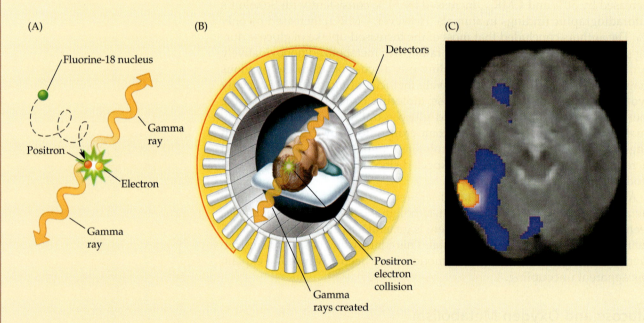

(A)

Fluorine-18 nucleus

Positron

Electron

Gamma ray

Gamma ray

(B)

Detectors

Positron-electron collision

Gamma rays created

(C)

Figure 7.4   Positron emission tomography (PET) imaging. Until the mid-1990s, the most common functional neuroimaging technique was PET, which relies on injection of a radioactive tracer into the bloodstream. As the tracer decays, it emits positrons, which travel a short distance before colliding with an electron (A). The collision results in a pair of emitted gamma rays that travel in opposite directions. The PET scanner (B) consists of a series of coincidence detectors that record the simultaneous arrival of these gamma rays. Depending on the tracer used, PET can be sensitive to several aspects of brain metabolism, including blood flow. The output of a PET scan indicates the number of events measured from each voxel during a long time period. These numbers can be converted to statistical maps, which then can be overlaid upon anatomical images, often from MRI. (C courtesy of Dr. David Madden, Duke University.)

BOX 7.1 *(continued)*

of brain metabolism, and for many years it was the mainstay of human functional neuroimaging. However, its dependence upon high-energy gamma radiation (or **ionizing radiation,** as named for its potential to break chemical bonds) presents problems for human studies. Radiation exposure in human research is carefully regulated, and subjects can participate in only a few PET scans. There are other drawbacks to PET imaging. Its spatial resolution is limited by the distance the positron travels away from the labeled molecule before it collides with an electron. This is dependent upon the particular isotope used; for example, the maximum distance that a positron emitted by ^{18}F will travel before encountering an electron is about 2.6 mm. Recall that it is the location of the gamma ray emission that is localized and not the location of the molecule of interest. More limiting, however, is the very poor tem-

poral resolution of PET imaging. Because many emissions must be detected before an image with sufficient signal-to-noise ratio can be produced, PET studies must collect data over a long period of time. For example, an image of blood flow based upon ^{15}O may take 90 seconds to acquire, while an image of glucose metabolism based upon ^{18}F may take 30 to 40 minutes to acquire. These acquisition times severely limit the temporal resolution of PET imaging and restrict the types of experimental designs that can be used.

When compared with PET imaging, MRI has several advantages. Because MRI does not involve ionizing radiation, subjects can be run repeatedly without the cumulative health risks of radiation exposure. Images with high signal-to-noise can be acquired in less than a second, and spatial resolution is limited primarily by the motion of the sample and signal-to-noise, not by the

ionizing radiation Electromagnetic radiation that has sufficient energy to separate electrons from electrically neutral atoms, turning them into ions.

inherent uncertainty in the measurement technique. But the potential resolution of MRI for anatomical studies should not be confused with the ability to resolve biological processes that influence the MRI signal. Even with the caveats described above, PET does directly image glucose or oxygen consumption. BOLD fMRI, for comparison, does not provide any direct information about metabolic processes themselves, but instead reports an indirect correlate of those processes. Thus, for many research questions about brain metabolism, PET imaging remains of critical importance.

genated hemoglobin from the capillaries supporting the active neural tissue and from the downstream venules. BOLD contrast following neuronal activity occurs not because the oxygenated hemoglobin increases the MR signal but because it displaces the deoxygenated hemoglobin that had been suppressing the MR signal intensity.

Here we consider three of the most influential explanations offered to explain the linkage between blood flow, glucose consumption, and oxygen utilization.

Watering the Garden for the Sake of One Thirsty Flower

Not all investigators accept the apparent uncoupling of $CMRO_2$ and CMR_{glu} during stimulation as indicative of anaerobic metabolism. In 1996 Malonek and Grinvald used a high-resolution optical imaging method in which the surface of the visual cortex in the cat is exposed to a light source and the reflected light is analyzed. Because different molecules (e.g., oxygenated and deoxygenated hemoglobin) absorb light of different wavelengths, the spectrum of the reflected light can be used to determine their presence at any given location in the cortex. They selectively activated small, spatially segregated populations of neurons in the visual cortex by presenting line gratings at particular orientations. The expected spatial pattern of neuronal activation across the visual cortex could then be compared to the spatial patterns of oxygenated and deoxygenated hemoglobin accumulation, allowing their measurements with high spatial and temporal resolution.

The results of the experiment showed that the evoked changes in hemoglobin and deoxygenated hemoglobin were quite distinct (Figure 7.5). The

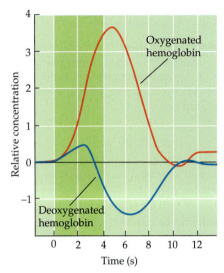

Figure 7.5 Changes in oxygenated and deoxygenated hemoglobin following neuronal stimulation. This figure shows that the concentration of deoxygenated hemoglobin increases rapidly at stimulus onset, peaking at about 2 s, and then declines to a minimum value about 6 s after onset. The oxygenated hemoglobin signal shows no decline, but begins rising shortly after stimulus onset and reaches a peak at about 5 to 6 s, with a slow decline to about 10 s. (Data from Malonek and Grinvald, 1996.)

deoxygenated hemoglobin–time curve showed a rapid increase that peaked about 2 s after the onset of the stimulus and then rapidly declined. By 6 s after the onset of the stimulus, the deoxygenated hemoglobin signal had declined to well below the prestimulus baseline level. In contrast, the oxygenated hemoglobin signal had a slightly delayed onset and then a much slower rise to a peak at about 5 to 6 s after stimulus onset. It was also much greater in amplitude than the deoxygenated hemoglobin signal. Moreover, unlike the weak deoxygenated hemoglobin signal, the spatial pattern of the oxygenated hemoglobin signal did not reflect the expected pattern of neuronal activity. Indeed, it was much more spatially extensive and extended into regions where there should have been no neuronal activity.

Three conclusions can be drawn from this experiment. First, the active neurons utilized whatever oxygen was already present to support their initial activity. This argues that increased metabolism at the onset of activation is oxidative. Second, there is an exquisite spatial correspondence at the onset of activity between neuronal activity and this initial increase in the deoxygenated hemoglobin signal. Third, the poor correspondence and greater spatial extent of the later oxygenated hemoglobin response indicates that the regulation of blood flow and oxygen delivery to the cortex is on a coarse spatial scale and mismatches metabolic needs. As Malonek and Grinvald put it, this is analogous to "watering the entire garden for the sake of one thirsty flower."

Thought Question

Why might the brain supply blood to a larger region than that of immediate neuronal activity?

These data suggest that the uncoupling reported by Fox and Raichle results not from an increase in anaerobic glycolysis but instead from a superfluous perfusion of oxygenated blood without a concomitant metabolic need. However, CMR_{glu} was not measured in this experiment, so whether the spatial pattern of OGI matched the pattern of neuronal activity could not be determined.

The Astrocyte–Neuron Lactate Shuttle Model

Other investigators have made a strong case that anaerobic glycolysis is present, at least transiently, in cerebral metabolism. Independent studies from two groups, Magistretti, Pellerin, and colleagues and Shulman, Rothman, and colleagues, have coalesced into an intriguing model that posits tight cooperation between neurons and their supporting astrocytes in managing the energy needs associated with increased neuronal activity (Figure 7.6). Astrocytes are glial cells that, among other functions, help regulate the extracellular environment. Astrocytes have fine processes that wrap around synaptic contacts in neurons and end feet that wrap around nearby capillaries. As discussed in the previous chapter, glutamate is the most prevalent excitatory neurotransmitter in the brain. Unchecked stimulation by glutamate, however, can be toxic to neurons. The central thesis of this model is that the increased release of glutamate by active neurons stimulates a highly efficient system in astrocytes that removes the glutamate from the extracellular space near synapses to stop its excitatory effects upon the postsynaptic membrane.

Glutamate is taken up by astrocytes via a high-affinity transporter that takes advantage of the electrochemical gradient for Na^+ and thus does not

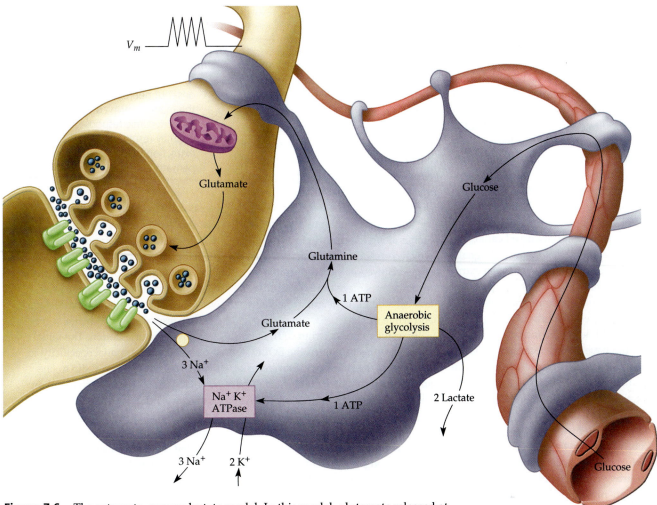

Figure 7.6 The astrocyte–neuron lactate model. In this model, glutamate released at the synapse following a change in membrane voltage (V_m) is quickly transported into an adjacent astrocyte where it is converted into glutamine for transport back to the neuron. The glutamate–glutamine conversion process is powered by one ATP from a fast anaerobic glycolysis process, which has two additional products: lactate, which is released into the extracellular space; and another ATP, which provides energy for the sodium–potassium pump at the astrocyte membrane.

require ATP to operate. However, three ions of Na^+ are cotransported into the cell with every molecule of glutamate. The astrocyte now has to solve two problems. The first is to remove the three ions of Na^+ to restore its electrochemical gradient. This is accomplished by the now familiar sodium–potassium pump, which transports the three Na^+ ions from the cell at the cost of one ATP. The second problem is to recycle the glutamate molecule so that it can be returned to the neuron, but not in its excitatory neurotransmitter form. This is accomplished through a reaction that converts glutamate into nonactive glutamine, again at the cost of one ATP. The glutamine is then transported out of the astrocyte and taken up by the neuron, converted back into glutamate, and then repackaged into synaptic vesicles, where it awaits another action potential for its release into the synaptic cleft.

The total cost to the astrocyte for this rapid removal and recycling of glutamate is two ATP per glutamate molecule. In this model, the cost is exactly balanced by the anaerobic glycolysis of glucose, which you will recall yields

BOX 7.2 The Initial Dip

Thus far, we have described the time course of the BOLD-contrast MR signal as an increase, or positive signal change, over time. One of the most interesting claims for BOLD fMRI is that this positive change is preceded by a smaller decrease in MR signal. This postulated decrease has been labeled the **initial dip,** and was first reported by Menon and colleagues in 1995. Building on the optical imaging work of Grinvald discussed earlier, they postulated that the BOLD signal confounded two factors, oxygen extraction and blood flow, that occur on different spatial and temporal scales. They hypothesized that fast imaging methods could detect the former, which would have a more focal spatial pattern than the latter. They presented a visual pattern that flashed for 10 s while collecting data using high-field (4 T) and fast-rate (TR of 100 ms) echo-planar imaging. To further improve signal-to-noise, they used a local surface coil, which increases detection power in nearby voxels. To detect voxels showing an initial dip, they compared each voxel's mean activity between 0.5 and 2.5 s to a prestimulus baseline period

using a *t*-test. For comparison, voxels showing a positive response were defined by a *t*-test comparing activity at 5 to 15 s to that at baseline.

The results verified that a small fraction of the active voxels showed an initial reduction in signal, the amplitude of which was less than half as large as the positive hemodynamic response (Figure 7.7A–C). The voxels showing the initial dip were found within gray matter along the calcarine sulcus, which corresponds to primary visual cortex. However, the later positive response was more spatially diffuse and extended into neighboring veins and white matter.

In a study conducted in 2001, Duong and colleagues examined the BOLD response in the primary visual cortex of anesthetized cats using high-field (4.7 T and 9.4 T) fMRI. The stimuli were drifting sine-wave gratings at different orientations. In the primary visual cortex, neurons are organized into columns that respond preferentially to stimuli of a particular orientation. By collecting data at very high spatial resolution (about 150 µm²), the researchers could identify individual orientation columns

initial dip The short-term decrease in MR signal immediately following the onset of neuronal activity, before the main positive component of the hemodynamic response. The initial dip may result from initial oxygen extraction before the later overcompensatory response.

(see Box 8.2 for related experiments examining ocular dominance columns in human subjects). Stimuli of perpendicular orientations (e.g., 45° and 135°) should activate different sets of orientation columns. The experimental test was whether the initial dip or the later positive response would better segregate voxels by orientation. The initial dip showed good spatial specificity, in that voxels with an initial dip to one orientation did not show an initial dip to the perpendicular orientation. In contrast, the later positive BOLD response was blurred over columns, such that most voxels showed positive BOLD activity to both orientations. The authors noted that the spatial specificity of the BOLD response was greatest over the first 2 s and decreased over time. This result suggests that the initial

(A)

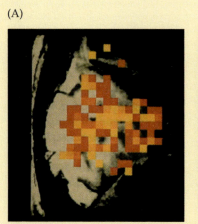

(B)

(C)

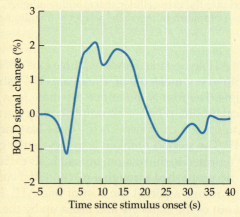

Figure 7.7 Spatial specificity of the BOLD initial dip. (A) A statistical map that shows all voxels in the visual cortex around the calcarine fissure that had a significant late positive hemodynamic response to visual stimulation. Note that the map of voxels that showed a significant early neg-ative response (i.e., the "initial dip") has fewer active voxels (B), suggesting that it may be more spatially specific. (C) The BOLD hemodynamic response across all voxels with an early negative response is shown. (From Menon et al., 1995.)

BOX 7.2 *(continued)*

dip may reflect oxygenation changes that are localized to capillaries, as first hypothesized by Menon and colleagues. However, the overcompensatory delivery of oxygenated blood that comprises the positive response causes more extensive changes in oxygenation within the venous drainage system.

Despite these intriguing results, the initial dip is a controversial topic for a simple reason: it is not reported in the vast majority of fMRI studies. So what could explain its infrequent observation? One likely factor is the rarity of high-field (e.g., ≥ 4 T) MR scanners for functional studies. The amplitude of the initial dip seems to scale dramatically with field strength. When measured at

1.5 T, the initial dip was only 12% of the magnitude of the positive response, which is only one-third of the proportion measured at 4 T. This result is consistent with the idea that the initial dip has a microvascular origin, since signal recorded from small blood vessels should scale more dramatically with field strength than signal recorded from large blood vessels. It may simply be more difficult to detect the initial dip at the field strengths most typical for fMRI. Another possible factor is that averaging over a large spatial region obscures the smaller-scale effects of the initial dip. Even in some studies where an initial dip was clearly present, it was reported to disappear if all voxels with a positive response were averaged.

While the evidence in support of the initial dip has strengthened in recent years, its underlying mechanisms still require further investigation. The hypothesis advocated by Menon and colleagues, that it represents an increase in oxygen extraction in advance of increased blood flow, remains consistent with the experimental data. But, recall that the BOLD signal depends not only on oxygen extraction but also on blood flow and blood volume. A transient decrease in flow or increase in volume would also result in a decrease in the BOLD signal. While these latter possibilities have not yet been ruled out, the oxygen extraction hypothesis provides the best current theoretical interpretation of the initial dip.

a net gain of two ATP for each molecule of glucose consumed. The astrocyte is then faced with one remaining problem: what to do with the lactate that accumulates as the end product of anaerobic glycolysis. The answer is to release the lactate into the extracellular space, where, due to its increased concentration, it diffuses into the neuron. Once inside the cytoplasm, the lactate is converted back into pyruvate through the action of the enzyme lactate dehydrogenase-1. The pyruvate is subsequently processed through the TCA cycle and electron transport chain to produce an additional 36 ATP that are used to support the energy costs of the neuron, as described previously.

In summary, the astrocyte–neuron lactate shuttle model proposes that an initial and rapid phase of anaerobic glycolysis is tightly coupled with the increase in excitatory glutamate release by neurons. In this way, it is consistent with the findings of Fox and Raichle. However, this model also predicts that oxygen is consumed in the normal way when the lactate produced in the anaerobic phase is converted to pyruvate in neurons and enters the TCA cycle. Thus, the model predicts only a transient shift to anaerobic glycolysis at the onset of stimulation. For this reason, it is interesting to note that recent studies by Mintun and colleagues using time-resolved PET have suggested that the uncoupling of $CMRO_2$ and CMR_{glu} observed by Fox and Raichle occurs early in stimulation and that these measures become coupled again as stimulation continues. This suggests that the brain may transiently utilize a fast but inefficient method for producing ATP when neuronal activity suddenly increases and glutamate must be removed from the synapse to avoid excitotoxic injury. However, as stimulation is sustained, the brain, using the lactate produced as an end product of anaerobic glycolysis, reverts to a slower but more efficient method of producing ATP through oxidation.

Transit Time and Oxygen Extraction

A third account for the uncoupling of glucose metabolism and oxygen utilization is presented in a formal biophysical model by Buxton and col-

balloon model A model of the interaction between changes in blood volume and changes in blood flow associated with neuronal activity.

leagues. This model also bears important similarities to an independent formulation by Gjedde. Like Grinvald and colleagues, these authors do not accept that the disparity between glucose consumption and oxygen utilization is evidence for anaerobic metabolism. This model is predicated upon four key assumptions. The first is that increased blood flow in response to neuronal activity is primarily accomplished by an increase in its velocity rather than by an increase in the number of capillaries through which the blood flows (i.e., no capillary recruitment). The second is that oxygen transport from blood to brain tissue is limited by several factors, and that the amount of oxygen extracted is proportional to transit time through the capillary bed. As blood velocity increases, the transit time decreases. The third assumption is that virtually all of the oxygen extracted from capillaries is metabolized, so there is no reserve pool of oxygen in brain tissue. The fourth assumption is that not all glucose that enters brain tissue is metabolized.

Buxton and colleagues argue that the likelihood of extracting an individual oxygen molecule (attached, of course, to hemoglobin) within a capillary has a fixed probability per unit time. Because of the increased blood velocity with neuronal activity, the resulting decrease in transit time reduces the overall likelihood that each oxygen molecule will be extracted. The rate of delivery of oxygen to tissue is thus a nonlinear function of flow velocity. Due to this nonlinearity, a disproportionately large increase in blood flow is required to cause even a small increase in the amount of oxygen extracted.

If transit time limits oxygen delivery, why doesn't it also limit glucose availability? Buxton states that the extraction of glucose is even more limited by transit time than that of oxygen, but, supported by data from Gjedde, he argues that less than half of the glucose extracted from capillaries is actually metabolized. Thus, the amount of glucose extracted from capillaries does not equal the amount metabolized in brain cells.

Implications for BOLD fMRI

The three formulations presented above account in different ways for the disparity between glucose consumption and oxygen utilization. The observations by Grinvald demonstrate that hemoglobin is delivered over an extensive region of cortex in response to the activation of a smaller neuronal region. This suggests that the coarseness in the control of blood flow to a cortical region limits the spatial resolution of fMRI. However, early decreases in fMRI signal, or initial dips (Box 7.2), would be colocalized with neuronal activity. In contrast, the astrocyte–neuron lactate shuttle model proposes a fast anaerobic response to neural activation and thus would not predict an initial dip. Indeed, definitive evidence for an initial dip would be inconsistent with the anaerobic glycolysis proposed in the lactate shuttle model.

The transit-time model of Buxton and colleagues did not attempt to account for the initial dip, but a later **balloon model** described the changes in blood volume that occur as a function of increased blood flow during brain activity. In this model, the increase in blood flow evoked by neuronal activation causes an inflow of blood into the venous system that is initially greater than its outflow. The result is increased blood volume in the venous system as it expands like a balloon to accommodate the increased inflow. In explorations of this model, Buxton and colleagues noted that it predicts that the initial increase in volume in small veins would be dominated by the presence of deoxygenated hemoglobin that was cleared first from the capillaries. This concentration of deoxygenated hemoglobin causes a loss of MR signal, and so the balloon model also predicts an initial dip. However, Buxton's interpretation is much different from that of Grinvald (and Menon and colleagues). Rather than reflecting a fast increase in deoxygenated hemoglobin caused by increased oxygen consumption in the vicinity of active neurons, Buxton's initial dip is a consequence of increased blood flow flushing deoxygenated hemoglobin from the capillaries into the veins at a faster inflow rate than outflow rate. If the Buxton et al. model is correct, the initial dip of the BOLD response, if observed, would not be a more spatially specific indicator of local neuronal firing.

The transit-time model of Buxton provides another challenge to the spatial resolution of fMRI using BOLD contrast. If the flow of oxygen-rich blood must be greatly increased so that only an additional few oxygen molecules can be extracted as fuel, the remaining hemoglobin-rich blood must enter the venous system, displacing deoxygenated hemoglobin and increasing the BOLD signal downstream from the active neurons. This possibility was captured in the question "Brain or vein?" that was posed by Frahm and colleagues in 1994. We emphasize this issue because of its importance to fMRI studies. Many reported areas of activation may be a consequence of venous drainage, not local neuronal activation, as any researcher who has found significant activation in the superior sagittal sinus will attest.

The Growth of BOLD fMRI

From the demonstrations of BOLD contrast by Ogawa and colleagues, it was clear that changes in blood oxygenation could be measured using MRI. The next step was to demonstrate that such measurements could be used to localize different functions in the human brain. The first functional studies used simple visual and motor tasks, such as watching a flashing checkerboard or squeezing one's hand repeatedly. Such simple tasks were not intended to provide new information about the organization of the brain; indeed, the locations of the visual and sensorimotor cortices had been known since the end of the nineteenth century! The primary goal of the first fMRI studies was instead to replicate well-established findings. If fMRI results were consistent with previous lesion or electrophysiological data, then there would be strong evidence for the future value of fMRI in studies of brain function. Before describing these early studies, we must resume our historical discussion from Chapter 1 so that they can be considered in the context of their times.

Evolution of Functional MRI

Few scientific discoveries are made in isolation. Most result from a combination of factors, often including economic and political influences, that together allow a nascent idea to flourish. The birth of fMRI was no exception. As evidence, consider that the paramagnetism of hemoglobin had been known for almost a half century before Thulborn and colleagues examined oxygenated and deoxygenated blood using MRI. It would be another decade after that test before the first fMRI studies were published. This slow pace of progress did not reflect a lack of interest in the brain. In contrast, there was considerable interest in scalp recordings of electrical potentials during the 1960s and 1970s and in PET imaging during the 1980s. The extended gestation and subsequent rapid growth of fMRI shown in the time line in Figure 7.8 resulted in large part from two external factors, both related to the clinical use of MRI: (1) improvements in pulse sequence design and scanner hardware, which reduced image collection time from many seconds to a few tens of milliseconds; and (2) the dramatic increase in the prevalence of MR scanners.

Figure 7.8 Milestones in the development of fMRI.

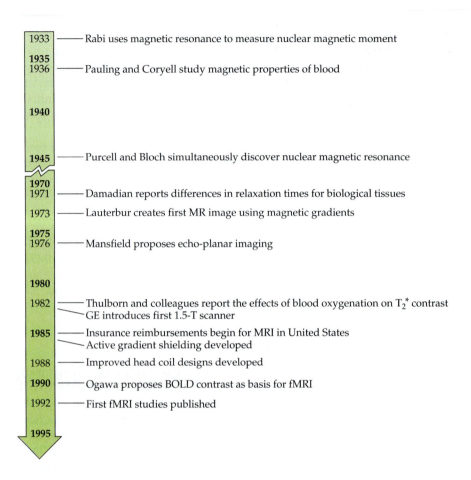

1933	Rabi uses magnetic resonance to measure nuclear magnetic moment
1935 1936	Pauling and Coryell study magnetic properties of blood
1940	
1945	Purcell and Bloch simultaneously discover nuclear magnetic resonance
1970 1971	Damadian reports differences in relaxation times for biological tissues
1973	Lauterbur creates first MR image using magnetic gradients
1975 1976	Mansfield proposes echo-planar imaging
1980	
1982	Thulborn and colleagues report the effects of blood oxygenation on T_2^* contrast
	GE introduces first 1.5-T scanner
1985	Insurance reimbursements begin for MRI in United States
	Active gradient shielding developed
1988	Improved head coil designs developed
1990	Ogawa proposes BOLD contrast as basis for fMRI
1992	First fMRI studies published
1995	

The first factor enabling fMRI was the development of pulse sequences and imaging hardware for rapid image acquisition. Early MR imaging was a slow process. The first MR image, for example, was acquired at a rate of more than 2 minutes per voxel. In modern imaging, where the brain may be composed of approximately 25,000 voxels, such a slow acquisition pace would correspond to approximately one volume per month! As discussed in Chapter 1, the development of echo-planar imaging (EPI), largely through the work of Peter Mansfield in the late 1970s, allowed an entire image to be collected following a single excitation pulse (Figure 7.9).

While the theoretical basis for EPI was developed relatively early, practical implementation of the theory was delayed by limitations in scanning hardware. The rapid changes in the gradient fields required by EPI could induce currents in metal parts within the scanner, introducing artifacts in recorded images. Rather than change scanner design to ameliorate this problem, manufacturers adopted other approaches, such as fast low (flip) angle shot, or FLASH, sequences, that did not tax scanner hardware as significantly as EPI. Not until about 1985 were active gradient-shielding techniques developed, largely through the work of Mansfield and colleagues, that incorporated an outer gradient winding in the opposite direction. The outer winding reduced eddy currents in the scanner hardware but added complexity and increased power requirements. Major manufacturers began adding actively shielded gradients to their standard scanner platforms over the following years. By the early 1990s, advances in gradient technology proposed by Turner and by Wong and colleagues provided the fast switching capability and high linearity, respectively, needed for EPI to be practical.

The second key factor was the increasing *clinical* applicability of structural MRI. Most of the relatively few scanners used in the 1970s were devoted to industrial applications, and almost none were being used in hospital settings. While clinical interest in MR imaging was lacking, there was substantial interest in computerized tomography (CT) scanners. Unlike standard X-ray imaging, which had remained largely unchanged since its discovery by Wilhelm Roentgen in 1895, CT imaging allowed clinicians to assess damage to soft-tissue structures (Figure 7.10A–C). CT scanners were expensive, typically requiring a capital commitment of more than $300,000, but the improved images they provided became an important part of the radiologist's arsenal, and by the early 1980s more than 5000 were in use worldwide. CT scans began to be demanded by doctors and patients alike, serving both to draw new patients to hospitals that possessed the latest equipment and to generate new income from the expensive procedures.

By the early 1980s, hospitals began considering the use of MRI as a complement to CT scanning, in part due to the enthusiasm of pioneers like Raymond Damadian (see Chapter 1). Several medical device companies, including Damadian's FONAR Corporation, General Electric (GE), and Varian, developed high-field scanners that promised image resolution that would far surpass that of CT. The first 1.5-T scanner was installed at Duke University by GE in 1982. This would remain the most common field strength for both clinical and research purposes for more than two decades.

Figure 7.9 One of the earliest EPI images. This cross section of a human finger represents one of the very first uses of echo-planar imaging to scan living human tissue. (From Mansfield and Maudsley, 1977.)

(A)

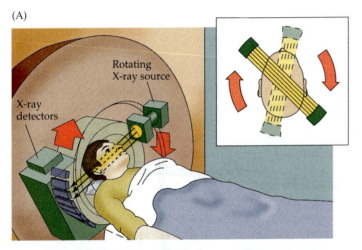

(B)

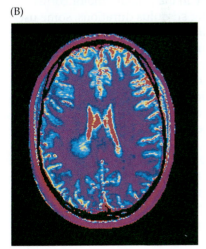

(C)

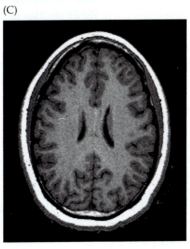

Figure 7.10 Computerized tomography imaging. CT uses a moving X-ray source to create a three-dimensional map of underlying tissue (A). Note that CT is sensitive to the same limitations on resolution and contrast as conventional X-rays (B). For comparison, a structural MRI image is shown in (C).

By 1985, MR scanning was sufficiently well established that insurance companies in the United States began reimbursing for MRI procedures. The cost of MRI scanners was still very high, often as much as $2 million, but hospitals were now able to recoup costs over many procedures. As had happened more than a decade earlier with CT, this new clinical demand sparked an explosion in the number of MRI scanners. By the year 2002, a mere 20 years after the introduction of the first high-field scanner, there were more than 10,000 such scanners worldwide. Although most were devoted to patient care during normal business hours, researchers at many institutions were able to use the scanners at night and on weekends for research into brain function. These research studies were often facilitated by supplemental hardware, such as gradient insert coils, that improved upon the hardware provided by the clinical manufacturers. The advances that facilitated the first fMRI studies, therefore, were developed in large part to meet the clinical demand for structural MRI.

Early fMRI Studies

The first BOLD fMRI studies were reported in 1992 by three groups. Kwong and colleagues used a gradient-echo EPI sequence at 1.5 T to study activity in the visual cortex. They evoked visual cortex activity by alternating 60-s periods of visual stimulation (e.g., the flashing of an LED pattern) with 60-s baseline periods of darkness. At the onset of the stimulation period, there was a sharp increase in MR signal around the calcarine fissure, increasing by about 3% within 10 s (Figure 7.11A–C). The activity increase was sustained for the duration of the visual stimulation, receding to the baseline level once darkness returned. These findings were replicated by a similar study published the following month by Ogawa and colleagues, who likewise evaluated changes in fMRI gradient-echo signal resulting from long-duration (e.g., 100 s) presentations of visual stimuli. Unlike the Kwong study, however, they used a pulse sequence that limited them to an effective TR of about 10 s, and they tested subjects at high field (4 T). Ogawa and colleagues manipulated TE to prove that the BOLD signal change depends upon T_2^* effects. At a very short TE of 8 ms, the stimulus effects previously seen at a TE of 40 ms disappeared. Since T_1-related effects should be independent of TE, as discussed in Chapter 5, the BOLD effect must depend on T_2^* effects. Nearly simultaneously, a third paper published in 1992 by Bandettini and colleagues reported similar effects, using a motor task in which subjects repeatedly touched their fingers to their thumb for a long block of time. Data recorded using gradient-echo EPI at 1.5 T showed significant activity in the primary motor cortex.

While most early fMRI studies used long stimulus durations, some used shorter stimulus events to examine vascular responses to a single, punctuate stimulus. The first such results were reported later in 1992 by Blamire and colleagues, who investigated changes in visual cortex activity following stimuli of different durations. They acquired images using a spin-echo EPI sequence at 2.1 T. The longer stimuli (10 s to 90 s) resulted in signal increases of about 10% over baseline. This finding was expected, based upon the studies described above. What was remarkable were the results from the short-duration stimuli. Even the shortest stimulus (2 s) evoked a significant 4% signal change in active voxels within the visual cortex (Figure 7.12). The authors noted that there was a short but measurable delay between the stimulus presentation and the MR signal change. On average, the first observable fMRI change in the primary visual cortex occurred about 3.5 s following the onset of the stimulus. The results shown in the figure repre-

(A)

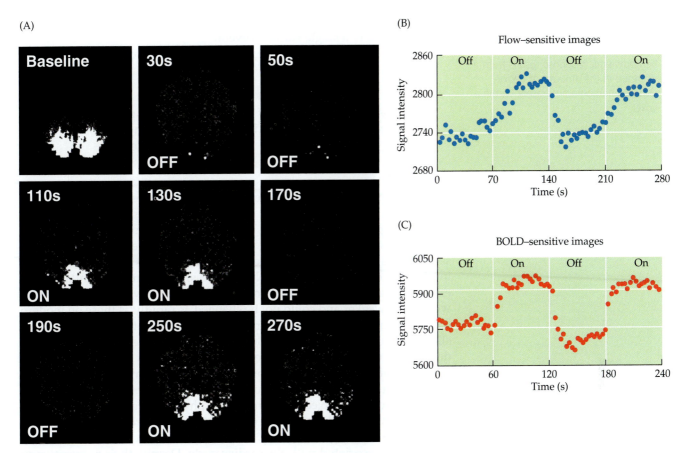

(B)

(C)

Figure 7.11   The first use of BOLD fMRI for functional mapping of the human brain. In this study, two fMRI techniques are used: flow–sensitive spin-echo inversion recovery (IR) and BOLD–sensitive gradient-echo (GE). (A) The area of activity for the flow–sensitive IR sequence. (B,C) The time courses of activity measured using each technique. Note the use of a long-interval blocked design, consistent with PET studies of its time. (From Kwong et al., 1992.)

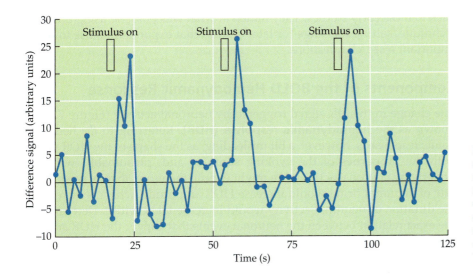

Figure 7.12   Changes in BOLD activity associated with presentations of single discrete events. This graph provides the first example of BOLD activity associated with single events. While event-related methods are extremely common in contemporary fMRI studies, their use did not become widespread until the late 1990s. (Data from Blamire et al., 1992.)

hemodynamic response (HDR) The change in MR signal on $T_2{}^*$ images following local neuronal activity. The hemodynamic response results from a decrease in the amount of deoxygenated hemoglobin present within a voxel.

sent the very first demonstration of the time course of hemodynamic activity in response to a single stimulus event.

> ### Thought Question
>
> Why is the finding of BOLD activity in response to short-duration stimuli important? What implications does it have for fMRI experimentation?

It is important to compare these early studies to current fMRI practice. At first glance, the procedures and equipment seem very similar. The field strengths reported above (i.e., 1.5 T, 2.1 T, 4.0 T) are similar to those of MRI scanners used now, more than a decade later. The use of EPI pulse sequences is also still common, though other sequences such as spiral imaging have grown in popularity. Nevertheless, there are substantial differences. The gradient fields that could be generated by the older scanners were much weaker and could not be changed as rapidly as those on modern scanners. Furthermore, the earlier studies collected data from one or a few slices, despite having relatively long TRs. Improvements in gradient coil design now enable the collection of more than 20 slices per second.

In addition to hardware improvements, there have been significant advances in strategies for fMRI analyses. None of these early studies corrected for possible subject head motion or physiological variation. Blamire and colleagues noted that voxels on the edge of the brain showed systematic oscillations in signal intensity, which they attributed to pulsatile motion of the brain associated with the cardiac cycle. Despite their recognition of this problem, no computational techniques were available for its solution. Today, however, the preprocessing of fMRI data to remove unwanted variability is an important aspect of fMRI analysis. In addition, the experimental designs used in these early studies were very simple, in that they evaluated only whether activity in a region of interest changed during a task as compared to a control condition. While this comparison is appropriate for simple visual or motor tasks, more-complex experimental questions require more-complex experimental designs.

Nevertheless, the basic elements of modern fMRI practice can be traced back to these early studies. They hinted at what was possible using this new technique, setting the stage for later studies that expanded its use to other important research questions.

Components of the BOLD Hemodynamic Response

The change in the MR signal triggered by neuronal activity (Figure 7.14) is known as the **hemodynamic response (HDR)**. Referring to *the* hemodynamic response is, however, a bit misleading, as the shape of the HDR varies with the properties of the evoking stimulus and, presumably, with the underlying neuronal activity. We might expect, therefore, that increasing the rate of neuronal firing would increase HDR amplitude, whereas increasing the duration of neuronal activity would increase HDR width. Determining the exact relation between the neuronal events that trigger the HDR and the shape of the HDR, however, is complicated by their differing dynamics. Cortical neuronal responses occur within tens of milliseconds following a sensory stimulus, but the first observable HDR changes do not occur until 1 to 2

BOX 7.3 Functional Studies Using Contrast Agents

BOLD contrast depends on the paramagnetic properties of deoxygenated hemoglobin, which induce changes in local magnetic fields that can be measured using T_2^* imaging. One potential way of increasing image contrast is to use exogenous **contrast agents** such as gadolinium diethylenetriaminepentaacetic acid (Gd-DTPA), highly paramagnetic substances that can be injected into the bloodstream but do not cross the intact blood–brain barrier. The agents used are well tolerated by most people, with mild headache and nausea as the most common side effects. Common contrast agents are shown in Table 7.1. Contrast agents have great importance for clinical imaging, especially in the detection of pathological tissue, including brain tumors. Under normal conditions, the diffusion of a contrast agent like Gd-DTPA through the bloodstream will reduce T_1 values of hydrogen protons in the blood, increasing signal within blood vessels but not elsewhere. But if there is damage to the blood–brain barrier due to brain pathology, the contrast agent may escape from the bloodstream and enter the surrounding tissue, resulting in increased signal on T_1-weighted images.

This effect upon T_1 relaxation, though clinically important, provides no information about brain function. Rather, it is the effect of contrast agents upon local magnetic field properties that enables functional studies. Because the injected contrast agent is highly paramagnetic and has a very strong magnetic moment, there will be a considerable inhomogeneity between the tissue outside of the blood vessel and the contrast-enhanced blood within. Remember from Chapter 5 that sharp gradients in magnetic field homogeneity can cause signal losses known as susceptibility artifacts, due to differential effects of the magnetic gradient upon spin precession. When a pulse sequence sensitive to T_2^* effects is used, these signal losses enable measurement of the local concentration of the contrast agent over time. Unlike BOLD contrast, which depends on both blood flow and oxygen extraction, exogenous contrast methods generally rely only on blood volume changes associated with functional activity. In addition, they have a limited lifetime due to their passage through the brain and subsequent dispersal through the vascular system. But, because the exogenous contrast agent is much more paramagnetic than deoxygenated hemoglobin, the signal change observed will be much larger, allowing meaningful data to be extracted from the first pass of the agent through the brain.

The first fMRI study to use exogenous contrast (and one of the first fMRI studies of any form) was reported by Belliveau and colleagues in 1991. They measured visual cortex activity using spin-echo EPI at 1.5 T following injection of a **bolus** of Gd-DTPA. In the test condition, subjects viewed a visual pattern that flashed at a rate of about 8 Hz, and in the control condition there was no visual stimulus. Based on electrophysiological data, this rate was known to robustly activate the primary visual cortex. The authors hypothesized that, following injection of the contrast agent, the raw MR signal would decrease due to increased magnetic susceptibility. Furthermore, the magnitude of this decrease should be greater for active brain regions due to local increases in blood volume. As shown in Figure 7.13A–C, there was a transient decrease in MR signal associated with passage of the contrast agent through the primary visual cortex. Note the delay of about 8 to 10 s between the injection of Gd-DTPA and the onset of the signal decrease. This delay reflects the time required for the contrast agent to travel from the injection site, which was the antecubital vein in the arm, through the heart to the primary visual cortex. Although decreases in signal intensity in the visual cortex were present in both the test and control conditions, the decrease was larger and occurred earlier for the flashing pattern than for darkness. From this result, the researchers concluded that blood volume had increased in the calcarine cortex and thus that neurons in that part of the brain are associated with visual perception.

contrast agent A substance injected into the body to increase image contrast.

bolus A quantity of a substance that is introduced into a system and then progresses through that system over time.

TABLE 7.1	**Properties of Common Contrast Agents Used for Structural MRI**		
Compound	Longitudinal relaxivity	Transverse relaxivity	Magnetic susceptibility
Gd-Cl2	1	1	1
Mn-Cl2	0.96	3.83	0.51
Gd-DTPA	0.52	0.5	1
Dy-DPTA	0.03	0.04	1.78
G-DTPA albumin	1.6	-	-
Iron oxide particle (3 nm)	0.41	0.63	40.7
Iron oxide particle (253 nm)	4.4	15.5	148

Source: Torchilin, 1995.

BOX 7.3 (continued)

(A)   (B)   (C)

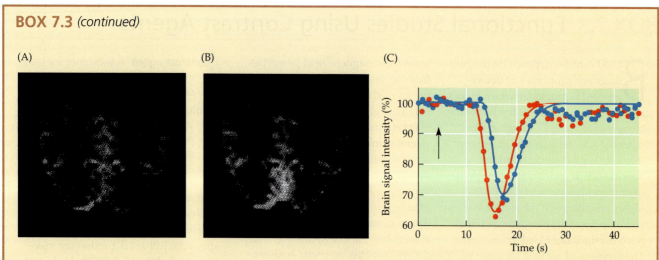

Figure 7.13 Functional MRI using exogenous contrast. This figure provides the first example of functional mapping of the human brain using MRI. Subjects were injected with the contrast agent Gd-DTPA and exposed to darkness or rapidly flashing lights. Compared with darkness (A), there was a significant increase in cerebral blood volume when the flashing lights were presented (B). The plot in (C) shows the passage of the contrast agent through the visual cortex, in conditions of visual stimulation (red circles) and darkness (blue circles). Note that in both cases there are significant decreases in MR signal due to the magnetic susceptibility effects of the contrast agent. However, the decrease occurs earlier and is larger in the activated condition. (From Belliveau et al., 1991.)

The power of exogenous contrast agents comes from the enormous signal changes they induce. Even in this early experiment, the signal change observed due to the contrast injection was about 30%. The difference between the test and control conditions was on the order of 5%. To appreciate the magnitude of such changes, compare them to the much smaller signal changes observed in BOLD fMRI, which are typically only a few percent. Furthermore, the clear differences observed between experimental conditions by Belliveau and colleagues were obtained without signal averaging. That is, the data shown in Figure 7.13 represent two trials, one test

and one control, from a single subject. Modern BOLD studies, for comparison, usually represent the average of many subjects with many trials per condition.

Despite this power, exogenous contrast agents are rarely used for fMRI research. One limitation can be seen in the time course of signal change. Because of the substantial transit delay of the agent, it is challenging to accurately measure the timing of brain activity. And since a single bolus is used, one measurement of signal change is obtained per trial. If one wants to study two types of trials, like Belliveau and colleagues, two injections are required. In general, as more conditions are

added, more injections are needed. These requirements preclude some types of analyses that are possible with endogenous BOLD contrast, such as the sorting of many trials based on accuracy or reaction time, fast event-related designs, evaluation of brain response as a function of stimulus sequence, and complex parametric studies. In addition, many subjects are less likely to participate in studies that require intravenous injection. So, while a number of researchers are actively investigating the use of contrast agents for fMRI (see Chapter 14), especially for studies in animals, nearly all current fMRI studies use endogenous BOLD contrast.

seconds later. Thus, the HDR is said to lag the neuronal events that initiate it. Throughout the remainder of the book, we will make frequent reference to different aspects of the HDR waveform, and so here we define some terms. Figure 7.15A and B provide an illustrative schematic of a typical HDR.

Remember that the BOLD signal in a voxel reflects the total amount of deoxygenated hemoglobin that is present, as well as noise resulting from several sources. As described in Box 7.2, some studies have reported an initial negative-going dip of 1 to 2 s duration that has been attributed to a transient increase in the amount of deoxygenated hemoglobin. After a short latency, the

(A)

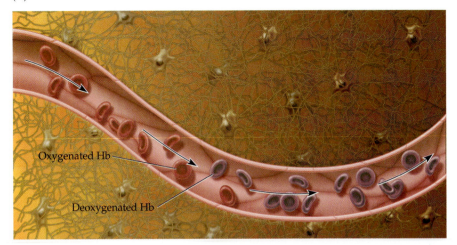

Oxygenated Hb

Deoxygenated Hb

(B)

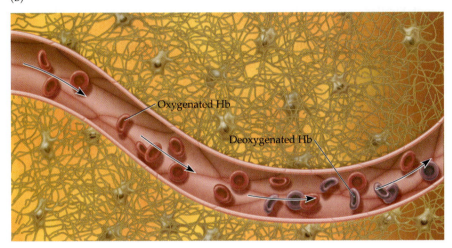

Oxygenated Hb

Deoxygenated Hb

Figure 7.14 Summary of BOLD signal generation. Under normal conditions, oxygenated hemoglobin is converted to deoxygenated hemoglobin at a constant rate within the capillary bed (A). But when neurons become active, there is an increase in the supply of oxygenated hemoglobin above that needed by the neurons (B). This results in a relative decrease in the amount of deoxygenated hemoglobin and a corresponding decrease in the signal loss due to T_2^* effects.

metabolic demands of increased neuronal activity over baseline levels result in an increased inflow of oxygenated blood. More oxygen is supplied to the area than is extracted, and this results in a decrease in the amount of deoxygenated hemoglobin within the voxel. If we monitor such an active voxel's activity using BOLD fMRI, we find that its signal increases above baseline at about 2 s following the onset of neuronal activity, growing to a maximum value at about 5 s for a short-duration stimulus. This maximum is known as the **peak** of the hemodynamic response. If the neuronal activity is extended across a block of time, the peak may be similarly extended into a plateau.

After reaching its peak, the BOLD signal decreases in amplitude to a below-baseline level and remains below baseline for an extended interval. This effect is known as the poststimulus **undershoot.** To understand the undershoot, we need to consider the changes in blood flow and blood volume separately (Figure 7.16). Following cessation of neuronal activity, blood flow decreases more rapidly than blood volume. If volume remained above baseline levels, while flow was at baseline, then a greater amount of deoxygenated hemoglobin would be present. Thus, the overall fMRI signal will be

peak The maximal amplitude of the hemodynamic response, occurring typically about 4 to 6 s following a short-duration event.

undershoot The decrease in MR signal amplitude below baseline due to the combination of reduced blood flow and increased blood volume.

Figure 7.15 Schematic representations of the fMRI BOLD hemodynamic response. Shown are representative waveforms for the hemodynamic response to a single short-duration event (A) and to a block of multiple consecutive events (B).

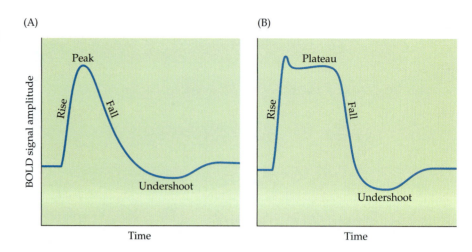

time course The change in MR signal over a series of fMRI images.

epoch A time segment extracted from a larger series of images, usually corresponding to the period in time surrounding an event of interest.

reduced below baseline levels. As blood volume slowly returns to normal levels, the fMRI signal will similarly increase to baseline, ending the undershoot. Similar ideas have been captured in the balloon model described earlier in this chapter.

Sample data from a single voxel showing its change in MR signal over time, or its **time course,** are provided in Figure 7.17A. In this experiment, the subject squeezed both hands whenever a brief flashing checkerboard was presented. There were long intervals between the stimuli so that there would be time for the hemodynamic response to return to baseline. Each line in Figure 7.17B presents the change in MR signal within a single voxel over a 21-s peristimulus **epoch,** from 3 s before the stimulus through 18 s after. Immediately apparent is the variability in the response over time. Even for very good responses, as shown in the figure, the noise in the data is of an amplitude similar to the hemodynamic response, making it difficult to identify the exact response evoked by each presentation of a stimulus. However,

Figure 7.16 Relative changes in cerebral blood flow and cerebral blood volume following neuronal activity. This figure shows data from an experiment in which the forepaw of a rat was stimulated for a period of 30 s and the resulting changes in cerebral blood flow (CBF) and cerebral blood volume (CBV) were measured. Note that following the stimulus offset, CBF returns quickly to baseline levels but CBV returns slowly. Elevated CBV relative to CBF causes an increase in the total amount of deoxyhemoglobin that is present, in turn causing the poststimulus undershoot in the BOLD signal. (Data from Mandeville et al., 1999.)

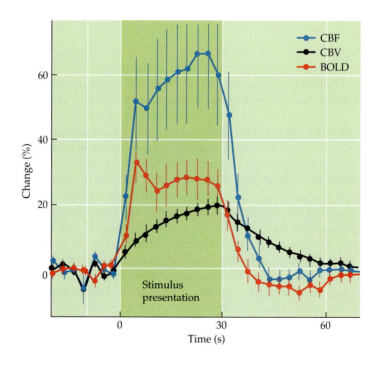

(A)

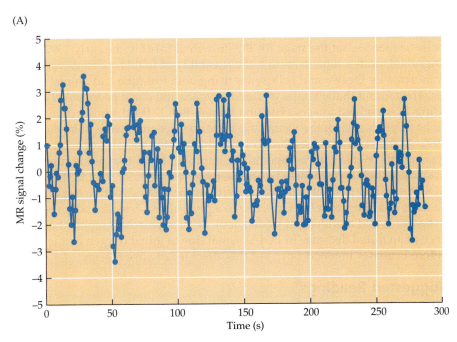

(B)

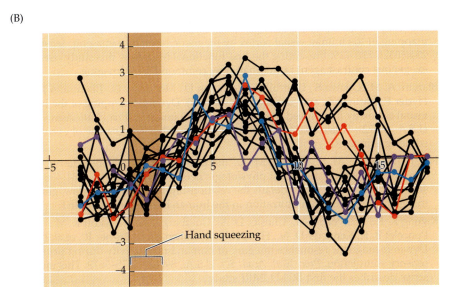

as data is combined across many evoked responses, a hemodynamic response similar to that shown in Figure 7.15A emerges.

Summary

Nearly all fMRI studies rely on an endogenous measure known as blood-oxygenation-level dependent (BOLD) contrast. The idea of using blood properties as indices of brain functions is more than a century old. Early research demonstrated that deoxygenated hemoglobin is paramagnetic while oxygenated hemoglobin is diamagnetic. Subsequent studies in the early 1980s revealed that the resulting differences in magnetic susceptibility could be measured using MRI. These results, in conjunction with the increased prevalence of MRI scanners and the development of high-speed pulse sequences, set the stage for the growth of fMRI in the early 1990s. Important studies demonstrating the feasibility of BOLD contrast were conducted by Ogawa and colleagues using both test tube and animal models. They found that changes in blood oxygenation could be visualized using T_2^*-weighted images. The first human BOLD fMRI studies investigated basic properties of the visual and motor cortices and were published in 1992. At the same time, researchers investigated the use of exogenous contrast agents. While contrast agents can improve signal-to-noise in functional studies, their invasiveness has made them less popular than BOLD. The BOLD response to brief neuronal activity, or the hemodynamic response, consists of a short onset delay, a rise to a peak after a few seconds, a return to baseline, and a prolonged undershoot. Some researchers report the presence of an initial decrease in BOLD signal due to initial oxygen extraction before increases in blood flow, but this effect is not always seen.

Suggested Readings

*Bandettini, P. A., Wong, E. C., Hinks, R. S., Tikofsky, R. S., and Hyde, J. S. (1992). Time course EPI of human brain function during task activation. *Magn. Reson. Med.*, 25: 390–397. This manuscript reports one of the first human fMRI studies.

*Belliveau J. W., Kennedy D. N., Jr., McKinstry R. C., Buchbinder B. R., Weisskoff R. M., Cohen M. S., Vevea J. M., Brady T. J., and Rosen B. R. (1991). Functional mapping of the human visual cortex by magnetic resonance imaging. *Science*, 254(5032): 716–719. Presenting the first functional MRI data, this study used an exogenous contrast agent rather than now common BOLD imaging.

*Blamire A. M., Ogawa S., Ugurbil K., Rothman D., McCarthy G., Ellermann J. M., Hyder F., Rattner Z., and Shulman R. G. (1992). Dynamic mapping of the human visual cortex by high-speed magnetic resonance imaging. *Proc. Natl. Acad. Sci. U.S.A.*, 89(22): 11069–11073. This early study describes the first use of event-related designs in fMRI.

*Fox, P. T., Raichle, M. E., Mintun, M. A., and Dence, C. (1988). Nonoxidative glucose consumption during focal physiologic neural activity. *Science*, 241(4864): 462–464. This classic paper details the relationship between blood flow, glucose metabolism, and oxygen utilization in the human brain studied by PET.

*Kwong K. K., Belliveau J. W., Chesler D. A., Goldberg I. E., Weisskoff R. M., Poncelet B. P., Kennedy D. N., Hoppel B. E., Cohen M. S., Turner R., et al. (1992). Dynamic magnetic resonance imaging of human brain activity during primary sensory stimulation. *Proc. Natl. Acad. Sci. U.S.A.*, 89(12): 5675–5679. This manuscript describes the first BOLD fMRI study.

*Magistretti, P. J., Pellerin, L., Rothman, D. L., and Shulman, R. G. (1999). Energy on demand. *Science*, 283(5401): 496–497. This paper provides a succinct review of the astrocyte–lactate shuttle hypothesis.

*Ogawa S., Lee T. M., Kay A. R., and Tank D. W. (1990a). Brain magnetic resonance imaging with contrast dependent on blood oxygenation. *Proc. Natl. Acad. Sci. U.S.A.*, 87(24): 9868–9872. This report provided the initial demonstration of the effects of blood oxygenation on T_2^* contrast, through studies of rats at high magnetic field.

*Ogawa S., Tank D. W., Menon R., Ellermann J. M., Kim S. G., Merkle H., and Ugurbil K. (1992). Intrinsic signal changes accompanying sensory stimulation: Functional brain mapping with magnetic resonance imaging. *Proc. Natl. Acad. Sci. U.S.A.*, 89(13): 5951–5955. One of the very earliest fMRI studies, this is of additional interest due to the difference between its methods and modern studies.

*Pauling, L., and Coryell, C. D. (1936). The magnetic properties and structure of hemoglobin, oxygenated hemoglobin, and carbonmonoxygenated hemoglobin. *Proc. Natl. Acad. Sci. U.S.A.*, 22(4): 210–236. This accessible manuscript from a future Nobel laureate describes the basic chemical and physical properties of hemoglobin.

Stehling M. K., Turner R., and Mansfield P. (1991). Echo-planar imaging: Magnetic resonance imaging in a fraction of a second. *Science,* 254(5028): 43–50. This early review article provides a good description of high-speed echo-planar imaging and some of its potential uses.

Indicates a reference that is a suggested reading in the field and is also cited in this chapter.

Chapter References

Buxton, R. B., and Frank, L. R. (1997). A model for the coupling between cerebral blood flow and oxygen metabolism during neural stimulation. *J. Cereb. Blood Flow Metab.*, 17(1): 64–72.

Buxton, R. B., Wong, E. C., and Frank, L. R. (1998). Dynamics of blood flow and oxygen metabolism during brain activation: The balloon model. *Magn. Reson. Med.*, 39: 855–864.

Chih, C. P., Lipton, P., and Roberts, E. L., Jr. (2001). Do active cerebral neurons really use lactate rather than glucose? *Trends Neurosci.*, 24(10): 573–578.

Duong T. Q., Kim D. S., Ugurbil K., and Kim S. G. (2001). Localized cerebral blood flow response at submillimeter columnar resolution. *Proc. Natl. Acad. Sci. U.S.A.*, 98(19): 10904–10909.

Fox, P. T., and Raichle, M. E. (1986). Focal physiological uncoupling of cerebral blood flow and oxidative metabolism during somatosensory stimulation in human subjects. *Proc. Natl. Acad. Sci. U.S.A.*, 83(4): 1140–1144.

Frahm, J., Merboldt, K. D., Hanicke, W., Kleinschmidt, A., and Boecker, H. (1994). Brain or vein—oxygenation or flow? On signal physiology in functional MRI of human brain activation. *NMR Biomed.*, 7(1–2): 45–53.

Gjedde, A., Marrett, S., and Vafaee, M. (2002). Oxidative and nonoxidative metabolism of excited neurons and astrocytes. *J. Cereb. Blood Flow Metab.*, 22(1): 1–14.

Harel, N., Lee, S. P., Nagaoka, T., Kim, D. S., and Kim, S. G. (2002). Origin of negative blood oxygenation level-dependent fMRI signals. *J. Cereb. Blood Flow Metabol.*, 22(8): 908–917.

Hyder, F., Rothman, D. L., and Shulman, R. G. (2002). Total neuroenergetics support localized brain activity: Implications for the interpretation of fMRI [Comment]. *Proc. Natl. Acad. Sci. U.S.A.*, 99(16): 10771–10776.

Jones M., Berwick J., Johnston D., and Mayhew J. (2001). Concurrent optical imaging spectroscopy and laser-Doppler flowmetry: The relationship between blood flow, oxygenation, and volume in rodent barrel cortex. *NeuroImage*, 13(6 Pt. 1): 1002–1015.

Magistretti, P. J., and Pellerin, L. (1999). Cellular mechanisms of brain energy metabolism and their relevance to functional brain imaging. *Philos. Trans. Royal Soc. London Ser. B Biol. Sci.*, 354(1387): 1155–1163.

Malonek, D., and Grinvald, A. (1996). Interactions between electrical activity and cortical microcirculation revealed by imaging spectroscopy: Implications for functional brain mapping. *Science,* 272(5261): 551–554.

Mandeville J. B., Marota J. J., Ayata C., Moskowitz M. A., Weisskoff R. M., and Rosen B. R. (1998). Dynamic functional imaging of relative cerebral blood volume during rat forepaw stimulation. *Magn. Reson. Med.*, 39(4): 615–624.

Mandeville J. B., Marota J. J., Kosofsky B. E., Keltner J. R., Weissleder R., Rosen B. R., and Weisskoff R. M. (1999). MRI measurement of the temporal evolution of relative CMRO(2) during rat forepaw stimulation. *Magn. Reson. Med.*, 42(5): 944–951.

Mansfield, P., and Maudsley, A. A. (1977). Medical imaging by NMR. *Br. J. Radiol.,* 50(591): 188–194.

Menon R. S., Ogawa S., Hu X., Strupp J. P., Anderson P., and Ugurbil K. (1995). BOLD based functional MRI at 4 Tesla includes a capillary bed contribution: Echo-planar imaging correlates with previous optical imaging using intrinsic signals. *Magn. Reson. Med.,* 33(3): 453–459.

Mintun, M. A., Vlassenko, A. G., Shulman, G. L., and Snyder, A. Z. (2002). Time-related increase of oxygen utilization in continuously activated human visual cortex. *NeuroImage,* 16(2): 531–537.

Ogawa, S., and Lee, T. M. (1990). Magnetic resonance imaging of blood vessels at high fields: In vivo and in vitro measurements and image simulation. *Magn. Reson. Med.,* 16(1): 9–18.

Ogawa S., Lee T. M., Nayak A. S., and Glynn P. (1990b). Oxygenation-sensitive contrast in magnetic resonance image of rodent brain at high magnetic fields. *Magn. Reson. Med.,* 14(1): 68–78.

Parri, R., and Crunelli, V. (2003). An astrocyte bridge from synapse to blood flow. *Nat. Neurosci.,* 6(1): 5–6.

Prichard, J., Rothman, D., Novotny, E., Petroff, O., Kuwabara, T., Avison, M., Howseman, A., Hanstock, C., and Shulman, R. (1991). Lactate rise detected by 1H NMR in human visual cortex during physiologic stimulation. *Proc. Natl. Acad. Sci. U.S.A.,* 88(13): 5829–5831.

Shulman, R. G., Hyder, F., and Rothman, D. L. (2001). Cerebral energetics and the glycogen shunt: Neurochemical basis of functional imaging. *Proc. Natl. Acad. Sci. U.S.A.,* 98(11): 6417–6422.

Shulman, R. G., Hyder, F., and Rothman, D. L. (2002). Biophysical basis of brain activity: Implications for neuroimaging. *Q. Rev. Biophys.,* 35(3): 287–325.

Shulman, R. G., and Rothman, D. L. (1998). Interpreting functional imaging studies in terms of neurotransmitter cycling. *Proc. Natl. Acad. Sci. U.S.A.,* 95(20): 11993–11998.

Silva, A. C., Lee, S. P., Iadecola, C., and Kim, S. G. (2000). Early temporal characteristics of cerebral blood flow and deoxyhemoglobin changes during somatosensory stimulation. *J. Cereb. Blood Flow Metab.,* 20(1): 201–206.

Smith, A. J., Blumenfeld, H., Behar, K. L., Rothman, D. L., Shulman, R. G., and Hyder, F. (2002). Cerebral energetics and spiking frequency: The neurophysiological basis of fMRI. *Proc. Natl. Acad. Sci. U.S.A.,* 99(16): 10765–10770.

Sokoloff, L., Reivich, M., Kennedy, C., Des Rosiers, M. H., Patlak, C. S., Pettigrew, K. D., Sakurada, O., and Shinohara, M. (1977). The ^{14}C-2-deoxyglucose method for the measurement of local cerebral glucose utilization. Theory, procedure, and normal values in the conscious and anaesthetized rat. *J. Neurochem.,* 28: 897–916.

Torchilin, V. P. (ed.) (1995). *Handbook of Targeted Delivery of Imaging Agents.* CRC Press, Boca Raton, FL.

Thulborn K. R., Waterton J. C., Matthews P. M., and Radda G. K. (1982). Oxygenation dependence of the transverse relaxation time of water protons in whole blood at high field. *Biochim. Biophys. Acta,* 714(2): 265–270.

Turner, R. (1988). Minimum inductance coils. *J. Phys. E Sci. Instrum.,* (21): 948–952.

Vanzetta, I., and Grinvald, A. (1999). Increased cortical oxidative metabolism due to sensory stimulation: Implications for functional brain imaging. *Science,* 286(5444): 1555–1558.

Wong, E. C., Jesmanowicz, A., and Hyde, J. S. (1991). Coil optimization for MRI by conjugate gradient descent. *Magn. Reson. Med.,* 21: 39–48.

Yacoub, E., and Hu, X. (2001). Detection of the early decrease in fMRI signal in the motor area. *Magn. Reson. Med.,* 45(2): 184–190.

8

Spatial and Temporal Properties of fMRI

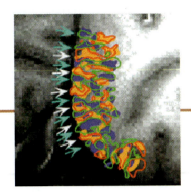

Neuronal activity associated with cognitive processes unfolds in both space and time. In investigating this activity using fMRI, we must consider its spatial and temporal properties. **Spatial resolution** refers to the ability to distinguish changes in a map across different spatial locations, while **temporal resolution** describes the ability to distinguish changes in activity at a single location over time. Both spatial and temporal resolution are determined by the sampling rates achievable by modern MRI scanners. Tremendous improvements in both spatial and temporal resolution of fMRI have been achieved in the past decade due to advances in scanner hardware. However, despite these technological advances, the ultimate limitation upon the functional resolution of fMRI is the spatial and temporal concordance of the BOLD signal with underlying neuronal activity. In this chapter, we will consider both technological and physiological limitations upon the spatial and temporal properties of fMRI.

We will also consider a third property, the **nonlinearity** of the BOLD response, which reflects the temporal dynamics of activity within a spatial location. To presage the following discussion, repeated activation of the same brain region within a short time interval evokes less activation with each repetition. Decreases in activity with repeated stimulation are known as nonlinearities or refractory effects.

Spatial Resolution of fMRI

The spatial resolution of an fMRI experiment is given by its voxel dimensions. Voxels are three-dimensional rectangular prisms whose dimensions are specified by three parameters: field of view, matrix size, and slice thickness. The field of view describes the extent of the imaging volume within a slice and is generally expressed in centimeters. The matrix size determines how many voxels are acquired in each dimension. Matrices used in fMRI are generally powers of 2, such as 64, 128, or 256, to facilitate use of the fast Fourier transform for image reconstruction. So, if the field of view for a pulse sequence is 24 by 24 cm, and the matrix size is 64 by 64, the resulting within-slice (in-plane) voxel size is 3.75 mm by 3.75 mm. Slice thickness provides the third dimension (through-plane) and is generally the same or larger than the in-plane voxel size (e.g., 5 mm). When the slice thickness is

spatial resolution The ability to distinguish changes in an image (or map) across different spatial locations.

temporal resolution The ability to distinguish changes in an image (or map) across time.

nonlinearity The property whereby the combined response to two or more events is not equivalent to the summation of the responses to the individual events in isolation.

BOX 8.1 Terminology of fMRI

The remainder of this book focuses on the design, analysis, and interpretation of BOLD fMRI experiments, along with the relation of fMRI to other neuroscience techniques. It is therefore necessary to introduce a number of key concepts that guide fMRI studies, and that recur throughout the following chapters. In order to familiarize you, these concepts are presented here as a prelude to more detailed discussions that will occur in later chapters.

Data Acquisition

Functional and structural MRI differ in more than just contrast sensitivity. The goal of structural MRI is to distinguish different types of tissue. Each structural image that is collected provides a snapshot of the underlying tissue, so a single image may be sufficient for mapping brain structure if contrast-to-noise is sufficiently high. Functional MRI has a very different goal: to relate changes in brain physiology *over time* to an experimental manipulation. A single functional image provides no information about brain activity. Only by examining changes across images over time can we infer that our experimental manipulation has an effect. For this reason, fMRI data are collected as a **time series,** a large number of images that are acquired in temporal order at a specified rate. This time series can then be examined for changes associated with the experimental stimuli, such as voxels that increased (or decreased) their activity following the presentation of a stimulus. Unlike structural imaging, which attempts to minimize noise within an image, functional imaging benefits from minimizing noise across successive images. Functional MRI analyses attempt to detect the small changes in MR signal associated with the BOLD effect while ignoring signal fluctuations due to other factors.

Functional MRI data are generally organized in a hierarchical fashion (Figure 8.1). The highest level is that of the subjects who participate in the experiment. It is common in fMRI studies to run 6 to 12 **subjects** in an experiment, with complex cognitive tasks running more subjects and simpler perceptual tasks running fewer. The number of subjects needed is dependent upon the power of the experimental design (see Box 9.2). Usually each subject participates in a single experimental **session** lasting 1 to 2 hours, but some experiments, such as those testing memory or drug effects, may require multiple sessions separated by days or weeks. Each experimental session includes collection of anatomical images and a number of **runs** of functional images, each lasting about 5 to 10 minutes. The session is broken into short runs for several reasons. First, subjects' fatigue is reduced, especially for studies that require sustained attention to a task. Second, there are more opportunities to identify and correct problems in the experiment, such as subjects' misunderstanding of instructions or an error in the image acquisition parameters. Third, frequent contact with subjects allows them to remain in control of their participation. Since most subjects are volunteers, they have the right to ask questions throughout the study, as well as to end the study at any time. Active communication with subjects during the experiment is not only preferable from an ethical standpoint but also has the advantage of reducing their stress levels and increasing the likelihood that the study will be completed.

Within each run, the functional data are acquired as a time series of **volumes.** In a typical experiment with a 1-second TR, there might be about 360 volumes acquired during a 6-minute run and perhaps 3600 volumes for the entire experiment. Note

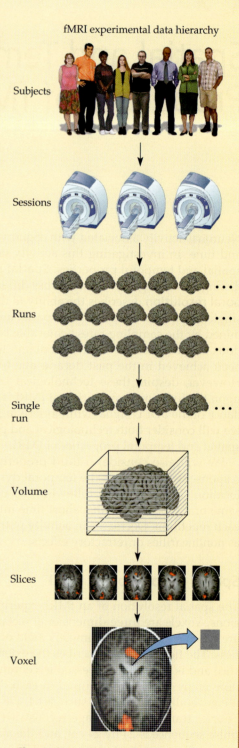

fMRI experimental data hierarchy

Subjects

Sessions

Runs

Single run

Volume

Slices

Voxel

Figure 8.1 How fMRI data are organized.

BOX 8.1 *(continued)*

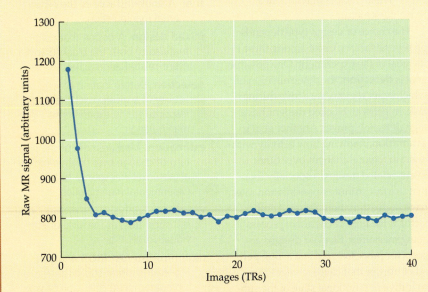

Figure 8.2   MR signal is elevated early in runs, before longitudinal magnetization reaches a steady state. Shown is a sample time course of activity in a single voxel for the first 40 images in a single run. Because of this increased activity, fMRI researchers often discard the first few images in a run. When they are removed before even being saved to disk, those images are known as "discarded data acquisitions," or disdaqs. Note that although the steady-state activity looks very flat at this scale, there is about a 4% variation across time points, much greater than the typical BOLD response.

that the overall MR signal is elevated in the first few volumes in each run, because the net magnetization has not yet reached a steady state (Figure 8.2). Therefore, the first few volumes are often excluded from further analysis. One term for these excluded volumes is **disdaqs,** a rough acronym for "discarded data acquisitions." Each of the remaining volumes is in turn composed of a variable number of slices, ranging from 1 to 4 in an experiment targeting a particular region, to 25 or more in a study designed to cover the entire brain. Note that each slice is acquired at a different point in time within the TR, but that all data *within* the slice are effectively acquired at the same time. Each slice consists of thousands of voxels that together form the image of the brain. Due to the Fourier approaches used for reconstructing MR data, slices usually consist of a 2^n-by-2^n matrix of voxels, such as 64×64 or 128×128. When

we acquire data for an fMRI experiment, we can think of that data as a four-dimensional matrix: *x* by *y* by slice (*z*) by time (e.g., $64 \times 64 \times 25 \times 3600$).

Experimental Design and Analysis

There are two basic types of fMRI studies: **blocked designs** and **event-related designs.** A blocked design presents two or more conditions in an alternating pattern. Most early fMRI studies used blocked designs. For example, in the Kwong and colleagues study described in the previous chapter, a bright visual pattern was presented for 60 s and then the display was dark for 60 s. This approach can be classified as an "ABABAB…" blocked design. Another common paradigm when comparing two different tasks is to present both in alternation with a baseline period. If a researcher were investigating brain regions

associated with listening to spoken English, three block types might be used: test blocks consisting of English speech, comparison blocks consisting of speech in a foreign language, and baseline blocks in which no speech is present. A typical order of blocks would be "ACB-CACBC…," where the test (A) and comparison (B) conditions alternate with the baseline condition (C). In most fMRI studies, each block is about 10 to 30 s in duration, and there may be many alter-

time series   A large number of fMRI images collected at different points in time.

subject   A participant in a research study.

session   A single visit to the scanner by a subject. For fMRI studies, each session usually includes both structural and functional scans.

run   An uninterrupted presentation of an experimental task, usually lasting 5 to 10 minutes for fMRI studies. It also refers to the set of functional images collected during that task presentation.

volume   A single image of the brain, itself consisting of multiple slices and voxels.

disdaqs   An abbreviation for "discarded data acquisitions"; it refers to images at the beginning of a functional run that are deleted without examination. This is done because MR signal is greatest in these first images, as the change in net magnetization following excitation has not yet reached a steady state.

blocked design   The separation of experimental conditions into distinct blocks, so that each condition is presented for an extended period of time.

event-related design   The presentation of discrete, short-duration events whose timing and order may be randomized.

BOX 8.1 *(continued)*

nations between different block types in a single run.

In an event-related design, stimuli are presented as individual events, or **trials.** The study by Blamire and colleagues in 1992 was the first to present event-related data. In slow event-related designs (i.e., interstimulus intervals greater than about 10 s), the hemodynamic response decays to baseline after each stimulus, which allows the response to each trial to be individuated. In fast-rate experiments, the events are presented sufficiently close together (i.e., less than 10 s) so that the hemodynamic response does not have time to decay to baseline between successive stimuli. For fast designs, special analysis procedures are required to separate the hemodynamic responses to different events. Some analysis techniques are possible with event-related designs but are incompatible with blocked designs. For example, individual trials can be sorted according to the subject's response time or accuracy. The effects of one trial type upon another, such as when examining the effects of a warning signal upon a subsequent behavioral response, can also be studied using a fast event-related design.

Nearly all fMRI studies fall into one of these two design categories. However, there is also growing interest in **mixed designs** that combine features from both types. In a mixed design, there are discrete stimulus events, but those events occur in the context of other

experimental factors that vary in a blocklike structure.

The choice of design type depends on several factors. Chief among these is the goal of the experiment. One possible goal is **detection,** the determination of which brain regions are active during a task. In general, blocked designs have high detection power. Another goal is **estimation,** knowing how activity within brain regions changes over time. Event-related designs, especially those that use fast stimulus-presentation rates, have high estimation power. Another factor is the type of cognitive process being measured. Blocked designs are good for processes that last a long period of time or that cause changes in a cognitive or emotional state of the subject, whereas event-related designs are stronger for discrete, short-term processes. While blocked and event-related designs have different strengths, their combination in a mixed design can provide the advantages of both. The choice of experimental design, as well as the effects of that choice upon experimental analyses, are discussed in considerable detail in Chapter 11.

With regard to the analysis of fMRI experiments, the key division is between **voxelwise analysis** and anatomical **region-of-interest (ROI) analysis.** In a voxelwise analysis, statistical tests are conducted on each voxel to evaluate its significance relative to the experimental hypothesis. Most fMRI studies use voxelwise approaches, and a number of soft-

trial A single instance of the experimental manipulation.

mixed design A design that contains features of both the blocked and event-related approaches.

detection Determination of whether activity of a given voxel changes in response to the experimental manipulation.

estimation Measurement of the pattern of change over time within an active voxel in response to the experimental manipulation.

voxelwise analysis The evaluation of statistical tests at the level of individual voxels.

region-of-interest (ROI) analysis The evaluation of statistical tests on a predetermined collection of voxels, often chosen to reflect a priori anatomical distinctions within the brain.

ware packages, both commercial and freely available, have been created to facilitate such analyses. In contrast, ROI analyses partition the brain into a smaller set of discrete regions, which are then individually analyzed for significance. The basic unit of an ROI approach is therefore not the voxel but a spatial set of voxels. ROI analyses can answer questions about the function of particular brain regions but are more time-consuming and labor-intensive than voxelwise analyses.

equal to the in-plane resolution, the voxels are cubic and the spatial resolution is said to be isotropic.

The size of the voxel used in a study may depend on the research question. Studies that examine the entire brain will use relatively large voxels, often around 4 to 5 mm on a side. In contrast, studies that examine a single brain region, such as the visual cortex, may use smaller voxels of 1 to 2 mm. For comparison, the letters making up this sentence are each about 2 to 3 mm in size. It is common to acquire anatomical images with smaller voxel dimensions (e.g., 1 mm × 1 mm in-plane), and functional data are often displayed on such high-resolution anatomical images. Note that the actual spatial resolution of the fMRI data is not affected by the images on which it is displayed, but depends solely on the voxel size used for functional acquisition.

It seems straightforward that increased spatial resolution carries advantages for fMRI studies. As the distance between adjacent voxels decreases, one is better able to distinguish boundaries between neighboring functional areas. So if fMRI data can be collected at any voxel size, why do researchers not always use the smallest possible? There are two primary challenges for using small voxels in fMRI: reduced signal compared to noise and increased acquisition time.

First, variation in the BOLD signal measured by fMRI depends upon the change in the total amount of deoxygenated hemoglobin within a voxel. So, if we reduce the size of our voxels by a factor of 2, the signal that we measure in each will be half as large, resulting in a smaller signal-to-noise ratio. In some brain regions, such as the primary motor or visual cortex, a finger flexion or a visual flash may evoke a very large brain response, and thus the reduced signal amplitude generated from small voxels may not be a problem. But in other brain regions, like the frontal lobe, a choice–response task may evoke much smaller changes in the brain, and larger voxels may improve the ability to detect those changes in the presence of noise. We will discuss the concepts of signal and noise in more detail in the following chapter.

Second, as voxel size decreases, the time needed to acquire a given volume of the brain increases. While slice acquisition rates will vary across scanners and pulse sequences, doubling the matrix size of a gradient-echo pulse sequence can double or even quadruple acquisition time. Increasing the through-plane resolution also increases acquisition time, in this case exactly proportionally to the resolution change. If one halves the slice thickness, then twice as many slices will be needed to cover the same volume, and twice the acquisition time will be required.

In designing an fMRI study, there are trade-offs among spatial coverage, spatial resolution, and the time required for acquisition. On most high-field MR scanners, functional images could be acquired at extremely small voxel sizes of less than a cubic millimeter. But those images would be acquired very slowly, and a large number would be required to cover the entire brain. For example, on a typical scanner, one might acquire 16 slices per second at 4 mm × 4 mm × 4 mm resolution, but only 1 slice per second at 1 mm × 1 mm × 1 mm resolution. The vertical extent of the cerebrum is about 110 mm or less, so at 4-mm resolution, about 27 slices would be necessary for full coverage. This imaging volume could be acquired in less than 2 s. At 1-mm resolution, 110 slices would be needed, but it would take about 110 s for their acquisition. Though extreme, this example points out the difficulty in using high spatial resolution for full-brain imaging. Increasing spatial resolution necessarily decreases temporal resolution. Conversely, increasing temporal resolution decreases spatial coverage. When planning an fMRI study, the researcher must weigh the relative importance of these factors in determining what pulse sequence to use for data acquisition.

All fMRI studies, especially those using relatively large voxels, suffer from **partial volume effects.** The MR signal measured at a given voxel reflects the sum of its entire volume. Even the smallest voxel may contain multiple types of tissue, each contributing part of the total volume. Figure 8.3 shows the possible contents of a single 4 mm × 4 mm × 5 mm voxel. In addition to the active neurons of interest and the local capillary bed, there may be other brain tissue that does not contribute to the measured activity. For example, voxels on the edge of the brain can contain gray matter, white matter, and

partial volume effects The combination, within a single voxel, of signal contributions from two or more distinct tissue types or functional regions.

Figure 8.3 Partial volume effects. A single voxel may contain many different types of tissue, including gray matter, white matter, cerebrospinal fluid, or blood vessels. The MR signal recorded from that voxel is the sum of signals recorded from all of these different tissue types. So, if a voxel on a T_1 image contains 25% cerebrospinal fluid (with low signal), 50% gray matter (with medium signal) and 25% white matter (with high signal), the MR signal recorded from the voxel will contain contributions from all three.

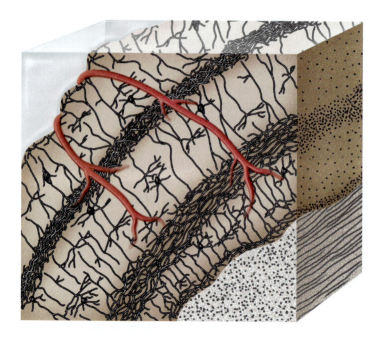

cerebrospinal fluid. Partial volume effects can significantly reduce the signal measured within a voxel using fMRI. If only part of the voxel is active, then the total BOLD signal will be smaller than if the entire voxel is active.

Spatial Specificity in the Vascular System

As stated previously, the ultimate functional resolution of fMRI depends on more than voxel size; it depends upon the concordance of hemodynamic and neuronal activity (see Chapter 15 for an expanded discussion of this issue). In an important study conducted in 2001, Logothetis and colleagues investigated the correspondence between the BOLD signal and electrophysiological measures, using simultaneous recordings in the primary visual cortex of monkeys. They found good spatial correspondence between the measures, especially between BOLD and local field potentials that reflect summated EPSPs and IPSPs. In 2000, a similar spatial correspondence was reported by Disbrow and colleagues, who used both fMRI and separate microelectrode recordings to map hand and face representations in the somatosensory cortex in the monkey. They found that the centroids of activity measured using fMRI generally were localized within the electrophysiologically mapped hand and face areas, but the areas mapped using fMRI were larger than those mapped with electrode recordings (Figure 8.4). The discrepancies observed between the measures were attributed to the filtering effects of the vascular system.

Let us consider the contributions of different parts of the vasculature to the BOLD effect. Recall that the BOLD signal results from the effects of deoxygenated hemoglobin, which is absent in fully oxygenated arterial blood. Thus, the BOLD signal only reflects the deoxygenated hemoglobin content of capillaries and veins. Because deoxygenated hemoglobin molecules are paramagnetic, they create magnetic field gradients within the vessel that extend into surrounding tissue. The primary mechanism for BOLD signal is the dephasing of spins within water molecules as they diffuse through these gradient fields. The spins located within the vessel itself give rise to the intravascular component of the BOLD signal, while the spins located in the surrounding tissue (i.e., parenchyma) give rise to the extravascular component

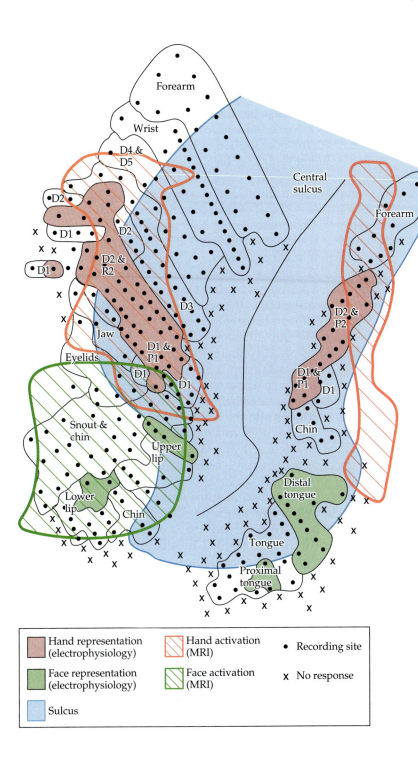

Figure 8.4   Spatial correspondence between fMRI and electrophysiological recordings. Both functional MRI and microelectrode recordings were used (in monkeys) to identify regions associated with motor/sensory responses. Note that the spatial extent of the regions mapped using fMRI (hatching) is much larger than that mapped using electrophysiology, although there is considerable overlap. (From Disbrow et al., 2000.)

Legend:
- Hand representation (electrophysiology)
- Face representation (electrophysiology)
- Sulcus
- Hand activation (MRI)
- Face activation (MRI)
- • Recording site
- x No response

of the BOLD signal. In a typical fMRI experiment using gradient-echo sequences, the BOLD signal reflects both intravascular and extravascular signal sources. Both of these signal components can arise from capillaries that are adjacent to and perfuse the active neurons. But because the paramagnetic deoxygenated hemoglobin is removed from the brain by the venous system, they can also arise from draining veins that are distant from the neuronal activity. Thus, the presence of signal changes in large draining veins limits the functional resolution of fMRI. These **large-vessel effects** can compromise studies that require high functional resolution (less than a centimeter).

large-vessel effects   Signal changes in veins that drain a functionally active region but are distant from the neuronal activity of interest.

Several characteristics are indicative of large-vessel effects. The simplest is magnitude of signal change. Because veins have much greater volume than capillaries, there can be a greater change in the amount of deoxygenated hemoglobin and thus in the total signal change. Systematic changes in the phase of the MR signal may also be observed, since large vessels have specific orientation within a voxel, unlike capillaries, which are randomly oriented (see Menon, 2002, for a description of how to overcome this problem). Voxels containing draining veins may be active across very different experimental conditions, since they may drain two distinct populations of neurons. A good example of such effects can be seen in the study of ocular dominance columns within the visual system (Box 8.2), in that adjacent voxels may have neurons with diametrically opposed responses. Finally, the initial negative response that is sometimes observed at high field is thought to represent oxygen extraction in the capillaries, so it will not be seen within voxels containing primarily distant large vessels (see Box 7.2).

Advanced acquisition techniques can be employed to exclude components of BOLD signal that are distant from the neuronal activities. These techniques take advantage of the different magnetic properties of large- and small-caliber vessels and the different diffusion properties of extravascular and intravascular spins. It is generally understood that the BOLD magnetic field gradient around the large vessels extends further in space, while that around the small vessels has a smaller spatial extent. More importantly, the magnetic field generated by the deoxygenated hemoglobin in large vessels has a more shallow gradient as it extends into the parenchyma (Figure 8.5A) than the steeper gradients generated within small vessels (Figure 8.5B). Thus, the magnetic field change experienced by extravascular spins traveling a given distance is different depending upon whether those spins are near large or small vessels.

Around large vessels, extravascular spins within diffusing water molecules experience relatively small magnetic field changes as they travel. Indeed, within the few tens of milliseconds that are typical for a BOLD fMRI acquisition, the magnetic field generated by deoxygenated hemoglobin within large vessels can often be approximated as a constant field inhomo-

Figure 8.5 Different effects of large and small vessels on extravascular spins. The magnetic field gradient created by deoxygenated hemoglobin within a blood vessel depends upon the diameter of the vessel. For large vessels (A), the gradient changes slowly over space, so diffusing extravascular spins experience a relatively constant magnetic field over time. Spin-echo imaging can be used to refocus the loss of phase coherence and eliminate the large-vessel signal. For small vessels (B), the gradient changes rapidly over space, so extravascular spins experience different magnetic fields as they diffuse. Loss of phase coherence cannot be recovered by spin-echo imaging, and this spin-echo imaging is sensitive to the small-vessel extravascular component of the BOLD signal.

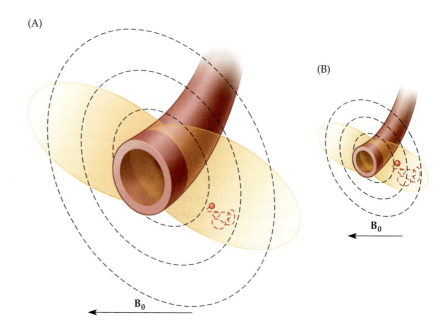

(A)

(B)

B_0

B_0

geneity over time. Recall that the refocusing 180° pulse in **spin-echo** sequences can reverse the loss of phase coherence resulting from a static field inhomogeneity; thus, we can use spin-echo acquisition strategies to remove the BOLD signal that arises from the extravascular compartment of large vessels. The situation is quite different for extravascular spins near small vessels. The steeper magnetic field gradients extending into the parenchyma outside of small vessels mean that spins in nearby water molecules experience a changing magnetic field inhomogeneity over time. The resultant loss of phase coherence cannot be completely refocused by the 180° pulse, and thus spin-echo sequences retain their sensitivity to the small-vessel extravascular component of the BOLD signal.

Spins within intravascular diffusing water molecules also experience a dynamic magnetic field inhomogeneity, as their diffusion distance is large compared to the spatial extent of the deoxygenated hemoglobin–induced magnetic field gradient. For this reason, spin-echo sequences are still sensitive to the intravascular BOLD signal in both large and small vessels. Thus, while spin-echo pulse sequences can eliminate the extravascular large-vessel component of the BOLD signal, another approach must be employed to eliminate the intravascular large-vessel BOLD signal. Because these intravascular spins are in flowing blood, they have a higher mobility (especially within large vessels), and thus motion-weighted image acquisition techniques can be used to isolate this population of fast-flowing spins. One such approach uses **diffusion-weighted** sequences to selectively suppress the intravascular component of large vessels (general approaches to diffusion weighting are discussed in Chapter 5, and advanced techniques are presented in Chapter 14).

Thus, the combined use of spin-echo and diffusion-weighted sequences can completely eliminate the signals from large vessels while preserving the small-vessel signals to achieve improved functional resolution. However, the overall effect of combining spin-echo and diffusion weighting is greatly reduced BOLD sensitivity. Such a combined approach may be practical only at high fields (>3 T), where the increase in overall signal can help offset the reduction in BOLD sensitivity.

What Spatial Resolution Is Needed?

From the previous discussion, we can conclude that the smallest spatial scale that can possibly be measured using BOLD fMRI is determined by the spatial properties of capillaries. Capillaries are very small, typically much less than a millimeter in length, and are generally separated from each other by tens to hundreds of microns. This suggests that the absolute lower limit for functional resolution of any hemodynamic measure of brain activity is about 100 microns. Even if the brain is sampled at a finer spatial resolution, the functional resolution would not be improved.

It is important to realize that the *right* spatial scale for an experiment depends on the question being asked. If you are a neurologist examining the effects of frontal lobe damage on intelligence tests, you may examine lesions that span 5 centimeters or more. If you are an electrophysiologist recording the firing of layer 4 neurons within the parietal lobe, you may need to localize the tip of your microelectrode within a few hundred microns. Table 8.1 provides a list of different spatial scales used in the study of the brain. It shows that research into the properties of the human brain spans about seven orders of magnitude, from large-scale anatomy to small-scale microbiology. The spatial resolution of fMRI is intermediate between these extremes, and fMRI is most suited for examining changes in brain function over millimeters to centimeters.

spin-echo (SE) imaging One of the two primary types of pulse sequences used in MRI; it uses a second 180° electromagnetic pulse to generate the MR signal changes that are measured at data acquisition.

diffusion weighting The application of magnetic gradients to cause changes in the MR signal that are dependent upon the amplitude and/or direction of diffusion.

TABLE 8.1 Different Spatial Scales in the Human Brain

Structure	Scale
Brain	100 mm
Gyri	10 mm
Dominance column	1 mm
Neuron	0.01 mm
Synapse	0.001 mm
Ion channel	0.00001 mm

BOX 8.2 Mapping of Ocular Dominance Columns Using fMRI

Neurons in the primary visual cortex of primates respond preferentially to visual stimuli from one eye. A large number of electrophysiological studies in nonhuman primates have demonstrated that these eye preferences are organized into vertical columns, with all neurons in a column sharing the same preference (Figure 8.6). The presence of **ocular dominance** columns in human visual cortex was verified using postmortem cytochrome oxidase staining in the early 1980s. Vascular responses have been shown by optical imaging to be localized within these columns, so hemodynamic techniques like fMRI could, in principle, map the columnar structure of the primary visual cortex. However, in humans the transition from one ocular dominance column to another occurs over about 1 millimeter of cortex, near the limit of spatial resolution for fMRI.

An early attempt to distinguish ocular dominance columns using fMRI was reported by Menon and colleagues in 1997. They used a FLASH pulse sequence on a high-field (4 T) scanner to acquire very-high-resolution (547 μm by 547 μm) images parallel to the calcarine sulcus in the primary visual cortex. On such slices, ocular dominance columns will often be oriented perpendicularly to the slice plane. The visual stimulus was a large red light-emitting diode (LED). To ensure monocular stimulation, subjects were instructed to open and close one eye at a time in a blocked pattern. The authors used a binocular stimulation condition to identify voxels corresponding to primary visual cortex. For each such voxel, they compared the relative

ocular dominance The degree to which a given neuron in the visual cortex responds more to stimuli presented to one eye than to stimuli presented to the other eye.

T_2^* blurring Distortions in T_2^* images that result from having a data acquisition window that is sufficiently long that significant T_2^* decay occurs over that interval.

signal change caused by stimuli presented to each eye. The results were consistent with previous data from other techniques, in that there were significant BOLD changes in the primary visual cortex that changed in dominance from one eye to another over about 1 mm of space (Figure 8.7). While its results were extremely interesting, this early study had several limitations, notably that the organization of the dominance columns was not replicated across multiple measurements. Without such replication, it is difficult to assess whether the observed fMRI data faithfully represents the true pattern of ocular dominance, especially since relatively few voxels showed ocular preferences.

In a later study conducted in 2001, Cheng and colleagues investigated whether dominance patterns measured using fMRI were stable across multiple sessions. They also used high-field (4 T) fMRI, but with a multishot gradient-echo echo-planar pulse sequence. Very-high-resolution voxels were used (470 μm by 470 μm). It is worth emphasizing that these high-resolution studies present a different set of challenges than standard fMRI. For example, here the authors acquired each slice through a series of 32 successive excitation pulses, resulting in a total time between successive volumes of nearly 10 s, even though only three slices were acquired. This multishot technique reduced the data acquisition time needed for each excitation, which in turn reduced **T_2^* blurring,** which results from

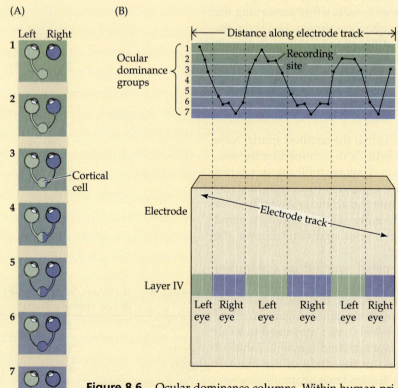

Figure 8.6 Ocular dominance columns. Within human primary visual cortex, neurons sensitive to input from one eye are organized into vertical columns.

BOX 8.2 *(continued)*

(A)

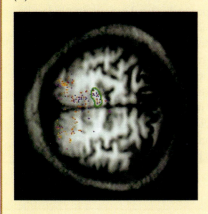

(B)

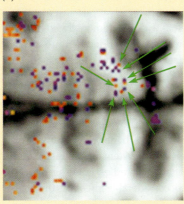

Figure 8.7 Early results suggesting the identification of ocular dominance columns in visual cortex using fMRI. Shown in (A) are voxels in human primary visual cortex that responded predominantly to stimulation from one eye or the other. Arrows in (B) indicate transitions between nearby voxels within the calcarine cortex. Voxels responding mostly to left-eye stimulation are shown in red, while voxels responding mostly to right-eye stimulation are shown in blue. In-plane voxel dimensions are approximately 0.5 mm on a side. (From Menon et al., 1997.)

the T_2^* decay that occurs during the acquisition window. To understand T_2^* blurring, remember that data acquisition (e.g., filling *k*-space) takes time, about 40 ms for a typical 64 × 64 image and much longer for very-high-resolution images. During this acquisition window, the spins are continuously undergoing T_2^* decay, so if the window is very long compared to the T_2^* value of the tissues being imaged, there will be virtually no signal toward the end of the acquisition window. This significant decay process can cause blurring for BOLD images, especially those that acquire an entire slice at very high resolution following a single excitation.

As a result of the long acquisition time, the authors also used very long block intervals of 2 minutes of monocular stimulation interleaved with 1 minute of darkness. Comparing the patterns evoked by monocular stimulation provided strong evidence for ocular dominance columns in primary visual cortex, notably in areas where the calcarine fissure ran parallel to the imaging plane, but not in areas identified with the secondary visual cortical area, V2 (Figure 8.8A–D). The mean width of columns was about 1.1 mm, consistent with the results from both earlier postmortem staining and from Menon and colleagues' study. Replicability analyses re-

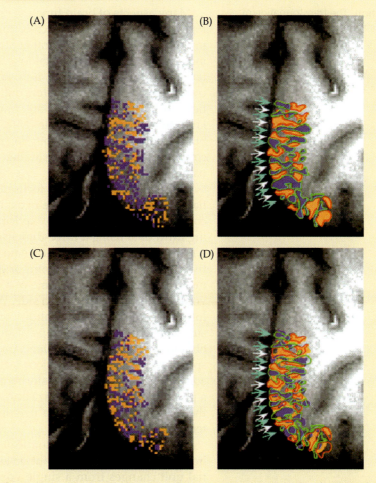

(A)   (B)

(C)   (D)

Figure 8.8 Ocular dominance columns in visual cortex. These results show repeatable measurements of ocular dominance columns across two sessions. The same subject participated in two sessions, shown in panels A and C. Note that the outlines of the areas of ocular dominance from the first session (B) correspond well to the results from the second session (D). (From Cheng et al., 2001.)

vealed that the observed patterns were significantly correlated for a given subject both between two experiments within the same session and across two different sessions.

The mapping of ocular dominance columns provides an example of the potential of very high-resolution fMRI. It has obvious value as a technical demonstration and will undoubtedly spur additional improvements in both pulse sequence design and image acquisition hardware. But does it add to the understanding of the brain? At first glance, these studies merely replicate a phenomenon that was first demonstrated in animals more than four decades ago and in humans more than two decades ago. The existence of ocular dominance columns was never in question, regardless of the outcome of the fMRI studies. Nevertheless, fMRI can provide an important contribution through the *in vivo* study of the human visual system, in contrast to *in vitro* or animal studies. For example, a topic of considerable interest is the presence or absence of attentional influences upon early visual processing. Understanding whether spatial attention influences activity in dominance columns will provide information about the organization of the visual system. It is important to emphasize that here, as in many areas of neuroscience, fMRI provides a source of information about the brain that can complement results derived from other techniques.

normalization The transformation of MRI data from an individual subject to match the spatial properties of a standardized image, such as an averaged brain derived from a sample of many individuals.

Many aspects of brain function vary over the spatial range of fMRI. Brain regions identified by cytoarchitectonic features, such as used by Brodmann in 1909, generally are several centimeters in size. While the visual cortex includes much of the occipital lobe, along with pathways extending into the temporal and parietal lobes, individual functional regions within the visual cortex extend in size from a few millimeters to a centimeter or more. Subcortical nuclei such as the caudate, putamen, and thalamus all are sufficiently large to encompass multiple fMRI voxels. Nevertheless, many aspects of brain structure, including both horizontal cortical layers and vertical cortical columns, exist on a much smaller scale and are very difficult to address using fMRI.

While this discussion has focused on effects of data acquisition upon spatial resolution, choices made in experimental analysis are also important. A common preprocessing step explicitly reduces spatial resolution by smoothing fMRI data using a three-dimensional Gaussian filter of several voxels in width (see Chapter 10). Typical smoothing parameters can increase the effective voxel size to $6 \times 6 \times 6$ mm or greater. Note that such a voxel contains more than 3 times the volume of a voxel 4 mm on a side, and 27 times the volume of a voxel 2 mm on a side. While smoothing can reduce spatial resolution, it can improve the validity of statistical tests and comparisons across subjects. Other analysis steps also reduce spatial resolution, albeit not as obviously as spatial smoothing. Any comparison across subjects will reduce spatial resolution, since subjects will differ in their anatomical structure. In addition, algorithms for transforming subjects to a common stereotaxic space, a process known as **normalization,** further reduce spatial resolution due to the difficulty in matching a person's individual anatomy to a stereotaxic template.

The decision to use anatomically based region-of-interest analyses has implications for spatial resolution as well. In an ROI analysis, the basic spatial unit changes from a single voxel to a region containing many voxels. Obviously, the ability to identify differences between adjacent voxels is lost, and thus spatial resolution is greatly reduced. However, to the extent that the chosen regions accurately map onto functional divisions within the brain, the functional resolution of the data may be greatly increased by signal averaging (since noise that is randomly distributed over space will be reduced). For example, the putamen is a relatively small structure within the basal ganglia that is associated with motor preparation, interval timing, and some cognitive processing. Since there are clear anatomical divisions between the putamen and the surrounding white matter, it is simple to create an ROI that includes the entire putamen. By considering the putamen as a whole, subregions within it cannot be distinguished; however, the ability to detect changes in the putamen as a whole will be greatly increased through spatial averaging. As a general rule, many analysis steps sacrifice spatial resolution in order to increase functional resolution.

Temporal Resolution of fMRI

For many experimental questions, it is important to determine the relative timing of brain activity. However, neuroscience techniques differ in their ability to measure relative timing. Recordings from microelectrodes within the brain can identify the firing of a single neuron as it occurs, localizing activity in time at the millisecond level, but these can only be made in non-human animals or in humans who are undergoing special tests associated with neurosurgical procedures. Lesion studies, in contrast, provide almost no information about the timing of brain activity. The ability to separate brain events in time is known as temporal resolution. FMRI is considered to have an intermediate level of temporal resolution, because it can discriminate events that are separated by intervals on the order of a few seconds. Just as the basic sampling unit for spatial resolution is the voxel, the basic sampling unit for temporal resolution in fMRI is repetition time, or TR. For typical pulse sequences used in fMRI, one image of the brain is acquired per TR. Depending upon the experiment, TR may range from very short (e.g., 500 ms) to very long (e.g., 4000 ms), with even more extreme values used in specialized experiments. While the value of TR contributes to the temporal resolution of an experiment, it is not the only factor.

Remember from the previous chapter that the fMRI BOLD hemodynamic response rises and falls over a period of more than 10 seconds, even if the duration of neuronal activity is very short (e.g., less than a second). So, when we collect fMRI data, we do not take snapshots of neuronal activity, but measure changes in the vascular system that provide an indirect estimate. Decreasing TR to better sample the fMRI hemodynamic response is beneficial because it improves our estimate of this response, which in turn improves the inferences we can make about neuronal activity.

We emphasize this framework because it suggests that there may be a preferred temporal resolution for a given experimental question. Consider the very simple event-related design in which a subject squeezes her hand whenever she sees a visual stimulus. If our goal is to determine whether an area of the brain becomes active due to hand motion (i.e., detection), a relatively slow sampling rate will suffice. At a 3-s TR, the hemodynamic response may be easily identified when compared to the prestimulus baseline, but its exact shape may be difficult to estimate (Figure 8.9A). Halving the TR to 1500 ms improves our estimate of the shape of the response and the timing of the peak but does not substantially change the measured amplitude (Figure 8.9B). Something very interesting becomes evident if we halve the TR again, to 750 ms. The measured hemodynamic response, though sampled twice as often, does not differ much in shape from the 1500-

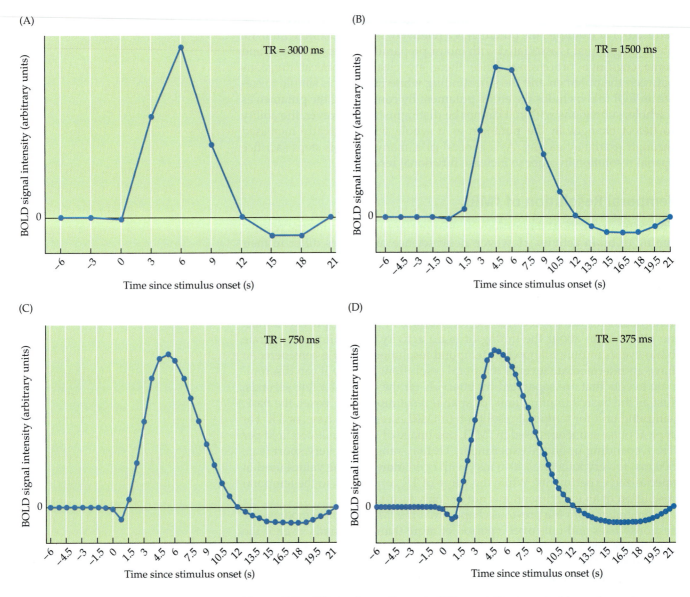

Figure 8.9 Effects of sampling rate (TR) upon the measured hemodynamic response. In each figure, an idealized hemodynamic response is sampled at a different rate.

ms condition (Figure 8.9C). Further reduction to 375 ms results in even less change in the measured shape of the hemodynamic response (Figure 8.9D).

> ## Thought Question
>
> How does the temporal resolution that is needed to detect significant activity change for long-interval blocked designs? Is the required TR larger or smaller than for event-related designs?

It seems counterintuitive that dramatic increases in sampling rate would have little effect upon temporal resolution. However, think about the effect of the additional samples on the estimate of the hemodynamic response. In the case of a 3-s TR, what do we know about the time points between samples (i.e., 1.5 s, 4.5 s, etc.)? Although they are not measured directly, a reasonable assumption might be that the hemodynamic amplitude at these points would be intermediate between the recorded samples. For now, we can consider simple linear interpolation, such that the midpoint would be given by the average of the two adjacent samples. At TRs greater than about 2 s, linear interpolation does not provide a good estimate of the values that would have been recorded from the intervening points. But as we shorten the TR to 1.5 s or less, even simple linear interpolation will accurately reproduce intermediate values, because the hemodynamic response has reproducible structure. The changes in blood flow and oxygen extraction that form the basis of BOLD contrast occur as a result of slow physical processes and do not themselves change rapidly over short time periods. Only if these physical processes varied dramatically within short intervals, say 100 ms, would increasing the sampling rate have a greater effect. Note that this example uses an event-related design, so that the hemodynamic response evolves over about 10 to 15 s. If a long-interval blocked design were used, then the changes in the hemodynamic response would be much slower and an even longer TR would be adequate. In summary, the temporal resolution of fMRI is determined both by the repetition time, TR, and by the limitations of the vascular system. For many experimental questions, temporal resolution of about 1 to 2 s is sufficient.

While decreasing the repetition time can improve temporal resolution, it can present some disadvantages to fMRI studies as well. In Chapter 3 we learned that one parameter of an MR pulse sequence is the flip angle, which reflects how far the net longitudinal magnetization is tipped toward the transverse plane by an RF pulse. Since the amount of measured MR signal is proportional to the projection of the magnetization vector on the transverse plane, large flip angles are associated with greater MR signal. For typical gradient-echo sequences with long TRs (i.e., greater than about 2 s), a flip angle of 90° can be used to recover maximal MR signal. But at shorter TRs, a smaller flip angle is required so that the magnetization will reach a steady state over repeated excitations. As a result, the amplitude of the transverse magnetization following excitation will be reduced at short TRs and less MR signal will be measured. Short repetition times also reduce spatial coverage. If a scanner can acquire 14 slices per second with a given pulse sequence, then only 7 slices could be acquired with a 500-ms TR, while 28 could be acquired with a 2000-ms TR.

Temporal resolution can be improved by using an **interleaved stimulus presentation,** in which the experimental stimuli are presented at different points within a TR on different trials. Note that this should not be confused with interleaved slice acquisition, which refers to the order of slice excitation within a TR. Figure 8.10A and B illustrates the basic approach. In a typical experiment with a 3-s TR, the experimental stimuli would be presented at TR onset, so the hemodynamic response is sampled at 3 s, 6 s, 9 s, etc., following stimulus presentation. In an interleaved design with three presentation times, the stimuli could be presented either at TR onset, one second into the TR, or two seconds into the TR. Thus, one-third of the trials would sample normally, one-third would sample at 1 s, 4 s, 7 s, and one-third would sample at 2 s, 5 s, 8 s, etc. By combining data across all three sets of trials, the hemodynamic response can be estimated with a temporal resolution of 1 s. In principle, additional delay conditions can be used, such as one-quarter, one-half, and three-quarters of a TR, to further increase temporal resolution.

interleaved stimulus presentation The presentation of events of interest at different points within a TR over trials (e.g., one-quarter, one-half, and three-quarters of TR in addition to TR onset), increasing the effective sampling rate of an experiment at the expense of fewer trials per condition.

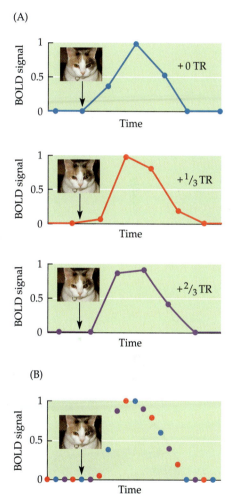

Figure 8.10 Use of interleaved stimulus presentation. In an experimental design with interleaved presentation, the experimental stimulus is presented at different points relative to the TR on different trials (A). Although the hemodynamic response may be sampled coarsely on each trial, the sampling occurs at different phases within the TR. Thus, combining across trials (B) fills in intermediate points, improving effective temporal resolution at a cost of increased experiment length.

reaction time The time required for someone to make a simple motor response to the presentation of a visual stimulus. Note that this is distinct from response time, which applies to situations in which someone must choose between two or more possible responses.

Interleaved presentation can therefore provide improved temporal resolution without limiting spatial coverage or reducing signal amplitude, and is thus an attractive option for many studies. Its primary disadvantage, however, lies in its reduction of the number of trials obtained for each delay condition, which increases their variability. If the data are highly variable, then interleaving may impair estimates of the hemodynamic response. Whether or not interleaved acquisition is used, therefore, depends upon the expected characteristics of the data and the goals of the experiment. Researchers must always balance improvements in temporal resolution against possibly diminished spatial coverage, spatial resolution, or experimental power.

The Timing of Brain Events

To understand the use of fMRI in studying the timing of mental processes, it is necessary to appreciate the different time scales over which such events occur. Imagine that you are driving a car and must quickly swerve to avoid an obstacle in the road (Figure 8.11). Within a millisecond or so after the image of the obstacle hits your eye, photoreceptors in the retina begin to release neurotransmitters. Over the next few milliseconds, the transmitters influence the activity in adjacent bipolar neurons, which in turn evoke action potentials in retinal ganglion cells that project to the lateral geniculate nucleus of the thalamus (as well as to a few noncortical targets). Transmission of visual information through the thalamus to the primary visual cortex requires a few tens of milliseconds, and significant electrical activity can be detected in secondary visual areas after about 100 ms. You will not turn the steering wheel until more than 200 ms have passed. The time needed to make such a simple movement in response to the occurrence of a stimulus, known as **reaction time,** has a lower limit of about 200 ms. (For comparison, in Olympic track events, runners who leave the starting blocks within 100 ms of the starter's pistol are penalized, because there has not been enough time for them to react to the stimulus.) By about 500 ms, you become aware of the

(A)

(B)

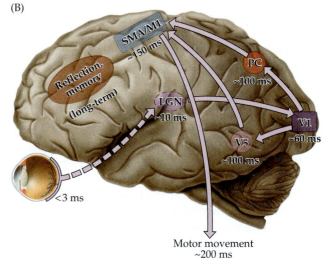

Figure 8.11 Timing of mental events. When a person makes a simple motor response, like turning a steering wheel to avoid an obstacle (A), a large number of different brain regions will become increasingly active. However, across these regions, the timing of activity may vary considerably (B). In regions that support basic sensory processing, neuronal activity may be present within about 100 ms of stimulus presentation. But in regions supporting more complex cognitive functions, activity may persist for tens of seconds.

stimulus and begin reflecting on the near accident. More-complex processes, like retrieving the memory of a similar event, may take several seconds, and changes in your emotional or physiological state may last for minutes or hours. Finally, there may be long-term effects, such as learned changes in your driving patterns, that persist for days, months, or even indefinitely.

A single stimulus can thus evoke changes in the brain that span more than eight orders of magnitude, from milliseconds to days. While this range is very large, most psychological experiments manipulate cognitive processes over periods of a few seconds, well within the range of fMRI. For example, response-selection studies typically present stimuli every few seconds, while short-term memory experiments may require the subject to remember an object for about 10 s. More difficult to study using fMRI are topics involving very small or very large time scales. A rough estimate of the lower limit of fMRI's temporal resolution for most conditions is a few hundred milliseconds. For example, there are well-known reentrant circuits running from higher visual processing regions back to the primary visual cortex. Attending to a visual stimulus has been shown to increase fMRI activity in the primary visual cortex, but that increase may result from either initial activity or a recurrence of activity due to feedback from other brain regions that occurs hundreds of milliseconds later (see Chapter 13).

Thought Question

How could experiments be designed to investigate feedback circuits in the brain using fMRI?

While there is no limit, in principle, that precludes fMRI studies of long time scales, practical factors make such studies challenging. One common manipulation is to change experimental instructions between runs, so that the participant does one task for several minutes and then another. This approach is necessary for many sorts of experimental questions, such as memory studies that separate stimulus learning from memory retrieval. When using such an approach, the researcher should monitor for problems like head motion and scanner drift that can cause systematic differences across runs. If the time scale needed is longer than an hour or two, as when examining long-term memory, then multiple scanner sessions will be necessary. Comparison of data across sessions raises many additional problems, since there may be differences in head position, fatigue level, and practice with the task. Nevertheless, it is important to emphasize that while the lower and upper bounds expressed here reflect the limitations common to most fMRI BOLD studies, with careful selection of imaging parameters and clever experimental design, these limits can be readily overcome.

The relation between timing and hemodynamic amplitude is critical for models of fMRI activity. Depending on the constraints of the vascular system, larger responses might take longer to reach their peak than smaller responses. Alternatively, a large-amplitude response might reflect greater neuronal activity, and thus greater metabolic demand, which could cause an earlier supply of oxygen and an earlier peak. While both arguments are plausible, neither is correct. For a given stimulus and brain region, the amplitude of the fMRI hemodynamic response appears to be independent of the timing of the response in both latency to onset and latency to peak (Figure 8.12). This means that if you measure the fMRI BOLD response in the auditory cortex to the presentation of a 2-s music video clip, there will be no

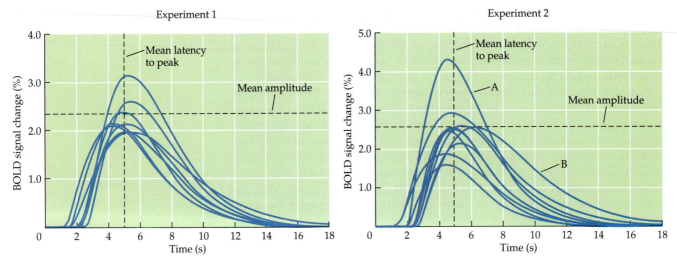

Figure 8.12 Amplitude and timing of the event-related fMRI hemodynamic response are uncorrelated. Two experiments were conducted in which hemodynamic responses in the visual cortex to a short-duration visual stimulus were measured. In both experiments, there was no correlation across subjects between the amplitude of the response and its time to peak. Note that in Experiment 2, the subject with the largest response (A) had an average time to peak, while the subject with the longest-latency response (B) had an average peak amplitude. (After Miezen et al., 2000.)

correlation across subjects between its amplitude and timing. However, if you measure the activity in that region for several different stimulus durations, the response at longer durations will be of both greater amplitude and increased latency. Likewise, if you compare activity in the auditory cortex to activity in another brain region (e.g., visual cortex), the two brain regions may differ in both amplitude and latency. These latter differences would reflect differences in neuronal processing as a function of stimulus duration or brain region, not differences in the hemodynamic response itself. In summary, changes in the amplitude of the fMRI hemodynamic response do not cause changes in the timing of the response, or vice versa, although external factors may affect both measures similarly.

Effects of Stimulus Duration

Over intervals from a few seconds to a few tens of seconds, the duration of the fMRI hemodynamic response provides a good estimate of the duration of neuronal activity. A good example of this was reported in 1999 by Menon and Kim, who investigated the role of the superior parietal lobe in mental rotation of complex objects. Decades of cognitive psychology studies have shown that the time needed to judge whether or not two similar objects are identical depends on the rotation angle between them. Thus, response time is twice as long for pairs that differ by 90° as for pairs that differ by 45°. Menon and Kim hypothesized that since the superior parietal lobe is critical for spatial processing, including mental rotation, its activity should extend in time for the entire rotation process. To test this idea, they measured the duration of the BOLD response in this region on each of 16 different trials that required objects to be rotated through different angles. They found that for each trial, the duration of the BOLD response matched well with the subject's response time (Figure 8.13A–C). The onset of the BOLD response did

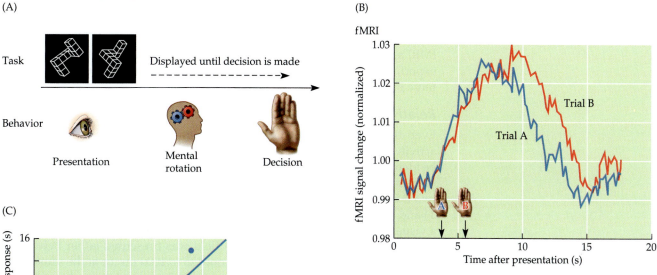

Figure 8.13 The width of the fMRI BOLD response increases with the duration of mental activity. Subjects were tested in a mental rotation task. Each trial measured how long it took the subjects to decide whether two stimuli were rotated versions of one another (A), then the fMRI hemodynamic response across trials was measured (B). The remarkable finding was that response time was a near perfect predictor of the width of the BOLD signal in the superior parietal cortex (C), which is important for spatial abilities, suggesting a good correspondence between duration of neuronal activity and the BOLD response. (After Menon and Kim, 1999.)

not differ across trials, suggesting that neuronal activity began at the start of the mental rotation process but stopped when mental rotation was complete.

Huettel and colleagues reported a similar result in a change detection task. In this task, two versions of the same picture were presented in rapid alternation, separated by a brief mask interval, for 40-s blocks. Each pair of photographs differed in one aspect, such as the position or color of a single object, and the subjects pressed a button when they identified what changed between them. Because the mask prevents the visual system from using motion transients to identify the changes, subjects cannot detect the changes automatically and the visual search may take anywhere from a few seconds to 30 seconds or more. The authors found that regions associated with visual search showed increases in BOLD activity that persisted for the duration of the search process, returning to baseline after the subjects found the change, even though the stimulus was visible to the subjects for the entire block. An interesting secondary result was the finding that areas that showed deactivations during the task (see Box 11.2) also showed differential activity based on the duration of search, decreasing in activity at the beginning of the block and increasing in activity after the subject found the change.

Recognize, however, that the duration of the *stimulus* or *behavior* does not necessarily correspond to the duration of the *neuronal activity*. Imagine seeing a photograph of a familiar face that is presented for 5 seconds. Neurons in the primary visual cortex will have their largest response over the first 100 ms or so, then become much less active. Neurons within face-sensitive regions in the inferior temporal lobe will be active at stimulus onset, as well

hemifield One half of a visual display, usually referring to the left or right half.

as throughout the 5-second period due to feedback from other brain regions. Some neurons within the frontal and parietal lobes may become active after the face disappears as you reflect upon what you just saw. While models for fMRI analysis are often constructed based upon stimulus duration, for most experimental questions the duration and timing of neuronal activity are more important.

Relative Timing across Brain Regions

Even though it is difficult to determine the absolute timing of neuronal activity based upon the fMRI BOLD signal, the relative timing of activity can be identified with great precision (Figure 8.14). In 1998 this was shown in an elegant study by Menon and colleagues, who investigated relative timing in two fMRI experiments using gradient-echo echo-planar fMRI at high field (4 T) and high temporal resolution (TR of 100 ms). Their first experiment used a visual checkerboard stimulus that was split into left and right **hemifields,** each presented for 2 s. The left hemifield was presented either before the right, with a delay interval ranging from 125 to 1000 ms, or at the same time. When they measured the difference in hemodynamic latency between the two hemispheres in the visual cortex, they found a near perfect correspondence with the presentation delay. The second experiment extended this result by introducing a motor reaction time task. Each trial began with the subjects watching a fixation cross at the center of the screen for 6 s. Then the screen turned bright yellow and a green start box and red target box

(A)

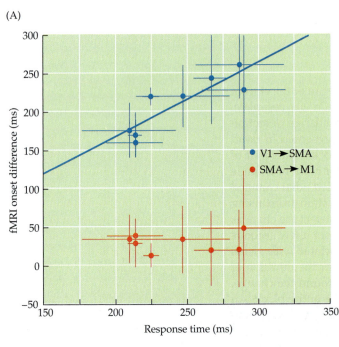

(B)

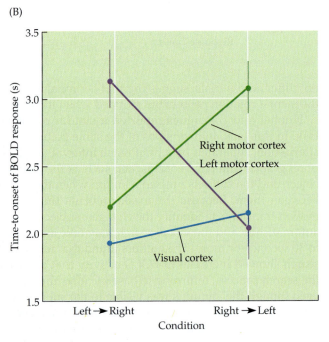

Figure 8.14 Using fMRI to identify the relative timing of activity across brain regions. (A) Subjects moved a target square across the display with a joystick when it changed color. The relative latency of the fMRI signal in different brain regions as a function of the subject's reaction time (RT) on the task was measured. The latency between BOLD activity in the primary visual cortex (V1) and in the supplementary motor area (SMA) increased roughly linearly with RT, while the latency between SMA and the primary motor cortex (M1) was unchanged with RT. This result suggests that processes influencing the speed of a response occur between V1 and SMA but not between SMA and M1. (B) In a similar approach subjects pressed a button with one hand at the onset of a 1.5-s-duration stimulus and a button with the other hand at offset. The order of activity between motor cortex regions depended on the order of responses, while activity in the visual cortex was independent of response order. (A after Menon et al., 1998; B after Miezin et al., 2000.)

appeared. The task was to use a joystick to move a cursor from the start box to the target box as quickly as possible. One second after the cursor was successfully moved, the screen returned to gray and the subjects returned the joystick back to its center. The authors investigated the timing of activity in three cortical regions: primary visual cortex (V1), primary motor cortex (M1), and the supplementary motor area (SMA). Activity in V1 was observed, on average, about 200 ms before activity in SMA, which in turn was about 30 ms before activity in M1.

> ### Thought Question
> How is it possible that researchers can identify timing differences of a few hundred milliseconds using fMRI if the hemodynamic response is delayed by a few seconds following the neuronal activity?

Especially remarkable were the effects of reaction time, which varied across subjects from about 200 to 300 ms, upon these differences. The difference between V1 and SMA activation was proportional to reaction time, suggesting that the pathway between them may be associated with decision or preparatory processes that differ between subjects (Figure 8.14A). However, the delay between SMA and M1 activation was constant across reaction times, indicating that that link supports more basic response-execution processes. To cognitive neuroscientists, such a result is extremely exciting because it suggests that variability in reaction time, which is the most commonly used measure in experimental psychology, can be restricted to particular brain regions. Note that the timing difference found between these regions using fMRI is larger than that calculated from electrophysiological studies, where a latency of around 100 ms between V1 and M1 is more typical. This discrepancy illustrates the basic problem with making inferences about the relative timing of neuronal activity across brain regions based upon fMRI data: differences in vascular properties also contribute to the timing of activity. This caveat, however, does not call into question the results of Menon and colleagues, because they demonstrated that the timing difference between regions depended on reaction time.

Within a single region, however, any vascular properties will be similar across timing conditions, allowing accurate estimation of small timing differences. In 2000, Miezin and colleagues investigated the issue of relative timing using a clever visuomotor task. They presented checkerboard stimuli in a rapid event-related paradigm. Each stimulus was presented for 1 s, and the time between stimuli was randomly varied, a technique called **jittering,** in this case with a mean of about 5 s. The subjects' task was to press a button with one hand when the stimulus appeared and press another button with the other hand when the stimulus disappeared. On one half of the trials, the right hand was used first, and on the other half, the left. They found that the estimated hemodynamic response in motor cortex corresponding to the onset of the stimulus was shifted earlier in time by about 0.75 to 1.0 s compared to the response to stimulus offset (Figure 8.14B). The fact that this shift was slightly less than the stimulus duration likely reflected preparation processes, since the subjects knew when the stimulus would disappear and could prepare for that button press. A subsequent power analysis suggested that timing differences as small as 100 ms could be reliably detected using such a paradigm.

jittering Randomizing the intervals between successive stimulus events over some range.

Figure 8.15 Maps of BOLD latency to peak in visual cortical regions. A 500-ms visual stimulus was presented and the latency to peak in voxels with significant BOLD activity was measured. Data are shown for two subjects. The color of each voxel indicates its latency, with voxels that had an early peak shown in blue and voxels with a late peak shown in red. Peak latency was shortest in voxels near the calcarine cortex (A,C), as shown in the left figures, and was longest in the fusiform gyrus, as shown in the right figures (B,D). (From Huettel et al., 2001b.)

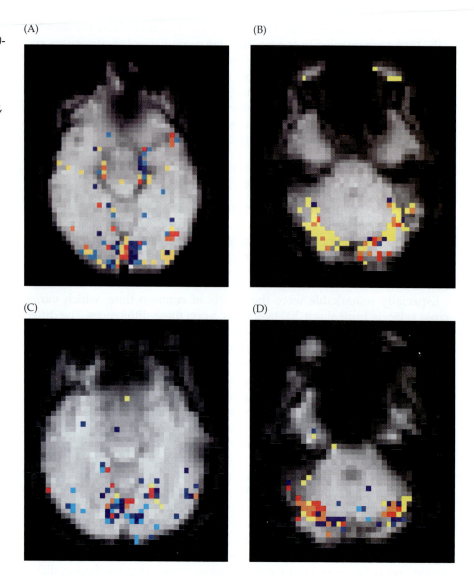

In summary, latency differences as small as a few hundred milliseconds can be measured between brain regions using fMRI (Figure 8.15). These differences may reflect changes in vascular response between brain regions and do not necessarily map directly to neuronal activity. In order to make inferences about relative timing of neuronal activity, researchers must selectively manipulate or measure one mental process while holding another constant. For example, decision processes may be proportional to response time, while low-level perceptual processes may be independent of response time, as in the study by Menon and colleagues. Comparisons within the same region do not suffer from such a problem, and thus very small intraregion timing differences can be identified.

Linearity of the Hemodynamic Response

So far we have considered the properties of the hemodynamic response to a single isolated stimulus. What happens when multiple stimuli are presented

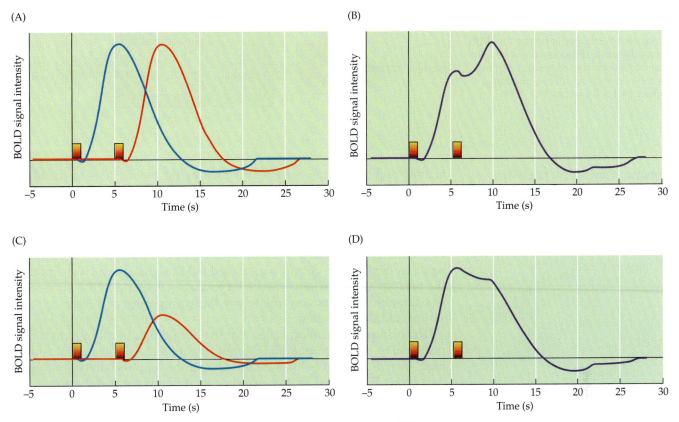

Figure 8.16 Linear and nonlinear addition of hemodynamic responses. If the same fMRI hemodynamic response were evoked by every stimulus (A), then the combined hemodynamic response to two stimuli would be a linear combination of two identical responses (B). But if the hemodynamic response were attenuated when stimuli were presented in rapid succession (C), then the combined response would be reduced in amplitude (D).

in succession? One possibility is that the same hemodynamic response is evoked for every stimulus, independently of the other stimuli presented, as shown in Figure 8.16A. If the stimuli are sufficiently close together that their hemodynamic responses overlap, then the measured total change in MR signal will be the sum of the individual responses (Figure 8.16B). This is known as a **linear system,** and its properties are discussed in the following section. Another possibility is that the hemodynamic response to a given stimulus depends on what other stimuli are presented (Figure 8.16C and D). If two stimuli are presented very close together, the combined response might be less than the sum of the two individual responses. Reductions in hemodynamic amplitude as a function of interstimulus interval are known as BOLD **refractory effects.** If refractory effects are present, then a linear model will overestimate the hemodynamic response to closely spaced stimuli, potentially reducing the effectiveness of experimental analyses. It is critical, therefore, to consider the evidence for and against the linearity of the fMRI hemodynamic response.

Properties of a Linear System

A basic framework for measurement of signal in fMRI is shown in Figure 8.17. Under this framework, when a stimulus is presented, it induces neuronal activity within a particular region of the brain. Since the neuronal

linear system A system that obeys the principles of scaling and superposition.

refractory effects Changes in the amplitude and timing of a response based on the characteristics of preceding responses.

Figure 8.17 The linear systems framework for fMRI. Boynton and colleagues investigated whether the fMRI hemodynamic response might be a linear transformation of neuronal input, combined with additive Gaussian noise. (After Boynton et al., 1996.)

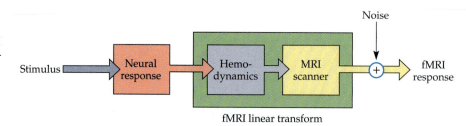

impulse A single input to a system. Impulses are assumed to be of infinitely short duration.

scaling A principle of linear systems that states that the magnitude of the system output must be proportional to the system input.

activity requires that oxygen be provided by the blood, there are resulting flow and volume changes in that brain region, as discussed in Chapters 6 and 7. The reduction in magnetic susceptibility associated with increased blood oxygenation then becomes measurable as BOLD contrast using fMRI. To reformulate this framework in terms of a linear system, we can consider the neuronal activity as a short-duration input, or **impulse,** to the hemodynamic system, whose output is measured in MR signal. For a given impulse, the hemodynamic system is assumed to always respond in the same manner. From this assumption follow two basic properties of a linear system: scaling and superposition.

The principle of **scaling** states that the output of a linear system is proportional to the magnitude of its input (Figure 8.18A). If the input is doubled, then the output is likewise doubled; if the input is halved, then so is the output. For fMRI data, this principle would indicate that changes in the relative amplitude of neuronal activity should lead to similar changes in the amplitude of the hemodynamic response. Now, why is this important?

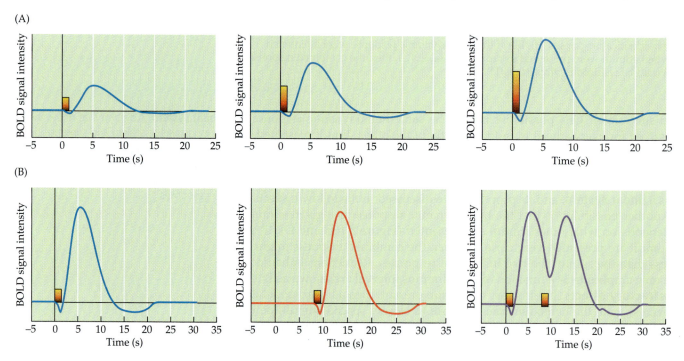

Figure 8.18 Scaling and superposition. (A) The principle of scaling states that the output of a linear system is proportional to the magnitude of the input. For fMRI, this implies that the amplitude of the hemodynamic response reflects the amount of underlying neuronal activity. (B) The principle of superposition states that the output of a linear system with more than one input is the sum of the responses to the individual inputs.

Remember that the goal of fMRI is to determine changes in neuronal activity, which must be inferred from the amplitude changes in the hemodynamic response. So, a study may present a test condition and a control condition, find that activity in the brain region of interest is twice as large in the test condition, and then infer that neuronal activity was similarly larger in that condition. If the hemodynamic amplitude were independent of the amplitude of neuronal activity, then no such inferences would be possible.

Whereas scaling refers to the amplitude of activity, the principle of **superposition** refers to the timing of activity (Figure 8.18B). Stated simply, superposition means that the total response to two or more events is the summation of the individual responses. If a single event generates a hemodynamic response, then two events presented in succession will generate a combined response equal to two individual responses added together. To understand the importance of superposition, consider a very simple experiment. You are interested in studying the brain activity associated with short-term memory of words, so you devise an experiment in which a word is presented, followed by a 2-s delay and then another word. The subject's task is to indicate whether or not the two words are the same. Since the two stimuli are both words, they will likely activate many of the same brain regions, and since they are presented so close together in time, their hemodynamic responses will overlap. How can you distinguish whether an area is active in response to the first word, the second word, or both? By assuming superposition, you can create models for what combined hemodynamic response would be expected in each condition. If an area is active in response to the first word but not the second, it will show an early rise to a peak at about 5 s, whereas if it is active only in response to the second word, the rise will occur 2 s later. If it is active in response to both words, there will be an intermediate but larger peak. Understanding the superposition of hemodynamic responses is critical for fMRI analyses.

It is important to recognize that although we are discussing the linearity of the hemodynamic response, nonlinearities may be present in the neuronal response as well. Many electrophysiological studies have demonstrated that evoked potentials, especially those related to primary sensory or motor processing, are reduced in amplitude when preceded by a similar potential within the previous second or two. Typical fMRI studies cannot distinguish between neuronal or vascular sources for nonlinearity without incorporating data on neuronal activity or employing adaptation methods.

Evidence for Rough Linearity

The first study of the linearity of the fMRI BOLD response was reported by Boynton and colleagues in 1996. They investigated the effects of duration of visual stimulation upon activity in the primary visual cortex, using an EPI gradient-echo sequence at 1.5 T. The durations tested were 3, 6, 12, and 24 s. The visual stimuli were checkerboard patterns that moved from right to left while flickering at a high rate (8 Hz). The contrast between dark and light squares on the checkerboard was manipulated over trials. To evaluate the scaling of the hemodynamic response, the authors examined the effects of two factors: stimulus contrast and stimulus duration. Their hypothesis was that these factors should have independent and additive effects on the BOLD signal if the hemodynamic response behaved as a linear system.

Boynton and colleagues found that for all stimulus durations, the amplitude of activity was greater at higher visual contrast levels but the hemodynamic response had the same basic shape. This confirmed the scaling principle of linearity. To test whether the superposition principle also held for

superposition A principle of linear systems that states that the total response to a set of inputs is equivalent to the summation of the independent responses to the inputs.

Figure 8.19 Evidence for the linearity of the fMRI hemodynamic response. Boynton and colleagues investigated whether the addition of the fMRI responses to several short-duration stimuli (blue lines) predicted the fMRI response to a longer-duration stimulus (red lines). The prediction fit the observed data well, save for an overestimation of the response given by the addition of 3-s stimuli. (After Boynton et al., 1996.)

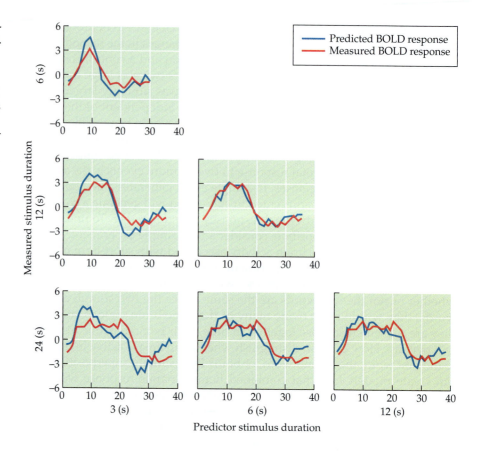

BOLD data, they investigated whether the response to a longer stimulus could be predicted by the sum of multiple shorter stimuli. Their results indicated linear superposition for most stimulus durations, such that the response to a 24-s stimulus was given by the addition of two 12-s stimuli or four 6-s stimuli (Figure 8.19). The one exception they noted was that the response given by the addition of 3-s stimuli was larger than predicted, and this discrepancy was attributed to neuronal adaptation effects (i.e., that the neurons themselves decrease in activity over the first few seconds of a stimulus). In total, these results provided strong evidence for the linearity of the hemodynamic response over stimulus durations ranging from a few to tens of seconds.

Following on the results of Boynton and colleagues, Dale and Buckner in 1997 investigated the linearity of the hemodynamic response to individual stimulus events, rather than extended stimulus blocks. They reasoned that neuronal adaptation effects could be eliminated by separating stimuli in time by an interval sufficiently long to allow complete neuronal recovery. To test whether complete linearity would be observed under such conditions, they presented clusters of one, two, or three stimuli at interstimulus intervals of either 2 or 5 s. The hemodynamic response to a second stimulus in a cluster was determined by subtracting the single-stimulus response from that to a pair of stimuli. Likewise, the response to the third stimulus was determined by subtracting the two-stimulus response from the three-stimulus response. If the principle of superposition holds for fMRI BOLD data, then all responses should have the same amplitude and shape regardless of where they occur in the cluster. Dale and Buckner's evidence supported this interpretation, in that the responses to the second and third trials in the set

(A)

(B)

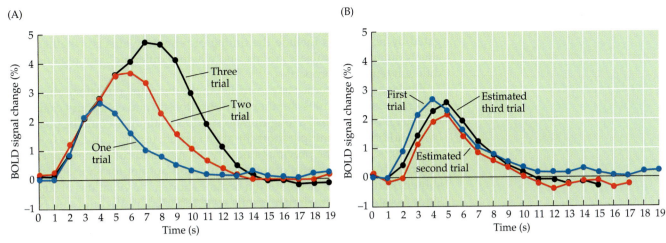

Figure 8.20 Linear addition of hemodynamic responses to individual stimulus events. (A) The hemodynamic responses evoked by presentation of one, two, or three identical stimuli (short-duration visual flashes) at short interstimulus intervals were measured. Shown here are data from a 2-s interval. The total hemodynamic response increased in a regular fashion as the number of stimuli in a trial increased. (B) By subtracting the one-stimulus trial from the two-stimulus trial, and the two-stimulus from the three-stimulus, the contributions of the second and third stimuli in a trial were estimated. To a first approximation, the responses to the second and third stimuli were similar to that to the first, suggesting that the BOLD response scales in a roughly linear fashion. (From Dale and Buckner, 1997.)

were generally similar to that of the first trial, (Figure 8.20) especially for pairs of trials at a 5-s interval. They concluded that the fMRI BOLD response adds across stimuli in a "roughly linear" fashion at intervals typical of experimental testing (e.g., a few seconds).

This finding, that individual trials evoke recognizable hemodynamic responses even when separated by relatively short intervals, has become extremely influential for design and analysis of fMRI studies. At first interpretation, it suggests that individual trials can be closely spaced to increase the number of trials presented and thus experimental power, without loss of response amplitude (see Chapter 11 for discussion of this issue). But, as the authors themselves note, there are significant limitations for such fast-rate studies. Primary among these are the deviations from linearity at short intervals. Close examination of the data from 2-s interstimulus intervals (see Figure 8.20B) reveals that the response to the second and third stimuli in a cluster are reduced in amplitude and increased in latency compared to the response to a single stimulus. In the best case, such nonlinearities would reduce the power of experimental analyses but would have little additional effect. But in the worst case, large nonlinearities could preclude the use of very short intervals (e.g., 1 second) between experimental stimuli.

Challenges to Linearity

Subsequent work on nonlinearities in the fMRI hemodynamic response investigated whether there is a **refractory period** following stimulus presentation during which subsequent stimuli evoke smaller hemodynamic responses. A preliminary suggestion based on the above results is that the fMRI hemodynamic response may be nonlinear at intervals of about 2 to 6 s but linear at longer intervals, since superposition was found at durations of 6 s but not 3 s, and better scaling was observed at intervals of 5 s than 2 s. Tests of refractory periods have been conducted using both blocked and event-related designs. Blocked designs (e.g., the 1996 Boynton and colleagues study) usually manip-

refractory period A time period following the presentation of a stimulus during which subsequent stimuli evoke a reduced response. For BOLD fMRI, the refractory periods for many types of stimuli last approximately 6 s.

ulate stimulus duration, and event-related designs (e.g., the 1997 Dale and Buckner study) usually manipulate interstimulus interval. The issues investigated by researchers include the timing of refractory effects, whether such effects differ across subject groups, and whether different brain regions have different refractory properties.

Blocked-design studies have verified that substantial refractory effects are present at short stimulus durations. In 1998 Robson and colleagues examined whether the response to a long-duration auditory stimulus could be predicted by the addition of multiple short-duration stimuli, testing durations from 100 ms to 25.5 s. As for the previous study by Boynton and colleagues, superposition held for stimuli of 6 s or more in duration but not for shorter-duration stimuli. Furthermore, as the stimuli became shorter, the violations of superposition became greater. Similar results were reported by Vazquez and Noll in 1998 for visual stimuli, with significant nonlinearities found for stimuli shorter than 4 s. Event-related studies have also supported the idea of a refractory period. Huettel and McCarthy presented short-duration visual checkerboard stimuli either singly or in pairs separated by a 1-s to 6-s interstimulus interval (Figure 8.21). A region of interest was identified in the primary visual cortex based on activity in response to a single stimulus, and that region was interrogated for all pairs of stimuli. The response to a second stimulus in a pair separated by 1 s was reduced by more than 40% from the normal response and was delayed in time by nearly 1 s. By 6 s, both the amplitude and latency of the hemodynamic response to the second stimulus in the pair had returned to near normal values. The finding of both amplitude and latency changes is consistent with the earlier work of Dale and Buckner, as well as with computational simulations of the hemodynamic response.

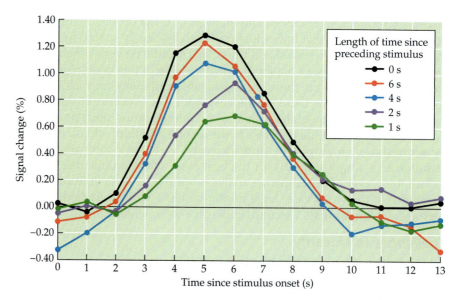

Figure 8.21 Nonlinearity of the hemodynamic response at short interstimulus intervals. Each trial consisted of a single visual stimulus or a pair of visual stimuli separated by a short interval. Single stimuli evoked a robust hemodynamic response (black line). At short interstimulus intervals (e.g., 1 to 2 s), the hemodynamic response was reduced in amplitude and increased in latency. These changes reflect the presence of refractory effects in the hemodynamic response. (After Huettel and McCarthy, 2000.)

Although the idea of rough linearity had permeated the literature, by the beginning of the twenty-first century the fMRI refractory period had become well accepted. Thus, experimental questions changed from whether it exists to how its properties might differ across individuals and brain regions. One of the first subject group comparisons was between young adults and healthy elderly adults. Given the many structural changes in the brain that accompany aging, including possible impairments in blood flow, it was predicted that refractory effects would be greater in elderly adults. This prediction, though sensible, turns out to be wrong. The magnitude of the refractory effect is similar for older and younger adults, as is the amplitude of the hemodynamic response itself. There is substantial interest in examining refractory effects in other subject groups. Patients with schizophrenia, for example, exhibit abnormal sensory habituation, as shown by electrophysiological measures. While neurologically normal adults show a significant decrease in electrophysiological responses when a stimulus is presented twice in rapid succession, a phenomenon known as sensory gating, schizophrenic adults have a much smaller decrease. Studying changes in the fMRI refractory period may lead to a better understanding of the neural systems associated with the sensory-gating deficits in schizophrenia.

Though sparse, some data exist that demonstrate differences in refractory effects across brain regions. Primary sensory or motor regions appear to have smaller refractory effects (i.e., are more linear) than a secondary regions. However, comparisons of refractory effects across brain regions may be confounded by differences in neuronal activity. In 2001, Birn and colleagues measured activity in the primary motor cortex and the SMA when subjects tapped their fingers for different durations. In the primary motor cortex, the hemodynamic response increased in amplitude with increasing duration, although there were violations of superposition for stimuli shorter than about 4 s. But in the SMA, which is involved with the planning of motor behavior, activation amplitude was similar across all stimulus durations. Huettel and colleagues showed in 2004 that a similar relation holds for visual stimuli: activity in the primary visual cortex scales with duration of a visual stimulus, but activity in the motion-sensitive region V5 is independent of duration. What is similar in both of these cases is that the secondary regions examined (SMA and V5) may be transiently active at the beginning of the stimulus, while the primary region may show sustained activity throughout stimulus presentation. It is therefore worth reemphasizing that refractory effects measured using fMRI may result from neuronal adaptation or from changes in vascular responsiveness, either of which could differ across brain regions.

Using Refractory Effects to Study Neuronal Adaptation

Though refractory effects are often seen as an impediment to fMRI research, through clever experimental design they can be used as indices of brain function. The basic idea comes from physiological studies of **adaptation.** If one repeatedly presents the same stimulus to a subject, as when giving a mild electric shock to a rat or showing a bright red balloon to a human infant, the response to that stimulus will diminish over time. After a number of presentations, the rat will stop jumping to the harmless shock and the infant will become bored with the balloon. When the response to a stimulus decreases with repeated presentation, the subject is said to have adapted to that stimulus. By changing the stimulus slightly, we can infer to which aspects of the stimulus the subject adapted. If we replace the red balloon with a red fire truck and the infant is still bored, then we can infer that she

adaptation A change in the response to a stimulus following its repeated presentation.

fMRI-adaptation (fMRI-A) A reduction in the BOLD response to the repeated presentation of a set of stimuli that differ along some attribute, indicating that the brain region being studied is insensitive (as measured by fMRI) to the stimulus attribute being varied.

adapted to the color red. But if she is now very interested in the fire truck, then she must have adapted to some other property such as shape. Similarly, many neurons in the visual system will preferentially fire for one type of visual stimulus, due to its particular shape, color, or way of movement. But with repeated presentations of that stimulus, the neuron's firing rate will decrease dramatically.

Given the presence of refractory effects, we can apply the principles of adaptation to fMRI. First, we repeatedly present a stimulus that evokes activity in a particular brain region. After a short period of repetition, we then present another stimulus that differs in some fashion. If the region being investigated contains neurons that respond differently to the new stimulus, it will show an increase in fMRI activity. But if the neurons do not distinguish between the old and new stimuli, the brain region remains adapted and fMRI activity will be at a low level.

This approach was first used by Grill-Spector and Malach in a series of experiments reported in 2001. They investigated whether neurons in the lateral occipital complex, which contains the lateral occipital lobe and the posterior fusiform gyrus, are sensitive to changes in higher-order properties of objects. For one of their experiments, they presented the same face repeatedly within a 10-s block. They compared the activation in this "identical face" condition to that measured in conditions where some property of the face was manipulated, such as position on the screen, viewpoint from left to right, illumination, size, or identity (i.e., different faces presented). Only one condition was varied within each block. It is important to recognize that roughly similar activity would be observed in these brain regions in response to any of the faces presented in isolation, so differential activity in the blocks could be attributed to refractory effects across multiple stimulus presentations.

The researchers found that activity in the fusiform gyrus, for example, was greatly reduced in response to repeated presentations of identical, size-varying, or position-varying faces, compared to repeated presentations of entirely different faces. In contrast, variation in direction of illumination or viewpoint caused a recovery from adaptation. From these results, the researchers concluded that the fusiform gyrus recognizes facial identity despite size or position manipulations, but does treat illumination or viewpoint manipulations as new stimuli. This approach, which is known as **fMRI-adaptation** or **fMRI-A,** has since been used in other domains, including for other visual features and for processing of number representations. For example, the recent 2003 study by Boynton and Finney demonstrated that refractory effects in the secondary (but not primary) visual cortex depend upon the orientation of visual line gratings. Likewise, Soon and colleagues (also in a 2003 study) have shown that refractory effects in face-sensitive cortex are greater for pairs of identical faces than for pairs of different faces, and we have shown a similar effect for motion stimuli in motion-sensitive visual cortex. Taken together, these studies indicate that BOLD refractory effects may provide information about the functional properties of neurons within a brain region.

Summary

Functional MRI has become a dominant neuroimaging technique in large part because of its spatial and temporal properties. The spatial resolution of an fMRI study determines our ability to separate adjacent brain regions with different functional properties. A key factor for spatial resolution is voxel size, which is typically about 3 to 5 mm for full-brain studies but can be less than 1 mm for studies targeted at a single brain region. However, using very small voxels has disadvantages, notably decreases in MR signal and increases in image acquisition time. Since the hemodynamic response measured by fMRI depends on increased blood flow, the BOLD effect can be measured in draining veins that are distant from the site of activity. Effective spatial resolution can be improved by removing these large-vessel effects. The temporal resolution of fMRI refers to the ability to estimate the timing of neuronal activity from the measured hemodynamic changes. The key pulse sequence parameter for temporal resolution is repetition time (TR), which is usually about 1 to 3 s. Depending upon the experimental design, decreasing TR below this range may have little effect upon experimental power. While the absolute timing of neuronal activity is difficult to determine using fMRI, the relative timing of activity between different stimuli or different brain regions can be determined within a few hundred milliseconds. Nonlinearities in the fMRI hemodynamic response reflect the temporal dynamics of activity in a single spatial location. If the same brain region becomes active twice in rapid succession, the hemodynamic response to the second event is reduced in amplitude compared with that evoked by a single event. This refractory period lasts about 6 s, with larger effects seen at durations less than about 2 s. While refractory effects present an analysis challenge for most studies, some researchers have taken advantage of these effects to study functional adaptation within a brain region.

Suggested Readings

*Boynton, G. M., Engel, S. A., Glover, G. H., and Heeger, D. J. (1996). Linear systems analysis of functional magnetic resonance imaging in human V1. *J. Neurosci.*, 16(13): 4207–4221. This early and influential study provides evidence supporting the idea that the fMRI BOLD signal results from a linear transformation of neuronal activity.

*Cheng, K., Waggoner, R. A., and Tanaka, K. (2001). Human ocular dominance columns as revealed by high-field functional magnetic resonance imaging. *Neuron*, 32(2): 359–374. An interesting demonstration of the power of fMRI to identify fine spatial detail in the human brain.

*Dale, A. M., and Buckner, R. L. (1997). Selective averaging of rapidly presented individual trials using fMRI. *Hum. Brain Mapping*, 5: 329–340. One of the early studies that provided evidence for the feasibility of event-related analyses.

*Huettel, S. A., and McCarthy, G. (2000). Evidence for a refractory period in the hemodynamic response to visual stimuli as measured by MRI. *NeuroImage*, 11(5): 547–553. A clear demonstration of BOLD refractory effects in the visual cortex.

Kim, S. G., and Ogawa, S. (2002). Insights into new techniques for high resolution functional MRI. *Curr. Opinion Neurobiol.*, 12(5): 607–615. A good review article that describes important issues relevant to the spatial properties of fMRI.

*Menon, R. S., and Kim, S. G. (1999). Spatial and temporal limits in cognitive neuroimaging with fMRI. *Trends Cogn. Sci.*, 3(6): 207–216. An interesting review of the properties of BOLD fMRI, with emphasis upon the form of the hemodynamic response.

*Menon, R. S., Luknowsky, D. C., and Gati, J. S. (1998). Mental chronometry using latency-resolved functional MRI. *Proc. Natl. Acad. Sci. U.S.A.*, 95(18): 10902–10907. This article provides striking early demonstrations of the power of fMRI to distinguish very small differences in timing between successive events.

*Indicates a reference that is a suggested reading in the field and is also cited in this chapter.

Chapter References

Birn, R. M., Saad, Z. S., and Bandettini, P. A. (2001). Spatial heterogeneity of the nonlinear dynamics in the fMRI BOLD response. *NeuroImage*, 14(4): 817–826.

Blamire A. M., Ogawa S., Ugurbil K., Rothman D., McCarthy G., Ellermann J. M., Hyder F., Rattner Z., and Shulman R. G. (1992). Dynamic mapping of the human visual cortex by high-speed magnetic resonance imaging. *Proc. Natl. Acad. Sci. U.S.A.,* 89(22): 11069–11073.

Boynton, G. M., and Finney, E. M. (2003). Orientation-specific adaptation in human visual cortex. *J. Neurosci.,* 23: 8781–8787.

Brodmann, K. (1909). *Vergleichende Lokalisationslehre der Grosshirnrinde in ihren Prinzipien dargestellt auf Grund des Zellenbaues.* Barth, Leipzig, Germany.

Buckner, R. L., Snyder, A. Z., Sanders, A. L., Raichle, M. E., and Morris, J. C. (2000). Functional brain imaging of young, nondemented, and demented older adults. *J. Cogn. Neurosci.,* 12 (Supplement 2): 24–34.

D'Esposito, M., Zarahn, E., Aguirre, G. K., and Rypma, B. (1999). The effect of normal aging on the coupling of neural activity to the BOLD HDR. *NeuroImage,* 10: 6–14.

Disbrow, E. A., Slutsky, D. A., Roberts, T. P., and Krubitzer, L. A. (2000). Functional MRI at 1.5 Tesla: A comparison of the blood oxygenation level-dependent signal and electrophysiology. *Proc. Natl. Acad. Sci. U.S.A.,* 97(17): 9718–9723.

Grill-Spector, K., and Malach, R. (2001). fMR-adaptation: A tool for studying the functional properties of human cortical neurons. *Acta Psychologica,* 107(1–3): 293–321.

Huettel, S. A., McKeown, M. J., Song, A. W., Hart, S., Spencer, D. D., Allison, T., and McCarthy, G. (2004). Linking hemodynamic and electrophysiological measures of brain activity: Evidence from functional MRI and intracranial field potentials. *Cerebral Cortex.,* 14: 165–173.

Huettel, S. A., Güzeldere, G., and McCarthy, G. (2001a). Dissociating the neural mechanisms of visual attention in change detection using functional MRI. *J. Cogn. Neurosci.,* 13: 1006–1018.

Huettel, S. A., Singerman, J., and McCarthy, G. (2001b). The effects of aging upon the hemodynamic response measured by functional MRI. *NeuroImage,* 13(1): 161–175.

Kwong, K. K., Belliveau, J. W., Chesler, D. A., Goldberg, I. E., Weisskoff, R. M., Poncelet, B. P., Kennedy, D. N., Hoppel, B. E., Cohen, M. S., Turner, R., et al. (1992). Dynamic magnetic resonance imaging of human brain activity during primary sensory stimulation. *Proc. Natl. Acad. Sci. U.S.A.,* 89(12): 5675–5679.

Logothetis, N. K., Pauls, J., Augath, M., Trinath, T., and Oeltermann, A. (2001). Neurophysiological investigation of the basis of the fMRI signal. *Nature,* 412(6843): 150–157.

Menon, R. S. (2002). Postacquisition suppression of large-vessel BOLD signals in high-resolution fMRI. *Magn. Reson. Med.,* 47: 1–9.

Menon, R. S., Ogawa, S., Strupp, J. P., and Ugurbil, K. (1997). Ocular dominance in human V1 demonstrated by functional magnetic resonance imaging. *J. Neurophysiol.,* 77(5): 2780–2787.

Miezin, F. M., Maccotta, L., Ollinger, J. M., Petersen, S. E., and Buckner, R. L. (2000). Characterizing the hemodynamic response: Effects of presentation rate, sampling procedure, and the possibility of ordering brain activity based on relative timing. *NeuroImage,* 11(6 Pt. 1): 735–759.

Obembe, O., Woldorff, M., Song, A., and Huettel, S. A. (2003). Adaptation of the fMRI BOLD signal in human motion area V5 is specific to the direction of stimulus motion. Abstract presented at Annual Meeting of the Society for Neuroscience, November 12.

Robson, M. D., Dorosz, J. L., and Gore, J. C. (1998). Measurements of the temporal fMRI response of the human auditory cortex to trains of tones. *NeuroImage,* 7: 185–198.

Soon, C.-S., Venkatraman, V., and Chee, M. W. L. (2003). Stimulus repetition and hemodynamic response refractoriness in event-related fMRI. *Hum. Brain Mapping,* 20: 1–12.

Vazquez, A. L., and Noll, D. C. (1998). Nonlinear aspects of the BOLD response in functional MRI. *NeuroImage,* 7: 108–118.

9

Signal and Noise in fMRI

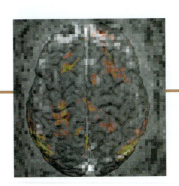

In BOLD fMRI experiments, small but meaningful changes in brain activity lie buried within highly variable measurements. Activation of neurons within a brain region results in a BOLD signal increase of only about a few percent. To understand how small an effect this is, consider the two brain images shown in Figure 9.1A and B. Both are T_2^*-weighted images taken from the same subject during performance of a hand squeezing task. The image in Figure 9.1A was taken while the subject was resting, while the image in Figure 9.1B was acquired a few seconds later at the maximum of the BOLD hemodynamic response evoked after she began squeezing her hand. Although these images appear nearly identical to the naked eye, there is actually an intensity change of about 5% in voxels within the primary motor cortex (Figure 9.1C and D), as shown on the plot of signal intensity changes over time (Figure 9.1E). This discrepancy illustrates the first fundamental problem of fMRI data analysis: *the measured BOLD signal change is very small compared to the total intensity of the MR signal.*

Small absolute effects are not necessarily difficult to measure: Thermometers can reliably identify temperature changes of a small fraction of a degree, while stopwatches can identify timing changes of a few milliseconds. Nor are they unimportant: A 1% increase in body temperature (approximately 4 K or 4°C, or about 7°F) would have likely fatal consequences. However, there is a second fundamental problem for fMRI data analysis: *the task-related BOLD signal change is very small compared to the total spatial and temporal variability across images.* Figure 9.1D shows a map of the percent signal change between two brain images. Readily apparent is the large variability across the image, especially in areas outside the brain or near its edges. Based on a single pair of images alone, it would be impossible to tell which increases in activity are due to the experimental task, and therefore meaningful, and which are due to other non-task-related sources and should be ignored.

In this chapter, we describe the sources of variability in fMRI data that can potentially mask the BOLD effect. Some variability results from temperature fluctuations in the MR scanner or the subject's body, which can cause artifactual changes in the recorded signal. While a potential problem, thermal variability tends to be highly random and independent of the experimental task. Thus, its effects can be minimized by averaging multiple data points. More problematic are physiological effects like head motion, heart

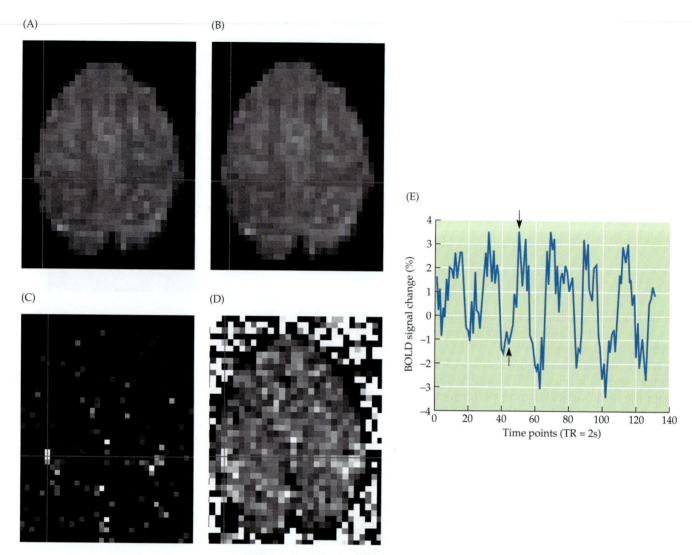

Figure 9.1 Changes in fMRI activity over time. Shown here are two BOLD fMRI images, one taken at time point 45, while the subject was resting (A), and the other taken at time point 50, while the subject was squeezing both hands (B). Even though this slice contains the hand regions of the primary motor cortex, the images appear nearly identical. The numerical difference between these images is shown in (C), and the percent signal change is shown in (D), scaled with white representing a +5% change and black representing a –5% change. The time course of the voxel indicated by the crosshairs is shown in (E), with arrows indicating the time points of (A) and (B).

rate, and respiration, all of which can occur together with an experimental manipulation. For example, the subject may move her head a small distance each time a visual stimulus is presented, due to the alerting or arousing properties of the image. Even if all of these problems are overcome, there may still be intrinsic variation in the brain regions that are active during performance of the task due to strategic, practice, or fatigue effects. There may even be variation in the BOLD effect itself, with the same stimulus evoking a 1% change on one trial but a 3% change on the next. Given these many sources of variability, even the most experienced fMRI researcher may consider it a wonder that one can identify any significant effects at all!

While nontask variability cannot be eliminated, understanding its possible causes can greatly improve strategies for experimental design and analysis. Many common imaging problems cause characteristic noise patterns in the data; the ability to recognize these patterns is an important part of any quality assurance plan. Also, when planning studies, understanding how much variability to expect allows the researcher to estimate the number of subjects needed to answer an experimental question. With costs for a single fMRI scanner session often approaching $1000, few researchers (or granting agencies) can afford many excess subjects.

Here, we discuss central concepts related to signal and noise in fMRI. We describe the sources of each and introduce the key idea of the signal-to-noise ratio. We then describe techniques for increasing signal-to-noise ratio through signal averaging, which underlies nearly all fMRI studies. Rather than presenting a stimulus once and examining the resulting BOLD changes, researchers present that stimulus many times under similar conditions in order to improve their estimate of the BOLD response.

Understanding Signal and Noise

Consider the following analogy. You are at a party and you ask your companion a question. At the same time that your friend replies, you also hear many other sounds. Other guests are holding conversations, music is playing, and the air conditioner fan is humming. If these other sounds are loud enough, your companion may have to speak more loudly or you may need to reduce the volume of the music in order to hear his reply. In this analogy, we can refer to your question as the stimulus, your companion's response to your question as the **signal,** and the other sounds that interfere with your ability to hear that response as **noise.** Note that what constitutes signal or noise depends upon your interests. If you wanted to eavesdrop on an adjacent conversation, you may stop listening to your friend. The new conversation would become the signal, and your friend's response would become noise. However, some sounds like the air conditioner's hum are unlikely to ever become signals.

We can use this analogy to think about fMRI. When we present a stimulus, we hope to measure a response in the brain, just as you expected to hear your companion's response to your question. However, in both cases the signal we hope to detect is mixed with other irrelevant sources of variability. We can improve our ability to detect the signal by increasing its amplitude or by decreasing the noise, that is, by increasing the **signal-to-noise ratio,** or **SNR.** In fMRI studies, the definition of the signal also depends upon our interests, as will be discussed in the next section. And, just like in the party environment, the noise may be decomposed into different sources. For these reasons, the term *signal-to-noise ratio* has different meanings in different contexts, and this can cause confusion. We will attempt to carefully delineate these different meanings so as to avoid this terminological confusion.

Signal and Noise Defined

Recall that in an fMRI experiment, only one physical quantity is measured, namely the magnitude of current in a detector coil measured by the MRI scanner hardware. This quantity is a composite of both signal and noise. The signal arises from changes in magnetization that we have heretofore referred to as the MR signal. The noise arises from thermal motions within the spin system and within the scanner hardware. Images reconstructed from this output of the detector coil current will similarly be composed of signal and noise. Because of the random nature of thermal noise, the noise component of the image will be equally distributed throughout the image. MR physi-

signal Meaningful changes in some quantity. For fMRI, an important class of signals includes changes in intensity associated with the BOLD response across a series of T_2^* images.

noise Nonmeaningful changes in some quantity. There are many sources of noise in fMRI studies, and some changes may be classified as either noises or signals depending upon the goals of the study.

signal-to-noise ratio (SNR) The relative strength of a signal compared to other sources of variability in the data.

raw signal-to-noise ratio (raw SNR)
The ratio between the MR signal intensity associated with a sample (e.g., the brain) and the thermal noise that is measured outside the sample.

contrast-to-noise ratio (CNR) The magnitude of the intensity difference between different quantities divided by the variability in their measurements.

contrast The intensity difference between different quantities being measured by an imaging system. It also can refer to the physical quantity being measured (e.g., T_1 contrast).

functional signal-to-noise ratio (functional SNR) The ratio between the intensity of a signal associated with changes in brain function and the variability in the data due to all sources of noise. Functional SNR is sometimes called dynamic CNR or functional CNR.

cists and engineers quantify this **raw signal-to-noise ratio (raw SNR)** by dividing the intensity of the image in a region that contains the sample (the signal) by the intensity of the image in a region that is outside of the sample (the noise). Raw SNR is used to evaluate the performance of the scanner hardware, and you would likely compare such measures of SNR if you were deciding which MRI scanner to purchase for your institution. Engineers strive to maximize raw SNR by using more-efficient detector coils and pulse sequences and by shielding the scanner from outside interference.

While a useful measure, raw SNR only provides part of the story. Since we want to create maps of brain anatomy or function, we need to be able to characterize differences in MR signal within different regions of the brain, and not just between the inside and outside of the brain. For this purpose, we introduce a new measure, the **contrast-to-noise ratio (CNR)**. As introduced in Chapter 1, the **contrast** of an MRI image refers to the physical property to which it is sensitive. So, an image sensitive to T_1 contrast will be bright for voxels with short T_1 values (like white matter) and dark for voxels with long T_1 values (like gray matter or cerebrospinal fluid). For anatomical images, the ability to identify differences between tissues depends upon the CNR, which is the intensity difference between the two tissues divided by the noise, as previously calculated.

Refer back to Figure 1.4 for a comparison of high-CNR and low-CNR images. On a T_1-weighted image with high CNR, a very clear boundary is observed between gray and white matter. This is especially evident for subcortical nuclei, which are visible at the center of Figure 1.4A. When CNR is reduced, it becomes more difficult to distinguish different tissue types (see Figure 1.4B). On this image, gray matter is still visible but often blurs into surrounding white matter. Subcortical nuclei, especially the thalamus, are very difficult to identify, and their edges have become indistinct. Roughly speaking, CNR describes the ease of seeing differences between tissues.

Two properties of CNR are important to understand. First, CNR is always relative to some comparison within an image. For example, T_1-weighted pulse sequences have very good ability to distinguish gray and white matter (high CNR), but only limited ability to distinguish cerebrospinal fluid and air (low CNR). Conversely, a proton-density pulse sequence can easily show differences between air and fluid, which differ dramatically in their density, but have less ability to distinguish gray and white matter. Second, CNR does not depend solely upon the absolute difference in intensity between two tissue types. Consider two structural images taken on different scanners. On the first image, gray-matter voxels have a mean intensity value of 150, white-matter voxels have a mean intensity value of 250, and the noise value is 100. On the second image, gray-matter voxels have a mean intensity value of 60, white-matter voxels have a mean intensity value of 70, and the noise value is 5. Which image would have a higher CNR? The mean intensity difference between gray and white matter is about 100 units in the first image and only 10 units in the second. But the variability is 20 times larger in the first image than the second. Consequently, the CNR in the second image will be about 2 times greater than that in the first image.

For most fMRI experiments, however, CNR is unimportant. Typical T_2^*-weighted images have intrinsically low contrast (see Figure 9.1). It is hard to identify boundaries between different types of tissue in functional images, much less to distinguish active and inactive regions. Instead, the important quantity for fMRI studies is **functional signal-to-noise ratio (functional SNR)**. (Some authors refer to this quantity as dynamic CNR or functional CNR). Here, we use the term *signal* to describe the difference between two states of the brain caused by an experimental manipulation. The term *noise* refers to the variability in those states *over time*.

It is important to recognize that functional SNR is different from CNR. CNR depends upon the intensity difference between voxels (i.e., across space). Functional SNR depends upon the intensity difference within a voxel, group of voxels, or region over time. The effects of increasing functional SNR are illustrated in Figure 9.2. Shown are activation plots for three voxels in and

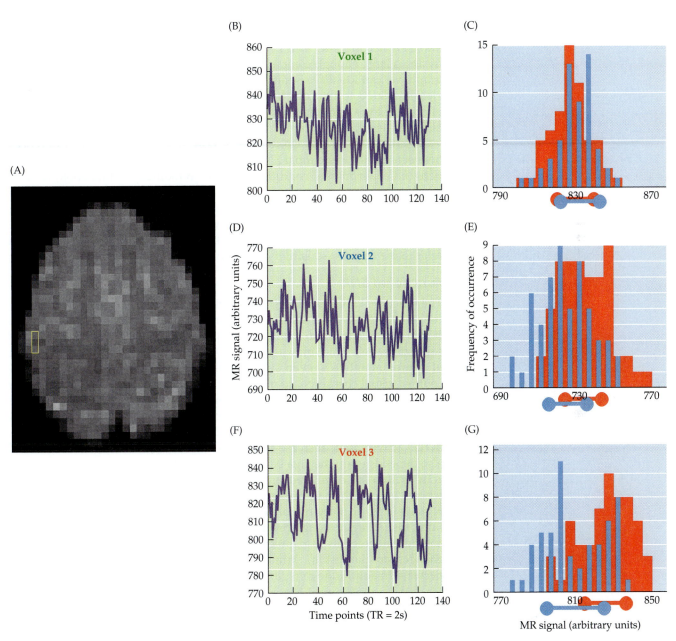

Figure 9.2   Voxels with low, medium, and high SNR. Shown in (A) are three adjacent voxels. As shown in (B), the uppermost voxel has little to no task-related signal change (low SNR), and the distributions of activity during task (red) and nontask (blue) periods are highly overlapping (C). (D) The middle voxel has a medium SNR, but there is still substantial overlap between the distributions (E). However, the lowermost voxel (F) has a very high SNR, and the distributions have much less overlap (G).

effect size The numerical difference between means divided by the standard deviation.

adjacent to the primary motor cortex, during performance of a blocked-design hand squeezing task. Note that the uppermost voxel shows little task-related activity, the middle voxel shows some task-related activity, and the bottom voxel shows clear and robust task-related activity. Plotted at right are simple histograms comparing time points during the hand squeezing blocks (in red) to those during resting blocks (in blue). For the upper voxel, the distributions overlap completely, indicating that hand squeezing had no effect upon activity in this voxel. In the middle voxel, the distributions begin to diverge, with more activity observed during task blocks. And in the lower voxel, there is a clear dissociation between the histograms. We can represent these histograms according to their means and standard deviations, which are indicated below each graph. If the difference between the means is large enough compared to the standard deviation, as in the bottom graph, we can identify significant activity. The concept of functional SNR is closely related to that of **effect size** in statistics. The statistical size of an effect is not the difference in percentage signal change but rather the difference between the conditions in units of standard deviation.

In summary, just as CNR reflects how easily we can see differences between tissues, functional SNR reflects how easily we can see differences between experimental conditions. For the remainder of this book, we will focus our discussion on the ability of fMRI experiments to detect meaningful changes in brain activity. Therefore, we will use the unmodified term *SNR* to denote functional SNR, while we will use *raw SNR* to describe the signal and noise directly measured by the detector coil. We will use *CNR* to refer to the contrast sensitivity of anatomical images.

Functional SNR

The functional SNR measured in an fMRI experiment may vary over a wide range. One factor that influences functional SNR is the amplitude of the BOLD signal. As shown in Figure 9.2, a simple motor task, like periodically squeezing one's hand, may generate BOLD changes in primary motor cortex of approximately 6%, even at 1.5 T. Likewise, periodic flashing of a high-contrast visual checkerboard may cause BOLD changes of 1 to 5% or more in the primary visual cortex. As the strength of the stimulus decreases, the resulting BOLD signal change also decreases. If the hand is squeezed less frequently, or if the checkerboard is blurred and flashed at a slower rate, BOLD activity may decrease to less than 1%. In addition, signal magnitude also depends upon the area being measured. Most experimental tasks evoke activity in a set of related brain regions. For example, pressing a button whenever a bright pattern appears on a screen will elicit activity in motor regions (e.g., primary motor cortex, supplementary motor cortex, cerebellum), visual regions (e.g., primary visual cortex, inferior temporal cortex), and decision regions (e.g., prefrontal cortex). As a rule of thumb, fMRI signal changes are largest in primary motor or sensory areas and generally decrease in amplitude in regions associated with higher cognitive function.

Thought Question
Why might the amplitude of the BOLD response typically be larger in primary sensory and motor cortices than in brain regions associated with complex cognitive processes?

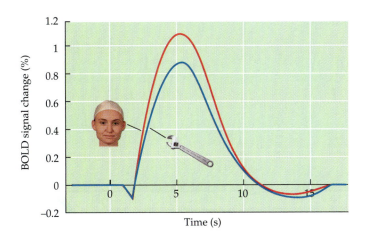

Figure 9.3 Using fMRI to examine relative activation. Activity in fMRI is rarely all or none, but is often a matter of degree. Shown are hypothetical responses of a face-sensitive region of the brain to faces and other objects. The response to each stimulus is large compared to the difference between them.

The examples in the previous section compared the BOLD signal evoked by an experimental condition to that of a resting condition. If a study compares two experimental conditions, as in a memory test comparing remembered and forgotten words, the differences between conditions are usually much smaller than the amplitude evoked by each condition itself compared to rest. This issue is illustrated in Figure 9.3. Consider the fusiform gyrus in the temporal lobe, which plays an important role in the perception of objects, including faces. If an fMRI subject views a single face presented in isolation, activity in the fusiform gyrus increases by about 1% over baseline. Although a face is a good stimulus for evoking fusiform activity, other complex stimuli, including tools, foods, and vehicles, also evoke activity in this brain region. If faces evoked, in one subject, a signal change of 1.1%, while tools evoked a signal change of 0.9%, the difference between the conditions would be a mere 0.2%. This example is not atypical, in that many fMRI experiments investigate differential activation of a single area by two or more stimulus types.

The second factor that determines functional SNR is the overall noise within the data. The noise in fMRI studies is composed of many sources, and it is usually quantified as the standard deviation of the voxel intensity over time. Noise is usually larger than the magnitude of the BOLD signal changes that we wish to measure. Some of the noise in fMRI data results from thermal fluctuations, as in all MR imaging. However, thermal noise only contributes a small portion of the noise in functional SNR. Other, more significant noise components include artifacts such as head motion, physiological variations related to heart rate and respiration, unrelated neural activity, and cognitive or behavioral variability in how the subject performs an experimental task. These sources are discussed individually in the following sections.

To demonstrate what fMRI data look like at different functional SNR levels, Figure 9.4 presents data from a simulated experiment that consisted of two alternations of task and nontask blocks. As SNR decreases, it becomes progressively more difficult to identify task-related changes in the data. At the highest value used, SNR = 4.0, the task and nontask blocks are clearly visible, but at the lowest value used, SNR = 0.5, the noise completely conceals any visible experimental effect.

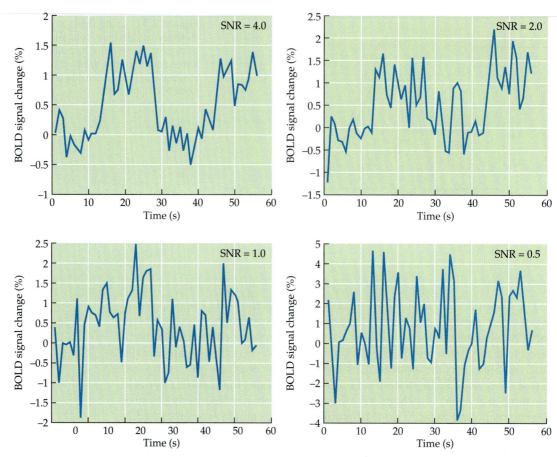

Figure 9.4 The effects of SNR upon fMRI data. Shown are simulated time courses of a blocked-design task at four different signal-to-noise levels (4.0, 2.0, 1.0, and 0.5). At high signal-to-noise levels, the transitions between blocks are obvious, but as SNR decreases, the blocks become harder to identify.

Sources of Noise in fMRI

power spectrum A representation of the strength of different frequency components within a signal. The Fourier transform converts a signal (i.e., changes in intensity over time) into its power spectrum.

At a given field strength, the overall signal is mostly determined by the amount of magnetization available. However, the behavior of noise is more complex. Noise in fMRI data has both temporal and spatial features. The temporal features can be seen in Figure 9.5, which presents the **power spectrum** of a single experimental run. A power spectrum shows what frequencies are present in a time series of data and is created using the Fourier transform. Peaks within a power spectrum can be thought of as regular oscillations in the intensity of the given voxel, reflecting changes over time due to the respiratory cycle, cardiac pulsations, or BOLD activity. These temporal components of fMRI noise are not distributed equally throughout the image, but rather have particular spatial distributions. Figure 9.6 displays an image of relative noise for a single run of an experiment in which subjects passively viewed high-contrast pictures. The most obvious feature of this image is that much of the anatomical structure of the brain is recovered, indicating that the variability inside the brain is much higher than the variability outside of the brain. If noise were constant across the image, then the image would be a uniform gray. Instead, the edges of the brain and even some of the interior structure are clearly recovered.

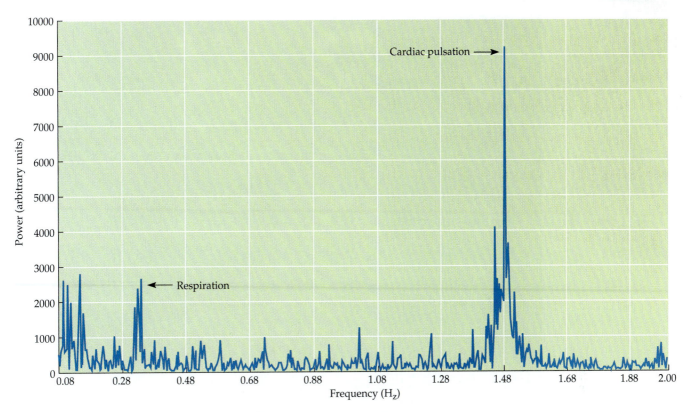

Figure 9.5   The power spectrum of an experimental voxel over a single run. The experimental task used an event-related design in which 1-s duration visual stimuli were separated by 9-s intervals. Visible are clear peaks at the respiratory and cardiac frequencies. The accuracy of these peaks was verified by physiological monitoring. To detect such high-frequency changes, a single slice was sampled at a TR of 250 ms. Note that the lowest frequencies are excluded from this plot because the very high power at low frequencies obscures the effects shown.

There are five main causes of temporal and spatial noise in fMRI: intrinsic thermal noise within the subject and the scanner electronics; system noise associated with imperfections in the scanner hardware; artifacts resulting from head motion, respiration, heart rate, and other physiological processes; variability in neuronal activity associated with non-task-related brain processes; and changes in behavioral performance and cognitive strategy. We discuss each of these sources of noise in the following sections.

Thermal Noise

All MR imaging, whether anatomical or functional, is subject to **thermal noise,** or changes in signal intensity over time due to thermal motion of electrons within the subject and within the scanner electronics. Thermal noise may also be called intrinsic noise. To understand the possible sources of thermal noise, recall from Chapter 2 the sequence of events that underlies acquisition of MRI data. Following its excitation, the sample (e.g., the brain), emits a radiofrequency signal that is detected by the receiver coil. The signal is then processed by a series of electronics hardware, replete with many conductors, resistors, and power amplifiers. Within each physical component in the receiver chain, free electrons collide with atoms, resulting in an exchange of energy. The higher the temperature of the sys-

thermal noise Fluctuations in MR signal intensity over space or time that are caused by thermal motion of electrons within the sample or scanner hardware.

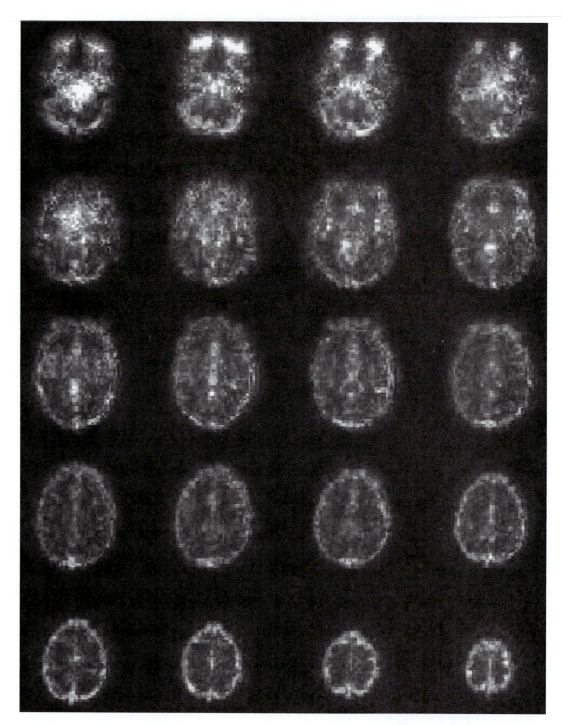

Figure 9.6　A map of noise across the brain. Shown is the standard deviation of a single experimental run during a simultaneous motor/visual task. Voxels with high standard deviation are shown in white, while voxels with low standard deviation are shown in black. Note that the standard deviation is not uniform across the image. Instead, it is greatest inside the brain, with areas of greatest standard deviation (i.e., highest noise) around the edges.

tem, the more frequent the collisions and the greater the distortion of the current signal. Thermal noise also depends on the frequency bandwidth of the receiver and the resistance in the detector coil. Theoretical formulations of thermal noise by Edelstein and colleagues have shown that it increases linearly with field strength. So thermal noise will be approximately twice as large at 3.0 T as at 1.5 T.

Because the magnitude of thermal contributions to the MR signal varies randomly over time, ideal thermal noise has no spatial structure. That is, the magnitude of thermal noise within a voxel is independent of its spatial location. However, the effect of a given magnitude of thermal noise does depend on the voxel's signal amplitude. Consider first a voxel within the brain. The voxel has very high raw signal and appears relatively bright on functional images. Thermal noise added during image acquisition may add or subtract from the measured intensity values, given high raw SNR, resulting in a Gaussian distribution of intensity values over time. Now consider a voxel in air outside of the brain. This voxel has negligible raw signal and appears to be very dark on functional images. Because there is no signal in the voxel, noise can only have an additive effect. That is, if the value of the voxel would be zero in the absence of noise, thermal noise will result in some small positive value. The resulting distribution will have a lower bound at zero and will be positively skewed. From a statistical perspective, the distribution of image intensities outside the brain has a Rayleigh distribution, not a Gaussian distribution as inside the brain. (A good discussion of the effects of raw signal upon noise distributions is found in the book by Buxton indicated in the references.)

System Noise

A second factor that contributes to variability in the measured fMRI signal is **system noise,** which generally describes variations or discrepancies in the function of the imaging hardware. Some common causes of system noise are static field inhomogeneities due to imperfect shimming, nonlinearities and instabilities in the gradient fields, and off-resonance or loading effects in the radiofrequency transmitter and receiver coils. Problems with the homogeneity of the main field cause spatial distortions or intensity variations across the images. One particularly important form of system noise is **scanner drift,** which results in slow changes in voxel intensity over time (Figure 9.7).

system noise Fluctuations in MR signal intensity over space or time that are caused by imperfect functioning of the scanner hardware.

scanner drift Slow changes in voxel intensity over time.

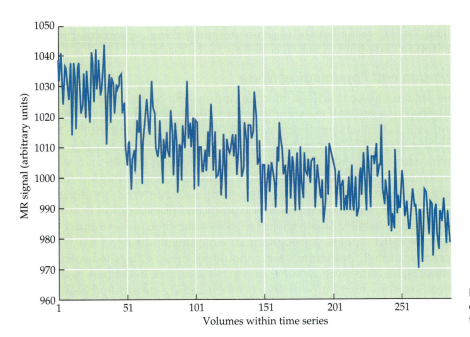

Figure 9.7 Scanner drift. Low-frequency changes in MR signal are collectively known as drift.

physiological noise Fluctuations in MR signal intensity over space and time due to physiological activity of the human body. Sources of physiological noise include motion, respiration, cardiac activity, and metabolic reactions.

Although drift can result from any of several different sources, a common cause is change in the resonant frequency of hydrogen protons associated with subtle changes in the strength of the static field. Even though it is powered by superconducting currents, the main magnet still experiences minute drifts in stability over time, often on the order of a few tenths of a part per million per day. Expressed in terms of field strength and resonant frequency, such drifts might reflect an alteration in the main field strength on the order of 0.005 of a Gauss and variation in the resonant frequency by a few Hertz. Small changes in the local strength of the magnetic field, if uncorrected, can lead to signal instability and spatial displacement. Similarly, gradient nonlinearities and instabilities affect the shape and location of the recorded images from one time point to another, leading to spatially dependent variations in noise over time. These two problems are discussed in detail in Chapter 4.

Scanner drift may result from factors other than system noise. In one of our subjects, we noticed an odd pattern of spatially correlated signal drift. Within the first run, voxels at the very back of the brain slowly but consistently increased in intensity, while those at the front of the brain steadily decreased in intensity. The cause of this puzzling change was revealed by examination of the position of the head over time. Over the course of the run, the head slowly moved downward, consistent with a slow leak in the vacuum pack that held the subject's head in place! Head movement can cause spatial distortions as well, notably on anatomical images collected using three-dimensional acquisition methods.

Problems with the radiofrequency coils can have several effects. If the frequency of the excitation pulse does not match the resonant frequency of the sample, excitation will be inefficient and intensity variation may be introduced, causing the MR signal to fluctuate over time. Another problem results from the fact that the receiver coil is coupled to the sample via mutual inductance, meaning that a change in the current or voltage distribution in the sample induces a corresponding change in the current and voltage carried by the receiver coil. Thus, the properties of the imaged object influence the noise measured in the receiver coil. Because induction of sample noise in the receiver coil reduces sensitivity, an optimum coupling scheme that matches impedance in the sample and the receiver coil is desired. This matching process is often referred to as achieving the dominant loading factor for the object being imaged (i.e., a particular subject's brain) so that optimal mutual coupling can be reached.

Motion and Physiological Noise

So far we have considered thermal and system noise, which result from intrinsic properties of the scanning system. If we scan an inert phantom (i.e., a plastic ball filled with fluid), we will still measure significant thermal and system noise. The human brain, though, is hardly inert. Muscles contract with each breath or heartbeat. Blood pulses through arteries and veins. The metabolic demands of neurons drive chemical reactions needed for subsequent activity. This activity, in all the senses of that word, results in variations in fMRI signal due to motion artifacts and **physiological noise.**

Signal variability due to subject motion is common and extremely disruptive for fMRI studies. Throughout an experiment, a subject may shift the position of their head; move their shoulders, arms, or legs to become more comfortable; and swallow more due to nervousness. In the best cases, small head motions may be partially corrected during data preprocessing (see Chapter 10), while in the worst cases, large motions may render data completely uninterpretable. Small-scale motions result from the regular oscillatory activity of the heart and lungs. This activity is much faster and more periodic than large-scale head motion, introducing a different set of challenges. If the rate of sampling is fast enough, it may be possible to characterize and minimize motion due to heart and lung activity during preprocessing (see the 1995 work of Hu and colleagues).

But in most fMRI studies, motion due to cardiac activity, in particular, is too fast to be sampled effectively (i.e., for TRs >500 ms), and if the TR is long enough (i.e., >2500 ms), respiratory activity may likewise be undersampled. Under those circumstances, the variabilities associated with these sources of motion are still present but become distributed throughout the fMRI time series in a manner that may be difficult to identify or correct. The misattribution of periodic noise sources by undersampling is known as **aliasing** (see Chapter 10). Respiration also introduces variability in the fMRI signal through systematic distortions in the magnetic field. As the subject breathes, the expansion of the lungs casts a magnetic susceptibility "shadow," influencing field strength and homogeneity of the magnetic field and altering signal intensity throughout the image (including areas outside of the brain itself), as demonstrated by Raj and colleagues in 2001.

It is important to recognize that the effects of motion in fMRI are usually not due to motion during image acquisition and resulting decrease in raw SNR. Recall from Chapter 5 that typical fMRI pulse sequences (e.g., spiral or echo-planar gradient-echo imaging) have very short TEs, often about 30 to 40 ms. There is little opportunity for motion to occur during such a short acquisition window. Motion causes problems because of variability across the time series of images, which is critical for functional SNR. A voxel near the edge of the brain, for example, may begin by containing mostly gray matter but end up, after motion, containing mostly cerebrospinal fluid. Note that if motion were completely random, then it would introduce noise that reduces SNR but that could be ameliorated with signal averaging. Motion is rarely random, though, and is often correlated with the experimental task, as, for example, when subjects hold their breath each time they press a response button. Motion also introduces both spatial correlations, since adjacent voxels move together, and temporal correlations, since movements are extended in time. We discuss strategies for preventing and correcting signal changes due to a common form of motion, head motion, in the following chapter.

While motion is a serious and damaging component of variability in fMRI, it is not the only one. Since the BOLD effect depends on the interaction between several physiological factors, including blood flow, blood volume, and oxygen metabolism, fluctuations in any of these factors will influence the observed signal. In 2001, Kruger and Glover investigated the spatial distribution of physiological noise, separating it into one component (σ_B) associated with variability in the transverse relaxation rate and another component (σ_{NB}) associated with cardiac and respiratory motion. Since the former component, like BOLD contrast itself, results from susceptibility-related signal changes, its magnitude depends upon TE. The latter component, in contrast, is independent of TE. Kruger and Glover found that the spatial distribution of these two components differed (Figure 9.8A–F). The former was much greater in gray matter than in white matter, while the latter was equally distributed throughout the brain. Furthermore, σ_B was typically about twice as large as σ_{NB}. These results suggest that physiological noise, rather than thermal or system noise, is the dominant source of variability in fMRI studies, especially at higher field strengths.

aliasing The sampling of a signal at a rate insufficient to resolve the highest frequencies that are present. The energy at those frequencies becomes artifactually expressed at lower frequencies, distorting the measured signal.

Figure 9.8 Distribution of physiological noise. For one subject, images showing anatomy (A), noise from all sources (B), physiological noise due to variation in blood flow and metabolic processes (C), and noise due to bulk head motion and cardiac and respiratory pulsations (D). Note that the noise in (C) is concentrated within gray matter, while that in (D) is more uniform, save for effects around the edge of the brain. For comparison are shown images from a phantom of noise from all sources (E) and physiological noise (F). Not surprisingly, physiological noise is negligible in the phantom. (From Kruger and Glover, 2001.)

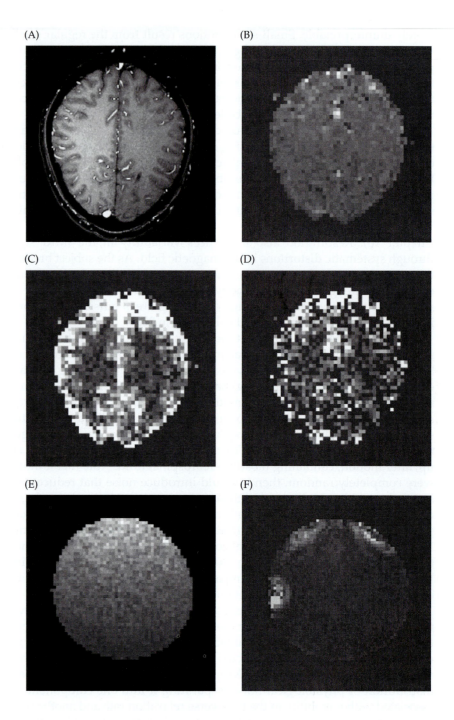

Non-Task-Related Neural Variability

In the party analogy described at the beginning of this chapter, we noted that after you had asked a question of your companion and awaited his answer, other conversations were occurring around you that were unrelated to your question and thus were constituents of the noise. However, unlike the other sources of noise discussed thus far, the words spoken in these other conversations were legitimate responses evoked by other questions asked by other speakers. These unrelated conversations, however, were not temporally synchronized to your question.

Let's consider an fMRI experiment in which we stroke the thumb with a brush to investigate which brain areas are activated by somatosensory stimuli. At the same time that the subject's brain experiences this discrete task-related sensory stimulus, the subject is also hearing the sounds of the scanner gradients, receiving varying visual stimuli as he/she looks around within the scanner, and activating brain systems associated with memory and mental imagery as he/she thinks about appointments for later that day. All of these stimuli—internal and external—activate neural processes that translate into varying metabolic demands and thus influence BOLD contrast. What makes us consider these activity-evoked BOLD changes as noise is that they are unrelated to the stimulus of interest. However, if we changed our experiment to investigate the response of the brain to these other stimulus events, we would find reliable regions of activation. For example, synchronizing our analysis to our subject's eye movements would reveal activation of a part of the brain called the frontal eye fields. This illustrates that the task-related responses in which we are interested occur within a highly active brain where routine neural processes are altering BOLD contrast at every moment. We can exploit the temporal synchrony between our stimulus of interest and evoked changes in BOLD contrast by signal averaging. We will discuss this important strategy for improving functional SNR at the end of this chapter.

Behavioral and Cognitive Variability

An often underappreciated source of noise in fMRI data comes from variability in how subjects perform the experimental task. In general, the more complex the task, the more performance will vary across time and across subjects. Consider three sorts of common experimental designs: passive viewing of a visual stimulus, pressing a button in response to an auditory stimulus, and remembering a set of digits over a delay interval. Even though these are all very simple designs, the mental operations they evoke will differ across trials.

The passive viewing design requires no experimental response of any form, which suggests that the evoked brain activity should be the same on every trial. However, this assumption fails to consider changes in arousal and attention over time. Arousal levels always wax and wane over the course of a scanner session, with accompanying changes in brain activity. Even when fully alert, subjects are often thinking about something other than the experimental task. As is discussed in Box 11.2, specific sets of brain regions have been implicated in daydreaming and other nontask processes.

Additional complications are introduced by tasks that require the subject to generate a response. The time it takes to execute a simple motor behavior, such as pressing a button or speaking a name in response to a stimulus, is known as **reaction time** or **response time,** depending on the experimental task. If the task simply requires detection of a stimulus, the behavioral measure is reaction time and is typically around a few hundred milliseconds. But if the task requires the subjects to make some judgment about a stimulus, such as whether or not they remember it from earlier in the experiment, then the behavioral measure is known as response time. Since response times require additional cognitive processes, they are always longer than reaction times. Depending on the experiment, response time may be as short as 300 ms or as long as several seconds. In any experiment, there will be both inter-subject and intrasubject variability in reaction or response time. One source of variability is a **speed–accuracy trade-off.** For almost all experimental

reaction time The time required for someone to make a simple motor response to the presentation of a stimulus. Note that this is distinct from response time, which applies to situations in which someone must choose between two or more possible responses.

response time The time required for someone to execute a choice between two or more possible responses. Note that this is distinct from reaction time, which applies to situations when only one possible response is present.

speed–accuracy trade-off The improvement in the speed of a response at the expense of accuracy, or vice versa, within an experimental task.

tasks, subjects can perform the task more accurately if they do it more slowly. Imagine that you are shown a series of photographs of faces and are asked to judge the emotion they are expressing. If you try to guess the emotion as quickly as possible, you will make many mistakes, especially on more complex emotions like disgust. Conversely, if you spend more time considering each face carefully, your accuracy will increase but your response times will slow.

Thought Question

How could differences in task performance confound fMRI studies that compare different subject groups, such as young and elderly adults?

Speed–accuracy trade-offs are important to consider when deciding what instructions to give subjects in an fMRI experiment. Since increasing one factor decreases the other, it is generally impossible for subjects to maximize both. That is, your subjects will not be able to respond as accurately as possible while doing so as fast as possible. For many experiments, therefore, it is reasonable to tell subjects, "Respond as quickly as you can while maintaining a low error rate." This reduces variability in error rate across subjects, especially if you provide feedback about errors and the target error rate. Alternatively, you can emphasize one factor but not the other. Accuracy should be emphasized when the characteristics of the response are critical. In a study comparing remembered words to forgotten words, for example, the response that the subject makes determines in which category a stimulus is placed. If the subject responds inaccurately, then the integrity of the analyses will be severely compromised. Speed should be emphasized when the processes of interest would change if the subject responded completely accurately. Tasks used in the study of attention often emphasize speed, because the effects of attention on behavior may disappear if the subject takes a long time to respond.

Shown in Figure 9.9A and B are histograms of response time data from a target detection task conducted as part of an fMRI experiment. While the input stimulus was similar on every trial, the output behavior differed considerably. On some trials, subjects responded in less than 500 ms, while on others, they did not respond for more than 1500 ms. Does the neuronal activity remain the same regardless of the time of the button press? To answer this question, we refer to the study from Menon and colleagues discussed in Chapter 8 (see Figure 8.14A). Recall that between some regions (i.e., from visual to supplementary motor), the relative timing of BOLD activity was dependent upon reaction time, but between others (e.g., from supplementary to primary motor), the BOLD timing was independent of reaction time. These results clearly indicate that the relation between reaction time and brain activity is location-dependent: Some cognitive processes are delayed with increasing response time while others are not. To deal with this issue, many research studies include reaction time, or some other behavioral measure, as a covariate in their analyses.

Strategy changes are a third source of task-induced variability. In many cognitive tasks, there may be more than one strategy that can be used to solve a task. A frequently used task in psychology experiments is learning a set of digits, like "36013," and remembering them over a few seconds. One

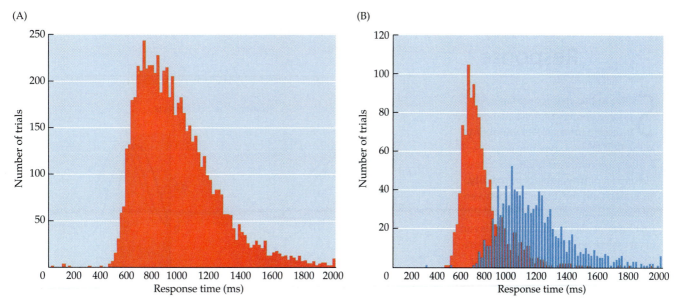

Figure 9.9   Variability in response time. (A) The distribution of response times across approximately 10,000 trials of a simple decision task. Note that the distribution is highly positively skewed, with a negative bound at about 400 ms and a mean of about 800 ms. (B) Distributions from two individual subjects. Note that even though these subjects were performing the same task, their patterns of performance across trials were very different.

strategy for doing this task is rehearsing, which involves repeating the set over and over again until it is time to make a response. Another common strategy is chunking, which involves breaking down the digit set into smaller, but memorable, numbers. A subject might, for example, remember "36013" by labeling "360" as the number of degrees in a circle and coding "13" as an unlucky number. Both strategies may be used by the same subject at different times within one experiment. Yet the strategies may be sufficiently distinct that they activate different brain regions, and thus the total activity would reflect some combination of the two.

Improving Functional SNR through Experimental Design

To improve functional SNR, we can attempt to increase the amplitude of the BOLD signal, decrease the noise, or do both. In this and the following sections, we will discuss three different strategies for doing so: improving experimental design, increasing field strength, and averaging data across trials.

Although hardware and computational approaches will dominate this discussion, it is important to recognize that very simple choices in the experimental design can have a large effect upon functional SNR. Consider an experiment designed to evoke BOLD activity in the primary visual cortex. Almost any visual stimulus will suffice, whether a simple checkerboard pattern or a picture of a face, a moving array of dots or a rotating visual scene. But even though all of these activate the primary visual cortex, they do not all activate it equally. High-contrast patterns with many visible sharp edges will induce very large activity, especially if flickered at a relatively rapid rate (e.g., about 10 Hz). But if the flicker frequency is much slower or faster, or if the contrast of the stimulus is reduced, then the measured BOLD activity

BOX 9.1 Intersubject Variability in the Hemodynamic Response

So far in this chapter we have considered sources of noise that contribute to **intrasubject variability** in the BOLD hemodynamic response. It is also important to evaluate the possible impact of **intersubject variability.** To understand the distinction between intrasubject and intersubject variability, first imagine that a single subject is run in an experiment that consists of 50 trials in which he/she squeezes his/her hand when he/she sees a shape appear. Even though the subject sees the same stimulus and performs the same action in each trial, the measured fMRI signal will be different on each trial due to the sources of intrasubject variability described in the previous sections. Now imagine that two different subjects are run in the same experiment. Each subject's data will have intrasubject variability that contributes to variability across trials, but there may be additional intersubject differences. For example, the shape of the hemodynamic response could be different, with one subject's response peaking at 5 s and the other's at 7 s. Intersubject variability has important consequences for statistical analyses.

The idea of intersubject variability in the shape of the hemodynamic response was tested by Aguirre and colleagues in 1998. They collected fMRI data from 40 subjects who participated in one or more sessions of a simple response task. During the scanner sessions, subjects watched a small cross in the center of the display. The cross flickered every 16 s, at which time the subjects pressed buttons with both thumbs. The 16-s interstimulus interval was chosen to allow the hemodynamic response to return to baseline between successive stimuli. The data were acquired using a gradient-echo EPI sequence at 1.5 T, with a TR of 2000 ms and a TE of 50 ms. The authors used an

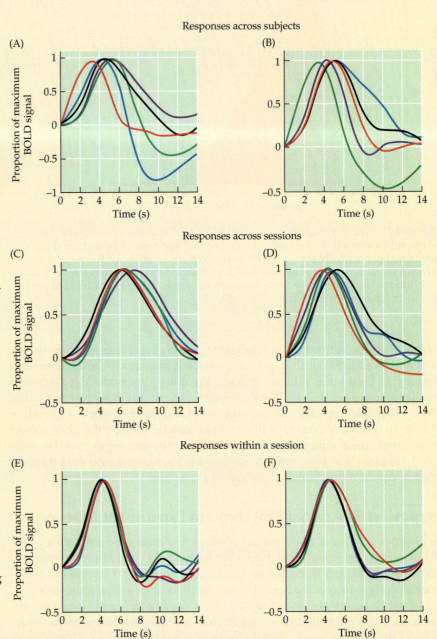

Figure 9.10 Variability in the hemodynamic response across subjects. The reproducibility of the fMRI hemodynamic response was examined. When hemodynamic responses across subjects (A and B) were compared, the shape of the response was highly variable. There was much less variability in the hemodynamic responses from a single subject collected across sessions (C and D) and even less variability in the responses collected within a single session (E and F). Note that each pair of charts shows two different sets of subjects, sessions, or responses. (After Aguirre et al., 1998.)

BOX 9.1 *(continued)*

intrasubject variability Variability in the fMRI data from a single subject associated with thermal, system, and physiological noise, as well as with variability in the pattern of brain activity during task performance.

intersubject variability Variability in fMRI data across a set of subjects; it includes the factors associated with intrasubject variability, along with between-subjects differences in task performance and physiology.

anatomical region-of-interest approach to identify the central sulcus and surrounding gray matter in each subject. The resulting ROIs included both the primary sensory cortex, which is immediately posterior to the central sulcus, and the primary motor cortex, which is immediately anterior. Within this ROI, they identified all voxels with significant power in the BOLD signal at the task frequency of 0.0625 Hz and its two succeeding harmonics (i.e., integer multiples of the task frequency) using a Fourier analysis. They then determined the average response in the active voxels across all trials and used that average as the estimated hemodynamic response for that subject. The experimental hypothesis to be tested was whether there was significant intersubject variability, defined as greater variability between different sessions of different subjects compared to different sessions of the same subject.

Across 32 subjects who each participated in a single session, there was considerable variability in the number of active voxels within the ROI (from 6 to 91), in the amplitude of the measured hemodynamic response (from 1 to 3%), and in the latency to peak response (from 3 to 6 s). The variability in the responses from different subjects was then compared to the variability in repeated sessions from the same subject. The results were striking (Figure 9.10A–F). Across

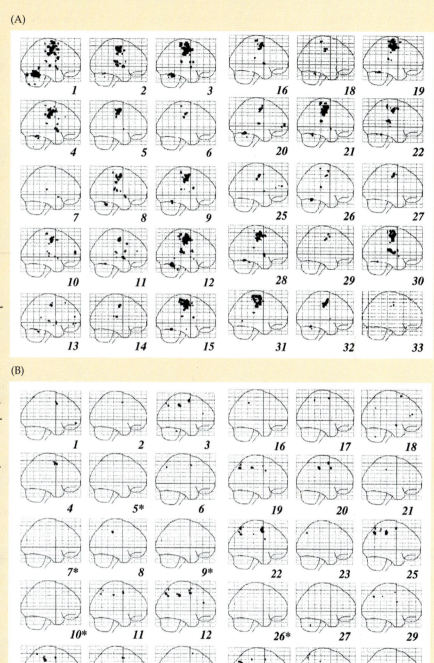

Figure 9.11 Reproducibility of fMRI activity across sessions. In what is likely a record, a single subject participated in 99 fMRI sessions, split among motor, visual, and cognitive paradigms. Even though the experimental procedures were repeated in exactly the same manner on every session, right down to repeating the quite familiar experimental instructions, the pattern of activity differed considerably across sessions (A, motor; B, cognitive). (From McGonigle et al., 2000.)

BOX 9.1 *(continued)*

multiple runs within a single scanner session, the hemodynamic responses recorded from a single subject showed very little variability (Figure 9.10E and F). A comparison of multiple sessions from the same subject across different days showed that the data variability increased by a factor of 3.5, but the hemodynamic response was still generally similar across the sessions (Figure 9.10C and D). However, across different subjects, there was more than 16 times as much variability as found in a single session, providing conclusive evidence for the presence of intersubject variability in the shape of the hemodynamic response (Figure 9.10A and B).

It is important to note that although the form of the hemodynamic response is generally similar for a given subject across different sessions, this similarity does not necessarily extend to the spatial extent of activation. That is, active voxels usually have the same time course across sessions, but the number of voxels that are active will differ. This point was illustrated in a heroic study conducted by Mc-Gonigle and colleagues in 2000, for which a single subject participated in 99 separate scanner sessions across a period of 2 months. Three blocked-design experimental tasks were used, each for 33 sessions: finger tapping, passive visual stimulation, and random-number generation. Every session was identically run on the same scanner, with the same room lighting and ambient sounds, with the same operator giving the same instructions. Indeed, the authors note that the subject had the same "I've done this before" thoughts before every session! When they compared the activation maps across sessions, the authors found that there were striking differences in the patterns of activation (Figure 9.11A and B). On some sessions, there were very clear activation foci in areas of interest, such as the motor cortex and the cerebellum for the finger tapping task. However, other sessions had almost no activation. Within the more cognitive random-number generation task, there was even greater variability in the overall pattern of activation that changed dramatically from session to session. These results demonstrate clearly that the data recorded from a single subject in a single research session are subject to considerable variability, even in very simple tasks that evoke robust fMRI activity.

---

will be smaller. Whenever possible, it is critical for researchers to select stimuli that will evoke large and reproducible signal changes.

Functional SNR can also be improved by minimizing the influence of noise components. Some aspects of noise prevention are the responsibility of the MR center and not the individual researcher. By ensuring that the MR scanner electronics are as stable as possible and by preventing extraneous radiofrequency signals from entering the scanner room, the research center can improve the stability of all data collected on that scanner. Researchers should become familiar with the quality assurance procedures at their MRI center so they can recognize such problems as they arise, even if they cannot prevent them from occurring.

Other issues can be addressed by individual researchers, especially through minimization of physiological and cognitive variability. The effects of head motion can be ameliorated with subject restraint and training, as we will discuss in Chapter 10. Training also improves understanding of the experimental task and allows subjects to attain a steady-state performance level before entering the scanner session. For many of our experimental tasks, we train our subjects in practice sessions ahead of time to minimize the learning effects or strategy changes that typically occur at the beginning of an experiment. Subjects are carefully instructed so that they know what is expected, especially with regard to what strategies they should adopt to perform a behavioral task.

Improving Functional SNR by Increasing Field Strength

In many circumstances, the primary determinant of functional SNR is the amount of net magnetization, which is proportional to the strength of the static magnetic field. Remember, however, that the signal we measure in fMRI does not depend solely on the net magnetization. Because the net magnetization must be tipped into the transverse plane to become measurable, other effects come into play, including T_1 and T_2 relaxation, pulse sequence parameters, motion-related contrast preparations (e.g., perfusion, diffusion), and susceptibility effects, all of which were discussed in Chapter 5. These latter factors temper the gains associated with strong magnetic fields, with important consequences for BOLD fMRI.

Raw SNR and Spatial Resolution

One solution for increasing the amplitude of the BOLD signal is to increase the scanner field strength. With increasing field strength, an increasing proportion of spins will align parallel with the static field, and thus net magnetization will increase. The fundamental rule relating field strength to theoretical signal is simple: As static field strength increases linearly, raw signal increases quadratically (i.e., with the square of the field strength). Thus, a 3.0-T scanner would measure 4 times as much raw signal as a 1.5-T scanner. In contrast, thermal noise scales linearly with the field strength, so a 3.0-T scanner measures 2 times as much thermal noise as a 1.5-T scanner. When we divide the quadratic increase in signal by the linear increase in noise, we find that the raw SNR only increases linearly with the field strength. (Recall from Chapter 1 the first whole-body fMRI scanner used by Damadian and colleagues in 1977 was named "Indomitable." The field strength of that scanner was only 0.05 T, resulting in a theoretical raw signal only about 1/900th and a raw SNR 1/30th as strong as in a modern 1.5-T scanner!)

Indeed, researchers have demonstrated these benefits using various experimental protocols. A very early study was reported in 1993 by Turner and colleagues, who compared visual cortex activity at 1.5 T and 4.0 T. They collected gradient-echo EPI images on both scanners using generally similar procedures. However, the TE was different between the scanners, namely 40 ms at 1.5 T and 25 ms at 4.0 T, because T_2^* increases with field strength, increasing susceptibility distortions at longer TEs. They used a simple blocked design that alternated blocks of flashing lights and darkness every 30 s (ten images). They found that the evoked MR signal was much larger at 4.0 T than at 1.5 T, with signal changes of 15% and 5%, respectively, within a selected set of voxels within visual cortex (Figure 9.12). These results suggest that raw SNR increases roughly linearly with the field strength.

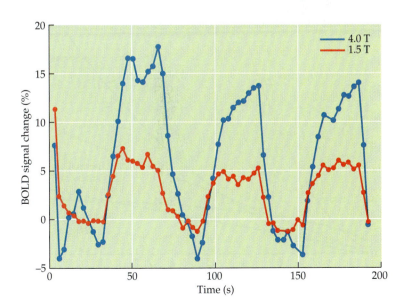

Figure 9.12 An early study of field strength effects in fMRI. Turner and colleagues measured changes in visual cortex activity at 1.5 T and 4.0 T. Approximately 3 times as much signal was recorded at the higher field strength.

partial volume effects The combination, within a single voxel, of signal contributions from two or more distinct tissue types or functional regions.

As raw SNR increases, so does the total signal recovered from each voxel. This allows the image to be parceled into smaller voxels while maintaining sufficient SNR within each, improving spatial resolution. Because many phenomena of interest, such as the ocular dominance columns we discussed in Box 8.2, have small spatial scale, an improvement in spatial resolution can greatly improve the functional resolution of an experiment. Studies of ocular dominance columns, for example, have been carried out at 4.0 T, and scanners with field strength approaching 9.0 T have been installed for human imaging. Reductions in voxel size also minimize **partial volume effects.** If a small voxel is primarily composed of active neural tissue that is responsive to the experimental task, it will generate a larger BOLD signal change than the same amount of active neural tissue located within a larger voxel. For this reason, decreasing voxel sizes can result in larger BOLD signal changes from active voxels.

Functional SNR and Spatial Extent

While raw SNR depends solely on the net magnetization and thermal noise within a voxel, functional SNR also includes physiological and neural variability, which we will collectively call physiological noise. The strength of the static field has different effects upon thermal and physiological noise. While thermal noise increases linearly with increasing field strength, physiological noise increases quadratically with field strength. So, as field strength increases from 1.5 T to 3.0 T, raw signal will quadruple, thermal noise will double, and physiological noise will quadruple. These relations suggest that at very high field strengths, physiological noise may become dominant, and thus the improvement of functional SNR with increasing field strength may be considerably less than linear (i.e., smaller than for raw SNR). As shown in Figure 9.13, at high field strengths, gains in signal are offset by similar increases in physiological variability, so functional SNR will not increase indefinitely. This conclusion is supported by Kruger, Glover, and their colleagues, who demonstrated that the relative contribution of physiological noise increases with field strength. They found that at

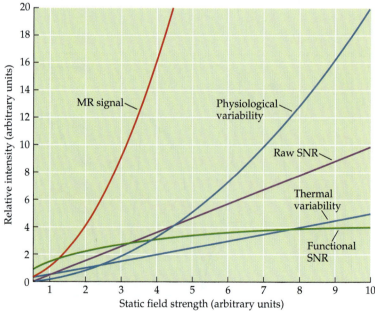

Figure 9.13 Changes in signal and noise with increasing static field strength. MR signal increases with the square of the field strength, while thermal noise increases linearly with field strength. The ratio of these quantities, raw SNR, thus increases linearly with field strength. However, because physiological noise increases with the square of field strength, functional SNR (which is dependent on both thermal and physiological noise) may reach an asymptote at high fields. Note that here the field strength is indicated in arbitrary units; the field strength beyond which such an asymptote would occur is not yet established.

1.5 T, physiological noise makes up about 40% of the total noise, but at 3.0 T, physiological noise composes more than 52%. At higher field strengths (e.g., 4.0 T), their calculations indicate that physiological noise could compose more than 60% of the total variation. As field strength increases above about 4.0 T, therefore, increases in physiological noise may counteract gains in signal (see Figure 9.13), setting an asymptotic upper limit for functional SNR.

A direct consequence of increased functional SNR is the increased spatial extent of activation (i.e., number of active voxels within a region). As functional SNR increases within a voxel, the probability of that voxel passing a threshold for statistical significance also increases. Thus, for a given experimental task, the spatial extent of activation can be used as an index of functional SNR. In their 1999 study, Yang and colleagues measured activity within the sensorimotor cortex while subjects performed a blocked-design finger tapping task at either 1.5 T or 4.0 T. Under optimum TR and TE parameters, there were approximately 70% more active voxels within the region at the higher field strength. However, when nonoptimal imaging parameters were used at 4.0 T, many fewer active voxels were identified, demonstrating the importance of other factors besides field strength for detection. Kruger and colleagues also found that spatial extent depends upon field strength, with about 40% more voxels active across the motor and visual cortices at 3.0 T compared to 1.5 T.

While the above studies used simple visual and motor tasks, a 2003 study by Krasnow and colleagues examined the effects of field strength on several different tasks, including perceptual, memory, and emotional processing paradigms. They compared activity at field strengths of 1.5 T and 3.0 T to evaluate whether more-complex tasks would evince similar increases in functional SNR with increasing field strength. They found that across brain regions there were substantial increases in the number of activated voxels with increasing field strength, with increases of 35 to 83% observed across regions in a cognitive task, suggesting that detection power throughout the brain improves with increasing field strength.

Spatial Specificity

Increasing field strength also influences the degree to which different vascular components contribute to the BOLD signal. Because the T_2^* value of blood decreases significantly with increasing field strength, the intravascular contribution, especially from the large vessels, would drop out at high field. For extravascular components, theoretical arguments by Ogawa have indicated that the spins near large vessels scale linearly with field strength, while those near small vessels increase quadratically (i.e., with the square of the field). Therefore, as field strength increases, the small-vessel extravascular component of the BOLD response increases faster than the large-vessel extravascular component. A schematic illustration of the different effects of field strength on these various BOLD signal components is given in Figure 9.14, suggesting that the extravascular component of small vessels would prevail at very high magnetic field.

Small vessels are more likely to be colocalized with the neuronal activity of interest, and thus the BOLD response may be more spatially specific at higher field strengths. In 2001, Kruger and colleagues investigated the effects of field strength (1.5 T vs. 3.0 T) upon functional SNR in different types of voxels in a combined visual and motor task. In addition to an overall increase in functional SNR, they found that functional SNR increased by

Figure 9.14 Effects of field strength upon the contributions of different vascular components to functional SNR. As field strength increases, the intravascular component of the BOLD signal drops out, leaving only the extravascular component. The small-vessel extravascular component increases more rapidly than that of large vessels, suggesting that BOLD fMRI may be more spatially specific to small vessels at high field strengths.

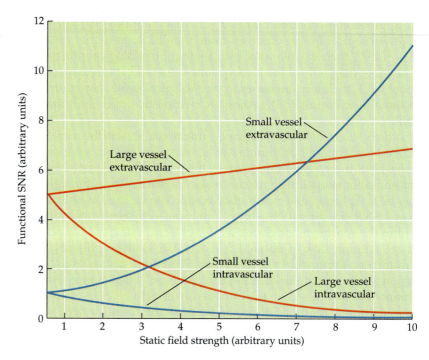

a factor of about 1.8 for small regions of activity that may correspond to large blood vessels, and by a factor of about 2.2 for larger regions of gray-matter activity, demonstrating the tendency of improved signal specificity to small vessels at high field in addition to the improved overall BOLD signal.

However, the extravascular component originating around large vessels would still be present despite its relatively reduced proportion in the overall BOLD signal (Figure 9.14). The presence of the large-vessel extravascular component at high field would still compromise spatial specificity. Thus, methods such as spin echo–based acquisition should be considered to reduce the large-vessel extravascular effect and regain spatial specificity.

The increased spatial specificity with field strength may appear to contradict the increased spatial extent discussed in the previous section. As the spatial extent of an activation increases, more voxels are labeled as being in a functional region, whereas increases in spatial specificity involve exclusion of voxels. No true contradiction exists, however. The former is an effect of increased functional SNR, which reflects our ability to determine whether or not a voxel's activity is predicted by our experimental hypotheses (see Chapter 12). We can use increased functional SNR in two ways. First, we will identify more voxels as active at the same statistical threshold. Or, by increasing our statistical threshold, we can improve our estimates of which voxels are active without changing the spatial extent of activation. Spatial specificity, on the other hand, is an effect of changes in the weighting of different vascular components. The large-vessel extravascular component does increase with field strength; it just does not increase as rapidly as the small-vessel extravascular component.

Thought Question

What do the effects illustrated in Figure 9.14 predict for studies of the fMRI initial dip (see Box 7.2)?

Signal and Noise in fMRI   **241**

Challenges of High-Field fMRI

It is also important to realize that as field strength increases, the MR properties of spin systems change. For example, the relaxation parameters T_1 and T_2^*, which both affect signal recorded in fMRI experiments, change with increasing field strength. The parameter T_1 increases with field strength (by about 30% from 1.5 T to 3.0 T), which could reduce the effective signal recovery at short TR values. The parameter T_2^* decreases with field strength (by about 25% in gray matter from 1.5 T to 3.0 T), which could reduce the time available to acquire signal. Researchers should be aware of these parameter changes and should account for them in pulse sequences. A more significant challenge comes from susceptibility artifacts that distort the uniformity of the magnetic field. Just as BOLD susceptibility effects increase with field strength, so too do signal losses in regions of the brain near air–tissue boundaries (Figure 9.15). These regions include the ventral frontal and temporal lobes, which are adjacent to air-filled sinuses. Without the use of specialized pulse sequences that can partially compensate for susceptibility-induced signal loss (see Chapter 14), imaging of these regions becomes more difficult or impossible at higher field strengths. Field inhomogeneity can also lead to geometric distortions that require specialized software and hardware for their correction.

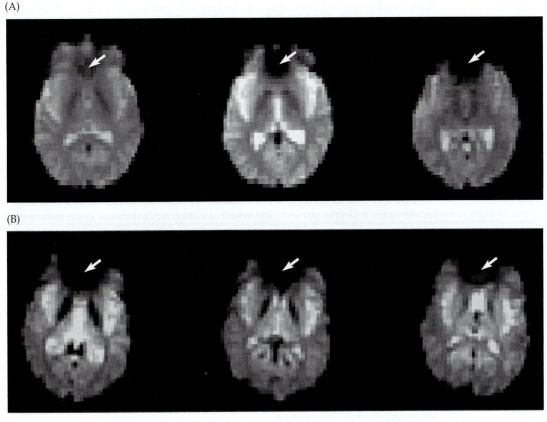

(A)

(B)

Figure 9.15 Susceptibility artifacts increase at higher field. While susceptibility artifacts at air–tissue boundaries are present on gradient-echo images at all field strengths, they increase in spatial extent at higher field strengths. Shown are images from three subjects, each of whom was scanned at both 1.5 T (A) and 4.0 T (B). Visible in all images are areas of signal loss in the ventral frontal lobe, which is indicated by the arrows. Note that the areas of signal loss are more extensive in the 4-T images.

signal averaging The combination of data from multiple instances of the same manipulation in order to improve functional SNR.

mean The average value of a set of observations.

standard error of the mean The uncertainty in the observed mean value, as calculated based upon both the standard deviation of the data and the number of data points.

Improving Functional SNR through Signal Averaging

The most powerful and widely used approach for improving the signal-to-noise ratio of fMRI data is also the simplest: **signal averaging.** Other terms for signal averaging include epoch averaging, event averaging, and trial averaging. The basic assumption of signal averaging is that the signal of interest is identical over repeated stimulus presentations, while the noise is random. With sufficient numbers of repetitions, the noise will tend to average out while the signal is preserved. Even a very weak signal is easily detected when averaged over many repetitions.

Signal averaging requires a reliable temporal relationship between the task event and the hemodynamic response. If subjects are required to make a complex decision about a visual stimulus, then it is possible that the neural activity associated with a decision outcome may vary over a period of seconds. The hemodynamic events associated with that neural activity might have a similar temporal variability. A signal average synchronized to the onset of the visual stimulus may result in an average hemodynamic response that has been blurred over time due to the temporal variability of the decision process. In this case, a signal average synchronized to the subject's button press may reduce that temporal variability. Also, the evoked stimulus is assumed to be constant across repetitions. If the signal diminishes over repetitions due to fatigue or habituation, then signal averaging will have limited value. Signal averaging does not require an explicit model of the noise, but it does require that the noise have a random relationship with the task event of interest. Artifacts or physiological noise synchronized to a stimulus or response event will be enhanced by signal averaging.

> ### Thought Question
> Recall the difference between detection of active voxels and estimation of the time course of activity. Which ability, detection or estimation, do you think would be most affected by signal averaging and why?

Note that we describe here the effects of signal averaging upon data collected from a single subject, for which averaging improves both estimation and detection power. However, intersubject averaging is also critical for fMRI studies. At the most general level, averaging across subjects provides additional data samples that improve the estimates of the effects of interest. Taken this way, intersubject averaging has similar salutary effects upon data stability as intrasubject averaging, and the following discussion can be easily extended to more than one subject. Yet combining data across subjects has a second, more important purpose: it allows researchers to make inferences about the representativeness of an experimental effect within the population. We consider statistical methods for combining data across subjects in Chapter 12.

Effects of Averaging on Estimation of the Hemodynamic Response

In statistical terms, the result of averaging multiple observations (e.g., time point 1 across trials) is known as the **mean,** and its uncertainty is known as the **standard error of the mean.** The fundamental rule of signal averaging can be

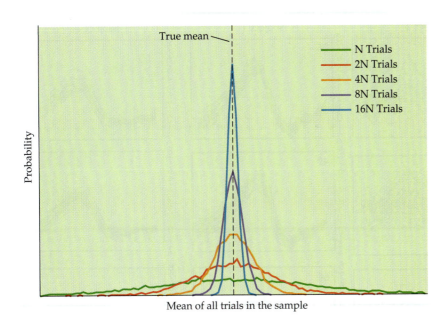

Figure 9.16   Reduction in the standard error of the mean with increasing number of trials sampled. As the number of trials in the sample increases, the precision with which the estimated mean of a sample improves, but only with the square root of the number of trials.

stated as follows: the standard error of the sample mean decreases with the square root of the number of independent observations (Figure 9.16). Let us consider the implication of this rule for fMRI data. Consider the MR signal observed in one voxel in a single trial. We can think of the data at each time point in the trial as composed of two parts, signal in the form of the hemodynamic response and additive Gaussian noise. As we know from Figure 9.4, the amplitude of the noise is generally much greater than the signal, so it is often difficult to see the hemodynamic response on single trials. Now, what happens to our data if we collect a second trial and then average it with the first? Since the noise follows a Gaussian (or normal) distribution, small values are more likely than extreme values. If there is a very large amount of noise at time point 1 in the first trial, it is unlikely that there will again be a large amount of noise at that time point in the second trial. Thus, extreme values will tend to be reduced. Using real numbers, if the noise has a standard deviation of 10 units on each trial, averaging 2 trials will reduce the noise by a factor of √2, to a standard deviation of about 7 units. Averaging 10 trials will reduce the noise by √10, to a standard deviation of about 3 units. The number of trials averaged can be thought of as the **sample size** for statistical purposes. In short, to double experimental SNR, one must collect four times as many trials.

Signal averaging, therefore, does not increase signal, but instead decreases noise. For fMRI data, as more trials are averaged, the amplitude of the hemodynamic response does not increase, but it can be characterized with better and better precision. The effects of signal averaging upon **estimation** of the hemodynamic response can be seen in Figure 9.17. In this experiment, we collected a very large number of experimental trials (>150) for each of two subjects in a visual stimulation task. In each trial, a single high-contrast checkerboard stimulus was presented for 500 ms. FMRI data were acquired using a gradient-echo echo-planar pulse sequence (TR: 1000 ms; TE: 40 ms) at 1.5 T. Within each subject, a region of interest in the medial occipital lobe was identified, and the mean activity within that region was measured in each of the 150+ trials. Each plot in the figure shows a set of 20 hemodynamic responses derived by averaging a different number of trials, from 1 to 64. So, the first

sample size   The number of observations that are made by an experiment. For fMRI data, sample size can refer to the number of trials for a given subject or to the number of subjects within an experiment.

estimation   Measurement of the pattern of change over time within an active voxel in response to the experimental manipulation.

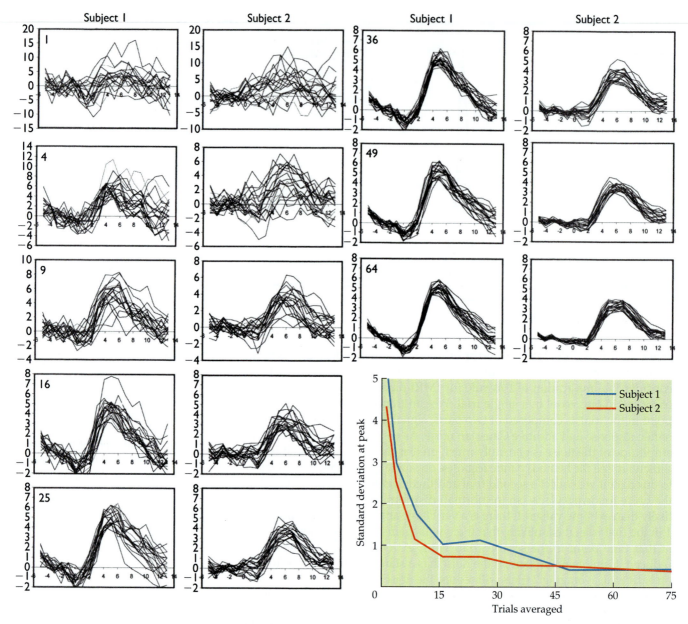

Figure 9.17 Effects of signal averaging upon the form of the hemodynamic response. As the number of trials in the sample increases, the precision of the hemodynamic response estimate increases and the noise in the response decreases. (From Huettel and McCarthy, 2001.)

plot shows 20 single-trial responses, the second shows a set of 20 samples each representing the average of 4 trials, and so forth. Note that the 8 plots increase incrementally in steps from 1^2 to 8^2 trials, representing equal decreases in the expected standard error of the mean.

Readily apparent are the substantial effects of signal averaging upon the stability of the hemodynamic response. If there is no signal averaging and individual trials are compared, as in the first plot, then the variability across samples is enormous. In some trials, there is an increase in activity of up to

15 MR units (about 3% in this experiment), while in others the activity actually decreases during the trial. So, it would be extremely difficult to characterize the hemodynamic response in this region from only a single trial. But after averaging only a few trials (e.g., 4 or 9), the response begins to take a recognizable form. It tends to rise and fall in a regular fashion, and the different samples of trials tend to be more similar to one another. After about 25 or 36 trials, the hemodynamic response is essentially the same in every sample. Again, signal averaging has no effect on the signal itself, so the expected hemodynamic response is similar regardless of how many trials are averaged. However, the larger the sample size, the less effect noise has upon the observed data. If the noise is truly random, we can calculate this effect of signal-averaging functional SNR by multiplying the initial SNR by the square root of the number of trials that are averaged. If our signal of interest is half the amplitude of the noise, our initial functional SNR is 0.5. However, if we average 25 trials, we improve the functional SNR by a factor of 5, resulting in an effective SNR of 2.5.

Recall from Chapter 8 that one model for fMRI data suggests that the measured MR signal can be thought of as the linear addition of signal (i.e., the hemodynamic response) and noise. The term *linear* in this context means that the effects of the two factors are independent; that is, the amount of noise at a given time point does not depend on the amount of signal at that time point. This assumption can be tested by comparing the variability in the fMRI signal in the prestimulus baseline to the variability around the peak of the response. In Figure 9.17, it is obvious that the variability is greater around the peak of the hemodynamic response than during the prestimulus baseline. In 2001, Huettel and colleagues quantified changes in variability by plotting the standard deviation at each time point relative to stimulus presentation. Variability near the peak of the hemodynamic response, compared to the prestimulus baseline, increased by a factor of about 3. These results indicate that variability in fMRI data does not merely result from the effects of additive noise, but instead is partly due to *variability in the fMRI signal itself*.

Effects of Averaging on Detection of Active Voxels

Detection of fMRI activity also improves with signal averaging. Most statistical tests use a thresholding approach, such that any voxel whose statistical value is greater than some predetermined threshold is labeled as significant, while values less than that threshold are nonsignificant. Although this labeling scheme is binary, the underlying statistics are distributed in a relatively continuous manner (Figure 9.18). Voxels near the center of cluster of activation tend to have the highest statistical values, while ones near the edges have the lowest. This continues outside of the nominally active region, such that nearby voxels tend to have positive statistical tests. To confirm that statistics are spatially graded, one merely has to lower the significance threshold, and the size, or **spatial extent,** of the active region will increase. If the threshold is raised, the spatial extent will decrease. In short, whether or not a voxel is labeled as active depends on only two factors, its statistical value (which in turn depends on SNR) and the threshold.

Given that functional SNR increases with signal averaging, the spatial extent of activation will also increase with signal averaging, as activity in some of the subthreshold voxels becomes detectable. This effect can be seen in Figure 9.19, which presents data from the visual stimulation task described in the preceding section. If only a few trials are averaged, then very few vox-

detection Determination of whether or not activity within a given voxel changes in response to the experimental manipulation.

spatial extent The number of active voxels within a cluster of activity (i.e., the size of the active region).

(A)

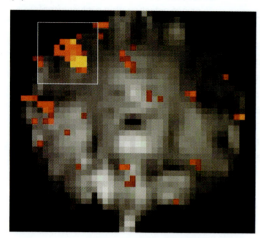

(B)

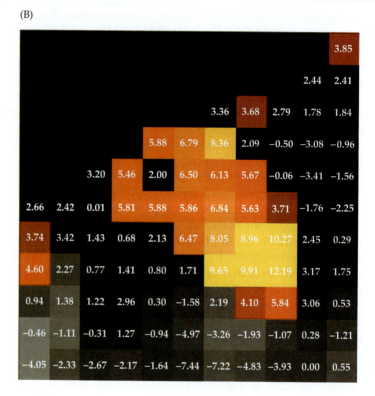

Figure 9.18 Distribution of statistical values across space. While activation maps of the brain (A) typically show in color only those voxels whose statistical value is greater than some threshold, the actual underlying statistics are often smoothly graded. Note in (B) that the activity focus highlighted in the white box in (A) contains the same voxels with high statistical values, along with others that are only slightly above threshold ($t > 3.6$). In fact, some voxels indicated as "inactive" on the color map have significance values quite near the threshold.

Type I error Rejecting the null hypothesis when it is in fact true. Also known as a false positive.

Type II error Accepting the null hypothesis when it is in fact false. Also known as an incorrect rejection or false negative.

els are active. For an average of 4 trials, for example, only one to two voxels were active in each subject. As the number of trials in the average increases, more and more voxels become active, until there are large regions of activity following 64 or more trials. When the number of active voxels was plotted as a function of the number of trials, the result was an exponential function that approached but did not reach an asymptote after more than 100 trials. Note that for these data, the topography of activity changes as the number of trials and thus the SNR increases. In subject 2, for example, voxels in the mid–calcarine cortex at the center of the image had above-threshold significance values after 16 trials, but voxels around the lingual gyrus at the bottom did not become significant until more than 64 trials. (Refer to the 2003 work of Saad and colleagues for a similar study using a blocked-design task.)

Most fMRI studies do not collect hundreds of independent trials per subject. More typical are designs with 20 to 50 trials per condition, and in rare cases even fewer are collected. Thus, many voxels that are really active during an experiment, but have low SNR, may not pass the statistical threshold. This illustrates an important point about fMRI studies, and most scientific research studies in general, namely that they are fundamentally conservative. More emphasis is placed upon ensuring that voxels that are labeled active are really active than upon identifying all active voxels. In terms that will be discussed in detail in Chapter 12, experiments typically try to avoid **Type I** errors at a cost of more-numerous **Type II** errors. Scientific conservatism works well for most fMRI studies. If we want to know whether the amygdala becomes active following presentation of a scary photograph, we do not need to show that every voxel in the amygdala is active, just that some of them are. Likewise, to demonstrate which brain regions are associated with a particular task, researchers list the foci of significant activation and in which structures they are contained.

But for some questions, accurate measurement of the spatial extent of activation is critical. One increasingly important use of fMRI is to map areas of particular interest, such as the language and motor cortices, in patients awaiting neurosurgery (see Box 12.2). If fMRI reveals that a patient's tumor abuts Broca's area, for example, then the neurosurgeon may decide that the risks of surgery (e.g., the inability to produce language) would be too great, and another course of treatment would be prescribed. In order to make such judgments, knowledge of the boundaries of the active area is necessary. In other studies, researchers may want to quantify differences in activity between two groups of subjects. For example, a study might investigate whether there are fewer active voxels within the frontal lobe in schizophrenia patients compared to neurologically normal subjects when they perform the Wisconsin Card Sorting Test.

Suppose that such a study found that the patients had fewer active voxels in a particular region of prefrontal cortex. Could you conclude, from those data alone, that schizophrenic subjects use less of the frontal lobe for this task than normal controls? To answer this question, recall that the likelihood that a voxel is detected by a statistical test is a function of its SNR. Differences in signal can cause SNR differences, of course, in that the schizophrenic subjects could indeed have less activity. However, differences in noise could also contribute to SNR differences. If the patient group had higher noise levels, for whatever reason, then their spatial extent of activity could be greatly reduced in the absence of any differences in signal. Stated another way, the two groups could have exactly the same areas of activity, but it could be more difficult to detect active voxels in one group than the other.

Huettel and colleagues investigated this issue in a comparison of visual processing between young adults and elderly adults. The amplitude of the hemodynamic response was identical between the groups for ROIs in both the calcarine and fusiform cortices. However, there were approximately twice as many active voxels in the young adult group as in the elderly. To determine whether this effect was likely to be real or an artifact of SNR differences, the SNR in each group was measured. The single-trial SNR was about 50% greater in the young than in the elderly. Based upon a simple simulation of the effects of SNR upon detection of active voxels, for the number of trials run in each group, SNR differences alone would predict about a 2:1 ratio of active voxels. Even more tellingly, the simulation suggested that had there been fewer experimental trials (e.g., about 30 to 35 compared to the 70 actually run), there would have been as much as 5 times as many active voxels in the young, due solely to the differences in noise between the groups. Similar results could occur for a variety of different comparisons, such as patient and nonpatient groups, patients on medication and off medication, or normal subjects in alert and fatigued states. It is critical, therefore, when averaging a small number of trials, to consider the activity measured to be a reflection of the SNR, which itself depends on other factors besides the activity of interest.

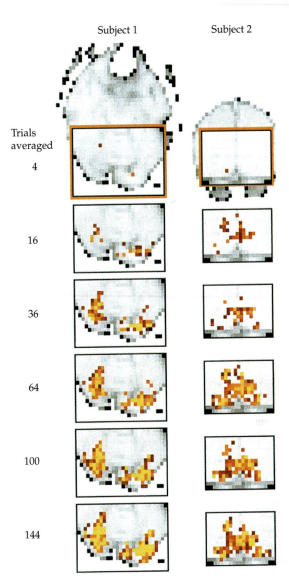

Figure 9.19 Spatial extent of fMRI activity increases with signal averaging. As the number of trials in the sample increases, the number of active voxels increases dramatically. (From Huettel and McCarthy, 2001.)

BOX 9.2 Power Analyses

Imagine that you are a newly minted assistant professor submitting your first grant on fMRI. You have spent weeks crafting a justification for your research program, clearly delineating the plan for a sequence of experiments, and carefully perfecting the design of each study. As you finish writing the grant, you come to the final section: the budget. You need to specify how many subjects you want to run in each experiment so you can request adequate support. Given the cost of each fMRI subject (around $1000), accurate estimation of the needed sample size is critical. If you run more subjects than needed, you will waste both time and money. If you run too few, you may not be able to answer the experimental questions. As you stare blankly at the budget pages, you ask yourself, "How do I calculate how much data I need to test my hypothesis?" To answer this question, a **power analysis** is needed. Power analyses estimate the likelihood of detecting a significant effect, if one truly exists, given the expected sizes of the effect and of the sample. Here we will explain power analyses and introduce some basic statistical concepts related to hypothesis testing (for additional detail, see Hays, 1994). Many of these concepts are elaborated on in Chapter 12 and are briefly introduced here to provide necessary background.

There are two types of mistakes you can make in any statistical test, including those used for fMRI. In one, you could decide that your test had significant results (i.e., the voxel was active) when no effect really existed. This is known as a Type I error. For most statistical tests, the likelihood of a Type I error, or α, is set ahead of time by the experimenter. The other mistake is that you could decide that the results of your test were not significant (i.e., the voxel was not active) even though there really was an effect. This is known as a Type II error, and its probability is represented by the symbol β. The goal of a power analysis is to determine the probability of detecting a real

effect, which is equivalent to $1 - \beta$. The quantity $1 - \beta$ defines the **power** of the statistical test.

One can calculate the power of a statistical test, given the Type I error rate, the expected SNR, and the sample size (see Equation 8.3). First, one must identify how large an effect will be needed for significance. Effect size, in a statistical sense, is not the numerical difference between the experimental conditions but is the numerical difference divided by the standard deviation (i.e., $\mu_0 - \mu_1 / \sigma_m$). Note that this is equivalent to SNR in the framework described earlier in the chapter. The needed effect size can be obtained from a statistical table (t-distribution) or from a statistical calculator. At an alpha value of 0.001, for example, an effect size of about 3.1 units is needed. Second, the expected effect size (z_a) for the sample must be calculated. Suppose that the expected difference between hemodynamic amplitudes in conditions 1 and 2 was 0.3% and that there was a 0.2% standard deviation in this value across 8 subjects. The expected effect size is the mean divided by the sample standard deviation, which is the standard deviation divided by the square root of the number of subjects. For the numbers above, the expected effect size is about 4.2 units. Third, the difference between the expected and needed effect sizes is calculated; in this case, $4.2 - 3.1 = 1.1$ units. Finally, this difference is converted back to a probability using a t-table, resulting in a β value of 0.12. The power of this test, or $1 - \beta$, would be 0.87.

$$power = 1 - \beta = 1 - p[z \leq (z_a + \frac{\mu_0 - \mu_1}{\sigma_m})]$$

One could restate the results of the power analysis in the following way: Given a sample size of 8 subjects, an expected change of 0.3%, and a standard deviation of 0.2%, there is an 87% chance that a real effect will be detected at an alpha value of 0.001. Based on such calculations, a researcher may decide that 87%

power analysis A calculation that estimates the likelihood of detecting an effect of a given size based upon the parameters of the experimental design.

power The probability of detecting an effect of the experimental manipulation.

is too low for comfort; about one out of eight experiments would show no effects. Recalculating the power analysis with 12 subjects increases the power to 0.98, and for 16 subjects the power is more than 0.998. These results suggest that running between 12 and 16 subjects in this experiment would make detection of real effects very likely. Although this example describes a power analysis to determine how many subjects should be run, power analyses can also be conducted to determine how many trials are needed per subject.

An important caveat for fMRI power analyses raised by Zarahn and Slifstein in 2001 argued that the use of raw signal units in power analyses may be inappropriate since the amount of raw fMRI signal change does not necessarily correspond to the amount of neural activity. For example, changing the alternation rate of a blocked design or changing a fast event-related design from periodic to randomized will affect the recorded fMRI hemodynamic response, even if the underlying neural activity is unchanged. The authors suggest that to conduct power analyses on underlying neural activity, rather than expected fMRI signal change in a particular experimental design, one must compare data from the desired paradigm to reference data taken from another, simpler paradigm, for which the pattern of neural activity can be estimated. While this approach may improve conceptualization of the units for power analyses, it does not change their basic properties, namely the calculation of the likelihood of detecting a given effect size for a given sample size.

Alternatives to Signal Averaging

In some instances, the amplitude of noise may be so large that too many trials would be required to sufficiently increase functional SNR through signal averaging. If the temporal properties of the noise can be well characterized—as when it occurs at a particular frequency—then it may be possible to remove the noise by applying a filter to the intensity time series for each voxel (see Chapter 10). Filters work particularly well when the frequency of the noise is very different from that of the signal of interest. For example, it may be possible to remove the effects of scanner drift from a voxel's time series by applying a high-pass filter that preserves the main frequency components of the hemodynamic response. Another, more advanced approach for removing noise from fMRI time series is the application of wavelet filtering. Wavelets are particularly useful for removing noise that contains sharp discontinuities. If sufficiently well characterized, some noise components can be modeled as so-called nuisance factors in regression models of fMRI time series, and thus removed from the statistical assessment of the signal.

Regression analysis is a powerful technique for functional MRI that will be discussed in detail in Chapter 12. We note here that regression analysis might appear to be an alternative to signal averaging, because it creates a hypothesis based upon an estimate of the hemodynamic changes that should occur over the entire time series. Yet, even though the data do not appear to be averaged in this latter approach, there is still an implicit effect of signal averaging. The more trials you include in the regression model, the more likely it is that you will detect active voxels. In fact, the effects of increasing the number of experimental observations are exactly the same regardless of whether there is explicit signal averaging.

Signal Averaging: Conclusions

In summary, averaging across multiple trials has two salutary effects on fMRI data: improving the estimation of the hemodynamic response and increasing the likelihood of detection of active voxels. As shown in Figures 9.17 and 9.19, both estimation precision and detection power tend to asymptote, so that adding 10 trials to an experiment with only 15 trials would have a substantial effect but adding 10 trials to one with 150 would do little. The diminishing-returns nature of signal averaging is related to the idea of the standard error of the mean discussed earlier. Since the standard error scales with the square root of the number of trials, incremental increases will have less and less effect. It is critical that you consider the numbers of trials conducted in the studies reported in the previous sections as merely rough guidelines. If your experimental questions rely on a very specific hypothesis about the shape of the hemodynamic response or on the detection of particular voxels within a small ROI, or if your task has low functional SNR (e.g., many cognitive tasks), then you will need more trials. Conversely, if the experimental task has very high functional SNR and very simple hypotheses to test, then fewer trials are necessary.

Summary

The ability to detect task-related variability, or signal, within non-task-related variability, or noise, is critical for fMRI. Three quantities are important: raw signal-to-noise ratio (raw SNR), contrast-to-noise ratio (CNR), and functional signal-to-noise ratio (functional SNR). Raw SNR depends on the magnitude of signal measured by the scanner compared to thermal noise. CNR depends on the intensity difference between two tissues of interest compared to the variability in those intensity values. Functional SNR determines our ability to detect signal changes associated with experimental effects of interest and is critical for many aspects of fMRI. While raw SNR scales linearly with the strength of the magnetic field, functional SNR scales less than linearly with field strength due to several sources of noise. Thermal and system variability in scanner hardware contribute to all types of MRI imaging but are much less important than physiological variability for fMRI, especially at high field strengths. The most common method for improving SNR in fMRI studies is signal averaging, the collection of multiple observations for each experimental condition. Signal averaging can substantially improve both estimation and detection power, but it can serve to mask potentially important effects.

Suggested Readings

*Aguirre, G. K., Zarahn, E., and D'Esposito, M. (1998). The variability of human, BOLD hemodynamic responses. *NeuroImage,* 8: 360–369. This influential paper provides important evidence for consistent differences in the form of the fMRI hemodynamic response across subjects.

*Huettel, S. A., and McCarthy, G. (2001). The effects of single-trial averaging upon the spatial extent of fMRI activation. *NeuroReport,* 12: 2411–2416. This short article documents the changes in hemodynamic response form and spatial extent of activation as more and more trials are averaged.

*Krasnow, B., Tamm, L., Greicius, M. D., Yang, T. T., Glover, G. H., Reiss, A. L., and Menon, V. (2003). Comparison of fMRI activation at 3 and 1.5 T during perceptual, cognitive, and affective processing. *NeuroImage,* 18: 813–826. Unlike most studies of field strength, which use simple visual or motor tasks, this report compares a variety of tasks at medium and high fields.

*Kruger, G., and Glover, G. H. (2001). Physiological noise in oxygenation-sensitive magnetic resonance imaging. *Magn. Reson. Med.,* 46: 631–637. Provides a clear description of different components of physiological noise.

*McGonigle, D. J., Howseman, A. M., Athwal, B. S., Friston, K. J., Frackowiak, R. S., and Holmes, A. P. (2000). Variability in fMRI: An examination of intersession differences. *NeuroImage,* 11: 708–734. This remarkable study describes a set of 99 fMRI sessions conducted on a single subject over a period of several months.

Parrish, T. B., Gitelman, D. R., LaBar, K. S., and Mesulam, M. M. (2000). Impact of signal-to-noise on functional MRI. *Magn. Reson. Med.,* 44: 925–932. A clear demonstration of how changes in signal-to-noise affect detection of activity; includes an example from a clinical patient.

Indicates a reference that is a suggested reading in the field and is also cited in this chapter.

Chapter References

Buxton, R. B. (2002). *Introduction to Functional Magnetic Resonance Imaging: Principles and Techniques.* Cambridge University Press, New York.

Edelstein, W. A., Glover, G. H., Hardy, C. J., and Redington, R. W. (1986). The intrinsic signal-to-noise ratio in NMR imaging. *Magn. Reson. Med.,* 3: 604–618.

Gati, J. S., Menon, R. S., Ugurbil, K., and Rutt, B. K. (1997). Experimental determination of the BOLD field strength dependence in vessels and tissue. *Magn. Reson. Med.,* 38: 296–302.

Hays, W. L. (1994). *Statistics* (5th ed.). Harcourt College, Fort Worth, TX.

Hu, X., Le, T. H., Parrish, T., and Erhard, P. (1995). Retrospective estimation and correction of physiological fluctuation in functional MRI. *Magn. Reson. Med.,* 34: 201–212.

Huettel, S. A., Singerman, J., and McCarthy, G. (2001). The effects of aging upon the hemodynamic response measured by functional MRI. *NeuroImage,* 13: 161–175.

Kruger, G., Kastrup, A., and Glover, G. H. (2001). Neuroimaging at 1.5 T and 3.0 T: Comparison of oxygenation-sensitive magnetic resonance imaging. *Magn. Reson. Med.,* 45: 595–604.

Ogawa, S., Kim, S.-G., Ugurbil, K., and Menon, R. S. (1998). On the characteristics of fMRI in the brain. *Ann. Rev. Biophys. Biomol. Struct.,* 27: 447–474.

Ogawa, S., Menon, R. S., Tank, D. W., Kim, S.-G., Merkle, H., Ellerman, J. M., and Ugurbil, K. (1993). Functional brain mapping by blood oxygenation level-dependent contrast magnetic resonance imaging. A comparison of signal characteristics with a biophysical model. *Biophys. J.,* 64: 803–812.

Raj, D., Anderson, A. W., and Gore, J. C. (2001). Respiratory effects in human functional magnetic resonance imaging due to bulk susceptibility changes. *Phys. Med. Biol.,* 46: 3331–3340.

Saad, Z. S., Ropella, K. M., DeYoe, E. A., and Bandettini, P. A. (2003). The spatial extent of the BOLD response. *NeuroImage,* 19: 132–144.

Turner, R., Jezzard, P., Wen, H., Kwong, K. K., Le Bihan, D., Zeffiro, T., and Balaban, R. S. (1993). Functional mapping of the human visual cortex at 4 and 1.5 Tesla using deoxygenation contrast EPI. *Magn. Reson. Med.,* 29: 277–279.

Wang, J., Alsop, D. C., Li, L., Listerud, J., Gonzalez-At, J. B., Schnall, M. D., and Detre, J. A. (2002). Comparison of quantitative perfusion imaging using arterial spin labeling at 1.5 and 4.0 Tesla. *Magn. Reson. Med.,* 48: 242–254.

Yang, Y., Wen, H., Mattay, V. S., Balaban, R. S., Frank, J. A., and Duyn, J. H. (1999). Comparison of 3D BOLD functional MRI with spiral acquisition at 1.5 and 4.0 T. *NeuroImage,* 9: 446–451.

Zarahn, E., and Slifstein, M. (2001). A reference effect approach for power analysis in fMRI. *NeuroImage,* 14: 768–779.

10

Preprocessing of fMRI Data

As described in the previous chapters, one can consider fMRI data as consisting of a three-dimensional matrix of volume elements (voxels) that is repeatedly sampled over time. So, a single experiment might have an imaging volume of $64 \times 64 \times 20$ voxels that is sampled every 2 seconds for a total of 10 minutes (300 time points per voxel). A straightforward way of analyzing such a data set would be to extract the raw time course for each voxel and compare each of these time courses to some hypothesis using a test of significance. While this approach indeed forms the basis of much of fMRI data analysis, as is discussed in Chapter 12, it contains some hidden assumptions. Notably, it assumes that each voxel represents a unique and unchanging location in the brain and that the sampling of that voxel occurs at a regular known rate. These assumptions, though seemingly plausible, are always incorrect. All fMRI data suffers from spatial and temporal inaccuracy caused by subject head motion, physiological oscillations like heartbeats and respiration, inhomogeneities in the static field, and/or differences in the timing of image acquisition. If uncorrected, this variability may reduce (or even eliminate) the detection power of an experiment.

Here, we discuss a series of computational procedures, known as **preprocessing** steps, that operate on fMRI data following image reconstruction but prior to statistical analysis. For example, researchers correct for head motion regardless of whether the experiment uses a blocked-design vision task or an event-related memory task. Preprocessing has two major goals. The first goal is to remove uninteresting variability from the data. In the prior chapter, we introduced a number of sources of variability that can be of large amplitude compared to the task-related signal. By reducing the total variance through preprocessing, we can increase **functional signal-to-noise ratio (SNR)**. The second goal is to prepare the data for statistical analysis. Spatial smoothing, for example, can be used to reduce the effective number of statistical tests while maintaining detection power. Many of the statistical analyses used in fMRI make assumptions that can be met by application of preprocessing techniques. The general framework for preprocessing is shown in Figure 10.1.

preprocessing Computational procedures that are applied to fMRI data following image reconstruction but before statistical analysis. Preprocessing steps are intended to reduce variability in the data that is not associated with the experimental task and to prepare the data for statistical testing.

functional signal-to-noise ratio (functional SNR) The ratio between the intensity of a signal associated with changes in brain function and the variability in the data due to all sources of noise. Functional SNR is sometimes called dynamic CNR or functional CNR.

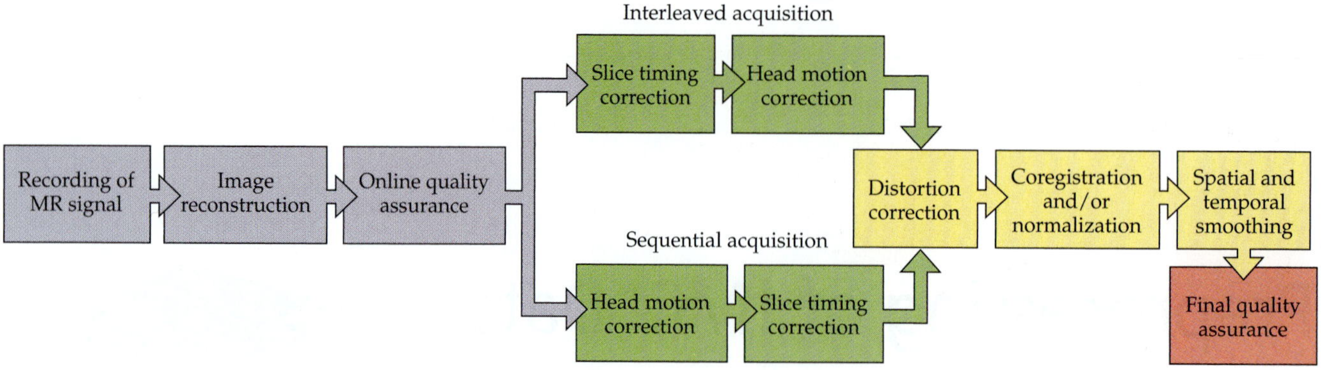

Figure 10.1 The basic framework for preprocessing of fMRI data. The steps between image reconstruction and data analysis are collectively known as preprocessing. The goals of preprocessing procedures are to reduce unwanted variability in the experimental data and to improve the validity of statistical analyses. Each step outlined above is discussed individually within this chapter.

Quality Assurance

quality assurance (QA) A set of procedures designed to identify problems with fMRI data so that they do not compromise experimental analyses.

An important and underutilized aspect of preprocessing is **quality assurance (QA)** testing. Due to the complexity of scanner instrumentation, many problems can (and will) arise on even the best-maintained scanner. If a subject's data are corrupted by extreme scanner noise, or by some problem with data acquisition, the subject may have to be excluded from experimental analyses. Given the substantial expense of each MR session, the loss of data carries a significant cost. Even more fearsome are unnoticed quality problems. The prevalence of automated statistical packages has made it possible for even the least experienced investigator to preprocess, analyze, and combine data across subjects without ever examining each subject's data. Without QA testing, unnoticed problems can propagate into the final results of an experiment, with potentially disastrous results.

The first rule of QA is simple: examine your data. Many common artifacts are readily visible in the raw images, even under cursory examination (Figure 10.2A and B). An effective way of viewing experimental data is as a time-series movie (or cine loop), in which an entire experimental run is shown, one volume after another, in a rapid sequence. Because our visual system is very good at picking up changes between successive images, many types of problems will pop out of the sequence. Radiofrequency noise, for example, can show up as repeating patterns on top of the data, while head motion can appear as rapid jerks. After repeatedly examining data from the same scanner, you will gain an implicit understanding of what "good data" should look like, and you will recognize experimental sessions with abnormally high noise levels.

Although visual inspection of fMRI data should be a regular part of any QA procedure, it is not in itself sufficient for ensuring data quality. Imagine that an acquisition or reconstruction error causes the loss of data from one slice of one image. That single bad image could, if included, cause severe artifacts in the final analysis, but to catch it would require visual examination of every slice in every volume. Rather than relying on visual inspection to catch all such errors, researchers can apply simple preprocessing tests to evaluate the quality of the data. At one extreme are tests designed to catch transient deviations, such as acquisition errors that result in loss of data. These include calculation of both the mean intensity of slices and the vol-

(A)

(B)

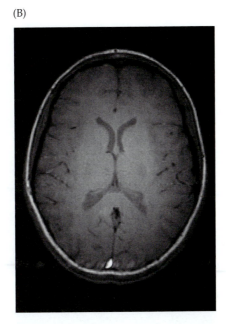

Figure 10.2 Common artifacts found in MR images. An important goal for quality assurance programs is the identification of image artifacts that can corrupt MR data. (A) Radiofrequency leakage resulting from an ungrounded electrical connection can cause "white pixels" in *k*-space, resulting in grating patterns on reconstructed images. (B) Variations in the local properties of the field can cause intensity variations across an image, such as the brightening of the center of the image compared to the periphery.

ume center of mass. Though crude, these measures are extremely effective at detecting aberrant data points, whether caused by lost slices, image intensity spikes, or extreme head motion. At the other extreme are tests designed to evaluate the overall quality of a data set. The simplest such measure is the calculation of the **raw SNR** for each data set, defined by mean intensity of the sample (i.e., brain) divided by the standard deviation of points outside the sample. Suppose that the first eight subjects in an experiment have mean intensity values of about 500 units and noise standard deviations of around 5 units, for raw SNRs of about 100, but the ninth subject has a noise standard deviation of 20 units and a correspondingly lower raw SNR. Such high variability likely indicates some problems with the data, whether subject-related like head motion or scanner-related like radiofrequency noise, that should be investigated further.

It is important to recognize that QA testing during preprocessing should be quick and reliable. The calculations described above, such as center of mass, mean intensity, and signal-to-noise, are extremely simple and require only a few lines of code. Because they run so quickly, they can even be done in real time at the scanner as the data are being acquired, which can allow the researcher to correct the underlying problem and salvage the session. Though not strictly part of preprocessing, regular QA tests of a single object, such as a **phantom,** can also facilitate detection of scanner problems. Phantoms are objects designed for testing MR systems (Figure 10.3). They are typically balls or cylinders filled with fluids, like saline solution or gel, although they can have internal structure (including some that attempt to mimic brain anatomy). Daily scanning of the same phantom with the same pulse sequences will indicate changes in the scanning environment, since the data should otherwise look identical across sessions.

In summary, quality assurance testing is the responsibility both of individual researchers and of imaging centers. Researchers should evaluate their data as they are collected, through visual examination and QA calculations. Imaging centers should keep track of problems that affect multiple investigators and should conduct regular QA testing to identify problems as early

raw signal-to-noise ratio (raw SNR) The ratio between the MR signal intensity associated with a sample (e.g., the brain) and the thermal noise that is measured outside the sample.

phantom An object used for testing MR systems. Most phantoms are filled with liquids or gels with known properties, so that problems with the scanner system can be readily identified.

(A)   (B)   (C)

(D)   (E)   (F)

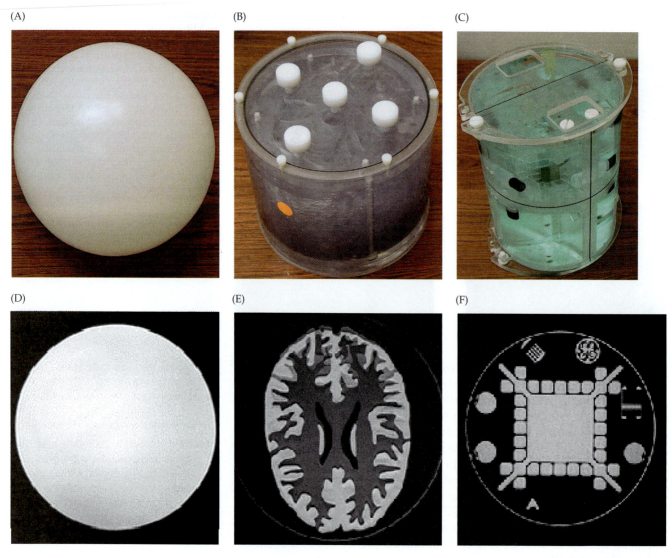

Figure 10.3   Examples of phantoms and their appearance on MR images. Phantoms are fluid- or gel-filled shapes that are used for testing MR scanners. They may be homogeneous (A, D), or have internal structure (B, C, E, F). (Phantoms courtesy of General Electric Corporation.)

interleaved slice acquisition The collection of data in an alternating order, so that data are first acquired from the odd-numbered slices and then from the even-numbered slices, to minimize the influence of excitation pulses upon adjacent slices.

as possible. All MR scanners are subject to image acquisition problems of one type or another. Without a diligent QA program, such problems will corrupt experimental data and frustrate investigators.

Slice Acquisition Time Correction

Most fMRI data are acquired using two-dimensional pulse sequences that acquire images one slice at a time, due to the use of spatial gradients that limit the influence of an excitation pulse to a single slice within the brain. A typical pulse sequence might acquire 24 slices or more to cover the entire brain within a TR of 1.5 to 3.0 s, depending on the capabilities of the scanner. Most pulse sequences use **interleaved slice acquisition,** such that the scanner first collects all of the odd slices and then collects all of the even slices to avoid cross-slice excitation. If there were 12 slices in the imaging volume, numbered from 1 at the bottom of the brain to 12 at the top, an interleaved acquisition sequence would collect the slices in the order 1-3-5-7-9-11-2-4-6-8-10-12. Less common is **ascending/descending slice acquisition,** in which the slices are collected consecutively: 1-2-3-4-5-6-7-8-9-10-11-12. Regardless of the order used, each slice is acquired at a different time point within the TR. Timing differences are especially problematic for interleaved sequences, in which spatially consecutive slices are not acquired successively. In virtually all fMRI scanning, the slices are acquired with equal spacing across the TR. Thus, assuming that the interleaved example above had a TR of 3 s and that slice 1 was acquired at 0 s, slice 2 would not be acquired until 1.5 s later, and slice 12 would be acquired 2.75 s after slice 1.

ascending/descending slice acquisition
The collection of data in consecutive order, so that slices are acquired sequentially from one end of the imaging volume to the other.

Thought Question

In most fMRI pulse sequences, the slices are equally spaced throughout a TR. Can you think of a type of experiment in which researchers might concentrate all of the slices at the beginning of the TR, so that there is a period of time in which no acquisition takes place? (Hint: Refer to Chapter 2 to consider what the subject experiences each time a slice is acquired.)

To illustrate how slice timing affects fMRI analyses, Figure 10.4 presents a typical interleaved imaging sequence consisting of 24 slices acquired with a

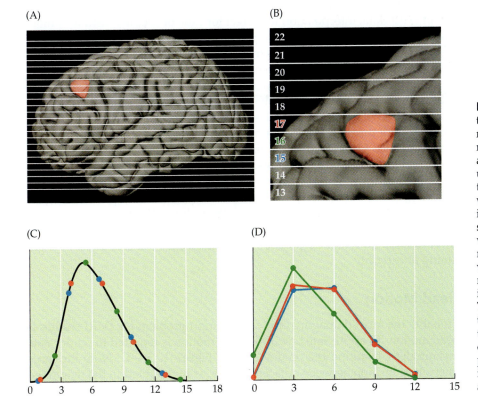

(A) (B) (C) (D)

Figure 10.4 Effects of slice acquisition time upon the hemodynamic response. Imagine that a single brain region, shown in red (A), is uniformly active following presentation of a stimulus. This region spans three slices, 15 to 17, within the imaging volume, which is acquired with a standard interleaved sequence (B). Because these slices are acquired at different times within the 3-s TR, the hemodynamic response within the slices will have very different time courses. The actual recorded signal from the different slices is shown in (C). When plotted for each TR, there are different time courses for the slices acquired early in the TR and the slice acquired later (D). The hemodynamic response in slice 16 appears to peak earlier than those in the surrounding slices, even though the underlying activity is identical.

temporal interpolation The estimation of the value of a signal at a time point that was not originally collected, using data from nearby time points.

3-s TR. The region of interest is shown in red in the frontal lobe (Figure 10.4A and B), and the hypothetical hemodynamic response in that region is plotted below (Figure 10.4C and D). Since the region of interest spans three slices—15, 16, and 17—the actual times at which it is sampled differ across slices. Slices 15 and 17 are sampled at 1 s and 1.125 s, respectively, whereas slice 16 is sampled at 2.5 s. So, for each slice, the measured time course will have a particular sampling delay, which can greatly influence the correspondence between observed data and experimental hypotheses. The consequences of slice-timing errors are much greater for event-related designs than for blocked designs, since the former depend upon accurate modeling of the timing of experimental events. Thus, correction for slice timing is necessary for many forms of event-related designs. In contrast, blocked designs measure changes in BOLD activity over long intervals (e.g., 20 seconds), so errors in determining block onset will have relatively little effect on the data and correction for slice timing is less critical.

To correct for slice-timing errors, some experimental analyses modify the predicted hemodynamic responses so that each slice is compared to a hemodynamic response function with slightly different timing. More common is correcting for slice timing using **temporal interpolation** during preprocessing. Interpolation uses information from nearby time points to estimate the amplitude of the MR signal at the onset of the TR. Several strategies for interpolation are used in fMRI, including linear, spline, and sinc functions. It is important to emphasize that no interpolation technique can perfectly recover the missing information from between samples. The accuracy of interpolation depends on two factors: the variability in the experimental data and the rate of sampling. If the experimental data change very rapidly over time (i.e., have high-frequency components) compared to the sampling rate, then interpolation will be unable to capture changes between data points. But if the data change very slowly compared to the sampling rate, then interpolation will be more effective. Given the typical temporal variation in fMRI data, interpolation to correct for time of slice acquisition is more effective for data acquired at relatively short TRs (e.g., 1 s) than for data acquired at long TRs (e.g., >3 s). Unfortunately, the need for accurate interpolation is greatest at long TRs because of the large intervals between successive acquisitions.

Slice-timing correction should be done before head-motion correction for data acquired using interleaved slice acquisition at a long TR. This is because small through-plane motions, as when part of a voxel moves from slice 12 to slice 13, will cause the timing of activity to be off by one-half of the TR value at affected time points. Thus, doing slice-timing correction first for interleaved sequences with long TRs will minimize timing errors, at a cost of increased sensitivity to head motion. For data acquired using an ascending/descending sequence or with a short TR, motion correction should be done before slice-timing correction. This will minimize motion effects associated with interpolation across adjacent voxels, at a cost of slight timing uncertainty.

Head Motion

Probably the most damaging (and frustrating!) problem for fMRI studies is head motion. To appreciate how little head motion is required to render data meaningless, examine the data shown in Figure 10.5A–C. Note the large intensity transition between adjacent voxels, as highlighted in the magnified

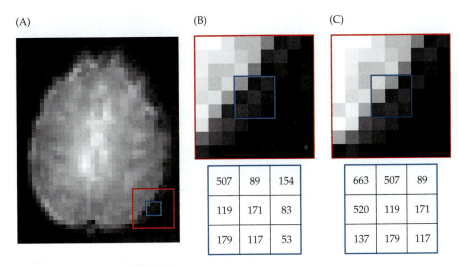

(A)   (B)   (C)

507	89	154
119	171	83
179	117	53

663	507	89
520	119	171
137	179	117

Figure 10.5   Effects of head motion on fMRI data. Large intensity transitions exist at tissue boundaries, including the edges of the brain (A). Here we demonstrate the effects of head motion upon voxel intensity. The magnified views show the position of the brain before head motion (B) and after a movement of one voxel to the right (C). The numerical intensity values for the voxels within the blue square are shown below. Note that the intensity in a given voxel may change by more than a factor of 5 due solely to head motion. This compares to a change of only 1 to 2% for real brain activity.

version in panel B. Now imagine that the subject moves his head almost imperceptibly, shifting by only 5 mm (i.e., the width of a single voxel) along a single axis. Even such a tiny movement has drastic effects upon the data, as shown in panel C. Remember that the scanner acquires images at absolute spatial locations, not relative to the brain's position. So if the subject moves his head by 5 mm, each voxel's time series will contain data from two different parts of the brain that are separated by exactly 5 mm. If those two parts of the brain have very different properties, as will certainly be the case at the edge of the brain, even this small head motion may cause very large changes in raw signal over time.

The basic problem introduced by head motion thus can be stated simply. FMRI analyses assume that each voxel represents a unique part of the brain; if the subject's head moves, then each voxel's time course is derived from more than one brain location. To consider the effects of head motion on statistical analyses, consider a blocked design similar to that used by Kwong and colleagues in 1992 (see Chapter 7), in which periods of darkness and light alternate every minute for 4 minutes. Suppose that the subject moves her head exactly one voxel to her left at the beginning of the last block, just after the lights come on. Voxels that had included the right edge of the brain will now include fluid around the right side of the brain, whereas voxels just outside the left side of the brain will now include gray matter. So, the overall signal will be artificially decreased on the right side of the brain and artificially increased on the left side. This phenomenon results in characteristic ringing patterns on one or both edges of the brain due to uncorrected head motion (Figure 10.6). One commonly observed form of head motion is a large, abrupt change in position between experimental runs (see Figure 10.9). Most fMRI experiments are partitioned into a number of relatively short (e.g., 4- to 8-minute) runs to reduce subject fatigue and, in some cases, to overcome hardware constraints on data acquisition. During the breaks between runs, subjects typically relax and talk to the experimenters, often resulting in considerable head motion. In many cases, different experimental conditions are separated across runs, so motion becomes more associated with one condition than another.

Within runs, subjects often make numerous small movements of the head. As subjects lie in a small space, unable to move around for a 1- to 2-hour ses-

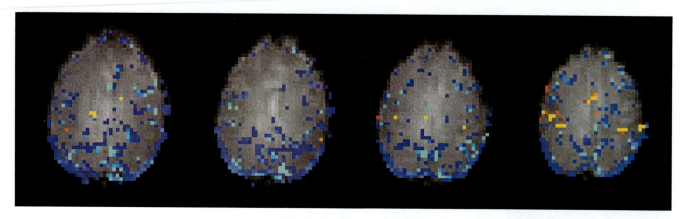

Figure 10.6 Edge effects of head motion in fMRI analyses. Because the intensity transitions in the brain are greatest at its edges, head motion often results in systematic rings of artifactual activation around the edges of the brain. Shown here are the results of a transient 4-s forward translation of two voxels at stimulus onset in one epoch. Note that the back of the brain, which changed from high intensity to low intensity as a result of the movement, exhibits a significant decrease in activity due entirely to the movement.

sion, they get increasingly tired and restless. If the experiment is set up so that one condition is at the beginning and another is at the end of the session, then the likelihood that fatigue-related motion will affect the analyses increases. The experimental stimuli themselves may cause head motion as well. Many experimental tasks require subjects to make motor responses, usually by moving a joystick or pressing a button, which may in turn induce head motion. If a picture is particularly alerting or arousing, it may surprise or shock the subjects into moving. Anyone who has been a subject in an MRI study has experienced momentary drowsiness…only to be startled into alertness by the next stimulus. Motion effects that are time-locked to stimulus presentation pose challenges for analysis and preprocessing techniques, since it becomes difficult to separate real brain activity from artifacts of motion. Within- and between-runs movements are sometimes corrected separately because of their different spatial properties.

Even though head motion is an inherently spatial problem, it can have consequences for activation timing. The examples in figures 10.5 and 10.6 considered in-plane motion, but motion frequently occurs between slice planes as well. Since most functional imaging sequences use interleaved slice acquisition, adjacent slices are acquired approximately one-half TR apart. For a long-TR imaging sequence, as is often used for full-brain imaging, head motion could result in misestimating the timing of activity by 1 to 2 seconds. A second timing problem is that motion within an acquisition also changes the pattern of spin excitation in the brain. Recall that for functional pulse sequences, like gradient-echo EPI, each slice experiences an excitation pulse at the beginning of the TR. But if the head moves within the acquisition of a single volume, then some of the slices may miss the excitation pulse. Those slices will recover more than other slices, because the time since the last excitation was longer, and thus will have different responses to subsequent excitations. A final consequence of head motion is the potential loss of data at the edges of the imaging volume. Most fMRI protocols use in-plane fields of view that are substantially larger than the brain, such as 20 or 24 cm. For such large fields of view, the resulting image is large enough that the head is surrounded by a few centimeters of air, and so it is unlikely that any in-plane movement would be large enough to move the brain outside of the imaging volume. More problematic is through-plane movement. Imagine that a researcher sets up the pulse sequence for one subject to have exactly enough axial 4-mm slices to fit the entire brain, from the top of the cerebrum to the bottom of the cerebellum. Later in the experiment, the subject moves his head slightly, about 4 mm, along the z-direction, and in doing so the top of his brain moves out of the imaging volume, so that data from that part of the brain is no longer acquired. In addition to all of the other problems with head motion described previously, this subject would have an irreversible loss of data from one slice. To prevent such data loss, additional slices should be acquired on the edges of the area of interest, whether the full brain or just a single region, so that small through-plane movements can be corrected.

Prevention of Head Motion

Like many other problems, head motion is more easily prevented than corrected. Most laboratories use head restraints of some form, such as bite bars, masks, vacuum packs, padding, or taping (Figure 10.7). The most effective

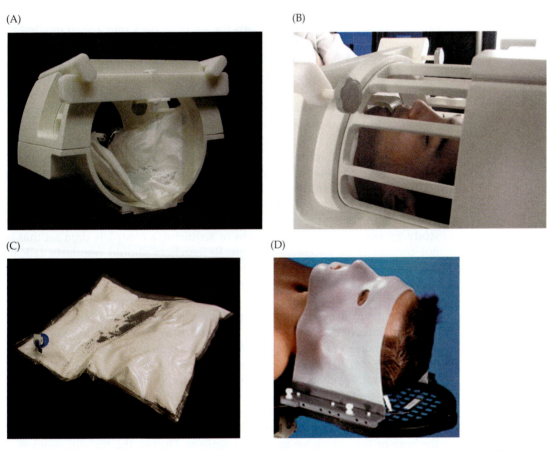

(A)

(B)

(C)

(D)

Figure 10.7 Head restraint systems. Because severe head motion can render fMRI data useless, several systems for head-immobilization exist. Shown in (A) is a standard volume head coil with two motion-restraint systems. Attached to the top of the head coil is a bite bar system, while at the bottom is a vacuum pack. When the bite bar is used (B), the subject clenches his/her teeth on a dental mold that has been cus-tomized to their bite pattern. This greatly restricts the effective motion of the head. Vacuum packs (C) contain many soft foam beads within a plastic casing. When air is pumped out, the pack hardens to form a shell around the contours of the subject's head. Thermoplastic masks (D) mold to the subject's face, and are anchored to a static support. (D from Med-Tec.)

262 Chapter Ten

mock scanner A simulated MRI scanner that does not have a magnetic field present, used for training research participants. Some mock scanners simulate scanner noises and measure subject head movement.

but difficult-to-use option is the bite bar (Figure 10.7A and B). As its name implies, a bite bar immobilizes the head by requiring subjects to clamp their teeth firmly on a dental mold, which in turn is solidly attached to the scanning hardware. With the jaw immobilized, potential head motion becomes very limited. However, while effective, bite bars can introduce subject compliance problems. Some subjects dislike using bite bars, which can both increase the likelihood that a participant ends a session prematurely and decrease the rate of subject recruitment. Despite these disadvantages, researchers at a number of institutions use bite bars successfully to minimize head motion. Better tolerated are systems that use moldable plastic or mesh to create a mask around the subject's head (Figure 10.7D). Such masks passively restrict head motion without requiring jaw clenching and are individually molded to each participant's physiognomy. The primary disadvantage of mask systems lies in the customization: it takes time to adjust the mask for each subject, especially with thermoplastic systems that must be heated and cooled before scanning. A secondary disadvantage is that some subjects may feel claustrophobic due to the high degree of immobilization.

Vacuum-pack systems combine good motion reduction with improved patient comfort (Figure 10.7C). The vacuum pack consists of a large number of soft beads within a flexible plastic casing. Once the subject is positioned in the scanner, the pack is fitted around the sides of the head and its air is pumped out. The loss of air hardens the vacuum pack into a shell molded to the contours of the skull. Since the face is left open, the risk of claustrophobia is not increased significantly. Many subjects, in fact, report preferring the vacuum system to no restraint at all because its head support allows them to relax their neck muscles. Although head motion, especially tilting the head forward, is not as restricted as it is with bite bars or face masks, the improved patient comfort makes vacuum packs a desirable option.

While restraint systems play an essential role in minimizing head motion, probably the most important factor is subject compliance. Because most fMRI subjects are research volunteers and not clinical patients, they receive no direct benefit from the session. Therefore, when subjects become uncomfortable, they may choose to terminate the session or to move to relieve soreness or pain. Working to maximize subjects' comfort and interest in the study greatly improves the chances of acquiring a complete data set that is not corrupted by excessive motion. Researchers should regularly talk to their subjects; even a simple "How are you doing?" after each run will help prevent anxiety and accompanying motion. We have also found that taping down subjects' foreheads greatly reduces head motion. Although a single piece of tape in itself cannot prevent a subject from moving his or her head, it provides feedback (in the form of changes in tension) when the subject moves. If a subject makes a slight motion, the tape provides him or her with a guide for how to return to the base position.

Head-motion effects can also be ameliorated through subject training. At our center, first-time subjects participate in training sessions within an MRI simulator, or **mock scanner,** that was constructed from the parts of a decommissioned scanner (Figure 10.8A). Recorded scanner noises are played within the bore of the simulator for added realism. During the training session, a three-dimensional tracking device (i. e., Polhemus sensor) is attached to the subject's head so that we can monitor head movements at millimeter resolution and caution the subject if head movements exceed a threshold (Figure 10.8B). We find that training in the simulator results in subjects who are more relaxed and comfortable during their real scanning sessions. Subjects who cannot tolerate confinement in the mock scanner, or who cannot avoid mov-

(A)

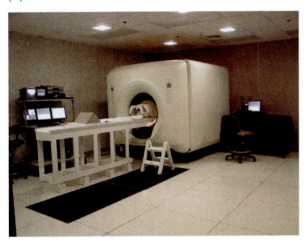

(B)

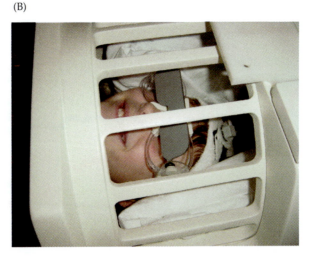

Figure 10.8   Use of a mock scanner system for prevention of head motion. By acclimating potential subjects to the MRI environment in a simulated or mock scanner (A), head motion and other subject compliance problems can be greatly reduced. (B) An adolescent subject with a Polhemus head-tracking system around her forehead. If she moves her head beyond a threshold amount, the movie that she is watching through the mirrored glasses will stop playing.

ing their heads over the course of the scanning session, can be excused from further participation in the study. In summary, prevention of head motion takes two basic forms: physical restraints that immobilize the head and adoption of training and communication procedures that reduce the likelihood of head motion.

Correction of Head Motion

When the head moves during an experiment, some of the images will be acquired with the brain in the wrong location. The goal of motion correction is to adjust the time series of images so that the brain is in the same position in every image. The general process for spatially aligning two image volumes is called **coregistration.** For motion correction, successive image volumes in the time series are coregistered to a single **reference volume.** Because the brain is the same in every image of the time series, a **rigid-body transformation** is used. Rigid-body transformations assume that the size and shape of the two objects to be coregistered are identical, and that one can be superimposed exactly upon the other by a combination of three **translations** (i.e., moving the entire image volume along the x-, y-, and z-axes) and three **rotations** (rotating the entire image volume through the x–y, x–z, and y–z planes). The assumption of rigid-body movements is generally plausible in fMRI studies, although inhomogeneities in the magnetic field may lead to differential scaling of images as a function of their position in the scanner.

To determine the likely amount of head motion, computer algorithms identify the set of translation and rotation parameters that provides the best match to a reference volume, such as the first image acquired in the session (Figure 10.9). The mathematical measure of how well one image matches another is determined by a similarity measure, or **cost function.** In the ideal case of perfect coregistration between the corrected volume and the reference volume, a voxel-by-voxel subtraction would yield a difference volume

coregistration   The spatial alignment of two images or image volumes.

reference volume   A target image volume to which other image volumes are to be aligned.

rigid-body transformation   A spatial transformation that does not change the size or shape of an object; it has three translational parameters and three rotational parameters.

translation   The movement of an object along an axis in space (in the absence of rotation).

rotation   The turning of an object around an axis in space (in the absence of translation).

cost function   A quantity that determines the amount of residual error in a comparison.

(A)

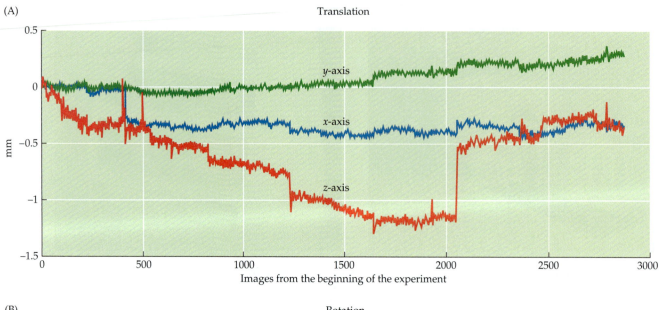

(B)

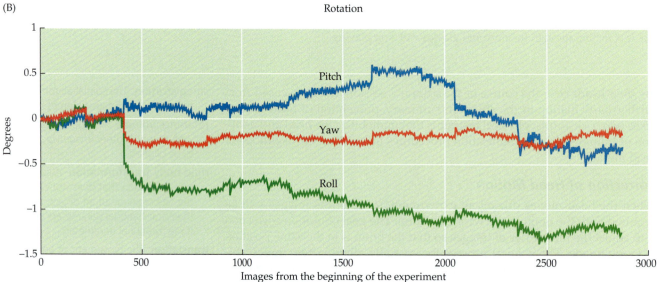

Figure 10.9 Plots of head motion over an experimental session. Shown are plots of translational (A) and rotational (B) head motion from a single fMRI session. This experiment consisted of seven runs, each of 410 images, with a TR of 1500 ms. Large motions between runs are visible as vertical lines on the plot (e.g., image 2050). Note that these are the *estimated* motion values, and thus can be influenced by a number of factors besides head motion itself, as indicated in the text.

of zero. A simple cost function, then, could be the sum of absolute intensity differences between voxels in the corrected and reference volumes. Since large differences are much more problematic than small differences, a more common cost function is the sum of squared intensity differences. Often, motion correction is done on smoothed images to minimize the effects of noise in the image upon the cost function. Regardless of the cost function chosen, the goal of motion correction is to find the rigid-body transformation at which the smallest value of the cost function is obtained.

One challenge to motion correction is that there are a very large number of possible ways in which the head can move. To illustrate this problem, consider a hypothetical subject who can translate her head by up to ±2.5 mm in any direction and can rotate her head by up to ±2.5° along any axis. For purposes of calculation, we will assume that she only can move her head in 0.1-mm increments and can only rotate it in 0.1° increments. For each of the six motion parameters, therefore, there are 50 possible values for her movement, and thus there are more than 15 billion possible combinations of movement parameters at each time point! It is computationally infeasible, therefore, to test all possible small movements and compute the cost functions for each of the thousands of volumes acquired in an experiment.

To overcome this problem, realignment algorithms use iterative approaches for head-motion correction. First, an initial guess is tested, followed by small deviations from that guess. If none of those attempts provides a good match, as indicated by the value of its cost function, then another educated guess is made based on the first tests. This process is repeated until a sufficiently good fit is obtained. Because testing all possible transformations is not possible, the solution obtained may not be the best solution available. For example, the coregistration algorithm may choose as a solution a transformation that minimizes the cost function compared to small deviations in all directions from that solution. However, a better solution with a smaller cost function may have been obtained by testing larger deviations. Converging upon a local minimum in the cost function rather than finding the true global minimum is a common problem in iterative numerical techniques.

Once a set of realignment parameters is determined, the next step is to resample the original data to estimate the values that would have been obtained had there been no head motion. This process is called **spatial interpolation** and is similar to the temporal interpolation described earlier in the chapter, in the section on slice acquisition time correction. However, whereas temporal interpolation only considers points in time (one dimension), spatial interpolation considers points in two or three dimensions. The simplest forms of interpolation are linear methods, such as bilinear for two dimensions or trilinear for three, which assume that each interpolated point should be a weighted average of all adjacent points. How much each neighboring point contributes is determined by how close it is to the new value. The primary advantage of linear methods is that they are very simple and can be quickly computed. A computationally intensive, but more accurate, approach is sinc interpolation. The sinc function is actually the Fourier transform of a rectangular or uniform function (see Figure 4.10). It is the optimal interpolation kernel for well-sampled images but may introduce artifacts if the data are not band-limited, that is, if there are important spatial frequencies in the brain that are not represented in the image. A good compromise is spline interpolation, which fits curves to the known data points in order to estimate unknown data. Common cubic spline interpolation methods create smooth curves by minimizing the second derivative of the connecting function. Spline techniques are intermediate in computational complexity between linear and sinc methods and provide good interpolation results for MRI data.While the standard approach is to minimize the effects of head motion during preprocessing using coregistration algorithms, it is also possible to isolate motion effects within experimental analyses. By including the calculated motion parameters as a term in the analysis model, variability related to head motion can be removed from the model. Since this approach

spatial interpolation The estimation of the intensity of an image at a spatial location that was not originally sampled, using data from nearby locations.

mutual information In the context of MRI, the amount of information about one image that is provided by knowledge of another image. For example, T_1 and T_2 images have different contrast and thus are very different on measures of squared deviation. However, the intensity of a voxel in a T_1 image can be predicted based on its intensity in a T_2 image, so T_1 and T_2 images of the same brain would have high mutual information.

shimming coils Electromagnetic coils that compensate for inhomogeneities in the static magnetic field.

magnetic field mapping The collection of explicit information about the strength of the magnetic field at different spatial locations.

reduces the amount of error (i.e., unaccounted-for variability) in the model, it can increase experimental power for detecting effects of interest. However, as already noted, head motion is often correlated with the experimental task, so including motion parameters in analysis models can also remove task-related activity.

It is important to recognize that algorithms for motion correction, whether conducted during preprocessing or analysis, are not perfect. Indeed, even if the head movement were known perfectly, spatial interpolation would introduce errors due to the limited resolution of functional images, resulting in residual motion effects within the corrected time series. Different cost functions are sensitive to different aspects of the data, and some are more likely than others to converge on local minima. For example, in 2001 Freire and Mangin reported that using the sum of squared differences between the reference and corrected volume as a cost function sensitizes the coregistration to the presence of large task-related BOLD activations in the time series of data. The resulting transformations thus shift the images in a manner systematic with the task and introduce spurious activations noticeable at high contrast borders (such as the edge of the images). Other cost functions that minimize the **mutual information** between the reference and corrected volume are less sensitive to these task-related effects. Mutual information is a measure roughly analogous to correlation that considers how well knowledge of a voxel's intensity in the reference volume predicts, or reduces the uncertainty about, the intensity of a voxel in the corrected image. Unlike the sum of squared deviations, mutual information does not assume that the intensities within the coregistered images must match. For this reason, mutual information is often used as a cost function when coregistering image volumes from different modalities, such as PET with MRI or CT with MRI.

Despite the problems enumerated in this section, measurement of head motion provides an important QA index, and correction of head motion may improve the quality of many fMRI data sets.

Distortion Correction

As we learned in Chapter 5, functional images often suffer from geometric or intensity distortions that preclude simple matching to the high-resolution structural images. The most common culprits for such distortions are inhomogeneities in the static or excitation fields. Static field inhomogeneities usually cause geometric distortions, although they can also lead to signal losses under severe conditions. Excitation field inhomogeneities usually cause intensity variations within the image. To ensure that images provide a true and undistorted representation of the functional neuroanatomy, researchers use specialized acquisition techniques and computational algorithms that correct the acquired images to account for these distortions.

A common method to prevent nonuniformity within the static magnetic field is magnetic field shimming. By adjusting many first-, second-, and higher-order magnetic field gradients generated by **shimming coils** (see Chapter 2), most field distortions can be corrected and a reasonably homogeneous field can be created. However, when shimming conditions cannot be optimized, especially at very high magnetic field, residual magnetic field inhomogeneity may remain significant enough to induce noticeable geometric distortions (Figure 10.10A). An alternative approach, called **magnetic field mapping,** can be adopted to provide explicit knowledge of the static magnetic field. A **field map** of the main magnetic field can be created by

(A)   (B)   (C)

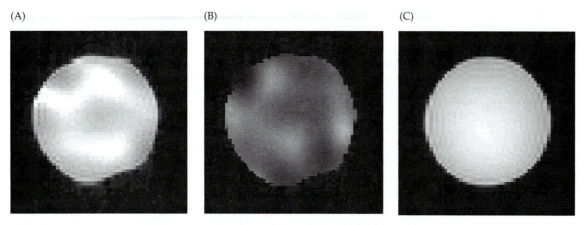

Figure 10.10   Correction of geometric distortions in functional images. In this image of a circular phantom (A), there is obvious geometric distortion. To correct for the distortion, a map of magnetic field intensity is acquired (B). The intensity map can be used to generate a corrected image (C).

acquiring two images of signal phase with slightly different echo times. The difference between the phase images (Figure 10.10B) is proportional to the strength of the field at any given location. If the field is completely uniform, then the phase difference induced by the different echo times will be the same in all voxels, and the resulting image will be a uniform gray. Field maps can be determined for a phantom or human brain and can be incorporated into the image reconstruction routine to correct for any geometric distortions (Figure 10.10C).

field map   An image of the intensity of the magnetic field across space.

> ## Thought Question
> Why does acquiring images of spin phase at two different echo times provide a measure of local magnetic field strength?

A common method to prevent nonuniformity in the excitation field is to construct very homogeneous volume transmitter and receiver coils. While the physical principles for producing such coils are well worked out (see Chapters 2 and 3 for additional discussion), in practice, even the best-constructed volume coils have residual intensity variations across space. This problem is exacerbated by the use of high-sensitivity surface coils, which by design introduce large, spatially dependent intensity variations. Thus, it would be useful to have explicit knowledge of the excitation field so intensity compensation algorithms could be applied post hoc based on such knowledge. To create a map of the excitation field, a large uniform object (e.g., a water-filled phantom) is placed in the center of the magnetic field. For each voxel in the phantom, the recorded signal depends upon two factors: the number of spins (e.g., hydrogen nuclei in a proton-density scan) and the strength of the excitation field at that location. The number of spins should be approximately constant across the phantom, since it is homogeneous; thus, any differences in intensity across the image will be due to variations in the strength of the excitation field.

bias field estimation A technique for estimating inhomogeneities in the magnetic field based upon intensity variation in collected images.

New techniques can correct for intensity variations even when the user does not have explicit knowledge of the imperfections in the static or excitation fields. These techniques can be especially useful when field maps are not available (i.e., for previously acquired images). One promising technique is based on **bias field estimation.** With this technique, we estimate the inhomogeneity using the distorted image itself, as we know that the distorted image is based on a transformation that changes the true data. This transformation is characterized by the bias field, which can be represented as a map of the intensity variations across space due to excitation field inhomogeneity. Because the measured data are a combination of the true data and the bias field, we cannot solve analytically for their individual contributions. Rather, we must estimate the bias field through numerical techniques. By making assumptions about the properties of the noise and the smoothness of the signal, we can determine the most likely pattern of distortions and thus recover an estimate of the true data. Common methods rely on Markov random field models and associated expectation-maximization algorithms to create a map of global and local signal gradients. While a detailed explanation of these methods is beyond the scope of this book, we refer interested readers to the Guillemaud and Brady reference listed at the end of the chapter.

An example of bias field correction is shown in Figure 10.11. The sagittal image shown (Figure 10.11A) has substantial signal loss at the base of the image around the neck. Each tissue type, whether bone, muscle, or fat, shows a similar gradient of intensity decreases toward the base of the image. The consistency of these decreases allows a bias field map to be estimated (Figure 10.11B). By enhancing the remaining signal in areas of significant loss, the algorithms compensate for this loss and produce a corrected image (Figure 10.11C). Bias field estimation and correction can substantially improve aspects of analysis that are dependent upon image uniformity, such

(A)

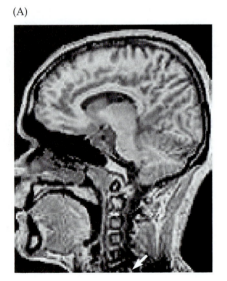

(B)

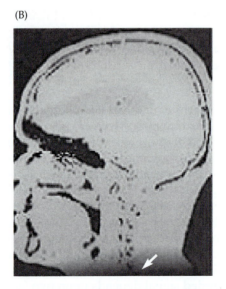

(C)

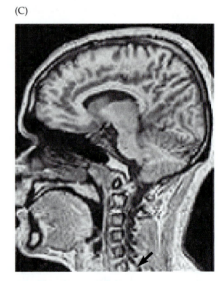

Figure 10.11 Bias field estimation and correction. There is a decrease in MR signal at the bottom (indicated by arrows) of this structural image (A). To correct for this signal loss, the relative intensity of the magnetic field is estimated (B), and a correction factor is applied to the original image. The low-signal region is corrected in the resulting image (C).

as tissue segmentation. For segmentation algorithms to be accurate, different tissue types need to have similar values throughout the brain. Large bias field differences can cause discrepancies in gray/white contrast in different locations. By estimating and correcting for such inhomogeneities, intensity values can be normalized throughout the brain, improving the accuracy of segmentation.

We note, however, that if there are too many local variations, the bias field does not always provide an accurate estimate of the field inhomogeneity. Under such conditions, the bias field correction could actually introduce errors in the segmentation of tissues of interest. Thus, field maps (whether for static field or excitation field) should always be acquired when high spatial and intensity fidelity is required, as for **retinotopic mapping** of the visual cortex.

Functional–Structural Coregistration and Normalization

The spatial and temporal corrections described in the previous sections ensure that each voxel contains data from a single brain region, as sampled at regular intervals throughout the time series. Such corrections are sufficient for analyses of the functional data from a single subject. Yet in most experiments, researchers want to address two questions that are difficult to answer with a single subject's functional data: how does activity map onto anatomy, and how consistent is that mapping across subjects? To answer these questions, we need to understand how our functional data correspond to the underlying neuroanatomy. Unfortunately, functional data typically are of low resolution and of little anatomical contrast, and they have geometric and intensity distortions, as we learned in the previous section. Because of these limitations, we often must map our functional data onto high-resolution and high-contrast structural images. To facilitate this mapping, coregistration algorithms link the functional images to high-resolution structural images from the same subject.

Even if brain activity can be well localized within a subject through coregistration, there remains the problem of comparing activity across individuals, whether in the same study or across studies. Some subjects have very large brains, while others have very small brains, and there is wide variation in shape, orientation, and gyral anatomy. For intersubject comparison to be feasible, each subject's brain must be transformed so that it is the same size and shape as all of the others. This process is called **normalization**. Coregistration and normalization are important preprocessing steps for most fMRI studies, especially those that use voxel-based (i.e., not anatomical region-of-interest) analyses.

Functional–Structural Coregistration

The differences between functional and structural images of the same brain region are striking. A typical functional image appears as a relatively undifferentiated and blurry blob, with only the ventricles and the barest outlines of gray matter distinguishable (Figure 10.12A). High-resolution structural images appear remarkably detailed by comparison, with clear sulcal outlines and distinct boundaries between gray and white matter (Figure 10.12B). This additional detail provides several advantages. Whereas anatomical boundaries are difficult, if not impossible, to identify on functional images (e.g., where is the Sylvian fissure in the functional image?), such boundaries are easily seen on structural images and regions of interest can

retinotopic mapping A technique for delineating functional regions within the visual cortex based upon their responses to stimuli presented at different retinal locations.

normalization The transformation of MRI data from an individual subject to match the spatial properties of a standardized image, such as an averaged brain derived from a sample of many individuals.

Figure 10.12 Comparison of functional and structural images. Functional (A) and structural (B) images have very different properties. Features that are readily visible on a structural image may be difficult to see or entirely absent on a lower-resolution, lower-contrast functional image of the same slice.

(A)

(B)

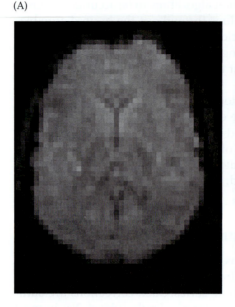

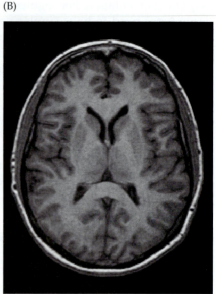

be easily located. Because the size, shape, and sulcal patterns of the brain are much more distinct on structural images, it also would be a great advantage if information from structural images could be used to guide normalization of functional images. Computational processes that map functional and structural images to each other are known as coregistration (Figure 10.13).

One may question the necessity of functional–structural coregistration, because both types of images are typically acquired in the same scanner session and should already be aligned. There are two reasons for this preprocessing step. The first occurs when the two types of images were acquired at different locations, either because different slices were wanted for each or because the subject moved slightly between their acquisitions. In either case, functional–structural coregistration is needed. As before, a rigid-body transformation may be conducted for coregistration in which a cost function is minimized. However, because structural and functional images often have different, sometimes even opposite, contrasts, some cost functions, such as the sum of squared differences, are not appropriate. Mutual information is often used for this purpose.

A second reason for functional–structural coregistration is image distortion. Some pulse sequences used to acquire functional images may introduce subtle geometric distortions; for example, echo-planar functional images may be slightly stretched along one axis relative to a high-resolution structural image obtained from the same subject in the same session. If present, these distortions cannot be corrected by the six-parameter rigid-body transformation that we use for motion correction. If the distortion is linear, such that all voxels are similarly stretched along one or more axes, then a nine-parameter linear transformation can be used, in which three additional parameters are introduced to account for scaling differences along the x-, y-, or z-axes. If the distortion is more complex, with regions of greater and lesser stretching, then more-complex warping algorithms must be employed.

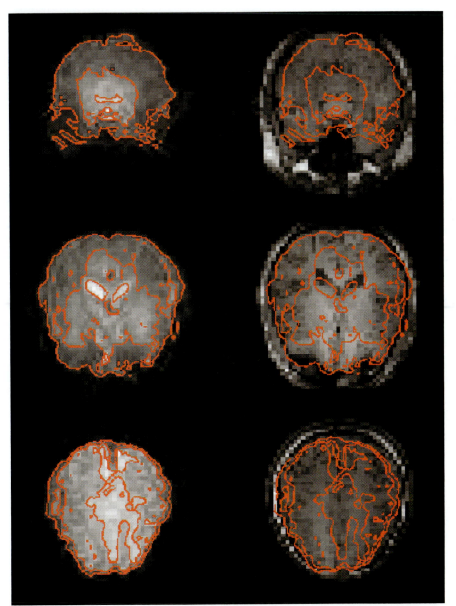

Figure 10.13 Coregistration of functional and structural images. The goal of coregistration is to align images from different modalities, such as a T_2^*-weighted functional volume (left column) with a T_1-weighted structural volume (right column). Successful coregistration relies upon identifying image boundaries (red lines) and matching those boundaries in the different image types.

Spatial Normalization

The human brain has remarkably variable morphology. The average adult brain is approximately 1300 cubic centimeters (cc) in volume, with values ranging from 1100 cc through 1500 cc based upon body size (Figure 10.14). Two subjects in the same fMRI experiment may thus differ in overall brain size by about 30%. As an aside, it is interesting to note that this difference is proportionally much smaller than the range of total body mass, which normally varies by about a factor of 2 or 3 among the adult population. There is also substantial variation in the shape of the adult human brain. Some people have brains that are longer and thinner, while others have brains that are shorter and fatter. The differences may be especially pronounced in particular regions. The organization of gyri and sulci is sufficiently variable that even major landmarks, like the calcarine sulcus, which divides the primary visual cortex, can have different positions and orientations across individuals.

(A)   (B)   (C)

(D)   (E)   (F)

(G)   (H)   (I)

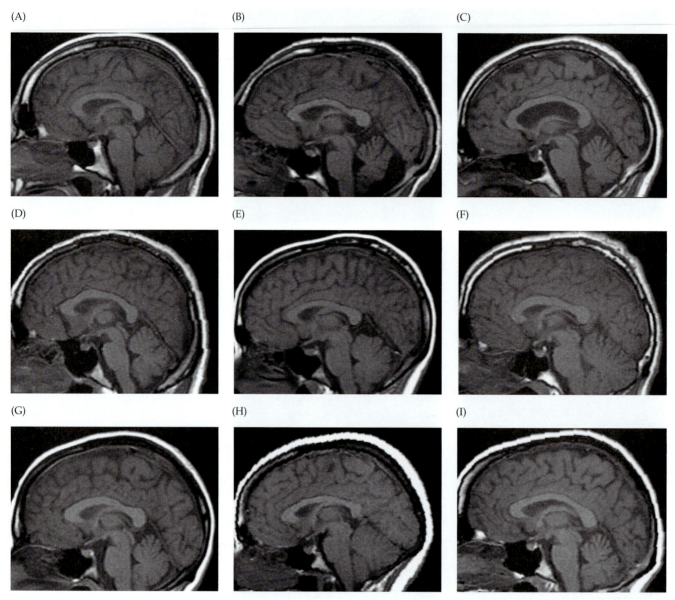

Figure 10.14 Examples of the variability in size and shape of the adult human brain. Each image provides a midsagittal view of the brain of a neurologically normal adult. Note the considerable variability in overall size, in relative height and width, and in the organization of internal structures. This variability poses problems for the normalization of experimental data into common stereotaxic space.

Normalization is a form of coregistration, except that here the image volumes to be coregistered differ fundamentally in shape and not as a result of image distortion. The goal of normalization is to compensate for these shape differences by mathematically stretching, squeezing, and warping each brain so that it is the same as every other brain. The concept of normalization should be familiar to anyone who has watched as computerized morphing programs transform one person's face into another's. Most fMRI analysis packages include modules that normalize data into a common space. Although these programs are largely automated, two guidelines are critical. First, always check the output of automated steps, as errors in normalization will propagate throughout the remainder of the analyses. Second, adjusting the data by hand to an approximate match before invoking the automated algorithm often improves the final output. Because of the assumptions that are made in the warping process, it is common for normalization algorithms to be caught in local minima, missing the best match between data and template. User adjustment can greatly reduce the chance of such problems.

Normalization of data within a study allows combination of data across individuals. Furthermore, if data within two different studies have been normalized in the same fashion, then the areas of activity found in each study can be compared. For this reason, many journals encourage the reporting of experimental data as coordinates within a common normalization scheme, or **stereotaxic space.** The most widely used stereotaxic space is **Talairach space,** which was created by the French physician Jean Talairach and colleagues and is based upon a simple stereotaxic framework derived from measurements on a single brain, that of an elderly woman. The origin of the space is set at the midpoint of the anterior commissure, with the x- and y-axes defined by the horizontal plane connecting the anterior and posterior commissures (Figure 10.15). While the standardization provided by this framework has been extraordinarily important for neuroscience, the use of a single brain presents many problems, notably that the brain used was unrepresentative of the population at large.

A better approach has come from recent attempts at probabilistic spaces based upon combining data from hundreds of individual scans. A commonly used space was created by the Montreal Neurological Institute and consists of an average of 152 T_1-weighted brain images. The MNI template has been scaled to match landmarks within the well-established Talairach atlas. Most normalization algorithms are based upon such probabilistic templates. To warp a given brain to a template, normalization algorithms determine the overall size of the brain, as well as its gross anatomical features. Some algorithms also require identification of key landmarks in the brain, such as major sulci; this may be done automatically or require user input.

stereotaxic space A precise mapping system (e.g., of the brain) using three-dimensional coordinates.

Talairach space The most commonly used space for normalization of fMRI data.

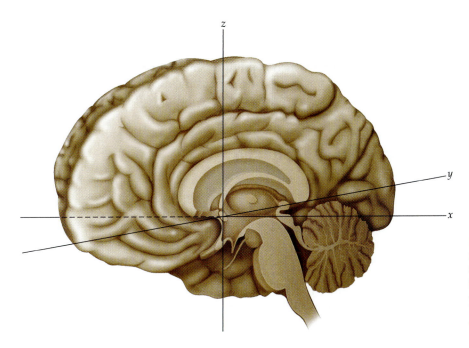

Figure 10.15 Typical coordinate axes for fMRI data. The most common axes for fMRI data define the x-axis as left to right and the y-axis by connecting the anterior and posterior commissures. The z-axis is perpendicular to the plane created by the other two lines.

cytoarchitecture The organization of the brain on the basis of cell structure.

filter Within the context of fMRI, an algorithm for removing temporal or spatial frequency components of data.

Even if normalization algorithms were able to transform two brains into the same stereotaxic framework, such success would not mean that the brains would have activation in exactly the same voxels. Remember that normalization is based upon gross morphological features of brains. These gross features do not necessarily indicate functional divisions between brain areas. More predictive of brain function are the regional cellular properties, or **cytoarchitecture,** which are usually not visible on MR images. Just as sulci and gyri are highly variable across individuals, so too are the boundaries between cytoarchitectonically distinct regions. (For an example of quantification of individual differences in the cytoarchitectonic organization of the human brain, consult the work of Rajkowska and Goldman-Rakic indicated in the references.)

Normalization is a powerful technique that enables the testing of complex hypotheses with improved statistical power, and its positive impact upon functional neuroimaging cannot be overstated. However, there are some caveats. Variability in brain features across individuals introduces theoretical constraints upon normalization. Nearly all normalization approaches are based on subject samples drawn from the standard population of fMRI participants: young, typically college-age, adults who are healthy and neurologically normal. Many subject groups systematically differ from this population in the properties of their brains. The brains of elderly individuals may have atrophy, manifested as sulcal widening and enlarged ventricles. Young children may have differently shaped brains, due to delayed maturation of some regions (e.g., frontal cortex), as well as different contrast associated with reduced neuronal myelination. Male and female brains also differ in subtle ways. Normalizing functional results across different subject groups may mask important group differences.

Variability in brain features across individuals also introduces practical constraints upon normalization. Many patient groups have a specific local pathology associated with their disorder, while patients with tumors may have brains that are apparently normal in most regions but have severe distortions in the lesion area. Since most normalization approaches attempt to minimize the differences between the subject's brain and some template, abnormal features may reduce the accuracy of the matching process. Some normalization approaches have been developed for nontypical subject populations, but this remains an area of considerable interest. Finally, by its very nature, normalization emphasizes that which is common among individuals and de-emphasizes that which is unique. Small but meaningful variations among individuals' functional neuroanatomy may be lost through this process. Investigators interested in individual differences may wish to consider alternatives to normalization.

Spatial and Temporal Filtering

Filters are used to remove or retain different frequency components that are present in a composite signal. Filters can operate on one-dimensional temporal data, such as a voxel's time course of intensity changes, and on two or three-dimensional spatial data, such as adjacent voxels in a BOLD-contrast image volume. In neuroimaging, filters are used to remove uninteresting variation in the data that can be safely attributed to noise sources, while preserving signals of interest. Filtering, then, can be used to increase functional SNR. Filters have other implications for statistical processing of fMRI data. By reducing the dimensionality of the data, filters can reduce the problem of multiple statistical comparisons. In this section, we will explore both uses of filters in fMRI preprocessing.

Temporal Filtering

The use of temporal filters can substantially improve the quality of fMRI data by improving functional SNR. To describe how temporal filters work, we will begin by reintroducing, from the previous chapter, the concept of the frequency spectrum of a signal. Consider the time series of data recorded from a single voxel, which describes the behavior of the voxel in the time domain. The same data can be converted, using a Fourier transform, to the frequency domain. The frequency range that is present in a sampled signal depends upon its sampling rate, which is given by the TR for fMRI data. The maximum frequency that can be identified, or the **Nyquist frequency,** is equal to one-half of the sampling rate. If the sampling rate is 0.5 Hz (TR of 2000 ms), for example, any frequencies in the underlying signal higher than 0.25 Hz would not be present in the sampled data. Instead, power at those frequencies would be aliased, or artifactually present at other frequency values. Because of the Nyquist limitation, we must sample the brain at twice the rate of any phenomenon of interest.

Nyquist frequency The highest frequency that can be identified in a digitally sampled signal; it is defined as one-half of the sampling rate.

task frequency The rate of presentation of a periodic experimental task.

> ## Thought Question
>
> Based on what you learned in earlier chapters, what disadvantages are there for collecting images at very high temporal resolution (short TR)?

In the example shown in Figure 10.16A–C, there is considerable power at about 0.025 Hz, which approximately corresponds to the **task frequency.**

(A)

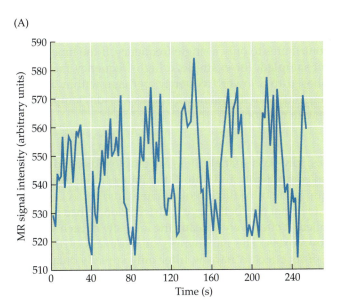

(B)

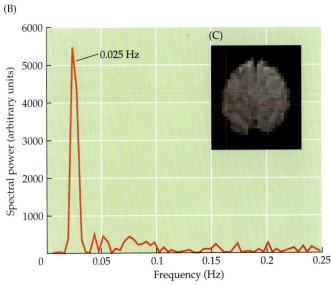

Figure 10.16 Comparison of the time and frequency domains for a single voxel. Shown are the raw time course (A) and power spectrum (B) from a single active voxel in the motor cortex (C). In this task, the subject alternated between squeezing his hands for 20 s and resting for 20 s. Visible in the power spectrum is the considerable power at the task frequency. (Note that the time course was normalized to a mean of zero before the power spectrum was calculated.)

matched filters The principle that the filter of the same frequency as the signal of interest provides maximal signal-to-noise ratio.

We emphasize that the two graphs show exactly the same data, only transformed from one domain to another. In our analyses, we want to keep information about changes in the data that occur at the task frequency but minimize changes in the data that occur at other frequencies. That is, we wish to reduce the contribution of noise that is isolated in particular frequency ranges. Suppose that we knew, based on physiological measurement, that a subject breathed every 4 seconds (0.25 Hz), on average, during this run (see Figure 9.5 for an example). Since we are not interested in breathing, but instead in the brain process occurring at the task frequency, we would like to remove the effects of breathing from the data. But how? To reduce the influence of breathing, we construct a temporal filter that selectively attenuates frequencies around 0.25 Hz but leaves other frequencies essentially intact. This is called a band-stop filter, since it attenuates a range or band of frequencies. A low-pass filter leaves low frequencies intact while attenuating high frequencies, and a high-pass filter stops only low frequencies.

The choice of filter depends on what sort of variability should be eliminated. Typical heart rates during an fMRI experiment vary, but are often between 1.0 and 1.5 Hz. The rate of respiration is slower, about 0.2 to 0.3 Hz. For comparison, a typical experimental design might present alternating blocks of 12 s of task and 12 s of rest, for a total presentation rate of 0.04 Hz. A low-pass filter that excluded frequencies above 0.2 Hz could remove physiological oscillations without significantly reducing the ability to detect the task effect of interest. However, if the experiment used a fast event-related design in which stimuli were presented more rapidly (i.e., every few seconds), the task and respiration would be at similar frequencies, and such filtering would be extremely difficult. Very-low-frequency changes are also observed in fMRI experiments, such as those related to scanner drift. These changes often take the form of near linear increases or decreases in absolute signal over the course of a several-minute experimental run. As noted in the prior discussion of head motion, such very slow changes can be extremely problematic for fMRI experiments, especially those using long-interval blocked designs. High-pass filtering of the data can remove slow driftlike trends. It is important to recognize that none of these factors, whether task, physiology, or drift, contributes to only a single frequency. If the time course is not sufficiently well sampled, for example, a high-frequency factor like heart rate could be aliased to a lower frequency, perhaps within the task range. All provide energy at many frequencies, and as a result, temporal filtering should be done with caution.

Spatial Filtering

In many fMRI analyses, low-pass spatial filters are employed to reduce the high-frequency spatial components and "blur" the images. The most common blurring technique is the introduction of a Gaussian filter. A Gaussian filter has the shape of a normal (or "bell-curve") distribution. When a Gaussian spatial filter is applied, it effectively spreads the intensity at each voxel in the image over nearby voxels. The narrowness or wideness of the filter refers to the distance of its effect: A narrow filter only spreads data over a few voxels, while a wide filter spreads data over many voxels. Spatial filter width for fMRI data is generally expressed in millimeters at half of the maximum value (full-width-half-maximum, or FWHM).

What are the advantages of spatially filtering fMRI data? The foremost advantage can be understood in terms of the principle of **matched filters,** which is that using a filter of the same frequency as the signal of interest maximizes SNR. This is similar to the concept of the band-stop filter for temporal data described in the previous section. In fMRI images, the width of the signal of interest can be understood in a literal sense: the typical spatial extent of regions of activity. If there were no spatial correlation in fMRI data, so that one could not predict whether a voxel would be active by whether its neighbors were active, then spatial filtering would reduce SNR. However, all fMRI data have spatial correlation, due both to functional similarity of adjacent brain regions and to blurring introduced by the vascular system. The cerebral cortex itself has a depth of about 5 mm, so activation of even a single cortical column can result in two or three active voxels, depending on their size. Additional spatial correlation is introduced when comparing across subjects. Because all subjects' brains differ from one another in shape and size, and potentially even in functional organization, areas of activity are rarely represented in exactly the same voxels. Instead, combining data across many subjects distributes activity across a range of voxels. By using a filter that matches the expected spatial correlation of the data, one can increase SNR considerably with minimal loss of spatial resolution.

A second advantage lies in improving the validity of statistical techniques. During the analysis of any fMRI data set, there will be an enormous number of statistical tests. In a typical functional imaging volume, there may be more than 100,000 voxels, each of which is evaluated for significance. If the threshold for significance is set at $\alpha < 0.05$, as is frequently done for psychological or medical experiments, then there should be more than 5000 voxels active due to chance alone. This is known as the **multiple comparison problem,** and is discussed in detail in Chapter 12. But if the data are spatially correlated, then there may be many fewer local maxima that exhibit significant activity (Figure 10.17A and B). In addition to its effects on false-positive rates, smoothing provides the additional benefit of improving the

multiple comparison problem The increase in the number of false-positive results (i.e., Type I errors) with increasing number of statistical tests. It is of particular consequence for voxelwise fMRI analyses, which may have many thousands of statistical tests.

(A)

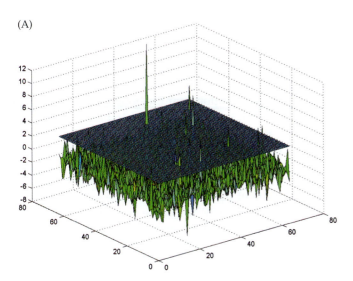

(B)

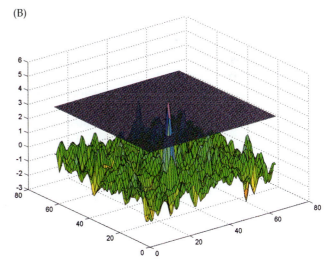

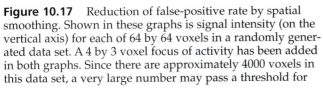

Figure 10.17 Reduction of false-positive rate by spatial smoothing. Shown in these graphs is signal intensity (on the vertical axis) for each of 64 by 64 voxels in a randomly generated data set. A 4 by 3 voxel focus of activity has been added in both graphs. Since there are approximately 4000 voxels in this data set, a very large number may pass a threshold for significance (e.g., alpha of 0.01), as shown in (A). Spatial smoothing will average data over adjacent voxels, reducing the likelihood that a cluster of voxels will pass the same threshold. As shown in (B), only the active cluster passes the significance threshold after smoothing (note the difference in z-axis scale between the graphs).

validity of experimental tests by making parameter errors more normal. Any derived parameter, such as the significance value measured at a single voxel, can be considered to be a combination of its true value along with some error. Many common statistical tests assume that error in measurement is normally distributed. Smoothing increases the normality of data, because averaging of multiple observations tends toward the normal distribution regardless of the properties of the individual observations (i.e., the central limit theorem). Therefore, smoothing can have a salutary effect upon fMRI statistical analyses.

The primary disadvantages of spatial filtering result from the necessarily imperfect match between filter width and activation extent. If the filter used is too large, then meaningful activations could be attenuated below the threshold for significance. This is especially problematic for functional structures that are very small, such as nuclei within the midbrain, where only a single voxel may be significantly active. If the filter used is too small, then it will have little positive effect on SNR, while reducing spatial resolution. Typical filter widths for fMRI are about 6 to 10 mm FWHM (i.e., about two to three voxels), although greater or lesser smoothing may be indicated by the noise level of the data. It is important to emphasize that spatial smoothing is beneficial for voxelwise analyses but has little effect on region-of-interest analyses. In ROI approaches, by definition, the experimenter constructs bounded functional regions for subsequent analysis. The edges of these regions are considered to be meaningful, so their blurring may introduce unwanted variability into the analysis.

Effects of Spatial Filtering on Functional SNR

It is important to recognize that functional SNR varies across space. Signal is greater in voxels highly associated with the task than in voxels with little to no task-related activity. Partial volume effects also reduce SNR in voxels near the edge of an activation. Noise varies over space as well, due to the many factors discussed in Chapter 9. Therefore, within any experiment, some voxels will have relatively high functional SNR and others will have low SNR. Parrish and colleagues conducted a set of simulations to determine the approximate SNR values needed to detect a BOLD signal change of a given amplitude, and how detection power changes with spatial filtering. They then applied those calculations to an fMRI time series measured for a clinical patient with a vascular malformation near the boundary between the parietal and occipital lobes. The time series consisted of 16 blocks and alternated between task and nontask conditions every 7 TRs.

The authors found that SNR varied across the brain. Without spatial filtering, almost no voxels had sufficient SNR for detection of a 1% BOLD signal change (Figure 10.18A), while a 2% change was detectable throughout most of the brain, save for the site of the malformation, the inferior frontal lobe, and the posterior midline (Figure 10.18B). The frontal lobe problem was due to signal loss around the air–tissue interface above the frontal sinus; this signal loss, known as a susceptibility artifact, is evident in many functional images throughout this book (see Figure 9.15). To investigate the effects of spatial filtering, the authors applied a 6-mm Gaussian filter and repeated their analysis. Detection power increased considerably throughout the brain. Where before there were large gaps above the malformation and frontal lobe, now there was sufficient power to detect a response through nearly all of the brain. Note that spatial filtering provides an increase in SNR at a cost of reduced spatial resolution.

(A)   (B)

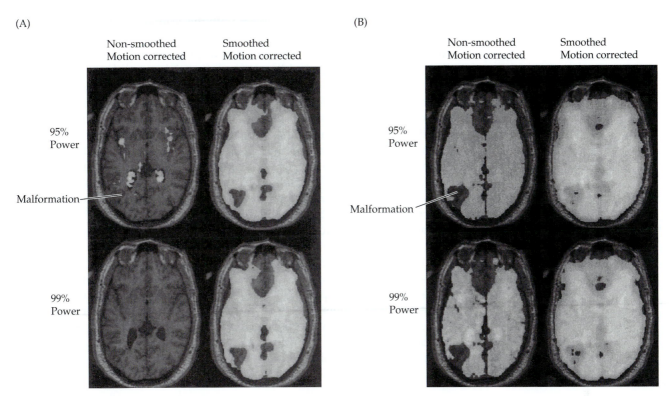

Figure 10.18   Differences in detection power throughout the brain. Researchers investigated the spatial distribution of detection power for fMRI signals of different amplitudes within data taken from a single patient. Voxels with sufficiently low noise for detection of a given signal change are indicated in white. Almost no voxels had noise levels sufficiently small for detection of a 1% signal change in the absence of spatial smoothing (A; left). With spatial smoothing, a 1% change was detectable in most regions, with the notable exceptions of the ventral frontal lobe and the area around the malformation (A; right). A 2% signal change, however, was detectable in most regions with or without spatial smoothing (B). (From Parrish et al., 2000.)

The results of Parrish and colleagues support a simple and intuitive conclusion: the ability to detect an activation of interest relies fundamentally on SNR, which may vary considerably across brain regions, subject groups, or tasks. SNR may be increased in several ways, such as by the noise reduction and signal averaging approaches discussed in the previous chapter or the preprocessing approaches discussed in this chapter. In a deep sense, spatial filtering has similarities to signal averaging, in that both combine data across observations. When a spatial filter is applied, data are combined across multiple voxels, while under signal averaging, data are combined across multiple trials. In both cases, the variability of the data can be reduced, increasing functional SNR.

Summary

Preprocessing procedures measure and/or remove unwanted variability in fMRI data in order to improve experimental analyses. Regular quality assurance tests are important for preventing and diagnosing data problems. By evaluating raw SNR, checking for common image acquisition problems, and examining distortions in the images, researchers can ensure that a hardware or software problem with the scanner can be quickly identified and corrected. Initial temporal and spatial preprocessing steps correct for variability both in the timing of slice acquisition and in the spatial position of voxels. The most insidious cause of spatial error is head motion, which if uncorrected can introduce severe artifacts into analyses.

Prevention of head motion typically relies on the combination of restrictive devices, like bite bars or masks, and subject training. Spatial errors resulting from inhomogeneities in the static magnetic field or radiofrequency coil can be corrected through mapping or estimation of the resulting distortion field. To improve spatial localization of activity, images may be transformed both by functional–structural coregistration and by normalization. FMRI coregistration matches functional data to higher-resolution structural images, enabling better anatomical localization of activity within a subject. Normalization mathematically warps subjects' brains to a standard stereotaxic framework, allowing better comparison across individuals within a study as well as reporting of data in common coordinates for comparison across studies. Functional resolution can be improved by judicious use of temporal and spatial filtering. Temporal filtering can remove selective noise components, like those introduced by physiological processes, and can correct for low-frequency scanner drift. Spatial filtering can increase functional SNR, reduce apparent noise, and increase the validity of comparisons across subjects. However, improperly applied filters can significantly reduce the quality of the data.

Suggested Readings

Della-Maggiore, V., and Chau, W. (2002). An empirical comparison of SPM preprocessing parameters to the analysis of fMRI data. *NeuroImage*, 17(1): 19–28. This intriguing article describes some methods for evaluating the value of different preprocessing steps.

Jezzard, P., Matthews, P. M., and Smith, S. M. (eds.) (2003). *Functional MRI: An Introduction to Methods*. Oxford University Press, Oxford. A wide-ranging book that contains several chapters on preprocessing steps in fMRI.

*Parrish, T. B., Gitelman, D. R., LaBar, K. S., and Mesulam, M. M. (2000). Impact of signal-to-noise on functional MRI. *Magn. Reson. Med.*, 44: 925–932. A clear demonstration of how changes in signal-to-noise affect detection of activity; includes an example from a clinical patient.

*Talairach, J., and Tournoux, P. (1988). *Co-Planar Stereotaxic Atlas of the Human Brain*. Thieme, New York. This atlas has become extraordinarily influential as a reference for brain anatomy and function.

Indicates a reference that is a suggested reading in the field and is also cited in this chapter.

Chapter References

Ashburner, J., and Friston, K. (1997). Multimodal image coregistration and partitioning—a unified framework. *NeuroImage*, 6(3): 209–217.

Cox, R. W. (1996). AFNI: Software for analysis and visualization of functional magnetic resonance neuroimages. *Comput. Biomed. Res.*, 29(3): 162–173.

Freire, L., and Mangin, J. F. (2001). Motion correction algorithms may create spurious brain activations in the absence of subject motion. *NeuroImage*, 14: 709–722.

Guillemaud, R., and Brady, M. (1997). Estimating the bias field of MR images. *IEEE Trans. Med. Imaging*, 16(3): 238–251.

Kwong, K. K., Belliveau, J. W., Chesler, D. A., Goldberg, I. E., Weisskoff, R. M., Poncelet, B. P., Kennedy, D. N., Hoppel, B. E., Cohen, M. S., Turner, R., et al. (1992). Dynamic magnetic resonance imaging of human brain activity during primary sensory stimulation. *Proc. Natl. Acad. Sci. U.S.A.*, 89(12): 5675–5679.

Rajkowska, G., and Goldman-Rakic, P. S. (1995). Cytoarchitectonic definition of prefrontal areas in the normal human cortex: II. Variability in locations of areas 9 and 46 and relationship to the Talairach Coordinate System. *Cereb. Cortex*, 5: 323–337.

Thulborn, K. R. (1999). Visual feedback to stabilize head position for fMRI. *Magn. Reson. Med.*, 41(5): 1039–1043.

Voyvodic, J. T. (1999). Real-time fMRI paradigm control, physiology, and behavior combined with near real-time statistical analysis. *NeuroImage*, 10(2): 91–106.

11

Experimental Design

All scientific research begins with a question. For cognitive neuroscience research, that question may be as broad as "What brain regions are associated with retrieval of information from long-term memory?" or as focused as "Does activity in the caudate nucleus precede or follow activity in the primary motor cortex?" From the experimental question, a researcher derives a **research hypothesis,** which is a statement about how a given manipulation should change some measurement. Hypotheses, like research questions, may be very general or very specific. An example of a general hypothesis for fMRI research is the statement "Activity in the frontal cortex will be reduced in depressed individuals." Hypotheses may also make specific claims about the nature of the fMRI measurement, such as "The activity in the middle frontal gyrus evoked by an n-back working memory task will decline proportionally to the degree of depression as measured by the Beck Depression Inventory." The key characteristic of a hypothesis is that it is falsifiable, that is, it can be tested experimentally. More specific hypotheses can be more easily falsified and are thus more informative.

To test a hypothesis, a scientist designs an **experiment.** Experiments, in the technical sense of the word, first manipulate some aspect of the world and then measure the outcome of that manipulation. The canonical example of an experiment is Galileo's test of the effects of mass on gravity. Galileo speculated that an object's acceleration due to gravitational effects does not depend on its mass. To test this hypothesis, he dropped two balls of different mass from a great height and found that they fell at the same rate. In this experiment, Galileo manipulated the mass of the objects being dropped and measured the relative time needed for them to fall a given distance. In modern fMRI experiments, scientists often manipulate some aspect of a stimulus, such as whether a picture is of a face or an object or whether a word is easy or difficult to remember, and then measure the change in BOLD signal within the brain. The way in which a scientist sets up the manipulations and measurements of an experiment is known as **experimental design.**

Scientists want to design their experiments in order to most efficiently answer meaningful questions about the world. All well-designed experi-

research hypothesis A proposition about the nature of the world that makes predictions about the results of an experiment. For a hypothesis to be well formed, it must be falsifiable.

experiment The controlled test of a hypothesis. Experiments manipulate one or more independent variables, measure one or more dependent variables, and evaluate those measurements using tests of statistical significance.

experimental design The organization of an experiment to allow effective testing of the research hypothesis.

variable A measured or manipulated quantity that varies within an experiment.

independent variables (IVs) Aspects of the experimental design that are intentionally manipulated by the experimenter and that are hypothesized to cause changes in the dependent variables.

conditions (or levels) Different values of the independent variable(s).

dependent variables (DVs) Quantities that are measured by the experimenter in order to evaluate the effects of the independent variables.

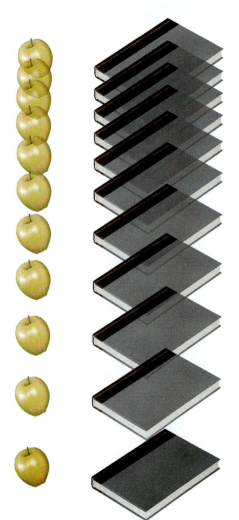

ments share several characteristics: they test specific hypotheses, they rule out alternative explanations for the data, and they minimize the cost of running the experiment. Advance planning to ensure good experimental design is especially important for fMRI experiments, given the significant resources they require in direct scanner costs and in the time spent by the experimenters, research assistants, and/or technologists in collecting and analyzing the data. If your experiment is inadequate for answering your hypotheses, all of that investment in time and money may be wasted. This chapter discusses the basic principles of experimental design for fMRI. Although we discuss the advantages and disadvantages of specific classes of experimental designs throughout the chapter, we want to emphasize a single overriding theme: the best experimental design is the one that lets you investigate *your* particular research question.

Basic Principles of Experimental Design

The fundamental element of an experiment is the **variable,** of which there are two types. **Independent variables (IVs)** are aspects of the experimental design that are expressly manipulated by the experimenter. The choice of IV depends upon the hypothesis to be tested. In Galileo's experiment, the IV was the mass of the objects, and there were two levels of mass (light and heavy). Different types of fMRI studies use different IVs. In a study of visual perception, one could use the variable *stimulus category* by showing subjects different types of objects (e.g., faces, houses, tools). A study of attention might manipulate whether or not subjects pay attention to a given object, so that one condition could be *attended* and the other *unattended.* And in a study of long-term memory, one could train subjects on a list of words one week before putting them in the scanner, and then compare *remembered* words to *novel* words that were not previously learned. The different values of an IV are often called **conditions** or **levels.**

Dependent variables (DVs) reflect the data measured by the experimenter. Different dependent variables provide different evidence for or against a hypothesis. Galileo compared how rapidly two objects fell; his dependent variable was relative time. Most fMRI studies use BOLD signal change as the primary dependent variable, although a few studies use other measures, as is described in Chapter 14. It is important to recognize that a single hypothesis can be evaluated using multiple dependent variables. For example, a common experiment in physics laboratories is to repeat Galileo's experiment while taking photographs of the falling masses at regular time intervals using a strobe-light system, as shown in Figure 11.1. The photographs provide information about the dependent variable, distance, from which velocity can be calculated. Similarly, a single hypothesis about the brain could be tested using fMRI, ERP (event-related potentials), magnetoencephalography (MEG), or lesion studies. Different neuroscience techniques provide different dependent measures, which can together provide converging evidence for a hypothesis.

Figure 11.1   A simple experiment. By dropping two objects of different masses and photographing their motion over time, an experimenter can verify that the independent variable, mass, has no effect upon the dependent variable, distance traveled over time.

> ### Thought Question
> The idea of converging evidence is a very important one in science. Why does the collection of data using different techniques (and thus different dependent variables) improve our ability to test research hypotheses?

Note that behavioral measures like response time and error rate can be considered as either DVs or IVs depending on the context. In most cases, researchers collect behavioral data in order to validate the experimental manipulations, as when examining whether attention (IV) decreases response time (DV). However, if one is interested in the effects of errors (IV) on BOLD signal (DV), the behavioral data may become the manipulated factor. In the remainder of this text, we will operationally define independent variables as those aspects of the experiment that serve as factors in an analysis, and dependent variables as those aspects that serve as data for the analysis.

Experimental variables, whether independent or dependent, may be categorical or continuous. A **categorical variable** can have one of a number of discrete values (Figure 11.2A). For example, if you want to map the hand regions of the motor cortex, you may set up an experiment in which the subject squeezes with either the left hand or the right hand. The IV in this experiment is *hand,* which obviously has only two values. But imagine that you are interested in measuring how activity in the motor cortex (DV) changes with pressure of squeezing (IV). Subjects could squeeze a sensor in their hand that measures how much force is exerted. In this experiment, force

(A)   (B)   (C)

Figure 11.2 Categorical vs. continuous variables. (A) A categorical variable is one that can take two or more discrete values. Thus, whether someone squeezes his or her left hand or right hand could be indicated by a categorical variable. (B) A continuous variable can take any of an infinite number of values, limited only by the precision of the measurement. How much force someone exerts when squeezing his or her hand could be indicated by a continuous variable. Note that some continuous variables can be converted into categorical variables. Color, for example, is at root a continuous variable (C) since it results from the frequency of visible light, which can take any of a range of values. However, we see discrete color categories even in a continuous spectrum.

continuous variable   A variable that can take any value within a range.

between-subjects   A manipulation in which different conditions are assigned to different subject groups.

within-subjects   A manipulation in which each subject participates in all experimental conditions.

would be a **continuous variable,** because it could take any value within a range (Figure 11.2B). Categorical independent variables are generally easier to work with in fMRI experiments, as they allow the use of treatment/control analyses, which are described in the next section. However, using continuous variables can in principle be much more powerful, and some experimental questions require them. One common procedure for fMRI studies is to discretize a continuous variable into a limited number of categories in order to simplify analyses. For example, consider an experiment that investigates whether response time influences the timing of activity in the basal ganglia. Response time is usually treated as a continuous variable that is measured in milliseconds. However, one could take all of the different trials in the experiment and classify them as "fast" or "slow" trials based on whether they were above or below the median. This procedure would change response time into a categorical variable.

An important distinction can also be made between two types of manipulations. In a **between-subjects** manipulation, different subject groups reflect different values of the IV. Note that the group difference may be some intrinsic qualifier, like males versus females or drug abusers versus abstainers, or it may be assigned by an experimental manipulation. In fMRI studies, between-subjects experiments are most common in examinations of the effects of a drug or disease state. To study the effects of schizophrenia upon executive processing in the frontal lobe, a researcher could run two groups of subjects, one with the disorder and one without. Designs that have different groups of subjects do different tasks are used less commonly, because differences in the composition of the groups, such as age, gender, or education, could confound the results. However, as discussed in the prior two chapters, there is large intersubject variability in fMRI studies. For this reason, most fMRI studies use **within-subjects** manipulations, where each subject participates in all experimental conditions. As a rule of thumb, experimental designs should be within-subjects whenever possible.

These concepts apply not just to fMRI studies but to any research program. For additional discussion of general principles of experimental design, we refer the interested student to the references section, where several comprehensive texts are listed.

Setting Up a Good Research Hypothesis

Underlying any experimental design is a research hypothesis, which has the following basic structure: "Manipulating the independent variable (IV) will cause changes in the measurement (DV)." The hypothesis is validated if we manipulate the IV and the DV changes as expected, but it is falsified if the DV does not change. A hypothesis can be made more precise by specifying how IVs and DVs should relate to each other. For instance, "*Increasing* the IV should cause a *decrease* in the DV." While hypotheses can be stated in many different ways, at root they all have this same underlying structure of cause and effect.

In fMRI studies, there are three distinct levels of research hypotheses, representing three different types of questions that can be asked (Figure 11.3). At the most specific level are hypotheses about *hemodynamic* activity in the brain. Such hypotheses reflect questions about the BOLD effect itself, without making inferences about its causes. Many of the studies of refractory effects discussed in Chapter 8 fall into this category, such as the 2002 study by Birn and colleagues that investigated changes in the linearity of the hemodynamic

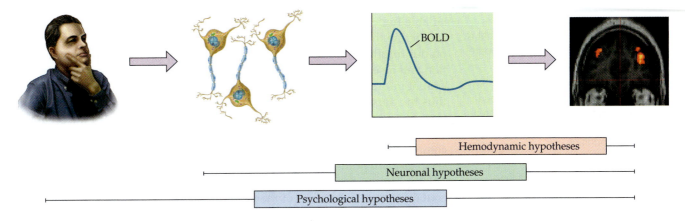

Figure 11.3 Constructing research hypotheses. Hypotheses are statements about the relations between independent and dependent variables. For fMRI experiments, there are three types of research hypotheses. The most basic are hemodynamic hypotheses, statements about hemodynamic activity measured by fMRI. More complex are neuronal hypotheses, which make claims about how underlying neuronal activity should affect fMRI data. Finally, psychological hypotheses attempt to relate some aspect of cognition to observed fMRI results. Psychological hypotheses are the most challenging to construct, but they can have the greatest influence on the study of the brain.

response in different brain regions. A second class of hypothesis addresses questions about *neuronal* activity. Since fMRI does not measure neuronal activity directly, researchers must estimate that activity by transforming the measured BOLD signal. An example of a neuronal hypothesis for fMRI would be: "Neuronal activity within the middle frontal gyrus increases with the number of items that must be held in memory." Note that although the fMRI measurement is still BOLD signal, the inference that is to be evaluated relates to the neuronal activity itself. The third type is *psychological* hypotheses. We can use fMRI to answer questions about psychological processes like attention, memory, or perception. One important hypothesis that has been studied using fMRI is "Encoding of items into memory and retrieval of items from memory are associated with activity in different hemispheres." Note that this hypothesis relies on very general concepts like encoding and retrieval that are not uniquely defined, in that reasonable people can (and do!) disagree over what those terms mean.

Psychological hypotheses can be the most difficult to construct, but they are often the most influential. An influential psychological hypothesis about the organization of the visual system was advanced by Ungerleider and Mishkin in 1982. They suggested that visual information might be processed in two distinct pathways, a ventral occipitotemporal pathway that processes object features ("what") and a dorsal occipitalparietal pathway that processes spatial properties ("where"). From this simple statement have come literally hundreds of neuroimaging and electrophysiological studies—extensions of the initial hypothesis to include dorsal and ventral divisions in the frontal lobe as well as debates over exactly what sorts of spatial/object information are represented. This particular hypothesis has become sufficiently well supported that it forms the basis of a **theory,** a generalizable set of rules that shapes thinking on a topic, in this case the visual system. It is important to recognize that this influential idea began with a simple and fal-

theory An organized set of ideas that guides thinking on a topic and that can be used to generate a variety of experimental hypotheses.

experimental condition A condition that contains the stimuli or task that is most relevant to the research hypothesis. Also called the task condition.

control condition A condition that provides a standard to which the experimental condition(s) can be compared. Also called the baseline condition or nontask condition.

epiphenomenal Being of secondary consequence to a causal chain of processes, but playing no causal role in the process of interest.

sifiable hypothesis. Psychological hypotheses are limited by how well we can define the concepts of interest. The "what/where" hypothesis depends on our intuitive understanding of the differences between spatial information and object information. However, some researchers have suggested that spatial information includes how objects can be manipulated spatially, and thus the dorsal stream represents "how" information, not "where" information. The resulting debate has spawned new hypotheses about the organization of the visual system, changing the very terms used by the scientific community.

To test a hypothesis, scientists set up an experiment. Given the hypothesis "Manipulating the IV will cause changes in the DV," the experiment must contain at least two values of the IV and must be able to measure changes in the DV. The simplest way to set up an experiment is to have two conditions that occur at different times. These are usually separated into an **experimental condition** and a **control condition,** which differ only in the effect of interest. The experimental condition is sometimes called the task condition, and the control condition is sometimes called the baseline condition or nontask condition. In Chapter 7 we discussed the first BOLD fMRI experiment, which was reported by Kwong and colleagues in 1992. They hypothesized that manipulating the amount of visual stimulation would change the BOLD activity level in the primary visual cortex. Their experimental condition consisted of bright flashing lights that the subjects watched using LED goggles, while their control condition was darkness. When different levels of BOLD activity between conditions were measured in the visual cortex, they attributed that difference to the IV of brightness.

Are fMRI Data Correlational?

A frequent criticism of fMRI data is that they are correlational, or **epiphenomenal,** implying that one cannot use them to make causal inferences and thus cannot conduct tests of experimental hypotheses (Figure 11.4A and B). This criticism is derived from the nature of the BOLD signal. As outlined in

(A)   (B)

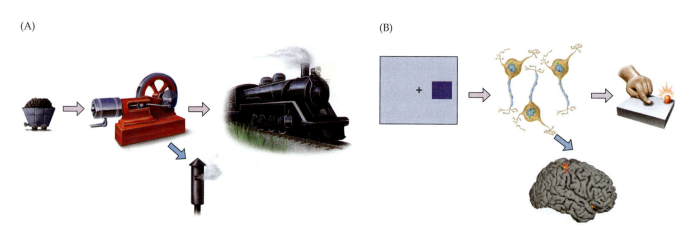

Figure 11.4 Causal chains and epiphenomena. We can think of many phenomena as part of a causal chain of events. (A) Feeding coal to a steam engine provides power that allows the train to move. The engine also emits steam as a by-product, which is then released via a whistle. Thus, the whistling noise is an epiphenomenon or a secondary consequence of the use of coal to power a steam engine. (B) Analogously, when you see a stimulus during an fMRI experiment, it causes your neurons to fire, which in turn evokes a behavioral response like pressing a button with your index finger. The neurons require oxygen to support their metabolism, and that supply of oxygen can be measured using fMRI. Note that the fMRI BOLD response is not part of the causal chain, although it still can be used as an index of the neuronal activity.

Chapter 6, current theories of brain function assume that information processing results from neuronal activity. Of primary importance are axonal action potentials and dendritic field potentials, but other aspects, including synaptic changes and neurotransmission, are also critical. So, when a physiologist implants an electrode into the brain and measures changes in its electrical potential, she assumes that such changes reflect some form of information processing, although the specific mental operations represented may be unknown. Hemodynamic changes, in contrast, do not necessarily reflect information processing. Remember from Chapter 7 that early studies showed that BOLD contrast could be evoked by physiological manipulations, such as CO_2 inspiration. These manipulations influenced the magnitude of the BOLD signal, presumably with little to no impact upon computations in the brain.

What does it mean for the BOLD signal to be epiphenomenal, that is, merely correlated with neuronal activity? From a strong hypothesis-testing perspective, one could use fMRI data to falsify hemodynamic hypotheses, as described in the previous section, but not neuronal or psychological hypotheses. But nearly all fMRI studies investigate psychological questions! Fortunately for fMRI researchers, the correlational objection rests on an overly strict definition of hypothesis testing. All hypotheses are based on the principle that the experimental manipulation *causes* changes in the dependent variable. However, the chain of causation does not have to be fully elaborated. Consider the form of many studies of drug effects. To examine whether a drug has a beneficial effect, a researcher gives the drug to one group of subjects and a placebo to another group. If the experimental group does better than the control group on some measure, such as lower incidence of cancer or increased performance on a memory test, then the beneficial-effect hypothesis is supported. Such a result does not mean that the drug is a direct cause of the dependent measure; it could influence other factors (e.g., mood) that more proximally cause the effect. Nor does it mean that no other manipulation could cause the effect. From this example, it is easy to recognize that all experiments, save perhaps those of low-level physics phenomena, have *implicit* causal structure.

In summary, *correlational* is not equivalent to *meaningless*. As critics correctly note, the mechanisms of BOLD activity are still not completely understood. Therefore, making inferences about neuronal activity based on BOLD data is made challenging by many factors, including scanner noise and limits in recording hardware, intersubject and intersession variability, and even uncertainty in the form of the evoked hemodynamic response. But the inability to completely explain *how* neuronal activity leads to BOLD signal does not call into question *that* the two are related. Consider a simple analogy. You are standing next to a train track, waiting for a steam locomotive. Within a few minutes, you hear the locomotive whistle far in the distance. Not being an engineer, in either sense of the word, you do not know what causes the whistling sound. Nor do you know whether the whistle is needed for the train to move or is completely unnecessary and epiphenomenal. Despite your profound lack of knowledge about the mechanism behind the whistle, you are certain about one fact: when you hear a whistle, it means that a train is coming.

Just as the whistle serves as a reliable predictor of the train, so too do BOLD fMRI data serve as a reliable predictor of neuronal activity. We return to this issue in Chapter 15, through discussion of some strategies used to improve the power of fMRI studies for making inferences about neuronal activity, including double dissociation approaches and combination of information across techniques.

subtraction In experimental design, the direct comparison of two conditions that are assumed to differ only in one property, the independent variable.

confounding factor Any property that covaries with the independent variable within the conducted experiment but could be distinguished from the independent variable using a different experimental design.

Confounding Factors

It is important for the researcher to make the experimental and control conditions as similar as possible. If the conditions differ in only one property, then any change in the dependent variable can be confidently attributed to the change in that property. This process is known as **subtraction,** since one can subtract the value of the dependent variable in the control condition from its value in the experimental condition to quantify the effect of the manipulation. But if the conditions differ in more than one way, then there could be multiple explanations for experimental effects. Any factor that covaries with the IV in an experiment is known as a **confounding factor.** Perhaps the most important aspect of experimental design, but the most difficult to master, is selecting good experimental and control conditions so as to minimize confounding factors.

FMRI studies with psychological hypotheses are particularly susceptible to confounding factors, since the concepts they address are often difficult to define. To understand why, consider the hypothesis that face perception relies on the fusiform gyrus within the inferior temporal lobe. The experimental condition seems obvious: present photographs of human faces (Figure 11.5A–C). But what is the appropriate control condition? One option would be to simply show nothing, making the design analogous to the Kwong study previously described. The experimental and control conditions would thus differ along the intended IV, in that the experimental condition would present faces while the control condition would not, but they would also differ in other factors. In this case, confounds would include brightness, presence of edges, nameability, and visual interest, among many.

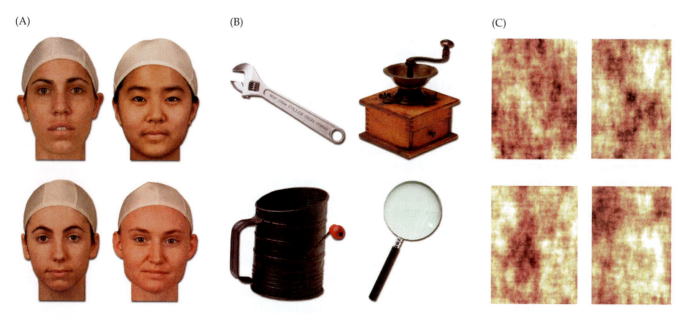

(A)   (B)   (C)

Figure 11.5 Selecting appropriate control stimuli. To study brain regions associated with face processing, you would want to manipulate the "faceness" of the stimuli in the experimental and control conditions. In the experimental condition, you could present a series of faces (A). However, many different control conditions are possible. One option is to present a series of simple objects in the control condition (B). The objects are visually interesting, like the faces, and have smaller parts that are nameable. Another possible control condition would be to present faces that have been transformed so that low-level visual properties are kept constant but the faces are no longer visible. (C) Shows faces that have been Fourier transformed, phase-scrambled, and inverse Fourier transformed. The same spatial frequency components are present, but they no longer form a face.

Another possible control condition would be to present faces that have been transformed in some way, so that parameters like brightness and spatial frequency composition are similar between the two conditions. Yet face perception means more than just the physical properties that make up the face. It also refers to seeing an image as a face as opposed to some other form of object. This psychological interpretation suggests another possible control condition, the presentation of random objects of generally similar complexity to the faces. Such a comparison would identify areas of the brain that respond more to the faces than to the otherwise similar objects.

An even more insidious type of confound in fMRI studies is the hidden causal factor. According to the oft-repeated mantra "Correlation does not imply causation," just because event A co-occurs with event B does not mean that A causes B or that B causes A. Failure to heed this warning can lead to confirmation of bad hypotheses. A classic example can be found in the link between ice cream consumption and violent crime: both are highest in summer months and lowest in winter months. Does this mean that eating ice cream causes crime, or vice versa? Of course not. Both variables are influenced by a third factor: temperature. This example will seem remedial to many students, but its basic logic holds even in more complex fMRI studies. Suppose that you are studying the effects of alcohol on motor cortex function. Your subjects watch a computer screen on which the letters "L" and "R" flash in a random sequence, and they squeeze their left or right hand when they see the corresponding letter. You find that BOLD signal in the motor cortex is reduced in subjects who drank alcohol compared to those who drank water. What do you conclude? One possibility, that alcohol reduces neuronal activity in the motor cortex, seems reasonable from the data. However, other interpretations should be considered. For example, the subjects may make many more mistakes under the influence of alcohol and squeeze their hands at the wrong times or not at all. The reduced BOLD activity may thus result from poor behavioral performance, not directly from the alcohol. Note that you cannot identify which factor, alcohol or behavioral performance, causes the reduced response with this single experiment. Additional experiments would be necessary to determine the true cause of the effect.

Several approaches can help to prevent confounding factors. It is important that factors that vary within your experiment do so randomly with respect to the independent variable. This is known as **randomization.** For example, if your study compares older and younger subjects, you should not have one researcher run all of the older subjects and another run all of the younger subjects, as that would introduce experimenter identity as a confounding factor. When factors cannot be made completely random, scientists often try to ensure that a potential confound is equally present for all conditions, which is called **counterbalancing.** Imagine that your subject pool for an experiment consists of four men and eight women. If you randomly assign people to the two conditions, you might end up with no men in one group. Instead, it may be better to divide the groups so that they have similar numbers of men and women. Similarly, if you have three different experimental runs, you could break up your subjects into three groups, one of which participates in the order 1-2-3, another in the order 2-3-1, and the third in the order 3-1-2. Such problems are especially important in fMRI studies where experimental conditions are broken into different runs, as when condition 1 occurs on runs 1 to 3 and condition 2 occurs on runs 4 to 6. On some tasks, subjects may get better over time (i.e., practice effects), and

randomization A process for removing confounding factors by ensuring that they vary randomly with respect to the independent variable.

counterbalancing A process for removing confounding factors by ensuring that they have equal influence upon the different conditions of the independent variable, usually by matching values across conditions.

BOX 11.1 An Example of fMRI Experimental Design

To see how scientists progress from research questions to experimental design, we will evaluate the design logic of an interesting study conducted by Zacks and colleagues in 2001. We will not discuss the results or their importance here, but should your interest be piqued, the study's full citation is available in the references at the end of the chapter. The authors were interested in how people parse a continuous stream of events, like watching a movie, into constituent parts. Early in the article describing the study, they stated their research question: "How does the human perceptual system extract these parts, their beginnings and endings, and the relationships among them from the flux of sensory data?" In the fMRI experiment designed to address this question, subjects watched a set of four movies of normal daily activities, like washing dishes or fertilizing a plant. The movies were simple single-camera recordings of a single actor performing the activity, with no breaks or cuts.

Every subject watched each movie three times. The first time, the subjects were instructed to passively view it and learn from it, but they did not know the upcoming task. On the second and third viewings, the subjects were instructed to press a button to mark conceptual boundaries between different components of the activity. For example, they might press the button when the actor picked up a watering can and then press it again when he began watering the plant. On one viewing the subjects were instructed to use a coarse criterion, marking the largest parts that seemed meaningful, and on the other they used a fine criterion, marking the smallest parts. Some subjects did the coarse marking first while others did the fine marking first, and each group was not told about the other condition until the final viewing (Figure 11.6). The authors measured

BOLD MRI activity at 1.5 T. They analyzed each subject's BOLD data from the passive viewing condition in epochs around the time points he or she marked in the other two viewings. The authors advanced the research hypothesis that "if segmentation is an ongoing component of normal perceptual processing, one should expect to see transient changes in neural activity correlated with perceptual event boundaries. . . . We predicted that we would observe differences between the response to fine and coarse segment boundaries during passive viewing."

From this description of the research study, we can identify the major components of the experimental design, beginning with the independent and dependent variables. The first independent variable was event boundary. The authors determined whether each fMRI data point was a boundary or not based on the subject's button press. Note that although the boundaries between events were created by the subjects, and thus

Figure 11.6 The experimental design of Zacks and colleagues. Subjects repeatedly watched short movies showing an actor performing a simple daily activity, like making a fence. The first time each movie was shown, subjects watched passively. On the second and third viewings, subjects were told that they should press a button at each boundary between adjacent events (e.g., when a board is cut or nailed into place), using either a fine or coarse criterion for segmentation. The order of the fine/coarse conditions was randomized across subjects, and subjects did not know about any of the segmentation conditions until immediately before each trial.

BOX 11.1 *(continued)*

could be considered a dependent variable in the context of a behavioral experiment, they served as an independent variable for the fMRI data. The second independent variable was segmentation instructions, which had three levels—none, coarse, and fine—that were partially counterbalanced across subjects. Both variables were categorical, since they had discrete values, and both were manipulated within subjects. The dependent variable was BOLD fMRI signal.

Based on these variables, we can next summarize the experimental hypotheses. First, manipulating whether or not a part of a video corresponds to an event boundary (IV) will influence the magnitude of BOLD signal change (DV). Second, manipulating whether that event boundary is created using coarse or fine criteria (IV) will influence the magnitude of BOLD signal change (DV). These are psychological hypotheses, since they make references to cognitive concepts (i.e., event boundary, coarseness of criteria) that are only operationally defined. Of note is the lack of specific predictions about the direction and magnitude of the BOLD signal change. While the authors predicted that there would be differences between the conditions, they did not predict whether the coarse or fine boundaries would evoke more activity. The absence of a directional prediction is not uncommon for fMRI studies, especially in exploratory studies that describe a novel phenomenon. As phenomena become better established, hypotheses become more precise.

Based on this cursory summary, we can evaluate whether the design of the experiment is adequate for answering its research question (Figure 11.7). First, are the independent variables appropriate? The use of subject-generated event boundaries seems very reasonable, in that it provides a better estimate of how each subject views the displays as compared to having other people rate them. Because the subjects do not know that they are going to respond to the videos until after they have finished viewing them for the first time, no bias is introduced by this independent variable. The second independent variable, segmentation, is partially counterbalanced, so that there should be no order effects for the coarse and fine conditions. However, there are several differences between the active and passive conditions, in addition to the independent variable of interest (segmentation). In the active conditions, subjects will be more familiar with the videos, have memories of their content, and have expectations about sequences of events. It would thus be problematic to compare the active segmentation conditions to passive viewing.

Second, is the dependent variable appropriate? The pulse sequence used can provide good BOLD contrast and thus can provide an appropriate dependent measure. Third, are the experimental hypotheses testable in this design? The primary hypothesis predicts a straightforward relation between the independent and dependent variables: that change in BOLD signal should preferentially occur at event boundaries compared to other time points. They are clearly falsifiable, in that it is possible for there to be no significant BOLD dif-

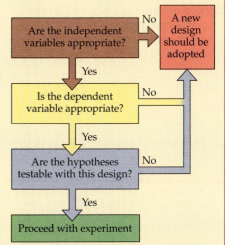

Figure 11.7 Questions to ask yourself when designing or evaluating a research study. These questions are critical for any study, regardless of whether it uses fMRI.

ferences associated with event boundaries or segmentation conditions. Based on this evaluation, the study appears to be well designed and capable of answering its stated experimental question. However, to learn how the authors answered that question, you will need to read the study!

This exercise is similar to, albeit more explicit than, the initial stages of the peer review process for manuscripts or grant applications. Conscientious reviewers attempt to understand whether the hypotheses and experimental design of a study are reasonable before considering the experimental results. We suggest that students conduct a similar evaluation of an fMRI study of their choosing.

---

thus their performance may be better on later runs. On other tasks, subjects might tire over time (i.e., fatigue effects), and their performance may worsen as the experiment goes on. Practice and fatigue effects can be minimized by randomizing or by counterbalancing the experimental conditions across time so that all conditions are affected similarly.

A good way to identify confounding factors is to participate in your own experiments as a pilot subject. You may recognize an unexpected confound when you adopt a different strategy than expected or when you find that the

block A time interval that contains trials from one condition.

blocked design The separation of experimental conditions into distinct blocks, so that each condition is presented for an extended period of time.

task is too easy or too difficult. Though one cannot always predict all possible confounding factors, the costs of fMRI experiments in time and money provide ample incentive for good experimental design. The best designs are able to efficiently answer the questions of interest and require a minimum number of experimental subjects and experimental trials per subject.

Blocked Designs

The simplest way to evaluate the effect of the independent variable on the dependent variable is to compare an experimental condition (in which the IV is present) to a control condition (in which it is absent or at a lower level). For example, imagine that you wanted to investigate whether listening to music improves studying for examinations. Your subjects listen to a list of 20 words read one at a time. For some subjects, during the first 10 words there is music playing in the background, while during the last 10 the room is quiet. To counterbalance the order of presentation, other subjects listen to music during the last 10 words but not the first 10. In this experiment, the trials from each condition are grouped together in time to form **blocks,** as shown in Figure 11.8A. As a general definition, the independent variable is considered to be at a constant level throughout a block, and transitions between blocks represent changes in the level of an independent variable. Here there are two blocks, music and quiet, combined within a single **blocked design.** The basic analysis of any blocked-design experiment, whether fMRI or not, involves

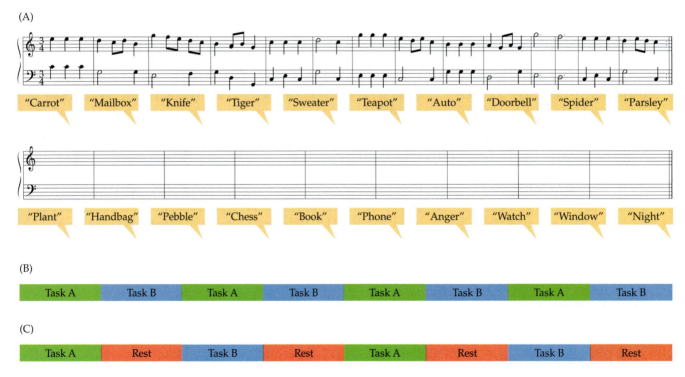

Figure 11.8 Basic principles of blocked designs. In a blocked fMRI design, the experimental tasks are separated into long-interval blocks. (A) A simple blocked design, in which subjects read a list of words presented one at a time. During the first block of 10 stimuli, the subjects hear music playing, while during the second block of 10 stimuli, no music is heard. Note that although each of these blocks contains multiple individual stimuli, in most blocked-design analyses it is assumed that the cognitive processes of interest are constant throughout the block. The most common blocked design alternates between two conditions (B), allowing identification of the difference in fMRI activity between them. For some research questions, a rest or baseline condition is introduced between the two blocks (C) so that activity independent to each condition can be measured.

comparing the dependent measure in each block condition, for example, that subjects remember 8 words on average while music is playing but only 6 on average when it is quiet. Unsurprisingly, such blocked designs, which are simple to create and straightforward to analyze, dominated the early years of fMRI (see Chapter 7).

To understand why blocked designs were first used, one must consider the context in which these early experiments took place. In the early 1990s, the magnitude of the BOLD change caused by neuronal activity was still unknown, and thus researchers adopted long block intervals to ensure that sufficient neuronal activity would be generated to evoke a measurable BOLD response. In addition, long task blocks had been necessary for PET imaging, which measures the total number of emission events following injection of a radioactive tracer (see Box 7.1). In a typical PET experiment using ^{15}O to measure blood flow, a tracer would be injected and then the subject would perform one condition of the task for 60 to 90 s. Then there would be a second injection of the tracer, followed by 60 to 90 s of a second condition. Although relatively few of the early fMRI researchers conducted studies using PET, they were familiar with its design limitations. Despite the many changes in how fMRI data are collected and analyzed, blocked designs have remained an important part of fMRI.

Setting Up a Blocked Design

The first issue to consider when creating a blocked design is the research question itself. Some experiments require long task blocks because the process of interest cannot be modulated over short intervals. If one is interested in studying vigilance or sustained attention, one could compare 30-s blocks in which subjects are concentrating on the task to 30-s blocks in which the subjects are not concentrating. Since active concentration may take some time to engage and disengage, using a blocked design will improve the subjects' ability to perform the task. Conversely, some experiments cannot use blocked designs due to the transience of the neuronal activity. Detection of infrequent targets, as in the common "oddball" or "n-back" paradigms, provides a good example. Imagine that you are watching a series of letters flashing rapidly on a computer screen. Your task is to press a button whenever you see an "X," which only appears 5% of the time. The oddball "X" cannot be presented repeatedly within a block, as that would change how subjects process it. An event-related or mixed design would instead be necessary.

Assuming that a blocked design is practical for an experiment, the researcher must next choose experimental conditions and determine the timing of the blocks. The former requirement relates to the IV, in that conditions must be selected that maximally influence the desired IV without introducing confounding factors. The latter requirement relates to the DV, since the properties of the hemodynamic response determine the length of the blocks and whether there should be spacing between them. The choice of conditions for the different blocks relates in an important way to the goals of the experiment. Imagine that you are interested in whether or not nouns and verbs are processed in different areas of the brain. One obvious design would use two conditions, nouns and verbs, each consisting of a series of words presented one at a time. Each condition could be presented for 30 s, and the conditions could alternate for the duration of the experiment. This **alternating design** (Figure 11.8B) is optimal for determining which voxels show differential activity as a function of the independent variable (i.e., the difference between the conditions). However, it does not provide any infor-

alternating design A blocked design in which two conditions are presented one after another for the duration of the experimental run.

control block A time interval that contains trials of the control condition.

null-task block A control block in which there are no task requirements for the subject. Also called a baseline block or nontask block.

mation about voxels that are active in both conditions or about the response to a single condition in isolation.

Another type of blocked design (Figure 11.8C) uses **control blocks,** such as watching a blank screen where there is nothing to read. Control blocks in which the subject does nothing are called **null-task blocks.** The presence of a control condition allows additional comparisons. Each experimental condition could be compared to the control condition to identify voxels that are activated by that condition independently. A comparison of noun reading and null-task blocks could find voxels associated with all aspects of noun reading, including perceiving letters, sounding out words, and imagining objects. Note that none of these processes would be identified by the direct noun–verb contrast. Another common comparison is to combine the experimental conditions and contrast the combination with the control condition. In the example above, one could identify all voxels that are more active in response to the presentation of words than to the null condition. This is especially useful if you plan to use a region-of-interest approach. The combined condition has increased experimental power compared to individual conditions, so it can be used to find brain regions active *across* the two conditions. Then, one can probe those regions to see whether any show differences *between* the experimental conditions.

Under the direct subtraction logic that guides block analyses, the use of additional control conditions does not preclude direct comparison of conditions, as in an alternating design. One could still compare BOLD activity during noun reading and verb reading, while ignoring any control condition. Additional conditions require additional time, however, and should not be added without necessity. Therefore, whenever you choose which conditions to include in a design, you should begin by evaluating whether a simple alternating design would be sufficient for answering your research questions. If not, consider what additional condition(s) would let you measure activity related to the general process of interest. Remember that control conditions may take many different forms. In the noun–verb example, possible controls could include a null-task condition, such as watching nonletter patterns or reading jumbled letter strings that do not form words. Depending on what aspect of reading is of interest, any of these control conditions might be reasonable.

After deciding on your experimental conditions, you should next consider the timing of your task blocks. FMRI experiments have used blocks as short as several seconds and as long as a minute or two. Within that large range, the experimenter has considerable flexibility in the choice of timing parameters. Most important to consider is the effect of block length on the experimental task. Are there time constraints that preclude very short or very long blocks? In many working memory experiments, for example, subjects must rehearse a changing set of items over time. If the block is too short or too long, such a task may be too easy or too difficult. As in many psychology experiments, fatigue effects (and to a lesser extent, practice effects) should be considered. Very demanding tasks may be difficult to sustain over extended periods of time, and subjects may do worse at the end of a long block. In general, block length should be chosen so that the same mental processes are evoked throughout. We discuss trade-offs in functional SNR associated with blocks of different lengths in the following section.

For most purposes, block length should be kept constant across the conditions. Remember that in an alternating design, the only statistical analysis that is possible is the difference between the two blocks. Even if one condition is labeled as the task and the other is called baseline, they are equally

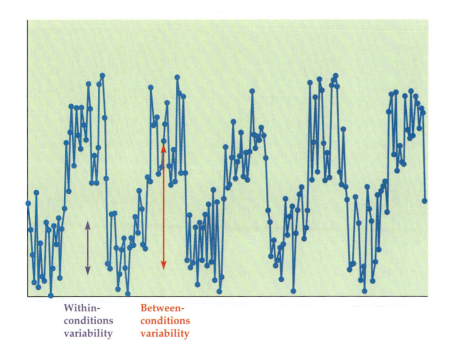

Figure 11.9 Within-conditions and between-conditions variability in blocked fMRI data. The goal of experimental design is to maximize the variability in the data that is due to the experimental manipulation (i.e., the between-conditions variability) while minimizing other sources of data variability (i.e., within-conditions variability). If the former is large compared to the latter, effects of interest can be identified.

Within-
conditions
variability

Between-
conditions
variability

important for the statistical comparison. To anticipate the discussion of analysis in Chapter 12, statistical comparisons between two conditions are determined by the magnitude of the difference between the conditions compared to the variability within conditions (i.e., shared standard deviation), as seen in Figure 11.9. Since the standard deviation of a data set decreases with the square root of the number of observations (i.e., time points in a block), the shared standard deviation will be largest when one block is very long and the other very short, while it will be smallest when the blocks are of equal length. So, for optimal statistical power, the blocks in an alternating design should generally be of equal length. However, if more than two conditions are used, then unequal block lengths or block numbers may be beneficial. If a primary comparison is something like the combination of condition 1 and condition 2 versus condition 3, then it may be worth assigning twice as many data points to condition 3. This commonly occurs in designs that use a null-task block along with two experimental conditions (i.e., 1-3-2-3-1-3-2-3-, etc). Also, if additional analyses will examine responses to individual events within an experimental block, as with the mixed designs described later in this chapter, then that block may be lengthened relative to a control block.

Advantages and Disadvantages of Blocked Designs

Though simple, blocked designs can be extremely powerful. For evaluating the strengths and weaknesses of an experimental design in fMRI, consider two factors: **detection,** or knowing which voxels are active, and **estimation,** or knowing the time course of an active voxel. These factors correspond roughly to spatial and temporal resolution. Detection power depends on the total variance in BOLD signal introduced by the experimental design, while estimation efficiency depends on the randomness of stimulus presentation. A central principle of creating fMRI experiments is that a design that is good at detection may not be good at estimation, or vice versa. (For a comprehensive and mathematically rigorous discussion of the trade-offs between detection and estimation, refer to the manuscripts by Liu and colleagues and by Birn and colleagues that are referenced at the end of this chapter.)

detection Determination of whether or not activity within a given voxel changes in response to the experimental manipulation.

estimation Measurement of the pattern of change over time within an active voxel in response to the experimental manipulation.

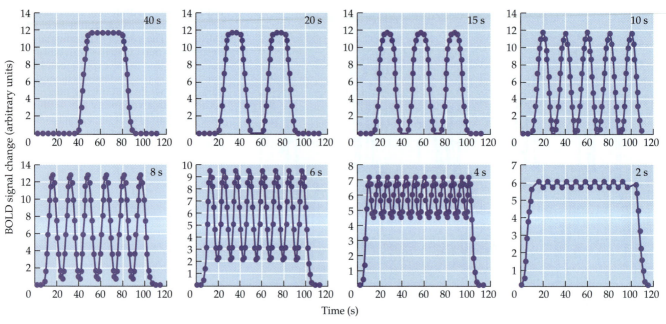

Figure 11.10 Effects of block interval on the fMRI hemodynamic response. These charts show simulated fMRI hemodynamic responses of voxels active only during the task block of an alternating on/off design. Note that as the block duration shortens below the width of the fMRI hemodynamic response, the response does not return to baseline. At very short block durations, there will be little to no difference between fMRI signal during active and inactive blocks. Note that the scales of the *y*-axes are reduced for block lengths of 8 s or less.

scanner drift Slow changes in voxel intensity over time.

Blocked designs are very good for detecting significant fMRI activity. The detection power of a blocked design is determined by the balance between two factors. First, the difference in BOLD signal between conditions should be as large as possible. Figure 11.10 shows a simulation of how the measured BOLD activity changes as the length of the blocks changes from very long (40 s) to very short (2 s). At long block lengths, a very large response is evoked during the task blocks and the response returns to baseline during the nontask blocks. Thus, there is maximal variability between the blocks. If the block length is sufficiently short (i.e., less than about 10 s) that the hemodynamic response cannot return to baseline during the nontask blocks, BOLD amplitude will be reduced. This reduces the total variability in the data, which in turn reduces the experimental power. In extreme cases, such as those with block lengths of only a few seconds, there will be almost no difference between task and nontask conditions. In summary, the use of long block intervals provides maximal BOLD amplitude changes between conditions.

Second, there should be as many transitions as possible between the conditions, to minimize the noise present at the task frequency. Remember that the noise in a BOLD time course has its highest power at low frequencies and lowest power at high frequencies. For example, at very low frequencies, there can be significant **scanner drift** associated with problems with the scanner hardware. If your design has very long (e.g., 180 s) experimental and control blocks, it will be difficult to know whether signal changes from one block to the next result from the experimental manipulation or from low-frequency noise. As the block length is reduced, the task frequency increases and thus the design is more immune to low-frequency noise.

Together, these factors indicate that the signal change at the task frequency will be greatest at relatively long block lengths, while the noise at the task frequency will be smallest at relatively short block lengths. As a rough guideline, block lengths of approximately the duration of the hemodynamic response (i.e., 10 s) provide large signal changes while reducing noise at the task frequency to an acceptable level. However, depending on the spectrum of the noise, detection power may increase at even shorter block intervals of 6 to 8 s (see McCarthy and colleagues, 1996, for an example). Longer blocks are often required for experiments that test cognitive processes like memory and attention, since it is difficult to ensure that those processes begin promptly at the block onset. It is important to recognize that if design constraints necessitate the use of very short block periods, those blocks should be treated like single events and their order should be randomized. This procedure is described in the section on event-related designs.

While their detection power can be very good, blocked designs are relatively insensitive to the shape of the hemodynamic response. We can understand this insensitivity by returning to the idea of **superposition,** which was introduced in Chapter 8. Setting aside refractory effects for the moment, the hemodynamic response to two identical stimuli presented in succession is equal to the sum of the individual responses. As more and more stimuli are presented in succession, each contributes to the total hemodynamic response. With task blocks of about 10 s or longer, which are greater than the width of the hemodynamic response to a single stimulus, every time point within the block contains a contribution from multiple stimuli, each at a different phase. The combined hemodynamic response thus rises rapidly at the onset of the task, thereafter remaining at a plateau value until the cessation of the block.

Since the plateau value represents contributions from all phases of the hemodynamic response, the particular shape of the response does not matter. Figure 11.11 shows four sample hemodynamic responses, each with a different shape, and how they would change as more events are presented. All four responses have the same total signal amplitude, as measured by the area under the curves. Consider the standard hemodynamic response shown in Figure 11.11A. As the length of the response block is increased from 2 to 32 events, each 1 s in duration and separated by 2 s, there is a consistent and smooth increase in overall hemodynamic amplitude, reaching a plateau at block lengths of about 12 s or longer. Now suppose that the hemodynamic response has a simple triangular form (Figure 11.11B). Obviously, this form differs considerably from that of the canonical hemodynamic response. But as the length of the block increases, the total hemodynamic response in panel B becomes more and more similar to that in panel A. As can be seen in the subsequent panels, the insensitivity of blocked designs to hemodynamic shape would hold if the hemodynamic response had two peaks (Figure 11.11C) and even if its values were completely randomized over the response duration (Figure 11.11D). For the same reasons, designs that use long stimulus blocks are also relatively insensitive to changes in the timing of the hemodynamic response.

Insensitivity to the shape and timing of the hemodynamic response has both advantages and disadvantages. The primary advantage is that it makes experimental analyses extraordinarily simple. When blocked, any hemodynamic response can be robustly modeled using a smoothed trapezoidal shape consisting of a rise, plateau, and fall. To evaluate the effect of the IV, the magnitude of the BOLD response during the task period can be compared to that during a baseline period. If there is no effect, the random differences in activity between the blocks would follow the *t*-distribution, so the magnitude of the *t*-statistic reveals the significance of the effect. Other

superposition A principle of linear systems that states that the total response to a set of inputs is equivalent to the summation of the independent responses to the inputs.

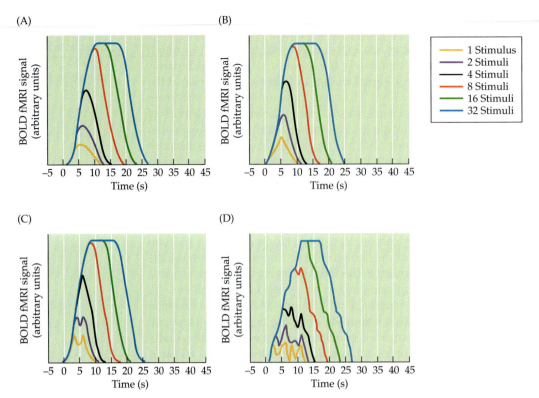

Figure 11.11 Insensitivity of blocked designs to the shape of the hemodynamic response. Each set of curves shows the simulated fMRI signal measured from blocks of 1, 2, 4, 8, 16, or 32 1-s stimuli. In (A), the base hemodynamic response shown in yellow has a standard form. As the number of stimuli in the blocks increases to 16 or more, the hemodynamic response reaches a plateau. Now consider the triangular waveform shown in (B). It is narrower than that in (A), so the response is different for small numbers of stimuli. But as more stimuli are averaged, the response approaches that of (A). Similar results can be seen for (C) and (D), which have very different hemodynamic responses. In fact, the hemodynamic response in (D) consists of the numerical values of the response in (A), but scrambled in a random order. So, if a single stimulus were present in the block, the BOLD data would look nothing like the standard hemodynamic response. Yet as increasing numbers of stimuli are averaged, the combined response will approach that of (A).

analyses are also possible, including power spectrum analyses, correlations, and explicit modeling of block waveforms (see Chapter 12 for more discussion). Balancing this advantage is a loss of estimation power. Imagine that you ran an experiment and recorded the data from the 32 stimulus curve in Figure 11.11A. You would be unable to estimate whether the hemodynamic response looked like that from panels A, B, or C, all of which result in nearly identical data. In fact, with sufficient noise, even the random hemodynamic response in panel D would be impossible to distinguish from the others.

> ### Thought Question
> Imagine that you recreated Figure 11.11 using a sample hemodynamic response that is delayed by a few seconds. Would the amplitude of the block be changed? Would its latency be changed?

In summary, blocked designs are simple and powerful. They are easy to create and can be easily explained to others. If the experimental and task

BOX 11.2 Baseline Activity in fMRI

The basic assumption of blocked designs is that block-related changes in BOLD signal result from differences between the experimental conditions. In the usual subtractive approach, there are two conditions: task and control. The task condition is assumed to consist of all of the neural processes present in the control condition, along with additional processes of interest. Consider the results from the following simple task, which were reported by Binder and colleagues in 1999. During task blocks, subjects listened to sequences consisting of low and high tones and pressed a button if a given sequence included two high tones (e.g., L-L-H-L-H). In control blocks, the subjects lay still in the scanner with their eyes closed. Each block lasted 24 s. Not surprisingly, the tone task evoked more fMRI BOLD activity than control blocks within the auditory, prefrontal, parietal, and motor cortices, among many other regions. These areas reflect regions that are associated with perception, decision, and response aspects of the task. The authors then looked for brain regions that were less active during the task blocks than during the rest blocks. Remarkably, a number of regions showed increased activity during rest, including the lateral parietal cortex (angular gyrus), the posterior cingulate or precuneus, the superior frontal gyrus, and the ventral prefrontal cortex. This pattern of results, which has been confirmed by many studies using both fMRI and PET, suggests that the assumptions of the subtractive method may be flawed. Some aspects of cognition may actually be inhibited during performance of psychological experiments, such that cognitive processes present in the control condition may not be present during the task condition. In the last few years, interpreting **deactivations,** or decreases in hemodynamic activity, has become an area of considerable interest.

deactivations Decreases in BOLD activity during task blocks compared to nontask blocks.

oxygen extraction fraction (OEF) The proportion of available oxygen that is removed from the blood.

What does it mean for fMRI activity to decrease during an experimental task? In answering this question, it is critical to recognize that blocked designs only provide information about the relative difference between two conditions, not about absolute levels of activity. Without a clear baseline to which both conditions can be compared, several different types of changes in absolute activity could result in similar changes in relative activity (Figure 11.12A–E). Gusnard and Raichle, in a 2001 comprehensive review of many research studies, suggest that the appropriate baseline condition for functional neuroimaging studies should be defined using the **oxygen extraction fraction (OEF),** which is largely stable across the brain (Figure 11.13). Even though some areas of the brain have greater blood flow than others, and some areas have higher oxygen requirements than others, the proportion of oxygen that is extracted when the subjects are resting with their eyes closed is spatially uniform, with only a few exceptions. Remember from Chapter 7 that the OEF decreases as part of the BOLD response due to an overcompensatory increase in blood flow. Thus, decreases from baseline OEF indicate increased neuronal activity, whereas increases indicate decreased neuronal activity.

By measuring the OEF at rest and during experimental conditions, whether directly using PET or indirectly via fMRI, researchers have identified a set of brain regions that show decreases in activity during performance of a wide range of experimental tasks. These regions in-

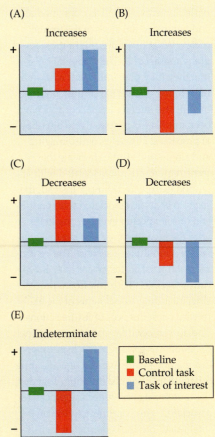

Figure 11.12 Possible origins of increases and decreases observed in fMRI. When experimental and control tasks are compared using a blocked design, there are several possible causes of observed increases or decreases in hemodynamic activity. First, an increase in activity during the experimental task could be observed when both tasks are either above baseline (A) or below baseline (B). Likewise, decreases in activity during the experimental task could be observed when both are above baseline (C) or below baseline (D). Note than in (A) and (C), either task could have a positive effect compared to baseline, but in (B) and (D), either could have a negative effect compared to baseline. If the tasks result in opposite activity (E), comparisons of the tasks with each other would be likely to yield a large effect, but neither may show a change versus baseline. (From Gusnard and Raichle, 2001.)

BOX 11.2 *(continued)*

clude medial and lateral aspects of the parietal cortex, as well as dorsomedial and ventromedial areas of the frontal cortex. What functions might these regions subserve? A likely possibility is that they may play important roles in the monitoring of external stimuli. Both the medial and lateral parietal cortices have been implicated in spatial and attentional processes. However, neuroimaging and single-unit studies indicate that these regions are not associated with attention to expected stimuli. Instead, they seem to be more associated with peripheral or unexpected events, consistent with the idea that they are part of a generalized monitoring system. The ventromedial frontal cortex, in contrast, is typically associated with emotional processing, including assessments of the likely reward consequences of future actions. The dorsomedial frontal cortex may mediate reflective thought, such as apperceiving one's state of mind or evaluating what others might be thinking. Together, the monitoring and reflecting processes associated with baseline activity can be integrated into the construct of "self-directed thought" (see Gusnard and Raichle for discussion of this idea).

To experience self-directed thought, close your eyes and relax for at least 10 seconds. If you are like most people, you will feel an initial sense of withdrawal from the world around you, followed by a growing sensitivity to external stimuli. You will notice sounds that had previously been outside your awareness. You will become sensitive to heretofore unnoticed muscle tension or joint pain. In short, the baseline state of brain activity is very different from that evoked by a demanding task, like reading this book. This difference was recognized by William James, who described introspection thusly: "When I try to remember or reflect, the movements [in the mind] in question, instead of being directed toward the periphery, seem to come from

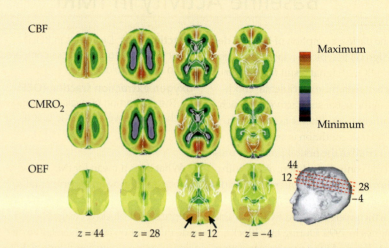

Figure 11.13   The oxygen extraction fraction (OEF) as a possible baseline for brain activity. Gusnard and Raichle suggest that the OEF, the proportion of available oxygen that is extracted from the blood, is highly stable across the brain and represents a good baseline for brain activity. Shown are four axial slices ($z = -4$, 12, 28, and 44 mm). Also shown here are relative cerebral blood flow (CBF) and cerebral metabolic rate for oxygen ($CMRO_2$); the ratio between these quantities gives the OEF. The arrows indicate the only regions of increased oxygen extraction relative to the remainder of the brain. These are in the visual cortex and likely reflect the fact that the subjects in this data set had their eyes closed. The baseline for these regions may reflect open eyes and normal visual stimulation. (From Gusnard and Raichle, 2001.)

the periphery inwards and feel like a sort of withdrawal from the outside world." (1890, p. 300)

Here, James emphasizes the essential difference between active and reflective states. The former is goal-directed, aimed at changing the surrounding environment or one's place in it. The latter is self-directed and passive, seeking information about the environment. James also notes his awareness of particular body motions during introspection, and how those physical movements might relate to the movement of thoughts. As in much of James's writing, his well-reasoned reflections anticipate the present discussion of baseline brain activity by more than a century. Rest or baseline conditions are not absent of mental processes. Instead, they contain particular types of processes associated with reflection, daydreaming, self-assessment, bodily attention, and emotion.

When designing an fMRI experiment, you must account for reflective processes in your choice of experimental and control conditions. Should the control condition have no explicit task requirements, subjects will naturally begin thinking about how they are doing in the experiment, what they will have for dinner, which friends they will see this evening, or even a dull pain in their lower back that they only now are beginning to notice. For this reason, rest or null-task conditions are not recommended, at least as the sole control condition. Instead, conditions should be chosen so that subjects are always performing some active task or attending to a changing environment. For example, if the experimental condition consists of judging the familiarity of remembered words, consider a control condition where subjects read words and indicate whether they are presented in capital or lowercase letters. Both conditions require attention and decision processes, thus precluding activity in the baseline system, but only the former invokes memory processes. Another suggested procedure is to explicitly include a null-task condition within your design to provide a baseline. By doing so, you can evaluate whether relative differences between your conditions reflect differential increases above baseline or an effect for one condition but not the other (see Figure 11.12). Understanding the effect of baseline processing upon fMRI data is important for any researcher, but it is especially critical for those who use blocked designs.

conditions are chosen carefully, then analysis becomes very straightforward. Blocked designs are very good at detecting voxels with significant activity, and they are also robust to uncertainty in the timing and shape of the hemodynamic response. However, because the experimental condition is extended in time, the brain activity it evokes may be highly heterogeneous over time, and some tasks may be inappropriate for blocked designs. They are also poor at estimating the time course of activity in active voxels.

Event-Related Designs

The second major class of fMRI experiments is characterized by the use of **event-related designs.** The central assumption of an event-related design is that the neural activity of interest will occur for short and discrete intervals, as when a brief flash of light evokes transient activity in the visual cortex. Stimuli that generate such short bursts of neural activity are known as **events** or trials. In most event-related designs, different conditions of the IV are associated with different events, similar to the relationship shown in Figure 11.14. Each event is separated in time from the previous event, with an **interstimulus interval,** or **ISI,** that can range from about 2 s to 20 s depending on the goals of the experiment. This differs from typical blocked designs, which may present many stimuli consecutively within a task block. Also unlike blocked designs, the different conditions are usually presented in a random order rather than an alternating pattern. Event-related designs have sometimes been called single-trial designs, to emphasize that stimuli are presented one at a time rather than within a block of trials. However, as data collection and analysis procedures have improved, analyses of changes in BOLD signal following only one stimulus presenta-

event-related design The presentation of discrete, short-duration events whose timing and order may be randomized.

event A single instance of the experimental manipulation. Also known as a trial.

interstimulus interval (ISI) The separation in time between successive stimuli. Usually refers to the time between the offset of one stimulus and the onset of the next, with the term *stimulus-onset asynchrony* (SOA) used to define the time between successive onsets.

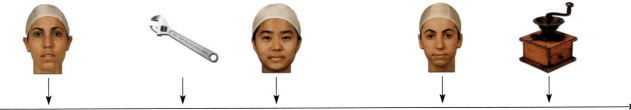

Time

Figure 11.14 Schematic diagram of an event-related fMRI design. The basic idea underlying event-related fMRI designs is that the processes of interest can be evoked transiently by brief presentations of individual stimulus events. Here, the relative timing of a series of stimuli is shown by their positions along the axis. In the design shown here, the activity in response to the face stimuli can be compared to the activity in response to the object stimuli.

electroencephalogram (EEG) The measurement of the electrical potential of the brain, usually through electrodes placed on the surface of the scalp.

time-locking Synchronization of analyses to events of interest, usually for the extraction of epochs.

signal averaging The combination of data from multiple instances of the same manipulation in order to improve functional SNR.

event-related potentials (ERPs) Small electrical changes in the brain that are associated with sensory or cognitive events.

tion have become possible, and thus the label *single-trial* should be reserved for such experiments.

Early Event-Related fMRI Studies

Event-related designs were rarely used in the early years of fMRI. Most research used long-interval blocked designs, with the notable exception of the 1992 study by Blamire and colleagues discussed in Chapter 7. Furthermore, even the few studies that measured the BOLD response to short-duration stimuli failed to conduct the additional analyses (i.e., trial averaging, latency measurements) that event-related designs afford. Within a few years, however, the design concepts drawn from PET were joined by ideas from another source, electrophysiology. Since the first recordings of electrical activity in the human brain by Hans Berger in the 1920s, researchers had known of tonic changes in the **electroencephalogram (EEG)** associated with different states of arousal or alertness. These changes were identified by comparing the EEG pattern during one state (e.g., deep sleep) to the pattern during another state (e.g., waking). By the late 1950s and early 1960s, researchers began investigating whether signals associated with specific sensory or cognitive events could be identified within the continuous EEG. By synchronizing or **time-locking** the EEG signal to the onset of a stimulus and **signal averaging** across many trials, they could extract small electrical changes known as **event-related potentials,** or **ERPs,** from the continuous EEG. Some ERPs, particularly those with short latencies (e.g., <100 ms), were associated with sensory processing. Others were associated with cognitive events. For example, the detection of an unexpected task-relevant stimulus evokes a systematic positive ERP deflection (now known as the P300) about 300 ms following the stimulus onset.

The key concepts underlying ERP studies, namely time-locking and signal averaging, became the basic principles of event-related fMRI. One of the first studies to compare event-related and blocked designs was reported by Buckner and colleagues in 1996. Their subjects were shown word stems, such as "ope-" or "fut-," and then were instructed to mentally generate completions of those stems (e.g., "opening," "future"). Previous blocked-design studies had shown that this task evokes activity in the visual and motor cortices, as well as in Broca's area, which is a language region within the left inferior prefrontal cortex. In runs of the blocked design, the word stems were presented about every 2 s within 30-s blocks that alternated with 30-s rest periods. Runs using the event-related design consisted of singly presented word stems that were followed by interstimulus intervals of about 15 s. Each subject participated in five to six runs of each type, with each run lasting 3 to 4.5 minutes. Note that many more words were presented in the blocked runs than in the event-related runs. During the task, BOLD fMRI data were recorded using an asymmetric spin-echo echo-planar pulse sequence at 1.5 T. Four subjects were tested at a TR of 2 s, and two were tested at a TR of 1 s. The authors hypothesized that similar patterns of activity would be elicited by both design types, which would validate the use of event-related designs. Furthermore, they anticipated that the event-related design could provide additional information about the timing of BOLD activity.

In their first analyses, Buckner and colleagues identified active voxels using the blocked presentation runs, and then evaluated the time course of activity in those voxels following single stimuli in the event-related runs. As expected, they found regions with block-related activity in the visual, motor, and left prefrontal cortices (Figure 11.15A). The critical test, however, was whether those same regions would show significant event-related activity.

(A)

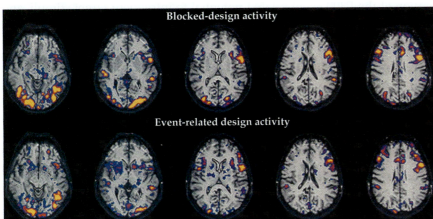

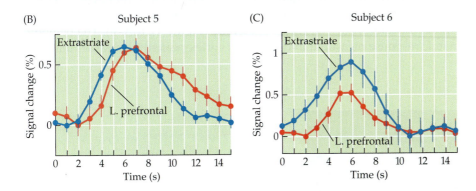

Figure 11.15 Results from one of the first comparisons of blocked and event-related designs. Subjects are shown word stems (e.g., "ora-") and then generate completed words (e.g., "orange"). They compared blocked and event-related versions of the same design and found generally similar patterns of activity (A), although more activity was observed in the blocked designs. Of additional interest was the suggestion that the event-related design could be used to identify latency differences between brain regions (B), although this result was not as clear in a second subject (C). (A from Buckner et al., 1996; B,C data from Buckner et al., 1996.)

They found that there was indeed reliable activity that was time-locked to the onset of the single events, although the amplitude of that activity (<1%) was less than that found for blocks of trials (2 to 3%). When all stimulus events were averaged, there were clear hemodynamic responses evident in the regions of interest. In one of two subjects whose data were sampled at a 1-s TR, there was a clear difference in the latency of the hemodynamic response between the visual and prefrontal cortex, such that the visual response was about 1 s earlier than the prefrontal (Figure 11.15B). A similar trend was observed in the other subject, but the results were not as clear (Figure 11.15C). It is interesting that, despite its prescience in experimental design, the analyses of this study were still grounded in the principles of blocked fMRI. To create their statistical map for the event-related runs, the authors defined individual time points following stimulus presentation to be part of either a nontask block (0 s to 3 s) or a task block (4 s through 11 s), and then conducted a subtractive analysis typical of a blocked design. Nevertheless, this early study clearly demonstrated the potential power of event-related designs for understanding cognitive function.

Another very early use of event-related fMRI to investigate a cognitive phenomenon was reported by McCarthy and colleagues in 1997. The researchers were interested in elucidating the brain regions associated with detection of an infrequently presented target stimulus. Their subjects watched a repetitive series of "O's," in which "X's" appeared very infrequently. The subjects counted the number of "X's" and reported that number to the experimenter after each run. Previous electrophysiological studies using this task had

epoch A time segment extracted from a larger series of images, usually corresponding to the period in time surrounding an event of interest.

averaged epoch The result of averaging a large number of epochs that are time-locked to similar events.

implicated the prefrontal cortex, parietal cortex, and hippocampus in the generation of the P300 event-related potential to infrequent target stimuli, and the authors hypothesized that these brain regions would also evince BOLD activity. Note that this hypothesis could not be tested using a blocked design, since that requires the target events to be randomly separated in time from one another. That is, if you presented a block of "O's" and then a block of "X's," the "X's" would no longer be unexpected and infrequent. To test their hypothesis, the authors collected gradient-echo echo-planar images at a TR of 1.5 s using a 1.5-T scanner. From the overall time series of volumes, they identified when the target "X's" occurred and then excised segments consisting of the six images before and nine images after each target. Segments of a time series that are time-locked to the presentation of an event are known as **epochs,** and the result of averaging all the epochs from one condition is an **averaged epoch.** The significance of each voxel at each time point in the epoch was determined by *t*-test (see Chapter 12).

The authors found that detection of an infrequent target evoked BOLD activity in the dorsolateral prefrontal cortex, chiefly in the right hemisphere, and in the lateral parietal cortex bilaterally (Figure 11.16A–F). The hemodynamic response measured in the parietal cortex peaked 1.5 s earlier than that

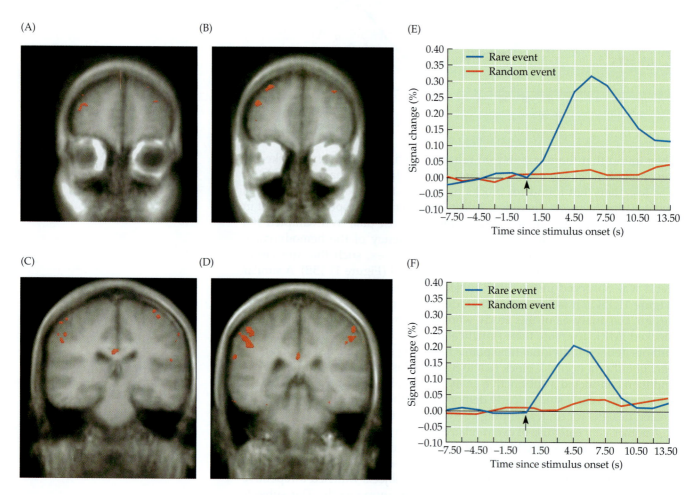

Figure 11.16 Use of event-related fMRI to study behavioral selection. Brain regions associated with selection of a response to a rare target stimulus are investigated. The target stimuli evoked activity in the dorsolateral prefrontal cortex (A and B) and in the lateral parietal cortex (C and D). Shown are the event-related responses evoked by these target stimuli in the prefrontal (E) and parietal (F) cortices. (A–D from McCarthy et al., 1997; E,F data from McCarthy et al., 1997.)

in the prefrontal cortex. No significant activity was found in the hippocampus, which may have reflected signal loss associated with magnetic susceptibility artifacts in ventral portions of the brain. Two aspects of the experimental design are worth noting, as they illustrate fundamental features of event-related fMRI. First, no matter what analysis is conducted, statistical tests must always evaluate BOLD activity associated with changes in the independent variable. Regardless of whether the analysis uses a simple *t*-test, as in the McCarthy and colleagues study, or correlation or general linear model approaches, the significance of the analysis depends on the difference in the BOLD signal evoked by the task condition and a control condition. The control condition may be implicit, perhaps merely the absence of the task condition, but it is always there (see Box 11.2). Second, some experimental questions can only be answered with event-related fMRI and not with blocked-design fMRI. Many cognitive processes, like attention, working memory, and target detection, may take on a fundamentally different character when repeated a number of times successively within a block. Researchers should always evaluate what design is necessary for eliciting activity of interest.

Principles of Event-Related fMRI

The first event-related experiments provided a new way to think about fMRI data. When stimuli were presented in a blocked design, the resulting BOLD signal was considered to reflect the magnitude of neural activity in one condition versus another. Thus, fMRI data were assumed to reflect *steady-state* brain activity at any moment in time. Event-related studies, in contrast, measured transient changes in brain activity associated with discrete stimuli. The pattern of changes *over time* became critical for experimental analyses. For this reason, high temporal resolution is more important for event-related studies than for blocked studies. Often in event-related studies, successive images are acquired with TRs of 1 to 2 s, in order to sample the hemodynamic response at a sufficiently fast rate. The temporal sensitivity of event-related designs has different consequences for detection and estimation. If the measured hemodynamic response differs from the hypothesized response, even by only a small amount (see Chapter 8), then the detection power of the experimental test will be greatly reduced. More positively, estimation of the time course of the hemodynamic response is often very good, especially when events are presented in relative isolation or when sophisticated deconvolution strategies are applied.

From the **linear systems** framework that was discussed in Chapter 8, one can consider stimulus events as **impulses,** each of which evokes a hemodynamic response. As first demonstrated by Boynton and colleagues in 1996, the amplitude and timing of a hemodynamic response depend upon both the intensity and the duration of the evoking stimulus. To the extent that the linear assumption holds (i.e., that the BOLD responses to successive stimuli do not interact), it is possible in principle to present events very rapidly and extract the hemodynamic response associated with individual events. Dale and Buckner investigated this issue in a 1997 study (see Chapter 8 for related experiments). They hypothesized that signal averaging could be applied to event-related designs even if the events were presented only a few seconds apart, despite the much slower (10 to 15 s) rise and fall of the hemodynamic response. The stimuli were flashing checkerboards of 1-s duration presented to either the left visual field or the right visual field (remember that a visual stimulus presented to the left evokes activity in the right visual cortex, and vice versa). Importantly, the order of presentation of the stimuli was ran-

linear system A system that obeys the principles of scaling and superposition.

impulse A single input to a system. Impulses are assumed to be of infinitely short duration.

domized, not alternated, because alternation at such short interstimulus intervals would have removed any effects (see Figure 11.10, for example).

> ### Thought Question
>
> How would the assumptions of event-related fMRI be violated if the neuronal activity in response to an event was not an impulse but instead had a long duration (e.g., 5 s)? How would the hemodynamic response change?

Figure 11.17 shows data from one of their experiments. At interstimulus intervals of only 2 s, robust activity for each trial type could be detected in the contralateral primary visual cortex. In fact, the observed activity was more easily detected at shorter intervals than at longer intervals. This seems counterintuitive, but remember that experimental power depends on the number of events that are averaged. In the 2-s condition, there were many more trials per experimental run than in the longer-interval conditions. When more trials are presented in rapid succession, the total variance in the BOLD signal increases, resulting in more experimental power. Dale and Buckner demonstrated that, provided that the events of interest are presented in a random order, areas of BOLD activity can be detected even using very short interstimulus intervals.

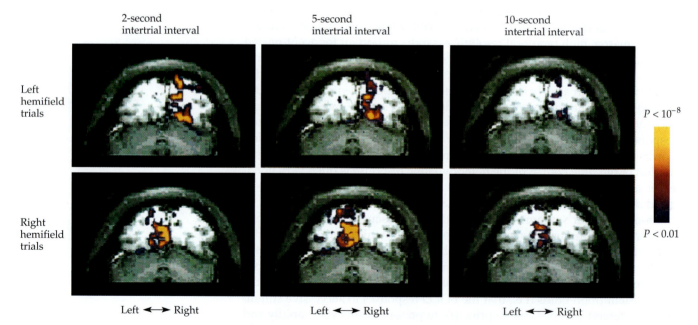

Figure 11.17 Rapid event-related fMRI with randomized stimulus presentation. FMRI activity associated with different stimulus types can be extracted from very rapid event-related designs, provided that the order of stimuli is randomized. In this experiment, visual stimuli were presented to either the left or right visual field with 2-s, 5-s, or 10-s intertrial intervals. Differential patterns of activity in response to the two stimulus types could be easily established at all intervals. Interestingly, the least activity was found at the longest intertrial interval, due to the much reduced number of experimental trials that were presented there compared to the shorter-interval conditions. (From Dale and Buckner, 1997.)

Now, does this study imply that short intervals are best for event-related studies? Not necessarily, in that its results focused on detection of areas of activity, not estimation of the time course of the hemodynamic response. Remember from Chapter 8 that hemodynamic refractory effects are present at interstimulus intervals of about 6 s or less. Thus, at shorter intervals, the evoked hemodynamic response may be of less amplitude than at long intervals (i.e., 15 s or greater). For this reason, researchers may use longer intervals between stimuli when attempting to measure the time course of the hemodynamic response. Another advantage of using long intervals is that, since the hemodynamic response has time to complete its rise and fall, they allow estimation of the baseline level of activity measured in the absence of stimulation. Typically, the baseline is identified by averaging the few time points that immediately precede each stimulus, creating a **prestimulus baseline.** This allows comparison not only between experimental conditions but also between each experimental condition and the baseline. In addition, some tasks may require long intervals due to their very nature, such as those involved in studying working memory, retrieval from long-term memory, decision making, or hemodynamic refractory effects. While sometimes necessary, the use of long intervals reduces the number of experimental trials, reducing detection power (e.g., see Figure 9.19). When designing a study, researchers should strive to reduce the interstimulus interval as much as possible to maximize the number of experimental trials collected.

Also important for event-related studies, especially those where only a single type of event is presented, is whether the interstimulus intervals are periodic or jittered. As the name implies, a **periodic event-related design** presents the events of interest at regular intervals. Slow (>15-s ISI) periodic designs are conceptually very simple, and their analysis is straightforward. Each event evokes a complete hemodynamic response, and events can be combined through selective averaging. Slow periodic designs are inefficient, however, due to their low density of events over time. Fast periodic designs would seemingly be more efficient, following the logic of the previous paragraph, but in fact may be even less practical. In 2001, Bandettini and Cox attempted to determine the best interstimulus interval for periodic presentation of a short-duration (2-s) stimulus. They found that at intermediate intervals of 10 to 12 s, substantial stimulus-related variability was present in the data, as visible in Figure 11.18A and B. However, as they shortened the interstimulus interval, the effects of the individual trials became less and less apparent. At the shortest interval tested, 2 s, there was a transient increase in BOLD activity at the beginning of the run but a plateau thereafter, precluding analysis of any individual trials.

Note that the difference between this study and that of Dale and Buckner, who found significant effects at 2 s, was that the latter presented two types of stimuli in random order. Randomization effectively jitters the time between successive onsets of the same stimulus, so that sometimes it will occur several times in a row and other times there will be a long interval between successive presentations. Without **jittering,** the BOLD signal will saturate to some maximal value with repeated presentations of the stimulus, becoming equivalent to a block of trials. However, the jittering must be sufficiently large relative to the period of the hemodynamic response to have a meaningful effect.

We emphasize that the timing constraints described here apply to the interval between successive *events* and not necessarily to the interval between successive *stimuli.* Imagine an experiment that presented two types

prestimulus baseline The calculation of a baseline value based on the BOLD signal present before events of interest.

periodic event-related design An experimental design in which events of interest occur at regular intervals.

jittering Randomizing the intervals between successive stimulus events over some range.

(A)

Visual cortex

(B)

Motor cortex

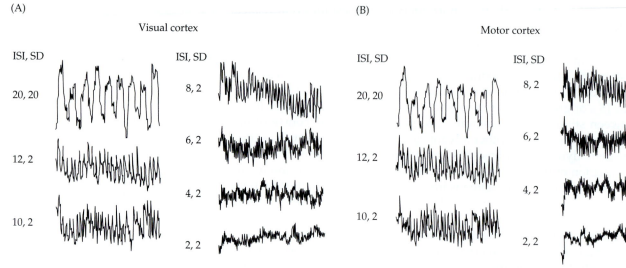

Figure 11.18 Effects of interstimulus interval upon event-related fMRI activity. As the interval between successive events decreases, the overlap between consecutive hemodynamic responses reduces the variability in the BOLD signal. Subjects performed a finger tapping task while watching a flashing visual stimulus. Activity within regions of interest in the visual cortex (A) and motor cortex (B) was measured under a number of different experimental conditions. When there was a long interstimulus interval (ISI) of 20 s and a long stimulus duration (SD) of 20 s, mimicking a blocked design, there was clear alternating activation in both regions. However, for short-duration events of 2 s, periodic activity was present at long ISIs of 10 to 12 s but not at short ISIs. (From Bandettini and Cox, 2000.)

semirandom design A type of event-related design in which the probability that an event will occur within a given time interval changes systematically over the course of the experiment.

of stimuli, words and nonword letter strings. If you knew that a given brain region responded to the words but not the nonwords, you could embed the words in a rapidly presented series of nonwords and the words would still evoke a large hemodynamic response. For that brain region, only the words would serve as events. However, for another brain region that responds equally to both words and nonwords, both types of stimuli would serve as events and BOLD activity would be at a steady state throughout the experiment. This logic is identical to that used in the study by McCarthy and colleagues described in the last section, and bears similarities to the fMRI-adaptation paradigms described in Chapter 8.

Semirandom Designs

In a periodic design, events are presented at a constant interstimulus interval, such as once every 16 s. In a randomized or jittered design, the interstimulus interval is determined by a fixed probability, expressed in terms of either the likelihood of a stimulus being presented at each time point (randomization) or the likelihood of a given ISI following each stimulus (jittering). While most event-related designs have used either a periodic or a jittered approach, a third type of design, **semirandom design,** has become increasingly popular (Figure 11.19A–C). In a semirandom design, stimulus probability varies systematically over time. One way to create such a design is to create "blocks" of stimulus probabilities. Imagine that your event is a flashing checkerboard presented for 500 ms, and you are sampling the brain at a TR of 1000 ms. You set up your experiment so that in the first 30-s block, each TR has a 25% chance of containing an event; in the next 60-s block, each TR has a 75% chance; and in the final 30 s, each TR has a 25% chance. The resulting design would look similar to Figure 11.19C. Another way to create a semirandom design is to have probability change smoothly over the exper-

(A)

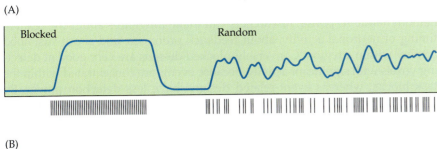

(B)

(C)

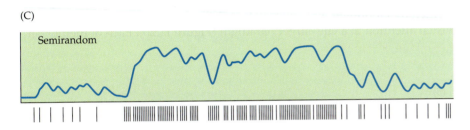

Figure 11.19 Semirandom designs that combine features of blocked and event-related designs. Each line reflects the presentation time of a single stimulus, such as a flash of a visual checkerboard, and the solid curves reflect the expected hemodynamic response. The semirandom design contains large-scale structure, in that some time intervals have high event-probability and some have low event-probability, with small-scale randomness. (A) and (B) combine a blocked epoch with random and semirandom periods, respectively, while (C) is a completely semirandom design. Note that these three designs have equal estimation efficiency and detection power. (From Liu et al., 2001.)

imental run (i.e., in a sinusoidal fashion) from some maximum to some minimum value. Although composed of individual events, semirandom designs are similar to blocked designs in that some time periods contain many events while others contain very few. As with blocked designs, this clustering increases the total variability in the BOLD signal.

Liu and colleagues conducted a number of simulations in 2001 to determine the relative advantages of semirandom designs compared to similar blocked or event-related designs. They found that although a semirandom design will always have slightly less detection power than a blocked design with the same number of events and blocks, due to its incomplete clustering, it will show substantial increases in estimation efficiency. More recent work by Liu and colleagues has extended these results to experiments with multiple trial types. Semirandom designs may be a good choice for experiments that value both detection and estimation. However, if the process of interest differs across ISIs, then the basic assumption of the semirandom design is violated. Known causes of ISI-related differences include hemodynamic refractory effects, especially at very short intervals, and changes in cognitive processes based on rate of presentation (i.e., a task may be simpler at slow rates than at fast rates). Nevertheless, semirandom design should be considered as a potentially valuable technique for optimizing trade-offs between detection and estimation.

Advantages and Disadvantages of Event-Related Designs

In general, the strengths of event-related designs mirror the weaknesses of blocked designs, and vice versa. While blocked designs are very poor at estimating the shape of the hemodynamic response, event-related designs have good estimation power. Estimation power is very important for many types of research questions. By characterizing the precise timing and waveform of the hemodynamic response, researchers can make inferences about the relative timing of neuronal activity, about feedback processes, and about sustained activity within a region. Conversely, blocked designs are very good at detecting voxels with significant activity, because events are concentrated within the task blocks, whereas event-related designs have less detection power. By using semirandom event-related designs, researchers can improve detection power somewhat, so that it approaches that of blocked designs. Yet decisions about experimental design cannot be made solely on the basis of the relative importance of detection and estimation. An increasing proportion of fMRI experiments value both factors, for example, those that seek to measure the difference in timing between two brain areas that are known to be active.

A more important criterion for choosing event-related designs comes from the experimental flexibility they provide. One form of flexibility is associated with the timing of events, in that researchers can use event-related methods to distinguish different brain processes associated with specific parts of a task, based on their relative timing. This flexibility is exemplified in an article written by Hopfinger and colleagues in 2000, that investigated the control of visual attention in a cue–target paradigm (Figure 11.20). Each of their experi-

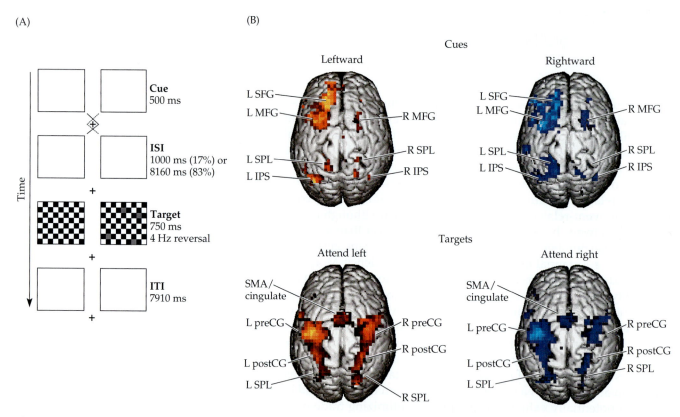

Figure 11.20 Use of an event-related design to separate different phases of an experimental task. One advantage of event-related designs is that they allow individuation of closely spaced aspects of a single trial. An event-related design was used to tease apart activity associated with an attention-directing cue from that associated with an attended or unattended target (A). Cues evoked activity in a network of frontal and inferior parietal regions, while targets evoked activity in motor, superior parietal, and ventrolateral frontal regions (B). Note that this analysis would have been impossible with a blocked design. Regions of activity include the superior frontal gyrus (SFG), middle frontal gyrus (MFG), superior parietal lobule (SPL), intraparietal sulcus (IPS), supplementary motor area (SMA), cingulate gyrus, the precentral gyrus (preCG), and postcentral gyrus (postCG). (From Hopfinger et al., 2000.)

mental trials began with the presentation for 500 ms of a cue that directed attention either to the left or right. Then, after a variable interval, checkerboard targets were presented simultaneously to the left and right of fixation for 750 ms. The subjects' task was to identify whether the checkerboard in the cued location contained any gray-colored checks. Event-related analyses were used to identify voxels that responded to the cue, to the targets, to both events, or to neither. They found that different sets of brain regions responded to the cues and targets, with superior frontal and inferior parietal regions most active in response to the cues and motor and ventrolateral frontal regions most active in response to the targets.

This interesting result would have been very difficult to obtain using a blocked design. Note that the nature of their cuing task precluded the separation of the different types of events into different blocks; each cue had to be followed by a target, which was in turn followed by a cue on the next trial, and so on. If the authors had alternated task and nontask blocks, thus combining both cues and targets into a single block, then both sets of regions would have been active during the task blocks. This illustrates one caveat of any fMRI study, and indeed of any neuroimaging study: All experimental tasks evoke multiple cognitive and perceptual processes. While no design can ensure a one-to-one relation between the task and the change in the dependent variable, event-related designs facilitate identification of cognitive processes associated with distinct time periods.

Event-related designs also provide researchers with latitude in their assignment of events to experimental conditions. The same events can be analyzed in different ways depending on the goals of the experiment. A researcher interested in how the presentation of an image affects its perception might present two types of images (e.g., faces and objects) in two orientations (e.g., right side up and upside down), each one at a time and in random order. The stimuli could be considered as one type of event, visual stimuli; two types of events, faces or objects; or even four distinct types. Note that this flexibility means that researchers can even choose their events based on experimental data, often known as **trial sorting.** (Note that, like many of the characteristics of event-related fMRI analyses, the basic concepts of trial sorting are derived from earlier electrophysiological studies.)

One of the most common sorting practices is categorizing events based on accuracy or response time. The pattern of data evoked on a given trial may be different based upon whether or not the subject responds correctly. For instance, some brain structures, such as the anterior cingulate gyrus, are more active on error trials than on correct trials. These differences may reflect cognitive processes like recognizing the mistake, adjusting response plans to prevent future errors, or reflecting on the cause of the error. Many experimenters remove error trials from their analyses, since the different processing on those trials may corrupt the effects of interest. If the total number of trials is sufficiently large, it may be possible to analyze correct and error trials independently. However, most experiments have relatively few error trials, and simple exclusion is usually preferred.

Even more exciting have been experiments that define their experimental conditions based solely on the subjects' responses. An early and influential example was reported by Brewer and colleagues in 1998, who investigated the brain regions associated with encoding information into memory. (We discuss a similar early study by Wagner and colleagues in the section covering fMRI research on memory in Chapter 13.) While in the fMRI scanner, their subjects saw a series of 96 pictures and judged whether each represented an indoor or outdoor scene. Thirty minutes later, after leaving the scanner, the subjects

trial sorting The post hoc assignment of events to conditions, often based on behavioral data.

mixed design A design that contains features of both blocked and event-related approaches.

were presented with the same 96 pictures, along with 32 new ones, and asked to judge whether each picture was distinctly remembered, somewhat familiar, or unrecognized. Note that the subjects had no advance warning of this memory test during the fMRI session. Based on the result of the memory test, the authors classified the presentation of each picture during scanning into remembered, familiar, or unrecognized conditions. Their fMRI analyses identified voxels whose activity was greater for pictures that were subsequently remembered and lesser for pictures that were later forgotten. The authors found that two regions, the right dorsolateral prefrontal cortex and bilateral parahippocampal cortex, were more active to the presentation of items that were remembered later. They concluded that these two regions compose a circuit involved in memory encoding. The power of these results comes from the use of post hoc trial sorting; subjects did not know that they were going to do a memory task, and there were no cues telling the subjects to remember some items and forget others. Instead, the researchers could infer the cognitive processes that were present during the earlier fMRI experiment based upon a later behavioral test. The reverse experiment is also possible, in that one can collect fMRI data during the recollection portion of the task and sort events based upon whether the subjects correctly recalled an earlier picture, as reported by Konishi and colleagues in 2000.

Trial sorting is at best very challenging in blocked designs. Removal of an entire block based on a single error trial is often impractical, and performance is often similar across different blocks due to averaging effects. Nor can differential effects of event timing or different components of a compound event be easily identified, due to the insensitivity of blocked designs to the shape of the hemodynamic response. For this reason, a large and increasing proportion of fMRI experiments have adopted event-related designs. Yet this flexibility comes with a price, albeit a small one. Event-related designs generally have lower detection power than similar blocked designs, resulting in part from their sensitivity to the shape of the hemodynamic response. If the wrong model for the fMRI hemodynamic response is used, then significant activations may be missed. Nevertheless, for a wide range of experimental tasks, event-related designs provide the best combination of flexibility and experimental power.

Mixed Designs

A third type of fMRI design combines the basic elements of blocked and event-related approaches. In a **mixed design,** stimuli are presented in discrete and regular blocks, but within each block are multiple types of events. This is illustrated in Figure 11.21. An important difference between mixed

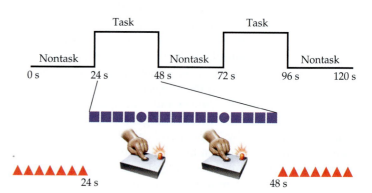

Figure 11.21 A sample mixed fMRI design. In a mixed design, events of interest are clustered within extended blocks. However, within each block the order of conditions is randomized. (After Huettel et al., 2004.)

designs and the other types of designs is that mixed designs allow analysis of IVs that change on different time scales. The task blocks, which may last for 20 to 30 s or more, are associated with sustained changes in task strategy, attention, or other cognitive processes. A subject may be attending to the left side of the visual display during one block and then attending to the right side for the next block. The different blocks induce different cognitive states in the subject, and thus blocked analyses can measure **state-related processes.** Note that this differs conceptually from the semirandom designs described earlier, even though both incorporate elements of blocked designs. When creating a mixed design, the researcher assumes that the grouping of events into a task block will cause the subject to adopt a particular cognitive state and maintain that state throughout the block. In contrast, the individual stimuli in a semirandom design are each assumed to evoke the same cognitive processes independent of the surrounding stimuli, with no higher-order states emerging. Thus, mixed designs are appropriate when one wants to examine sustained brain activity, while semirandom designs are preferred for optimal detection of transient brain activity.

As in an event-related design, the stimuli presented rapidly within the block will evoke separable short-term changes in the brain. For example, a subject may have been directed, when attending to the left, to quickly press a button to identify each stimulus. The particular processes evoked may differ depending on what stimulus is presented, as when comparing an object presented on the attended left to an object presented on the unattended right. Thus, the individual events within a mixed design's blocks reflect **item-related processes.** Note that state- and item-related processes are not necessarily related within a task; the brain structures responsible for attending to the left or right are not the same as those responsible for pressing buttons in response to targets. Mixed designs are thus extremely powerful for research questions that involve both a long-term cognitive process and short-term implementations of cognitive processes on individual trials.

state-related processes Changes in the brain that are assumed to reflect distinct modes, or states, of function. State-related processes are more easily measured with blocked designs.

item-related processes Changes in the brain that are assumed to be caused by the properties of individual stimuli, or items. Item-related processes are more easily measured with event-related designs.

> ## Thought Question
> Mixed designs can also be used to study transient processes that occur at the onset and offset of blocks. What sorts of cognitive processes are likely to occur at the beginning and end of task blocks?

The value of mixed designs can be seen in a study of recognition memory reported in 2001 by Donaldson and colleagues. They wanted to identify brain regions associated with two types of memory processes: general processes associated with attempted retrieval of items from memory regardless of their content, and specific processes associated with successful or unsuccessful retrieval. They used a mixed design with 105-s task blocks separated by 30-s nontask blocks. During each task block, 42 events were presented, randomized among three types: words that had been studied in a practice session beforehand, words that had not previously been studied, and fixation trials where the subject stared at a crosshair in the middle of the display. By randomly including fixation trials among the words presented, the authors effectively jittered the ISIs for the other stimulus types. Donaldson and colleagues collected BOLD fMRI data on a 1.5-T scanner using an asymmetric spin-echo pulse sequence. They found that a large number of regions showed event-related activity, including motor and visual regions,

(A)

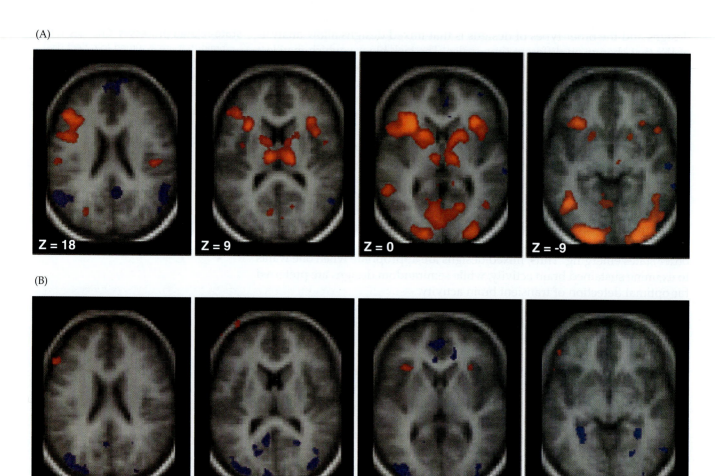

(B)

Figure 11.22   Transient and sustained activity measured using a mixed design. These data show patterns of event-related (A) and blocked (B) fMRI activity within a single mixed-design memory task. (From Donaldson et al., 2001.)

the frontal cortex, the insula, the thalamus, and the basal ganglia (Figure 11.22). A smaller set of regions had sustained increases in activity during the task blocks compared to the nontask blocks, including parts of the middle, inferior, and medial frontal gyri, as well as the insula (Figure 11.22B). When compared across types of processing, some regions seemed to be associated with both, notably the frontal and insular cortices, while other regions were associated independently with one type or the other.

While Donaldson and colleagues used a mixed design to distinguish between two different sets of brain regions, these designs can also be used to better understand activity in a single brain region. For example, fMRI studies have implicated the dorsolateral prefrontal cortex in two types of psychological processes: maintenance of stimulus information in short-term or working memory, and inhibition of a prepared behavior combined with selection of an unprepared behavior. These two types of processes have different fMRI signatures. Maintenance of information over time is, by its nature, a sustained process. Most fMRI studies that investigate maintenance, therefore, have used blocked designs or long-interval event-related designs. Behavioral inhibition and selection, by contrast, is a transient process, and most fMRI studies investigating it have used event-related designs. To investigate sustained and transient prefrontal activity within a single study, Huettel and colleagues used a mixed design in which infrequent target events were presented within task blocks, which alternated with perceptually similar nontask blocks (design shown in Figure 11.21). As this task had no explicit maintenance requirements, the authors hypothesized that any sustained activity must result from extended response-preparation processes and not maintenance. BOLD fMRI images were collected using a spiral gradient-echo series at 1.5 T. The dorsolateral prefrontal cortex showed event-related but not blocked activity, indicating that it was associated with transient but not sustained processes for the task demands tested.

It is important to recognize—as noted by Donaldson and colleagues in their coda—that state-related activity does not necessarily result in increased activity during one block type compared to another block type. Changes in a cognitive state could instead have modulatory effects upon event-related activity, so that the hemodynamic response to individual events within the block increases in amplitude. Consider a design in which task blocks involve attention to stimuli while nontask blocks do not. Within a region associated with the control of attention, there might be increased, steady-state activity throughout the task block. But in a region whose activity is influenced by attention, there might be larger hemodynamic responses to events within unattended blocks than within attended blocks. Mixed designs thus have great utility for many types of cognitive questions, but require analysis strategies targeted to the expected activity of interest.

Summary

The important issues in fMRI experimental design are the creation of a research hypothesis, the choice of experimental conditions to test that hypothesis, and the presentation of stimuli to manipulate the experimental conditions over time. When selecting conditions for an experiment, it is important to avoid confounding factors, or variables that unintentionally covary with the independent variable of interest. There are two main types of fMRI experimental designs: blocked and event-related (Table 11.1). In a blocked design, each condition is presented continuously for an extended time interval and the different conditions are usually alternated over time. Some blocked-design studies incorporate a baseline period without an experimental task, to account for specific brain regions that are often more

TABLE 11.1 Advantages and Disadvantages of Each Type of fMRI Experimental Design

	Advantages	Disadvantages
Blocked	Excellent detection power Useful for examining state changes Simple analysis	Poor estimation power Insensitive to shape of hemodynamic response Potential problems with selection of conditions
Event-related	Good estimation power Allow determination of change from baseline Very flexible analysis strategies Best for post hoc trial sorting	Can have reduced detection power Sensitive to errors in predicted HDR Refractory effects can influence analyses
Mixed or semirandom	Best combination of detection and estimation Can dissociate transient and sustained components of activity	Most complicated analyses Relies on assumptions of linearity

active in baseline conditions. Event-related designs present stimuli one at a time rather than together in a block. Long-interval periodic event-related designs are useful when a prestimulus baseline is necessary but otherwise have poor experimental power. Jittered event-related designs, where the time between stimuli varies randomly, are preferable for most studies, and they increase in power with decreasing interstimulus interval. Semirandom designs with some periods of frequent stimulus presentation and other periods of infrequent presentation can potentially increase experimental power but require more-complex analyses. True mixed designs combine blocked and event-related analyses and are used for comparison of long-term sustained activity with short-term transient activity.

In fMRI studies, there is no optimal experimental design. The fundamental rule when designing your study is that you should choose the design that best suits your experimental question. An optimal semirandom design is useless if the brain activity of interest cannot be initiated and terminated over short intervals, just as a blocked design cannot be used if the conditions cannot be separated into different blocks. When designing a research study, the most important factor to consider is the simplest: with which design will my experimental manipulation evoke differential BOLD activity?

Suggested Readings

*Buckner, R. L., Bandettini, P. A., O'Craven, K. M., Savoy, R. L., Petersen, S. E., Raichle, M. E., and Rosen, B. R. (1996). Detection of cortical activation during averaged single trials of a cognitive task using functional magnetic resonance imaging. *Proc. Natl. Acad. Sci. U.S.A.*, 93: 14878–14883. This early study anticipates the later power of event-related fMRI analyses.

*Gusnard, D. A., and Raichle, M. E. (2001). Searching for a baseline: Functional imaging and the resting human brain. *Nat. Rev. Neurosci.*, 2(10): 685–694. This review article provides an overview of the issues involved with comparing activation across conditions in neuroimaging studies, and also describes possible functions for regions that have shown consistent decreases in activity during experimental tasks.

*Hopfinger, J. B., Buonocore, M. H., and Mangun, G. R. (2000). The neural mechanisms of top-down attentional control. *Nat. Neurosci.*, 3: 284–291. This influential article delineates networks associated with different aspects of attentional control.

Keppel, G. (1991). *Design and Analysis: A Researcher's Handbook.* Prentice-Hall, Englewood Cliffs, NJ. A classic, readable textbook on experimental design.

*Liu, T. T., Frank, L. R., Wong, E. C., and Buxton, R. B. (2001). Detection power, estimation efficiency, and predictability in event-related fMRI. *NeuroImage*, 13: 759–773. Though challenging, this article provides detailed mathematical comparisons of the relative strengths and weaknesses of different experimental designs.

*Zacks, J. M., Braver, T. S., Sheridan, M. A., Donaldson, D. I., Snyder, A. Z., Ollinger, J. M., Buckner, R. L., and Raichle, M. E. (2001). Human brain activity time-locked to perceptual event boundaries. *Nat. Neurosci.*, 4: 651–655. An interesting research article that investigates how people partition continuous events into discrete periods.

Indicates a reference that is a suggested reading in the field and is also cited in this chapter.

Chapter References

Bandettini, P. A., and Cox, R. W. (2000). Event-related fMRI contrast when using constant interstimulus interval: Theory and experiment. *Magn. Reson. Med.,* 43(4): 540–548.

Binder, J. R., Frost, J. A., Hammeke, T. A., Bellgowan, P. S., Rao, S. M., and Cox, R. W. (1999). Conceptual processing during the conscious resting state. A functional MRI study. *J. Cogn. Neurosci.,* 11(1): 80–95.

Birn, R. M., Cox, R. W., and Bandettini, P. A. (2002). Detection versus estimation in event-related fMRI: Choosing the optimal stimulus timing. *NeuroImage,* 15: 252–264.

Blamire, A. M., Ogawa, S., Ugurbil, K., Rothman, D., McCarthy, G., Ellermann, J. M., Hyder, F., Rattner, Z., and Shulman, R. G. (1992). Dynamic mapping of the human visual cortex by high-speed magnetic resonance imaging. *Proc. Natl. Acad. Sci. U.S.A.,* 89: 11069–11073.

Boynton, G. M., Engel, S. A., Glover, G. H., and Heeger, D. J. (1996). Linear systems analysis of functional magnetic resonance imaging in human V1. *J. Neurosci.,* 16: 4207–4221.

Brewer, J. B., Zhao, Z., Desmond, J. E., Glover, G. H., and Gabrieli, J. D. (1998). Making memories: Brain activity that predicts how well visual experience will be remembered. *Science,* 281: 1185–1187.

Dale, A. M., and Buckner, R. L. (1997). Selective averaging of rapidly presented individual trials using fMRI. *Hum. Brain Mapping,* 5: 329–340.

Donaldson, D. I., Petersen, S. E., Ollinger, J. M., and Buckner, R. L. (2001). Dissociating state and item components of recognition memory using fMRI. *NeuroImage,* 13: 129–142.

Huettel, S. A., Misiurek, J., Jurkowski, A., and McCarthy, G. (2004). Dynamic and strategic aspects of executive processing. *Brain Res.,* in press.

James, W. (1890). *The Principles of Psychology.* Dover, New York.

Konishi, S., Wheeler, M. E., Donaldson, D. I., and Buckner, R. L. (2000). Neural correlates of episodic retrieval success. *NeuroImage,* 12: 276–286.

Liu, T. T., (2004). Efficiency, power, and entropy in event-related fMRI with multiple trial types: Part II: Design of experiments. *NeuroImage,* 21: 401–413.

McCarthy, G., Luby, M., Gore, J., and Goldman-Rakic, P. (1997). Infrequent events transiently activate human prefrontal and parietal cortex as measured by functional MRI. *J. Neurophysiol.,* 77: 1630–1634.

McCarthy, G., Puce, A., Luby, M., Belger, A., and Allison, T. (1996). Magnetic resonance imaging studies of functional brain activation: Analysis and interpretation. *Electroencephalogr. Clin. Neurophysiol. Suppl.,* 47: 15–31.

Raichle, M. E., MacLeod, A. M., Snyder, A. Z., Powers, W. J., Gusnard, D. A., and Shulman, G. L. (2001). A default mode of brain function. *Proc. Natl. Acad. Sci. U.S.A.,* 98: 676–682.

Sutton, S., Braren, M., Zubin, J., and John, E. R. (1965). Evoked-potential correlates of stimulus uncertainty. *Science,* 150: 1187–1188.

Ungerleider, L. G., and Mishkin, M. (1982). Two cortical visual systems. In *Analysis of Visual Behavior* (D. J. Ingle, M. A. Goodale, and R. J. W. Mansfield, eds.), pp. 549–586. MIT Press, Cambridge, MA.

12

Statistical Analysis

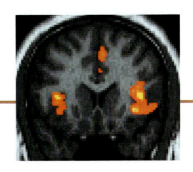

You have just completed data collection for the first subject of your first fMRI experiment. After careful consideration, you decided to use a simple two-condition blocked design. During task blocks, a series of famous names (e.g., Bill Clinton, Michael Jordan) flashed across the screen, while during nontask blocks, the names were of people unknown to the subject. You hypothesized that the task condition would be associated with greater activity in the fusiform gyrus, which is critical for face processing, because subjects would imagine the faces that go with the famous names. So, to evaluate this hypothesis, you calculated that the mean activity in the fusiform gyrus was 500 units in the famous-names block and 498 units in the unknown-names blocks. As you stare at these numbers, you realize that your hypothesis remains unanswered. The averages are numerically different, to be sure, but is the difference meaningful?

This example illustrates the use of **descriptive statistics,** or summaries of a data set. Any set of numbers can be described using statistics like the mean, median, or standard deviation. But regardless of the experiment, the recorded data do not provide a complete and unerring description of the world. Instead, the data represent but a single **sample,** or one set of observations out of the many that might have occurred in the experiment. If our subject had performed the task differently, or if we had selected a different subject, our data could have been very different. It is possible that the numerical difference between blocks that we measured in this subject was due to random variation, such that it would disappear if the subject was run a second time. As experimenters, we want to do more than just describe our observations; we want to make inferences about the underlying processes that cause the data. Stated another way, we do not want to know merely whether the fMRI activity in the task block was greater than that in the nontask block *within the particular data we recorded.* Instead, we want to know whether the difference between conditions would be reliable across repeated observations from the same subject, from the same group of subjects, or from the population at large. To make such judgments, we must use **inferential statistics** that provide estimates of our certainty in the experimental hypothesis.

descriptive statistics Statistics that summarize the sample data but do not allow inferences about the larger population.

sample (1) A set of observations drawn from a larger population of potential observations. (2) An object to be imaged using magnetic resonance.

inferential statistics Statistics that make inferences about the characteristics of a population based upon data obtained from a smaller sample.

research hypothesis A proposition about the nature of the world that makes predictions about the results of an experiment. For a hypothesis to be well formed, it must be falsifiable.

null hypothesis The proposition that the experimental manipulation will have no effect upon the experimental data. Most statistical analyses evaluate the probability that the null hypothesis is true, i.e., that the observed data reflect chance processes.

significance testing The process of evaluating whether the null hypothesis is true. Also known as hypothesis testing.

Recall from the previous chapter that experiments should be designed to test a **research hypothesis,** often symbolized H_1, that states a possible relation between independent and dependent variables. Although often only one hypothesis is stated, all experiments are designed to discriminate between two possible hypotheses, the research hypothesis and another, **null hypothesis** (H_0) that usually states that the manipulation has no effect. For the experiment example above, the null hypothesis (H_0) would be "Reading famous versus unknown names has no effect upon fMRI activity in the fusiform gyrus." All well-formed hypotheses must be falsifiable, in that either the research or the null hypothesis, but not both, must be true. This can be seen by examining the typical mathematical form of the hypotheses:

$$H_1: \text{Condition 1} \neq \text{Condition 2}$$

$$H_0: \text{Condition 1} = \text{Condition 2}$$

Since the null hypothesis assumes that the independent variable has no effect, it predicts that the observed values of the dependent variable will be similarly distributed between the conditions. In the blocked design in our example, we might expect the data obtained in the two conditions to have been drawn from the same distribution (i.e., mean intensity + Gaussian noise), with any differences due to random chance. As loose examples, if the mean fMRI response across different nontask blocks ranged from 450 to 550 units, a value of 500 in a task block would be consistent with chance expectation. But if typical values for nontask blocks were from 497.95 to 498.05 units, then a task value of 500 would be unlikely to be due to chance. The process of evaluating whether differences between conditions are likely to be due to chance is known as **significance testing.**

In the following sections, we explore a number of different approaches to significance testing of fMRI data. All the approaches differ in their assumptions and goals, but they share some common features. First, they express significance as the probability that the results could occur under the null hypothesis. The color maps that form the basis of many figures in fMRI manuscripts almost always express this probability, often with dull colors as relatively high probabilities that the difference is due to chance and bright colors as low probabilities that the difference is due to chance (Figure 12.1A

(A)   (B)

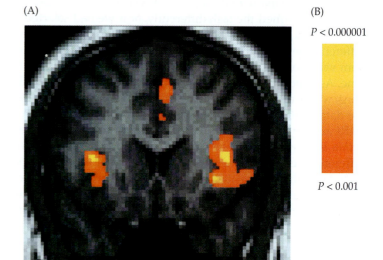

$P < 0.000001$

$P < 0.001$

Figure 12.1 Statistical maps of fMRI data. Functional MRI data are usually displayed using a background anatomical MRI image with an overlaid statistical map (A). In the statistical map, voxels whose activity passes some threshold value are shown in color, with the intensity of the color corresponding to the significance value (B). More extreme significance values (lower probabilities) are usually shown in brighter colors. It is critical to recognize that the colors represent the output of some statistical test, not absolute data values.

and B). Second, voxels whose probability levels are below a threshold probability, known as an **alpha value,** are labeled as significant, while voxels whose probability is above the threshold are labeled as nonsignificant. The alpha value provides the probability of a **Type I error,** or deciding that the null hypothesis is false when it is really true (Figure 12.2). In terms of fMRI analyses, a Type I error means that a voxel was labeled as active when it was not (i.e., a false positive). Since fMRI studies may involve statistical tests on thousands of voxels, it is challenging to decide upon an appropriate alpha value. Third, the approaches are generally conservative, in that they emphasize excluding inactive voxels more than detecting all active voxels. This results in high rates of **Type II error,** or accepting the null hypothesis when it is really false (i.e., a false negative).

Just as no single experimental design is appropriate for all research questions, no single analysis approach can be used for all experiments. The correct method for any given experiment depends on the nature of the experimental design, the hypotheses to be tested, and the type of error to be minimized. Therefore, in this chapter we discuss a number of different approaches to fMRI data analysis. We begin with simple analyses such as *t*- and correlation tests and progress to the commonly used general linear model, which subsumes those simpler tests. We discuss key issues specific to fMRI studies, including choosing an appropriate alpha value based on the number of voxels tested and combining data across multiple subjects. We also describe a different approach to fMRI data, region-of-interest analysis, that has considerable power in elucidating the function of anatomical regions. Throughout, we emphasize the theory behind the different analysis approaches, so that the researcher can make an informed selection for a given experiment. For equations and guidelines on implementing particular tests, we refer the reader to the statistical textbooks indicated in the references section.

Basic Statistical Tests

The simplest and oldest of all statistical tests can be used on the data in Figure 12.3. Shown are the BOLD changes in a motor cortex voxel associated with brief hand movements during the presentation of a 3-s duration stimulus. Following every presentation of a stimulus, there was an increase in signal that lasted about 10 s. How do we know whether this voxel is significantly active? In this case, we can use the venerable **interocular trauma test,** which can be stated succinctly: the comparison is significant if the data, when plotted, hit you between the eyes. In the plotted data, the effect of the independent variable is obvious, because every time the stimulus was presented there was a very large change in the dependent variable. If only all fMRI data were so simple to analyze! As discussed in Chapter 9, the signal-to-noise ratio in most fMRI experiments is quite low, so effects are very rarely so easy to spot in the raw data. Researchers must instead use signal averaging and significance testing to evaluate whether the experimental manipulation has any effect.

The particular statistical test to be used for a given experiment depends on the hypothesis to be tested. When evaluating whether a voxel has different mean signal levels in two experimental conditions, the common *t*-test is appropriate. If a hypothesis makes specific predictions about the form of the activity change, as when using a model for the expected hemodynamic response, then a correlation test may be useful. For periodic designs, notably

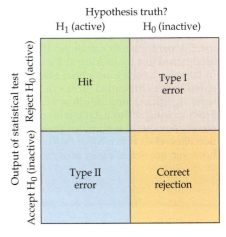

Figure 12.2 Types of experimental errors. When testing research hypotheses, there are four possible outcomes. The experimenter may reject the null hypothesis when it should be rejected; this is sometimes called a "hit," and in fMRI it corresponds to successfully identifying an active voxel. Rejecting the null hypothesis when it is in fact true is known as a Type I error, and corresponds in fMRI to labeling a voxel as active when it is not. Accepting the null hypothesis when it is in fact false is a Type II error; in fMRI, this is labeling a voxel as inactive when it is active. Type II errors are common in fMRI. Finally, accepting the null hypothesis when it is indeed true is called a "correct rejection."

alpha value An a priori probability (e.g., 0.001) chosen as the threshold for statistical significance. If the probability that the data would be obtained under the null hypothesis is less than the alpha value, the data are considered to be statistically significant.

Type I error Rejecting the null hypothesis when it is in fact true. Also known as a false positive.

Type II error Accepting the null hypothesis when it is in fact false. Also known as an incorrect rejection or false negative.

interocular trauma test An intuitive test of significance based on highly visible effects of the experimental manipulation. It states that data are significant if, when plotted, they hit you between the eyes.

Figure 12.3   Use of the interocular trauma test for statistical significance. For some data, the effect of the experimental manipulation can be readily ascertained just by looking at the data. In this voxel, each time a brief visual stimulus was presented (arrows), there were significant increases in activity. From looking at these data, it is completely obvious that stimulus presentation elicited an effect. Most fMRI data, however, are not so easily analyzed!

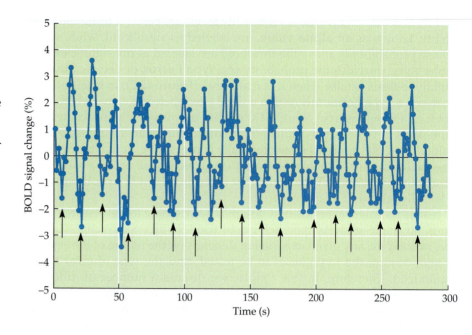

subtraction   In experimental design, the direct comparison of two conditions that are assumed to differ only in one property, the independent variable.

distribution   The pattern of variation of a variable under some conditions. For example, the normal distribution has a characteristic bell shape.

those with alternating blocks, Fourier analyses are useful for identifying regular changes in the fMRI data occurring at the task frequency. These tests allow testing of hypotheses that compare two conditions. For more-complex comparisons, the general linear model may be used, as discussed later in this chapter.

The t-Test

In a standard two-condition blocked design, the null hypothesis is simple: the difference between the conditions has no effect on the fMRI data. As described in the introduction to this chapter, a simpleminded way to compare the conditions would be to calculate the difference between their means (i.e., 500 units vs. 498 units). This comparison follows the logic of **subtraction** advanced in the previous chapter. However, a difference between condition means, by itself, is uninformative. It is necessary to evaluate any difference in means in the context of their variability. So, under the null hypothesis, any difference between the mean of the fMRI data recorded in Condition 1 and the mean of the data recorded in Condition 2 is due to random chance. The *t*-distribution describes the expected difference between two random samples drawn from the same **distribution** (Figure 12.4). The mean of the *t*-distribu-

Figure 12.4   The Student's *t*-distribution. A commonly used statistical distribution, especially for blocked-design fMRI, is the Student's *t*-distribution. The *t*-distribution describes the expected difference between two samples drawn from the same normal distribution. It resembles the normal distribution at larger sample sizes ($n > 30$), but at smaller sample sizes it is narrower near the center and has more of its values near the tails.

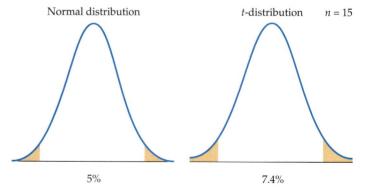

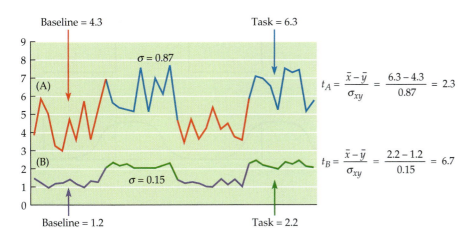

Baseline = 4.3 ‖ Task = 6.3

$$t_A = \frac{\bar{x} - \bar{y}}{\sigma_{xy}} = \frac{6.3 - 4.3}{0.87} = 2.3$$

$$t_B = \frac{\bar{x} - \bar{y}}{\sigma_{xy}} = \frac{2.2 - 1.2}{0.15} = 6.7$$

σ = 0.87

σ = 0.15

Baseline = 1.2 ‖ Task = 2.2

Figure 12.5 Conducting a *t*-test. The *t*-test compares the size of an effect (i.e., the difference between blocks) to the variability in the data (i.e., the shared standard deviation). Shown here are two simulated fMRI time courses. In plot A, the effect of the experimental manipulation is 2 units in amplitude, but the variability is relatively high, so the *t*-statistic is about 2.3. In plot B, the manipulation only has a 1-unit effect, but the variability is much smaller, and the resulting *t*-statistic, 6.7 is much higher.

tion is zero, since the two samples should on average have the same mean value, and the standard deviation of the *t*-distribution (i.e., the standard error of the mean) is the sample standard deviation divided by the square root of the sample size. Note that the *t*-distribution looks generally similar to the normal distribution, but at small sample sizes it has slightly more extreme values. When the sample size is very large, however, the shape of the *t*-distribution approaches the shape of the normal distribution.

To conduct a **t-test** (Equation 12.1 and Figure 12.5), the researcher calculates the means for all data points in the two conditions and divides their difference by the shared standard deviation (σ_{xy}):

$$t = \frac{\bar{x} - \bar{y}}{\sigma_{xy}} = \frac{\bar{x} - \bar{y}}{\sqrt{\sigma_x^2 + \sigma_y^2}} \qquad [12.1]$$

The resulting *t*-statistic can then be converted to a probability value based on the **degrees of freedom (df)**, or the number of unconstrained data points. For many statistical tests, the number of degrees of freedom is equal to the number of data points minus 1. As an example, for a sample of 20 data points with a known mean value, there are 19 degrees of freedom, since if you know 19 of the data points and the mean, you can calculate the 20th data point. Once the probability of the *t*-test has been determined using a statistical table or calculator, the researcher compares that probability to the alpha value for the experiment. For example, imagine that 25 time points in each condition are collected and that the difference between the means was 7 MR units and the standard deviation was 2 MR units. The resulting *t*-statistic will have a value of 3.5. The researcher wants to evaluate this statistic against the experiment's alpha value, which had been set at 0.01. With 48 degrees of freedom (i.e., 24 from each group), we can calculate that there is less than a 0.001 chance that the data in these conditions were drawn from the same distribution. This probability is lower than the threshold alpha value, and thus the null hypothesis could be rejected.

A primary challenge in setting up *t*-tests for blocked designs lies in deciding which fMRI time points belong to which experimental conditions. This problem is illustrated in Figure 12.6A–D. Consider a standard alternating blocked-design fMRI study with two conditions each of 20 s in duration. If you repeated this design two times and collected fMRI data with a 1-s TR, then you would have a total of 80 time points in the data set. Which time points should be assigned to condition A and which should be assigned to condition B? An obvious first option would be to assign the first 20 points to

t-test A test for statistical significance based on the Student's *t*-distribution. The *t*-test typically evaluates whether the mean values of two sets of observations are sufficiently different to preclude their being drawn from the same distribution.

degrees of freedom (df) The number of independent observations within a data set. For many statistical tests, there are *n* – 1 degrees of freedom associated with *n* data points.

Figure 12.6 Assigning time points in a blocked design to *t*-conditions. Although *t*-tests are commonly used for blocked designs, they do pose some challenges. Consider the simple alternating blocked design shown in (A). If we convolve this design with a hemodynamic response, we get the pattern of activity shown in (B). Because of the hemodynamic latency, the fMRI data do not correspond well to the timing of the original experimental design. By introducing a lag to the design (C), we can better fit the true timing of activity, although the transition periods between the blocks are still analyzed. Excluding the block transitions (D) can further distinguish experimental conditions.

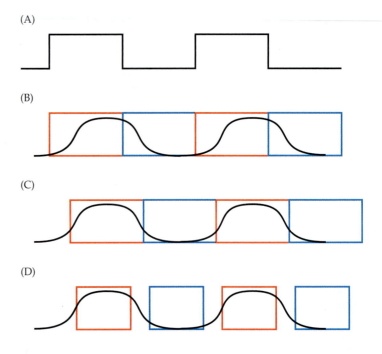

A, the next 20 to B, and so forth. But remember from Chapter 7 that the BOLD fMRI response lags behind neuronal activity. Therefore, a better approach would account for this lag by delaying the onset of all blocks (e.g., by about 6 s). But even this approach is imperfect. Because changes in the BOLD response are not instantaneous, there will be transition periods at the onset of each block where the measured fMRI signal will be changing from low to high or from high to low. By excluding these highly variable transition periods and sampling only the latter parts of each block, the researcher can select time points where the BOLD response has reached a steady state, maximizing the power of the *t*-test.

Although the *t*-test assumes that its data are drawn from normal distributions with equal variability, one of its strengths for fMRI is that it is relatively insensitive to violations of these assumptions. In even a short fMRI study, there will be at least a few tens of time points collected per voxel, and many studies collect hundreds of data points in each condition. At these sample sizes, deviations from normality have no meaningful effect on the outcome of the test. Likewise, with large samples, the conditions may have very different numbers of time points or have different variability without compromising the outcome of the *t*-test. While the *t*-test may be statistically valid for fMRI data, several potential concerns do exist. Any systematic difference between the experimental conditions, whether associated with meaningful BOLD activity or with uninteresting artifacts like scanner drift or head motion, could result in a significant *t*-test (Figure 12.7). This is especially a problem for blocked studies that have only a few cycles of the task and non-task conditions. The *t*-test is also inappropriate for answering questions about the timing of activity, since it combines across all time points within a condition.

While this discussion has focused on blocked designs, *t*-tests are also useful for some analyses of event-related designs. Remember that the basic role of the *t*-test is to identify differences in the means of two samples of data. If

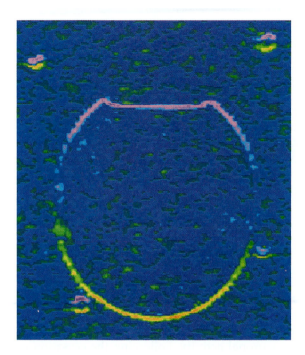

Figure 12.7 Effects of scanner drift on *t*-tests. Shown here is an activation map of a phantom, with positively significant voxels shown in the green-to-yellow color map and negatively significant voxels shown in the blue-to-pink color map. The position of the phantom "moved" slightly along the frequency-encoding direction (top to bottom) due to slow changes in the center frequency of the scanner over time. Even though there was no true activity, this motion within the images was significant according to the *t*-test conducted.

a research question focuses on specific data points within an event-related design, then a *t*-test may be appropriate. Many event-related designs, especially those studying working memory or attention, evaluate the magnitude of fMRI activity at a given time point. In an experiment conducted by Jha and McCarthy in 2000, subjects were shown photographs of one or more faces, to be remembered over a long delay interval of up to 27 s. One of the research questions was whether remembering more faces would result in increased activity during the delay interval, suggesting that the brain region being tested was involved in memory maintenance processes. The authors used a *t*-test to compare activity when subjects remembered multiple faces to when they remembered only a single face, at each time point within the delay interval. They found that there were significant differences at time points early in the interval, due to the presentation of the faces to be remembered. However, these differences disappeared as the interval progressed. The authors concluded, based on the nonsignificant *t*-tests, that memory maintenance had no effect on fMRI activity. In summary, regardless of the experimental design, if the research question can be answered by evaluating whether or not two samples have statistically different means, then a *t*-test may be appropriate.

While the *t*-test evaluates differences between the *means* of two distributions, it is insensitive to differences in their *variability* or *shape*. To find such differences, a **Kolmogorov–Smirnov (K–S test)** can be used. The K–S test converts each distribution to a cumulative distribution function, which plots the proportion of the data at or below each possible value of the dependent variable. The statistic of interest in the K–S test, D_k, is the maximal difference between the cumulative distributions at any value of the dependent variable. The flexibility of the K–S test comes with a price: greatly reduced sensitivity to changes in sample means compared to the *t*-test. Thus, the *t*-test should be used when the experimental hypothesis predicts that the manipulation should have an additive effect on the dependent variable, while the

Kolmogorov–Smirnov (K–S) test A test for statistical significance that evaluates whether two samples are drawn from the same distribution. The K–S test is sensitive to differences in variability and skew between distributions, but it is much less sensitive to differences in mean than the *t*-test.

K–S test should be restricted to situations where the manipulation is expected to have an effect on the variability of the dependent variable.

> **Thought Question**
>
> The K–S test is rarely used in fMRI because few experimental manipulations are designed to increase the variability of fMRI data. Can you think of an experimental manipulation that would increase the variability of fMRI data, but not its mean?

correlation analysis A type of statistical test that evaluates the strength of the relation between two variables. For fMRI studies, correlation analyses typically evaluate the correspondence between a predicted hemodynamic response and the observed data.

correlation coefficient (or *r*-value) A number between –1 and 1 that expresses the strength of the correlation between two variables.

Correlation Analysis

While the *t*-test and K–S test can be applied to many fMRI studies, neither analysis uses any information about the shape of the hemodynamic response. Indeed, when excluding transitions between task blocks, information about the shape of the response is explicitly removed. Nevertheless, the fMRI signal does contain important timing information. As discussed in Chapter 7, the fMRI hemodynamic response takes about 5 s to rise to its maximum after the onset of neuronal activity. Following the cessation of neuronal activity, the hemodynamic response falls over an additional 5 to 10 s and then stabilizes at a below-baseline level for an extended interval. The consistency of the hemodynamic response allows prediction of the change in fMRI activity that should be evoked in an active voxel. Using a **correlation analysis,** a researcher can quantify the correspondence between the predicted hemodynamic response and the observed data. Correlation analyses were first reported in fMRI by Bandettini and colleagues in 1993 and have since been an important part of fMRI analyses.

Conducting a correlation analysis on fMRI data is very simple. First, identify two epochs, ideally of equal length, that correspond to the experimental data and to a predicted hemodynamic response. Second, calculate the covariance in the data, as indicated by the numerator of Equation 12.2:

$$r = \frac{1}{n-1} \times \frac{\sum (x - \bar{x})(y - \bar{y})}{\sigma_x \sigma_y}$$ [12.2]

Note that the covariance may be either positive or negative. If the covariance is positive, values of the experimental data were large when values of the predicted data were large, or they were small when small. But if the covariance is negative, the values of the experimental data tended to be small when the values of the predicted data were large, or vice versa. Third, normalize the covariance by dividing by the product of the standard deviations of the two epochs. The resulting **correlation coefficient,** or *r*-value, can have values ranging from 1.0 to –1.0, or from perfect positive correlation to perfect negative correlation. A correlation of 0 indicates that the experimental data are unrelated to the prediction. As with the statistics discussed in the previous section, the significance of the correlation coefficient can be evaluated using statistical tables based on the degrees of freedom; a correlation of 0.5 is more likely to be significant when based on 1000 data points than when based on 10. This basic correlation analysis is then repeated for every voxel in the brain to create the map of significant activity.

Given the differences between correlation and *t*-tests, it may surprise you that when they are applied to the same data set, they give identical results.

Remember that the *t*-test evaluates whether data in one condition differ from data in another condition. Exactly the same test could be conducted by correlating the experimental data with a boxcar waveform (i.e., within task blocks the response will be 1, while in nontask blocks the response will be 0). This similarity is often seen in graphical descriptions of experimental designs, in which the different conditions are plotted as different values along the *y*-axis, and can be demonstrated using any sample data set and Equations 12.1 and 12.2. For any value of *r*, there is a corresponding value of *t*, given the degrees of freedom in the data. Note also that both tests measure signal change divided by nonsignal variability, with the *t*-test using the difference between means and the correlation test using the more general measure of covariation. Thus, the power of the correlation coefficient (like the *t*-test) rests on having maximal variability in the signal of interest compared to experimental noise. Furthermore, if the values of either the experimental or predicted data are distributed in a highly non-normal fashion, then the correlation statistic may not be meaningful. This may occur in fMRI studies if there are very long prestimulus or poststimulus baseline periods, so that most data points in the prediction epoch are near zero.

Correlation analyses are often used in conjunction with signal averaging, but in principle, signal averaging is unnecessary. One could use the entire experimental session as a single time course, then compare that time course to a prediction composed of many individual hemodynamic responses. Indeed, this idea forms the basis of the general linear model, described later in this chapter. However, signal averaging can have very salutary effects upon correlation analyses in fMRI. If there are low-frequency changes in the data, as result from scanner drift, then the overall correlation between data and prediction may be greatly reduced. Averaging across stimulus epochs before doing the correlation analysis minimizes the influence of low-frequency changes.

Signal averaging can also inform the choice of the predicted hemodynamic response. One way to generate the predicted hemodynamic response is to use an empirical function derived from another experiment. As the fMRI hemodynamic response is generally similar across subjects, the simplicity of using a canonical function may be attractive. However, recall from Chapters 9 and 10 that the characteristics of the hemodynamic response may differ across subjects, brain regions, and stimuli. Such differences can reduce the significance of correlation tests. One way of overcoming this problem is to generate a unique hemodynamic response for each subject, based on a screening run, partial data set, or region/voxel of interest. More-complex approaches begin by using the correlation with a canonical response to identify a region of interest, then interrogating those voxels for their hemodynamic response, and then repeating these steps until they converge to a solution. If the initial predicted hemodynamic response is reasonably well correlated with the actual data, then such iterative or bootstrapping approaches can be very effective.

Fourier Analysis

As discussed in Chapter 11, a blocked-design fMRI task presents stimulus conditions at regular intervals. As a consequence, the MR signal within an active voxel regularly rises during task blocks and falls during nontask blocks. The periodic nature of this signal change can be quantified using a **Fourier transform.** The Fourier transform expresses a temporally (or spatially) varying signal as the linear sum of a series of sine waves of different

Fourier transform A mathematical technique for converting a signal (i.e., changes in intensity over time) into its power spectrum.

time domain The expression of a signal in terms of its intensity at different points in time.

frequency domain The expression of a signal in terms of its power at different frequencies.

frequencies, amplitudes, and phases. A plot of the magnitude of each sine-wave component necessary to recreate the original signal is called a power spectrum. Thus, the power spectrum itself is another way of representing the original data. In the language of signal processing, the raw fMRI time series data are in the **time domain,** meaning that they show the relative intensity of the signal at each time sample. The power spectrum represents the same data in the **frequency domain,** indicating the intensity of the signal at each component frequency. If a task-related signal rises and falls at a known frequency, then a peak will occur at that frequency in the power spectrum (see Figure 10.16). We discussed in Chapter 10 the use of the Fourier transform to remove unwanted variability from the data, and here we extend that discussion to consider its use for statistical analysis of task-related variability.

In practice, the frequencies that can be measured by a Fourier analysis depend upon how often the BOLD time series is sampled. The basic rule of sampling, the Nyquist sampling theorem, states that to accurately measure a given frequency, you must sample at a minimum of twice that frequency. Thus, the Fourier transform of n time points sampled at a given TR contains $n/2$ frequencies ranging from 0 Hz to $1/(2 \times \text{TR})$ Hz, which are represented along the x-axis of the power spectrum. The first frequency component, at 0 Hz, represents the mean intensity of the signal and is often called the DC component, after the electrical term for direct current (i.e., a constant-voltage power source). Since fMRI time courses generally are represented in arbitrary units with positive values proportional to the amount of current through the receiver coil, the DC component is generally positive and very large. Also present in almost all fMRI data, even from very stable scanners, is substantial low-frequency power associated with scanner drift, among other factors (see Chapter 9). There are also slow physiological changes due to vascular oscillations, although such effects are incompletely understood. Because of this power at low frequencies, very long block lengths are not ideal for fMRI.

Substantial high-frequency (i.e., >0.5 Hz) power is rare in fMRI experiments, save for that associated with heart rate, even when the sampling rate is sufficiently fast. At fast stimulus-presentation rates, the sluggishness of the fMRI hemodynamic response tends to smooth the data considerably, serving to filter high-frequency components of the data. So, even if your two conditions alternated at a rate of 2 Hz, there would be no hemodynamic changes at that rate to be measured.

While Fourier approaches can be used for standard alternating blocked designs, more-complex designs are also possible. Imagine an experiment in which you wish to identify differential activity evoked by faces, animals, and objects. You could create blocks of faces that recur with a period of 12 s, blocks of animals with a period of 14 s, and blocks of objects with a period of 16 s, and then combine all of these blocks into a single stimulus series with each stimulus category appearing at its specific frequency (Figure 12.8). Voxels that are activated by faces should have a peak in the power spectrum at 1/12 s, or 0.083 Hz; voxels activated by animals should have a peak at 0.071 Hz; and voxels activated by objects should have a peak at 0.063 Hz. Voxels that are activated by both faces and objects should have two spectral peaks, at both 0.083 and 0.063 Hz. Using blocks that overlap in time, as in this example, can be much more efficient than conducting a series of separate experiments.

Combining sine waves at the magnitude specified in a power spectrum is not sufficient to accurately recreate the original raw data. Imagine that a

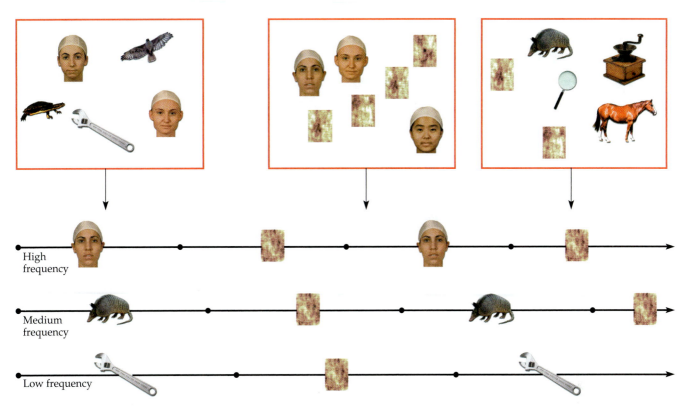

Figure 12.8 The use of overlapping blocks with different frequencies. If several different classes of stimuli are presented at different frequencies, a Fourier transform can be used to separate activity associated with each. Here, faces are presented at the highest frequency, animals are presented at an intermediate frequency, and objects are presented at the lowest frequency. Each is presented individually in an alternating blocked design, with scrambled objects as the control condition. Note that what subjects see changes at different points in the task, as shown at top. Some of the time, all three categories will be present, while at other times, only one or two of the categories will be visible.

power spectrum informs us that our original data were composed of two sine waves, one at 4 Hz and the other at 5 Hz. In principle, we should be able to add a 4-Hz sine wave and a 5-Hz sine wave with the appropriate magnitudes as indicated in the power spectrum and recreate our raw data. However, if we change the phase angle of one or both of these component sine waves, we can create many different waveforms. Happily for us, the Fourier transform also provides a phase spectrum, which specifies the phase angle that each sine-wave component must be shifted in order to recreate the original data. This is advantageous in fMRI studies where the sluggishness of the hemodynamic response causes a lag in the onset and offset of the stimulus blocks. The phase angle at the task frequency provides a frequency domain measurement of this time lag. This phase lag can be compared for voxels in different brain regions and can thus provide a measure of differential hemodynamic latency.

Differences in the phase of the BOLD signal at the task frequency can be purposively introduced by manipulating the task timing. Figure 12.9 shows data from a study mapping the motor cortex in a single patient (see Box 12.2

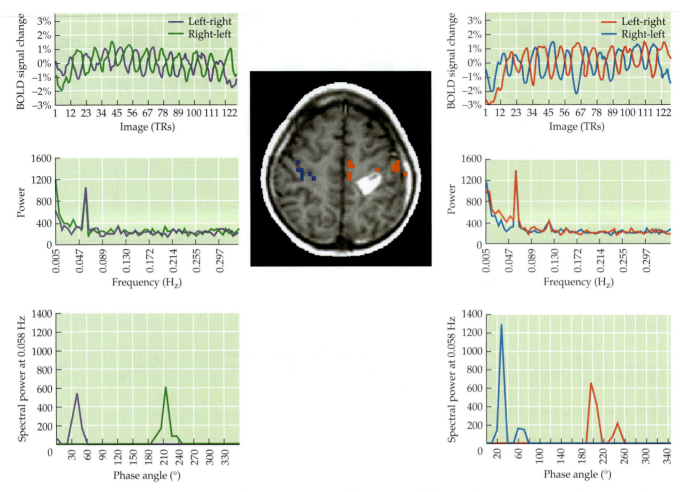

Figure 12.9 Use of frequency and phase information in cortical mapping. This patient, who had an arteriovenous malformation (AVM) in the left hemisphere (right side of image), participated in blocked-design motor squeeze tasks that began either with a left-hand squeeze or a right-hand squeeze. The raw data are shown in the upper graphs, the power spectra are shown in the middle graphs, and the phase at the task frequency (peak in spectra) is shown at bottom. Note that although both hemispheres had peaks at about the same frequencies, the phases are different, allowing dissociation of right-hand and left-hand activity.

for related information). The task alternated squeezing the left and right hands (blocks of about 9 s), beginning with each hand on one-half of the runs. Since both types of runs, left-first and right-first, had the same block lengths, they both had maximal power at the same task frequency (about 0.057 Hz). However, the responses at that frequency were 180° out of phase. Thus, by manipulating the phase of stimulus presentation across runs, we can introduce known phase changes into our BOLD data that can help distinguish true task-related activity from noise that may occur at the task frequency. Active voxels can be identified as those that both increase in power at the task frequency and change phase consistent with the experimental manipulation.

In summary, the Fourier transform is an important tool for analyses of periodic fMRI data. It is most commonly used with alternating blocked designs, but it can be used with any design in which different conditions occur at different frequencies. It provides two measures at each frequency component, power and phase. Power can be used to evaluate whether significant activity is present at a frequency, and phase can be used to evaluate the timing of that activity.

Displaying Statistical Results

The goal of most fMRI statistical tests, regardless of their complexity, is to evaluate the probability that each voxel is consistent with the null hypothesis. When statistical tests from all voxels in the brain are combined, the result is a **statistical map,** or **statistical parameter map,** of brain activity. The statistical map is usually color-coded according to the probability value for each voxel. For example, if the alpha value for an experiment were set at 0.01, a voxel with a near alpha probability value of 0.009 might be displayed in a dark red, while a voxel with an extremely low probability value of 0.000001 might be shown as a bright yellow. The association between probability values (or another statistic) and the colors that label them is known as a **color map.** In general, researchers use darker, desaturated colors to indicate low significance levels and brighter, highly saturated colors to indicate high significance levels. The statistical map is usually displayed on top of a **base image** that illustrates brain anatomy. However, it is important not to confuse the properties of a base anatomical image with those of the overlaid statistical map. The former is usually of high resolution and has contrast dependent on a physical property of the brain (e.g., T_1), while the latter is a calculated statistical map reflecting the correspondence of the data to an experimental hypothesis. (Note that although the vast majority of color maps display statistical significance, other properties such as percent signal change or latency can also be displayed; see, e.g., Figure 8.15).

There are many options for displaying fMRI data, each with advantages and disadvantages. The most common option is the single anatomical slice with overlaid color map (Figure 12.10A). In many experiments, the anatomical images are acquired at the same slice locations as the functional images, so little additional processing is necessary. Single slices are also generally easy to read, as foci of activity are highly visible. But given the variability in brain anatomy across subjects, it may be challenging to identify which gyrus or sulcus is active. Depending on the areas of interest, one slice orientation may be better than another. Gyri and sulci that run from left to right (e.g., the central sulcus) are difficult to identify in coronal slices, while those running from front to back (e.g., most frontal gyri) are harder to interpret in axial slices. Another limitation of single-slice displays is the choice of slices to include. Rarely will all collected slices be displayed in a single poster, manuscript, or lecture slide, due to their sheer number. Instead, the researcher will display selected slices that illustrate the major activation locations found in the study. When showing single slices, it is critical to explicitly label the left and right hemispheres, due to the axial symmetry of the human brain. Historically, MRI data have been displayed in **radiological convention,** such that the left side of the image corresponds to the right side of the brain and vice versa. This convention results from the way in which radiologists typically interact with patients, who are generally facing them or lying in scanners with their feet toward them. Displaying fMRI data in normal or **neurological convention** (i.e., based on a surgeon looking from the head to the feet) has become increasingly common in recent years.

While statistical maps are often calculated and displayed as two-dimensional slices, they also can be displayed in three-dimensional perspective

statistical map (or statistical parameter map) In fMRI, the labeling of all voxels within the image according to the outcome of a statistical test.

color map The association between numerical values of a parameter and a set of colors.

base image The image on which a statistical map is displayed, often a high-resolution anatomical image.

radiological convention The practice of displaying images of the brain so that the left side of the image is the right side of the brain and vice versa, as if one were facing the subject.

neurological convention The practice of displaying images of the brain so that the left and right sides of the image correspond to the same sides of the brain, as if one were behind the subject.

rendered image A display of MRI data in three-dimensional perspective.

glass-brain view A two-dimensional projection of fMRI data, as if the brain were made transparent and only the activations were visible.

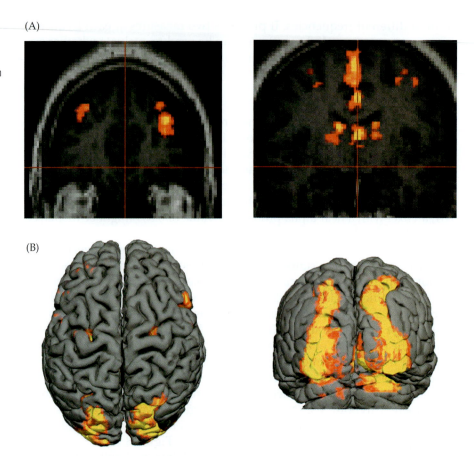

Figure 12.10 Two- and three-dimensional representations of fMRI data. Statistical maps of fMRI data are typically shown either as two-dimensional slices (A) or as three-dimensional rendered brains (B). (B from Huettel et al., 2001, created using FreeSurfer, CorTechs/Martinos Imaging Center, Boston, MA.)

(Figure 12.10B). Such displays are often called **rendered images.** The major advantage of three-dimensional rendering is that one can easily identify the locations of brain activity, especially with regard to prominent gyri and sulci. Such images are also more easily interpreted by naïve viewers who are more familiar with the general shape and external structure of the brain than with specific internal features. Hidden, however, are internal nuclei, such as the basal ganglia and thalamus, as well as internal cortical regions like the hippocampus, cingulate, and insula. It is also more difficult to show both hemispheres simultaneously in a single image, so authors often include more than one rendered image within a single figure. To overcome the problems introduced by the opacity of rendered images, some analysis programs generate transparent or semitransparent images, sometimes called **glass-brain views** (Figure 12.11A). These project all foci of activity onto an outline of the brain, allowing the researcher to see all of the activations at once. As with any projective display technique, a single glass-brain view is considerably underdetermined, in that many possible sets of activations could lead to the displayed image. For this reason, most programs generate a set of three orthogonal views of the brain, so that by comparing among them researchers can localize activations.

(A)   (B)

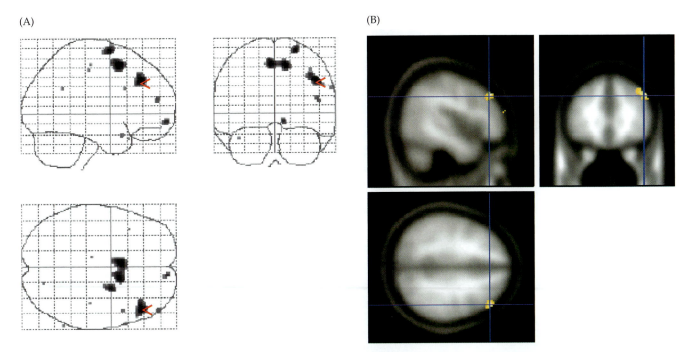

Figure 12.11 Glass-brain views of fMRI data. One common way to visualize fMRI data is to use a "glass-brain" view (A), which shows the three orthogonal projections of the original data. The red arrow (<) is at the same location in each brain view. All activations are visible in each orientation, although it can be difficult to identify their anatomical locations. For this reason, glass-brain views are more useful for working with data than for final display. Use of projection views in conjunction with anatomical or reference slices (B) makes identification of activation foci much easier. (Images created using SPM; Wellcome Department of Cognitive Neurology, London, UK.)

Rendering a brain image can be very computationally intensive, especially if the analysis program generates a smooth high-resolution surface based on an anatomical image. Many researchers, therefore, use simple two-dimensional or glass-brain displays when working with data from an experiment, and only create the high-quality rendered images when making final figures for a manuscript. Besides standard surface views, several other types of rendered images are available. To illustrate activity that lies within deep cortical sulci, the outer cortical layer can be removed or de-emphasized. For applications where precise distinctions between adjacent brain regions must be made, researchers may display fMRI data on **inflated brains** or **flat maps** (Figure 12.12). This is most common for retinotopic mapping of the visual system. Remember that the cortex is basically a single folded sheet about 5 mm in depth. As its name implies, an inflated brain recovers this structure by expanding the cortical surface like a balloon while maintaining its basic shape. A flat map is obtained by cutting the inflated surface at different points and then laying out the cortical sheet in two dimensions. Since no changes in depth are visible in these techniques, the original gyral and sulcal patterns are marked using different colors or brightness levels. When a three-dimensional object like the brain is transformed into a two-dimensional map, there are by necessity some local distortions. Compare, for example, globes and world maps; the latter either have cuts between adjacent areas (e.g., Goode's interrupted map) or distortions in size (e.g., Mercator projections). Similarly, minimization of distortion is a significant problem for the generation of flat maps of the brain.

inflated brain A transformation of the cortical sheet into a balloonlike structure, removing gyral and sulcal folds so that activation can be more easily viewed.

flat map An unfolded and flattened representation of the cortical sheet to allow viewing of topographic changes over cortical space. Flat maps are most commonly used in fMRI to illustrate the organization of the visual cortex.

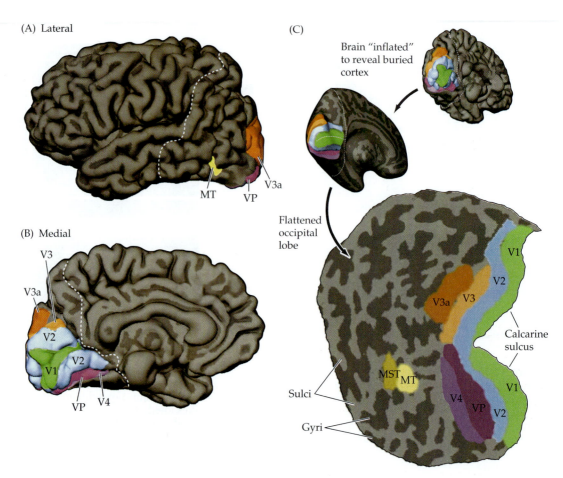

(A) Lateral

(B) Medial

(C)

Brain "inflated" to reveal buried cortex

Flattened occipital lobe

Figure 12.12 Flat map views of the brain surface. Flat map views of the brain can be useful for determining the topographic organization of the cortex. The most common use of flattened views is for retinotopic mapping of the visual cortex. After identifying areas of activation, as shown here on lateral (A) and medial (B) views of the visual cortex, researchers inflate, cut, and flatten the cortical surface (C) to show the spatial distribution of active regions. (After Sereno et al., 1995.)

The General Linear Model

Chapter 8 introduced the idea of representing fMRI data in a linear model. The formula for a linear model is given in Equation 12.3:

$$y = a_0 + a_1 x_1 + a_2 x_2 + \ldots + a_n x_n + e \qquad [12.3]$$

model factors A set of hypothesized changes in BOLD activity associated with the manipulations of the independent variables or with other known sources of variability.

parameter weights For most fMRI analyses, quantities that reflect the relative contribution of the different model factors to the observed data within a given voxel.

The basic idea behind a linear model is that the observed data (y) is equal to a weighted combination of several **model factors** (x_i) plus an additive error term (e). The **parameter weights** (a_i) indicate how much each factor contributes to the overall data. The term a_0 reflects the total contribution of all factors that are held constant throughout the experiment. For fMRI data, this would include the raw T_2^* values recorded in particular voxels in the absence of BOLD activation, as well as any activity that is constant throughout the experiment. In solving the linear model equation, the researcher has only one known quantity, the experimental data. The model factors represent hypothesized components of the data, but may or may not be meaningful. Given the data and a specified set of model factors, the researcher can

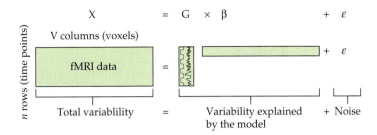

Figure 12.13   Basic principles of the general linear model in fMRI. The general linear model attempts to find the set of experimental parameters (β) for a design matrix (G) that best accounts for the original data (X).

calculate what combination of weights serves to minimize the error term. The minimum error term after solving the linear model is known as the **residual.** When there is only one dependent variable (e.g., predicting income based on age and education), Equation 12.3 is known as a univariate multiple regression model. But the same equation can be extended to include a large number of dependent variables, such as the many time points within an fMRI study, through the **general linear model.**

Figure 12.13 illustrates the use of the general linear model in fMRI. The experimental data are represented as a two-dimensional matrix consisting of n time points by V voxels. Note that the spatial structure of the fMRI data is not used in the general linear model, since the values of the parameter weights and error term are calculated independently for all voxels. The voxels are instead arranged along one dimension for ease of calculation. The **design matrix,** which specifies the linear model to be evaluated, consists of M model factors, each n time points in length (Figure 12.14). Depending on the analysis strategy, the mean value for each voxel may be subtracted during preprocessing or a constant term may be included in the model. The parameter matrix contains M rows and V columns, such that each cell indicates the amplitude of one of the model factors for a given voxel. Finally, the error term is an n-by-V matrix. In some notation systems, the design matrix is denoted as G and the parameter matrix is denoted as β.

After setting up the general linear model for a given experiment, the researcher calculates what combination of weights, when multiplied by the design matrix, gives the smallest error term. To understand this process, consider a simple experiment where the subject squeezes her hand every 20 s while fMRI data are recorded with a TR of 1 s over 60 time points. You hypothesize that active voxels should show three distinct hemodynamic responses, one following each of the three hand squeezes. You then enter this hypothesis as a single column in the design matrix. The general linear model evaluates how much this hypothetical time course contributed to the real data, compared to variability outside of the model. Since fMRI data consist of many time points, the residual error for a given voxel must be combined across all time points into a single value. As discussed earlier, the formula for combining many error values into one summary statistic is known as a **cost function.** In the general linear model, the standard cost function is **least-squares error,** or the sum of all squared residuals. To test the significance of a model factor for a given voxel, the amplitude of its associated parameter is divided by the residual error. Under the null hypothesis, this quantity should follow the F distribution, and so its statistical significance can be evaluated as a function of the available degrees of freedom.

residual The variability in the data that remains unexplained after accounting for the model factors.

general linear model A class of statistical tests that assume that the experimental data are composed of the linear combination of different model factors, along with uncorrelated noise.

design matrix In fMRI implementations of the general linear model, the specification of how the model factors change over time.

cost function A quantity that determines the amount of residual error in a comparison.

least-squares error A commonly used cost function, the sum of the squared residuals.

Model parameters

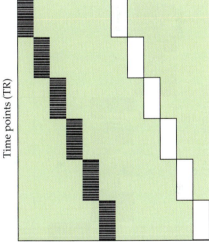

Figure 12.14   A design matrix for the general linear model. The set of model functions that attempts to explain the experimental data using the general linear model is known as the design matrix. In the experiment illustrated here, subjects listened to a series of tones with constant pitch. Presented randomly within the series were rare deviant tones with a higher pitch. The expected fMRI signal over time for each run is shown in the six columns to the left, with white indicating maximum signal and black indicating minimal signal. The six columns to the right reflect constant values included to remove the mean signal change for each run. Note that each run consists of roughly 200 brain images.

TABLE 12.1 Some of the Major Statistical Packages Available for the Analysis of fMRI Data

Package	Availability	Web site
AFNI	Freely available	afni.nimh.nih.gov/afni/
Brain Voyager	Commercial	www.brainvoyager.com
MEDx	Commercial	medx.sensor.com
SPM	Freely available	www.fil.ion.ucl.ac.uk/spm/
Stimulate	Freely available	www.cmrr.umn.edu/stimulate/
VoxBo	Freely available	www.voxbo.org

This example may seem conceptually similar to the correlation analysis described earlier in the chapter. In both cases, the significance is based on how well the experimental data fit a predicted hemodynamic response. This similarity is not coincidental. If only one model factor is used, then the general linear model is identical to the correlation analysis. The *t*-test can also be easily conducted in this framework by using a model factor with only two levels, one for each of the two conditions. The Fourier transform is also equivalent to a general linear model, although expressing it in terms of a design matrix would be very complex, in that it partitions variability within the raw data according to a number of independent frequency components.

The general linear model provides the theoretical framework that underlies most fMRI studies, regardless of their design. All major fMRI statistical packages include routines for its analysis, with the specific implementation dependent on the program (Table 12.1). However, each shares the same set of simple algorithms and assumptions. In short, the general linear model assumes that the raw data can be modeled as the sum of separate factors, each of which may vary independently across voxels, along with additive Gaussian noise that is also independently and identically distributed. In the following sections, we evaluate the implications of these assumptions for constructing and testing models for fMRI data.

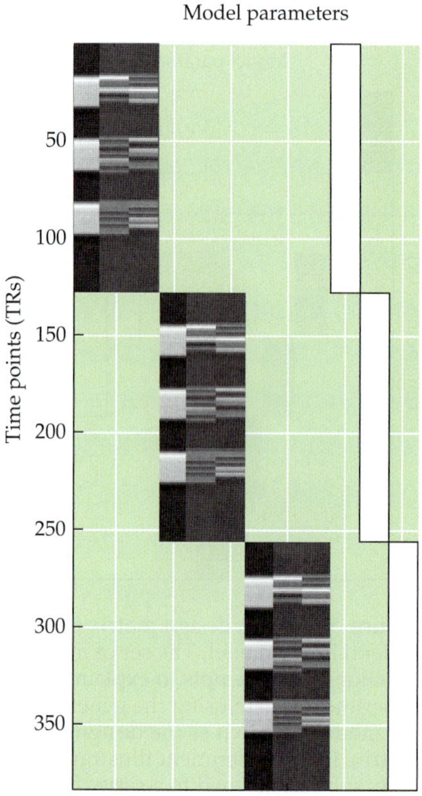

Constructing a Design Matrix

There are four basic components to the general linear model: empirical data, a design matrix, parameter weights, and residual error. Of these, the data are obtained experimentally, the design matrix is constructed by the experimenter based on the study design, and the parameter weights and residual error are calculated during analysis. Thus, the success of a general linear model analysis rests solely upon the validity of the experimenter-created design matrix. The design matrix consists of one or more model factors that represent possible contributors to the fMRI time course. As an example, consider the mixed blocked/event-related designs discussed at the end of Chapter 11. One such design might include task blocks consisting of two trial types, A and B, and nontask blocks where the subject rests. A design matrix describing these data could include one column for the blocked task versus rest factor, along with two more columns representing the individual trial types (Figure 12.15). Each of these columns should represent a prediction about how hemodynamic activity would change should a voxel be associated with that factor. So, the blocked factor would have alternating periods of low and high activity with smooth transitions between them. The event-related factors would have short-duration hemodynamic responses that are time-locked to the different trial types.

Figure 12.15 A design matrix for a mixed design. Here, three design columns are present for each run. The first represents a blocked effect, while the second and third represent event-related effects associated with two different stimulus classes. The three columns at far right reflect constant values included to remove the mean signal change for each run.

In graphical depictions of fMRI design matrices, the predicted value of a factor at each point in time is usually scaled on a dark–light color map. Black indicates that the factor is predicted to have no effect at that time point, while white indicates that it should have its largest effect. Model factors associated with specific hypotheses are known as **experimental factors.** There are two types of experimental factors. **Covariates** are factors that can take any of a continuous range of values, where the value of the factor represents the amount of some known quantity. The most common covariates in fMRI design matrices are predicted hemodynamic responses. Others include response time and physiological changes like the respiratory cycle. **Indicators** are factors that have integral values that indicate a qualitative level. For fMRI, these may include experimental conditions, as in the *t*-test; subject treatment or demographic conditions; accuracy of a trial; and many other factors. Covariates and indicators are mathematically equivalent within the general linear model; the latter have a restricted set of values, while the former can vary freely.

In addition to the expected model factors, the design matrix often includes additional factors associated with known nonexperimental sources of variability. These are known as **nuisance factors.** Suppose that the MR scanner on which this study is conducted often has a linear drift during experimental sessions. An additional factor could be introduced into the design matrix to account for this drift. Or, if the subject's respiration was measured during the session, the design matrix could include a factor for artifacts associated with the repeated breathing. Of course, these factors have nothing to do with the experimental hypotheses, in that the experiment was not designed to test scanner drift or subject respiration. So why are they included in the design matrix?

Nuisance factors serve two related purposes in experimental analyses. First, they can reduce the amount of residual variation included in the error term. If the intensity of a voxel were to drift by a few percentage points through the course of a run, the overall variability in the voxel would be very large, compared to the BOLD effect of interest. But if a linear factor were added to the design matrix, much of that variability would be assigned to that factor rather than to the error term, increasing the significance of the results. Second, assigning known variability to nuisance factors improves the validity of the general linear model. The model assumes that residuals are independent and identically distributed as Gaussian noise, which may not be the case if a regular source of variation is excluded from the design matrix. It is therefore critical to include all anticipated changes in the BOLD signal, whether of interest or not. However, wanton inclusion of extra factors is not recommended. Each additional column in the design matrix reduces the number of degrees of freedom available. In the limiting case, one could reproduce perfectly any set of n time points with a combination of $n - 1$ different model factors. Since the significance of any individual factor is evaluated as a function of the number of available degrees of freedom, it is in the researcher's interest for the number of factors to be as small as possible. In practice, however, the inclusion of a limited number of nuisance factors makes statistical testing more conservative, due to the reduced number of degrees of freedom, but can improve the validity of the general linear model.

In creating a design matrix, the experimenter should be careful to avoid including model factors that are themselves correlated. The inclusion of such **collinear factors** can complicate the interpretation of the results, as variance

experimental factors Model factors that are associated with specific experimental hypotheses.

covariates Experimental factors that can take any of a continuous range of values.

indicators Experimental factors that have integral values to indicate a qualitative level.

nuisance factors Model factors that are associated with known sources of variability that are not related to the experimental hypotheses.

collinear factors Model factors that are highly correlated with one another. The inclusion of collinear factors reduces the validity of general linear model analyses.

attributable to one such factor may become confused with variance associated with another.

Modeling BOLD Signal Changes

While the general linear model can be an extremely powerful tool for analysis of fMRI data, its validity rests on a series of assumptions. The first, and most important, of these is that the design matrix should contain factors that accurately reflect BOLD changes due to neuronal activity of interest. Consider a simple experiment where subjects see a picture of an object and then must retrieve a specific, elaborated memory of a past event associated with that object. The pictures are presented infrequently, with interstimulus intervals ranging between 20 and 30 seconds. To investigate what voxels are active when subjects remember past events, the researcher sets up a column of the design matrix with standard hemodynamic responses at the onset of each picture. But after completing the general linear model analysis, the researcher is surprised that visual cortical areas are active but memory-related areas are not. What could cause such a result? Imagine that you are the subject in this experiment, and you have been instructed to remember a detailed episode from your past based upon the picture on the screen. The first picture is a balloon. Now, recall a particular event in your life. If you are like most people, it took you between 5 and 15 seconds (or even longer, depending on the complexity of the memory) to recall and re-experience a particular event. A brain region associated with the recollection process would be unlikely to have transient BOLD activity that peaked at 5 seconds; instead, its activity would be extended in time for perhaps tens of seconds. In order to detect memory-related activity, therefore, the design matrix would have to model extended BOLD changes, not standard short-duration hemodynamic responses.

This example illustrates the importance of thinking about the columns of the design matrix as predictions of the BOLD time course based upon hypothesized neuronal activity. The basic assumption of the design matrix is that the BOLD response can be estimated by convolving a hemodynamic response with the times of stimulus presentation. While this is often appropriate, the design matrix is intended to test hypotheses about hemodynamic activity, not about stimuli. Before creating your design matrix for an experiment, you should think carefully about the separate types of brain processes that are evoked in your experiment, along with their timing and duration. In tasks where several processes are likely to be evoked sequentially, researchers often identify different phases of the task. These phases may be explicit, as when subjects view an attentional cue, which must be remembered over a delay interval, followed by a target that requires a response. The resulting design matrix could have separate columns corresponding to those three phases. Or they may be implicit, established by the experimenter based on an expectation of what the subjects will do on the task. If the task was to remember a complex display of shapes presented for 10 s, the researcher might distinguish between two phases: a beginning encoding phase (2 s), where the subjects study the display; and a rehearsal phase (8 s), during which time the subjects commit particular aspects of the display to memory. It is worth emphasizing that no fMRI statistical analysis can be valid when the statistical test, here determined by the predictions of BOLD activity in the design matrix, does not reflect the actual changes in the brain associated with the experimental hypotheses.

Most analyses model BOLD activity based upon a standard hemodynamic response. However, more-complex design matrices can be created to potentially improve the generalizability of the statistical model. To model small differences in hemodynamic onset or in the shape of the hemodynamic response, the design model can include additional factors known as time and dispersion derivatives. The hemodynamic response itself can be replaced with a small number of basis functions, such as low-frequency sine and cosine waveforms or gamma functions. Since a wide range of hemodynamic responses can be expressed using a combination of multiple basis functions, this approach can detect voxels whose activity does not follow the standard response, such as those with a wider response or with a later peak. However, the outcomes of such tests are much more complex and challenging to interpret.

Statistical models can ameliorate the effects of intersubject variability in the BOLD response (see Box 9.1) by using subject-specific hemodynamic response functions. Aguirre and colleagues demonstrated this in 1998 by evaluating the mean correlation across subjects between the measured data and several models of the hemodynamic response, including a gamma function, a Poisson function, and the first eigenvector of part of their data set. Note that gamma and Poisson functions describe mathematical shapes that roughly match that of the hemodynamic response, and an eigenvector is a component of the data that explains some proportion of its variability. They found that the gamma function and eigenvector were generally good models for the observed data, with mean correlations of about 0.83, while the Poisson function had a mediocre mean correlation of 0.49. As the authors noted, however, even a correlation of 0.83 explains less than 70% of the variance in the data, so there is considerable room for improvement. They then tested the effects of using subject-specific functions by evaluating data from four of their subjects who had each participated in five runs within a single session. They used the first run to generate an estimated hemodynamic response for that subject, then measured the correlation between that response and the responses measured on subsequent runs. The mean correlation rose to more than 0.96, which accounts for about 92% of the variance in the data. By using subject-specific hemodynamic responses, rather than a generic response function, the authors achieved a substantial increase in experimental power.

Finally, a frequent source of confusion when thinking about the use of the general linear model in fMRI is the idea of linearity itself. Remember from Chapter 8 that the BOLD response does not obey the assumptions of linearity at short interstimulus intervals. So, how can it be analyzed using the general linear model? This confusion rests upon two distinct ideas about linearity. The hemodynamic response is nonlinear with respect to stimulus presentation, because the combined response to two stimuli in succession is less than the sum of the responses to the two stimuli independently. But, stimulus presentation is not itself important in the general linear model. What is important is that the overall BOLD time course, whatever its form with respect to the stimuli, adds linearly with other sources of variability in the data. So, refractory effects in the BOLD response can be incorporated directly into the experimental design matrix without compromising the validity of the model. One way to do this is to adjust the columns of the design matrix directly by including interaction effects. Another method identified by Friston and colleagues in 1998 is to use Volterra kernels, which allow modeling of the influence of a stimulus upon subsequent stimuli, to specify a second column in the design matrix. Without such corrections, the design matrix may not accurately capture the desired BOLD time course.

homoscedastic Having the property that the distributions of noise are similar for all experimental conditions.

heteroscedastic Having the property that the distributions of noise are different across experimental conditions.

multiple comparison problem The increase in the number of false-positive results (i.e., Type I errors) with increasing number of statistical tests. It is of particular consequence for voxelwise fMRI analyses, which may have many thousands of statistical tests.

Additional Assumptions

Provided that the design matrix is appropriate for testing the experimental hypotheses, several other conditions must be met for the general linear model to be appropriate. In this section, we document these assumptions, along with their implications for fMRI studies. We emphasize that, although the general linear model framework has proven to be an effective tool for answering many questions about the brain, its limitations have spurred many researchers to investigate alternative approaches to fMRI data analysis (refer to Box 12.1).

> ### Thought Question
>
> One criticism of general linear model approaches is that the models themselves are not tested. That is, just because a model explains a significant proportion of the variability in the data, it is not necessarily the best model. What would happen, for example, if the design matrix in Figure 12.15 omitted the event-related columns? What sorts of erroneous conclusions could be drawn?

One assumption that has been the source of considerable debate is the use of the same design matrix throughout the brain. Although each voxel will have a different set of parameter weights, the model used to calculate those weights is identical. But we know that the properties of the hemodynamic response, especially its latency, may differ across brain regions. A model factor that is correct for one region may thus be incorrect for another, reducing the amount of variation explained by the model and increasing the residual error. The use of multiple basis functions provides some flexibility, compared to using a single canonical hemodynamic response, but again complicates interpretation of the results. One way of overcoming the problem of regional variability is to combine a general linear model approach with region-of-interest analyses, as discussed later in this chapter.

The residual variation is assumed to be distributed as Gaussian noise with similar properties at all *time points*. In other words, the amount of noise in a voxel does not depend on the task condition. That is, the data should be **homoscedastic**. If there is more noise in one condition than another, the data are **heteroscedastic**. Although the general linear model assumes the former, this assumption may not always be valid. Noise levels are higher during BOLD activity than during rest (see the work by Huettel and colleagues discussed in Chapter 9), although whether such changes are due to hemodynamic variability or to variability in neuronal processing remains unknown. This does not imply that all *voxels* must have similar noise properties. A voxel that contains a major blood vessel or that is near the edge of the brain may have much higher noise than most others in the brain. However, within that voxel, the residuals should be equally variable at all time points.

Another assumption is that that all voxels are analyzed independently, even though adjacent voxels tend to have very similar properties. In fact, introducing correlation between adjacent voxels through spatial smoothing is a common step during preprocessing. While the general linear model framework cannot account for spatial correlation, the significance values it generates can be adjusted at later stages of analyses, as discussed later in this chapter. Likewise, the model assumes that each time point is independent of all others, in that the residuals should be similarly distributed throughout. Scanner drift, thermal variation, head motion, and many other factors can cause the overall MR signal to change dramatically across time points, influencing the amplitude of the residual error. It is critical, therefore, to attempt to remove such unwanted variability before it reaches the error term, either during preprocessing or by including appropriate nuisance factors.

In summary, the general linear model has become the dominant statistical framework for fMRI analyses. The *t*-test, correlation test, and power spectrum analysis all represent special cases of this framework, each incorporating simplifying assumptions. The power of the general linear model comes from its flexibility. By incorporating appropriate model factors into the design matrix, a researcher may test nearly any experimental hypothesis. However, the choice of design matrix is critical for the validity of the analysis. If an inappropriate model is specified, either through the inclusion of incorrect model factors or the exclusion of existing nuisance factors, then the analysis may give incorrect or null results.

Corrections for Multiple Comparisons

A typical fMRI data set contains about 20,000 voxels within the brain and several times that number outside of the brain. Imagine, for the moment, that of those many voxels, you are only interested in one, a single voxel within the gray matter adjacent to the right calcarine sulcus. Your experiment is a simple event-related visual task, and you calculate a *t*-statistic of 2.5 based on the voxel's correlation with a predicted BOLD response. The chance that such an extreme *t*-statistic could occur under the null hypothesis, based upon the 20 degrees of freedom in the test, was only about 1 in 50 ($P = 0.02$), less than your alpha value of 0.05. Given such a low probability, you confidently reject the null hypothesis for that voxel. Flush with the excitement of a significant result, you decide to analyze the remaining voxels. You run all of the voxels through the correlation test, calculate a *t*-value for each, and compare those *t*-values to your alpha value. Now, about a thousand voxels in the brain are active, distributed in seemingly random fashion (Figure 12.16A–C). Even worse, a few thousand voxels outside the brain appear to be active! You stare at the computer screen in disbelief. Why are so many voxels active?

This example illustrates one of the central problems of fMRI data analysis, that of **multiple comparisons.** Stated succinctly, the greater the number of statistical tests conducted, the greater the chance of a false-positive result. To illustrate this point, we created a random data set ($64 \times 64 \times 20$ voxels) where the intensity of each voxel at each time point was distributed as Gaussian noise. We then conducted a *t*-test on these data, comparing one set of 20 time points (Condition 1) to another set of 20 time points (Condition 2). Both conditions consisted of random data, so any difference between them

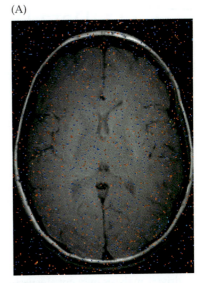

(A)

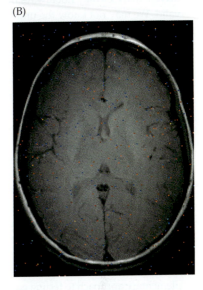

(B)

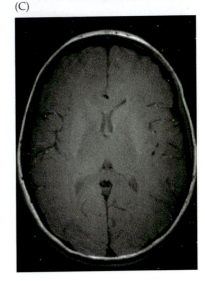

(C)

Figure 12.16 The problem of multiple comparisons. A simple analysis of random data at three different significance levels ($P = 0.05$, 0.01, and 0.001) was conducted. Note that since the data were random, any activation was due merely to chance. In this slice, which contains roughly 64,000 voxels, about 1600 had significant positive activation at a threshold of 0.05 (A), about 360 had positive activation at a threshold of 0.01 (B), and 32 still had significant activity at a threshold of 0.001 (C).

BOX 12.1 Data-Driven Analyses

A potential problem with the standard analysis methods described in the rest of this chapter is that they require an accurate estimate of the fMRI signal that should result from the performance of the task. When we test a voxel's time course to see if it is active, we are really testing how well that time course matches the idealized waveform that an active voxel should exhibit. Such approaches are known as **hypothesis-driven analyses,** and they are common for fMRI studies. However, the assumptions of hypothesis-driven analyses may not always be valid. We may not know the underlying brain activation, because the subject may not have been doing the task correctly or may have been daydreaming and not doing it at all. We may not know the appropriate hemodynamic response for that subject or for that part of the brain. Furthermore, if our fMRI experiment is very complex, involving watching a movie or using a driving simulator, it may be impossible to be able to specify a priori the waveform of an activated voxel. In summary, even if we can create a model of the expected neuronal activity, we may have no way to ensure that our model is correct.

Data-driven analyses provide a complementary approach to testing each voxel's time course against a hypothesis. When conducting a data-driven analysis, the researcher explores the structure of the data in the hope that task-related activations will emerge. For this reason, data-driven techniques are also known as exploratory analyses. Two popular data-driven techniques are **independent components analysis (ICA)** and **clustering.** In an ICA fMRI analysis, it is assumed that the data can be modeled by identifying sets of voxels whose activity both varies together over time and is maximally different from the activity in other sets (see McKeown and colleagues,

1998). The time courses of activity associated with each set are called components. The voxels contributing to each component need not be contiguous; for example, a component associated with motor processing may include distinct foci of activity in many motor regions. Also, each voxel may participate in more than one component. The goal of ICA is to partition the original data into a set of spatial patterns, so that when the contribution from each pattern is summed together, they accurately estimate the data (Figure 12.17). Note that an ICA analysis can be conducted completely blind with respect to the experimental task or hypotheses.

In a clustering analysis, researchers create mathematical estimates of the similarity between the time courses of different voxels so that the voxels can be segregated into distinct clusters. A very

hypothesis-driven analyses The evaluation of activity based on testing of the validity of the null hypothesis.

data-driven analyses Exploratory techniques that examine the intrinsic structure of the data.

independent components analysis (ICA) An important class of data-driven analysis that identifies spatially stationary sets of voxels whose activity varies together over time and is maximally distinguishable from that of other sets.

clustering A data-driven technique that looks for clusters of voxels with similar time courses.

exciting form of clustering analysis was reported by Cordes and colleagues, who investigated patterns of activity in resting-state data (see also work by Biswal

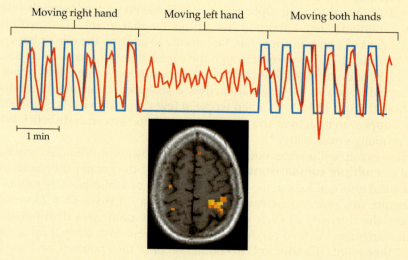

Figure 12.17 Independent components analysis (ICA) of motor cortex. This subject participated in a motor movement task with three phases: rotating the right hand at the wrist, rotating the left hand at the wrist, and rotating both hands simultaneously. The times of hand movement are shown in blue, and the identified ICA component is shown in red. The voxels corresponding to that component are shown in the figure below. Note that these voxels were identified only by examination of the data themselves, not by hypothesis testing. (Data courtesy of Dr. Martin McKeown, University of British Columbia.)

BOX 12.1 *(continued)*

and colleagues discussed in detail in Chapter 13). That is, they looked for correspondences across voxels in data collected while the subject was not performing any experimental task. They determined clusters of contiguous voxels whose activity was highly correlated at low frequencies (<0.1 Hz). They found clear regions of activity in the primary motor and sensory cortices, the frontal lobes, the thalamus, and Broca's area. These areas show a high degree of coactivation, which has been interpreted by many to suggest functional interconnectivity.

Data-driven methods are sometimes referred to as model-free analyses, since they do not depend on estimates of the hemodynamic response. This reference is erroneous, though, because all data-driven methods rely on at least some underlying assumptions, although those assumptions tend to be less stringent than those of the general linear model. A primary challenge lies in deciding how many components or clusters to isolate from a given data set. As more components are included, more of the variance in the original data is explained, but the

components become more difficult to interpret. Most data-driven methods also assume that all voxels have similar statistical properties, although it can be easily shown that this assumption is false (see Chapter 9). Voxels at the edges of the brain tend to have markedly different statistical properties than voxels completely in gray matter, which in turn are different from voxels in white matter. Small groups of voxels whose time course of activity differs from the rest of the voxels may therefore skew the results of any method attempting to fit the overall structure of the data. In some applications, the voxels are first segmented into broad categories like "gray matter" and "white matter" so that a data-driven method can be applied only to voxels that have similar statistical properties. Data-driven methods may also accentuate intersubject variability. While it is possible to isolate ICA time courses that are similar across subjects, the validity of such intersubject comparison is unclear.

Data-driven analyses have been shown to give comparable results to traditional hypothesis-based approaches when the two are compared directly,

and in some cases (e.g., when subjects do not perform the task consistently), they have proved superior at identifying accurate maps of activity. For this reason, methods that attempt to combine the strengths of hypothesis- and data-driven approaches may prove powerful. For instance, McKeown and colleagues have shown that ICA components can be used to determine reasonable task-related regressors in a general linear model framework and to estimate trial-to-trial variability to determine the effects of signal averaging. Conversely, incorporating knowledge about the spatial properties of true fMRI activation will improve future data-driven analyses. We know that some sources of noise in fMRI data, such as artifacts from large blood vessels, have different spatial properties compared to areas of meaningful activity. Augmenting current data-driven methods with techniques that look at both the spatial and temporal aspects of the fMRI signal, as determined by hypothesis-driven analyses, may provide a powerful means to more accurately determine brain activity from fMRI data.

was due solely to chance. At an alpha value of 0.05, there were about 4000 active voxels; at an alpha of 0.01, there were about 800 active voxels; and at an alpha of 0.001, there were still 80 active voxels. All of these voxels are false positives, since there was no signal present in the original data. In any data set with random noise, the number of false-positive results for n statistical tests is simply $n \times \alpha$. The probability of having no false-positive results is given by Equation 12.4:

$$P \text{ (no Type I error)} = (1 - \alpha)^n \qquad [12.4]$$

Note that for the sorts of alpha values typically used in social science experiments (e.g., 0.05, 0.01), this probability approaches zero for even small fMRI data sets. If you analyzed only a single slice of 4096 voxels at $\alpha < 0.01$, the odds of having no false positives is 1.3×10^{-18}, or one quintillion to one. Stated differently, you are certain to make at least one Type I error of labeling a voxel as active when it is not.

The standard strategy for overcoming the problem of multiple comparisons is reducing the alpha value, so that voxels are less likely to pass the significance threshold due to chance. A common and stringent method for doing so

(A)   (B)   (C)

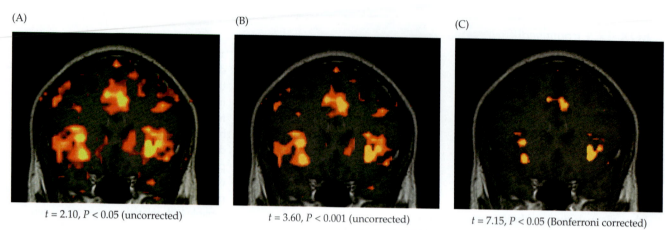

$t = 2.10, P < 0.05$ (uncorrected) $t = 3.60, P < 0.001$ (uncorrected) $t = 7.15, P < 0.05$ (Bonferroni corrected)

Figure 12.18 Effects of Bonferroni correction on fMRI data. Shown are data from a single subject at three different levels of significance. At the lowest P value of 0.05, there is substantial activity, including some clear regions of activity and scattered noise. At an intermediate P value of 0.001, the activity is much reduced. After Bonferroni correction to an adjusted P value of 0.05 (unadjusted $P = 0.000001$), the most active regions are still present, but many of the other potentially meaningful regions of activity are lost.

Bonferroni correction A stringent correction for multiple comparisons in which the alpha value is decreased proportionally to the number of independent statistical tests.

is **Bonferroni correction,** in which the alpha value is decreased proportionally to the number of independent statistical tests, as seen in Equation 12.5:

$$\alpha_{bon} = \alpha / n \qquad [12.5]$$

If 4096 voxels are being tested, applying Bonferroni correction reduces the alpha value from 0.01 to 0.000002. At this new, much stricter level, there is only a 0.01 probability that *any* voxel will pass the statistical threshold solely due to chance. In principle, Bonferroni correction effectively controls for Type I error, increasing the researcher's confidence that positive statistical tests correspond to meaningful activation. Yet in practice it has severe disadvantages. While it decreases Type I error, it also increases the probability of Type II error, or failing to detect voxels with real activity (Figure 12.18). For many research questions, especially those that are novel or exploratory or have clinical relevance, an increased rate of Type II error may be unacceptable. Imagine that you have conducted an fMRI study to identify cortex necessary for language processing in a patient about to undergo neurosurgery (refer to Box 12.2). A very conservative threshold might identify some active voxels, but it risks missing other truly active voxels with lower significance values. In such a situation, Type II errors could lead to the resection of functional tissue and thus would have a real consequence for the patient's outcome.

Some researchers developed more-sensitive techniques that strike a balance between Type I and Type II error. In 2002, Genovese and colleagues proposed a method for correcting alpha to control the false discovery rate, or the proportion of statistically active voxels that results from chance variation. The resulting correction is less stringent than Bonferroni, while allowing interpretation of the likelihood that an active voxel is meaningful.

Random Field Theory

Bonferroni correction adjusts the alpha value based on the number of *independent* statistical tests. Usually, this is taken to be the number of voxels; if there are 20,000 voxels, there are 20,000 tests. But it is not the case that voxels are completely independent. Time courses in adjacent voxels tend to be highly correlated, for many reasons. Many sources of noise, notably head motion, affect voxels within a brain region similarly. BOLD activity itself often spans large regions, especially if large-vessel effects are present in the data. And explicit spatial smoothing during preprocessing ensures that no voxel is independent of its neighbors. Given these many sources of inter-voxel dependence in fMRI data, Bonferroni correction greatly overestimates the number of independent statistical tests, resulting in a corrected alpha value that is much too conservative. Techniques have been proposed that modify the denominator in Equation 12.5 based upon the degree of correlation between activated voxels, effectively reducing the stringency of the Bonferroni correction factor.

To determine a better correction factor, Worsley and colleagues applied the theory of **Gaussian random fields** to fMRI data. Random field theory estimates the number of independent statistical tests based upon the spatial correlation, or **smoothness,** of the experimental data (see Figure 10.17). Although smoothness depends heavily on the properties of the Gaussian filter used in preprocessing, intrinsic correlations also matter, and thus it is typically calculated by the statistical program used for analysis. Based on the smoothness, which is expressed in voxels, the number of independent tests in a data set can be calculated. If a data set consisting of $x \times y \times z$ voxels had smoothness with full-width-half-maximum of V voxels, the number of independent comparisons (R) would be given by:

$$R = (x \times y \times z)/V^3 \qquad [12.6]$$

The independent comparisons are sometimes known as **resolution elements** or **resels.** With even small to moderate amounts of smoothness in the data, the number of resels will be much less than the original number of voxels. At a smoothness of 3 voxels, there would be 1/27 as many resels as voxels. From the number of resels (and secondarily from the shape of the brain volume), one can estimate how many clusters of activity should be found by chance at a given statistical threshold. This number is known as the **Euler characteristic** of the data. Note that for smooth data, the effect of threshold upon the Euler characteristic is not monotonic. At very low statistical thresholds, those only slightly above chance, there will be very few clusters. However, these clusters will be very large and interconnected since much of the brain will be labeled as active. At medium thresholds (i.e., at thresholds of about $P \sim 0.15$ for typical studies), there will be a very large number of smaller clusters merely by chance. But as the threshold increases, only very few small clusters should be present by chance. To calculate a new significance threshold, one determines the threshold whose Euler characteristic corresponds to the desired alpha value (e.g, 0.05). That is, given the number of resels in the data, at what threshold will there only be a 0.05 probability of seeing a cluster of activation simply by chance? For smoothed data, this threshold will always be much less than that of the Bonferroni correction, resulting in a less conservative test of significance.

Cluster-Size Thresholding

Another approach for correction of multiple comparisons evaluates the size of any active clusters, not just their number. If only a single isolated voxel is active, then that voxel's activity may result from mere chance. It is much less likely, however, that a group of contiguous voxels will all be active by

Gaussian random fields A branch of mathematics that deals with the properties of smooth, spatially extended data. Application of random field theory to fMRI data can help ameliorate the multiple comparisons problem.

smoothness The degree to which the time courses of nearby voxels are temporally correlated.

resolution elements (or resels) The independent statistical tests within an fMRI volume.

Euler characteristic The number of clusters of significant activity due to chance that can be expected based upon the number of resels and the smoothness of the data.

cluster-size thresholding The adoption of a minimum size, in voxels, for a cluster of active voxels to be labeled as significant.

chance. This can be seen by careful examination of the data from Figure 10.17. While about 200 voxels in this figure are active due to chance, very few clusters of two or more adjacent voxels are present. Using **cluster-size thresholding,** first introduced in separate 1995 studies by Xiong and colleagues and Forman and colleagues, a researcher adopts a relatively liberal alpha value (e.g., $P < 0.01$) for voxelwise comparisons, and then increases the conservatism of the test by only counting clusters as significant if they are as large as some threshold. The size of cluster to use in a given experiment depends upon the desired alpha value and the number of voxels in the data set. Typical cluster-size thresholds for fMRI data are around three to six voxels. Tables of specific thresholds were reported in the Xiong and Forman studies, and software analysis packages often suggest appropriate thresholds for a given data set.

Cluster-size thresholding works because as cluster size C increases, the number of such clusters (n_C) increases much more slowly than the probability that a given cluster is active. In a single slice of 4096 voxels (64×64), there are approximately 16,000 distinct clusters of two contiguous voxels and approximately 55,000 clusters of three contiguous voxels. (In three-dimensional data, several times as many clusters are present at each size.) If the alpha value for the cluster (α_C) is set to 0.001, the expected number of false-positive voxels is 4096×0.001, or about 4. For the same alpha value, the joint probability of two given voxels being active is just 0.001×0.001, which comes out to one in one million. Thus, the expected number of false-positive clusters of two contiguous voxels is $16,000 \times 0.000001$, or 0.016. Finally, the joint probability of any three voxels being active is $0.001 \times 0.001 \times 0.001$, which comes out to one in one billion. So, the expected number of false-positive clusters of three contiguous voxels is about $55,000 \times 0.000000001$, resulting in an expectation of 0.000055 false-positive clusters.

In summary, the likelihood of a false-positive result decreases with increasing cluster size. The effects of cluster-size thresholding upon the false-positive rate are indicated in Equation 12.7 (compare to Equation 12.4):

$$P \text{ (no Type I error, cluster)} = (1 - \alpha_C)^{n_C} \qquad [12.7]$$

By reducing the alpha value used in an experiment, cluster-size thresholding will often reduce the number of Type II errors, or misses of true activity. However, it makes several assumptions that, if violated, introduce potentially severe disadvantages. First, by definition, thresholding assumes that all areas of significant activity extend over a large number of voxels. This precludes small but meaningful activations. If your cluster-size threshold is six voxels, then detecting an active brain region of only four voxels in size becomes extremely unlikely. Second, it assumes that activation foci are generally convex, or spherical, when calculating probabilities. If an active region has a very nonspherical shape, as when running linearly along the edge of a gyrus, then cluster size analyses may not be appropriate. Third, the above logic assumes that activity in adjacent voxels is uncorrelated, so that the probability of n voxels all being active is given by α^n. This assumption is incorrect for fMRI data, as noted earlier. Cluster-size calculations can be adjusted based upon the intrinsic correlation of fMRI data, either through estimates of their smoothness or by measuring the number of active clusters in a null fMRI data set (i.e., one without an experimental task). For example, if spatial smoothing and random field theory are applied, such adjustments should be made.

region-of-interest (ROI) analysis Evaluating statistical tests on a predetermined collection of voxels, often chosen to reflect a priori anatomical distinctions within the brain.

Region-of-Interest Analyses

Voxelwise analyses look for significant effects in many different voxels, often encompassing the entire brain. This approach is preferred for a wide range of research hypotheses, especially those related to a particular cognitive process. Yet some hypotheses require a more targeted analysis approach. If you are interested in a particular brain region, you may form your hypothesis about that region, rather than the entire brain, e.g., "Is the caudate nucleus active during recall of a word from memory?" In this example, the caudate nucleus becomes an anatomical region of interest, whose identity is defined based upon anatomical criteria (Figure 12.19A and B). In a deep sense, the basic question addressed by a voxelwise analysis, "What brain regions evince a particular pattern of fMRI activity?" is the inverse of the question posed by a **region-of-interest (ROI) analysis,** namely "What pattern of activity occurs in a particular brain region?"

For most studies, researchers establish the ROIs based upon a priori expectations about the likely involvement of different brain areas in a task. A researcher interested in studying motor function might draw an ROI that encompasses the anatomical extent of the precentral gyrus, which contains the primary motor cortex. That ROI is considered to be a homogenous and indivisible unit, at least for the purposes of the ROI analysis. Usually, ROIs

(A)

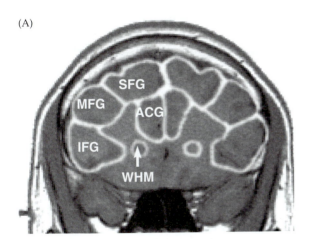

(B)

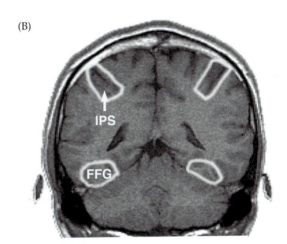

Figure 12.19 Region-of-interest analysis. Region-of-interest (ROI) analyses divide the brain into sections based upon anatomical or functional criteria. (A) The inferior (IFG), middle (MFG), and superior frontal gyri (SFG), and the anterior cingulate gyrus (ACG), as well as a white-matter control region (WHM). (B) The intraparietal sulcus (IPS) and the fusiform gyrus (FFG). These ROIs were drawn based upon anatomical criteria. (From Jha and McCarthy, 2000.)

anatomical ROI Region of interest that is chosen based on anatomical criteria.

are drawn on structural T_1 or T_2 images collected at the beginning of a scanner session. The structural images are used for two reasons: they typically have higher resolution, often four times that of the functional images in each in-plane dimension; and they have much greater tissue contrast. They are then coregistered to the functional data. In most ROI approaches, the researcher draws the edges of a particular brain area, such as the sulci that demarcate a gyrus of interest, and then selects all circumscribed voxels. If **anatomical ROIs** are chosen beforehand and are drawn without consultation with functional activity maps, then they can provide an unbiased estimate of activity within a given brain area.

ROI analyses have several advantages over voxelwise methods. First, because there are always many fewer ROIs than voxels, the total number of statistical comparisons is greatly reduced, minimizing the need for correction for multiple comparisons. For example, in a study of motor cortex, a researcher might draw two ROIs to encompass the primary motor cortex in each hemisphere. This number pales in comparison to the tens of thousands of voxels within the brain. Second, each ROI combines data from many voxels, so there will be a corresponding increase in signal-to-noise to the extent that the ROI is functionally homogenous. This spatial signal averaging complements temporal signal averaging common to both types of analysis. Another advantage is that ROI approaches allow identification of brain topography, as reflected in changes in activity level across slices. Comparisons across ROIs, whether in different regions in the same slice or in the same region across slices, can be used to create simple and easily understood parametric activity maps. Finally, ROI approaches ameliorate many of the problems of comparing data across subjects. Because brain regions are drawn on a subject-specific basis, they can be compared across subjects, thus eliminating inaccuracies introduced by normalization of an individual's anatomy to a reference brain.

Both practical and theoretical problems constrain the universal use of ROI approaches. Simply put, drawing ROIs can be extremely challenging. There are some automated programs that attempt to partition the brain into anatomical regions based on segmentation algorithms and templates of typical brain structure. Though much progress has been made, variation among subjects in the size, shape, and local organization of the brain has impeded the development of any program that is both universally valid and fully automated. Most ROI creation, therefore, uses a nonautomated, highly labor-intensive approach. Using specialized computer tools, researchers draw ROIs by hand directly on the structural images, referring to brain atlases as guides for the anatomy. The subjective nature of ROI drawing requires attention to correspondence between different drawers; statistical evaluation of their agreement is necessary. Of great interest are ROI creation programs that combine the best features of automated and by-hand approaches. These programs require the user to identify anatomical landmarks, such as some major sulci, and based upon those landmarks, the programs partition the brain into ROIs. This combination provides a good compromise between accuracy and speed of creation.

While ROI analyses provide important information about the functional properties of particular brain regions, they introduce a new problem: the potential mismatching of anatomical and functional regions of the brain. The idea that anatomically distinct regions of the brain are likely to have different functional properties is not new. An early and influential mapping of the brain was created by the German physician and neurobiologist Korbinian

Brodmann, who parsed the human cerebral cortex into nearly 50 anatomically distinct regions, known as **Brodmann areas** (see Figure 6.22). It is important to note that Brodmann's areas were defined by their **cytoarchitecture**—differences in the size, type, and distribution of neurons within a brain region—and do not necessarily correspond to specific gyri or sulci. Functional MRI, at least at the spatial resolution typical of human studies, provides no information about cytoarchitectonic features of the brain; thus, Brodmann areas cannot be directly determined for a particular MRI subject.

Even with perfect mapping of anatomy, however, there would remain the problem of linking anatomical regions to functional divisions within the brain. Visual processing, for example, relies on defined occipitotemporal and occipitoparietal pathways that cross many anatomical regions. No one region could account for a complex function like vision. This problem can be partially overcome by drawing several ROIs that encompass different anatomical components of a functional network. Conversely, a single anatomical region may contain multiple functional regions. If only a small subdivision of the anatomical ROI is activated by your task, then your functional SNR may be reduced by the inclusion of many inactive voxels. In this case, it may be beneficial to subdivide the anatomical ROI. One approach we have used is to slice the ROI along its long axis and plot the spatial distribution of activity. Such an approach, however, greatly increases the number of ROIs and once again raises the statistical issue of multiple comparisons.

Due to the variability in function within any anatomical region, ROI approaches to fMRI should therefore be combined with voxelwise approaches whenever possible. One potential combined approach is to use the anatomical ROI as a grouping factor. An investigator can then count and compare the number of activated voxels identified in a voxelwise analysis that occur within the ROI for each experimental condition. The investigator can also remove the active voxels from the ROI and then examine the average time course of BOLD intensity in the remaining voxels. This approach can be used to search for voxels that may have a different temporal pattern of activation than that modeled in the general linear model.

We have thus far discussed regions of interest drawn on the basis of an individual's anatomy. Another powerful approach is to create **functional ROIs,** which include only voxels that were activated by a particular stimulus. For example, in her 1997 studies of face processing in the fusiform gyrus, Kanwisher and her colleagues first identified voxels differentially activated by faces compared to other complex visual stimuli in a screening task. These face-activated voxels then defined a functional "face area" ROI that the researchers used to evaluate the effects of other experimental manipulations on face processing.

Intersubject Analyses

So far, we have focused on the issue of identifying areas of activity within a single subject's data. Yet nearly all fMRI experiments collect data from multiple subjects, and most have samples of 10 or more subjects. How then can one combine data from multiple subjects to better test experimental hypotheses? Combining data across subjects presents several challenges. It is difficult to match anatomical locations across subjects, given the wide variability in shape and size of the adult human brain. Most experiments overcome this challenge by normalizing all subjects' data to a common stereotaxic space during preprocessing, as described in Chapter 10. In conjunction with spatial

Brodmann areas Divisions of the brain based on the influential cytoarchitectonic criteria of Korbinian Brodmann.

cytoarchitecture The organization of the brain on the basis of cell structure.

functional ROI Region of interest that is chosen based on functional criteria, such as the output of a voxelwise analysis.

fixed-effects analysis Intersubject analysis that assumes that the effect of the experimental manipulation is fixed across subjects, with differences between subjects caused by random noise.

random-effects analysis Intersubject analysis that treats the effect of the experimental manipulation as variable across subjects, so that it could have a different effect upon different subjects.

smoothing, normalization greatly reduces anatomical differences across subjects, at a cost of functional resolution. Less common, but very useful, are ROI analyses for identifying particular brain regions based on each subject's anatomy, as described in the preceding section. Even if one is confident that the same brain region is identified in all subjects, whether by normalization or ROI, a theoretical problem remains: combining data from that region into a single statistical test.

There are two common statistical approaches for fMRI studies. For simplicity of exposition, we will consider how each approach affects the analysis of a single experiment with eight subjects who participated in two blocks with 10 data points in each. However, the basic concepts discussed here apply to any number of subjects, to any number of data points in any design, and to any statistical test. The first, and most obvious, analysis approach involves combining all data points from all subjects into a single analysis. The 80 data points in the task condition and the 80 data points in the control condition could be compared using a t-test with 158 degrees of freedom. A variant of this approach would be to average the time courses across subjects, resulting in a single time course. The result of this average could then be evaluated for significance using a t-test with 18 degrees of freedom. The latter variant has fewer degrees of freedom, but the data within each group would be more consistent due to intersubject averaging. These approaches are known as **fixed-effects analyses** (Figure 12.20A), because they assume that the experimental effect is fixed, or constant across subjects, save for the influence of random noise. Applied to fMRI data, fixed-effects models assume that the experimental manipulation has the same effect upon BOLD signal in every subject.

Though popular, fixed-effects analyses have an important disadvantage: they restrict statistical inferences to the particular sample of subjects collected in the study. Suppose that in two of your subjects you measure a very large effect, while in the other six there is no effect at all. After averaging across the subjects, you compare your conditions by t-test and find that they differ significantly. You immediately recognize that this significant result seems inconsistent with the data, given that there was no effect in 75% of your subjects. This contradiction results from the sensitivity of fixed-effects models to extreme results from individual subjects. Under the assumption that the experimental manipulation affects all subjects similarly, the best estimate for its true effect is the mean value across subjects.

In order to make inferences about the population from which subjects are drawn, one must incorporate into the experimental analyses information about the distribution of the effect across subjects. Each subject can be considered as one of many possible subjects who could have participated in the experiment. The experimental manipulation could have a different effect on each of these potential subjects; that is, some could have a large BOLD response, while others could have a small BOLD response. For our research hypothesis to be applicable to the larger population, a two-stage **random-effects analysis** must be conducted. In the first stage, summary statistics are calculated in the comparison of interest for each subject independently. If a voxelwise approach is used, then statistical maps are created for every subject. In the second stage, the distribution of the individual subjects' statistics is itself tested for significance. This can be done using a t-test that evaluates whether the individual subjects' summary statistics are drawn from a distribution with a mean of zero. If this second-stage statistical test is significant at the established alpha value, then it can be concluded that the experimental manipulation would have an effect on the population from which the subjects were drawn (Figure 12.20B). Note that the

(A)

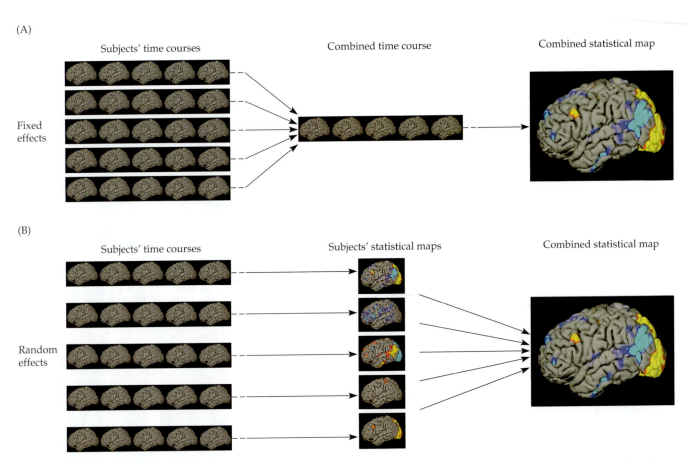

Figure 12.20   Conceptual outline of fixed- and random-effects analyses. (A) In a fixed-effects analysis, the experimental effect is assumed to be constant (i.e., fixed) across the subject population, so the experimental manipulation has the same effect on all subjects. The data are combined across subjects and then undergo testing for significance. (B) In a ran-dom-effects analysis, the experimental effect is considered to vary across subjects. Statistical maps are created for each subject, and then the output of those statistical tests is subjected to a second level of analysis. The advantage of random-effects analyses is that they allow inference to the population from which the subjects were drawn.

subject population for many fMRI studies may itself be unrepresentative, in that subjects tend to be college-age, intelligent, physically healthy, and neuro-logically normal. The use of random-effects analyses does not allow extension of results to those individuals who are not within the subject population (e.g., the elderly, children, patient groups).

> ## Thought Question
>
> Given the limitations of random-effects analyses discussed here, what sorts of experiments are necessary for fMRI results to be applicable to a wide range of subject groups? What problems (e.g., from Chapter 9) would be associated with such studies?

In summary, fixed-effects analyses allow inferences about the subjects who were run in a particular study, while random-effects analyses allow inferences about the population from which the subjects were drawn. Random-effects analyses can be conducted with minimal additional computa-

BOX 12.2 Real-Time Analysis in Presurgical Patients

A common clinical application of fMRI is as a diagnostic tool for identifying functional areas that need to be preserved during neurosurgery. For many patients with brain tumors, vascular malformations, intractable epilepsy, or other types of pathology, surgical removal of the diseased portion of the brain provides the best clinical outcome. However, surgery may not be indicated for all subjects, and the amount of tissue to be removed may depend upon its functional properties. If tissue removal would result in damage to brain regions essential for human language function, memory, or primary sensory or motor processing, it could have a devastating effect on the patient's subsequent quality of life. For example, damage to the left temporal lobe may render him or her unable to comprehend speech. Thus, when deciding upon the course of treatment for a given patient, neurosurgeons want to be able to evaluate the likely functional consequences of removal of a particular brain region. **Cortical mapping** plays an important role in this evaluative process.

Since the 1950s, cortical mapping has typically been done during the surgery itself by temporarily probing selected brain regions using direct electrical stimulation of the cerebral cortex (see Chapter 15). This process involves placing a stimulating electrode on different parts of the exposed cortical surface. By sending a small electrical current through the electrode, the surgeon can inhibit or excite local neuronal activity. In most cases, direct stimulation impairs the function of a brain region; for example, stimulation of language areas may render patients temporarily unable to speak. In other cases, stimulation may actually cause the patient to hear sounds or see colors, motion, or shapes, if the electrode is near primary sensory areas. Although direct electrical stimulation is

widely used, it has some disadvantages. The procedure is highly invasive and time-consuming, the patient must be awakened during surgery, the range of functions that can be investigated is limited, and the only cortical areas that can be measured are those near the exposed surface of the brain.

To overcome these disadvantages, a number of hospitals have begun investigating the use of fMRI for cortical mapping in surgical patients (Figure 12.21A and B). The advantages of fMRI are straightforward. It can be used to map functions anywhere in the brain, including within deep-brain structures difficult to reach using electrodes. It is noninvasive and can be conducted in advance of surgery to aid in surgical planning. And experimental tasks can be tailored to a wide range of cognitive, motor, and perceptual functions. Combining functional and conventional anatomical MRI in the same scanning session can provide maps of important functional areas superimposed on high-resolution images that show detailed anatomical structure and sites of tissue pathology. Multiple brain functions can usually be mapped within a 30- to 40-minute scanning session, providing neurosurgeons with important information to aid in weighing treatment options and in planning the surgical approach to the lesion. FMRI can also be used in conjunction with traditional electrophysiological approaches, by guiding the placement of electrodes for subsequent intraoperative testing.

Despite its obvious potential, diagnostic fMRI has still seen limited use, primarily because its analysis and interpretation is technically demanding. Whereas most fMRI research involves pooling results from many subjects, as described in the previous section, diagnostic fMRI must produce interpretable activation maps in every individual. It is critical, therefore, that each scan pro-

(A)

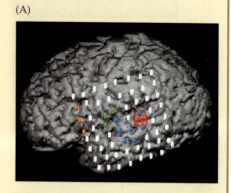

(B)

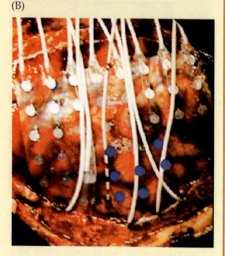

Figure 12.21 Cortical mapping of function. This patient was undergoing cortical mapping in preparation for neurosurgery. The subject underwent both direct electrical stimulation and fMRI. On the reconstruction of the patient's brain in (A), the locations of the electrodes in the grid in (B) are shown as white circles. The electrodes are highlighted according to effects that direct stimulation had on different tasks: orange, speech arrest; green, induced mouth or face movements; and blue, deficits in auditory comprehension and object naming. The locus of fMRI activity during a language comprehension task is shown on the brain surface in red. Note the overlap, albeit incomplete, between the fMRI and electrophysiological data.

BOX 12.2 *(continued)*

duce high-quality MR images with good functional resolution.

An important factor in achieving reliable diagnostic fMRI capabilities has been the development of **real-time analysis** methods. In a real-time analysis, the fMRI data are reconstructed, preprocessed (if needed), and statistically analyzed immediately following acquisition of each image. Thus, the desired functional maps are available at the conclusion of the scanning session. Real-time analyses can be very useful for standard fMRI experiments, because they provide a way to monitor the quality of the results. If the subject moves his head excessively or is unable to perform the experimental task, real-time analyses can catch the problem during the session so that it can be corrected. Real-time generation of statistical maps can also make scanning more efficient by allowing each scan to run only as long as necessary to reach a satisfactory confidence level. For clinical cortical mapping, the ability to assess task performance and activation map quality while the patient is still in the scanner is crucial. Rapid and efficient data processing also allows immediate planning of time-sensitive treatments.

Given the range of statistical approaches available for analyzing standard fMRI data, as discussed earlier in this chapter, it is not surprising that a similar range of analysis strategies have been used for real-time fMRI cortical mapping. Head motion is the most common cause of poor results, so some approaches correct for head motion during scanning. Other approaches emphasize on-line detection of motion so that the MR operator can repeat unsuccessful scans. Since the primary goal of cortical mapping is detection of active voxels, the experimental tasks used are generally simple and powerful blocked designs that can be analyzed using *t*-tests or correlation analyses. Use of fast computer resources and efficient software for analyses is critical.

Even when an fMRI activation map is successfully obtained, interpreting its significance presents another challenge. Many studies comparing fMRI and electrical stimulation mapping in the same patients have shown that these two approaches generally agree, but enough differences remain to make it difficult to make surgical treatment decisions based on the fMRI results alone. Also, it is difficult to assess which areas of fMRI activi-

cortical mapping The mapping of function to different areas of the cerebral cortex, in order to guide plans for clinical treatment.

real-time analysis A set of computational steps designed for rapid analysis of fMRI data, so that statistical tests are conducted immediately following acquisition of the images.

ty, as defined by a statistically significant BOLD hemodynamic response, are actually essential for a particular function. Just because an area is active during an fMRI experiment does not mean that its removal will impair the studied function. Nor do traditional fMRI maps indicate how close to the border of an active area the surgeon can cut without damaging the associated brain function. Nevertheless, fMRI holds considerable promise for improving clinical cortical mapping. Careful clinical trials will be needed to establish confidence criteria for interpreting fMRI maps and determining which analysis methods provide the most accurate and reliable diagnostic results. Such studies are likely to lead to an increased role for fMRI clinically and will also result in improvements relevant to research applications of fMRI.

tion, and most statistical packages now include them within standard analysis procedures. While studies using fixed-effects models are still published, many reviewers for journals and granting agencies have recognized the importance of random-effects models and evaluate manuscripts and grants accordingly. Thus, random-effects analyses are strongly recommended for fMRI studies.

Summary

Since fMRI studies rely on the detection of a weak signal in the presence of substantial noise, careful statistical analysis is necessary. Most fMRI analyses are based on hypothesis testing. The researcher sets up two hypotheses, an experimental hypothesis with some prediction about the data and a null hypothesis based on random chance. The probability that the data could have occurred under the null hypothesis is compared to a threshold alpha value, and if the alpha value is exceeded, then the result is declared significant. Two types of errors are possible in hypothesis testing. Type I errors occur when a nonsignificant result is declared significant (a false positive), while Type II errors occur when a significant result is missed (a false negative). FMRI analyses typically attempt to exclude Type I errors, but as a result they are prone to Type II errors. Significantly active voxels are displayed on statistical maps, usually with the degree of significance indicated using a color scale.

A number of basic statistical tests exist for testing single hypotheses using fMRI. Nearly all are variants of the general linear model, which treats the data as a linear summation of a number of dissociable factors. When using the general linear model to analyze fMRI data, an experimenter creates a design matrix that lists factors of interest (model factors) as well as other known, but uninteresting, sources of variability in the data (nuisance factors). The general linear model provides a powerful and flexible tool for data analysis, but some of its assumptions may not hold for fMRI data. Researchers have developed new data-driven analyses that seek to characterize relations among voxels over time, without creating an a priori statistical hypothesis. Regardless of the analysis approach used, a central problem for fMRI studies is the vast number of statistical tests they require, which leads to false-positive results. Standard corrections like the Bonferroni method are too strict and may eliminate true activations. One approach is to use information about spatial properties of activation, either through Gaussian random field theory or cluster-size thresholds. Another approach is to reduce the number of tests through region-of-interest analyses, which allow targeted studies of anatomical areas. Finally, for all statistical analyses, data should be combined across subjects to increase experimental power. Random-effects approaches enable inference to the population from which the subjects were drawn and are preferred over traditional fixed-effects analyses.

Suggested Readings

*Brodmann, K. (1909). *Vergleichende Lokalisationslehre der Grosshirnrinde in ihren Prinzipien dargestellt auf Grund des Zellenbaues.* Barth, Leipzig, Germany. A remarkably detailed collection of anatomical studies of human and animal cortices. An English-language translation by L. J. Garey from Imperial College Press is now available.

Friston, K. J., Holmes, A. P., Worsley, K. J., Poline, J. P., Frith, C. D., and Frackowiak, R. S. J. (1995). Statistical parametric maps in functional imaging: A general linear approach. *Hum. Brain Mapping,* 5: 189–210. Describes the use of the general linear model for analysis of PET and fMRI data; forms the basis for the popular SPM approach to data analysis.

*McKeown, M. J., Makeig, S., Brown, G. G., Jung, T. P., Kindermann, S. S., Bell, A. J., and Sejnowski, T. J. (1998). Analysis of fMRI data by blind separation into independent spatial components. *Hum. Brain Mapping,* 6: 160–188. Provides the theoretical framework for the application of independent components analysis (ICA) to fMRI.

*Worsley, K. J., Marrett, S., Neelin, P., Vandal, A. C., Friston, K. J., and Evans, A. C. (1995). A unified statistical approach for determining significant signals in images of cerebral activation. *Hum. Brain Mapping,* 4: 58–73. This paper establishes the mathematical underpinnings for spatial comparisons of functional brain images.

*Indicates a reference that is a suggested reading in the field and is also cited in this chapter.

Chapter References

Aguirre, G. K., Zarahn, E., and D'Esposito, M. (1998a). A critique of the use of the Kolmogorov–Smirnov (KS) statistic for the analysis of BOLD fMRI data. *Magn. Reson. Med.,* 39: 500–505.

Aguirre, G. K., Zarahn, E., and D'Esposito, M. (1998b). The variability of human, BOLD hemodynamic responses. *NeuroImage,* 8: 360–369.

Bandettini, P. A., Jesmanowicz, A., Wong, E. C., and Hyde, J. S. (1993). Processing strategies for time-course data sets in functional MRI of the human brain. *Magn. Reson. Med.,* 30: 161–173.

Biswal, B. B., Van Kylen, J., and Hyde, J. S. (1997). Simultaneous assessment of flow and BOLD signal in resting state functional connectivity maps. *NMR Biomed.,* 10(4–5): 165–170.

Biswal, B., Yetkin, F. Z., Haughton, V. M., and Hyde, J. S. (1995). Functional connectivity in the motor cortex of resting human brain using echo-planar MRI. *Magn. Reson. Med.,* 34(4): 537–541.

Cordes, D., Haughton, V., Carew, J. D., Arfanakis, K., and Maravilla, K. (2002). Hierarchical clustering to measure connectivity in fMRI resting-state data. *Magn. Reson. Imaging,* 20: 305–317.

Cox, R. W. (1996). AFNI: Software for analysis and visualization of functional magnetic resonance neuroimages. *Comput. Biomed. Res.,* 29: 162–173.

Forman, S. D., Cohen, J. D., Fitzgerald, M., Eddy, W. F., Mintun, M. A., and Noll, D. C. (1995). Improved assessment of significant activation in functional magnetic resonance imaging (fMRI): Use of a cluster-size threshold. *Magn. Reson. Med.,* 33: 636–647.

Freedman, D., Pisani, R., and Purves, R. (1997). *Statistics.* Norton, New York.

Friston, K. J., Josephs, O., Rees, G., and Turner, R. (1998). Nonlinear event-related responses in fMRI. *Magn. Reson. Med.,* 39(1): 41–52.

Genovese, C. R., Lazar, N. A., and Nichols, T. (2002). Thresholding of statistical maps in functional neuroimaging using the false discovery rate. *NeuroImage,* 15: 870–878.

Hays, W. L. (1994). *Statistics* (5th ed.). Harcourt College, Fort Worth, TX.

Huettel, S. A., Güzeldere, G., and McCarthy, G. (2001). Dissociating the neural mechanisms of visual attention in change detection using functional MRI. *J. Cogn. Neurosci.,* 13(7): 1006–1018.

Jha, A. P., and McCarthy, G. (2000). The influence of memory load upon delay-interval activity in a working-memory task: An event-related functional MRI study. *J. Cogn. Neurosci.,* 12(Suppl. 2): 90–105.

Kanwisher, N., McDermott, J., and Chun, M. (1997). The fusiform face area: A module in human extrastriate cortex specialized for the perception of faces. *J. Neurosc.,* 17: 4302–4311.

McKeown, M. J. (2000). Detection of consistently task-related activations in fMRI data with hybrid independent component analysis. *NeuroImage,* 11: 24–35.

McKeown, M. J., Varadarajan, V., Huettel, S., and McCarthy, G. (2002). Deterministic and stochastic features of fMRI data: Implications for analysis of event-related experiments. *J. Neurosci. Methods,* 118: 103–113.

Schlosser, M. J., Luby, M., Spencer, D. D., Awad, I. A., and McCarthy, G. (1999). Comparative localization of auditory comprehension by using functional magnetic resonance imaging and cortical stimulation. *J. Neurosurg.,* 91: 626–635.

Voyvodic, J. T. (1999). Real-time fMRI paradigm control, physiology, and behavior combined with near real-time statistical analysis. *NeuroImage,* 10(2): 91–106.

Xiong, J., Gao, J., Lancaster, J. L., and Fox, P. T. (1995). Clustered pixels analysis for functional MRI activation studies of the human brain. *Hum. Brain Mapping,* 3: 287–301.

13

Applications of fMRI

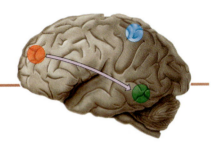

The success of any research technique can be judged by the importance of the research questions it has been used to answer. In that sense, the success of fMRI to date is undeniable. Investigators have used fMRI to answer questions rooted in a wide range of academic disciplines, including cognitive neuroscience, psychology, neurobiology, psychiatry, radiology, and many others. With increasing breadth of investigation has come a complementary depth of inquiry. As of the publication date of this book, more than 5000 articles describing fMRI research have been published in academic journals. To merely list all of the topics to which fMRI has been applied, much less to discuss those topics in any detail, would be an epic undertaking, one beyond the scope of any single review. Indeed, there have been more than 250 published review articles that discuss fMRI research.

Thus forsaking comprehensiveness, we review in this chapter selected key applications of fMRI. We have two goals. First, we identify three sets of advantages that result from the application of fMRI to research into brain function. Second, we document specific advances made within a small set of topic areas: attention, memory, executive function, and consciousness. These topic areas are hardly exhaustive, and we could easily have chosen a completely different set that included such subjects as language, emotion, sensory and motor functions, and development. It is our hope that the studies discussed in this chapter will illustrate how practicing scientists use fMRI as a tool for understanding the brain, and that the interested reader will be able to extend the concepts discussed to other domains.

Translational Research

According to some critics, fMRI studies have provided little information beyond that already given by previous research methods (Figure 13.1A–D). It is hardly surprising, they would say, that watching a flashing checkerboard results in activity in the occipital visual cortex or that flexing the fingers of one's hand activates the primary motor cortex. While not yielding this point, assume for a moment that this criticism was true and fMRI *only* provided a measure of well-known functional brain anatomy. Would it still

Figure 13.1 Development of understanding of the visual system. The basic organization of the visual system has been recognized for centuries. Shown in (A) is a schematic diagram of the eyes, the optic nerve, and the optic chiasm, from an eleventh-century Egyptian text. (B) By the eighteenth century, the crossing of information at the optic chiasm was well recognized, as shown in this drawing from 1750 by the English surgeon John Taylor. (C) Anatomical studies of nonhuman animals further revealed the system's retinotopic organization, demonstrating that foveal and peripheral parts of the visual field are represented in different anatomical locations, as shown in this 1879 drawing by Hermann Munk. Key components of the visual system, including the lateral geniculate nucleus of the thalamus and primary visual cortex, can also be identified using fMRI. (D) These areas were active when the subject *imagined* a flashing checkerboard. The optic tracts are indicated by arrows. (A–C from Finger, 1994; D from Chen et al., 1998.)

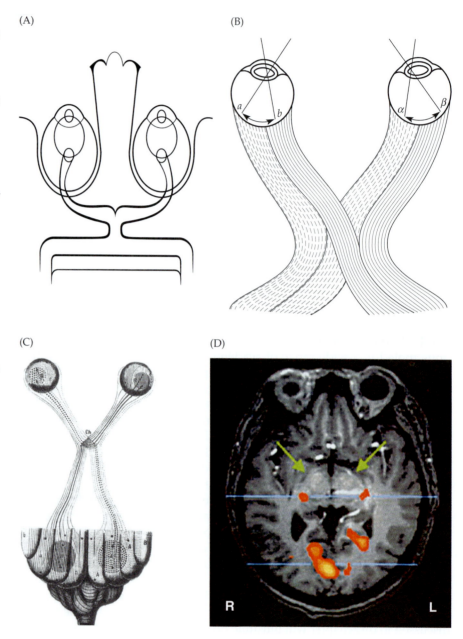

have value as a tool in neuroscience research? We argue an emphatic yes. In providing a noninvasive measure of functional activity, fMRI allows us to readily test that functional activity over a wide range of conditions. If finger movements activate the primary motor cortex, then consider a study that uses fMRI to observe the motor cortex over the course of learning a complex sequence of finger movements, or a study that observes motor cortex activity as a subject recovers the use of their hand following a stroke.

The possibilities grow as more-complex cognitive functions can be monitored with fMRI. For example, several studies have demonstrated activation of the hippocampus during the retrieval of an episodic memory. This is not surprising, as the relationship between the hippocampus and memory has been well established by many prior methods, most prominently human and animal lesion studies. However, with this demonstration, studies can now use hippocampal fMRI activation for a psychological study that examines the efficacy of different retrieval strategies, or for a study that examines memory retrieval during childhood development or in normal aging, or for a study of the effects of a drug that may influence the rate of cognitive decline in Alzheimer's disease, or even for a study that evaluates the integrity of the hippocampus prior to a planned resection for temporal lobe epilepsy. Here, rather than using fMRI as a tool to identify the functions of as yet uncharted brain regions, fMRI is used as an outcome measure to quantify how function is altered by a host of experimental manipulations and/or intrinsic factors, such as attention, learning, disease progression, life span changes, or genetics.

Recent studies suggest that fMRI can also be used as a **surrogate marker** that substitutes for a clinical endpoint, such as the progression of a disease or the effectiveness of a drug therapy. Indeed, researchers are now investigating whether fMRI measures of functional activity in response to pharmacological manipulations can improve in development of novel compounds for a host of neurological and psychiatric diseases. These applications demonstrate the value of fMRI research in **translational medicine,** that aspect of clinical research that spans basic science and clinical practice.

> ## Thought Question
> What other applications might fMRI have for improving clinical practice?

FMRI is an excellent tool in research programs that translate between human and nonhuman animal biomedical research. Animal researchers can utilize tools that have much greater functional resolution than fMRI, but that added resolution is often achieved through invasive methods that could not be used in humans. Animals can be studied using a host of pharmacological interventions, invasive electrophysiological methods, and experimental lesions. With genetic manipulations that delete, or knock out, specific genes from an animal's genome, the influence of genetics upon a particular brain function can also be examined. Animals can also be studied using the same imaging methods described in this book. In many areas of study, investigators use similar experimental tasks in both humans and animals.

For example, fear conditioning is a standard manipulation used to study emotion. In a typical fear conditioning paradigm in a mouse or rat, a tone is paired with a foot shock. In such situations, the mouse or rat engages in freezing behavior. After a sufficient number of pairings of tone and shock, the tone alone will elicit freezing behavior. Extensive animal research by LeDoux and his colleagues established the central role of the amygdala (see Box 6.2) in a network of brain structures and pathways mediating conditioned fear, and has served as a model for such human diseases as depression and anxiety disorders. The fear conditioning paradigm in animals has enabled a host of additional studies, including many that probe the genetics of conditioned fear using knockout mice. But what links these animal models back to human diseases? A 1998 study by LaBar and colleagues investigated fear conditioning in human subjects using a virtually identical paradigm to that used in rats and mice, with fMRI providing the outcome

surrogate marker A measurement that provides information about the clinical progression of a disease or condition.

translational medicine The practice of modifying clinical practice based on findings from basic science research and of modifying the direction of basic science research based on evidence from clinical studies.

Figure 13.2 Translational medicine. The ultimate goal of most medical research is to facilitate improvements in health care and treatment. FMRI research can play an important role in this process. Imagine that a researcher observes that a mouse strain displays behavior that is suggestive of a human clinical disorder. FMRI can be used to build upon animal research by identifying candidate brain areas in humans that may be associated with the disorder, and can further be used to test subjects with the clinical disorder of interest. FMRI can also be used to evaluate the effects of proposed drug treatments on both the brain and the behavior, resulting in validation of new treatments or guidance for future animal studies.

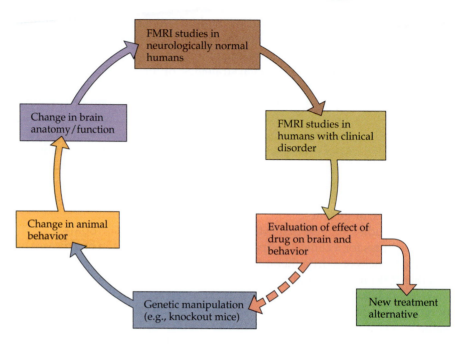

measure. Strong activation of the amygdala was obtained in response to the conditioned fear stimulus, and it persisted into the extinction phase of the study, when the shock was no longer presented. This study and the many others that followed clearly established the role of the amygdala in emotional processing in humans, and thus provide a strong link between the human and animal studies. Moreover, a subsequent 2001 study by Sheline and colleagues used fMRI to demonstrate that patients suffering from depression had an exaggerated response in the left amygdala when viewing faces, particularly those depicting a fearful expression. Treatment of these patients with the antidepressant medication sertraline reduced the amygdala's response to stimuli. Such studies demonstrate the power of fMRI to close the loop between basic research in animals and clinical treatment in humans (Figure 13.2).

Studying Human-Specific Topic Areas

The examples in the previous section illustrate the potential value of using fMRI even when studying functional neuroanatomy that was established using another technique. While such examples are important, many fMRI studies investigate processes that are much more difficult to study using other techniques. An important class of such processes includes those that are primarily characteristic of human cognition. No dividing line exists between those aspects of cognition that are "human" and those that are shared with other animals. However, even the most dogged supporter of animal cognition would have difficulty arguing against the premise that some mental processes are more typical of the human mind while others are more generally present across multiple species. For example, most people can readily generate a mental image of a familiar location, such as their home or workplace. The quality of this image undoubtedly varies across individuals, as some people report having only impoverished mental images while others report constructing elaborate and detail-filled scenes that they can manipulate or transform. Nevertheless, if you are interested in mental imagery, you can study it in humans simply by asking them to imagine something. Now consider trying to study mental imagery in nonhuman animals. Even putting aside whether imagery exists as a mental process for a chimpanzee or rat, it would be difficult at best to convince an animal to generate a mental image, much less to transform it on command.

A number of specific topics have been studied primarily in human subjects and have thus been important areas of fMRI research. These topics can be generally described as those dealing with **higher cognition**. One class of higher cognitive functions requires the symbolic encoding of information and includes functions like language, episodic or autobiographical memory, conceptual categorization, and calculation. These processes are very different between language-using humans and nonhuman animals, though the study of animals may still be important (e.g., examining numerosity judgments by chimpanzees as a precursor to calculation). Another class contains functions related to internal mental states, such as goal setting, decision making, consciousness, and emotion. While there is no longer any doubt that animals can have mental representations (e.g., spatial maps, abstract relations between stimuli), the contents of those states are likely to be very different from those of humans. Some topics must be studied in humans because we are interested in their expression as part of the human condition. For instance, to understand human social behaviors such as emotional responses to others' aversive eye movements or decision making in group situations, one must test people in the relevant social situations. Likewise, to understand changes in the mind and brain associated with human development, experiments that use similar tasks across the life span are necessary.

In contrast, many mental processes seem to be common across species. Chimpanzees have been taught to learn abstract rules, rats are quite good at interval timing, and trained pigeons have become world-class visual discriminators. Even though the tasks that tap these abilities may be quite complex, animals can, with sufficient training, learn to perform them. A good example of this is controlled visual attention, which is discussed later in this chapter. Because attention reflects an internal mental state, it may seem more suited to study in humans, who can verbally report where they are attending when it is different from where they are looking. Yet monkeys can be taught to attend to peripheral spatial locations while maintaining fixation at the center of a display. Through sophisticated behavioral paradigms (and much patience), researchers using electrophysiological recording with nonhuman primates have mapped out the primary components of brain systems involved with visuospatial attention.

While some of the most significant advances in the understanding of these higher cognitive functions have come from fMRI, we emphasize that other techniques remain extremely important. As described earlier in this section, even characteristically human processes share aspects of much simpler behaviors. To understand visual imagery, one must understand the organization of the visual system, for which electrophysiological and lesion studies have been central. Likewise, the understanding of language, that most human of all faculties, requires investigation of motor production systems, auditory comprehension systems, and even temporal sequencing systems, all of which are present in many organisms. Even for topics that may be restricted to human populations, fMRI is hardly the only option, as lesion, drug, and electrophysiological studies remain critical for many research questions.

higher cognition The set of processes that are considered to be more representative of the mental function of humans than of nonhuman animals. Examples include consciousness, executive function, abstract reasoning, and autobiographical memory.

phrenology The belief that bumps and indentations on the skull provide information about the magnitude of some trait supported by the underlying brain region.

Identifying Functional Relations among Brain Regions

The power of fMRI for generating maps of brain function has played an important role in popularizing cognitive neuroscience, both by making neuroimaging accessible to more researchers and by attracting new interest from the general public. To understand just how dramatic this popularization has been, consider that during the late 1980s only a handful of laboratories were using PET to create functional images of the brain. Now, hundreds of institutions have scanners that are used to collect fMRI data, with that number growing every year.

The popular impact of fMRI research comes in large part from the attractiveness of the images created. For an example, imagine that you are sitting (along with one of the authors of this textbook) in the audience of a research conference in the mid-1990s, shortly after the inception of fMRI. The potential use of neuroimaging would already be known to most of the psychologists in the audience, due in part to popularly aimed works like Posner and Raichle's 1994 book, *Images of Mind*. Yet at this time, few of the audience members use neuroimaging in their own laboratories. At the end of the session, the final speaker describes preliminary results using a new technique called "functional magnetic resonance imaging." After a short explanation of the research methods (including an experimental design that confounds the effect of interest with several other factors!), the speaker shows a slide of BOLD activation overlaid upon high-resolution anatomical images. The slide is visually compelling and full of structure, and you look at the maps of activity with interest. A few moments later, you tear your eyes away and observe the reactions of those around you. The entire audience is staring intently at the slide, with their gazes transfixed by the images. Despite the limitations of this study, the images it generated have an almost visceral effect.

Given the power of functional images of the brain to instill wonder in even a sophisticated audience, it is unsurprising that they have rapidly permeated the popular consciousness (Figure 13.3). On a nearly daily basis, news agencies proclaim the discovery of the brain area for this or that higher-level function. Yet the very power of fMRI images raises an important caveat, specifically that one must avoid mistaking the quality of the image for the quality of the idea it represents. Because fMRI is a spatially localizing technique, it can create the false impression that complex psychological functions are localized in small bits of brain tissue. When reading about an fMRI study evaluating working memory, for example, it is tempting to conclude that "working memory" is a well-defined psychological process, that it is controlled by a specific area of the brain, and that the controlling area is located *here*. The idea that single brain functions are mapped to discrete brain regions is a highly attractive one, as witnessed by the popular acceptance of **phrenology** two centuries ago. However, it is clear in most fMRI studies that many often spatially disparate brain regions are activated by the same task. This strongly suggests that complex functions are reflected by the coordinated activity of many discrete brain regions.

From Coactivation to Connectivity

FMRI holds significant promise for elucidating the functional relations among brain regions because of its spatial coverage. Most fMRI studies collect data from the entire brain every few seconds, providing complete spatial coverage at moderate temporal resolution. Advanced pulse sequences now allow collection of more than 20 slices per second, enabling roughly 1-Hz

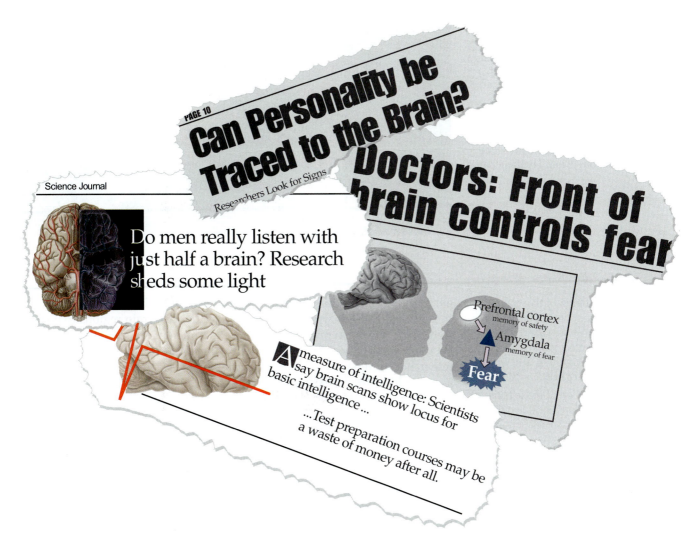

Figure 13.3 Functional MRI studies have elicited substantial media coverage, for better or worse. Many fMRI studies have been picked up by the popular media. While this has led to increased visibility for neuroimaging, as well as increased recognition of the influence of the brain upon behavior, many stories emphasize sensationalism over accuracy. Media reports of fMRI studies share some common properties. Anatomical regions are often generalized, because the intended audience knows neither the anatomy nor the jargon used to describe it (e.g., the frontopolar cortex vs. the prefrontal cortex). Complex concepts like personality, intelligence, and emotion are linked to specific areas, even when the research study describes activation in terms of brain systems. The study's results are applied to common behavior, for example, how one can become a better parent or stock market investor. And there is often a focus on studies of individual differences or social psychology that tap into common stereotypes about behavior.

sampling of whole-brain activity. Even if fMRI cannot characterize the activity within a single brain region as completely as electrophysiological techniques, which may sample at 1000 Hz or faster, its spatial coverage makes it superior at describing functional relations between regions. In this section we discuss the theoretical principles that allow inferences about functional relations, and we describe the methodological implementation of these principles in Box 13.1.

The simplest relationship among regions is **coactivation,** in which two or more distinct brain regions show simultaneous activity during an experimental task (Figure 13.4). A classic example of coactivation can be seen in motor tasks. Squeezing your left hand will result in activity in the precentral

coactivation The simultaneous activity of two or more brain regions within a single experimental task. Coactivation of brain regions does not imply that the regions are functionally connected.

Figure 13.4 Coactivation of brain regions. Any complex experimental task will evoke activity in several brain regions simultaneously. The regions indicated in this color map had significantly greater activity during a rest condition than during a visual search task with similar perceptual characteristics. Even though these regions are coactive, they do not necessarily serve the same function. (From Huettel et al., 2001.)

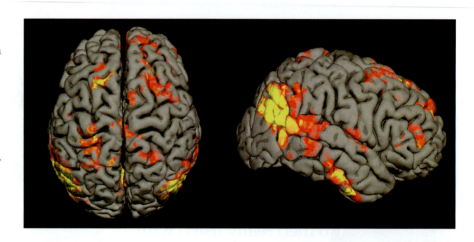

connectivity The form of the relations between different brain regions, including whether they are directly or indirectly connected, whether one region influences another, and whether feedback processes exist.

network A description of the relations of a set of brain regions, including their connectivity and causal relations.

gyrus in the right hemisphere and in the cerebellum in the left hemisphere. Voxel-based fMRI analyses are designed to identify brain regions that show significant activity in response to some experimental manipulation, and thus by their very nature provide coactivation data. It is common for fMRI researchers to report that a given experimental task evoked concurrent activity in multiple brain regions (e.g., that a working memory task evoked activity in the prefrontal and parietal cortices) and to infer from this that these regions are part of a single functional system. (See Box 11.2 for additional discussion of coactivity during rest/baseline conditions.)

However, while coactivity tells you that two brain regions are related, it tells you nothing about the form of that relation, or the **connectivity** between brain regions. Consider the simple task of encoding a set of three faces into working memory. If subjects perform this task while being scanned using fMRI, there will be a set of coactive regions including the dorsolateral prefrontal cortex, superior parietal cortex, and fusiform gyrus. What can we conclude from this coactivity? One inference might be that top-down influences from the prefrontal cortex guide activity in the other regions. Another possibility is that visual processing in the temporal and parietal lobes may lead to prefrontal activity in a bottom-up fashion. Or, activity in all three regions may be triggered by signals from yet another source. Because of the inherent causal uncertainty in any single map of the brain, fMRI research has often been dismissed as being merely descriptive (i.e., describing patterns of coactivation) rather than mechanistic (i.e., explaining how the brain accomplishes a complex behavior). Patterns of coactive regions are often erroneously summarized as **networks** of brain activity. This misuses the term *network*, which should be restricted to descriptions of structural and connective relations that include the causal flow of information. For descriptions of simple associations among regions (i.e., with unknown connectivity and causality), we reserve the term *system*.

Nevertheless, fMRI *can* be used to build more-sophisticated models of connectivity. Some aspects of connectivity can be deduced by measuring the covariance in activity among regions across a number of experimental conditions. Consider a simple example that consists of three brain regions, A, B, and C, and two experimental conditions, X and Y (Figure 13.5). In condition X, brain regions A and C are coactivated, but B is not active. In condition Y, brain regions B and C are coactivated, but A is not active. From these results,

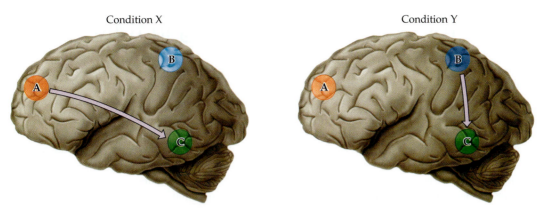

Condition X   Condition Y

Figure 13.5   Using coactivity to make inferences about connectivity. By looking at patterns of coactivity across different experimental conditions, inferences about connectivity (i.e., the influence of brain areas upon each other) can be made. If one condition activates areas A and C, and another condition activates areas B and C, then one can begin to make inferences about the necessity and sufficiency of activity in one region for activity in another region.

there is a **double dissociation** between regions A and B, since one manipulation has an effect on A but not B and another on B but not A. This allows the inference that these regions have different functional properties. Furthermore, the information about region C provides information about connectivity. The observed pattern of associations and dissociations supports the hypothesis that regions A and B are functionally related to C but not to each other. Furthermore, because the presence of activation at C does not always predict the activation of A and B, the pattern of data suggests (but does not prove) directionality and causality. That is, A causes C to become active, and B causes C to become active. This conclusion would be strengthened if there was a measurable temporal delay (or phase lag) such that the measured activation of A or B preceded that of C, although differences in the latency of hemodynamic timing throughout the brain can reduce the impact of such results. Of course, this example simplifies typical fMRI data, which often have a much more complex set of interrelations, but its basic logic underlies many of the more complex techniques introduced in Box 13.1.

double dissociation   The demonstration that two experimental manipulations have different effects on two dependent variables. One manipulation affects the first variable but not the second, and the other manipulation affects the second but not the first.

> ### Thought Question
>
> Many scientists believe that the demonstration of a double dissociation is a necessary step for establishing a clear relation between the independent and dependent variables. Given what you know so far, what do double dissociations tell you that single dissociations do not?

Ideally, we would like models of connectivity to include information about unidirectional connections (i.e., A causes B) as well as feedback connections (i.e., A causes B, which in turn influences A). In order to constrain the possible functional connections within a model, researchers incorporate information about the anatomical connections between brain regions. Although most connections between brain regions are highly reciprocal,

BOX 13.1 Methods for Connectivity Mapping in fMRI

Most fMRI analysis approaches generate **statistical maps** that identify whether a given voxel (or ROI) exhibits significant task-related signal changes. These analyses are conducted independently on all voxels so that each can be tested for significance. However, activity maps do not provide information about the relations among brain regions, save that regions are coactive. Coactivation in an fMRI study does not necessitate that two regions share a single function. For example, in a task that involves squeezing your hand when a bright light flashes, your motor and visual cortices could be simultaneously active, even though they serve very different functions. Yet because fMRI data are collected over time, they *do* contain substantial information suggesting how regions may be functionally related. Several approaches have been developed to generate **functional connectivity maps,** which describe the pattern of functional relations among brain regions, independent of particular task-induced activation. These include cross-correlation, partial least squares, iterative connectivity mapping, and structural equation modeling, all of which are discussed in this box, as well as independent components analysis (ICA), which was discussed in Box 12.1. Additional approaches excluded here for space considerations include multidimensional scaling, hierarchical clustering, and integration with data from **diffusion tensor imaging (DTI)** or **transcranial magnetic stimulation (TMS).** For a discussion of research using these latter approaches, we refer the reader to the 2002 review article by Passingham and colleagues cited in the Suggested Readings.

Because the fMRI signal has temporal structure, information about the coherence of activity over time can be used to guide connectivity mapping. It is worth noting that this approach has been used for many decades in the measurement of high-frequency oscillations activity in the EEG waveform, as was first identified by Hans Berger in the late 1920s. By placing electrodes on the scalp, Berger discovered a regular change in electrical potential at about 10 Hz, which was later named the alpha rhythm. Subsequent EEG studies identified regular oscillatory activity at bands of higher frequencies (e.g., beta, ~20 Hz; and gamma, >30 Hz) and lower frequencies (e.g., delta, <4 Hz; and theta, 4 to 7 Hz).

A similar approach was pioneered for fMRI by Biswal and colleagues in 1995, who measured fMRI activity in the sensorimotor cortex during a rest condition in which subjects performed no motor task. They used a gradient-echo EPI pulse sequence with a TR of 250 ms to rapidly sample a single slice within the brain. Cross-correlation analyses identified voxels whose BOLD activity time courses were significantly correlated with each other, even though no overt task was being performed. Such a correlation between two voxels would suggest that the voxels were functionally related. Note that this study, along with most other early studies, used a single time course derived from a voxel or ROI to seed the correlation analysis. The result was a single map showing connectivity with that seed location. More-advanced analyses, such as the partial least squares approach developed by McIntosh and colleagues for PET and now applied to fMRI, provide sets of maps showing patterns of commonality and difference across experimental conditions.

In 1997, Biswal and colleagues found that time courses of activity in voxels within the sensorimotor cortex were significantly correlated at low frequencies (<0.08 Hz), both within a single hemisphere and across hemispheres. However, there was little correlation between voxels within the sensorimotor cortex and those in other regions. Interestingly, the resulting functional connectivity map matched traditional activation maps obtained during motor movement tasks. In a later study comparing BOLD and flow-dependent imaging (Figure 13.6), the authors found better matching between connectivity and activation maps for BOLD imaging than for flow imaging. This suggests that similar brain processes may underlie low-frequency oscillations and task-related BOLD signals. Subsequent studies by other groups, including a 1999 study by Xiong and colleagues, confirmed these results and extended them to additional brain regions. Although the exact mechanism of low-frequency BOLD oscillations is not yet known, both spontaneous neuronal activity along pathways that connect the regions and shared control of blood supply are likely contributions.

While analyses of data from resting or **null-task blocks** provide important information about functional connectivity, they face several limitations. The most critical of these potential problems is that the characteristics of the resting state are unconstrained (see Box 11.2). Imagine that you are a subject in one of these studies. As you enter the scanner, the experimenter instructs you to close your eyes and relax during the session; you are to remain still without thinking about anything in particular. Such a task, of course, is impossible. One cannot shut off active thought in the same way that one closes a running faucet; indeed, the very act of remembering the task instructions violates them. For this reason, a number of researchers have investigated methods of extracting functional connectivity maps from data that contain task-related activity. Data-driven analyses, like those discussed in Box 12.1, provide one important set of tools for this process. In 2000, Arfanakis and colleagues collected data from the same set

BOX 13.1 *(continued)*

(A) BOLD

Task

(B) Flow

(C)

Rest

(D)

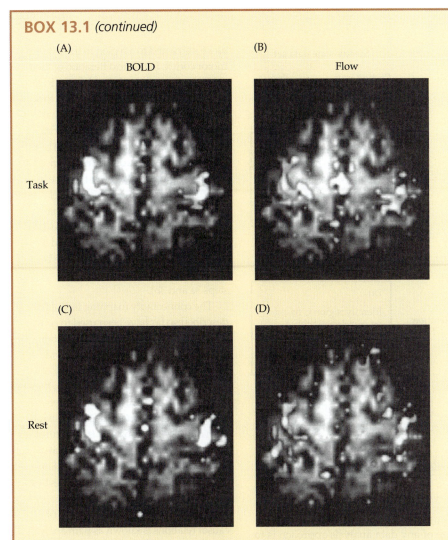

statistical map (or statistical parameter map) In fMRI, the labeling of all voxels within the image according to the outcome of a statistical test.

functional connectivity map An image or diagram of the pattern of connectivity between different regions of the brain, independent of activity associated with experimental tasks.

diffusion tensor imaging (DTI) The collection of images that provide information about the magnitude and direction of molecular diffusion. It is often used to create maps of fractional anisotropy.

transcranial magnetic stimulation A technique for temporarily stimulating a brain region to disrupt its function. It uses an electromagnetic coil placed close to the scalp; when current passes through the coil, it generates a magnetic field in the nearby brain tissue, producing localized electric currents.

null-task block A control block in which there are no task requirements for the subject. Also called a baseline block or nontask block.

Figure 13.6 BOLD imaging provides information about connectivity between regions. (A) FMRI data using BOLD-sensitive and (B) blood-flow-sensitive imaging was collected during performance of a bilateral finger tapping task. Both techniques found significant activity in the motor cortex. Resting-state data was collected using each type of imaging. Low-frequency oscillations that signal functional connectivity between regions were identified. The BOLD resting data clearly indicated that the hand areas of the motor cortex were functionally connected (C), matching the activation data, while the flow resting data exhibited much less functional connectivity (D). (From Biswal et al., 1997.)

of subjects in both resting and task conditions. The experimental tasks included finger tapping, passive viewing of a visual display, and auditory language comprehension, each presented in a 32-s-on/32-s-off blocked design. The authors used ICA to remove components of the data that had a significant cross-correlation with a hypothesized hemodynamic response and were located within a priori regions of interest. Using methods similar to those of Biswal and colleagues, the authors generated connectivity maps for each of the three tasks, based on both resting data and task data processed to remove task-related components. The connectivity maps were remarkably similar despite the different active task re-

quirements, indicating that functional connectivity can be measured even when a task is present.

A novel extension of this technique was proposed by Hampson and colleagues in 2002. They collected separate data sets from the same subjects in two types of runs: resting and task. In the resting runs, nothing was presented and no response was required. The task runs used a blocked design in which the subjects listened to either a reading of a story or silence. The authors used an iterative comparison method that generated connectivity hypotheses based upon one data set and tested those hypotheses in the other data set. The basic approach is shown in Figure 13.7. First, the authors used a standard blocked analysis on the

BOX 13.1 *(continued)*

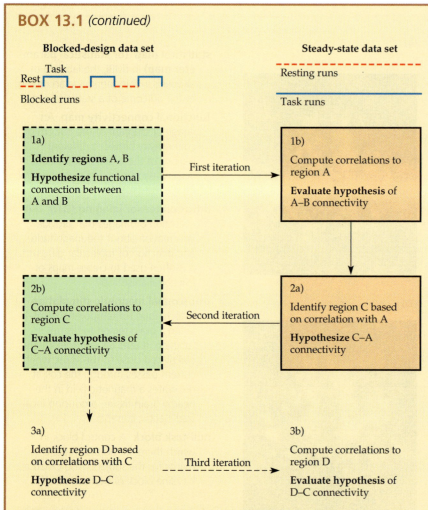

Figure 13.7 An iterative procedure for identifying functional connectivity between brain regions. A central challenge of any data analysis approach is to combine hypothesis testing and hypothesis formation, since using the same data for both purposes can introduce bias. One way to overcome this problem is to collect two data sets from the same subjects, such as a blocked-design language comprehension task and a steady-state null task. Working back and forth between these data sets, researchers can identify regions of activity during the task and evaluate hypotheses about their connectivity with other regions. (From Hampson et al., 2002.)

task data set to create a task-related activity map. As expected, they found significant activity in Broca's area and Wernicke's area. This resulted in the hypothesis that these two regions are functionally related. To test this hypothesis, they used Broca's area as the seed for a connectivity analysis. The voxel time courses from the resting data set were low-pass filtered to remove frequencies greater than 0.08 Hz and then correlated with the mean activity from Broca's area. Strong connectivity was found from Broca's area to the corresponding anatomical region in the right hemisphere, while weaker connectivity was noted both to Wer-

nicke's area and to a region in the left premotor cortex. In the next iteration of their analysis, the authors defined a new ROI in the left premotor cortex based on this connectivity map. The hypothesis that Broca's area and the left premotor cortex are functionally connected was then tested, using both the auditory and silence conditions of the task data set independently. Both revealed significant correlations between these regions. Note that this iterative approach, in which one data set generates hypotheses to be tested by the other data set, could in principle be extended to additional brain regions (e.g., steps 3a and 3b).

The connectivity mapping techniques described so far have been used to confirm functional relations between brain regions. However, they do not provide information about the directionality of those relations, that is, whether area X influences activity in area Y, or vice versa. A powerful technique used to investigate such questions of causality is **structural equation modeling (SEM),** which attempts to determine what combination of causal relations between variables best accounts for the observed data. The process of evaluating potential sets of causal relations is known as path analysis. Applications of SEM to fMRI often use models that are constrained by the known anatomy, with pathways in the model reflecting connecting pathways between brain regions. The first use of SEM in fMRI was reported in 1997 by Buchel and Friston, who studied the effects of attention upon processing in the visual cortex. They found that attention increased the connectivity between extrastriate visual areas and the posterior parietal cortex, with the prefrontal cortex one potential source of this attentional control effect. More recent studies have used SEM both to evaluate models of connectivity between regions and to

BOX 13.1 *(continued)*

measure the effects of other factors upon that connectivity (see Figure 13.8).

Functional connectivity studies of the type described here are necessary to move fMRI studies from descriptive toward mechanistic explanations of complex behavior. However, it is important to understand that the models of connectivity provided by these formal techniques are only that—models. Additional data must be sought to verify that the supposed functional relationships actually exist. These data could be sought in human lesion studies in subjects in whom a stroke or surgical excision has damaged or removed a key component of the network model generated on the basis of SEM. Another approach might involve comparing different groups of subjects with known or presumed differences in the pattern of connectivity. For example, in 1998, Horwitz and colleagues used PET data to develop a functional connectivity model that linked the left angular gyrus and extrastriate occipital and temporal cortex in single-word reading in normal individuals. This model was then tested in a population of dyslexic subjects, where a functional disconnection was observed. Such demonstrations serve to validate both a particular model derived from normal individuals and the functional connectivity approach in general.

In summary, fMRI provides sufficient spatial and temporal resolution to identify connectivity across brain regions. Simple correlation approaches can be used to reveal regions that are functionally related, even in data sets collected in the absence of an experimental task. More-complex hypothesis testing and modeling approaches introduce anatomical information into the analyses and allow measurement of the relative strength and directionality of the relations between regions. It is important to recognize that the success of connectivity mapping rests on a simple principle: the anatomical and functional specialization of the brain. Even though every region of the brain projects to many others, and even a simple task may evoke activity in a wide range of regions, considerable specialization remains. In 2002, Passingham and colleagues introduced the idea that each region has a unique **connectional fingerprint,** representing its pattern of connectivity with other regions. We believe that this concept is a useful one, as it emphasizes that neuroscience analysis approaches should be constrained by anatomical considerations. Although all voxels may be treated similarly by standard fMRI analysis methods, they have different anatomical (and functional) properties. Connectivity mapping has the potential to elucidate these properties, thereby greatly improving the inferences that can be made within fMRI experiments.

structural equation modeling (SEM)
  A mathematical technique for elucidating the causal relations between a set of variables. In fMRI studies, SEM can be used to create models of the connectivity between different brain areas.

connectional fingerprint The pattern of anatomical connections to and from a given brain region. The term *fingerprint* conveys that connectivity patterns are unique to particular brain regions.

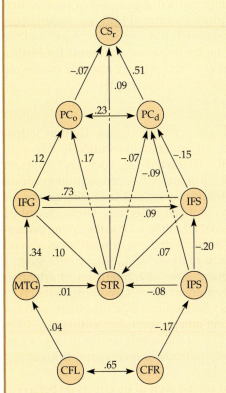

Figure 13.8 Measurement of connectivity between brain regions. Subjects learned a set of arbitrary associations between visual patterns and finger movements while in the fMRI scanner. Structural equation modeling was used to identify the relations between activity in different brain regions across the entire fMRI time series (path coefficients indicate how large a change was evoked in the target region by a one-unit change in the source region). The paths between regions were chosen based on anatomical considerations. The regions shown here include the left and right calcarine fissures (CFL, CFR), the middle temporal gyrus (MTG), the anterior striatum (STR), the intraparietal sulcus (IPS), the inferior frontal gyrus (IFG), the inferior frontal sulcus (IFS), the opercular and dorsal parts of the precentral gyrus (PCo, PCd), and the rostral bank of the central sulcus (CSr). (From Toni et al., 2002.)

there are a number of relatively unidirectional pathways or loops, especially between cortical and subcortical regions. The connection between the prefrontal cortex and the basal ganglia forms one such pathway, as the prefrontal cortex has heavy projections to the basal ganglia but receives little direct input in return. Instead, the basal ganglia project to the thalamus, which itself projects back to the prefrontal cortex. By incorporating information about these pathways into models of brain function, researchers can improve the models from simple patterns of coactive systems to more detailed and directional networks. Diffusion tensor imaging, which is described in Chapter 14, has become an important tool in this process.

Topic Areas

In the remainder of this chapter, we discuss some of the key research topics to which fMRI has been most profitably applied. Again, we emphasize that this set of topics is by no means complete. Functional MRI has made important contributions to many areas of research not considered here, and we urge the interested reader to select topics of personal interest for further exploration. Additional citations for review and primary research articles are included in the references section at the end of this chapter.

Attention

Discussions of attention invariably begin with definitions. Though "attention" seems to be something that we all understand intuitively, our intuitions seem somehow inadequate for characterizing such an important process. It is curious, therefore, that the commonly cited definition comes from the psychologist/philosopher William James, whose writing echoes his extraordinary capability for intuition and self-reflection. James described attention thusly: "Every one knows what attention is. It is the taking possession by the mind, in clear and vivid form, of one out of what seem several simultaneously possible objects or trains of thought." (1890, pp. 403–404)

We begin this section by considering three characteristics of attention identified by James. First, he described attention as something that acts to bring the representation of one object (whether real or imagined) into the focus of consciousness, while excluding others. Second, attention can either be voluntarily initiated by the individual or reflexively drawn to an external object. Third, attention can be directed to objects or their properties, not just to locations in space.

The importance of visual attention can be seen in its effects on behavior. When subjects attend to a location in space or to an object feature, they make judgments about that spatial location or feature more rapidly and more accurately. An event-related fMRI study of spatial attention conducted by Small and colleagues in 2003 investigated whether these improvements in behavioral performance were correlated with activity in particular brain regions. Subjects watched a display consisting of a center diamond and two flanking squares. At the beginning of the trial, either one side of the diamond flashed to point at one of the squares (cue trial) or both sides of the diamond flashed (neutral trial). The cue predicted the location of a later target 80% of the time. The authors hypothesized that brain regions associated with shifting attention would be most active when a valid cue significantly speeded response time to the later target. Note that their comparison was between identical stimuli (validly cued trials) that were sorted based upon whether that trial's response time was faster (by more than one standard error) than that to neutral cues. This procedure is similar to the *post hoc* **trial sorting** introduced in Chapter 11 that is most commonly conducted in memory experiments. They found that BOLD activity within the posterior cingulate and ventromedial frontal cortices significantly increased on fast-response-time trials, while activity in the intraparietal sulcus decreased on fast-response-time trials. The authors concluded that these regions are associated with the reallocation of spatial attention based upon motivational biases. These results are particularly compelling because they cannot be attributed to stimulus or design differences between the conditions, since all trials were visually similar.

While this study identified areas that may be central to modulatory control of attention, other studies have evaluated how particular brain areas are influenced by attention. A very important research question is whether attention can modulate activity in the primary visual cortex (V1). A number of electrophysiological studies had indicated that attention does not affect activity in V1, but instead acts at later stages of visual processing. However, some early fMRI studies found that attention had significant effects on activity in V1. To reconcile these disparate findings, in 1999 Martinez and colleagues reported data from separate fMRI and **event-related potential (ERP)** experiments. Their ERP results indicated that although attention does modulate fMRI activity in the primary visual cortex, it does not affect early visual processing. Instead, the most likely effect of attention upon activity in V1 is through later, re-entrant feedback from other visual cortical regions. Because the temporal resolution of fMRI precludes easy distinction between early (e.g., 60 ms) and late (e.g., >200 ms) electrical activity, other techniques remain critical for study of the timing of attentional effects. In particular, the combination of fMRI and ERP studies holds promise for overcoming the **inverse problem** that precludes accurate spatial localization using electrophysiological methods (Figure 13.9). This possibility is discussed at greater length in Chapter 15.

A second important issue that has been studied using fMRI is how top-down, controlled attention and bottom-up, reflexive attention may be sup-

trial sorting The *post hoc* assignment of events to conditions, often based on behavioral data.

inverse problem The mathematical impossibility of determining the distribution of electrical sources within an object based upon the measurement of electrical or magnetic fields at the surface of the object.

event-related potentials (ERPs) Small electrical changes in the brain that are associated with sensory or cognitive events.

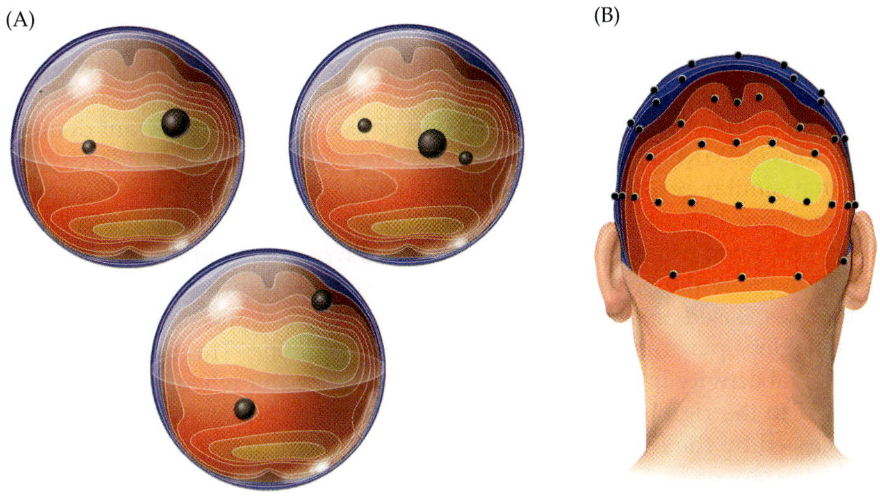

Figure 13.9 The inverse problem in ERP source localization. Scalp-recorded electrophysiological techniques (EEG, ERP) have difficulty mapping patterns of activity across the brain, due to the inverse problem (A). Three distributions of sources within a sphere are indicated. Because the brain is highly conductive, each source contributes to the total activity measured at surface electrodes. Although the activation sources differ in location, number, and intensity, they all evoke the same electrical activity measured on the surface. Procedures for localizing sources of activity, known as electrical dipole modeling, rely on assumptions about the number and location of those sources. (B) A typical scalp voltage map recorded in an ERP experiment of visual attention. Combined fMRI and ERP studies can be used to improve inferences about the sources of the ERP generators. (ERP data courtesy of Dr. Joseph Hopfinger, University of North Carolina, Chapel Hill.)

Figure 13.10 Attention to spatial locations and object properties. Controlled visual attention evokes activity in a similar set of brain regions across different tasks. (A) The subject attends for an object that is presented in a particular spatial location, whereas in (B), the subject attends for an object that moves in a particular direction. Both types of tasks evoke fMRI activity in extrastriate regions in the ventral (fusiform and MT) and dorsal (intra-parietal sulcus) streams, as well as in the frontal cortex (frontal eye fields). (From Corbetta and Shulman, 2002.)

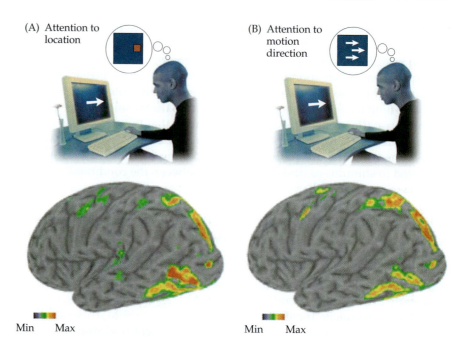

(A) Attention to location

(B) Attention to motion direction

Min   Max

Min   Max

hemifield One half of a visual display, usually referring to the left or right half.

ported by distinct brain systems. Corbetta and Shulman, in a 2002 review article based upon their earlier fMRI studies, demonstrated that top-down visual attention evokes activity in dorsal parietal and/or dorsal frontal brain regions regardless of whether it is directed toward a spatial location or an object with a particular direction of motion (Figure 13.10). In contrast, fMRI studies of bottom-up attention (including those using tasks discussed later in this chapter) find activity in lateral parietal and ventral frontal regions, primarily within the right hemisphere. Corbetta and Shulman suggested that top-down and bottom-up attention rely upon separate dorsal and lateral parietofrontal systems, respectively, consistent with the results from Hopfinger and colleagues discussed in Chapter 11. It is important to recognize the value of fMRI for this sort of large-scale mapping of brain systems. Because fMRI can collect data simultaneously from the entire brain, it allows researchers to map patterns of activity across regions.

The studies discussed so far focused on spatial attention, but fMRI has also provided new information about attention to objects. Early fMRI studies demonstrated that attention to a particular object class increases BOLD activity in areas sensitive to that type of object. Though important demonstrations of fMRI, such studies were more replicative than groundbreaking, in that similar results could be shown using other techniques. However, more-recent studies have investigated higher-level properties of object attention. One good example comes from the 2003 work of Handy and colleagues studying how the presentation of manipulable tools influences attentional processes. Based on their earlier ERP studies, they hypothesized that the left parietal lobe plays an important role in motor planning. This hypothesis predicts that activity in response to tools would be greater when they were presented to the right of fixation (or right **hemifield**) and were subsequently processed by the left hemisphere. They used fMRI to test this hypothesis. Subjects passively viewed pictures of tools and animals presented either to the left or right of fixation, while watching for an infrequent superimposed target, a black grating. As hypothesized, there was greater activity in the parietal cortex in response to tools presented to the right hemifield compared to those presented to the left hemifield. However, the parietal brain regions active in response to tools were not the same as those associated with spatial attention. Based on this result, the authors suggested that attention to manipulable objects and attention to spatial locations rely on different brain systems, a result that could not have been anticipated from the previous ERP data.

While James thought of attention as something that brings the representation of an object into consciousness, it is not necessary for an object to be consciously perceived for it to influence behavior. In the phenomenon known as **visual extinction,** which typically results from right parietal lobe damage, patients can identify singly presented objects regardless of their location. But if two objects are presented, one to the left and one to the right, the patients can only identify the object presented on the right. Even though patients only report seeing one of the objects, the other object still can affect behavior. In 2000, Rees and colleagues used fMRI to examine brain activity in a patient with visual extinction. They showed him pictures of houses and faces on the left, right, or left and right sides of a display and asked him to press a button to indicate on which side(s) stimuli were presented. His behavioral results showed clear evidence for extinction, in that he had 98% accuracy on unilateral trials but only 3% accuracy on bilateral trials. However, the fMRI results revealed activity in the primary visual cortex for both consciously seen and extinguished stimuli, although activity was greater for the former. This suggests that activity in the primary visual cortex can occur in the absence of visual awareness.

In addicted individuals, attention can be drawn preferentially to stimuli that are associated with their disorder. As examples, smokers will attend to an image of a hand holding a cigarette, while alcoholics will attend to images of friends drinking at a bar. An early PET study conducted in 1996 by Grant and colleagues showed that images of cocaine abuse increased activity in prefrontal and limbic brain regions of abusers. Subsequent fMRI studies by Schneider and colleagues in 2001, and by Due and colleagues in 2002, also found limbic activation in samples of alcoholics and smokers, respectively, although the latter study also reported that attention to irrelevant smoking cues evoked activity in regions associated with detection of relevant targets. An important tool for investigating changes in attention (and decision making) associated with disorders like addiction will be **virtual reality** (Figure 13.11). By presenting stimuli in highly realistic environments, researchers can increase the effect of those stimuli on behavioral, emotional, and attentional processes.

To conclude, we want to emphasize two methodological advances that have had great effect upon the study of attention using fMRI. The first is that of fast-rate event-related fMRI, as introduced in Chapter 11. Attention has long been known to be a transient phenomenon, noted even by James, who commented on the difficulty of sustaining attention for more than a few seconds. Because of this transience, many attention experiments use cue–target paradigms in which attention is cued to a particular location and then a target is presented either at that location or at another location. Usually the cue–target interval is kept very short, spanning only a few seconds. For sample experiments, see the study by Hopfinger and colleagues presented in Chapter 11, and the study by Small and colleagues described earlier in this section. Neuroimaging techniques with low temporal resolution, such as

visual extinction The loss of experience of a visual stimulus due to simultaneous presentation of another stimulus in another part of the visual field.

virtual reality Computer simulations of real-world experiences, often presented using immersive visual displays and manipulated using specialized tools.

(A)

(B)

(C)

Figure 13.11 Virtual reality and fMRI. An important goal for many types of experiments is ecological validity, or the degree to which the task faithfully replicates real-world challenges. Many fMRI researchers are using virtual-reality environments to study phenomena like attention, perception, spatial navigation, phobias, addiction, and even motor behavior. For example, looking around a bar (A) induces attention to drug-related stimuli and craving in smokers and alcoholics. Realistic environments (B) can be used to study route learning, spatial memory, and imagery. Interactive environments (C) allow the study of motor behavior and action planning, even when actual motion is restricted. (A, B courtesy of Dr. Steve Baumann, Psychology Software Tools; C courtesy of Dr. Martin McKeown, University of British Columbia.)

 retinotopic mapping A technique for delineating functional regions within the visual cortex based upon their responses to stimuli presented at different retinal locations.

PET or blocked-design fMRI, cannot separate these events. However, event-related fMRI with randomized trial types can be used to dissociate cue-related and target-related activity (see the 1998 article by Burock and colleagues, and the 2000 article by Hinrichs and colleagues, for examples).

The second advance is the development of fMRI paradigms for in vivo topographic mapping of sensory cortices. Functional mapping of the visual system is often called **retinotopic mapping,** because retinal eccentricity and angle are used to define boundaries between adjacent regions. Once functional regions are mapped in a given subject, then the effects of attention upon those regions can be identified. This can be seen in a 1999 report by Somers and colleagues, who mapped a set of eight distinct regions within the visual cortex and then investigated the effects of foveal (i.e., near center of gaze) or extrafoveal attention upon BOLD activity in those regions. They found that attention had strong effects on activity in these regions, some of which have been investigated by subsequent experiments. These results demonstrate the power of fMRI for both spatial localization of function and subsequent analysis of how that function changes in response to manipulations like attention.

Memory

The study of memory long predates fMRI. Behavioral techniques for understanding and improving memory have been known for several millennia. Schools of oration in ancient Rome, for example, taught the use of complex schemes for place–object associations (i.e., the "method of loci") so that orators could more easily memorize long and complex speeches. Experimental studies of memory began almost concurrently with the birth of psychology as a discipline, through the pioneering work of the German philosopher/psychologist Hermann Ebbinghaus in the 1880s. Lesion studies of memory have provided clear evidence for the mnemonic functions of particular brain structures, most famously noted in patient H.M., who lost the ability to form new long-term memories following resection of much of his medial temporal lobes more than 50 years ago.

Given this rich history, it is important to identify areas of research where fMRI has made a clear contribution. We highlight three such advances. First, fMRI studies have provided new evidence for the functional organization of human memory systems, complementing substantial previous work done with rodents and nonhuman primates. Second, the use of event-related fMRI in conjunction with trial sorting has allowed researchers to identify links between brain activity and behavioral outcomes. Third, the use of whole-brain imaging has demonstrated that memory is mediated by a distributed system rather than a few selected brain regions.

A fundamental division in memory research is between processes that support the **encoding** of information into long-term memory and those that support the **retrieval** of information from memory. Processes associated with explicitly encoded information are called **declarative memory** processes, and a further distinction can be made between episodic and semantic components of declarative memory. **Episodic memory** supports the recall of past occurrences of specific events, while **semantic memory** supports the recall of facts independently of past events. There are many other aspects of memory that are not declarative processes, including procedural memories, motor skills, short-term rehearsal, and classical conditioning, among others. We exclude these latter aspects from this discussion, primarily for space considerations, and secondarily because most fMRI studies of long-term memory have used tasks that tap declarative processes. We refer those interested in other forms of memory to the relevant review chapter by Squire and Knowlton for a clear introduction.

One of the first examples of the power of fMRI for elucidating the functional organization of brain systems for memory was reported by Gabrieli and colleagues in 1997. They investigated encoding and retrieval processes in separate runs within the same scanning session. The encoding run alternated task blocks of novel, to-be-remembered photographs of scenes with a control block of two familiar pictures presented repeatedly. The retrieval run alternated blocks where 90% of the pictures were remembered from a study session before the experiment and blocks where 90% of the pictures had not been previously seen. They found that different areas of the medial temporal lobe were active in response to encoding and retrieval. Although the specific division advanced by the authors has been modified based on subsequent research, the demonstration that encoding and retrieval processes were dissociable in the human brain served to catalyze subsequent work.

A powerful technique for studying brain systems for encoding is the subsequent memory paradigm (see Paller and Wagner for a review), which had been used in previous ERP studies in the 1980s. In this approach, the brain

encoding The conversion of information, such as stimuli in the sensory environment, into a mental representation suitable for storage in long-term memory.

retrieval The accessing of information from long-term memory stores so that it can guide thought or behavior.

declarative memory Processes that support the conscious encoding and retrieval of information about facts and events.

episodic memory Processes that support the conscious encoding and retrieval of information about occurrences of particular events.

semantic memory Processes that support the conscious encoding and retrieval of information about facts, independent of particular events.

response on each trial is sorted based on whether the stimulus was remembered or forgotten at a later test. In a 1998 study by Wagner and colleagues, subjects were scanned using fMRI while they judged whether each word in a rapidly presented series was abstract or concrete. Each of their six runs contained 40 abstract words, 40 concrete words, and 40 fixation trials (no word), presented in a random order for 750 ms with an ISI of 1250 ms. Shortly after the end of the scanner session, the subjects took a memory test consisting of 960 items, half that they had seen in the scanner and half that were new. Based on this test, the authors identified encoding trials that were subsequently remembered with high confidence and encoding trials that were subsequently forgotten. Using an event-related analysis, they found greater activity in response to remembered items compared to forgotten items in the left inferior prefrontal cortex (Figure 13.12A–C), the parahippocampal gyrus, and the fusiform gyrus. The authors speculated that the degree of engagement of these regions during encoding determines the strength of the subse-

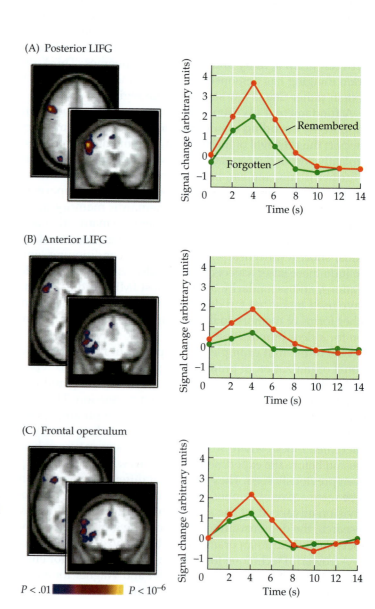

(A) Posterior LIFG

(B) Anterior LIFG

(C) Frontal operculum

$P < .01$ $P < 10^{-6}$

Figure 13.12 The use of trial sorting in the study of memory. With the advent of event-related fMRI, a number of investigators have begun using trial sorting based on item-specific effects, such as whether a word is later remembered or forgotten. Activity in several brain regions, notably the posterior (A) and anterior (B) left inferior frontal gyri (LIFG) but also the frontal operculum (C), predicts whether subjects were able to remember a particular stimulus. (From Wagner et al., 1998.)

quent memory trace. A similar procedure was used in 1999 by Henson and colleagues to investigate differences between conscious recollection (i.e., "remembering") and feelings of familiarity (i.e., "knowing"). They found that a region in the left frontal lobe showed increased activity in response to words that were subsequently given a "remember" judgment compared to those that were given a "know" judgment.

Studies of retrieval of information from memory have also benefited from advances in fMRI methods. Using event-related designs, combined with the trial sorting practices described earlier, researchers can identify distinct brain systems associated with different aspects of retrieval (see Buckner and Wheeler for a comprehensive review). Attempting to retrieve an item from memory evokes activity in the left-lateralized posterior frontal cortex, seemingly independently of the content of the object to be remembered or the success of the attempt. Anterior regions of the frontal cortex are also active, although the role of these regions is less clear, perhaps involving self-monitoring of the retrieval process. In contrast, the success of memory retrieval seems to depend on activity in the medial temporal lobe, parietal cortex, and anterior frontal cortex, as shown by a number of fMRI studies. Retrieval also evokes activity in corresponding sensory cortices. That is, retrieval of spatial information evokes activity in the parietal cortex; retrieval of objects, scenes, and faces evokes activity in the ventral temporal cortex; retrieval of auditory information evokes activity in the superior temporal cortex; and so forth. This specialization based upon content is known as **domain specificity.** While domain specificity in the sensory cortices is well established, specialization in frontal regions remains an important area of study.

Finally, functional neuroimaging, and fMRI in particular, has become a key tool for the study of distributed memory systems in the brain. Within the last decade, neuroimaging studies using PET and fMRI have generated large-scale models describing the functional organization of aspects of memory in the human brain (e.g., the HERA [hemispheric encoding / retrieval asymmetry] model of Tulving and colleagues). Yet despite these successes, describing distributed systems for memory using fMRI poses several challenges. Within a single process like "retrieval" is packed a multitude of subprocesses, including understanding instructions, accessing long-term stores, selecting candidate memories for reactivation, inhibiting inappropriate memories, and reporting the retrieved episode. These processes may be confounded in many studies. Memory is intimately tied to experience; as evidence, the word *remember* means literally "to bring into the mind again." As discussed later in the section on consciousness, the use of fMRI to study experiential phenomena suffers from a host of challenges.

Many aspects of memory, especially those dealing with motor skills, are difficult to measure given the constraints of the MRI environment. To tap such processes, creative experimental designs will be necessary. For example, to study memory for motor movements using fMRI, one might need to use imagined (rather than real) movements. In addition, some of the key regions involved in memory—those within the medial temporal lobe—can be difficult to image using conventional fMRI due to susceptibility artifacts, especially at higher field strengths. Advances in pulse sequence design, as described in Chapter 14, will help overcome this limitation. Finally, combining information from fMRI and other techniques remains critical, especially for understanding disorders that have substantial effects upon memory (e.g., Alzheimer's disease, dementia, strokes).

domain specificity The segregation of functional regions in the brain according to the type of information that they process.

executive function The top-down control of cognition based on goals and context.

prefrontal cortex The parts of the frontal lobe anterior to regions that support motor processes.

sequence effects Changes in behavior in response to a stimulus based on the context formed by preceding stimuli.

Executive Function

An increasingly important area of cognitive neuroscience is the study of **executive function,** which can be defined as the top-down control of thoughts and behavior based on goals and context. Just like *attention* and *memory*, the term *executive function* hardly reflects a unitary process. Postulated subcomponents include selecting among potential actions, monitoring performance for mistakes, maintaining information in working memory, switching from task to task, and preventing distracting stimuli from influencing behavior. At one level, it may seem that the breadth of topics considered to be executive poses a challenge for fMRI studies. After all, how can we map out the brain areas that support a function if we cannot even define it? It is counterintuitive, therefore, that fMRI has played a particularly important role in the understanding of executive function, perhaps greater than that for any other topic discussed in this chapter. To illustrate why, we detail the key properties of executive function and how they match the strengths of fMRI.

Because fMRI can be easily used to study spatially extensive cognitive processes, it is ideally suited for studying executive function. Like the study of attention, research into executive function involves both understanding brain regions that exert top-down control and assessing the effects of that control upon other brain regions. Note, however, that executive processes differ from attentional processes in that the former act upon other cognitive processes while the latter act upon representations of objects or spatial locations. The brain region most associated with executive function is the **prefrontal cortex,** which is heavily interconnected with other parts of the brain, notably the thalamus, basal ganglia, medial temporal cortex, and secondary sensory and motor cortices. For a good overview of prefrontal control processes, see the review article by Miller and Cohen indicated in the references section.

A second reason for the growth of fMRI studies in this area results from the tasks used to study executive function. More than any other area of cognitive neuroscience (and indeed of psychology), the study of executive function has generated a veritable Cambrian explosion of different experimental paradigms, all sharing a loose relation to control processes. Figure 13.13 illustrates a small sample of common tasks to emphasize one shared feature: because all contain infrequent events of interest, they adapt well to event-related fMRI. In the oddball task, for example, the subjects watch or listen to a series of stimuli (e.g., squares) and respond only when a infrequent target stimulus (e.g., a circle) is presented. Because of the very nature of the task, blocking the target events in time would mean that they were no longer infrequent, changing the cognitive processes they evoke. Event-related techniques are necessary for research into the influences of one trial upon the next, or **sequence effects.** In 2002, Huettel and colleagues used a classification task in which two stimuli (i.e., a circle and a square) were presented with equal probability, each requiring a different button-press response (Figure 13.14A). Although the overall sequence was random, short-term patterns like five circles in a row arose by chance. FMRI activity within regions of the lateral prefrontal cortex was evoked by stimuli that broke these short-term patterns (Figure 13.14B), with the magnitude of that activity increasing with increasing pattern length (Figure 13.14C). This effect, that the activity in response to a stimulus depends upon its context, could not be identified using blocked designs that collapse across adjacent stimuli.

Nevertheless, blocked fMRI designs can provide very useful information for studies of executive processing. While the tasks illustrated in Figure

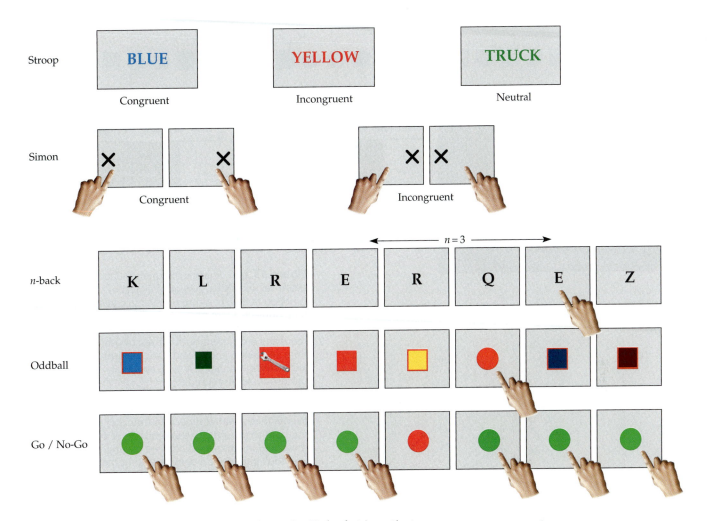

Figure 13.13 Common executive processing tasks. Tasks that investigate executive processing often require the participant to make different responses based on context. In some cases, the contextual information interferes with responding, as in the Stroop task, in which subjects must name the ink color while ignoring the irrelevant word names. In the Simon task, subjects press buttons based upon the position of stimuli; subjects are faster when the assigned response hand matches the stimulus position. Other tasks require subjects to make infrequent responses, either based on stimuli held in working memory (the *n*-back task; shown here is a 3-back task) or to a particular target (the oddball task). In the go/no-go paradigm, subjects respond to most stimuli but must inhibit responses to others.

13.13 evoke transient fMRI activity, perhaps related to moment-to-moment response selection or behavioral monitoring processes, the performance of such tasks itself evokes sustained executive processes that can be studied using blocked designs. Blocked *n*-back tasks, in particular, have been used in a number of studies investigating the manipulation of information in working memory. Because of the importance of both event-related and blocked approaches for different components of executive function, mixed designs will likely be important for future studies.

While most fMRI executive processing research uses tasks derived from other modalities, like oddball or delayed-match-to-sample, a new and growing area of research employs event-related tasks derived from real-world sit-

(A)

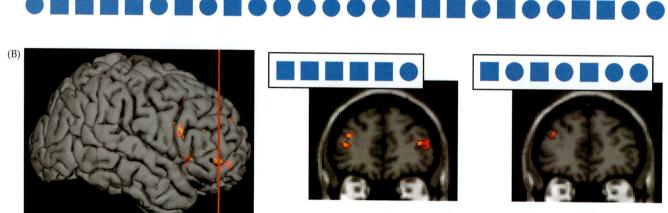

(B)

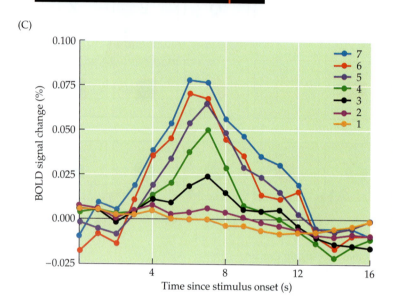

(C)

Figure 13.14 Studying sequence effects using event-related fMRI. A central aspect of executive function is the changing of behavior based upon context. Subjects were presented with a random series of two stimuli (excerpt shown in A), each stimulus requiring a different button press. Within that random sequence, short-term patterns arose by chance, and activity in response to events that violated the patterns was measured. Shown in (B) are coronal slices at the plane shown at left; the areas in the lateral prefrontal cortex were more active in response to events that violated repeating (middle) and alternating patterns (right). The magnitude of activity in these regions increased with increasing length of the previous pattern (C), demonstrating the profound effect that context has upon executive function. (From Huettel et al., 2002.)

ecological validity The degree to which the processes studied in an experiment are similar to those produced in the natural environment.

uations. The degree to which an experiment maps onto real-world situations is known as its **ecological validity.** As an example, in most psychological experiments, research subjects may receive some payment for performing a decision or memory task, but their payment is not directly correlated to that performance. Yet outside of the laboratory, our actions often have very real consequences, as when we decide at which restaurant to eat or we remember (or forget) a loved one's birthday. Some topics, like memory, may be best studied using tasks with low ecological validity but high experimental control. However, it is difficult, if not impossible, to map the brain systems underlying decision making without using stimuli (like real monetary payments) that evoke meaningful decisions. In 2002, Pochon and colleagues studied the interaction between executive processes and reward by testing subjects in an *n*-back task in which different trials had different reward values (totaling to $285, across all trials). Their fMRI results demonstrated that different sets of brain regions were sensitive to task difficulty and to task reward, as shown in Figure 13.15A–D. The use of fMRI to study the brain systems for processing expectancy for rewards has become increasingly

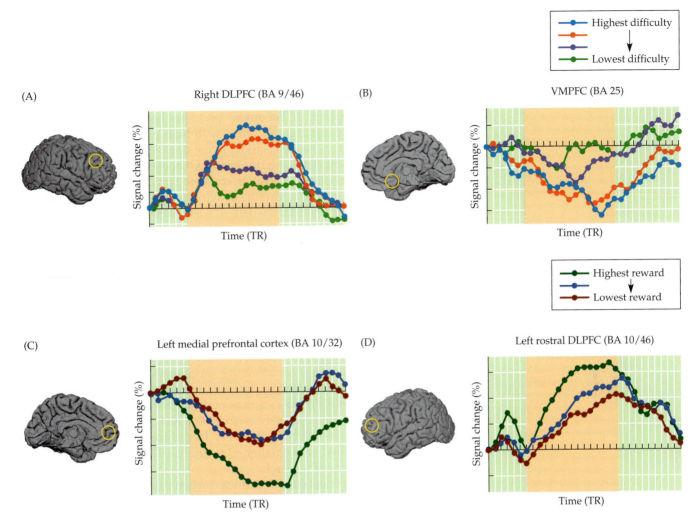

Figure 13.15 Different regions show increases in activity for task difficulty and reward. An fMRI *n*-back task with both difficulty and reward varying over trials was conducted. A system of prefrontal, parietal, and cerebellar regions showed changes in activity with task difficulty. For example, activity in the right dorsolateral prefrontal cortex (DLPFC) increased with increasing difficulty (A), while activity in the bilateral ventromedial prefrontal cortex (VMPFC) decreased with task difficulty (B). A different set of regions including the frontal, cingular, insular, and temporal cortices and the basal ganglia showed changes in activity associated with reward. In the left medial prefrontal cortex, activity decreased with increasing reward (C), while in the left rostral dorsolateral prefrontal cortex, activity increased with increasing reward (D). (From Pochon et al., 2002.)

common over the past several years, as researchers have extended results from single-unit studies in primates to fMRI studies in humans (see Montague and Berns for a review).

game theory A set of mathematical approaches for studying choices made by individuals in cooperative or competitive social situations.

Thought Question

Why are studies with high ecological validity preferred to those with low ecological validity?

Another way to improve ecological validity is to cloak decisions in social contexts, as by having subjects cooperate or compete with other individuals. A small but growing number of studies have used **game theory,** a mathe-

meta-analysis The statistical analysis of data collected from multiple experiments.

matical framework relating choices in social situations to expected rewards. In a 2003 fMRI study by Sanfey and colleagues, subjects played an "ultimatum game" with a series of human and computer opponents. In this game, each opponent makes a monetary offer to the subject; some offers are fair and some are unfair. The subject chooses whether to accept or reject each offer; however, the consequences of rejecting an offer ($0) are always worse than those of accepting it. Yet many previous behavioral studies have revealed that people reject unfair offers with high probability. The authors found that unfair offers evoked activity in the dorsolateral prefrontal cortex, anterior cingulate gyrus, and anterior insula. Of note was a trade-off between activity in the prefrontal and insular cortices. For unfair offers that were accepted, there was greater prefrontal activity than insular activity, while for unfair offers that were rejected, the pattern was reversed. This study points to the potential utility of fMRI for studies typically thought to be the domain of economics rather than psychology. A number of laboratories have begun exploring ways in which people inside the MRI scanner can interact with other individuals, so that the neural correlates of social behavior, including social decision making, can be explored.

Finally, because of the number of different executive processing tasks that have been used, synthesis of information across experiments is extremely important. One experimenter may describe activity in terms of response selection, another in terms of working memory, and another in terms of task switching, even when they are all doing variations of the oddball task. An important tool for synthesizing findings across the literature is **meta-analysis,** or combining results from a number of different studies (usually already published) into a single new analysis. In 2000, Cabeza and Nyberg reported a comprehensive meta-analysis of a very large number of fMRI and PET studies (Figure 13.16A), and smaller meta-analyses have been reported for many individual areas of research.

Meta-analyses are most easily conducted when studies report their results in a common form. Neuroimaging approaches, like both PET and fMRI, typically report their results in one or both of two forms: the spatial coordinates of activity within a stereotaxic space (e.g., Montreal Neurological Institute, Talairach) or the containing region in a cytoarchitectonic system (e.g., Brodmann's areas). If a study found activity in the middle frontal gyrus, for example, it might report that activity as occurring at coordinates $x = -42$, $y = 32$, and $z = 32$, or that it was present in Brodmann's area 46. By looking for commonalities across multiple studies, researchers can uncover general principles that span multiple tasks. For example, in their meta-analysis of executive function studies conducted using PET and fMRI, Duncan and Owen combined data from 20 separate experiments (Figure 13.16B). Although the exact foci of activity differed across studies, the authors found that they tended to cluster in three primary regions: the mid-dorsolateral frontal cortex, mid-ventrolateral frontal cortex, and dorsal anterior cingulate cortex. One important caveat for meta-analytic strategies is that, by reducing neuroimaging data to a set of activation locations, they ignore other information from the original studies, such as the timing of activity.

In summary, the study of executive processing faces particular challenges. Executive functions are supported by distributed brain systems, and the tasks used to study executive processing are often complex, rapidly presented, open-ended, and/or realistic. The strengths of fMRI are well suited to meet these challenges. Because of the difficulty in defining executive processes, we anticipate that collection of converging data across many studies using different paradigms will play a large role in future advances.

(A)

Working Memory		Frontal										Cingulate				Parietal			Temporal								Occip			Subcort		
Study	Contrast	10	9	46	11	47	45	44	6	8	4	32	24	23	31	7	40	39	38	ins	42	22	21	20	mt	37	19	18	17	bg	th	cb
Object																																
Haxby 95	face: hold 21 sec – sm	○				○						□						○				○										
Courtney 97	face: hold 8 sec (regressor)		□	□		□	□	□																	□		□	□				*
Courtney 96	face: hold 3 – sm		●	●	●	●	○					*	*															□				*
Smith 95-1	shape: hold – match						○					*	*															○				
Petrides 93a	shape: SOP – match		○	□					●			*					□										□					
Belger 98-1	shape: hold – ctrl		●	□																							□					
Elliot 98b	shape/col conj: hold – sm						○	○				□				□	○										□	□	□		○	○
Klingberg 97	patt: altern match – simple		●						◼								●															
Owen 98	patt: 1 back – sm								●	□									□			●	●			○						
McCarthy 96	*shape: det rep – sm*			□			○																									

Perception		Frontal										Cingulate				Parietal			Temporal								Occip			Subcort		
Study	Contrast	10	9	46	11	47	45	44	6	8	4	32	24	23	31	7	40	39	38	ins	42	22	21	20	mt	37	19	18	17	bg	th	cb
Face																																
Grady 94-1	face: match – sm																										□	□	□			
Haxby 94	face: face match – sm				●	●	●																					□				
Haxby 95	face: hold 1 sec – sm		●	●	●	●	□													○					●			□				□
Sergent 92a	face: gender – gratings																											●				
N. Kapur 95a	face: gender – rest																								●			□	□			
Puce 95	face: face – scrambled																							□			□	□				
Clark 96	face: match – sm															●											●					
Puce 96	face: face – left																										□	□				
Kanwisher 97a	*face: face – obj*																										□					
McCarthy 97	*(obj + face) – obj*																										□					
Clark 98	face: novel/targ – scrambled																										●					

(B)

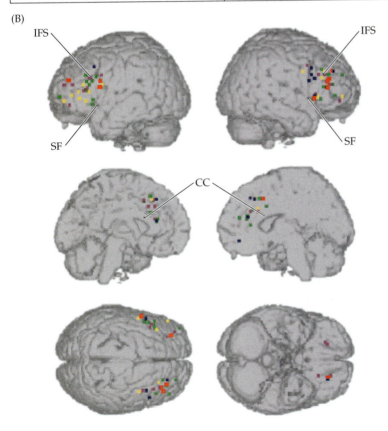

Figure 13.16 (A) Meta-analysis across anatomical regions. Meta-analyses combine data from multiple studies in order to improve detection power or generalizability of the results. One form of meta-analysis for neuroimaging data codes studies by whether they found activity in particular anatomical regions, here broken down by Brodmann areas. The upper table shows a meta-analysis of one type of executive function research, studies of working memory, which show activity predominantly in frontal, cingulate, and parietal regions. For comparison, the lower table shows studies of perception, which most frequently show activity in temporal and occipital regions. (B) Voxel-based meta-analysis. Another way of doing meta-analyses of neuroimaging data is to map activation coordinates. In the meta-analysis reported by Duncan and Owen, a number of different executive processing studies are mapped onto a standardized brain, revealing clusters of activity in the dorsolateral prefrontal cortex (around the inferior frontal sulcus; IFS), ventrolateral prefrontal cortex (above the Sylvian fissure; SF), and anterior cingulate cortex (CC). (A from Cabeza and Nyberg, 2000; B from Duncan and Owen, 2000.)

BOX 13.2 Use of fMRI in Nonhuman Primates

The fMRI studies described so far in this book have been restricted to human subjects. Yet in principle, other animals could serve as research subjects. Within the past few years, a handful of laboratories have begun fMRI studies of nonhuman primates, primarily using the rhesus monkey (*Macaca mulatta*) and other macaques. Although fMRI is not necessary for in vivo study of the animal brain, given the power of intracranial electrophysiology, it does provide some important advantages (see the commentary written by Paradiso in 1999 for additional discussion). First, and most importantly, it can link human and animal research. In all fields of science, methodological advances can cause divisions that are based on techniques rather than topic. Researchers who conduct electrophysiological studies of decision making in monkeys may communicate with other monkey electrophysiologists but not with researchers using human neuroimaging. Studies using fMRI in monkeys can bridge the gap between human fMRI and monkey electrophysiology, allowing their results to be more easily integrated. This may be particularly important for domains like vision, whose basic neural organization was established primarily using animal electrophysiology.

Second, it provides information that can complement the limitations of existing techniques. In many ways, intracranial electrophysiology is considered to provide the clearest evidence for the function of a brain region, in that implanted electrodes can provide direct information about neuronal activity. However, each electrode records signals from only a small brain region (in some cases a single neuron), and therefore breadth of spatial coverage is sacrificed. Using fMRI to guide subsequent electrode placement could substantially improve the efficiency of electrophysiological re-

search. And, since fMRI does not require surgery (e.g., to implant electrodes), it may have some ethical advantages for some forms of exploratory research. Animal fMRI studies can also inform human fMRI studies, even though both brain anatomy and cognitive function differ between species. More data can be collected in animal fMRI studies than is typical for human research, given that the same animal could participate in a large number of experimental sessions. Thus, functional SNR could potentially be much higher in animal fMRI, benefiting studies with more experimental conditions or with parametric changes in an independent variable. FMRI in monkeys also provides an opportunity to introduce other concurrent manipulations, such as simultaneous electrophysiological recording, use of contrast agents, or evaluation of drug effects. While these manipulations may not be practical in human volunteers, they may be conducted under the guidelines for acceptable care and use of laboratory animals.

The first studies using fMRI in nonhuman primates were reported by 1998, by two groups who simultaneously conducted very similar experiments. Stefanacci and colleagues recorded fMRI BOLD data from the visual cortex of a rhesus monkey during a passive viewing task. The animal lay in a prone position within a specially designed "chair," which was itself contained within a local gradient coil inside a standard clinical 1.5-T MRI scanner (Figure 13.17). The animal's head was fixed into place using a headpost, so that it could look down the bore onto a display screen in front of it. Of note was the use of a mock scanner environment over a period of a month to familiarize the monkey with the confinement and noise levels of the scanner. During the scanning sessions, the monkey watched a video movie that was presented in a 16-s-on/16-s-off blocked design. The monkey also periodically

received a squirt of juice as reward for staying still during the session. Scanning procedures were generally similar to those used in human studies: gradient-echo EPI with a 1-s TR and a 40-ms TE. The authors found significant activation in occipital visual regions, as well as in higher visual regions within the superior temporal gyrus. A second study by Dubowitz and colleagues used a very similar apparatus and visual stimulation paradigm. Their results mirrored those of Stefanacci and colleagues, in that they were able to identify regions of significant activity in the visual cortex.

Though highly exploratory, these early studies demonstrated the feasibility of collecting BOLD fMRI data in monkeys. Subsequent studies from these groups and others replicated these results, while suggesting topics for future research. One area that holds particular promise is the use of exogenous contrast agents to increase SNR. Recall from Chapter 7 that injection of a highly paramagnetic substance into the bloodstream causes susceptibility-related signal loss on T_2^*-weighted images. Because the magnitude of this signal loss depends upon the total amount of the contrast agent that is present in a voxel, it serves as an index of local cerebral blood volume. While exogenous contrast agents are not practical for most human fMRI studies, given the noninvasiveness of standard BOLD measurement, they may offer significant advantages for studies in nonhuman animals. As an example, a 2002 study by Leite and colleagues demonstrated that the use of an exogenous contrast agent (monocrystalline iron oxide nanoparticles, or MIONs) increased functional sensitivity by a factor of 2 to 3 over BOLD contrast, depending upon the experimental design. Another important research domain lies in using animal fMRI models to improve understanding of the basic principles of BOLD fMRI.

BOX 13.2 *(continued)*

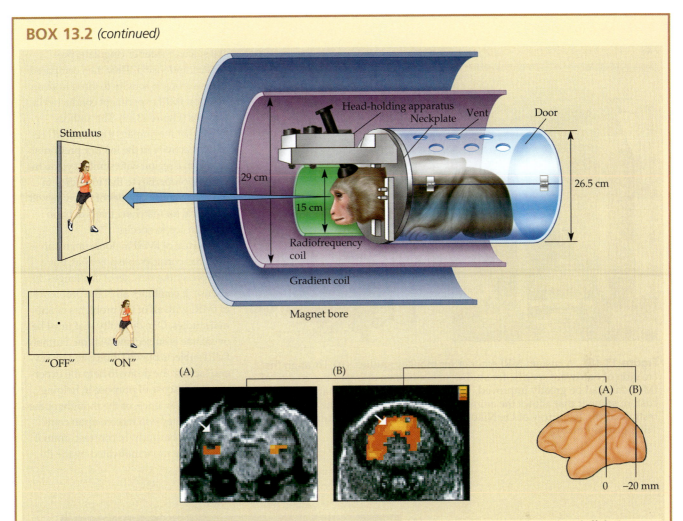

Figure 13.17 Collecting fMRI data in the monkey. Using fMRI with nonhuman animals poses problems, particularly when they are awake and performing a task. This figure shows one of the first successful fMRI experiments using monkeys. A rhesus macaque monkey was placed in a special primate chair that was turned sideways to fit into the bore of a standard human 1.5-T scanner (top). The animal watched a movie presented in a blocked on/off design. Significant BOLD activity was found in the temporal (A) and occipital (B) lobes. Researchers noted that there were substantial problems with head motion, due in part to the use of scanning and restraint hardware that were not designed specifically for monkey fMRI. (From Stefanacci et al., 1998.)

In a series of experiments, Logothetis and colleagues have investigated the relation between hemodynamic and electrophysiological measures of brain activity, using concurrent fMRI and ERP/EEG measures. While we discuss the results of these studies in detail in Chapter 15, one of their technical advances should be noted here, namely a custom vertical-bore MRI scanner designed specifically for use with monkeys (Figure 13.18). Several other institutions have installed monkey-specific scanners in recent years.

Although nearly all fMRI studies in monkeys have studied basic sensory functioning, studies of more-advanced cognitive processes are also possible. A very interesting study of executive function, reported by Nakahara and colleagues in 2002, investigated the brain regions involved in shifting between response sets. An important hallmark of human prefrontal cortex damage is an inability to shift from one mode of responding to another, as demonstrated by behavioral impairments in the Wisconsin Card Sorting Test. In order to study set shifting in monkeys, Nakahara and colleagues developed a modified version of this test that two macaque monkeys (*Macaca fuscata*) performed within a standard clinical scanner. The authors found significant activity in response to category shifts in the monkeys' inferior prefrontal cortex, as well as in the intrapari-

BOX 13.2 *(continued)*

(A)

(B)

Figure 13.18   A custom MRI scanner for monkey studies. (A) Through the creation of hardware specific for studies of nonhuman animals, the quality of fMRI data can be greatly improved. Logothetis and colleagues have created a custom scanner that allows the animal to remain upright with the head restrained (B). (Courtesy of Dr. Nikos Logothetis, Max Planck Institute, Tübingen, Germany.)

etal sulcus, posterior cingulate, precuneus, and insula. They then compared these regions of activity to those from an identical fMRI experiment conducted in humans (Figure 13.19). The authors found that the humans also showed significant activity in the inferior prefrontal cortex, in a region with similar cytoarchitectonic properties to that identified in monkeys. Future studies of this type will be critical for matching maps of brain function across species.

The use of fMRI in nonhuman animals has considerable potential, but it also presents a new set of challenges. In a sense, it combines all of the problems of fMRI with all of the problems of animal studies. One difficulty that must be overcome is subject motivation. Human fMRI subjects may be motivated by several factors: the desire to help the experimenter, a sense of purpose in helping to advance science, or the thought of the payment they will receive upon completion of the study. In contrast, animal subjects are more motivated by the di-

Figure 13.19   Comparison of fMRI in monkey and human. A potentially exciting use of fMRI in monkeys is for direct comparison to human data. Data was collected from both macaque monkeys (A) and humans (B) in a variant of the Wisconsin Card Sorting Test (height of slices, z, shown in mm). In both species, there was significant activity in the bilateral inferior frontal cortex in response to stimuli that require a shift from one response set to another. This result suggests that these regions may be functionally homologous between the species. Note that the brain images are shown at different scales; the human brain has more than 10 times the volume of the macaque brain. (From Nakahara et al., 2002.)

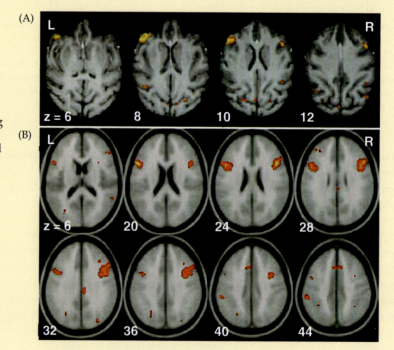

BOX 13.2 *(continued)*

rect rewards given for experimental compliance, such as squirts of juice. Though juice is a good reward system for behavioral studies, it is not ideal for fMRI. Swallowing a sip of juice requires contraction of muscles in the jaw and throat, which in turn causes both distortions in the local magnetic field and head motion. Even with a periodic reward, an animal may have difficulty remaining still. For example, in the study by Stefanacci and colleagues, a number of the experimental runs were severely corrupted by large head motions. The authors noted that this head motion may have been exacerbated by the limitations of using a clinical MRI scanner with a primate chair inserted within the bore, so dedicated monkey scanners

have the potential to minimize such problems.

Finally, we note that animal models themselves have limitations. Monkeys are similar to humans in overall brain organization, but they are expensive to maintain and test, and relatively few institutions have large colonies. A less expensive option is to move to rodents, as is most typical for behavioral neuroscientific studies. Rats are cheaper, are common, and perform many tasks well, but they have extremely small brains (about 2 cc). Most genetic manipulations have been performed in mice, making them good candidates for studies of the effects of specific genes upon brain function, but their brains are much smaller still (about 0.4 cc). To emphasize the

problem of scale involved with imaging a rodent brain, consider that at a voxel size typical for human studies, only about 30 voxels would be needed to contain the entire brain of a rat, and only about 6 would be needed for the brain of a mouse. Yet despite these limitations, several fMRI studies in rodents have been conducted using ultra-high-field scanners. These studies have generated exquisite maps of sensory cortices, as exemplified by the work of Xu and colleagues in the olfactory bulb of the rat. Thus, fMRI studies of nonhuman primates and other animals are likely to become increasingly important, both for improving understanding of brain function and for clarifying the basic physiological mechanisms of fMRI.

Consciousness

Of all the terms used by psychologists, the idea of consciousness is the most poorly defined. It can mean wakefulness, as in "He regained consciousness within a few minutes of the accident." It can describe the belief system of a group of people: "The idea of personal freedom began to enter the popular consciousness following the revolution." Or it can mean something in between, like personal awareness: "I became conscious of the ringing phone, and walked across the room to answer it." It is the last of these conceptions, that of personal subjective experience, that has proven the most vexing for scientists.

To understand why consciousness is so difficult to study, look up from this book and out at the world around you. Depending on your location, you may see desks in a classroom, stacks of books in a library, or, if you are fortunate enough to be reading this book outside on a warm spring afternoon, white clouds drifting across a blue sky. Now pick an object, any object. What is its color? As you are staring at the object, a series of physical processes take place. Photons from an external light source, whether the sun or a nearby lamp, reflect off of the object. Some of those photons collide with photoreceptors in your eye, where they induce chemical changes in particular photopigments, depending upon their frequency. This results in electrical activity within the photoreceptors, which in turn propagates from the eye via the thalamus to the primary visual cortex, and from there on to higher cortical centers for vision. Though the details are amazingly complex, it is important to recognize that the series of processes that take place when you see the color blue are different from those when you see the color red. By mapping these two sets of processes, one could, in principle, recognize those aspects of brain function that differ according to what color is consciously experienced. However, consciousness poses a second, much more insidious problem. Think about the physical steps that seem to all add up to your experience of blue. Which of those steps make it possible for *you* to actually

easy problem A research question that can be addressed, in principle, using existing experimental methods.

hard problem A research question that cannot be answered, even in principle, by existing experimental methods and scientific principles.

neural correlates Patterns of brain activity that covary with another phenomenon, such as a mental state or behavior.

binocular rivalry The alternation of images presented independently to each eye.

experience blueness? Put another way, how can low-level information processing in the brain actually translate into your awareness of the world around you?

The philosopher David Chalmers has labeled these two problems of consciousness as **easy problems** and **hard problems.** Here, *easy* and *hard* do not refer to complexity or difficulty, in the same sense that a 1-digit multiplication problem is easy and a 10,000-digit multiplication problem is hard. Instead, these terms refer to the sorts of methods that can be applied for their solution. Easy problems are those dealing with the mechanisms of biological processes; they are easy because they can be explained in terms of lower-level physical principles. This chapter, and indeed this entire book, is filled with examples of fMRI being applied to easy problems. The hard problems of consciousness are those that relate to personal experience. No scientific principles exist that state how the firing of a neuron or the release of a neurotransmitter can generate a feeling, emotion, or sensation. How then can fMRI be applied to address the hard problems of consciousness? One approach that has been pursued by many investigators rests on the idea of **neural correlates** of consciousness; a neural correlate is a marker in the brain that may index consciousness, even if the causal relations between them are unknown (see also Box 1.1). By looking for neural correlates of consciousness, researchers can transform hard problems into easy ones, bypassing questions about how subjective experience can arise from objective, physical activity. As will be evident from the following examples, nearly all fMRI studies of consciousness have focused on visual experience.

> ### Thought Question
>
> Do you believe that there are aspects of the mind that cannot be addressed by science, even in principle? How would you defend your position against someone with the opposite perspective?

Thus, the basic framework used by most fMRI studies of consciousness is simple. The experimenter induces a change in the experience of the subject, then measures the patterns of activity associated with those changes. Ideally, this change in experience is accompanied by minimal perceptual changes, to reduce the likelihood of confounding factors. A good example of this approach is found in a clever study conducted by Tong and colleagues in 1998, which investigated the effects of **binocular rivalry** upon activity in extrastriate visual cortex (Figure 13.20). Binocular rivalry occurs when the two eyes see different visual displays, as when one sees a horizontal bar and the other a vertical bar. Rather than combine the displays into a single image (e.g., a plus symbol), the visual system switches between the two rivalrous images, usually every few seconds, so that sometimes you see one image and sometimes the other. The subjects in this study viewed pictures of faces in one eye and houses in the other eye and indicated when the display switched from one stimulus type to the other (Figure 13.20A).

While the physical display does not change during these switches, the contents of conscious experience do change, and those changes evoked systematic variation in visual cortical activity. Face-to-house switches were associated with decreased activity in the fusiform gyrus and increased activ-

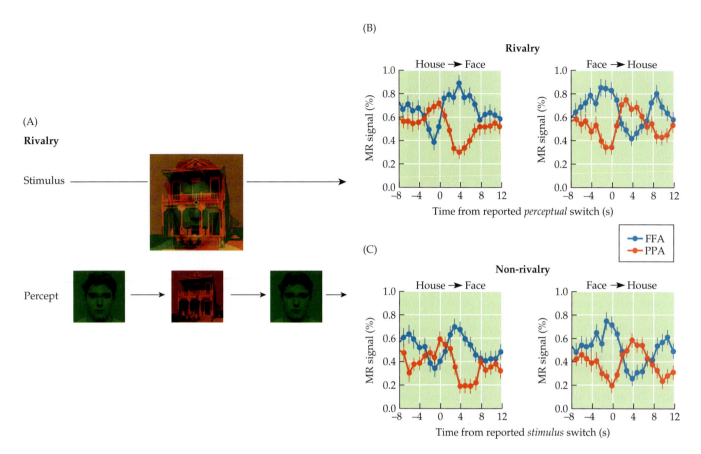

Figure 13.20   Relating brain activity to perceptual experience. One way to investigate the neural correlates of consciousness is to relate changes in brain activity to changes in experience. In this figure, a binocular rivalry paradigm is used (A), in which one eye saw a face and the other eye saw a house, so that the subject's perception alternated frequently between faces and houses. fMRI activity in face-selective regions (FFA) and place-selective regions (PPA) followed the subject's report of rivalrous switches from one stimulus type to another, as shown in (B). The time courses of activity in response to perceptual switches (where the stimulus did not change) were similar to those in a control condition in which the display in both eyes actually alternated between houses and faces (C). (From Tong et al., 1998.)

ity in the parahippocampal gyrus, while house-to-face switches resulted in the opposite pattern of activity (Figure 13.20B). These activity changes therefore represent a correlate of conscious experience, not merely a passive reflection of visual input. A control condition compared these results to real alternations between faces and houses in a non-rivalry paradigm, with the timing of switches matched to the rivalry condition. It found that subjective switches and real switches evoked very similar patterns of activity (Figure 13.20C). Note that this particular design could not be implemented with PET, because the brain must be sampled at a faster rate than the frequency of switching. Similar approaches have been used for studies of attention, illusory perception, emotion, and imagery.

A second framework adopts the reverse approach: using **subthreshold stimuli,** the experimenter identifies what sorts of brain changes can occur in the absence of conscious experience. To present visual stimuli without inducing awareness, researchers often use a masking paradigm, in which the stimuli of interest are shown for only a short duration (<50 ms) and are followed by a complex visual image. In 1998, Whalen and colleagues used such a mask-

subthreshold stimuli Stimuli presented below the threshold for detection. In psychophysics, the threshold is also known as the limen, and thus subthreshold stimuli are also known as subliminal stimuli.

(A)

(B)

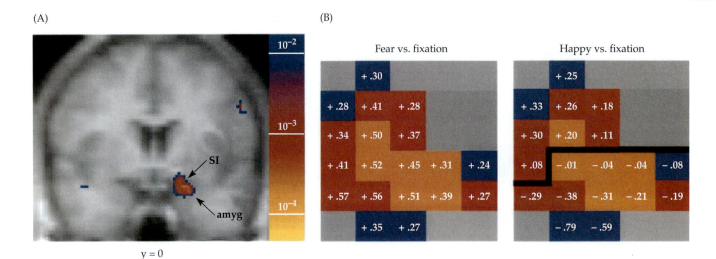

y = 0

Figure 13.21 Activation in the amygdala in response to unconsciously perceived faces. Subjects viewed face stimuli with fearful or happy expressions for a very short duration (33 ms), followed by a masking neutral-expression face (167 ms). Subjects reported seeing only the neutral-expression faces, and not any of the emotional faces. However, fMRI activity in the amygdala (A), a region important for emotion, was significantly greater for fearful faces than for happy faces. The activity also extended into the adjacent substantia innominata (SI). When researchers looked at specific voxels within the amygdala (B), they found an interesting dissocia-tion between its dorsal and ventral parts. In the dorsal part of the amygdala, there was significant activity in response to both fearful and happy faces, although there was more activi-ty following the fearful-face stimuli. But in the ventral part, there was no activity in response to the happy-face stimuli. The researchers suggested that this represents a functional division based on emotional content within the amygdala. The colors represent significance levels for the fearful-versus-happy comparison, and the numbers represent the percent BOLD signal change in the indicated condition. (From Whalen et al., 1998.)

ing approach for their fMRI study of unconscious processing of emotional expressions. They presented faces with an emotional expression (happy or fearful) for 33 ms, followed immediately by faces with a neutral expression for 167 ms. When questioned after the experiment, most of the subjects reported no knowledge of the emotional faces. Yet there was more activity in the amyg-dala, a medial temporal structure that supports emotional processing, in response to the fearful faces than to the happy faces (Figure 13.21A and B).

An interesting comparison between subthreshold and superthreshold perception was reported in 2001 by Beck and colleagues, who employed a change blindness paradigm to examine processing in dorsal and ventral pathways. Normally, the human visual system is very good at detecting changes, a fact capitalized upon by innumerable warning systems. If a change is hidden by a visual mask or is cloaked by attention elsewhere, however, it becomes extremely difficult to detect (for interesting examples, see the work of Rensink and of Simons, and their colleagues). Beck and col-leagues required subjects to perform a difficult letter judgment task while simultaneously attending to changes in adjacent visual stimuli (faces and outdoor scenes). They used fMRI to compare activity between trials where changes were detected (change detection) and trials where changes occurred but were not detected (change blindness). They found that change detection evoked activity in the fusiform gyrus, parietal cortex, and dorsolateral pre-frontal cortex, while change blindness only evoked weak activity in the fusiform gyrus and neighboring visual areas. These results suggest that activity in the dorsal visual pathway may be necessary for visual awareness, complementing studies of the ventral visual pathway like that by Tong and colleagues described earlier.

FMRI studies can also be used to improve understanding of disorders of consciousness. Patients with lesions to part of the primary visual cortex report that they cannot see stimuli presented in the part of the visual field corresponding to their lesion. However, in some cases they can guess characteristics of the stimuli with considerable accuracy. This phenomenon has been given the evocative name **blindsight** to describe the dissociation between the patients' experience and apparent information processing by the visual system. In 2001, using fMRI, Goebel and colleagues demonstrated that stimuli presented within the blindsight area evoke activity in higher visual regions. While stimuli evoked no BOLD activity in the damaged V1 area, a rotating spiral evoked activity in motion area V5 and objects evoked activity in the lateral occipital cortex and fusiform gyrus. These fMRI results extend the decades-old patient studies by showing that activity in extrastriate regions is not sufficient for visual awareness; activity in the primary visual cortex is also required. Another interesting disorder is Charles Bonnet syndrome, in which patients with visual impairments experience vivid and animated hallucinations, such as mosaic patterns of lines, common animals, or fantastic creatures. Using event-related fMRI, ffytche and colleagues showed that there were significant increases in activity in the fusiform gyrus during the period of hallucination, and there were suggestions that the content of the hallucinations governed the location of activity. These two studies point to the potential value of combined fMRI and lesion studies for refining theories about consciousness.

blindsight A phenomenon in which individuals with cortical damage have no experience of visual stimuli within the damaged part of the visual field, but can nevertheless report the characteristics of those stimuli under particular conditions.

Summary

Functional MRI studies have made substantial contributions to the understanding of the mind and brain. Replication of existing results, as early studies typically accomplished, validated the feasibility of fMRI research. But as fMRI became more established, replication gave way to extension. Researchers asked new questions about human cognition or functional relations between brain regions that were difficult to answer with earlier methods. By the late 1990s, fMRI had made profound contributions to the democratization of cognitive neuroscience, making the brain more accessible to researchers and the public alike. While fMRI has had a substantial impact on a number of topic areas, perhaps the most visible advances have been made in the understanding of higher cognitive processes, including attention, memory, and executive function. Each of these domains has been shaped by results from fMRI, although other techniques remain of considerable interest. Even that most nebulous of all psychological topics, consciousness, has been attacked with some success. Despite many studies, however, fundamental questions remain about how fMRI can illuminate the relation between cognitive functions and brain activity.

Suggested Readings

Brett, M., Johnsrude, I. S., and Owen, A. M. (2002). The problem of functional localization in the human brain. *Nat. Rev. Neurosci.*, 3: 243–249. The authors describe, in clear language, the technical and theoretical issues facing attempts to localize brain activity using neuroimaging.

*Buckner, R. L., and Wheeler, M. E. (2001). The cognitive neuroscience of remembering. *Nat. Rev. Neurosci.*, 2: 624–634. A comprehensive review of studies of memory retrieval, including many using fMRI.

Gazzaniga, M. S., Ivry, R. B., and Mangun, G. R. (2002). *Cognitive Neuroscience.* Norton, New York. This accessible textbook provides a good introduction to the field of cognitive neuroscience, including all of the topics discussed in this chapter.

*Nakahara, K., Hayashi, T., Konishi, S., and Miyashita, Y. (2002). Functional MRI of macaque monkeys performing a cognitive set-shifting task. *Science,* 295: 1532–1536. This report contains an extremely interesting comparison between human and monkey fMRI data.

*Passingham, R. E., Stephan, K. E., and Kotter, R. (2002). The anatomical basis of functional localization in the cortex. *Nat. Rev. Neurosci.,* 3: 606–616. An interesting and provocative review of the relation between anatomical connectivity and brain function.

Rees, G., Kreiman, G., and Koch, C. (2002). Neural correlates of consciousness in humans. *Nat. Rev. Neurosci.,* 3: 264–270. A good review article describing attempts to map correlates of consciousness, notably of visual experience.

Indicates a reference that is a suggested reading in the field and is also cited in this chapter.

Chapter References

Arfanakis, K., Cordes, D., Haughton, V. M., Moritz, C. H., Quigley, M. A., and Meyerand, M. E. (2000). Combining independent component analysis and correlation analysis to probe interregional connectivity in fMRI task activation datasets. *Magn. Reson. Imaging,* 18: 921–930.

Beck, D. M., Rees, G., Frith, C. D., and Lavie, N. (2001). Neural correlates of change detection and change blindness. *Nat. Neurosci.,* 4: 645–650.

Biswal, B. B., Van Kylen, J., and Hyde, J. S. (1997). Simultaneous assessment of flow and BOLD signals in resting-state functional connectivity maps. *NMR Biomed.,* 10: 165–170.

Biswal, B., Yetkin, F. Z., Haughton, V. M., and Hyde, J. S. (1995). Functional connectivity in the motor cortex of resting human brain using echo-planar MRI. *Magn. Reson. Med.,* 34: 537–541.

Buchel, C., and Friston, K. J. (1997). Modulation of connectivity in visual pathways by attention: Cortical interactions evaluated with structural equation modelling and fMRI. *Cereb. Cortex,* 7: 768–778.

Buckner, R. L. (2000). Neuroimaging of memory. In *The New Cognitive Neurosciences,* M. S. Gazzaniga (ed.), pp. 817–828. MIT Press, Cambridge, MA.

Burock, M. A., Buckner, R. L., Woldorff, M. G., Rosen, B. R., and Dale, A. M. (1998). Randomized event-related experimental designs allow for extremely rapid presentation rates using functional MRI. *NeuroReport,* 9: 3735–3739.

Cabeza, R., and Nyberg, L. (2000). Imaging cognition II: An empirical review of 275 PET and fMRI studies. *J. Cogn. Neurosci.,* 12: 1–47.

Chalmers, D. J. (1996). Facing up to the problem of consciousness. In *Toward a Science of Consciousness,* S. R. Hameroff, A. W. Kaszniak, and A. C. Scott (eds.), pp. 5–28. MIT Press, Cambridge, MA.

Chen, W., Kato, T., Zhu, X. H., Ogawa, S., Tank, D. W., and Ugurbil, K. (1998). Human primary visual cortex and lateral geniculate nucleus activation during visual imagery. *NeuroReport,* 9: 3669–3674.

Corbetta, M., and Shulman, G. L. (2002). Control of goal-directed and stimulus-driven attention in the brain. *Nat. Rev. Neurosci.,* 3: 201–215.

Dubowitz, D. J., Chen, D. –Y., Atkinson, D. J., Grieve, K. L., Gillikin, B., Bradley, W. G., and Anderson, R. A. (1998). Functional magnetic resonance imaging in macaque cortex. *NeuroReport,* 9: 2213–2218.

Dubowitz, D. J., Chen, D., Atkinson, D. J., Scandeng, M., Martinez, A., Andersen, M. B., Andersen, R. A., and Bradley, W. G. (2001). Direct comparison of visual cortex activation in human and non-human primates using functional magnetic resonance imaging. *J. Neurosci.,* 107: 71–80.

Due, D. L., Huettel, S. A., Hall, W. G., and Rubin, D. C. (2002). Smoking cues elicit activation in mesolimbic and visuospatial neural circuits: Evidence from fMRI. *Am. J. Psychiatry*, 159: 954–960.

Duncan, J., and Owen, A. M. (2000). Common regions of the human frontal lobe recruited by diverse cognitive demands. *Trends Neurosci.*, 23: 475–483.

ffytche, D. H., Howard, R. J., Brammer, M. J., David, A., Woodruff, P., and William, S. (1998). The anatomy of conscious vision: An fMRI study of visual hallucinations. *Nat. Neurosci.*, 1: 738–740.

Finger, S. (1994). *Origins of Neuroscience.* Oxford University Press, New York.

Gabrieli, J. D., Brewer, J. B., Desmond, J. E., and Glover, G. H. (1997). Separate neural bases of two fundamental memory processes in the human medial temporal lobe. *Science*, 276: 264–266.

Goebel, R., Muckli, L., Zanella, F. E., Singer, W., and Stoerig, P. (2001). Sustained extrastriate cortical activation without visual awareness revealed by fMRI studies of hemianopic patients. *Vis. Res.*, 41: 1459–1474.

Grant, S., London, E. D., Newlin, D. B., Villemagne, V. L., Liu, X., Contoreggi, C., Phillips, R. L., Kimes, A. S., and Margolin, A. (1996). Activation of memory circuits during cue-elicited cocaine craving. *Proc. Natl. Acad. Sci. U.S.A.*, 93: 12040–12045.

Hampson, M., Peterson, B. S., Skudlarski, P., Gatenby, J. C., and Gore, J. C. (2002). Detection of functional connectivity using temporal correlations in MR images. *Hum. Brain Mapping*, 15: 247–262.

Handy, T. C., Grafton, S. T., Shroff, N. M., Ketay, S., and Gazzaniga, M. S. (2003). Graspable objects grab attention when the potential for action is recognized. *Nat. Neurosci.*, 6: 421–427.

Henson, R. N., Rugg, M. D., Shallice, T., Josephs, O., and Dolan, R. J. (1999). Recollection and familiarity in recognition memory: An event-related functional magnetic resonance imaging study. *J. Neurosci.*, 19: 3962–3972.

Hinrichs, H., Scholz, M., Tempelmann, C., Woldorff, M. G., Dale, A. M., and Heinze, H. J. (2000). Deconvolution of event-related fMRI responses in fast-rate experimental designs: Tracking amplitude variations [erratum appears in *J. Cogn. Neurosci.*, 2000, 12(6), following table of contents]. *J. Cogn. Neurosci.*, 12: 76–89.

Hopfinger, J. B., Buonocore, M. H., and Mangun, G. R. (2000). The neural mechanisms of top-down attentional control. *Nat. Neurosci.*, 3: 284–291.

Horwitz, B., Rumsey, J. M., and Donohue, B. C. (1998). Functional connectivity of the angular gyrus in normal reading and dyslexia. *Proc. Natl. Acad. Sci. U.S.A.*, 95: 8939–8944.

Huettel, S. A., Güzeldere, G., and McCarthy, G. (2001). Dissociating the neural mechanisms of visual attention in change detection using functional MRI. *J. Cogn. Neurosci.*, 13: 1006–1018.

Huettel, S. A., Mack, P. B., and McCarthy, G. (2002). Perceiving patterns in random series: Dynamic processing of sequence in prefrontal cortex. *Nat. Neurosci.*, 5: 485–490.

James, W. (1890). *The Principles of Psychology.* Dover, New York.

LaBar, K. S., Gatenby, J. C., Gore, J. C., LeDoux, J. E., and Phelps, E. A. (1998). Human amygdala activation during conditioned fear acquisition and extinction: A mixed-trial fMRI study. *Neuron*, 20: 937–945.

Leite, F. P., Tsao, D., Vanduffel, W., Fize, D., Sasaki, Y., Wald, L. L., Dale, A. M., Kwong, K. K., Orban, G. A., Rosen, B. R., Tootell, R. B., and Mandeville, J. B. (2002). Repeated fMRI using iron oxide contrast agent in awake behaving macaques at 3 Tesla. *NeuroImage*, 16: 283–294.

Logothetis, N. K., Pauls, J., Augath, M., Trinath, T., and Oeltermann, A. (2001). Neurophysiological investigation of the basis of the fMRI signal. *Nature*, 412: 150–157.

Mandeville, J. B., Marota, J. J., Kosofsky, B. E., Keltner, J. R., Weissleder, R., Rosen, B. R., and Weisskoff, R. M. (1998). Dynamic functional imaging of relative cerebral blood volume during rat forepaw stimulation. *Magn. Reson. Med.*, 39: 615–624.

Martinez, A., Anllo-Vento, L., Sereno, M. I., Frank, L. R., Buxton, R. B., Dubowitz, D. J., Wong, E. C., Hinrichs, H., Heinze, H. J., and Hillyard, S. A. (1999). Involvement of striate and extrastriate visual cortical areas in spatial attention. *Nat. Neurosci.*, 2: 364–369.

McIntosh, A. R., Bookstein, F. L., Haxby, J. V., and Grady, C. L. (1996). Spatial pattern analysis of functional brain images using partial least squares. *NeuroImage*, 3: 143–157.

Miller, E. K., and Cohen, J. D. (2001). An integrative theory of prefrontal cortex function. *Annu. Rev. Neurosci.*, 24: 167–202.

Montague, P. R., and Berns, G. S. (2002). Neural economics and the biological substrates of valuation. *Neuron*, 36: 265–284.

Paller, K. A., and Wagner, A. D. (2002). Observing the transformation of experience into memory. *Trends Cogn. Sci.*, 6: 93–102.

Paradiso, M. A. (1999). Monkey business builds a bridge to the human brain. *Nat. Neurosci.*, 2: 491–492.

Pochon, J. B., Levy, R., Fossati, P., Lehericy, S., Poline, J. B., Pillon, B., Le Bihan, D., and Dubois, B. (2002). The neural system that bridges reward and cognition in humans: An fMRI study. *Proc. Natl. Acad. Sci. U.S.A.*, 99: 5660–5674.

Posner, M. I., and Raichle, M. E. (1994). *Images of Mind.* Scientific American Library, New York.

Ranganath, C., and Rainer, G. (2003). Neural mechanisms for detecting and remembering novel events. *Nat. Rev. Neurosci.*, 4: 193–202.

Rees, G., Wojciulik, E., Clarke, K., Husain, M., Frith, C., and Driver, J. (2000). Unconscious activation of visual cortex in the damaged right hemisphere of a parietal patient with extinction. *Brain*, 123: 1624–1633.

Rensink, R. A., O'Regan, J. K., and Clark, J. J. (1997). To see or not to see: The need for attention to perceive changes in scenes. *Psychol. Sci.*, 8: 368–373.

Sanfey, A. G., Rilling, J. K., Aronson, J. A., Nystrom, L. E., and Cohen, J. D. (2003). The neural basis of economic decision-making in the Ultimatum Game. *Science*, 300: 1755–1758.

Schneider, F., Habel, U., Wagner, M., Franke, P., Salloum, J. B., Shah, N. J., Toni, I., Sulzbach, C., Honig, K., Maier, W., Gaebel, W., and Zilles, K. (2001). Subcortical correlates of craving in recently abstinent alcoholic patients. *Am. J. Psychiatry*, 158: 1075–1083.

Sheline, Y. I., Barch, D. M., Donnelly, J. M., Ollinger, J. M., Snyder, A. Z., and Mintun, M. A. (2001). Increased amygdala response to masked emotional faces in depressed subjects resolves with antidepressant treatment: An fMRI study. *Biol. Psychiatry*, 50: 651–658.

Simons, D. J., and Chabris, C. F. (1999). Gorillas in our midst: Sustained inattentional blindness for dynamic events. *Perception*, 28: 1059–1074.

Small, D. M., Gitelman, D. R., Gregory, M. D., Nobre, A. C., Parrish, T. B., and Mesulam, M. M. (2003). The posterior cingulate and medial prefrontal cortex mediate the anticipatory allocation of spatial attention. *NeuroImage*, 18: 633–641.

Somers, D. C., Dale, A. M., Seiffert, A. E., and Tootell, R. B. (1999). Functional MRI reveals spatially specific attentional modulation in human primary visual cortex. *Proc. Natl. Acad. Sci. U.S.A.*, 96: 1663–1668.

Squire, L. R., and Knowlton, B. J. (2000). The medial temporal lobe, the hippocampus, and the memory systems of the brain. In *The New Cognitive Neurosciences*, M. S. Gazzaniga (ed.), pp. 765–779. MIT Press, Cambridge, MA.

Stefanacci, L., Reber, P., Costanza, J., Wong, E., Buxton, R., Zola, S., Squire, L., and Albright, T. (1998). fMRI of monkey visual cortex. *Neuron*, 20: 1051–1057.

Tong, F., Nakayama, K., Vaighan, J. T., and Kanwisher, N. (1998). Binocular rivalry and visual awareness in human extrastriate cortex. *Neuron*, 21: 753–759.

Tong, F. (2003). Primary visual cortex and visual awareness. *Nat. Rev. Neurosci.,* 4: 219–229.

Toni, I., Rowe, J., Stephan, K. E., and Passingham, R. E. (2002). Changes of cortico-striatal effective connectivity during visuomotor learning. *Cereb. Cortex,* 12: 1040–1047.

Tulving, E., Kapur, S., Craik, F. I., Moscovitch, M., and Houle, S. (1994). Hemispheric encoding/retrieval asymmetry in episodic memory: Positron emission tomography findings. *Proc. Natl. Acad. Sci. U.S.A.,* 91: 2016–2020.

Wagner, A. D., Schacter, D. L., Rotte, M., Koutstaal, W., Maril, A., Dale, A. M., Rosen, B. R., and Buckner, R. L. (1998). Building memories: Remembering and forgetting of verbal experiences as predicted by brain activity. *Science,* 281: 1188–1191.

Whalen, P. J., Rauch, S. L., Etcoff, N. L., McInerney, S. C., Lee, M. B., and Jenike, M. A. (1998). Masked presentations of emotional facial expressions modulate amygdala activity without explicit knowledge. *J. Neurosci.,* 18: 411–418.

Xiong, J., Parsons, L. M., Gao, J., and Fox, P. T. (1999). Interregional connectivity to primary motor cortex revealed using MRI resting state images. *Hum. Brain Mapping,* 8: 151–156.

Xu, F., Kida, I., Hyder, F., and Shulman, R. G. (2000). Assessment and discrimination of odor stimuli in rat olfactory bulb by dynamic fMRI. *Proc. Natl. Acad. Sci. U.S.A.,* 97: 10601–10606.

14

Advanced fMRI Methods

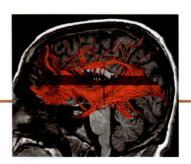

From their infancy in the early 1990s, fMRI methods have dramatically evolved. Many early studies acquired only one or two images, at slice acquisition rates as slow as one per 10 seconds. A primary goal of early studies was to provide proof-of-concept results, such as showing that the occipital lobe becomes active during a visual stimulation task, rather than to generate novel findings that were unexpected based on existing knowledge. Now, as fMRI research enters a period of adolescence, there has been an explosion of interest in studying a wide variety of cognitive processes beyond simple sensation, from attention to memory to decision making to consciousness. Fast event-related designs combined with advanced pulse sequences have enabled acquisition and analysis of subsecond changes throughout the brain. Though this growth has been extraordinary, it is important to recognize that fMRI remains a relatively young technique. Just like an adolescent, its grasp reaches out to an ever widening world, while its thoughts are directed inward toward its own limitations.

In this chapter, we present some of the major recent advances in image acquisition and analysis that promise to benefit future fMRI research. These advances have been driven by the desire to collect images at the highest possible spatial resolution and with the fastest possible acquisition speed, while maintaining sufficient spatial fidelity and functional SNR. We therefore have organized the discussion in this chapter thematically, separating advances that challenge the spatial limits of fMRI from those that test its temporal limits. It is important to recognize that the methods discussed in this chapter reflect but partial snapshots of promising research breakthroughs. Given the enormous number of laboratories that are currently pushing the bounds of fMRI, it would be impossible to document all advances. Our goal, instead, is to orient the reader to the likely directions of future progress, while conveying some of the breathlessness of the current pace of research. Not only do many important research questions remain unanswered, but we still do not know what limits (if any) restrict the questions that can be asked. It is truly a remarkable time to be doing fMRI research.

ultrahigh-resolution MRI The acquisition of MR images with voxel sizes on the order of tens of micrometers. Applications of ultrahigh-resolution MRI to animal tissue are known as MR microscopy.

Spatial Resolution and Spatial Fidelity

Although the most striking advantage of MRI over previous neuroimaging methods is its excellent spatial resolution, the possibility of further improvements has driven recent developments in pulse sequence design and imaging hardware. Increases in spatial resolution for anatomical MRI result in advantages for fMRI research. Remember that although BOLD fMRI measures a vascular response in the brain that may span a few centimeters, the vascular response is evoked by neuronal activity that may be organized on a sub-millimeter scale. The spatially restricted neuronal activity, not the more widespread vascular response, controls the flow of information in the brain. Therefore, improvements in the resolution of MRI down to the cellular level may have significant consequences for functional studies. We will refer to studies that attempt to resolve image details on the order of tens of micrometers as **ultrahigh-resolution MRI** or **MR microscopy.** Although we discuss here how ultrahigh-resolution MRI benefits research into brain structure and function, it has had significant consequences for other fields of science as well, including studies of gene expression, animal phenotype characterization, and stem cell migration. Because of the many advantages of ultrahigh-resolution MRI, laboratories investigating a number of diverse and interesting questions have pushed its spatial limits such that fine resolution at a cellular level is achievable.

Imagine the possibility of imaging a single neuron! To understand the challenge of such a task, consider that a typical fMRI voxel has dimensions of about 4 mm on a side, roughly similar to the size of the word "the" in this book. Yet within that tiny voxel exist more than a million neurons. The cell body, or soma, of a given neuron may be only a few tens of micrometers in diameter, while its axon may stretch only a few millimeters. Despite the challenges posed by such an extreme scale, there have been some promising results in anatomical MRI. In 1999, Dodd and colleagues, for example, used iron oxide as a contrast agent for imaging T cells, which are important components of the immune system. A single T cell is approximately 5 μm in diameter, or $1/200$ of a millimeter. In order to scan these cells directly, resolution on the order of 1 to 2 μm would be necessary. However, if highly paramagnetic iron oxide is introduced into the cells, much larger regions of susceptibility-induced signal loss will be measured on T_2^*-sensitive images. In a sense, this effect is very similar to the BOLD mechanism described in Chapter 7, but on a much smaller scale. The resulting susceptibility effects can be used as indicators of iron oxide and thus of the position of the cells. Using a small-bore scanner at 4.7 T, Dodd and colleagues collected images with extremely high resolution (voxel dimensions of about 25 μm on a side), and the position of T cells became clearly visible.

While this result, along with those from similar studies, has been extremely promising, it is important to note its limitations. Chief among them is that the use of iron oxide contrast does not allow identification of structure within a cell, as can be obtained with electron microscopes, but instead provides information about the location of cells. Note also that voxel volume decreases with the cube of spatial resolution, such that a voxel 0.5 mm on a side has only $1/8$ the volume of one that is 1 mm on a side. A 25-μm voxel, like that obtained by Dodd and colleagues, has only $1/_{64,000}$ the volume of a 1-mm voxel. Since the total MR signal measured from a voxel is roughly proportional to its volume, the MR signal at ultrahigh spatial resolution is extraordinarily weak compared to that at normal spatial scales. As a result, most of the ultrahigh-resolution MRI images have been acquired ex vivo or in vitro on small-bore high-field MRI scanners.

> ## Thought Question
>
> Based on what you learned in Chapter 9 about the sources of noise in MRI, what problems would you encounter when attempting ultrahigh-resolution MRI in vivo?

Ultrahigh-resolution MRI has become an increasingly important tool for understanding brain anatomy. In recent years, spatial resolution on the order of a few tens of micrometers has been regularly achieved, providing similar resolution to that available with traditional light-microscopic techniques. A sample ultrahigh-resolution image is shown in Figure 14.1. One important advantage of MRI over other similar approaches is the relative ease of quantitative analyses. Many researchers use **volumetric** and **morphometric** techniques to measure properties of size and shape, respectively. Based on the tissue contrast used for the MR images (e.g., T_1), researchers can outline a given brain structure in two sets of animals (e.g., normal and genetic knockout mice) and then investigate changes in brain anatomy associated with the group difference. The results can be readily stored in a database for use by other investigators, such as the Biomedical Informatics Research Network (www.nbirn.net). Because the MRI data are collected electronically, they are more easily analyzed and disseminated than are traditional microscopic slides.

We emphasize, however, that ultrahigh-resolution images are typically only acquired at very high field strengths and long acquisition times and are most commonly used for imaging small animals. There are two primary reasons for this limitation. First, field homogeneity becomes increasingly important with increasing strength of the static field, such that it is very difficult to ensure the stability across space of an extremely strong magnetic field. Very-high-field MRI scanners with bore sizes large enough to accommodate human imaging are extremely expensive and difficult to maintain and are thus very uncommon. Typical small-bore scanners for rodent imaging may have field strengths of 7 T or greater but **magnet diameters** of only

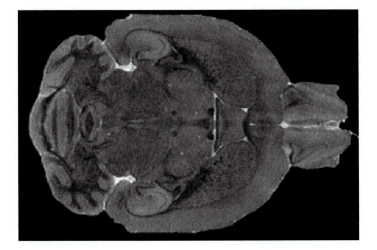

Figure 14.1 An ultrahigh-resolution MR microscopy image. Shown is an image of a male C57BL/6J mouse brain, collected at 43-μm isotropic resolution. To appreciate the spatial resolution of this image, consider that approximately one million of its voxels would fit within a single 4 mm × 4 mm × 5 mm human fMRI voxel. (Courtesy of Dr. G. Allan Johnson, Center for In-vivo Microscopy, Duke University.)

effective bore size The clearance within the bore of the MRI scanner that limits the maximum size of the sample that can be scanned.

phased array A method for arranging multiple surface detector coils to improve spatial coverage while maintaining high sensitivity.

multiple-channel imaging (or parallel imaging) The use of multiple receiver channels to acquire data following a single excitation pulse.

8 to 30 cm. For comparison, typical whole-body MRI scanners have magnet diameters of about 90 to 100 cm. Once outfitted with other imaging hardware, the **effective bore sizes** for small-animal scanners may only be 4 to 20 cm, while human scanners have effective bore sizes of about 60 cm. Second, acquisition of sufficient MR signal for acceptable raw SNR requires an extremely long scan time, which may not be tolerable for human participants. Images of the sort shown in Figure 14.1 may require more than 24 hours of collection time, for example, and even relatively rapid acquisition methods require a few hours per subject. While the results from animal models cannot always be extrapolated to humans, the technical advances associated with ultrahigh-resolution MRI studies have offered insight into problems associated with high-field fMRI in humans. In the past few years, several human scanners at 7 T and above have been successfully installed, providing exciting new results and presenting new challenges.

In the following sections, we discuss some of the state-of-the-art imaging techniques that are being developed for improving the spatial characteristics of the functional signal. We begin with hardware improvements that enhance the reception of signal using multiple channels in parallel, and then consider new techniques for measuring hemodynamic changes in the brain. While BOLD contrast has been extraordinarily useful for fMRI studies, its reliance on T_2^* imaging makes it vulnerable to susceptibility-induced signal losses in the ventral frontal and temporal lobes adjacent to the sinuses. We therefore discuss strategies for compensating for these losses through modification of standard pulse sequences. We end with an explanation of new methods for doing fMRI that do not rely on BOLD contrast. Because the BOLD signal may not always be colocalized with neuronal activity, these new methods have become increasingly important.

Multiple-Channel Acquisition

Throughout this book, we have concentrated on single-channel reception methods. As discussed in Chapters 3 and 4, the precession of net magnetization within the transverse plane induces a current in a nearby receiver coil. Changes in this current over time allow reconstruction of the spatial properties of the sample. While use of a single coil is most common, it is also possible to acquire data from multiple coils in parallel, such as in a **phased array** design, as described in Chapter 2. This is known as **multiple-channel acquisition** or **parallel imaging.** The use of multiple-channel acquisition has two advantages. One is to increase the spatial resolution and raw SNR without increasing acquisition time; the other is to reduce the duration of the readout window and thus minimize spatial distortion without compromising SNR.

To illustrate an example of increasing spatial resolution using multiple-channel acquisition, consider the schematic reception system shown in Figure 14.2A. Here, the four receiver coils simultaneously but independently cover the four quadrants of the imaging volume, each with a matrix size of $n \times n$ (e.g., 128×128). By simply combining all four images, an image with a large field of view that contains the entire sample can be obtained with a matrix size of $2n \times 2n$ (e.g., 256×256), illustrated in Figure 14.2B. Note here that the imaging matrix dimensions are doubled, without any increase in imaging time. Such an implementation is conceptually straightforward; however, each individual image usually contains signal from other quadrants due to aliasing that results from spatial subsampling. In addition, the signal intensity of the final image (Figure 14.2C) varies severely in space, depending upon the voxel position with respect to the individual

(A)

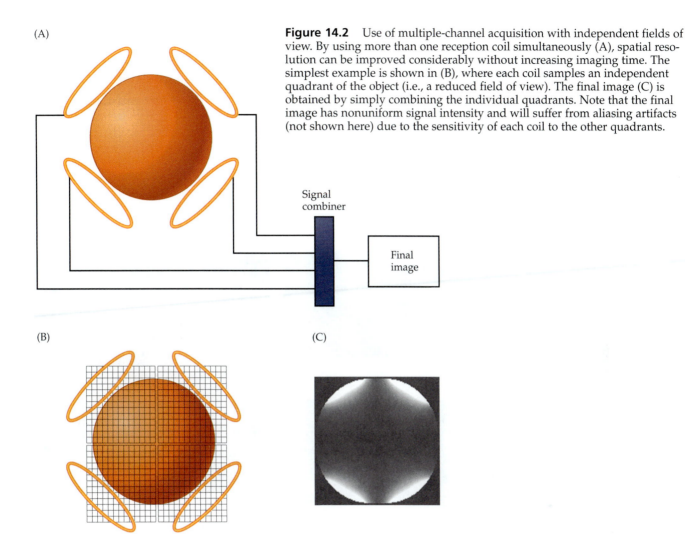

Figure 14.2   Use of multiple-channel acquisition with independent fields of view. By using more than one reception coil simultaneously (A), spatial resolution can be improved considerably without increasing imaging time. The simplest example is shown in (B), where each coil samples an independent quadrant of the object (i.e., a reduced field of view). The final image (C) is obtained by simply combining the individual quadrants. Note that the final image has nonuniform signal intensity and will suffer from aliasing artifacts (not shown here) due to the sensitivity of each coil to the other quadrants.

Signal combiner

Final image

(B)

(C)

surface coils. For fMRI, this could result in different functional SNR across the brain.

Multiple-channel imaging can also be used to increase spatial resolution by collecting data from coils with overlapping fields of view (Figure 14.3). During the imaging session, all channels acquire data with larger coverage in k-space to reach higher resolution. To keep the time of data acquisition short, the k-space data are subsampled for individual coils (Figure 14.3A), resulting in the severely aliased images shown in Figure 14.3B. By incorporating field maps from individual coils (Figure 14.3C) and using an iterative reconstruction process to remove aliasing artifacts, a final image with uniform spatial coverage and high spatial resolution can be achieved (Figure 14.3D). The relation between the number of coils and the matrix size can be expressed more generally in the following way. Assuming the number of receiver coils is M, the number of sampling points for each coil is P, and the number of voxels desired in the final reconstructed image is n^2, we must use enough coils so that $M \times P > n^2$. Thus, as M coils are used, the matrix size could increase by a factor of up to $\sqrt{M}$ for a given acquisition time, as demonstrated by Sodickson and colleagues and also by Pruessmann and colleagues. In addition to increasing spatial resolution, multiple-channel

(A)

(B)

(D)

(C)

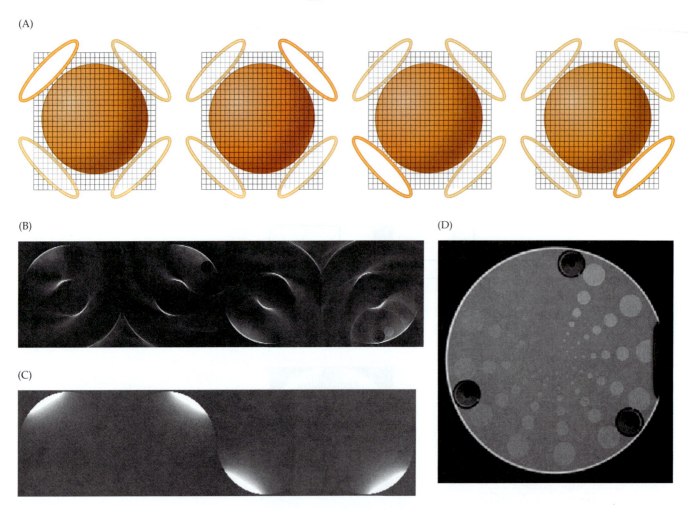

Figure 14.3 Use of multiple-channel acquisition with overlapping fields of view. If multiple receiver coils are each used to sample the entire object (A), the resulting images (B) will be distorted by the differential sensitivity of the coils across space. By obtaining field maps from individual coils to determine their spatial sensitivity (C), such information can be incorporated into the reconstruction process, resulting in a final uniform image with improved spatial resolution (D).

acquisition can also increase raw SNR. When multiple coils are targeted at the same brain region, images from individual channels can be combined to increase the magnitude of the signal. Figure 14.4 demonstrates the use of a four-channel phased-array coil targeted at human visual cortex. The resulting increase in raw SNR could be used for better segmentation of gray and white matter within these regions.

Fast imaging sequences have long readout or data acquisition windows following each excitation, during which time phase errors accumulate. As discussed in Chapter 4, these phase errors often lead to spatial distortions. Such distortions can be effectively minimized if the duration of the readout window can be shortened; however, shortening the readout window reduces the imaging matrix and thus spatial resolution. But by using multiple-channel imaging, the readout duration can be shortened without reduc-

(A) Four-channel phased-array surface coil

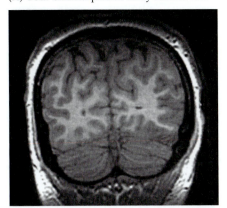

(B) Standard quadrature volume coil

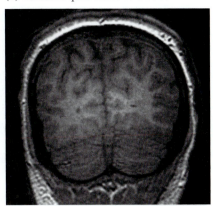

Figure 14.4 Effects of multiple-channel acquisition upon raw SNR. (A) An image collected using a four-channel phased-array surface coil, while (B) is an image collected using a standard volume coil. Both images were acquired on the same 4-T scanner in the same subject. The raw SNR is much improved by the use of four-channel parallel acquisition, as shown here in (A) by the better contrast between gray and white matter. The improved raw SNR facilitates tissue segmentation and also allows acquisition of higher-resolution images without increasing acquisition time.

ing the imaging matrix. For example, by using four receiver coils for data acquisition, a 256×256 imaging matrix can be acquired in the same amount of time as a single coil can collect a 128×128 imaging matrix. In principle, the duration of the readout window can be shortened by up to a factor of M, given M receiver coils. An example of reduced image distortion in multi-channel EPI is illustrated in Figure 14.5, demonstrating the value of multiple-channel imaging for preserving the spatial fidelity of an image.

Susceptibility Compensation and Weighting

As discussed in Chapter 9, an increasing proportion of fMRI experiments are being performed at high-field scanners to increase functional SNR. Despite this advantage, high-field scanning poses significant challenges for fMRI. Major problems for BOLD fMRI studies are **susceptibility artifacts,** which manifest as signal losses and spatial distortions in ventral brain areas that are near interfaces between air and brain tissue. Susceptibility artifacts are present on any T_2^*-weighted image and are exacerbated by fast imaging

susceptibility artifacts Signal losses on T_2^*-dependent images due to magnetic field inhomogeneities in regions where air and tissue are adjacent.

(A)

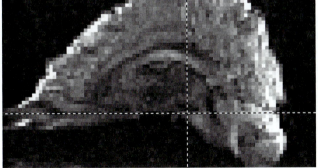

(B)

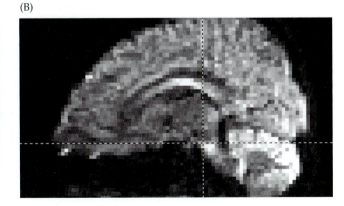

Figure 14.5 Effects of multiple-channel acquisition upon spatial fidelity. Distortions often present in images acquired using a single reception channel (A) can be reduced by using multiple-channel acquisition (B). The improved spatial fidelity, especially in areas with susceptibility artifacts, results from the use of a shortened data acquisition window in multiple-channel imaging. Both images are of the same slice in the same subject at the same spatial resolution (2.5 mm × 2.5 mm). (Courtesy of Dr. Susumu Mori, Johns Hopkins University.)

Figure 14.6 Effects of susceptibility compensation. Shown in (A) are two representative axial slices acquired using gradient-echo echo-planar imaging. Visible is the typical pattern of susceptibility-induced signal losses in frontal and inferior temporal regions (indicated by arrows). (B) The same slices, here acquired using a single-shot susceptibility compensation sequence. Much greater signal is present in the regions of susceptibility artifact, and anatomical details are clearly visible within those regions. Both pairs of images were collected at 4 T from the same subject.

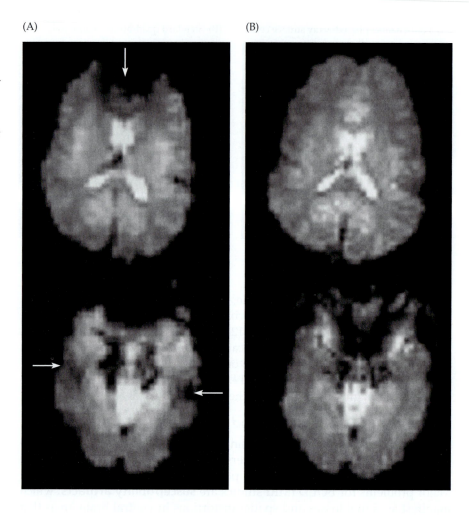
(A)   (B)

linear gradient A magnetic field gradient whose strength varies linearly across space.

methods, long TEs, and high-field scanning. The areas of most common distortion are shown in Figure 14.6A. Note the near complete signal loss in the ventral frontal lobe and in the lateral inferior temporal lobe; the former is immediately above the sphenoid sinus, while the latter is above the auditory canals. Susceptibility artifacts have had a significant impact upon functional brain mapping. Because no fMRI signal can be measured from these regions, they are often excluded from characterization of functional brain systems. Nevertheless, evidence from other modalities has shown that these areas are important for many cognitive and perceptive processes, including memory, emotion, attention, language, and olfaction. It is thus critically important to develop methods for recovering fMRI signal from these regions.

Several research groups have developed methods for recovering signal from these regions. One approach that ameliorates, but does not eliminate, susceptibility artifacts is to use thinner slices (i.e., <1.5 mm) to reduce the field change through the slice. This approach reduces both SNR and spatial coverage to levels that are not practical for most fMRI studies, and therefore it is not commonly used. A second method is to use multiple **linear gradients** to compensate for the susceptibility-induced field distortions. This approach was originally proposed for anatomical imaging by Frahm and colleagues in 1988 and was later adopted by a number of other groups for both anatomical and functional imaging. Despite its effectiveness in recovering signal, this approach is not feasible for most fMRI experiments because it requires multiple excitations for a single image. As many as 16 excitations may be needed to generate a uniform image, greatly increasing the effective TR of the experiment. Compensation by multiple linear gradients, therefore, has had little effect upon fMRI studies.

More efficient susceptibility compensation methods have been implemented that use **higher-order gradients** to correct for field inhomogeneities, reducing the number of gradients needed to a more tolerable level. For example, early work by Cho and colleagues proposed using an excitation pulse with a quadratic profile to better match real field inhomogeneities. This development reduced the number of excitations to two: a quadratic profile, for regions with signal loss; and a standard uniform profile, for regions without signal loss. More recently implemented single-shot methods provide much-improved signal recovery with minimal cost to temporal resolution, as implemented by Song for EPI and Glover and colleagues for spiral imaging. The effectiveness of the EPI implementation at 4 T is illustrated in Figure 14.6B.

While macroscopic susceptibility effects, such as seen at ventral brain regions, lead to significant signal losses and global geometric distortions, and thus should be minimized or compensated, microscopic susceptibility effects may reveal useful information about brain function. For example, microscopic **susceptibility-weighted imaging (SWI)** methods have been developed to image venous vasculature and capillaries, creating images of the venous system known as **venograms** (Figure 14.7). Venograms differ from the angiograms described in Chapter 5 in that they do not use flow information to create imaging contrast. Instead, venograms use phase dis-

higher-order gradient A magnetic field gradient whose strength changes in a nonlinear fashion, such as in a quadratic manner, across space.

susceptibility-weighted imaging (SWI) A class of techniques for creating images of the venous system based on microscopic susceptibility effects.

venogram An image of the venous system.

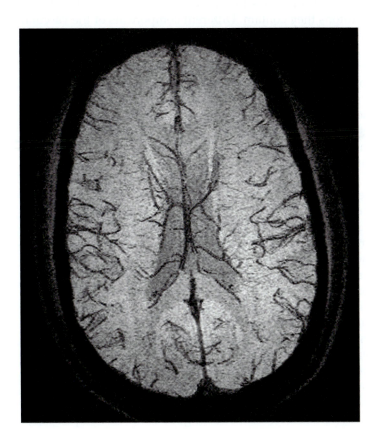

Figure 14.7 A venogram. This image illustrates the pattern of large and small veins present within a single axial slice. Venograms use phase discrepancies caused by local susceptibility effects to map out the venous system. (Courtesy of Dr. Todd Parrish, Northwestern University, and Dr. E. Mark Haacke, Wayne State University.)

diffusion weighting The application of magnetic gradients to cause changes in the MR signal that are dependent upon the amplitude and/or direction of diffusion.

b factor The degree of diffusion weighting applied within a pulse sequence.

apparent diffusion coefficient (ADC) The quantification of diffusivity assuming isotropic diffusion.

crepancies associated with slight differences in resonance frequency caused by local susceptibility effects, which generates greater contrast for the vascular system than found in intensity-based susceptibility imaging, such as BOLD. Only the venous system can be imaged in this manner, since blood in the arterial system is oxygenated and has minimal effect on susceptibility images. Venograms have the sensitivity to image small vessels, on the order of 100 µm. Since the BOLD signal results from changes in venous and capillary networks, the ability to map the venous system provides critical information about its origins.

Improving BOLD Contrast

The previous sections described techniques for improving the spatial resolution, coverage, and fidelity of fMRI. However, these improvements are not in themselves sufficient for ensuring accurate localization of fMRI signal to the initiating neuronal activity. There still remains a fundamental gap between our understanding of the underlying neuronal events and the measured fMRI BOLD response. As discussed in Chapter 9, the contributing sources of the BOLD signal are complex. Given the measured BOLD signal within a voxel, what do we know about the activity of neurons in that part of the brain? Many laboratories are actively investigating the spatial correspondence between BOLD contrast and neuronal activity. While it is possible to use intracranial recording data for spatial validation of BOLD data, as is discussed in Chapter 15, such data are often not available. It is therefore critical to develop noninvasive validation approaches.

One method that may improve understanding of the spatial origins of the BOLD signal is **diffusion weighting** (see Chapter 5). Diffusion weighting adjusts the contributions of voxels to the total MR signal according to the mobility of the protons they contain. Different components of the vascular system have different proton mobility, and thus diffusion-weighted imaging can help visualize the vascular origins of the BOLD signal. Protons within large vessels, for example, move quickly through space along the axis of the vessel due to flow, while those within capillaries move slowly and in more directions due to the random geometry of the capillaries. Note that diffusion weighting influences all motion of the protons, including blood flow, and not solely diffusion due to thermal effects. For this reason, a more accurate description of this technique would be "mobility-weighted imaging."

By adding different diffusion-weighting components to the acquisition pulse sequence, one can selectively reduce the influence of large-vessel contributions to the BOLD signal (Figure 14.8A–D) in an attempt to improve functional resolution. The amount of diffusion weighting introduced by a pulse sequence is known as the **b factor,** with typical units of seconds per millimeter squared. The squared term in the units represents the fact that the average movement by diffusion is essentially random, so the distance traveled increases proportionally to the square root of time, compared to blood flow, in which particles move at a relatively constant rate and direction over time. Larger b factors remove increasing amounts of the intravascular large-vessel signal (Figure 14.8C). Note that the map of diffusion rates, or static **apparent diffusion coefficient (ADC),** across active voxels shows substantial large-scale variability (Figure 14.8D), suggesting that much of the BOLD signal results from large-vessel effects. One problem raised by diffusion-weighted imaging techniques is correlating the amount of diffusion weighting with the size of the affected vessels. For instance, diffusion-weighted acquisitions are often not effective in removing the extravascular parenchy-

(A)

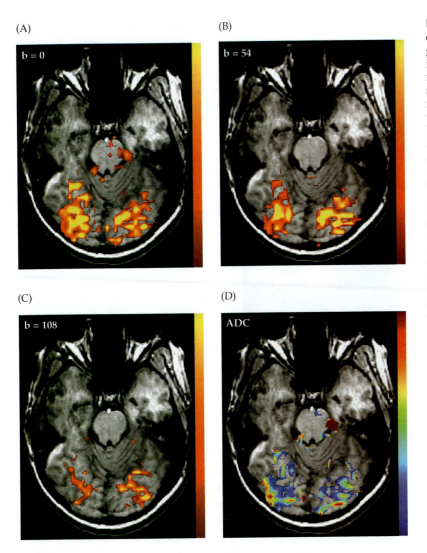

(B)

(C)

(D)

Figure 14.8 BOLD maps acquired at different b factors and the resulting ADC map. A single subject passively viewed objects presented in a blocked design, while BOLD contrast was measured at 4 T using different values of diffusion weighting. Shown at upper left (A) is a map of BOLD activity with no diffusion weighting (b = 0); this is equivalent to normal BOLD contrast measured in most fMRI studies. As diffusion weighting increases to b factors of 54 (B) and 108 s/mm² (C), the region of significant activity reduces in extent due to the elimination of signal from large blood vessels. The data from the three different diffusion-weighting values can be combined into a single map of static ADC contrast (D), where red indicates voxels with high spin mobility due to the presence of large vessels and blue indicates voxels with low spin mobility that may reflect largely capillaries. The colormaps for (A–C) reflect *t*-values of 3.6 to 8.0 (and greater), while the color map for (D) reflects ADC values of 0.4 to 4.0×10^{-3} mm²/s.

mal component of the large-vein signal, since it usually has small diffusion coefficients. This results in corona-shaped activation patterns surrounding the large vessel. While promising, diffusion-weighted protocols for attenuating unwanted signals face challenges in both the strength and selectivity of their effects.

Another approach for potentially improving the spatial specificity of the BOLD signal takes advantage of the **initial dip** in the BOLD signal. Recall from Box 7.2 that the initial dip is a transient negative BOLD signal that may result from the focal increase in oxygen consumption within capillaries adjacent to active neurons, immediately following the onset of neuronal activity. Thus, the initial dip could potentially be better localized to neuronal activity than the conventional later positive BOLD signal. In 2000, Kim and colleagues compared the spatial specificity of the initial dip and positive BOLD response by investigating the columnar organization of cat visual cortex (Figure 14.9A–C). They presented visual gratings at specific orientations while collecting BOLD images at very high spatial resolution; for comparison, the scale bar in Figure 14.9A is 1 mm in length. By plotting the amplitude of the initial dip over space, they identified regions of visual cortex that

initial dip The short-term decrease in MR signal immediately following the onset of neuronal activity, before the main positive component of the hemodynamic response. The initial dip may result from initial oxygen extraction before the later overcompensatory response.

(A)

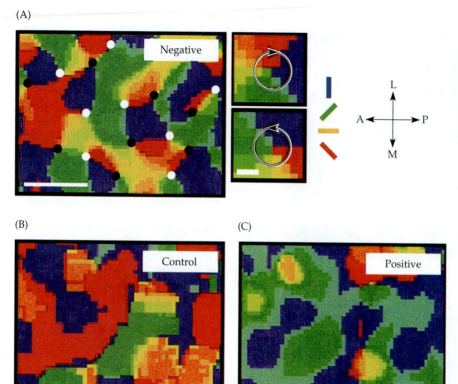

(B)

(C)

Figure 14.9 Demonstration of orientation columns in cat visual cortex. The orientation selectivity of cat visual cortex using different components of the BOLD signal was measured. Shown in (A) is a map of orientation columns generated using the initial dip. Note the very clear columnar organization, with the characteristic pinwheel structure observed at the points indicated by the dots (and shown in the inset). For comparison, the positive response showed much less orientation specificity (C) and was more similar to a control analysis using data collected before stimulus presentation (B). (From Kim et al., 2000.)

perfusion imaging A technique for measuring blood flow through capillaries using MRI.

arterial spin labeling (ASL) A family of perfusion imaging techniques that measure blood flow by labeling spins with excitation pulses and then waiting for the labeled spins to enter the imaging plane before data acquisition.

were sensitive to stimuli of a particular orientation. As shown in the inset of the figure, a characteristic pinwheel structure was observed around the intersection of multiple orientation columns, such that adjacent voxels had different orientation specificity. However, the activation pattern obtained using the positive BOLD response showed much less spatial specificity (Figure 14.9C). To date, the most convincing evidence for the initial dip has come from high-field studies in animals that allow sufficiently high spatial resolution to investigate the fine details of cortical columnar structure. With the increasing availability of ultrahigh-field human scanners (e.g., 7 T and above), the use of the initial dip to localize human columnar structure may become practical.

Non-BOLD Contrasts

A fundamental limitation of BOLD imaging is that it is not exclusively sensitive to the microvasculature surrounding and supporting the neuronal activity of interest. However, changes in the properties of the microvasculature can be measured using other contrast techniques. Three such alternative contrasts are discussed here: perfusion imaging, vascular-space-occupancy imaging, and diffusion imaging.

Perfusion imaging detects the entry of blood into voxels (see Chapter 5 for methods). Through the use of **arterial spin labeling (ASL),** perfusion-weighted images can be made sensitive to blood flow from upstream arterial networks into the microvasculature. Because perfusion imaging is sensitive to capillary activity, perfusion contrast with optimized timing parameters may have better functional resolution than BOLD contrast. A sample com-

(A)   (B)   (C)

(D)   (E)   (F)

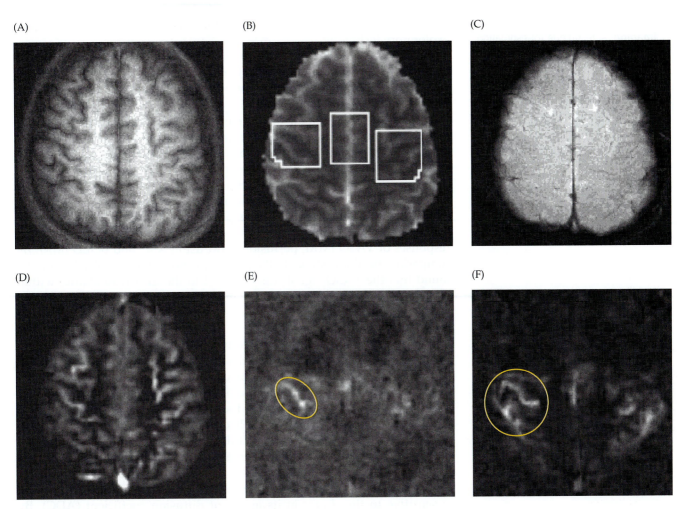

Figure 14.10   Comparison of perfusion and BOLD contrasts. Shown are an anatomical reference image (A), a T_1 image with regions of interest in motor cortical areas (B), and a T_2 image (C). The resting-state perfusion map is shown in (D). During a simple motor task, there were significant increases in perfusion within the regions of interest, as shown in (E). The perfusion-related increases generally were similar to those obtained using BOLD contrast (F), but were more spatially specific. In all images, absolute signal intensity is shown using a grayscale color map. (From Luh et al., 2000.)

parison between optimized perfusion and BOLD contrasts is shown in Figure 14.10A–F, which indicates that cerebral blood flow contrast measured using ASL imaging is more spatially localized than blood oxygenation contrast measured using BOLD imaging. Similar results have been obtained in animal models in studies that resolved the columnar organization within cat visual cortex. Perfusion imaging does have a significant limitation, however, which precludes its use in some fMRI experimental designs. Because the labeled blood must travel from the labeling plane (e.g., in the neck) to the capillaries in the imaging plane, the temporal resolution of perfusion imaging is lower than that of BOLD imaging. Moreover, the travel time is not known a priori and must be determined experimentally. If too short an interval is used, the labeled spins may not have reached the capillary bed. But if too long an interval is used, T_1 recovery effects will reduce or eliminate altogether the perfusion signal. Perfusion imaging, therefore, may have its greatest success answering well-formed questions about the detection of activity

vascular-space-occupancy (VASO) imaging A technique for estimating cerebral blood volume through nulling of intravascular signal and measurement of changes in parenchymal signal.

intravoxel incoherent motion (IVIM) The uncorrelated motion of spins within a voxel.

dynamic IVIM imaging A technique for generating images based on changes in IVIM. It can be used to generate images sensitive to hemodynamic changes within capillaries.

within targeted brain regions, rather than as a generally applicable or exploratory technique.

Another recent technique that may improve the spatial specificity of fMRI is **vascular-space-occupancy (VASO) imaging,** as developed by van Zijl and colleagues. Because the T_1 of spins within the blood vessels differs from the T_1 of spins in the parenchyma, an inversion pulse (see Figure 5.7) can be used to selectively eliminate the signal from within the blood while sparing the parenchymal signal. Using this inversion preparation technique, VASO imaging provides a measure of the total extravascular signal. Under the assumption that the total brain volume remains constant, a decrease in parenchymal signal between experimental conditions would indicate an increase in cerebral blood volume. Lu and colleagues demonstrated the feasibility of VASO imaging in a 2003 experiment that compared brain activation using a visual stimulation task, while measuring the hemodynamic responses of VASO fMRI, perfusion fMRI using ASL, and BOLD fMRI. By comparing the VASO signal to the perfusion and BOLD signals, the authors found that the VASO signal was confined to the microvasculature within cortical gray matter. These properties make VASO imaging ideal for improving the spatial specificity of fMRI, although further validation of this new technique will be necessary.

While static diffusion-weighting techniques may be valuable for improving BOLD contrast, as discussed in the previous section, dynamic diffusion contrasts hold potential as a replacement for BOLD imaging. Some researchers have investigated the use of dynamic diffusion-weighting techniques that are sensitive to task-induced **intravoxel incoherent motion (IVIM).** Le Bihan and colleagues applied this term to their technique for creating static images of perfusion. IVIM imaging was extended to measure brain function by Song and colleagues, who interleaved several b factors within each acquisition to change the amount of diffusion weighting over time (Figure 14.11). The resulting time series in each voxel has contrast that is sensitive to the *change* in its apparent diffusion coefficient (ADC). By choosing an appropriate range of b factors, the experimenter can make the resulting time course sensitive to task-induced changes in vessels with a particular size, such as capillaries.

Dynamic IVIM imaging has several advantages over BOLD imaging for spatial localization. Because it detects relative mobility rather than magnetic susceptibility, its spatial specificity does not depend on field strength. Compared to spin-echo BOLD or measurement of the initial dip, it has high functional SNR. Dynamic IVIM imaging does not require labeling of blood and subsequent transit time to the imaging plane, and thus it does compromise temporal resolution and spatial coverage. Dynamic IVIM can also eliminate the extravascular large-vessel signal, because the mobility of extravascular spins near large vessels does not change over time. And, by using a b factor of 0 with one of the excitation pulses, it can be collected concurrently with standard BOLD contrast, albeit with a time penalty proportional to the number of b factors used. Thus, current implementations of dynamic IVIM are not suited for event-related fMRI designs. However, methods in development for acquisition of multiple b factors within a single shot will eliminate this time penalty, and may have more general applicability.

A close relative of the aforementioned ADC contrast uses very high b factors (400 to 1600 s/mm^2) to eliminate all vascular contributions to the MR signal, and thus make it exclusively sensitive to ADC changes in the parenchyma. As described earlier in this section, ADC values normally increase during neu-

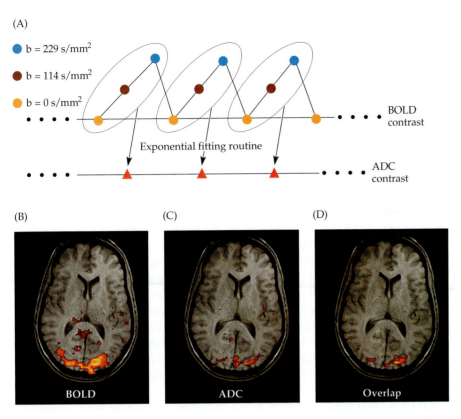

(A)

- b = 229 s/mm²
- b = 114 s/mm²
- b = 0 s/mm²

BOLD contrast

Exponential fitting routine

ADC contrast

(B)   (C)   (D)

BOLD   ADC   Overlap

Figure 14.11 Simultaneous acquisition of BOLD and ADC contrasts. By varying the amount of diffusion weighting over time, both BOLD and ADC contrasts can be obtained within a single fMRI run, as shown in (A). Successive images were acquired at 4 T using this approach, with b factors of 0, 144, or 229 s/mm². The data from the b factor of 0 are simply normal BOLD images, and a BOLD map can be generated from them (B). The change in activity across the three b factors can be used to generate an ADC map (C). The overlap between ADC and BOLD extraneous activations has improved spatial specificity compared to either measure independently (D).

ronal activity when small b factors are applied. However, when very high b factors are used, there is a systematic decrease of ADC during neuronal activity. In 2001, Darquie and colleagues suggested that this paradoxical decrease results from cell swelling that is induced by neuronal activation, although this mechanism is still under considerable investigation. Preliminary data from Michelich and MacFall collected using a visual stimulation task at 4 T suggest that different brain regions exhibit ADC increases and decreases using b values of 300 and 1570 s/mm² (Figure 14.12). Significant uncertainty remains in the source of the high-b-factor ADC signal, its spatial and temporal properties, and the optimal approaches to image acquisition

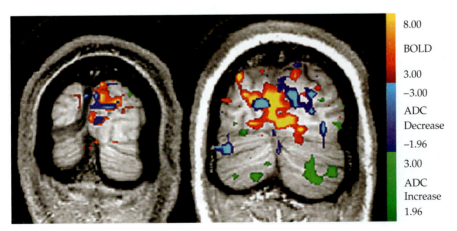

8.00

BOLD

3.00

−3.00

ADC Decrease

−1.96

3.00

ADC Increase

1.96

Figure 14.12 The removal of vascular contributions to MR signal using very high b factors. Shown here are data collected from two slices at 4 T with very high b factors (300 and 1570 s/mm²). Regions showing decreases in ADC activity (blue color map) are spatially adjacent to regions showing BOLD activity (red color map). ADC increases were observed (green color map) in other brain regions. The cause of the high-b-factor ADC effect has not been established, but may reflect cell swelling induced by neuronal activation. (Courtesy of Dr. Charles Michelich and Dr. James MacFall, Brain Imaging and Analysis Center, Duke University.)

isotropic Having similar properties in all directions.

anisotropic Having different properties in different directions; often referenced in the context of anisotropic diffusion, where molecules tend to diffuse along one axis but not others.

diffusion tensor imaging (DTI) The collection of images that provide information about the magnitude and direction of molecular diffusion. It is often used to create maps of fractional anisotropy.

and paradigm design. These problems will have to be solved before high-b-factor ADC can be widely used in fMRI studies.

Spatial Connectivity

As discussed in the previous chapter, a complete description of brain activation should include not only activated brain areas but also their connectivity. The properties of water diffusion can be used to provide information about anatomical connectivity. If unconstrained, water molecules will diffuse randomly in all directions. This is called **isotropic** diffusion. However, if the motion of water molecules is constrained by the structure of their environment, they may diffuse in some directions more than others (see Figure 5.18). This is called **anisotropic** diffusion. Within the brain, axonal fiber tracts constrain the diffusion of water molecules so that molecules within them move along the primary axis of the tract. This fact can be exploited using **diffusion tensor imaging,** or **DTI,** which provides information about the location and orientation of white-matter tracts in the brain. Diffusion tensor data represent each voxel as a three-dimensional ellipsoid reflecting the rate of diffusion along the three principal axes (Figure 14.13A and B). Note that the voxels along fiber pathways, which are visible as white matter in Figure 14.13A, tend to form lines along the pathway. By connecting the long axis of each ellipsoid between given starting and end positions, we can trace the structure of fiber tracts, as illustrated in Figure 14.14A–C. A number of groups have been responsible for the development of DTI, including Mori and colleagues, Basser and colleagues, and Poupon and colleagues.

DTI has been used primarily to evaluate the integrity of white matter in the brain, as when investigating deficits due to aging, injury, or disease. However, it also provides information about functional connectivity. Because brain regions that are connected functionally are also likely to be connected anatomically, areas of functional activity may show direct or indirect connecting pathways on DTI images. Functionally defined brain regions can be used as seed points for DTI algorithms, to identify tracts linking these regions to other areas of the brain. In principle, BOLD activity maps could be used to generate seed points for fiber tracking, thereby investigating functional connectivity. However, because BOLD activity may be more spatially extensive than the underlying neuronal activation, seed points selected based upon BOLD activity alone may lead to inaccurate connectivity maps. For example,

Figure 14.13 Fiber tracking using diffusion tensor imaging. DTI allows measurement of the relative motion of water molecules within the voxel. (A) An image showing, in three dimensions, a diffusion map of white-matter voxels. Each voxel is represented by an ellipsoid whose dimensions reflect the rate of diffusion, with spheres reflecting isotropic diffusion and narrow ellipses showing diffusion along a preferred axis. White-matter tracts can be reconstructed from these data using algorithms that find continuous tracks of diffusion across voxels, as indicated schematically for a hypothetical 5-by-6 set of voxels (B). Visible in red is a curve obtained by tracing diffusion axes across adjacent voxels. (A courtesy of Dr. Guido Gerig, University of North Carolina at Chapel Hill.)

(A)   (B)

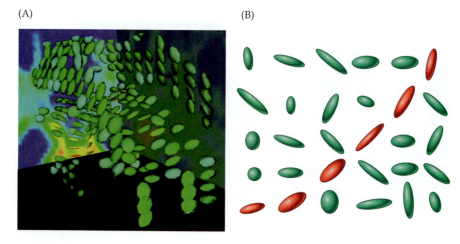

(A)

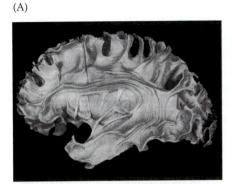

(B)

Figure 14.14 Comparison of anatomical and DTI fiber tracts. Diffusion tensor imaging can be used to reconstruct axonal tracts connecting different brain regions. Shown here are the white-matter radiations in a sagittal drawing of the brain (A); a two-dimensional map of fiber tracts obtained using DTI, shown at the midline of a solid brain (B); and a three-dimensional map of fiber tracts displayed on a glass brain (C). (A from Ludwig and Klionger, 1956; B courtesy of Dr. Susumu Mori, Johns Hopkins University.)

(C)

preliminary studies from Song and colleagues have compared the effectiveness of BOLD and dynamic ADC contrasts for generating seed points for fiber tracking (Figure 14.15). The BOLD activation (shown in blue) does not allow accurate selection of seed points. The ADC activation revealed by dynamic IVIM imaging (shown in red) can be used to create seed points for fiber tracking, as shown in green. Collection of fMRI data and DTI data within a single experiment holds great promise for bridging the gap between neuroimaging and neuroanatomical techniques for understanding brain function.

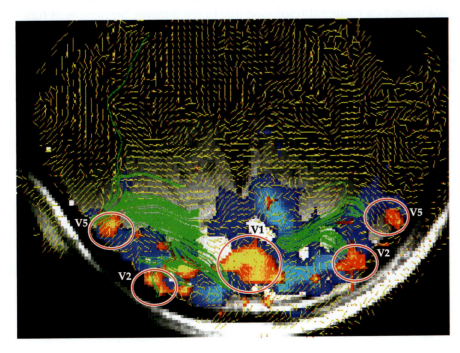

Figure 14.15 Combined use of DTI, ADC fMRI, and BOLD fMRI. Fiber tracking using diffusion tensor imaging can provide important information about the functional properties of different brain regions. In yellow is shown the diffusion tensor vector field; straight lines across multiple vectors indicate fiber tracts. Tracts between visual areas are shown in green. Note that although BOLD contrast shows activity in an extended set of brain regions (blue), ADC contrast shows activity in a smaller set of regions (red) that more closely correspond to the connecting tracts. These activated areas likely correspond to visual processing areas V1, V2, and V5, representing primary, secondary, and motion-sensitive cortices.

electroencephalography (EEG) The measurement of the electrical potential of the brain, usually through electrodes placed on the surface of the scalp.

magnetoencephalography (MEG) A noninvasive functional neuroimaging technique that measures very small changes in magnetic fields caused by the electrical activity of neurons, with potentially high spatial and temporal resolution.

Temporal Resolution

Just as a number of new and exciting methods have been developed for improving the spatial resolution and fidelity of fMRI, novel approaches to improve temporal resolution have also been advanced. Because of the relatively coarse sampling rate of fMRI, improvements in its temporal resolution are particularly valuable. Electrophysiological techniques like **electroencephalography (EEG)** and **magnetoencephalography (MEG)** can detect changes in the brain with roughly millisecond resolution, whereas fMRI samples the brain approximately once per second or slower. Temporal resolution in fMRI is limited by three factors (see Chapter 8 for an extended discussion). First, although individual slices can be acquired within a few tens of milliseconds, 20 or more slices are required to sample the entire brain with reasonable spatial resolution. Thus, the time between successive acquisitions of the entire brain is much longer than the acquisition time for a single slice. Second, the net magnetization of voxels requires time to recover between successive excitations. Thus, even if one wanted to repeatedly sample a single slice as rapidly as possible, the functional SNR in that slice would be greatly reduced at very short repetition times. Third, the most common functional contrast mechanism, BOLD, does not image neuronal activity directly, but instead measures hemodynamic correlates of that activity. The uncertain delay between neuronal activity and its hemodynamic expression reduces temporal resolution. Unless these limitations are overcome, a number of important research questions will remain outside the purview of fMRI.

In the second part of this chapter, we discuss some of the primary advances in pulse sequence development and experimental design that contribute to improved temporal resolution. Not discussed here are improvements in image acquisition rate that have resulted from improvements in MR scanners, notably through the development of more-efficient gradient systems. We note that although hardware improvements have contributed greatly to fast imaging methods, further advances will have a relatively limited impact on temporal resolution due to the intrinsic limitations of functional SNR. For images to be collected faster and with greater SNR, new strategies for their acquisition will be needed.

Multiple-Channel Acquisition

Recall that the use of multiple detector coils can improve spatial resolution without increasing imaging time (as shown in Figure 14.4), or reduce spatial distortions while maintaining the imaging matrix (as shown in Figure 14.5). However, if improved temporal resolution is desired instead, then multiple-channel acquisition can also improve temporal resolution without sacrificing spatial resolution or spatial coverage. Just as the unique spatial information provided by each channel can increase resolution over a single channel, the same data can be acquired in less time using multiple channels simultaneously. Normally, a single coil is used to acquire an $n \times n$ image. Four independent coils can also be used to collect that same image, each acquiring $n/2 \times n/2$ data points. Since each coil only acquires one-quarter of the original data, the image can be collected in one-quarter of the time. The temporal reduction factor could be smaller if the multiple coils overlap spatially. In general, if there are M receiver coils each sampling P points, the requirement for redundancy means that there must be more samples than voxels in the image: $MP > n^2$. Thus, temporal resolution improves proportionally to the number of receiver coils used, that is, by a factor up to M. This improvement is in image acquisition time only and does not affect the recovery of the net magnetization nor the delay introduced by the hemodynamic response. Note that the addition of coils has different effects on spatial resolution and temporal resolution. Because spatial resolution is measured in squared units within a slice (mm^2), it increases proportionally to the change in the square root of the number of coils. But temporal resolution is measured in linear units (s), and it improves linearly with the number of coils.

Partial k-Space Imaging

Chapter 5 introduced popular fMRI pulse sequences, notably gradient-echo echo-planar imaging (EPI) and gradient-echo spiral imaging. These pulse sequences rely on very rapid changes in magnetic gradients to enable collection of k-space data. While the speed of data acquisition using these sequences can be increased by increasing the strength of the magnetic gradients, such increases push ever closer to the physiological limits governing human tolerance to the change in magnetic field strength over time (dB/dt) and the specific absorption rate (SAR) for radiofrequency energy. Achieving further increases in imaging speed with additional hardware improvements will be more challenging, due to safety limits imposed by the FDA and other regulatory agencies. Thus, researchers have looked for ways to improve image acquisition rates by changing how k-space data are collected. One key area of development is **partial k-space imaging,** in which k-space is incompletely sampled during each acquisition. As less time is spent sampling k-space, images can be collected more rapidly.

In order to sample k-space more rapidly, a partial k-space pulse sequence collects data from only some points within the matrix, but not others. Since the center of k-space contains the preponderance of MR signal, it is usually sampled. The missing peripheral k-space samples are then filled with zero values so that the reconstructed image will have the desired matrix size. Nevertheless, effective spatial resolution is reduced, since higher spatial frequencies in the data are excluded from the sampling (see Figure 4.6). Note that the blurring effect of the zero-filling method in k-space is equivalent to a sinc interpolation in imaging space. For most applications, therefore, sampling the center of k-space and zero-filling the remainder of the matrix does not provide acceptable results.

Variations on this approach have been developed that use more principled methods than zero-filling for assigning values to nonsampled locations in k-space. One frequently used method is known as **keyhole imaging.** Only the center portion of k-space is sampled on each trial, and peripheral regions are filled in with previously acquired data. This eliminates the apparent blurring effects due to zero-filling, although there is no real gain in high-spatial-frequency functional information. Another approach, **conjugate mirroring,** samples only part of k-space on each trial, filling in the missing regions using the conjugate symmetry principle. That is, because of the symmetry of k-space, the same image information is normally sampled at two different k-space points. Conjugate mirroring only samples one of these points and then estimates the other. The k-space coverage patterns for both of these techniques are illustrated in Figure 14.16A and B. Using both methods, fMRI images can be collected at very high temporal resolution with excellent spatial resolution. In one implementation of conjugate mirroring at 3 T, researchers were able to collect isotropic 1-mm^3 slices through the human brain, at an acquisition rate of a few tens of milliseconds per slice

partial *k*-space imaging A technique for reducing data acquisition time (and thus increasing temporal resolution) by collecting only part of the *k*-space data following each excitation and filling the uncollected portions of *k*-space with estimated data.

keyhole imaging A partial *k*-space imaging technique in which only the center of *k*-space is collected following each excitation, in order to maximize raw SNR while minimizing acquisition time.

conjugate mirroring A partial *k*-space imaging technique in which data collected from one half of *k*-space is used to determine data from the other half.

Figure 14.16 Reducing imaging acquisition time through partial *k*-space imaging. Shown are two common methods for reducing *k*-space coverage to gain temporal resolution while maintaining the same imaging matrix and spatial resolution. (A) A keyhole pattern, where the center of *k*-space (shown in orange) is acquired for each image while the periphery of *k*-space (in blue) is filled with previously acquired data. The use of previously acquired data avoids the blurring effect induced by zero-filling methods. (B) A conjugate mirroring technique, in which data are acquired from one half of *k*-space (in orange) and mirrored into the other half (in blue). Note that the conjugate mirroring technique acquires data from slightly more than half of *k*-space to ensure that the center is well represented to maximize raw SNR.

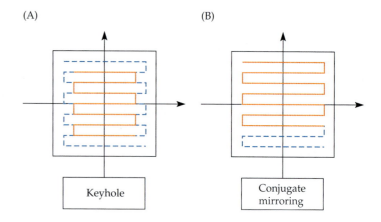

(Figure 14.17A and B). This roughly matches the size of cortical columns and may reflect near optimal resolution for fMRI.

Thought Question

What might be a disadvantage of conjugate mirroring? As a hint, consider what factors contribute to the raw MR signal measured at each point in *k*-space. Why would it be better to collect two samples of the *k*-space data than just one sample?

Because keyhole and conjugate mirroring techniques fully sample the center of *k*-space, most of the MR signal (and thus raw SNR) is preserved. But when one is attempting to measure BOLD signal change within a small region, the raw SNR may not be the most important factor. High-spatial-frequency changes that reflect small regions of functional activity may be more

Figure 14.17 Fast partial *k*-space fMRI with cubic millimeter resolution. Use of a partial *k*-space acquisition strategy can greatly improve the speed of image acquisition. (A) is at $1 \times 1 \times 10$ mm resolution, while (B) is at $1 \times 1 \times 1$ mm resolution. These single-shot images were collected at roughly the same speed as normal fMRI images, despite having much higher resolution. The subject participated in a bimanual finger tapping task. (Courtesy of Dr. Andrzej Jesmanowicz and Dr. James S. Hyde, Medical College of Wisconsin.)

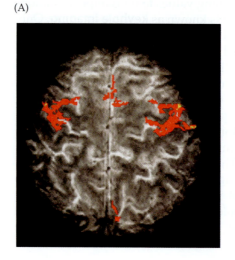 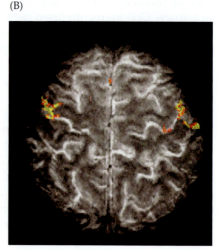

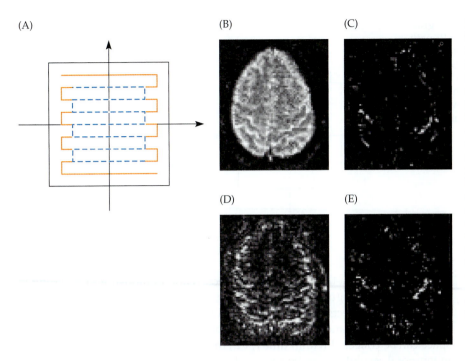

(A) (B) (C)

(D) (E)

Figure 14.18 Rapid fMRI using outer *k*-space imaging. Outer *k*-space imaging records data from the periphery of *k*-space on each image (A, orange) while filling the center of *k*-space with previously acquired data (A, blue). The potential value of this technique for fMRI is that the peripheral points may contribute more to high-spatial-frequency effects, such as small BOLD activations. (B) A standard EPI image from a time series of volumes, and the BOLD significance map from that time series is shown in (C). For comparison, (D) shows an EPI image acquired using outer *k*-space filling, with its significance map shown in (E). Note the substantial difference between the two types of EPI images, with the image in (D) completely lacking low spatial frequencies, but also note the similarity in the activation maps. (Data courtesy of Dr. Gary Glover, Stanford University.)

important than low-spatial-frequency changes that reflect the overall MR signal. In order to assess the detailed spatial characteristics of small activations, it is often important to acquire data from peripheral regions of *k*-space that correspond to high-spatial-frequency components. A method known as **outer *k*-space (OK) imaging** has been proposed by Glover and colleagues to preserve potentially important changes in functional activity. The principle of outer *k*-space imaging is illustrated in Figure 14.18A–E. OK imaging can be thought of as the complement of the keyhole technique described in the last paragraph, in that the former samples only the peripheral portions of *k*-space while the latter samples only the center of *k*-space.

Partial sampling of *k*-space is analogous to the idea of filtering introduced earlier for signals in the time domain. If only part of *k*-space is sampled, then spatial frequencies outside the sampling range are effectively filtered. Thus, keyhole imaging is analogous to a low-pass spatial filter, while OK imaging is analogous to a high-pass filter. Recall from Chapter 10 that the correct filter to use for a given signal depends on the frequency of that signal, according to the principle of **matched filters.** If characteristics of the spatial pattern of activation are known, then an optimally matched *k*-space trajectory can be constructed that fully maintains the spatial integrity of the activation while maximizing temporal resolution.

Efficient k-Space Trajectories

Echo-planar imaging is the most popular fast imaging method for fMRI, but it does not optimally use the scanner gradients. Traditional EPI implementations alternate between the x- and y-gradients to traverse a stepwise path through *k*-space (see Figure 5.22). Because the amplitude of the gradient determines the velocity of the *k*-space trajectory, turning on only one gradient at any given time limits the speed at which *k*-space data can be acquired. To overcome this limitation and increase the speed of slice acquisition, pulse sequences have been developed that use both the x- and y-gradients simultaneously. A simple

outer *k*-space (OK) imaging A partial *k*-space imaging technique in which only the periphery of *k*-space is collected following each excitation, in order to ensure that high-spatial-frequency components of the MR signal are present.

matched filters The principle that the filter of the same frequency as the signal of interest provides maximal signal-to-noise ratio.

Figure 14.19 Simultaneous use of x- and y-gradients to speed image acquisition. A typical EPI path through k-space uses the x-gradient to collect a single line of k-space in time t (A). Through the use of both the x- and y-gradients at the same time to traverse a diagonal path through k-space, the time that it takes to fill up the entire k-space can be reduced by a factor of $\sqrt{2}$, effectively increasing temporal resolution without sacrificing spatial resolution (B).

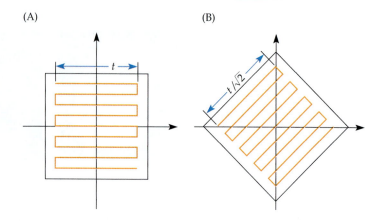

spiral imaging A technique for fast image acquisition that uses sinusoidally changing gradients to trace a corkscrew trajectory through k-space.

spiral-out trajectory A corkscrew path that begins at the center of k-space and ends at the periphery. It is the most common form of spiral imaging.

spiral-in trajectory A corkscrew path that begins at the periphery of k-space and ends at the center. Spiral-in imaging has the advantage that data acquisition can begin before time TE and thus the total time needed to collect an image is reduced.

version of such a method, originally proposed and demonstrated by Wong in 1992, is shown in Figure 14.19A and B. In a standard EPI sequence, turning on the x-gradient collects a single horizontal line of k-space within time t. However, if both the x- and y-gradients are turned on, a single diagonal line of k-space can be collected within time $t/\sqrt{2}$; thus an overall improvement of $1/\sqrt{2}$ in temporal resolution can be achieved.

Another approach for data acquisition using both gradients at the same time is **spiral imaging.** Traditional spiral imaging techniques employ a **spiral-out trajectory,** which always starts from the center of k-space (Figure 14.20A). In spiral-out imaging, no gradient precedes collection of the center of k-space, and therefore the center cannot be missed due to gradient problems. Furthermore, because the gradients are very weak in the center, flow artifacts are minimized. However, spiral-out imaging also has disadvantages, chiefly the necessity for a time gap between the excitation and the beginning of the data acquisition (i.e., TE) to ensure sufficient T_2^* sensitivity. As a result, the total imaging time for spiral-out acquisition is the sum of the TE (often about 30 to 40 ms) and the length of the readout window (an additional 30 ms or more).

How could the acquisition time for spiral imaging acquisition be further improved? One effective strategy, as demonstrated in recent reports by Glover and Law in 2001 and by Guo and Song in 2003, is to acquire data during the wasted gap time. A **spiral-in trajectory** begins data acquisition in the periphery of k-space immediately following excitation and completes data acquisition in the center of k-space at time TE (Figure 14.20B). This ensures sufficient T_2^* weighting while minimizing the time between successive excitation pulses. Thus, the rate of slice acquisition can be greatly improved, in some cases by up to a factor of 2. A typical implementation of a spiral-in pulse sequence with a 64×64 matrix allows acquisition of approximately 24 slices each second (with a TE of 30 ms). Using such a sequence, it is possible to acquire data from the entire brain with approximately 1-s temporal resolution. As spiral imaging techniques become more established, we expect that they will come to replace echo-planar sequences as the pulse sequence of choice for fMRI studies.

Improved Experimental Designs

It is important to recognize that temporal resolution cannot be manipulated arbitrarily. A number of physical limitations constrain the possible temporal

(A)

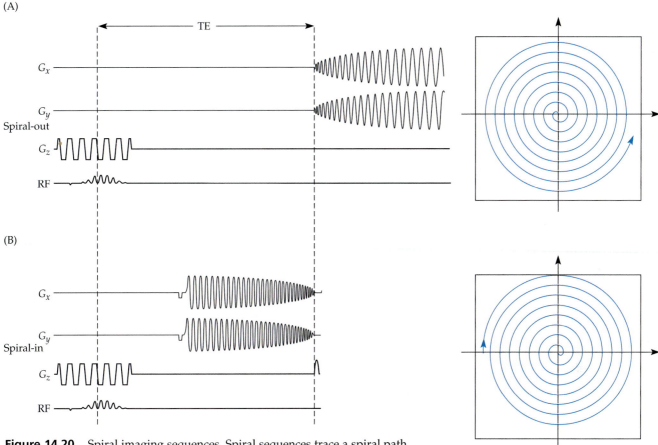

(B)

Figure 14.20   Spiral imaging sequences. Spiral sequences trace a spiral path through *k*-space, allowing more-efficient use of the gradients and more-rapid data acquisition. In the conventional spiral-out sequence (A), the gradients are turned on at time TE, but in the spiral-in technique (B), the gradients are turned on earlier so that the center of *k*-space is reached at time TE. The spiral-in sequence can thus acquire data more rapidly than the spiral-out sequence per unit time.

resolution that can be obtained using fMRI. Some of these limitations result from current imaging hardware and may change over time. As examples, typical static field strengths of MR scanners may increase, albeit slowly, as will the capabilities of gradient systems. In addition, improved receiver characteristics will allow higher sampling frequencies. However, there are also limitations that are intrinsic to the fMRI technique. The T_1 and T_2^* properties of brain voxels restrict the maximum SNR that can be achieved at a given temporal resolution, just as the net magnetization of a voxel restricts the maximum SNR that can be achieved at a given spatial resolution. That is, as TR decreases, the raw SNR also decreases. At very short TRs (e.g., below 200 ms), the resulting decrease in functional SNR may preclude identification of BOLD changes. It is critical, therefore, to optimize experimental designs so that temporal resolution can be maximized.

We previously described the technique known as **interleaved stimulus presentation** (see Figure 8.10) as an approach for improving the effective sampling rate for a given TR. By jittering the time of stimulus presentation within the TR, one can sample hemodynamic time courses at different latencies relative to the stimulus onset on different trials. These multiple time

interleaved stimulus presentation   The presentation of events of interest at different points within a TR over trials (e.g., one-quarter, one-half, and three-quarters of TR in addition to TR onset), increasing the effective sampling rate of an experiment at the expense of fewer trials per condition.

BOX 14.1 Direct MRI of Neuronal Activity

All of the fMRI contrast techniques described heretofore in this book have relied on indirect measures of neuronal activity. BOLD contrast relies on relative oxygenation, diffusion contrast relies on movement of water molecules, and perfusion relies on blood flow. Yet none of these measures are themselves thought to mediate information processing in the brain. Ideally, we would want to bypass all of these indirect markers and measure the activity of neurons directly, whether singly, as in single-unit recording, or collectively, as in field-potential measures. Can MRI be used to image neuronal activity directly? At present the answer to this question is a qualified no. The electrical activity of neurons is weak, temporally transient, and spatially inhomogeneous. Detection even of large effects will be challenging, at best. However, there have been tantalizing results from recent studies that suggest that direct neuronal imaging may be possible.

A study conducted by Joy and colleagues in 1989 provided intriguing results. The authors used spin-echo imaging to assess phase changes associated with the field perturbation of electrical currents, both in phantoms and in peripheral human nerves. Their results showed that physiological currents in biological systems may be detected by acquiring phase maps during stimulation. Since neuronal action potentials are essentially electrical depolarizations akin to current changes in a wire, these results suggested that it may be possible to image neuronal activity directly using MRI. However, the results have not been confirmed by further studies, and the application of this technique to neurons in the brain may be more challenging than to peripheral nerves.

New methods for using MRI to detect minute electrical activity have been proposed. One candidate technique involves the measurement of **Lorentz forces,** which arise from the movement of charged particles through a magnetic field. As the particles move through the field, they experience a force that is perpendicular to both the local magnetic field and the particles' direction of motion. This force acts to displace the particles; if the particles are within a conductor, the conductor will be displaced within the external medium. Similarly, the components of neurons that contain moving electrical charges, such as active axons, will experience small displacing forces. The resulting displacements can be measured using MRI, hence the term **Lorentz effect imaging (LEI).** Preliminary results in gel phantoms were reported in 2001 by Song and Takahashi.

If we assume that the Lorentz force is only along the x-direction, the displacement-induced phase change in a nearby voxel can be estimated by Equation 14.1:

$$\phi = \int_0^T \gamma G \Delta x \, dt \qquad [14.1]$$

Here, G is the strength of the encoding and decoding gradient, Δx the displace-

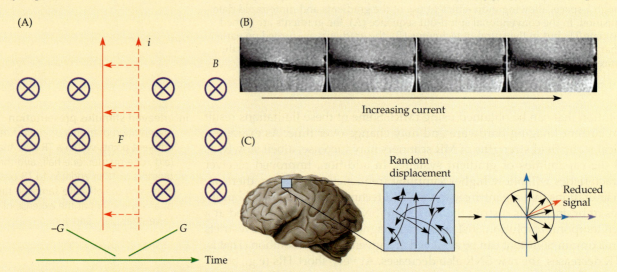

Figure 14.21 Lorentz effect imaging (LEI). Lorentz effect imaging relies on the behavior of a current-carrying wire in a magnetic field. The wire is subject to a lateral force F perpendicular to both the direction of the field B shown in (A) and the direction of the moving charges i. This force is known as the Lorentz force. (B) Shows results from a phantom containing a wire carrying different amounts of charge; from left, 0 µA, 100 µA, 200 µA, and 500 µA. Note that the magnitude of the distortion increases with increasing current. The potential application of LEI to fMRI is shown in (C). Within an active voxel, the electrical currents will be largely randomly oriented. The random orientation means that the direction of the Lorentz effect will differ across electrical sources, resulting in a signal loss due to loss of phase coherence that is analogous to the T_2^* effect.

BOX 14.1 *(continued)*

Lorentz force The force on a moving charge within a magnetic field. Lorentz forces cause spatial displacements in conductors (e.g., wires, neuronal axons) if those conductors are placed in MRI scanners.

Lorentz effect imaging (LEI) A potential technique for direct visualization of electrical activity (e.g., of neurons) using MRI.

ment, T the duration of the encoding/decoding gradients, and γ the gyromagnetic ratio. Note that even for very small displacements, this phase shift could be significant when the product GT is large enough. If the phase shifts are coherent within the voxel, then phase images could be used to detect the Lorentz effect. However, given the random direction of neuronal currents and the elastic nature of brain tissue, the phase shifts are likely to be incoherent within the voxel. As such, the result of the Lorentz effect upon MR images would be a loss of signal intensity. Proof-of-concept experiments conducted on phantoms using G of 50 mT/m and T of 2 ms have suggested that the LEI technique may have a spatial accuracy on the order of 10 μm, given a raw SNR of 100 (Figure 14.21A–C). With improvements in imaging hardware and with increased signal averaging, this technique may become useful for detecting spatial displacements induced by neuronal electrical currents.

Assuming that rapidly changing magnetic fields are more likely to be associated with electrical activity of neurons, in 2002 Bodurka and Bandettini attempted to selectively detect rapidly changing fields while suppressing slowly changing fields. The initial concept was tested on a phantom with implanted wires. The timing of transient currents in the wires was modulated relative to a 180° excitation pulse. Very small phase differences were detected, demonstrat-

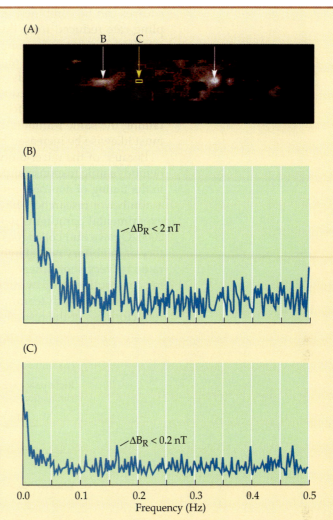

Figure 14.22 Detection of minute electrical activity using MRI. Using a wire-containing phantom, researchers investigated whether very small transient electrical currents could be detected by collecting images sensitive to phase changes. The location of the wires within the phantom are shown as white arrows in (A), and the on/off frequency of the currents was 0.16 Hz. The Fourier spectrum of the voxel that contained the wire indicated by the left arrow revealed a current-induced field shift (ΔB_R) of 2 nanoTesla (B). In a voxel 12.5 mm from the left wire (indicated by yellow arrow), they detected a field shift of 200 picoTesla (C), or about one ten-billionth the strength of a standard MR scanner. These results suggest that MRI can be used, in principle, to detect field changes of strength similar to neuronal activity. (From Bodurka and Bandettini, 2002.)

ing the feasibility of the approach (Figure 14.22A–C). To illustrate the potential importance of this effect, the magnetic field changes measured were as brief as only 40 ms in duration and as small as only 2×10^{-10} T (200 pT). These magnetic changes are about 10 billion times smaller than typical static field strengths, illustrating the profound technical require-

ments of direct neuronal imaging. We emphasize that studies of direct current imaging have heretofore been conducted in phantoms and will undoubtedly be more difficult to conduct in human subjects. Nevertheless, the successes so far point to the eventual development of these remarkable techniques as an alternative to vascular-based fMRI.

courses can be combined into a single time course with the effective sampling rate reduced from the actual TR by a factor equal to the number of interleaved steps. For example, with an actual TR of 2000 ms and 10 jittering steps, one could sample at an effective rate of 200 ms. As we discussed in Chapter 8, the primary disadvantage of interleaved stimulus presentation is that the length of data acquisition increases with the gain in temporal resolution. To increase the effective sampling rate by a factor of 10 while maintaining the same number of samples per condition, the experiment length must likewise be increased by a factor of 10.

Because of the uncertainty associated with the relation between the fMRI hemodynamic response and neuronal activity, millisecond-level distinctions in the timing of neuronal activity are challenging for fMRI studies. However, a number of researchers have investigated whether clever manipulation of experimental paradigms will allow probing of very fast neuronal events. In 2000, Ogawa and colleagues reported a technique that induces either excitatory or inhibitory neural interactions by presenting consecutive stimuli separated by very short intervals, on the order of tens of milliseconds. By applying consecutive forepaw stimulations with variable interstimulus intervals to the rat, the research team was able to detect the inhibition due to neuronal refractoriness of the response to the second stimulus (Figure 14.23A and B).

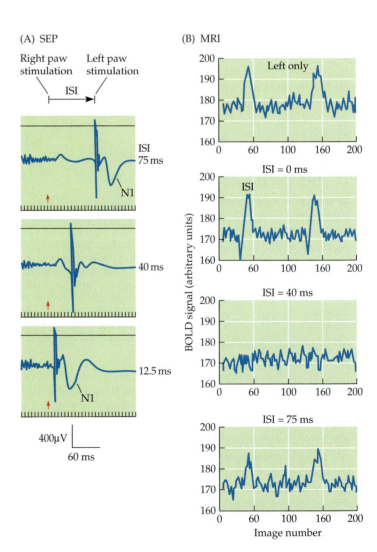

Figure 14.23 Using neural interactions to improve the temporal resolution of fMRI. The electrophysiological and BOLD responses in the somatosensory cortex to bilateral stimulation of the rat forepaws were investigated. (A) Shows electrophysiological responses in the right somatosensory cortex. Normally, a somatosensory evoked potential (SEP; N1) is present following stimulation of the left forepaw (e.g., in 12.5- and 75-ms interstimulus interval conditions). But when the right stimulation precedes the left by about 40 ms, then there is suppression of the electrical activity. Importantly, that suppression is also present in the BOLD effect (B), suggesting that the use of fMRI suppression designs may be able to resolve very small differences in event timing, on the order of tens of milliseconds. (From Ogawa et al., 2000.)

Such an inhibition effect is subsequently manifested in the BOLD signal. This manipulation provides improved temporal resolution for neuronal events without physically increasing the sampling interval, as neuronal *interactions* on the order of milliseconds can lead to very different hemodynamic responses. Similar effects have been used to make spatial judgments about brain regions in fMRI-adaptation paradigms (see Chapter 8).

Summary

Nearly all fMRI studies share the same constraints. They sample the brain with a spatial resolution of a few millimeters and a temporal resolution of a few seconds. The resulting images are sensitive to BOLD contrast, which is an indirect measure of neuronal activity. Though a vast array of research questions can be answered despite these limitations, advances in the spatial and temporal resolution of fMRI will expand its applicability. Many of the advances so far have been driven by hardware improvements, notably by increasing the strength of the static and gradient fields and by using more-advanced receiver coil arrangements. However, further improvements will need to come from better acquisition strategies and pulse sequence designs. Spatial resolution will be improved through better understanding of the spatial origins of the BOLD signal, including comparison to other forms of contrast. Spatial fidelity may be improved by new pulse sequences that have been developed to recover MR signal in areas affected by susceptibility artifacts. Temporal resolution will be improved by new *k*-space acquisition methods, including partial *k*-space imaging and efficient data collection with spiral sequences. Improvements in experimental design will also contribute to better temporal resolution. Finally, some research groups have provided evidence for MR measurement of minute electrical currents, which may lead the way to direct MR imaging of neuronal activity.

Suggested Readings

*Dodd, S. J., Williams, M., Suhan, J. P., Williams, D. S., Koretsky, A. P., and Ho, C. (1999). Detection of single mammalian cells by high-resolution magnetic resonance imaging. *Biophys. J.,* 76: 103–109. One of the first papers to demonstrate the feasibility of single-cell MRI.

*Glover, G. H., and Law, C. S. (2001). Spiral-in/out BOLD fMRI for increased SNR and reduced susceptibility artifacts. *Magn. Reson. Med.,* 46(3): 515–522. The first demonstration of simultaneous image acquisition using both spiral-in and spiral-out trajectories to recover susceptibility-induced signal losses with high temporal efficiency.

Johnson, G. A., Cofer, G. P., Gewalt, S. L., and Hedlund, L. W. (2002). Morphologic phenotyping with MR microscopy: The visible mouse. *Radiology,* 222: 789–793. This manuscript discusses advances in MR microscopy and their applications.

*Kim, D. S., Duong, T. Q., and Kim, S. G. (2000). High-resolution mapping of iso-orientation columns by fMRI. *Nat. Neurosci.,* 3(2): 164–169. Demonstrates that selective use of the initial dip in the BOLD response improves spatial localization of orientation columns within the visual cortex.

Logothetis, N. K., Guggenberger, H., Peled, S., and Pauls, J. (1999). Functional imaging of the monkey brain. *Nat. Neurosci.,* 2(6): 555–562. An important paper demonstrating improved neuronal localization using functional imaging in monkeys.

*Luh, W. M., Wong, E. C., Bandettini, P. A., Ward, B. D., and Hyde, J. S. (2000). Comparison of simultaneously measured perfusion and BOLD signal increases during brain activation with T_1-based tissue identification. *Magn. Reson. Med.,*

44(1): 137–143. This manuscript demonstrates how ASL perfusion imaging may provide superior spatial localization compared to traditional BOLD fMRI.

*Ogawa, S., Lee, T. M., Stepnoski, R., Chen, W., Zhu, X. H., and Ugurbil, K. (2000). An approach to probe neural systems interaction by functional MRI at neural time scale down to milliseconds. *Proc. Natl. Acad. Sci. U.S.A.*, 97: 11026–11031. A convincing demonstration of how improved paradigm design may allow probing of neuronal events on the order of milliseconds using fMRI. The results expand the utility of fMRI for imaging neuronal interactions.

Song, A. W., Wong, E. C., Tan, S. G., and Hyde, J. S. (1996). Diffusion weighted fMRI at 1.5 T. *Magn. Reson. Med.*, 35: 155–158. This early study applies diffusion-weighting methodology to fMRI to investigate the signal origins of BOLD contrast.

Indicates a reference that is a suggested reading in the field and is also cited in this chapter.

Chapter References

Allison, T., Puce, A., Spencer, D. D., and McCarthy, G. (1999). Electrophysiological studies of human face perception. I: Potentials generated in occipitotemporal cortex by face and non-face stimuli. *Cereb. Cortex*, 9(5): 415–430.

Basser, P. J., Pajevic, S., Pierpaoli, C., Duda, J., and Aldroubi, A. (2000). In vivo fiber tractography using DT-MRI data. *Magn. Reson. Med.*, 44(4): 625–632.

Bodurka, J., and Bandettini, P. A. (2002). Toward direct mapping of neuronal activity: MRI detection of ultraweak, transient magnetic field changes. *Magn. Reson. Med.*, 47: 1052–1058.

Bulte, J. W., Zhang, S., van Gelderen, P., Herynek, V., Jordan, E. K., Duncan, I. D., and Frank, J. A. (1999). Neurotransplantation of magnetically labeled oligodendrocyte progenitors: Magnetic resonance tracking of cell migration and myelination. *Proc. Natl. Acad. Sci. U.S.A.*, 96: 15256–15261.

Chen, N. K., and Wyrwicz, A. M. (1999). Removal of intravoxel dephasing artifact in gradient-echo images using a field-map based RF refocusing technique. *Magn. Reson. Med.*, 42: 807–812.

Cho, Z. H., and Ro, Y. M. (1992). Reduction of susceptibility artifact in gradient-echo imaging. *Magn. Reson. Med.*, 23: 193–196.

Constable, R. T. (1995). Functional MR imaging using gradient-echo echo-planar imaging in the presence of large static field inhomogeneities. *J. Magn. Reson. Imaging*, 5: 746–752.

Constable, R. T., and Spencer, D. D. (1999). Composite image formation in z-shimmed functional MR imaging. *Magn. Reson. Med.*, 42: 110–117.

Darquie, A., Poline, J. B., Poupon, C., Saint-Jalmes, H., and Le Bihan, D. (2001). Transient decrease in water diffusion observed in human occipital cortex during visual stimulation. *Proc. Natl. Acad. Sci. U.S.A.*, 98: 9391–9395.

Detre, J. A., and Wang, J. (2002). Technical aspects and utility of fMRI using BOLD and ASL. *Clin. Neurophysiol.*, 113(5): 621–634.

Disbrow, E. A., Slutsky, D. A., Roberts, T. P., and Krubitzer, L. A. (2000). Functional MRI at 1.5 Tesla: A comparison of the blood oxygenation level-dependent signal and electrophysiology. *Proc. Natl. Acad. Sci. U.S.A.*, 97(17): 9718–9723.

Duong, T. Q., Kim, D. S., Ugurbil, K., and Kim, S. G. (2001). Localized cerebral blood flow response at submillimeter columnar resolution. *Proc. Natl. Acad. Sci. U.S.A.*, 98(19): 10904–10909.

Frahm, J., Merboldt, K. D., and Hanicke, W. (1988). Direct FLASH MR imaging of magnetic field inhomogeneities by gradient compensation. *Magn. Reson. Med.*, 6: 474–480.

Guo, H., and Song, A. W. (2003). Single-shot spiral image acquisition with embedded z-shimming for susceptibility signal recovery. *J. Magn. Reson. Imaging*, 18(3): 389–395.

Hu, X. (1994). On the "keyhole" technique. *J. Magn. Reson. Imaging*, 4(2): 231.

Jesmanowicz, A., Bandettini, P. A., and Hyde, J. S. (1998). Single-shot half *k*-space high-resolution gradient-recalled EPI for fMRI at 3 Tesla. *Magn. Reson. Med.,* 40(5): 754–762.

Joy, M., Scott, G., and Henkelman, M. (1989). In vivo detection of applied electric currents by magnetic resonance imaging. *Magn. Reson. Imaging,* 7(1): 89–94.

Lai, S., Reichenbach, J. R., and Haacke, E. M. (1996). Commutator filter: A novel technique for the identification of structures producing significant susceptibility inhomogeneities and its application to functional MRI. *Magn. Reson. Med.,* 36(5): 781–787.

Le Bihan, D., Breton, E., Lallemand, D., Grenier, P., Cabanis, E., and Laval-Jeantet, M. (1986). MR imaging of intravoxel incoherent motions: Application to diffusion and perfusion in neurologic disorders. *Radiology,* 161(2): 401–407.

Lu, H., Golay, X., Pekar, J. J., and van Zijl, P. C. M. (2003). Functional magnetic resonance imaging based on changes in vascular space occupancy. *Magn. Reson. Med.,* 50(2): 263–274.

Ludwig, E., and Klionger, J. (1956). *Atlas Cerebri Humani.* Little, Brown and Co., Boston, MA.

Mao, J., and Song, A. W. (1999). Intravoxel rephasing of spins dephased by susceptibility effect for EPI sequences. *Proc. ISMRM,* 1982.

Moore, A., Josephson, J., Bhorade, R. M., Basilion, J. P., and Weissleder, R. (2001). Human transferring receptor gene as a marker gene for MR imaging, *Radiology,* 221: 244–250.

Ordidge, R. J., Gorell, J. M., Deniau, J. C., Knight, R. A., and Helpern, J. A. (1994). Assessment of relative brain iron concentrations using T_2-weighted and T_2^*-weighted MRI at 3 Tesla. *Magn. Reson. Med.,* 32: 335–341.

Poupon, C., Clark, C. A., Frouin, V., Regis, J., Bloch, I., Le Bihan, D., and Mangin, J. (2000). Regularization of diffusion-based direction maps for the tracking of brain white matter fascicles. *NeuroImage,* 12(2): 184–195.

Pruessmann, K. P., Weiger, M., Scheidegger, M. B., and Boesiger, P. (1999). SENSE: Sensitivity encoding for fast MRI. *Magn. Reson. Med.,* 42: 952–962.

Sodickson, D. K., and Manning, W. J. (1997). Simultaneous acquisition of spatial harmonics (SMASH): Fast imaging with radiofrequency coil arrays. *Magn. Reson. Med.,* 38: 591–603.

Song, A. W. (2001). Single-shot EPI with signal recovery from susceptibility-induced losses. *Magn. Reson. Med.,* 46: 407–411.

Song, A. W., Harshbarger, T., Li, T., Kim, K. H., Mori, S., and Kim, D. S. (2003). Functional activation using ADC contrast allows better spatial localization to the neuronal activity: Evidence using DTI fiber tracking. *NeuroImage,* 20: 955–961.

Song, A. W., and Takahashi, A. M. (2001). Lorentz effect imaging. *Magn. Reson. Imaging,* 19(6): 763–767.

Stenger, V. A., Boada, F. E., and Noll, D. C. (1999). Gradient compensation method for the reduction of susceptibility artifacts for spiral fMRI data acquisition. *Proc. ISMRM,* 538.

Ugurbil, K., Garwood, M., Ellerman, J., Hendrich, K., Hinke, R., Hu, X., Kim, S.-G., Menon, R., Merkle, H., Ogawa, S., and Salmi, R. (1993). Imaging at high magnetic field: Initial experience at 4T. *Magn. Reson. Q.,* 9: 259–277.

van Vaals, J. J., Brummer, M. E., Dixon, W. T., Tuithof, H. H., Engels, H., Nelson, R. C., Gerety, B. M., Chezmar, J. L., and den Boer, J. A. (1993). "Keyhole" method for accelerating imaging of contrast agent uptake. *J. Magn. Reson. Imaging,* 3(4): 671–675.

Wong, E. C. (1992). Diagonal single shot EPI. *Proc. ISMRM,* 4521.

Xue, R., van Zijl, P. C., Crain, B. J., Solaiyappan, M., and Mori, S. (1999). In vivo three-dimensional reconstruction of rat brain axonal projections by diffusion tensor imaging. *Magn. Reson. Med.,* 42(6): 1123–1127.

Yang, Q. X., Dardzinski, B. J., Li, S., Eslinger, P. J., and Smith, M. B. (1997). Multi-gradient echo with susceptibility compensation (MGESIC): Demonstration of fMRI in the olfactory cortex at 3T. *Magn. Reson. Med.*, 37: 331–335.

Yang, Y., Engelien, W., Pan, H., Su, S., Silbersweig, D. A., and Stern, E. (2000). A CBF-based event-related brain activation paradigm: Characterization of impulse-response function and comparison to BOLD. *NeuroImage*, 12(3): 287–297.

Yang, Y., Frank, J. A., Hou, L., Ye, F. Q., McLaughlin, A. C., and Duyn, J. H. (1998). Multi-slice imaging of quantitative cerebral perfusion with pulsed arterial spin labeling, *Magn. Reson. Med.*, 39: 825–832.

15

Converging Operations

In this final chapter, we consider more broadly the relations between fMRI and other methods used to study brain function. We adopt the broad perspective of a neuroscientist whose interest lies not in the technical intricacies of specific methods but rather in using those methods to understand brain function. Our discussion begins with the assertion that no single technique yet available (even one as multifaceted and powerful as fMRI) is sufficient to fully explicate how perceptual, motor, and cognitive processes are instantiated within the brain. All techniques have weaknesses that limit the scope of their interpretative power. Indeed, one important motive that we had in writing this book was to make plain those limitations as they apply to fMRI in its current practice. To overcome the weakness of individual techniques, students of brain function should employ **converging operations** in their research programs. That is, they should bring corroborating and complementary evidence from multiple techniques to bear on a single research question. By employing converging operations, researchers can increase the explanatory power of their findings.

In the sections that follow, we describe techniques that have been used frequently in concert with fMRI. Our goal is to present these techniques in sufficient detail that their strengths and weaknesses can be appreciated. These techniques are organized under two broad headings: those that change the state of neuronal activity in the brain and those that observe the state of neuronal activity in the brain. Before turning to these complementary techniques, however, we first consider the research program of cognitive neuroscience generally and functional brain mapping more specifically. No matter how advanced the methods, it is ultimately the precision of the research questions that determines the rate of scientific progress.

Cognitive Neuroscience

Cognitive neuroscience seeks to understand how complex behavior is produced by the functional repertoire of the brain. Like cognitive science, it studies mental processes that mediate between the sensory input that a system experiences and the behavior that a system produces. Like neuroscience, it seeks mechanistic explanations for behavior in the activity of neu-

converging operations The use of two or more techniques to provide complementary evidence used to test an experimental hypothesis or scientific theory.

construct An abstract concept that explains behavior but which itself is not directly observable. Attention is an example of a psychological construct.

isomorphic Having an identical form. A physiological measurement that is isomorphic with a psychological construct would have the same sign and temporal dynamics as the construct.

localization of function The idea that the brain may have distinct regions that support particular mental processes.

rons and in the context of evolution. Given these similarities, one straightforward strategy for cognitive neuroscientists would be to use fMRI and other techniques to localize the mental processes identified by cognitive science to particular brain regions. Once the region that supports a given process is identified, its underlying neural circuitry can be studied in greater detail (perhaps using molecular, neurophysiological, and computational methods). If only brain mapping were so easy!

While the strategy introduced in the previous paragraph is purposefully oversimplified, it captures much of the logic used by many cognitive neuroscience studies. Is there anything unreasonable about this simple approach? One potential problem concerns the questionable biological reality of the postulated mental processes, or **constructs,** to be studied. Many cognitive scientists are attracted to functional neuroimaging precisely because it seems to provide the means to validate abstract psychological constructs. That is, if an experiment demonstrates that brain activity covaries with manipulations of a postulated construct, the construct is assumed to exist. However, there is no requirement that any psychological construct necessarily exist as a biological entity. Indeed, a model of a cognitive process may have considerable explanatory power without any of its parts corresponding to real brain regions or patterns of brain activity.

The history of science is replete with psychological constructs that were once dominant but have been discredited and forgotten. Imagine that fMRI were available in Gall's time. Would it have made sense to conduct an fMRI experiment to search for neural activity associated with approbativeness, a phrenological faculty associated with one's personal vanity? Or imagine that fMRI were available in Vienna in 1920. Would it have made sense to conduct an fMRI experiment to search for the neural locus of the id? Or imagine that fMRI is available in your laboratory now. Does it make sense to conduct an fMRI study to search for the neural substrate of working memory, or altruism, or emotional intelligence? At one time or another, all of the above constructs have been used to explain complex behavior. Some are no longer credible, others are hotly debated, while others still have widespread currency.

A second potential problem results from assuming that a unitary psychological concept must be realized by a unitary biological entity. One might conclude, on the basis of a blob of active voxels found using fMRI or a new ERP component, that a construct as abstract and multifaceted as emotional intelligence is actually a discrete brain process instantiated in a particular gyrus. Yet this is unlikely to be the case. Complex constructs emerge from the activity of large numbers of more basic functions, and the mapping of any complex construct to a discrete anatomical focus seems improbable.

Third, the course of neural activity need not be **isomorphic** with the presumed behavior of the construct. Does increased attention have to be manifest as an increased BOLD signal? Or could attention decrease BOLD activity in a brain region? Does maintaining a memory over a 20-second period require neurons to continually fire for 20 seconds? While many fMRI statistical analyses assume isomorphism between stimuli and the evoked neural activity, this assumption has been called into question by many studies.

Fourth, the very nature of most physiological methods in cognitive neuroscience ensures that researchers find evidence for **localization of function.** All of the many techniques discussed in this chapter provide data that are spatially differentiated. Thus, it is not surprising that studies using these techniques often conclude that the psychological construct tested is localized to a small network of spatially discrete regions. A cognitive function that was equally distributed throughout brain tissue would be nearly invisible to the physiological techniques described in this book.

Finally, investigators often implicitly assume that, within some limits, functions are localized in the same brain regions of different individuals. In many fMRI studies, great effort is expended to normalize each individual's brain anatomy to a common standardized brain space or atlas (see Chapter 10). Normalization improves the statistical reliability of the inferences we draw from imaging data, while providing a degree of comfort to scientists who are suspicious of single observations. Similar methods have been devised to standardize electrophysiological and lesion data into common coordinate systems. While normalization methods have been extraordinarily useful for many research questions, they are not appropriate for functions that are located in different regions across individuals. For example, the hemispheric laterality of language can vary with handedness or as a result of early brain injury. If a subject group contained some left-handed and some right-handed individuals, a group statistical analysis might reveal a widespread system of activation even though each subject had a highly focal pattern. When studying questions related to language function, therefore, investigators often select subjects with an eye toward minimizing suspected differences in brain organization (e.g., choosing only right-handed individuals).

Strategies for Research in Cognitive Neuroscience

In contrast to the idealized strategy discussed earlier in this chapter, the real practice of cognitive neuroscience is messy, iterative, and incremental. A research hypothesis may be initiated by a concept from psychology, like the distinction between short-term and long-term memory. Or, the spark may come from a neurological observation, for example, that bilateral lesions of the medial temporal lobe lead to a permanent inability for an individual to create new memories. Following the initial hypothesis is a cycle of testing, refinements of the hypothesis, and more testing.

Physiological data, and in particular fMRI, can play an important role in this bootstrapping process, by breaking down complex behavior into functional subcomponents. One strategy is to assume that processes that occur at different anatomical loci or at different temporal latencies are different. Following this logic, if you run the perfect experiment to isolate your favorite psychological construct, and you reliably identify several discrete foci of activity, then your construct must have several subcomponents. You can then perform additional experiments to try to dissociate these subcomponents on the basis of psychological manipulations. A related strategy reverses the emphasis. You can test a wide range of experimental manipulations to see which alter the activity of a single brain region. To what stimuli is this area sensitive? Does its activity change with learning? Must a stimulus be attended for activity to be evoked, or is activity evoked automatically? How does activity change if the subject is given extensive experience with nonpreferred stimuli?

By continually testing and revising hypotheses about brain function, cognitive neuroscientists can transform an ill-defined psychological construct into a clear theory whose components are associated with specific brain structures. In the following sections, we describe the various techniques used by cognitive neuroscientists to test their hypotheses. Within each section, we describe the technique, its applications, and its relation to fMRI research. We hope to convey how converging studies using these seemingly

direct cortical stimulation Applying small currents directly to brain tissue to excite or disrupt neural activity. Direct cortical stimulation is usually conducted in humans to localize critical brain regions in the context of neurosurgery.

microstimulation Applying currents through microelectrodes to stimulate activity in a small number of neurons.

transcranial magnetic stimulation (TMS) A technique for temporarily stimulating a brain region to disrupt its function. TMS uses an electromagnetic coil placed close to the scalp; when current passes through the coil, it generates a magnetic field in the nearby brain tissue, producing localized electrical currents.

equipotentiality The concept that a function is so widely distributed within the brain that it depends upon the activity of the brain as a whole. Equipotentiality is the antithesis to localization of function.

disparate techniques provide the best opportunity for advances in our understanding of brain function.

Changing Neuronal Activity

Any scientific method can be described by what it measures and how that measure relates to some process of interest. Some methods directly measure a process of interest by quantifying its output. For example, if you are interested in the effects of an experimental manipulation upon the voltage across a wire, you can measure the voltage change directly using a voltmeter attached to electrodes on the wire. Analogously, to measure voltage changes associated with neuronal activity, you can place electrodes directly on the brain surface. Other methods are indirect and measure another process that is correlated with, but not necessarily caused by, the process of interest. Most brain imaging methods, including fMRI, provide indirect measures of neuronal activity. If the correlation between the measured process and the process of interest is high and reliable, then indirect measures can be very valuable. However, if these processes are only weakly correlated, or can be dissociated by the activities of yet other (often unknown) processes, then the value of indirect methods is diminished.

For research questions about psychological constructs, all methods of measuring brain activity are indirect (see Figures 11.3 and 11.4). Even when neuronal activity is measured directly, as in some electrophysiological techniques, it does not necessarily reflect the psychological construct of interest. For this reason, neuroimaging and electrophysiological techniques are commonly criticized as revealing correlations, not causation. That is, while they can demonstrate an association between a brain region and a psychological construct, they cannot establish that the brain region is necessary for the construct. Rephrasing this point as a question: If an investigator demonstrates with fMRI that the performance of a working memory task activates a specific region of the dorsolateral prefrontal cortex, would the removal of that activated cortex impair working memory? To answer such a question, cognitive neuroscientists must manipulate neuronal activity and then measure the effects of that manipulation upon behavior.

Direct Cortical Stimulation

An extremely important technique for establishing the necessity of a brain region for a cognitive construct is cortical stimulation, or the application of electrical current to evoke neuronal activity. Three primary stimulation techniques are in use today. In **direct cortical stimulation,** electrical current is introduced through relatively large electrodes that are placed on the surface of the brain or directly into brain tissue. Many modern animal studies use **microstimulation** techniques that activate only a small number of neurons. And, through the introduction of a focal magnetic field from outside the skull, a process known as **transcranial magnetic stimulation (TMS)** (described later in this chapter), activity can be evoked in neurons within a large brain region.

The first scientific studies of direct cortical stimulation were reported in the 1870s, as part of a period of transition in the understanding of brain function. Before this time, the dominant concept of brain organization had been the idea of **equipotentiality,** that cognitive functions were equally distributed throughout the cortex. This idea had been based in large part upon the work of the French physiologist Pierre Flourens, who lesioned the brains of rabbits and pigeons and observed the effects on behavior. Lesions to subcortical structures caused specific functional damage (e.g., lesioning the medulla impaired respiration), but damage to the cortex never was functionally specific. Based on these results and those from other laboratories using other species, Flourens became a vocal opponent of the idea of localization of function in the cortex and of its advocates (e.g., Gall). However, by Flourens's death in 1867, evidence had begun to accumulate in favor of cortical localization, notably Broca's 1861 observation of aphasia caused by a circumscribed left frontal lesion. Within this changing climate, the German physiologists Gustav Fritsch and Eduard Hitzig reported that direct cortical stimulation of anterior regions of the cortex in the dog caused muscular movements of the contralateral side. Stimulation of other brain regions produced no such movement. Their results precipitated an explosion of interest in cortical stimulation, and researchers such as the British scientist David Ferrier soon mapped much of the sensory and motor cortices. By the 1876 publication of Ferrier's influential book *The Function of the Brain,* the evidence against equipotentiality had become overwhelming.

Today, direct cortical stimulation is most frequently used to map areas of critical function (e.g., language, motor abilities) in patients awaiting or undergoing neurosurgery. Based on a map that delineates critical functional regions, neurosurgeons may change the path taken through the brain surface to remove a deep tumor or may remove more or less tissue during a resection. This minimizes the chance that the patient will suffer from motor, language, or other deficits following surgery. An early pioneer of this approach was the American-born neurosurgeon Wilder Penfield, who helped found the Montreal Neurological Institute. During the 1940s and 1950s, Penfield and his colleagues methodically mapped the human brain in awake patients undergoing surgery. In addition to the sensory and motor cortices, Penfield studied brain regions involved in language processing and memory. Within the discipline of neurosurgery, direct cortical stimulation remains the standard for functional brain mapping.

In the modern practice of direct cortical stimulation, a pair of stimulating electrodes are placed on the surface of the cortex (Figure 15.1A). One electrode, designated the **anode,** provides a source of electrical current, while the second electrode, designated the **cathode,** provides a sink to which the current will flow. The stimulation usually consists of trains of weak (1 to 10 μA), rapidly presented (50 Hz) current pulses, each 100 to 500 μs in duration. During stimulation, brain tissue in the current path from the anode to the cathode is depolarized. Stimulation mapping is often conducted during the surgery itself. The surgeon moves the electrodes to different locations on the

anode A source of positive charge or ions, and an attractor for free electrons.

cathode An attractor for positive charge or ions, and a source of free electrons.

(A)

(B)

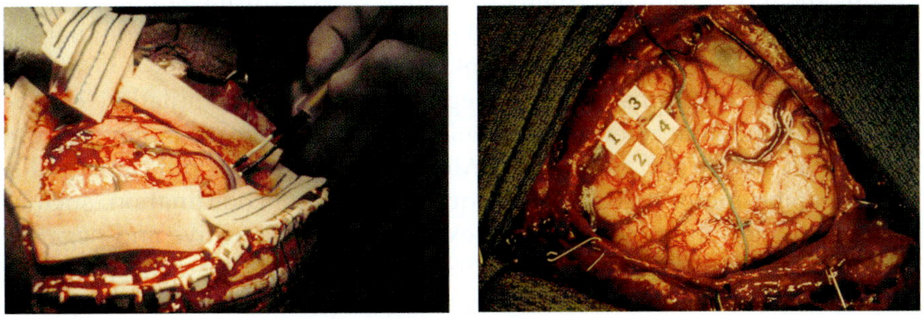

Figure 15.1 Direct cortical stimulation. In some neurosurgical procedures, it is important to localize particular functional brain regions that might be located near the planned excision. In direct cortical stimulation performed during surgery, a surgeon places a pair of stimulating electrodes on the surface of the brain while testing the patient for language comprehension, speech, sensation, or movement. In (A), the surgeon's gloved hand can be seen holding the cathode and anode above the brain's surface. In (B), functional areas of the brain are marked by sterile tickets that indicate what function was evoked or interrupted at that site. (Courtesy of Dr. Dennis D. Spencer, Yale University; photographs by Joseph Jasiorkowski.)

Figure 15.2 An 8 by 8 grid of electrodes embedded in a sylastic grid and placed on the exposed cortical surface of the human brain. (Courtesy of Dr. Dennis D. Spencer, Yale University; photograph by Joseph Jasiorkowski.)

exposed cortical surface, tests the effect of stimulation on the function(s) of interest, and then places numbered sterile paper tickets as markers of function (Figure 15.1B). If sensory or language functions are being tested, the patient needs to be awake and cooperative during that part of the procedure. Some muscular twitches evoked by stimulation can be observed with patients who are under light anesthesia.

In patients with some forms of epilepsy, grids of electrodes are sometimes implanted subdurally over a period of days or weeks (Figure 15.2). The grids are typically constructed of a flexible sylastic sheet into which small electrodes are embedded. A typical grid may consist of an 8 by 8 array of electrodes, each separated by 1 cm and therefore covering 49 cm^2 of cortex. By recording the frequency and locations of seizures within this grid, the patient's doctors can determine whether a particular surgical excision would reduce seizure frequency or eliminate the seizures entirely. In these circumstances, direct cortical stimulation mapping is sometimes performed using these electrode grids. Electrical current is systematically introduced between adjacent pairs of electrodes while the subject is engaged in a language, motor, or perceptual task. As patients are conscious, alert, and comfortable during these extraoperative stimulation studies, much useful information has been obtained about higher cognitive function in this setting.

Functional Consequences of Direct Cortical Stimulation

The consequences of direct cortical stimulation differ across brain regions. In some regions, stimulation evokes a positive response; for example, stimulation of that part of the primary motor cortex responsible for hand movement might evoke flexion of the fingers in the contralateral hand, and stimulation of the mouth region may cause the lips to twitch or the tongue to move. Positive responses provide particularly strong evidence of the causal role of a brain region for an action or percept. In other regions, stimulation might inhibit activity. Stimulation of a small region of the left inferior frontal region (i.e., Broca's area) can cause speech arrest, even though patients can still move their mouth and tongue on command. After the stimulation ends, patients report that they knew what they wanted to say but had been unable to say it. During stimulation of Wernicke's area in the posterior temporal cortex, patients remain able to speak but they may not be able to understand the speech of others, carry out spoken commands, or complete simple sentences. Or, stimulation may have no effects at all. This may occur because the current density is too weak to depolarize nearby neurons (and thus increasing current may yield a response), or it may result from a failure to test the specific process supported by that region. For example, as described in the following paragraph, stimulation of some regions of the fusiform gyrus in the temporal lobe produces an inability to recognize familiar faces while preserving the ability to name familiar objects. If an investigator was testing the recognition of visually presented objects during stimulation but never included faces in the test set, he might mistakenly conclude that the fusiform gyrus was functionally silent.

Sometimes both positive and negative effects of stimulation can be obtained at the same site. Stimulation of the supplementary motor area can evoke both simple and complex coordinated motor actions but can also disrupt ongoing motor activity that requires bimanual coordination, such as twiddling one's thumbs. A striking example of both positive and negative effects of stimulation comes from a 1999 study by Puce and colleagues, who stimulated electrode sites on intracranial grids within the fusiform gyrus.

Before stimulation, the researchers showed the subjects photographs of familiar and famous faces, whom the subjects were able to identify. The faces, but not other stimulus categories, evoked large changes in electrical potential in electrodes within the fusiform gyrus. The investigators then stimulated those electrodes. Several of the subjects became prosopagnosic during the duration of the stimulation; that is, they could no longer recognize the faces, although they could recognize common objects. Once the stimulation ended, they could once again recognize these individuals. While the disruption of face recognition by stimulation was a noteworthy finding, there was the possibility that the effect was not specific to faces. Perhaps the disruption would have also occurred for any object that had a specific ellipsoidal shape, was of the category of living things, or had bilateral symmetry. However, in two of the subjects, stimulation evoked a vivid hallucination of a face. This remarkable positive effect of stimulation provided strong evidence that the observed disruption was specific to faces.

homotopic The cortex in one cerebral hemisphere that corresponds to the same region in the other hemisphere.

> ### Thought Question
>
> Can you think of a circumstance where the evocation of a complex behavior by cortical stimulation of a brain region may not be evidence of a causal role of that region in that behavior?

While direct cortical stimulation is a potentially powerful technique, it has several limitations. First, it is invasive and may precipitate a seizure, particularly in patients who suffer from epilepsy. This risk underscores the fact that direct cortical stimulation can only be performed in a clinical context. Second, at high current levels, current sufficient to depolarize neurons may spread from the stimulating electrodes and excite brain regions at some distance. This can introduce uncertainty in the interpretation of the localization results. For this reason, the cathode and anode are usually kept in close proximity, and the investigator gradually increases the stimulating current so that the threshold at which a stimulation effect is first observed can be monitored. Third, positive or negative effects of stimulation do not necessarily indicate that the surgical removal of the stimulated region will cause corresponding deficits. For example, a 1986 stimulation study by Luders and colleagues revealed the existence of a basal temporal language area in the left fusiform gyrus, whose stimulation leads to the inability to speak or understand language. Despite these striking deficits, surgical removal of this region does not typically lead to the same severe and lasting language deficits that would occur with removal of Wernicke's or Broca's area. Why does damage to some brain areas lead to functional deficits, while damage to others results only in mild or transient deficits? As we will consider in the discussion of lesion studies later in the chapter, this may reflect the ability of the brain to reorganize some functions following damage, perhaps by engaging **homotopic** regions in the opposite hemisphere.

Several published studies have directly compared direct cortical stimulation and fMRI. In 1999, Schlosser and colleagues tested patients who were about to undergo surgery in the language-dominant temporal lobe (see Figure 12.21). To help guide the neurosurgeon, localization of temporal lobe language regions was attempted preoperatively using fMRI, and direct cortical stimulation was later performed either extraoperatively or intraopera-

repetitive TMS (rTMS) A series of closely spaced TMS stimulation pulses.

tively. The fMRI study used a blocked design in which native English-speaking subjects passively listened to speech that alternated between familiar (English) and unfamiliar (Turkish) languages. The same speaker was used throughout, and basic auditory properties were controlled between the two conditions. Thus, the subject heard a near continuous stream of speech, but his comprehension of speech varied between blocks. Greater activation was observed in response to the English speech in the lateral temporal (i.e., Wernicke's area) and inferior frontal (i.e., Broca's area) cortices in the language-dominant hemisphere of most subjects tested.

Direct cortical stimulation was also used to localize the lateral temporal language region in 14 of the fMRI subjects. At electrode locations near the locations of fMRI activity, cortical stimulation interfered with auditory comprehension, object naming, or speech production tasks in 12 subjects. Stimulation therefore validated the results obtained from the fMRI task. However, while the correspondence between temporal lobe language areas identified by fMRI and by direct cortical stimulation was generally good, differences were noted in the spatial extent of activation using these different methods. As noted in Chapter 7, the spatial extent of fMRI activation may overestimate the area in which neuronal activation occurs, and so some discrepancies in spatial extent might be expected. However, because the spatial limits of the activation may influence the extent of a surgical resection, better methods to identify the boundaries of fMRI activation must be developed (see Box 12.2). Nevertheless, the results of Schlosser and colleagues suggest that information from direct cortical stimulation may provide important evidence that complements that obtained by fMRI studies.

Transcranial Magnetic Stimulation

Heretofore, we have discussed invasive methods for direct cortical stimulation that involve opening the skull to place electrodes against the brain. An alternative method, transcranial magnetic stimulation (TMS), was introduced in the 1980s. In TMS studies, an electrical coil is placed on the outside of the skull and rapidly charged with current (Figure 15.3A). This generates a strong magnetic field (as large as 2 T) that lasts less than a millisecond. This field extends through the skull and into the brain, where it produces an electrical current by electromagnetic induction (Figure 15.3B). The configuration of the coil influences the focality of the field and, thus, the spread of the electrical current. One popular coil design has the shape of a figure eight, for which the field is maximal near the midway point between the coils. TMS can be used to deliver a single brief electrical pulse to the brain, or it can be used to deliver a series of pulses for durations that span seconds to minutes (**repetitive TMS**, or **rTMS**). In addition to its value for functional brain studies, rTMS has also shown promise in the treatment of disorders such as depression, perhaps by increasing dopamine levels in the frontal cortex.

> ### Thought Question
> How is TMS related to the discussion of the effects of dB/dT explored in Chapter 2?

As currently practiced, TMS is considered a safe and noninvasive method and has been used in more than 2000 published studies of both normal vol-

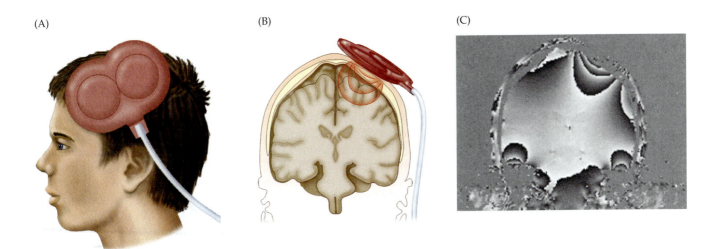

Figure 15.3 Transcranial magnetic stimulation (TMS). In TMS, an electromagnetic coil is placed on the surface of the skull (A). Rapidly reversing the flow of a very strong current within the coil induces a current field in the brain (B). The magnetic field lines associated with a TMS pulse can be seen in the upper right of this coronal MRI phase map (C). (C from Drs. Daryl Bohning and Mark George, Medical University of South Carolina.)

unteers and patients. Indeed, one of the authors of this textbook was a volunteer subject in one of the first studies performed to test the safety of the single-pulse TMS method. It should be noted, however, that prior to the establishment of safe operating limits and procedures, rTMS evoked seizures in a small number of presumably normal subjects who had no prior history of seizure disorders. Also, due to current spread, the actual brain regions stimulated are even more uncertain than in the direct cortical stimulation studies discussed earlier. In 1997 Bohning and colleagues used MRI phase maps to visualize the distribution within the brain of the magnetic field induced by TMS (Figure 15.3C) to help localize the sites of stimulation.

TMS has been used creatively in a large number of studies of brain function. By manipulating the latency at which a pulse is applied to a given brain region, researchers can interrupt processing at different points in time. For example, in 2003, Mottaghy and colleagues used single-pulse TMS to study verbal working memory in a two-back task (see Figure 13.13 for a depiction of the *n*-back task). The delay between the task stimulus and the delivery of the TMS was varied over a range of 140 to 500 ms. The authors found that working memory processes were impaired by shorter-latency TMS delivered to the parietal cortex and by longer-latency TMS delivered to the frontal cortex. This suggested that the flow of information was from parietal to frontal sites. Within the frontal lobe, TMS delivered to the right hemisphere caused disruption at earlier delays than in the left frontal region, suggesting a flow of information from right to left hemispheres. It is important to note that the delivery of TMS did not disrupt a choice reaction time control task that did not have a working memory component. Thus, the effects of TMS were specific to working memory processes and specific to particular time points.

One of the most promising uses of TMS has been to determine whether regions activated in fMRI studies are essential for task performance. For example, in 2002 Rushworth and colleagues used fMRI to identify regions of the frontal lobe that were activated during two forms of task switching. In the response-switching condition, subjects switched between rules for selecting a response, while in the visual-switching condition, subjects switched between rules for selecting a stimulus. For each trial in each condition, the subject either kept or switched the rule from the previous trial. Although the two conditions evoked fMRI activity in different sets of brain regions, both activated the medial frontal cortex in the region of the pre-supplementary motor area (pre-SMA). The authors thus hypothesized that this region plays an important role in task switching. To test this hypothesis, the authors later stimulated the pre-SMA using rTMS. This disrupted both tasks, but only on trials when the subject switched from the previous task rule. When the TMS stimulator was moved over motor cortex adjacent to the region of fMRI activity, stimulation had no effect on the task. Taken with the fMRI results, these TMS data provide important converging evidence that the pre-SMA is a critical brain region in task switching and, furthermore, that its role is limited to the time of a switch. While combined or parallel use of TMS and fMRI is still in its infancy, such studies will become increasingly important in coming years.

Brain Lesions

The most venerable approach for studying the function of the brain is the observation of functional changes associated with brain lesions. Shortly after Broca's 1861 discovery, many other functional changes associated with brain lesions in humans were reported. In 1868, Dr. John Harlow described his observations of Phineas Gage, a railroad foreman in Cavendish, Vermont, who in 1848 had suffered a horrible accident in which an explosive charge blasted an iron tamping rod through his left cheekbone and out of the top of his head. Gage not only survived the accident (and was able to walk and speak within minutes) but lived for another 12 years. However, the frontal lobe injury caused a dramatic change in personality. His prior well-balanced and responsible bearing was replaced by a profane and irresponsible demeanor in which he showed little regard for others. Gage's case was one of the first cases in which a profound alteration of personality was linked to a lesion within a specific brain region. Many early researchers, including the German neurologist Hermann Munk, created controlled, experimental lesions in animals to make important discoveries about the organization of the cerebral cortex. Other scientists, like David Ferrier, used both lesion and cortical stimulation studies in animals in their research.

Lesion studies in both humans and animals are still an important method for the study of brain function. Like cortical stimulation, which can be considered to create a transient and reversible lesion, lesion studies provide information about the necessity of a brain region for a particular function. Yet by themselves, lesion studies have several disadvantages. Studies in humans depend primarily upon naturally occurring lesions, such as those produced by a stroke, that can be large and extend across many functional brain regions. This variability makes it difficult or impossible for investigators to assemble a group of patients with identical lesions. Furthermore, natural lesions often involve damage to white-matter pathways, impairing functions that are supported by distant brain regions that were undamaged but became disconnected. These problems can be ameliorated by studying patients with well-defined surgical lesions, such as patients who have received a temporal lobectomy to relieve intractable epileptic seizures. However, these patients have suffered for many years from a preexisting neurological disorder and often continue to take powerful drugs that may alter normal brain function.

Lesion studies can also have interpretive difficulties. Unlike the positive results sometimes observed with direct cortical stimulation, lesions do not *produce* complex behaviors. Thus, the loss of function following a brain lesion does not guarantee that the damaged brain tissue was the locus for that particular function. For example, a large lesion in the primary visual cortex would impair not only basic visual perception but also many higher-order functions like object recognition, reading, and eye gaze perception. It would be absurd to suggest that all of these visually based functions resided in the primary visual cortex, yet this region was clearly essential for every one of them. For this reason, investigators who employ the lesion approach systematically compare the pattern of associations and dissociations between lesions in different brain regions and performance on different experimental tasks.

To this end, several groups around the world have established large databases, or **registries,** of individuals who have brain lesions and who have been studied in a large number of different tasks. One example is the Cognitive Neuroscience Patient Registry developed by Antonio and Hanna Damasio and their many collaborators at the University of Iowa. Another is the patient registry developed by Robert Knight and his colleagues at the University of California, Berkeley. By evaluating the effects of damage to different brain regions, as determined by quantitative reconstructions of lesions across many subjects, researchers can identify patient groups who share a particular functional impairment. Figure 15.4 presents an example of this approach. By recording lesion characteristics from a large group of subjects, impairments across a spectrum of tasks can be mapped to particular regions of damage.

Lesion studies have considerable value for dissection of complex tasks into their subcomponents. In 1955, Teuber introduced the concept of the **double dissociation** (see Chapter 13 for a discussion of similar logic applied to fMRI). By demonstrating that a lesion to brain structure A impairs function X but not function Y, a researcher establishes a **single dissociation** between the functions. But with the additional result that that a second lesion to structure B disrupts function Y while leaving function X intact, the researcher has established a double dissociation, and can make more-specific inferences about brain function. Consider the following example. An investigator creates a model for face processing that hypothesizes the existence of separate functions for retrieving face identity and for the recognition of emotional facial expression. A single dissociation would demonstrate that damage to a specific brain region (e.g., the ventral temporal lobe) impairs judgments of face identity but not judgments of emotional expressions. This result is consistent with the model, but it might also have resulted from other factors, such as higher functional SNR on one task than the other. More-powerful support for this model would come from the second demonstration that damage to a different brain region (e.g., the right frontoparietal region) impairs judgments of emotional expressions but not of identity. Readers interested in additional discussion of lesion interpretation in the context of neuropsychological theory, including caveats concerning double dissociation, should refer to the book by Shallice listed in the suggested readings.

registry A patient database. A registry might include information about the locations of brain lesions in a large population of individuals who might then be asked to participate in experimental studies.

double dissociation The demonstration that two experimental manipulations have different effects on two dependent variables. One manipulation affects the first variable but not the second, and the other manipulation affects the second but not the first.

single dissociation The demonstration that an experimental manipulation has an effect upon one variable but not upon a second variable.

Left dorsal prefrontal

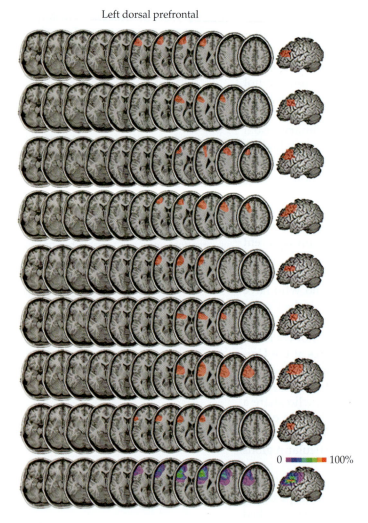

0 ▰▰▰▰▰ 100%

Figure 15.4 Lesion maps from a patient registry. Shown are the extent of lesions in the left dorsal prefrontal cortex for eight subjects. The lesions are indicated by red shading on a stack of axial slices and on a surface reconstruction. The bottom row shows a color-coded summary that indicates the degree of lesion overlap in this sample. (Courtesy of Dr. Robert Knight, University of California, Berkeley.)

plasticity The change in the normal functional properties of brain tissue following injury or experience.

recovery of function The improvement in a previously impaired ability over time, due to functional or structural changes within the brain.

Combined Lesion and fMRI Studies

Evidence from lesion studies can greatly extend the interpretive power of fMRI. When a process both evokes fMRI activity in a brain region and is disrupted when that region is lesioned, researchers can more readily conclude that the process relies on the brain region for its execution. The benefits of converging lesion and fMRI studies are thus similar to those of combined direct cortical stimulation and fMRI studies, as discussed earlier.

Most studies that have combined lesion analysis and fMRI in the same individual have investigated the influence of a developmental lesion upon a well-localized function, such as language processes in the left hemisphere. For example, in 2002, Staudt and colleagues studied five individuals who had suffered left hemisphere lesions around the time of birth. When tested in language activation tasks, these individuals showed a pattern of right hemisphere activation that was virtually the mirror result of the left hemisphere activation pattern obtained in age-matched controls without brain lesions. From these fMRI results, the authors argued that early damage to left hemisphere regions supporting language results in the recruitment of homotopic regions in the undamaged right hemisphere. Another example comes from the 1997 work of Schlosser and colleagues, who studied a 19-year-old patient with a large arteriovenous malformation in her right frontal and rostral parietal lobes. As a result, she had experienced poor motor control of the left side of her body (i.e., hemiparesis) since childhood. While she had no motor control over her left hand, sensation was preserved. An fMRI study was conducted using a blocked design in which the left and right hands were alternately stroked by a brush. Strong activation was obtained in response to both right- and left-hand sensation, but, as illustrated in Figure 15.5, stroking the left hand activated the primary sensory region of the *ipsilateral* left hemisphere. That is, her brain was reorganized so that sensations from both sides of the body were (at least partially) represented in the same hemisphere. These fMRI studies provide strong evidence for the functional **plasticity** of the human cortex in response to early brain injury.

Combined fMRI and lesion methods have also been used to study **recovery of function** in individuals who acquired lesions in adulthood from stroke or other brain injury. Using fMRI, TMS, and magnetoencephalography, in 1998, Rossini and colleagues investigated changes in the brain of a poststroke patient who had recovered significant motor function. Their results suggested that the sensorimotor cortex in the affected hemisphere was enlarged, and shifted posteriorly, compared to the other hemisphere. In a similar study conducted in 1997, Cramer and colleagues used fMRI to study 10 patients who had recovered good motor function following stroke.

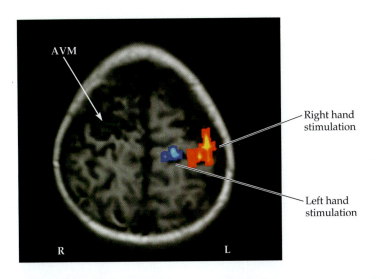

Figure 15.5 Evidence for functional plasticity from combined lesion/fMRI studies. Shown are the patterns of fMRI activations evoked by stroking the right hand (red) and left hand (blue) in a patient with a large arteriovenous malformation (AVM) in the right hemisphere. Note that the response to the left hand occurs in the left, or ipsilesional, hemisphere. (From Schlosser et al., 1997.)

When the patients performed a finger tapping task, activity in the sensorimotor cortex of the unaffected hemisphere was *increased* relative to controls. Increased activation was also found in the SMA and cerebellum. These results suggest that recovery of motor function after stroke involves the increased participation of homotopic regions of the unaffected hemisphere and midline motor regions. While some activation was obtained in the affected hemisphere of the stroke patients, it was restricted to the edge of the cortical infarct. Because of its localization power and noninvasiveness, fMRI can be used both to complement lesion studies in order to understand brain organization and to supplement lesion data in order to investigate functional changes associated with the lesions.

Thought Question

What properties of fMRI may make it a poor choice for assessing function in patients with vascular lesions?

Probabilistic Brain Atlases

To this point, we have discussed two forms of lesions: those in which brain tissue has been excised surgically and those where focal damage or injury has made the existing tissue nonviable. In many diseases that affect the brain (e.g., Alzheimer's disease, schizophrenia), such frank and focal lesions do not occur. Rather, regions within the brain of an afflicted individual may exhibit tissue volume loss that progresses over the course of the illness. As with lesions due to stroke or surgery, volume loss in particular regions may impair specific cognitive functions, and thus fMRI studies in these patient groups may be valuable as a prognostic indicator.

New image processing techniques take advantage of large MRI databases and advanced computational methods to determine which regions vary between normal and diseased brains. Recall that in Chapter 10, we discussed how preprocessing fMRI data often involves the warping of the brains from individual subjects into a stereotaxic space to simplify statistical

Figure 15.6 Variability in brain anatomy. Overlaid upon the rendered brains are maps of the variability in brain anatomy in the cortex of control and schizophrenic subjects (both males and females). Areas of high variability across individuals are shown in red-purple, while areas of low variability across individuals are shown in blue. Increased variability is observed in the frontal cortex for both male and female schizophrenics. (Courtesy of Drs. Katherine Narr and Arthur Toga, Laboratory of Neuroimaging, University of California, Los Angeles.)

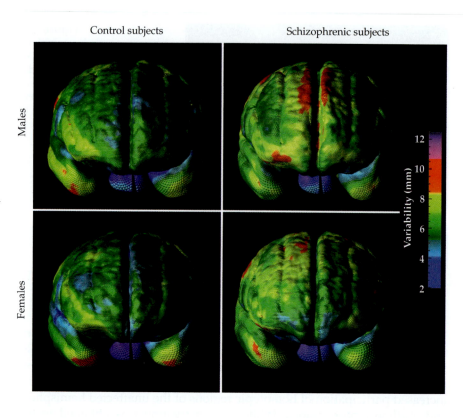

polymorphism A common variation in a gene or segment of DNA.

imaging genomics A new field that investigates the effect of genetic variation upon brain structure and function.

analyses across subjects. The degree to which a brain must be warped to match a normalized space is itself of interest, because it provides a quantitative measure of regional brain variability. Investigators are using such measures to study structural differences between the diseased and normal brain. Figure 15.6 illustrates the relative variability of samples of brains from schizophrenic individuals and from normal controls. Note that the brains of the schizophrenic individuals show greater variability (red-purple colors) in several regions of the frontal lobes, including the midline. This finding corroborates fMRI results from many groups across a variety of tasks that have demonstrated that schizophrenic subjects show abnormal fMRI activation patterns in the prefrontal cortex. Readers interested in learning more about the use of probabilistic brain atlases to study human disease are referred to the article by Toga and colleagues in the suggested readings.

Brain Imaging and Genomics

For a growing number of neurological and psychiatric disorders, there are variations, or **polymorphisms,** in some genes that signal increased risk for an individual developing the disease. As researchers begin to investigate the effects of these polymorphisms upon brain function, a new field has emerged that has been named by Hariri and Weinberger as **imaging genomics.**

An early and notable study conducted by Bookheimer and colleagues in 2000 used fMRI to investigate memory processes in people with and without genetic risk factors for dementia. In their study, 30 individuals were tested, all of whom were neurologically normal and had memory scores within the normal range for their age. However, 16 of the individuals carried the epsilon 4 allele of the apolipoprotein E gene (*APOE-4*), which is associated with an increased risk of developing Alzheimer's disease in individuals experiencing cognitive decline. The remaining 14 individuals carried the epsilon 3 allele (*APOE-3*) and thus were not at increased risk. When participating in an fMRI experiment of retrieval of items from memory, the *APOE-4* group showed increased activation of the hippocampus, the parietal cortex, and the prefrontal cortex. These structures have been implicated as important to memory by many experiments. When a subgroup of subjects were tested on memory tests two years later, the decline in their memory performance was predicted by the degree of increased activation. That is, *APOE-4* individuals who had increased fMRI activity in these regions were more likely to have later memory impairments. These results suggest that fMRI can detect subtle patterns of damage that may result in later functional deficits, even prior to the development of clinically apparent memory deficits or disease onset. Also of interest is the suggestion that increased fMRI activation may reflect compensatory processes that offset the functional consequences of the incipient disease.

In 2002, Hariri and colleagues examined individuals with a variation in a gene related to the neurotransmitter serotonin. This variation had previously been linked to increased behavioral measures of anxiety, but the relation was weak and unreliable across different studies. The researchers used fMRI to test two groups of subjects, one with the genetic variation and one without, all of whom were healthy and had no neurological or psychiatric disorders. The subjects viewed pictures of faces that depicted fearful or angry expressions. Previous research had established that these pictures evoke significant activity in the amygdala, a region of the brain associated with emotional processing. However, despite the fact that the groups did not differ on anxiety- or fear-related traits, the subjects with the genetic variation showed a greater response in the right amygdala to the fearful and angry faces. This study demonstrated the power of fMRI to probe the functional consequences of genetic variation. Readers interested in this fascinating new field should consult the suggested readings.

In summary, information about brain structure provided by stimulation, lesion, or TMS studies complements information about brain function provided by fMRI. Inferences made using one technique are improved by converging studies using the other. Questions about causality that are raised by fMRI results can be answered using lesion studies, just as fMRI can answer questions about large-scale systems and recovery of function that are raised by lesion data. Furthermore, fMRI can assess the functional consequences of statistical differences in brain structure and in genetic variation. As a result, techniques that examine the consequences of changes in neuronal activity will continue to be critical for research programs in cognitive neuroscience.

Measuring Neuronal Activity

The first electrophysiological studies were conducted in 1848 by the German physiologist Emil Du Bois-Reymond, who discovered that nerves in a frog exhibit **action potentials.** Shortly afterwards, Hermann von Helmholtz used action potentials to measure the speed of conduction along the frog's nerve. It is a scientific irony that Du Bois-Reymond and Helmholtz were both students of the physiologist Johannes Müller, who believed in the vitalist ideas that activity of the nervous system was ephemeral and thus could not be measured experimentally. The studies of Du Bois-Reymond, Helmholtz, and their contemporaries such as Julius Bernstein did much to explain neural trans-

action potential A wave of depolarization that travels down a neuronal axon.

BOX 15.1 Electrogenesis

In Chapter 6, we introduced the sequence of events associated with the depolarization of a small segment of the neuronal membrane. While that discussion was in the context of the resulting metabolic demands, whose supply forms the basis of the fMRI BOLD signal, here we consider the electrophysiological consequences of membrane depolarization. Recall that the movement of ions through membrane channels supports information processing through the **integrative** and **signaling** activity of neurons. In this context, integration refers to the spatiotemporal summation of **excitatory postsynaptic potentials (EPSPs)** and **inhibitory postsynaptic potentials (IPSPs)** on the neuron's dendritic arbors and cell body. EPSPs and IPSPs vary in magnitude and duration depending upon the strength and timing of the synaptic input. If the spatiotemporal summation of EPSPs and IPSPs can be considered a computation performed upon a pattern of synaptic input, then the action potential is the output of this computation. Unlike postsynaptic potentials, action potentials are all-or-none; if the summation of EPSPs and IPSPs at the axon hillock surpasses a threshold, a self-propagating action potential will be triggered. But if the threshold is not surpassed, no action potential will occur. Because the action potential carries information to other interconnected neurons, we refer to action potentials as the signaling component of information processing in the brain.

What do we mean by *electrophysiological*? What properties of ions, membranes, and channels involve electricity? Atoms normally have as many negatively charged electrons as they have positively charged protons, and thus they are electrically neutral, having no net charge. However, if an atom gains or loses one or more electrons, it becomes an electrically charged **ion**.

Na^+ is a positively charged sodium ion because it has lost an electron, while Cl^- is a negatively charged chlorine ion because it has gained an electron. Due to the selective permeability of a neuron's membrane and the action of ionic **pumps,** there is an unequal distribution of ions across the neuronal membrane and thus an unequal distribution of charge. An electrode placed inside of a neuron at rest would record a large potential difference compared to an electrode outside of the neuron, with the interior of the membrane about -70 mV relative to the outside.

Let's consider the sequence of events associated with the depolarization of a small patch of a neuron's membrane. First, there is an inward positive current caused by inflow of positive sodium ions, creating a relative deficit in positive charge within the surrounding extracellular space. The depolarized patch of membrane thus becomes a **current sink** and attracts positively charged ions (Figure 15.7). The inrushing positive charge flows within the neuron and away from the depolarized membrane, creating an intracellular accumulation of positive charge. This, in turn, causes an outward positive current from the unexcited portions of the neuronal membrane. This outward flow constitutes a **current source,** from which the positive ions flow back through the extracellular space toward the sink. To conserve charge, the efflux from the source is equal to the influx at the sink. The strong current flow within the restricted intracellular space of the neuron is called the **primary current,** while the relatively weak return flow through the much larger extracellular conductive medium (or **volume conductor**) is called the **volume current.** While the primary current is confined to the intracellular space of the neuron, the volume currents extend throughout the conductive medium that contains the neuron.

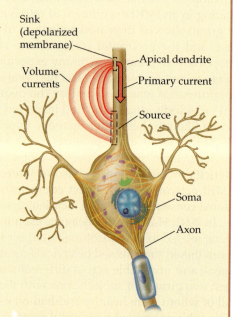

Figure 15.7 Current flow in a depolarized neuron. The patch of depolarization caused by synaptic activity becomes a current sink where current enters the neuron in the form of positively charged Na^+ ions. The buildup of positive charge within the neuron causes a current flow within the neuron called the primary current. To conserve charge, positive current flow exits the unexcited portions of the neuron's membrane, creating a current source. In the extracellular space, return or volume currents flow back toward the sink. Although most dense nearest the neuron, these volume currents extend throughout the brain. When viewed from a distance, the close apposition of the current source and sink approximates a current dipole.

The charge at the current source generates an electric field that is directed radially outward and whose strength decays with the inverse square of distance. That is, doubling the distance from the current source increases the area occupied by the electric field by a factor of 4, and thus the intensity of the electric field is only one-fourth as strong. The

BOX 15.1 *(continued)*

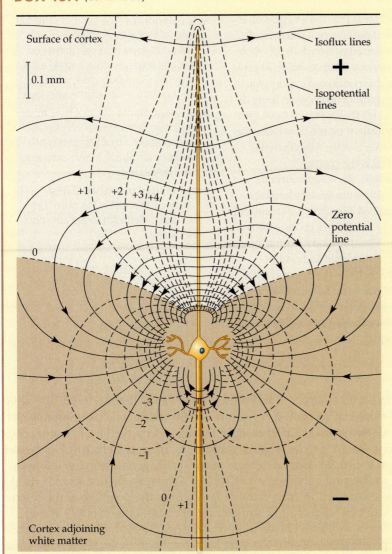

Figure 15.8 The extracellular electric field in the brain associated with neuronal activity. Shown is a representation of the consequences of the depolarization of the soma of a pyramidal cell. The volume currents are shown as solid isoflux lines, while the isopotential lines are shown as dashed. The zero potential line occurs where the flux lines begin to bend inward toward the sink. Relative to the zero potential line, positive potentials are measured above the line and negative potentials are measured below. Note that the field weakens with increasing distance from the neuron. (After Cruetzfeldt, 1974.)

integrative activity The collection of inputs from other neurons through dendritic or somatic connections.

signaling activity The transmission of the outcome of an integrative process from one neuron to another.

excitatory postsynaptic potential (EPSP) A depolarization of the post-synaptic cell membrane.

inhibitory postsynaptic potential (IPSP) A hyperpolarization of the postsynaptic cell membrane.

ion A charged atom.

pump A transport system that moves ions across a cell membrane against their concentration gradient.

current sink An attractor of positive ions. A depolarized patch of neuronal membrane is a current sink because positively charged ions will flow toward it.

current source A source of positive ions.

primary current The current flow within a neuron caused by the inflow of ions through ionic channels opened by synaptic activity.

volume conductor A continuously conductive medium. The brain, meninges, skull, and scalp constitute a volume conductor throughout which currents created by ionic flow can be measured.

volume current The return current through the extracellular medium that balances the primary current within a neuron.

current dipole A positive and negative point charge separated by an infinitesimal distance. A current dipole is used as a simple and convenient model for the electromagnetic fields produced by an activated neuron.

charge at the current sink generates an electrical field that is directed radially inward. Because the distance on the neuron between the source and sink is very small, we can idealize this close apposition of positive and negative point sources as a **current dipole.** The electrical field produced by a dipole is simply the vector sums of the outward- and inward-oriented radial electric fields of the current source and sink. The electric field generated by the current dipole can be conceptualized as a set of flux lines through the volume conductor that connect the point charges (Figure 15.8).

A potential difference can be measured in volts (or, more typically for brain electrophysiology, microvolts) between locations in the electric field. Isopotential

BOX 15.1 *(continued)*

lines, along which the voltage is constant, can be drawn perpendicular to the electric field lines. Because the charges at the source and sink are equal and opposite, the zero potential line is located at the point where the outward-directed field from the source begins to bend inward to the sink. The isopotential lines on the outward-directed side of the field measure positive voltages, while the isopotential lines on the inward-directed side of the field measure negative voltages. In the case of a depolarized neuron, the electric field produced by the source and sink can be measured by electrodes at different points in the extracellular space. For example, if depolarization occurred in the **apical dendrites,** then an electrode near the dendrites would record a negative potential relative to an electrode near the soma. If the soma was depolarized, as

shown in Figure 15.8, the reverse would occur. The dipole is a convenient model for a depolarized neuron. Indeed, when observed from a distance, the fields generated by the coordinated activity of a larger ensemble of neurons can be modeled as though they were produced by a single **equivalent dipole.** This forms the basis for several of the techniques described later in this chapter.

In principle, the volume currents associated with neuronal depolarization can be detected anywhere within the volume conductor. Indeed, because the conductive medium around a neuron includes the entire brain and skull, neuronal activity can be detected with electrodes placed on the scalp. We will return to a discussion of scalp-recorded **event-related potentials,** or **ERPs,** later in this chapter.

apical dendrites The dendrites that are distant from the neuronal cell body. For typical pyramidal cells in the cortex, the apical dendrites extend to the superficial layers of cortex, while the cell bodies are located in deeper layers.

equivalent dipole A simplifying model that represents the electromagnetic field produced by a population of neurons as though it were produced by a single dipole.

event-related potentials (ERPs) Small electrical changes in the brain that are associated with sensory or cognitive events.

---

electroencephalogram (EEG) The measurement of the electrical potential of the brain, usually through electrodes placed on the surface of the scalp.

electrogenesis The explanation for electrophysiological phenomena such as EEG or evoked potentials based upon ionic current flows instigated by synaptic activity.

single-unit recording Collection of data about the electrophysiological activity (e.g., action potentials) of a single neuron.

field potentials Changes in electrical potential over space associated with postsynaptic neuronal activity.

magnetoencephalography (MEG) A noninvasive functional neuroimaging technique that measures very small changes in magnetic fields caused by the electrical activity of neurons, with potentially high spatial and temporal resolution.

mission in peripheral nerves and muscle fibers. However, not until 1875 were the first electrical recordings of brain activity published by the physician Richard Caton of Liverpool. Strongly influenced by the studies of his contemporary David Ferrier, Caton wanted to measure electrical potential changes in the cortex. Because these electrical changes were extremely weak, he used a reflecting galvanometer that had a mirror attached to its coils. As the voltage changed in the cortex of an animal, the position of the mirror moved only very slightly, but sufficiently to cause a much larger change in the position of a reflected beam of light. This primitive amplification method made it possible to observe the very small voltages associated with brain activity. A half century later, the Austrian psychiatrist Hans Berger extended Caton's work by measuring continuous changes in voltage on the scalp over time. The technique that he developed became known as electroencephalography, and its measure became known as the **electroencephalogram (EEG).**

Many different electrophysiological methods exist for studying different facets of neuronal electrical activity, or **electrogenesis** (Box 15.1). At one extreme, these methods can measure changes in ionic conductances at an isolated patch of a single neuron's membrane, while at the other extreme, they can measure the synchronized activity of millions of neurons. We begin our examination of direct measures of neuronal activity with a discussion of the recording of action potentials from individual neurons, a technique known as single-cell or **single-unit recording.** We then discuss the recording of summated **field potentials** associated with postsynaptic activity. Field potentials can be measured in different ways at different scales, using both intracranial electrodes and scalp electrodes. We conclude with a consideration of **magnetoencephalography (MEG),** a technique that records the magnetic fields associated with neuronal activity.

Single-Unit Recording

The most direct measure of neuronal electrical activity is the action potential. The primitive methods used by Du Bois-Reymond to record the action potential in 1848 were greatly advanced by the introduction of the microelectrode in the first half of the 20th century. Microelectrodes are placed either inside of a neuron or next to the neuron's cell body in the extracellular space. Studies measuring the rate of action potentials using microelectrodes, a technique known as single-unit recording, have generated some of the most important discoveries in all of neuroscience.

The value of single-unit recording was powerfully demonstrated in studies initiated in the late 1950s by David Hubel and Torsten Wiesel, who were working at that time in the laboratory of Steven Kuffler at Johns Hopkins University. Using single-cell recording, Kuffler had previously demonstrated that retinal ganglion cells had a center-surround organization. That is, these cells increased their activity when a light was flashed in the center of a **receptive field** and decreased their activity when a light was flashed in the periphery of their receptive field. Hubel and Wiesel extended those studies into the visual cortex (Figure 15.9). By presenting more-complex stimuli, such as lines and edges, Hubel and Wiesel discovered that some cells in the primary visual cortex had receptive fields very different from those of retinal ganglion cells. **Simple cells** had a more rectangular receptive field with adjacent rectangular inhibitory regions, as if combining the output of a line of ganglion cells, and their rate of firing varied with the orientation of the visible line or edge. A similar approach was used to identify a second population of **complex cells,** which responded best to lines of a particular orientation, regardless of their position within the receptive field. Later studies building upon this work described many important properties of the visual cortex, including its columnar arrangement and its changes during development. For these fundamental discoveries, Hubel and Wiesel received the Nobel Prize in Physiology or Medicine in 1981.

receptive field The part of the visual field that, when stimulated, will result in an increase in firing of a particular neuron.

simple cell A neuron in the visual cortex that responds with increased firing to a stimulus with a preferred orientation in its receptive field and with decreased firing to a stimulus in the region surrounding its receptive field.

complex cell A neuron in the visual cortex with a larger receptive field than a simple cell and that responds to a stimulus with preferred orientation anywhere within its receptive field.

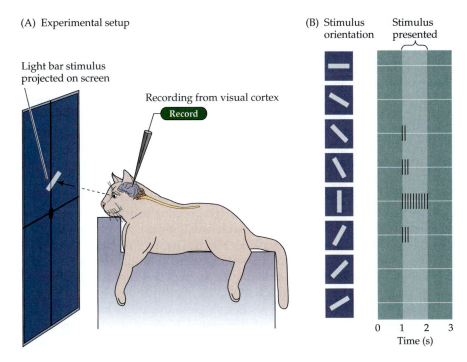

(A) Experimental setup

Light bar stimulus projected on screen

Recording from visual cortex

Record

(B) Stimulus orientation — Stimulus presented

0 1 2 3
Time (s)

Figure 15.9 Single-unit recording. This figure illustrates the recording of a simple cell from the visual cortex of the cat. The cat views slits of light, the orientation of which the experimenters systematically vary. The single-unit discharge is shown for each orientation. The preferred vertical orientation is determined by the abrupt burst of action potentials for this stimulus. Some degree of generalization can be seen by the response of the cells to slightly off-vertical orientations.

Figure 15.10 Single-unit recording in an oculomotor delayed response task. Monkeys were trained to fixate at the center of a display while a target stimulus was illuminated for 500 ms at one of eight peripheral locations. Following offset of the target, the monkey maintained fixation for an additional 3-s delay period. Any eye movement during the presentation of the target or during the delay period caused the trial to be aborted. At the conclusion of the delay period, the fixation cross disappeared and the monkey made a saccade to the remembered location of the visual target and, if correct, received a juice reward. Plotted in the surrounding panels are the single-unit responses from a neuron in the principal sulcus in the prefrontal cortex. Within each of these eight panels, the first pair of vertical lines demarcates the interval during which the visual cue was presented. The last vertical line indicates the offset of the delay period. (From Chafee and Goldman-Rakic, 1998.)

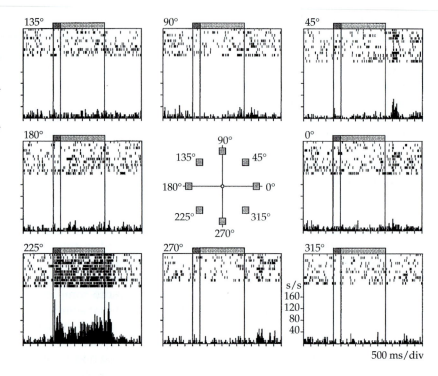

raster A depiction of the firing rate of action potentials by a neuron in which time is represented along the horizontal axis and a dot indicates the occurrence of an action potential.

A more recent example of the value of single-unit recording in cognitive neuroscience is provided by the work of Patricia Goldman-Rakic and her colleagues, who explored the properties of neurons in the monkey's prefrontal cortex during an oculomotor delayed response task. Monkeys were required to remember the location of a visual target that was briefly presented in the periphery, and to make an eye movement to the remembered location at the end of a delay period. The results shown in Figure 15.10 are from Chafee and Goldman-Rakic's 1998 study and illustrate a typical outcome for a neuron in the dorsolateral prefrontal cortex. Shown are eight location panels, each containing a series of rows, or **rasters,** in which a black dot indicates the occurrence of an action potential. Each of the rasters corresponds to one trial of the delayed response task. At the bottom of each panel is a histogram that indicates the number of times the neuron fired at a particular time during the task across all trials. The spatial specificity of this neuron was striking, in that significant firing was only observed when the target was presented at the lower-left location. Even more remarkable was the fact that the neuron fired robustly throughout the delay interval, when the monkey was maintaining the target location in memory. Because there was little to no neuronal activity in the other seven locations, Chafee and Goldman-Rakic suggested that this neuron was coding the specific location of the remembered stimulus and was not responding in a general way to the delay interval. Other neurons in the same small region of cortex responded selectively to the other visual target locations. Due to the spatial selectivity of these neurons (like the primary visual cortex neurons discussed in the previous paragraph), Goldman-Rakic described these to-be-remembered spatial locations as their memory fields.

Because of the clarity of such results, single-unit studies have generated great excitement for the study of the neural basis of working memory. Many fMRI studies have used similar delayed response tasks to demonstrate sustained BOLD activation of the prefrontal cortex and other brain regions. For example, Courtney and colleagues used fMRI in 1997 to demonstrate sustained activity within the dorsolateral prefrontal cortex during an 8-s delay interval between the presentation of to-be-remembered pictures of faces and a test face. Similarly, in 1998, Belger and colleagues presented subjects with a series of delayed-response trials in which the nature of the items to be remembered varied on alternating trials. On spatial trials, the subject was shown successively three white dots in different spatial locations. After a delay of 3500 ms with no stimulus present, a test dot was shown and the subject indicated whether or not it matched one of the remembered locations. On shape trials, the subject was shown successively three complex polygons and, again, was required to indicate after a stimulus-free delay whether a test polygon matched any of the remembered set. Control trials were similarly constructed, but the "memory set" stimuli stayed on the screen throughout the delay interval and thus the subject made a simple discrimination when the test item appeared that did not depend upon memory. As in the study by Courtney and colleagues, strong BOLD activation was observed in the dorsolateral prefrontal cortex in the memory trials but not the control trials. The strength of the activation also varied with the stimulus materials, with primarily right hemisphere activation occurring for the spatial memory trials and bilateral activity occurring for the shape trials. Activation also occurred in the parietal lobe and intraparietal sulcus.

These are but two examples from a major area of fMRI research that was initiated largely on the basis of single-unit studies. Interested readers are directed to the reviews by Miller and Cohen and by Curtis and D'Esposito in the suggested readings. A more thorough discussion of BOLD activation during such executive processing tasks can be found in Chapter 13.

Limitations of Single-Unit Recording

As can be appreciated from these two examples, single-unit recording has high spatial resolution, as it can identify adjacent neurons that differ in their receptive or memory fields. Moreover, the temporal resolution of single-unit recording is exquisite. Because the responses evoked by closely spaced stimuli are clearly discriminable, Chafee and Goldman-Rakic were able to classify neurons on the basis of their responses to the target cue, the delay interval, or the response cue. Both the temporal and spatial resolution of single-unit recording are several orders of magnitude better than what can be obtained using fMRI. Given these advantages, it is unsurprising that single-unit recording has an outstanding record of accomplishment in neuroscience.

However, while the strengths of the single-unit recording technique far outweigh its weaknesses, the latter are still notable. Most significant is the fact that single-unit recording is an invasive technique that requires the brain to be penetrated by the recording electrode. Although single-unit recordings have been made on a limited basis in humans undergoing neurosurgery, its application is primarily restricted to animals. A second limitation is that single-unit recording does not establish a causal relationship between the firing pattern of the neuron and the presumed underlying process. Thus, while it appears that the neuron illustrated in Figure 15.10 is coding the spatial location of the target and therefore is critical to working memory, the result demonstrates only a correlation. Would the removal of that single neuron render the animal incapable of remembering that specific spatial

PSP Any postsynaptic potential, excitatory or inhibitory, that results from synaptic activity.

location? It is unlikely that working memory would be so dependent upon a single neuron among the billions that comprise the monkey's brain.

One way to establish a causal relation between a brain region and a cognitive construct under study is to disable the brain region and observe whether the process of interest can proceed without the participation of the neurons populating the region. Techniques for disabling brain activity were discussed earlier in this chapter and include permanent or temporary brain lesions and transcranial magnetic stimulation. As an example, many lesion studies in monkeys have firmly established that damage to the prefrontal cortex, whether permanent and caused by surgical lesions or reversible and caused by local cooling, produces a selective deficit in working memory performance. Thus, the integration of converging data from single-unit recordings and lesion studies makes a much stronger case that these neurons play a causal role in working memory processes than does either result alone.

A second way to establish a causal relation is to artificially control the firing of the neuron and observe its effect on behavior. Such an approach has been taken by Newsome and colleagues, who have altered the output of neurons in extrastriate visual cortex in the monkey using electrical microstimulation. For example, neurons within motion-sensitive visual cortex (MT/V5) fire more frequently when a stimulus with a preferred direction of motion is presented. In a 1994 study, Salzman and colleagues trained monkeys on a psychophysical task in which rewards are given for correctly indicating the correlated direction of moving dots. To make the task difficult, dots with random motion are added to dilute the proportion of dots moving in a correlated direction. Predictably, when the display contains a large proportion of dots moving in random directions, the performance of the monkeys degrades. However, when neurons with the correct preferred direction were electrically stimulated during the presentation of the moving dots, the monkeys' performance improved. These data demonstrate that increased neuronal firing provides a code for direction preference that can cause monkeys to make particular judgments in a behavioral task.

Finally, while single-unit studies are difficult to conduct simultaneously with neuroimaging techniques like fMRI, research using both techniques can be conducted in parallel or in series. Many laboratories are combining exploratory fMRI studies with confirmatory single-unit studies or are using human fMRI to test hypotheses generated using single-unit recording. A good example of the value obtained by combining these methodologies can be found in the review by Miller and Cohen in the suggested readings.

Field Potentials

The term field potential refers to the summation of extracellular excitatory and inhibitory postsynaptic potentials (we shall use the shorthand **PSP** to refer collectively to EPSPs and IPSPs). Because the configuration of sources and sinks changes from moment to moment with the strength and pattern of synaptic inputs, field potentials change on an instant-by-instant basis to reflect this input. For this reason, the change in voltage over time reflected by field potentials has high temporal fidelity to the changing neuronal activity. Field potentials can be recorded by electrodes located anywhere within a conductive volume, including electrodes placed directly on the cortical surface, electrodes that penetrate deep structures in the brain, and electrodes placed on the surface of the intact scalp. In each of these cases, the electrode measures summated PSPs, and so in their essence all of these techniques are based upon the same principles. However, the relative proximity of the electrode to the sinks and sources that produce the extracellular volume currents has both practical and theoretical consequences that differentiate intracranial and scalp recordings.

Field potentials measured on all of these spatial scales have provided useful complementary information for fMRI studies. However, it is the prospect of combining scalp-recorded field potentials with fMRI measurements that has excited the greatest interest. If field potential recording could provide information about the sequence of neural events while fMRI could provide information about the location of neural activity, then combining these methods could potentially provide an unparalleled description of the spatiotemporal activity of neurons during cognitive tasks. Despite this promise, technical and theoretical limitations have retarded progress in achieving fusion between the techniques. We describe these challenges in this and the following section.

Four facts about postsynaptic potentials are relevant to our present interest. First, unlike the very brief (<1 ms) duration of a typical action potential, individual PSPs can be tens of milliseconds in duration. Second, hundreds or even thousands of synapses may make contact with the dendritic arbors and soma of a single neuron, and PSPs can occur at many synapses in close temporal succession. Third, as explained in Box 15.1, the volume currents associated with individual PSPs extend into the extracellular space with a strength that diminishes rapidly with increasing distance from their source and sink. Fourth, the volume currents associated with individual PSPs summate in the extracellular space.

In principle, because field potentials represent the summation of activity across a large population of neurons, an electrode placed into the brain will record the space-weighted sum of *all* of the PSPs produced at every synapse of every neuron in the brain! However, the contribution of an individual PSP to a field potential is strongly influenced by the geometry and timing of synaptic activity, as we will discuss next. A third factor, the distance between the source–sink associated with that PSP and the recording electrode, is discussed in the following section.

Because a single extracellular field potential reflects the activity of many neurons, the geometric arrangement of the sources and sinks influences both its magnitude and shape. If all active neurons in a region have the same orientation and spatial arrangement of sources and sinks, the extracellular volume currents they generate will summate to form a strong field. However, imagine that the same neurons were geometrically rearranged so that every other neuron was physically reversed in its orientation. The dipoles formed by adjacent source–sink pairs would now have opposite polarity, and the resulting extracellular fields would largely cancel. Cancellation could also occur if the dipoles had completely random orientations. The timing of the synaptic input to a population of neurons also affects the resulting extracellular field potential. If the synaptic input occurs at the same time, such as when a number of signals are time-locked to an external sensory stimulus, then greater summation will occur than if the input is not synchronous. Thus, field potential recording is biased toward fields produced by synchronous inputs on regularly arranged neurons, such as caused by simultaneous sensory input to a layer of pyramidal cells in the cortex.

Localizing the Neural Generators of Field Potentials

If an electrode placed anywhere in the brain will record the sum of all EPSPs and IPSPs of all synapses in the brain at any instant, how can field potential recording be used to localize active neurons? The answer is com-

inverse problem The mathematical impossibility of determining the distribution of electrical sources within an object based upon the measurement of electrical or magnetic fields at the surface of the object.

near field The strong electric field that occurs near the current source–sink where small changes in distance result in large changes in field strength.

far field The weak electric field distant from the current source–sink where small changes in distance result in very small changes in field strength.

plex and relies on different biophysical concepts than those discussed for fMRI. Remember that field potentials are measured as the difference in voltage (or electrical potential) between pairs of electrodes. For intracranial electrode recordings, one electrode might be placed in the brain and a second electrode might placed outside of the brain (e.g., on the scalp, chin, or earlobe). This external electrode is sometimes called the reference electrode, because it is relatively inactive when compared to the electrode in the brain. In another arrangement, both electrodes may be placed in the brain and the difference in their activity may be of interest. Regardless of the arrangement, the basic principles of field potential measurement are the same. Because the volume currents associated with PSPs extend throughout the conductive medium (i.e., brain, fluid, scalp), differences in potential may be measured between any two points that are not on the same isopotential line. The magnitude of the measured potential difference depends on the spatial configuration of the electrodes relative to the location of the dipole generator.

Although an electrode in the brain might record a potential difference relative to a distant electrode outside of the brain, there is no localizing information in that single measurement. From a single electrode pair, a nearby dipole generating a weak field cannot be distinguished from a distant dipole generating a very strong field. To localize the neuronal generator, one must make several measurements of the field to estimate its shape. This process is illustrated in Figure 15.11.

Thought Question

What would have resulted in the example shown in Figure 15.11 if the electrode's vertical trajectory was not directly through the dipole's center, but was off to the left or the right? Would your conclusion about the localization of the dipole change?

The approach of localizing active neural tissue by mapping its electric field works well as long as there is only one spatially focal population of active neurons (i.e., one equivalent dipole). If several distinct populations of neurons are active (i.e., multiple equivalent dipoles), their electric fields summate and their locations cannot be determined with certainty from the combined field. This is known as the **inverse problem** (see Figure 13.9 for an example). However, due to the quadratic decay of electric field strength with distance, a given dipole will have very different effects on nearby electrodes (i.e., those in its **near field**) depending upon their distance. However, the dipole will contribute similarly to distant electrodes (i.e., those in its **far field**), because their relative distance is similar. Thus, to constrain inferences about the location of the dipoles generating an electrical field, we need to sample that field across a large number of electrodes. FMRI can play an important role in this process by identifying candidate areas of brain activity that may be modeled as equivalent dipole sources.

In the following sections, we consider implementations of field potential recordings using intracranial and scalp electrodes. In our discussion of scalp recordings, we return again to the issue of dipole fields, because the great distance of scalp electrodes from all dipoles within the brain complicates the localization of neuronal activity.

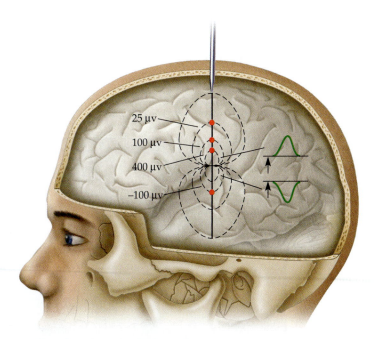

Figure 15.11 Localization of the generator of a field potential. Imagine that a stimulus evokes activity in a single ideal dipole located 5 cm below the skull's surface (isopotential, but not flux, lines shown here). To locate the dipole, researchers lower an electrode along a vertical trajectory. A second electrode is placed on the earlobe to serve as a reference, and all measurements of potential difference, or voltage, are made between the electrode within the brain and this reference. On the first measurement, the electrode is lowered 4 cm into the brain, the stimulus is presented, and a waveform is measured with a peak potential difference of 100 μV. This single measurement is insufficient to localize the dipole. If the electrode is next raised 2 cm upward from this starting location so that it is now 2 cm deep, a potential difference of 25 μV is measured. Because the potential difference is smaller, the researchers conclude that they have moved the electrode farther away from the dipole. They reverse direction and move the electrode down 2.5 cm, to a position 4.5 cm into the brain. They now record a potential difference of 400 μV. By plotting their voltage measurements by distance, they recognize that the measurements follow an inverse square relationship and that the dipole must be located 5 cm deep. If the researchers lower their electrode past the zero isopotential line, an abrupt change in polarity occurs.

Intracranially Recorded Field Potentials

At any instant, there are immeasurable numbers of active dipoles within the brain. The spontaneous fluctuation of field potentials caused by these dipoles is known as the electroencephalogram, or EEG. However, much of the EEG activity may be unrelated to processing of the particular sensory or cognitive events of interest and can therefore be considered physiological noise. This noise can be reduced by application of the same signal averaging techniques as used for event-related fMRI (see Chapter 9). If a sufficient number of trials are averaged, local field fluctuations that are unsynchronized and thus unrelated to the stimulus event will average to zero. Thus, with signal averaging, only the field potentials associated with the synchronizing event will remain. The discussions in these sections focus on signal-averaged field potentials that are time-locked to a stimulus, or **evoked potentials.**

Evoked potential recordings have been used in many seminal studies of the sensory and motor organization of the brain. In the late 1930s, Clinton Woolsey and colleagues measured evoked potentials from electrodes placed on the surface of the sensory cortex (of cats and monkeys) to exquisitely delineate its somatotopic organization. Although evoked potential mapping

evoked potential A field potential that occurs in response to a sensory stimulus.

BOX 15.2　Localization of Function Using Field Potential Recordings

Because the volume currents associated with synaptic activity extend throughout the surrounding conductive medium, field potentials can be recorded inside the brain or on the surface of the brain or skull. However, because the volume currents are denser nearer to the active neurons, the spatial resolution of field potential measurement is greatest at nearby locations. In this box, we demonstrate how field potentials evoked by a discrete stimulus (a brief electrical pulse to the median nerve at the wrist) are manifest at different recording scales—from an array of penetrating electrodes in monkey somatosensory cortex (15.12A), to a surface array of electrodes on the pial surface of the human brain that spans the central sulcus (15.12B), and to an array of electrodes on the intact scalp of a human (Figure 15.12C).

Shown in the upper left panel of Figure 15.12A is a sagittal view of the central sulcus. The primary motor cortex (Brodmann area 4) is on the precentral bank of the central sulcus, while the primary sensory cortex is located on the posterior bank of the central sulcus (area 3b) and the crown of the postcentral gyrus (area 1). The neurons in area 3b are oriented tangentially, or horizontally, to the cortical surface, with their apical dendrites oriented anteriorly in the direction of area 4. The neurons in area 1 are oriented radially, or vertically, with their apical dendrites oriented upwards toward the crown of the postcentral gyrus. The dots

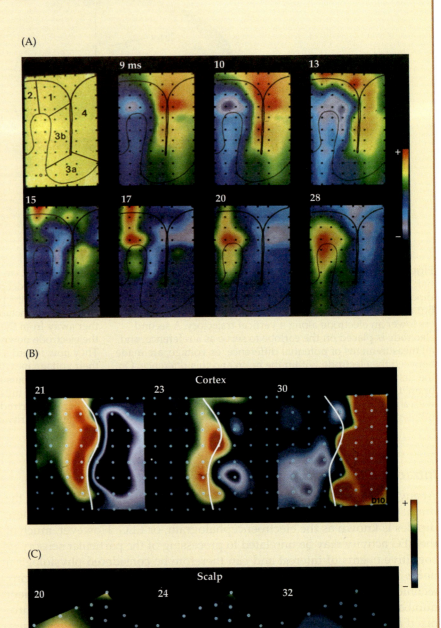

Figure 15.12　A comparison of field potential recordings made intracranially in the monkey (A), intracranially in the human (B), and on the surface of the human scalp (C). Anterior brain regions are shown to the right in (A) and to the left in (B) and (C).

BOX 15.2 *(continued)*

in this panel indicate locations from which field potential measurements were made. The color contour maps indicate the distribution of voltage at seven different time points after the stimulus is presented.

At 9 ms after a brief stimulation to the median nerve of the arm, the cell bodies of the area 3b somatosensory neurons become depolarized (cool colors) while the apical dendrites become polarized (hot colors). The tangential orientation of this dipolar field is obvious by the close horizontal apposition of the red and purple blobs. By 13 ms, the cell bodies in the area 1 somatosensory neurons become depolarized. This creates a vertically oriented dipole, with positive voltages recorded directly above the crown of the postcentral gyrus and negative voltages recorded below. This radial dipole begins to fade by 17 ms. However, at 17 ms, the activation of the area 3b neurons now extends to the apical dendrites. The sink–source relationship between the apical dendrites and the soma now reverses, and the polarity of the field reverses. The reversal of the field can be appreciated by compar-

ing the positions of the hot and cool colors at 10 and 20 ms.

This same sequence of events can be observed in field potential recordings from the cortical surface, as shown in (B). These recordings were made with electrode arrays similar to that shown in 15.2. Unlike the monkey electrodes, which penetrate the brain in columns, these electrodes in the human brain are lying on the surface. The anterior brain is to the left in each panel. Because of the larger size of the human body, initial depolarization of the cell bodies of somatosensory neurons in area 3b occurs at about 20-ms latency, at which time a positive current flows from the source in the apical dendrites to the sink at the cell body. This is recorded as a positive evoked potential (P20) at the level of the apical dendrites and anterior electrode locations. A negative evoked potential (N20) is simultaneously recorded at the level of the soma and at posterior electrode locations. The neurons in area 1 are activated about 5 ms later, at which time a positive evoked potential (P25) is recorded directly above their apical den-

drites. This occurs somewhat medial to the main axis of the area 3b dipole. And, as in the monkey, the field generated by the 3b neurons reverses polarity, as is evident at 30 ms. Finally, the same sequence of events can be recorded with electrodes placed on the scalp surface, as indicated in C.

These cortical and scalp recordings demonstrate some facts about localizing neurons from field potential maps. As in our simple example in Figure 15.13, the actual location of the area 3b neurons is marked by the isopotential line. Because these neurons are oriented horizontally, the largest positive and negative fields are located anterior and posterior, respectively, to the neurons. Thus, it is the shape of the field and not its maximum amplitude that is used to localize the area 3b neurons. This situation is different for the radially oriented area 1 neurons. As their associated dipolar field is oriented vertically, the neurons are located directly below the maximum field potential. Thus, the shape and orientation of the dipolar fields are important in localizing the active neurons.

in animals has gradually given way to single-unit studies, it is still used in human studies today, usually in the context of epilepsy seizure monitoring or localization of function during neurosurgery. Good examples of the value of evoked potential mapping have come from the study of the somatosensory cortex. In 1979 Woolsey published a topographic map of the human somatosensory cortex derived from both evoked potential and direct cortical stimulation techniques, and in 1982 Allison used evoked potential mapping to demonstrate the sequence of electrophysiological events that occur in the somatosensory cortex in response to stimulation of nerves in the hand. Wood and colleagues in 1988 used this description to devise a technique for localizing the somatosensory cortex in humans during neurosurgery by recording the shape of the field produced on the cortical surface.

Because of the spatial and temporal resolution of intracranial recording of field potentials, it can be used to localize and temporally sequence synaptic events of different populations of neurons. This is illustrated in the examples shown in Box 15.2, which depict how field potential recording can discriminate different synaptic events occurring in two different populations of neurons activated by a somatosensory stimulus over a time interval of just a few milliseconds. The examples also demonstrate the effect of changing scale from fine penetrating electrodes to subdural grids to scalp electrodes on the recording of the field potentials generated by the same sequence of synaptic events.

Using the techniques developed in 1995 by Allison and Wood, Puce and colleagues compared evoked potential and fMRI techniques for localizing the hand region of the somatosensory cortex. The correspondence of localization by both techniques was quite good, suggesting that fMRI methods performed preoperatively may replace the necessity for cortical surface evoked potential studies performed intraoperatively. This conclusion was similar to that described earlier in the chapter for comparisons of direct cortical stimulation and fMRI. However, while useful for localization, the coarse temporal resolution of the fMRI data precluded distinction of separate populations of neurons within the somatosensory cortex that had been previously identified using intracranial field potential recordings. Nor could fMRI provide information about the time course of synaptic events.

While the earliest field potential recordings using intracranial electrodes in humans investigated basic sensory processes, this technique has also been used to investigate human perception and cognition. When the eliciting event is considered to be a perceptual or cognitive event and not a simple sensory stimulus, the term *event-related potential*, or *ERP,* is often applied. Despite the change in terminology, ERP studies obey the same biophysical principles as other measurements of field potentials. As an example, in 1980 Halgren and colleagues studied ERPs recorded from multicontact depth electrodes in humans who were engaged in an oddball target detection task (see Figure 13.13). Because the ERPs recorded in the hippocampus exhibited sharp changes in amplitude and field polarity, the researchers concluded that the target events elicited activity in hippocampal neurons. Note that fMRI studies using this task have demonstrated that target detection evokes activity in a distributed set of brain regions, not just the hippocampus. While it is difficult to investigate large-scale brain systems in a single intracranial ERP study, subsequent work by Halgren and others has measured the characteristics of activity of several other discrete regions activated by this prototypical executive function task.

Higher perceptual processes have been investigated by Allison and colleagues, who measured ERPs from intracranial electrodes with the areas of the ventral occipitotemporal lobe associated with complex vision. In their studies, patients are shown exemplars of many different stimulus categories, including letter strings, geometric shapes, cars, fruits and vegetables, and faces, and nonobject scrambled displays that matched the spatial frequency characteristics of other stimulus categories. Figure 15.13A and B demonstrate that faces, but not other stimulus categories, evoked focal ERPs from the surface of the fusiform gyrus. It is from this same region that direct cortical stimulation produced transient prosopagnosia and face hallucinations in some patients, as described earlier in this chapter. In 1997, Puce and colleagues compared the location of this face-specific region to that identified by fMRI. This study was conducted in two patients in whom both procedures were done, although not simultaneously. Good correspondence was obtained between the location of the face-specific ERPs and fMRI activation by faces. Some fMRI activity was found in other regions of the ventral extrastriate cortex where no electrodes had been located. Because of the limited temporal resolution of fMRI, the authors could not determine what sources of neuronal activity generated the BOLD response. This latter fact is of critical interest because localized neuronal activity can persist for hundreds of milliseconds after the first ERP changes are observed.

(A)

(B)

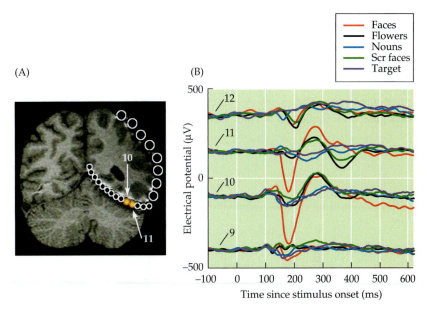

Figure 15.13 Intracranial recording of field potentials. (A) A coronal MR image that illustrates the locations of subdural electrodes in a single patient. The electrodes were contained within a sylastic strip with an interelectrode distance of 5 mm that crosses the surface of the fusiform gyrus (electrodes 10 and 11). Signal-averaged field potentials are superimposed for several stimulus categories. Large focal negative field potentials with a latency of about 200 ms were evoked by the faces (red line) but not by the other stimulus categories (B). These face-specific ERPs were largest in the fusiform gyrus. Note, however, that electrodes only 5 mm distant from either side of these two electrodes did not record face-specific potentials.

So, if we know that fMRI and ERP activity are both present in a brain region, how can we know which of the sequence of field potentials measured in that location is the eliciting event for the BOLD signal? To address this question, we will continue to consider activity in the fusiform gyrus associated with the processing of faces. Within this region there is both an early face-specific potential, known as the N200 because it occurs about 200 ms after stimulus onset, and a later face-specific potential, which occurs after about 600 to 800 ms (the onset of this activity can be seen in Figure 15.13B for Electrode 10). One possible interpretation for these two forms of activity is that the early potential reflects the initial perceptual processing of the face, while the later potential represents recurrent or feedback influences from higher brain regions. Under this idea, different functional processes are not separated in space but are separated in time.

To evaluate whether this model of fusiform function is correct, one must manipulate some aspect of the stimulus that would affect one functional process but not the other. For example, recognition of the identity of a face may be supported by completely different brain regions, but the results of that distant processing may cause top-down activation of the fusiform gyrus. So, an experimenter could manipulate over trials the identity of the presented faces (or manipulate attention to face identity, or memory for face identity, etc.). If the fMRI activation in the fusiform reflects the later potential, then variation in face identity may cause changes in the BOLD signal and in the later evoked potential, but not in the N200. Because a psycholog-

BOX 15.3 Neuronal Activity and BOLD fMRI

Both single-unit firing and field potentials provide direct, albeit different, measures of the informational transactions of neurons. While we have emphasized so far in this chapter that these measures complement fMRI data, it is important to recognize that the direct relation between neuronal activity and the BOLD response remains unknown. Is there a strong correlation between BOLD fMRI measurements and these direct measures of neuronal activity? How might the integrative and signaling aspects of neuronal activity individually contribute to the BOLD signal? One might expect that both electrophysiological measures would have similar influences upon the BOLD response, since the EPSPs that trigger action potentials also generate field potentials. However, summated IPSPs generate field potentials as well, but inhibit the firing of action potentials, so there are clear circumstances in which different electrophysiological measures could have different contributions. We will thus consider separately single-unit (or multiunit) and field potential measures of neuronal activity.

Few studies have directly compared electrophysiological and BOLD fMRI measures. Most studies have compared data from different species. For example, in 2000 Rees and colleagues reported a positive correlation between BOLD fMRI activity in humans and single-unit activity in monkeys across parametric manipulations of perceived motion. However, in a landmark 2001 study, Logothetis and colleagues compared simultaneously recorded fMRI and electrophysiological measures in the primary visual cortex of the monkey. The monkeys viewed a rotating visual checkerboard pattern while being scanned in a 4.7-T scanner using gradient-echo echo-planar imaging. Single-unit, multiunit, and local field poten-

tial recordings were obtained simultaneously with fMRI in 619 sessions performed with 10 monkeys. The results are shown in Figure 15.14. Single-unit activi-

ty occurred transiently at the onset of the stimulus and did not persist over time, while the local field potentials showed both transient and persistent activity.

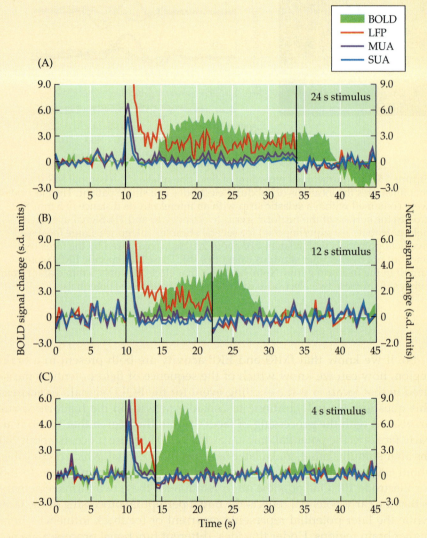

Figure 15.14 The relation between BOLD and neuronal activity. The time course of BOLD activation evoked by visual stimulation is shown as a solid green histogram, while the time course of multiunit activity (MUA) is shown in purple, the time course of single-unit activity (SUA) is shown in blue, and the time course of local field potentials (LFP) is shown in red. The onset and offset of the visual stimulus is shown as vertical gray bars and varies from 24 to 12 to 4 s in the top, middle, and bottom panels, respectively. Note that the BOLD activity and the local field potential activity are extended in time throughout stimulus presentation, while the single- and multiunit activity rapidly return to baseline. These results suggest that postsynaptic activity that generates local field potentials may be a primary contributor to the BOLD response. (From Logothetis et al., 2001.)

BOX 15.3 *(continued)*

The local field potential activity better predicted the BOLD signal change than did the multiunit activity, although the latter still provided some predictive information. The authors concluded that the BOLD contrast mechanism reflects primarily the input and intracortical processing in a given area, that which we have characterized as the integrative aspect of neuronal processing, rather than its output reflected in action potential firing. Given this result, recall from Chapter 6 our discussion of Attwell and Laughlin's energy budget for the brain. On the basis of the large number of synapses per neuron in primates, they hypothesized that compared to lower animals, a greater proportion of the brain's energy budget would be required to restore postsynaptic concentration gradients. The results from the study of Logothetis and colleagues support this conjecture.

Support for the relation between field potential recordings and BOLD fMRI was obtained in a 2004 study of human subjects by Huettel and colleagues. As in the study by Logothetis and colleagues, the duration of a visual stimulus was manipulated and the time course of the BOLD signal was compared to the time courses of the intracranially recorded field potentials.

Because of the logistical challenges involved with the study of human subjects, different subject groups participated in the electrophysiological and fMRI conditions. Field potentials were measured in a group of nine patients who had subdural grids and electrode strips implanted in the visual cortex as part of an evaluation for possible surgery to relieve seizure disorders. Because simultaneous measures were not obtained, the field potential responses were combined across electrodes in each of three anatomically defined regions of the visual cortex: the pericalcarine cortex (including V1), fusiform gyrus, and lateral temporal occipital cortex (likely including the motion-sensitive region MT/V5). A total of 74 electrodes were identified across these three regions. BOLD FMRI data from the same regions was recorded at 4 T from a sample of 12 neurologically normal young adult subjects.

The results from the pericalcarine region showed a strong relation between stimulus duration, the amplitude and duration of the field potentials, and the duration of the BOLD response. These data therefore confirm the results from this same region reported by Logothetis and colleagues. However, in other visual cortical regions, the relation between electrophysiological and BOLD measures was less clear. In the lateral occipitotemporal cortex, neither the field potentials nor the BOLD response were systematically altered by stimulus duration. And in the fusiform gyrus, the BOLD fMRI response increased with increasing stimulus duration, as was found for the pericalcarine region, but the field potentials were unaffected by stimulus duration. Thus, for the fusiform, dissociation between BOLD and field potential measures was obtained. The reason for this dissociation is not known. One possibility is that the techniques measure different components of neuronal activity. The potentials measured in the fusiform gyrus may reflect more-distant current sources, or the BOLD changes in the fusiform may be distant from the precipitating neuronal events. If true, however, this possibility does not clarify the issue, as a robust BOLD response that varied with stimulus duration was measured in the fusiform. Another possibility is that another aspect of neuronal activity, such as the synchronicity across neurons within a region, plays a key role in the BOLD response. Future studies directly comparing fMRI and electrophysiological measures will be necessary to extend the results discussed in this section to additional brain regions, stimulus conditions, and subject populations.

---

ical construct may be associated with some aspects of neural activity (e.g., BOLD signal change) but not others (e.g., N200), converging operations are critical. For example, a researcher who observes an fMRI response in the fusiform gyrus to judgments of face identity might infer that this response reflects neuronal activity at the time of the most prominent face-specific ERP, that is, at 200 ms. Thus, fMRI data, considered in isolation, may lead to the premature conclusion that judgments of face identity occur early in time within the fusiform gyrus. Although hypothetical, this example reflects current debates concerning the sequence of events associated with face processing in the brain, including the effects of directed attention, face memory, and emotional face expression. As great care must be taken in interpreting the timing of events when only fMRI evidence is available, intracranial electrode recordings can provide an important complementary source of information.

Figure 15.15   Scalp recording of electrical field potentials. This subject is wearing a cap in which electrodes are sewn at standardized spatial locations. The white plastic holders containing the electrodes are visible on the cap's surface. The scalp under each electrode is gently abraded to remove dead skin and oils and then a conductive gel is injected through a hole in the plastic holder to bridge the gap between the scalp and electrode. This creates a continuous electrical connection between the scalp and the electrode surface. The potential difference between each electrode and its reference are amplified 20,000 to 50,000 times by a bank of amplifiers, as shown on the left. The resulting time-varying signal is known as the electroencephalogram, or EEG. The EEG signal is recorded by a computer and signal-averaged with respect to stimulus or response events. The resulting averages are called scalp-recorded evoked potentials or event-related potentials.

ERP component   A stereotypic feature of an ERP waveform, such as a peak or trough at a particular latency, that has a presumed functional significance.

Scalp-Recorded Field Potentials

Because the skull and scalp are conductive, the field potentials generated in the brain can be recorded from arrays of electrodes placed on the scalp. Unlike intracranial field potential studies, which can only be conducted within a limited clinical context, scalp-recorded field potential studies are conducted with normal volunteer subjects in hundreds of laboratories around the world. In a modern field potential study, electrodes are placed at standard locations on the scalp surface so that results from different laboratories can be compared. Electrodes can be attached to the scalp one at a time using adhesives, or stretch caps into which electrodes have been sewn at the standard locations can be placed on the head (Figure 15.15). A typical electrode cap might include 32 or 64 electrodes, and some may have 128 or more electrodes.

Many researchers are interested in identifying **ERP components** that are associated with various aspects of language comprehension, memory, executive processing, attention, face perception, and dozens of other processes. ERP components are deflections in the signal-averaged ERP waveforms that occur at particular latencies relative to particular stimulus or cognitive events and have a stereotypic distribution of voltage at standard electrode sites. Based upon these components, researchers have developed process models that take advantage of the high temporal resolution of ERPs to predict the sequence of functional operations that occurs during complex behaviors. As we noted in our introduction to cognitive neuroscience earlier in this chapter, these process models may have considerable value for understanding the mind, even if information is lacking about where these operations occur within the brain. This makes ERP recording a valuable tool for cognitive neuroscience research. However, our interest in scalp ERPs here is motivated by its potential complementarity with fMRI.

If we know the precise spatial configuration and strength of the equivalent dipoles active at a particular instant, then it is possible to compute the exact scalp distribution of potential that would result. This mathematically tractable process is known as the **forward solution.** Furthermore, we also established that the temporal sequence of neuronal events, even those separated by mere milliseconds, changes the scalp distribution of the electric fields in predictable ways. If fMRI can tell us the exact location of all brain regions activated by a stimulus, and if we know the orientation of the active neurons in those regions, *and* if we know the precise time course of activity in those regions, then we should be able to calculate the resulting scalp electric fields using forward solution techniques.

While this would be an impressive technical feat, its successful implementation depends upon us already knowing everything about the spatiotemporal sequence of neuronal activity. What if you measured the electric field at the scalp? Could you then calculate the spatial configuration of neural generators and the temporal sequence of their activation? This reverse operation, computing the spatial configuration of dipoles from knowledge of the scalp distribution of voltage, is known as the inverse problem (see Figure 13.9). If the inverse problem could be solved, the need for localizing techniques like fMRI would be greatly reduced, as scalp-recorded ERP studies would provide complete information about both temporal and spatial properties of neuronal activity.

If we know for certain that only one dipole is active, we can solve for its location from an adequate sample of its potential distribution on the scalp. However, in the more likely event that many dipoles are simultaneously active, this approach will not work, because different configurations of dipoles can create the same distribution of voltage at the scalp. Thus, the inverse problem has no unique solution. The inverse problem applies to all field potential recording, not just scalp ERPs. However, in intracranial recording we can move our electrode so close to the active neurons (i.e., in the near field) that the contribution from distant dipoles is negligible, so that it appears as though only one equivalent dipole is active. For scalp recording, all electrodes on the scalp are essentially in the far field of all dipoles in the brain. This problem is compounded by the presence of the skull, which has a much higher electrical resistance than the brain and which greatly reduces the spatial resolution of scalp-recorded ERPs. Despite the nonuniqueness of the inverse problem, many powerful techniques have been developed to approximate a solution by incorporating simplifying assumptions. Readers interested in additional details on this topic are directed to the paper by Baillet and colleagues listed in the suggested readings.

What if, however, the spatial configuration of dipoles was known in advance? Under such conditions it would be possible to use the scalp ERP data to estimate the moment-by-moment changes in the strength of those dipoles and thus generate a time course of activity for each brain region. It has been asserted that fMRI activations may provide the locations of the dipole generators and thus that scalp-recorded ERPs can provide the information about their time course. In 1998, the validity of this approach was tested by Liu and colleagues using Monte Carlo simulations. Their modeling attempted to account for two potential problems in combined fMRI and electrophysiological measurement: that some active neural generators would not be represented by an fMRI activation and that an fMRI activation might not be associated with neural activity. The results of their simulations were encouraging, and the authors suggested that fMRI can be useful for seeding models of dipole structure.

forward solution The direct calculation of the electric and magnetic fields that would occur at an array of sensors based upon a given distribution of dipoles with known orientations and magnitudes.

Figure 15.16 Magnetoencephalography (MEG). Shown is a modern MEG system with 248 MEG sensors plus additional channels for noise reduction and simultaneous EEG recording. The sensors are located in the helmet close to the subject's head. The SQUID sensor devices require cryogens contained in the large thermoslike dewar to maintain superconductivity. (Courtesy of Dr. Ken Squires, 4D Neuroimaging.)

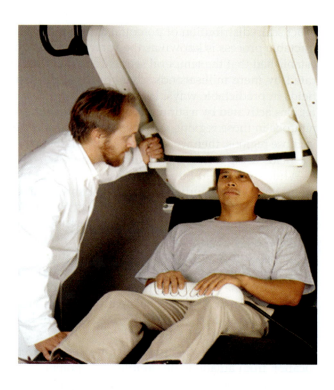

evoked magnetic fields (EMFs)
A change in the MEG that occurs in response to a particular stimulus. An EMF is the magnetic equivalent of an evoked potential or event-related potential in EEG.

Magnetoencephalography

In the prior section on field potentials, we explained how electrophysiological methods could be used to localize neuronal activity by measuring electrical field potentials. Yet a current flowing through space gives rise not only to an *electric* field but also to a *magnetic* field. The neuroscience technique for measuring these magnetic fields is magnetoencephalography, or MEG. The magnetic signals produced by neuronal activity are extremely weak, on the order of 100 femtoTesla or fT (an fT is 10^{-15} Tesla). To record these weak fields, MEG scanners use very sensitive coils known as superconducting quantum interference devices, or SQUIDs, that detect magnetic flux. In early studies, a single SQUID sensor attached to a gantry was moved systematically about the skull to make sequential measurements of the magnetic flux. In modern MEG systems, hundreds of sensors are housed in a helmetlike device and measurements are made simultaneously (Figure 15.16).

Despite the difference in instrumentation, MEG studies are very similar in practice to scalp-recorded electric field potential studies (i.e., both EEG and ERPs). Just as ERPs can be obtained by time-locked averaging of the EEG waveform, **evoked magnetic fields,** or **EMFs,** can be identified by time-locked averaging of the MEG waveform. EMFs that correspond to many well-studied ERP phenomena have been identified. Nevertheless, MEG recording has a significant advantage when compared to scalp-recorded ERPs. Because magnetic fields are unimpeded by the high resistance of the skull, they can be measured with higher spatial resolution than electric fields. In that sense, MEG and EMF measurements are more similar to direct cortical recordings than to scalp recordings. However, despite MEG's superior spatial resolution, it is not immune to the inverse problem.

Unlike electrophysiological methods that depend on volume currents, MEG depends mainly on the primary current that extends along the long axis of the neuron and is very sensitive to the neuron's orientation. In a spherical medium, like that approximated by the skull, the magnetic fields generated by a radially oriented dipole cannot be detected outside of the head. Thus, if the primary current does not have a component that is tangential to the surface of the skull, it cannot be detected by MEG. This can be both an advantage and a disadvantage. It is an advantage in that radially oriented neuronal populations can be ignored in modeling the generators of magnetic fields, and thus the models are simpler. It is a disadvantage in that MEG does not provide a complete description of neuronal activity. For this reason, MEG and EEG measurements are often obtained simultaneously.

Similar strategies have been advanced for combining EMF and fMRI studies as have been developed for combining ERP and fMRI. For example, Ahlfors and colleagues combined fMRI with MEG in a study reported in 1999 that examined the neural response to a sudden change in perceived motion. They used fMRI to identify several motion-sensitive regions within the visual cortex, including area MT+ (homologous to the motion-sensitive region V5 discussed earlier), as well as the primary (V1) and secondary (V2) visual cortices. The fMRI-derived location of the MT+ activation was very consistent with a dipole model created to account for the peak in the EMF waveform in the time range of 130 to 170 ms. This same MT+ region was also consistent with EMF activity at about 260 ms. EMF responses from V1 and V2 were very small, and the dipole modeling for these regions peaked at about 200 to 260 ms. As these activations were longer in latency than the initial activity for area MT+, they may reflect feedback from other areas. This latter conclusion based upon the EMFs is important, because activity in V1 and V2 may be considered on the basis of fMRI alone to be early in the anatomical sequence of motion-processing areas.

The combined use of EMF or ERPs and fMRI is at a very early stage of development. Despite significant obstacles related to ambiguities in dipole modeling solutions, the addition of fMRI data to constrain the modeling of neural generators and to infer their time courses of activation holds much promise. The temporal ordering of neuronal activity in a widespread pattern of fMRI activations would be a tremendous leap forward in the development of network brain models of complex sensory, motor, and cognitive tasks.

Advice for the Beginning Researcher

We conclude by summarizing themes we have developed throughout this textbook. Although we offer them here as advice for the novice scientist, we believe their principles are important for all students and faculty, whether beginning researchers or experienced investigators.

From the many studies described in this book, it is clear that neuroimaging in general, and fMRI in particular, provides an extraordinarily powerful and flexible tool for answering questions about brain function. Technological developments will continue to improve the spatial and temporal resolution of fMRI, further extending its interpretive reach. Yet, although the emphasis of this book has been upon a particular *technique*, we stress that science should be driven not by techniques but by *questions*. No method, regardless of its technical wizardry, is valuable unless it can answer interesting and important questions. Therefore, although scientists should master experimental techniques, just as a craftsman should become expert with his or her tools, scientists should not become defined by the tools they use. All techniques have limitations, and the conscientious scientist should draw from multiple techniques so that those limitations do not affect investigation of the driving research questions. For this reason, we advocate that researchers employ a multimodal, converging operations approach that combines different techniques.

Regardless of the technique, if there is one piece of advice that all scientists should heed, it is this: immerse yourself in your data. Understand the processes that generate your data, by examining both the technique and the experimental design. For fMRI, in particular, the processes that generate the data are not trivial to understand, and they require diligent work for their mastery. As a result, it is tempting to think that the physical and biophysical foundations of fMRI are hard but that the questions to be asked and the experimental designs needed to answer them are easy. We could not disagree more with this perspective. The most difficult part of any fMRI study is the design of an experiment that will give you meaningful answers. Understanding how the data are generated is critical precisely because it facilitates effective experimental design. Even though tremendous advances in MR physics and engineering have made it very easy to acquire fMRI data, those advances should not be squandered on trivial questions or wasted on bad experimental designs. With this last point in mind, new researchers should remember that skepticism is a valued part of science, and it should be applied as liberally to one's own results as to others'. Do not blindly trust canned analytical techniques, because all statistical approaches, like all research techniques, have strengths and weaknesses. Always evaluate whether your approach is the right one for your experimental question.

Finally, one trend more than any other defines modern research: the growth of interdisciplinary science. Like many fMRI researchers, we work regularly with psychologists, psychiatrists, physicists, radiologists, and neurobiologists, as well as scientists and clinicians from many other disciplines. Each of these fields has much to contribute to future fMRI research, and scientists should incorporate ideas from all of them into their research programs. As fMRI becomes more established and its physiological mechanisms become better validated, it will become an increasingly important clinical tool. As many of the technical advances described in Chapter 14 become implemented, its applications in biomedical engineering will become prevalent. And as its integration with other neuroscientific approaches becomes increasingly feasible, cognitive neuroscientists will answer an increasingly wide range of research questions. In writing this textbook, we have been amazed by how far its concepts reach, frequently exclaiming to ourselves, "It's all connected!" as we discover a new link to another discipline. In this textbook, we hope to have conveyed some of the excitement of these discoveries.

Summary

The field of cognitive neuroscience is presently in a data-driven phase where experimental observations are accruing at a rapid pace. In part, this reflects the vitality of a young field where only recently have powerful techniques—such as fMRI—that are appropriate to the nature of its questions become widely available. However, without the development of theoretical foundations that incorporate these observations and that could underlie future experiments, progress will be slow. The development of these theoretical foundations will require the reasoned integration of data from many methods, a process known as converging operations. Two classes of techniques are used by cognitive neuroscientists. The first class includes approaches that change neuronal activity, like direct cortical stimulation,

TMS, genetics, and lesion studies. These techniques can inform inferences about the necessity of a brain region for a given cognitive process, providing important complementary evidence for fMRI studies. The second class of processes includes approaches that measure neuronal activity, notably electrophysiological studies of single-unit activity, local electrical field potentials, and local magnetic field changes. These approaches have superior temporal resolution compared to fMRI but have problems with localization of neuronal generators. Combined fMRI and electrophysiological studies thus have promise for improving functional resolution, although many technical challenges remain. Researchers should adjust their experimental strategies, including techniques and experimental designs, based upon their experimental questions. This interdisciplinary approach is the future of cognitive neuroscience, and indeed of all of science.

Suggested Readings

Allison, T., Wood, C. C., and McCarthy, G. (1986). The central nervous system. In *Psychophysiology: Systems, Processes and Applications: A Handbook* (E. Donchin, S. Porges, and M. Coles, eds.), p. 5–25. Guilford Press, New York. An introduction to the physiology of field potentials with a philosophical consideration of their use in localizing sensory, motor, and cognitive function.

*Baillet, S., Mosher, J. C., and Leahy, R. M. (2001). Electromagnetic brain mapping. *IEEE Signal Processing Magazine*, November, 14–30. A very accessible review of the use of mathematical techniques to localize neuronal generators of electrical and magnetic fields.

Brazier, M. A. B. (1988). *A History of Neurophysiology in the 19th Century.* Raven Press, New York. A fascinating history of the use and development of electrophysiological methods in neuroscience.

*Curtis, C. E., and D'Esposito, M. D. (2003). Persistent activity in the prefrontal cortex during working memory. *Trends Cognitive Sci.,* 7(9): 415–423. A review of recent data concerning prefrontal activation in working memory tasks.

Hämäläinen, M., Hari, R., Ilmoniemi, R., Knuutila, J., and Lounasmaa, O. (1993). Magnetoencephalography. Theory, instrumentation and applications to the non-invasive study of human brain function. *Rev. Modern Phys.,* 65: 413–497. An excellent and comprehensive review of MEG, including neurophysiology, instrumentation, and modeling.

*Hariri, A. R., and Weinberger, D. R. (2003). Imaging genomics. *Br. Med. Bull.,* 65: 259–270. A brief introduction to a newly emerging field that looks for structural and functional brain changes associated with genetic variation.

Logothetis, N. K. (2003). The underpinnings of the BOLD functional magnetic resonance imaging signal. *J. Neurosci.,* 23(10): 3963–3971. A recent review of the relationship between neuronal activity and BOLD-contrast fMRI.

*Miller, E. K., and Cohen, J. D. (2001). An integrative theory of prefrontal cortex function. *Annu. Rev. Neurosci.,* 24: 167–202. A review of prefrontal cortical function that emphasizes complementary results from single-unit neurophysiology in monkeys and fMRI in humans.

*Shallice, T. (1988). *From Neuropsychology to Mental Structure.* Cambridge University Press, Cambridge. A classic text that considers at length the interpretative issues associated with lesion studies in humans.

* Toga, A. W., Thompson, P. M., Mega, M. S., Narr, K. L., and Blanton, R. E. (2001). Probabilistic approaches for atlasing normal and disease-specific brain variability. *Anat. Embryol.,* 204(4): 267–282. An interesting review of the use of probabilistic brain atlases to identify disease-related changes in brain morphometry.

Indicates a reference that is a suggested reading in the field and is also cited in this chapter.

Chapter References

Ahlfors, S. P., Simpson, G. V., Dale, A. M., Belliveau, J. W., Liu, A. K., Korvenoja, A., Virtanen, J., Huotilainen, M., Tootell, R. B., Aronen, H. J., and Ilmoniemi, R. J. (1999). Spatiotemporal activity of a cortical network for processing visual motion revealed by MEG and fMRI. *J. Neurophysiol.,* 82(5): 2545–2555.

Allison, T. (1982). Scalp and cortical recordings of initial somatosensory cortex activity to median nerve stimulation in man. *Ann. N.Y. Acad. Sci.,* 388: 671–678.

Allison, T., Puce, A., Spencer, D. D., and McCarthy, G. (1999). Electrophysiological studies of human face perception. I: Potentials generated in occipitotemporal cortex by face and non-face stimuli. *Cereb. Cortex,* 9(5): 415–430.

Belger, A., Puce, A., Krystal, J. H., Gore, J. C., Goldman-Rakic, P. S., and McCarthy, G. (1998). Dissociation of mnemonic and perceptual processes during spatial and non-spatial working memory using fMRI. *Hum. Brain Mapping,* 6: 14–32.

Berger, H. (1929). Über das Elektroenkephalogram des Menschen. *Arch. Psychiatr. Nervenkr.,* 87: 527–570.

Bohning, D. E., Pecheny, A. P., Epstein, C. M., Speer, A. M., Vincent, D. J., Dannels, W., and George, M. S. (1997). Mapping transcranial magnetic stimulation (TMS) fields in vivo with MRI. *NeuroReport,* 8(11): 2535–2538.

Bookheimer, S. Y., Strojwas, M. H., Cohen, M. S., Saunders, A. M., Pericak-Vance, M. A., Mozziotta, J. C., and Small, G. W. (2000). Patterns of brain activation in people at risk for Alzheimer's disease. *N. Engl. J. Med.,* 343(7): 450–456.

Broca, P. (1861). Remarques sur le siége de la faculté du langage articulé, suivies d'une observation d'aphemie (perte de la parole). *Bulletins de la société anatomique de Paris,* année 36, 2ème serie, tome 6: 330–357.

Caton, R. (1875). The electric currents of the brain. *Br. Med. J.,* 2: 278.

Chafee, M. V., and Goldman-Rakic, P. S. (1998). Matching patterns of activity in primate prefrontal area 8a and parietal area 7ip neurons during a spatial working memory task. *J. Neurophysiol.,* 79: 2919–2940.

Cohen, D. (1972). Magnetoencephalography: Evidence of magnetic fields produced by alpha rhythm currents. *Science,* 161: 664–666.

Courtney, S. M., Ungerleider, L. G., Keil, K., and Haxby, J. V. (1997). Transient and sustained activity in a distributed neural network for working memory. *Nature,* 386: 608–611.

Cramer, S. C., Nelles, G., Benson, R. R., Kaplan, J. D., Parker, R. A., Kwong, K. K., Kennedy, D. N., Finklestein, S. P., and Rosen, B. R. (1997). A functional MRI study of subjects recovered from hemiparetic stroke. *Stroke,* 28: 2518–2527.

Cruetzfeldt, O. (1974). The neuronal generation of the EEG. In *Handbook of Electroencephalography and Clinical Neurophysiology,* Vol. 2, Part C (A. Remond, ed.). Elsevier, Amsterdam.

Dale, A. M., Liu, A. K., Fischl, B. R., Buckner, R. L., Belliveau, J. W., Lewine, J. D., and Halgren, E. (2000). Dynamic statistical parametric mapping: Combining fMRI and MEG for high-resolution imaging of cortical activity. *Neuron,* 26(1): 55–67.

Di Russo, F., Martinez, A., and Hillyard, S. A. (2003). Source analysis of event-related cortical activity during visuo-spatial attention. *Cereb. Cortex,* 13(5): 486–499.

Du Bois-Reymond, E. (1848). *Untersuchungen über thierische Elektricität, Erster Band.* Georg Reimer, Berlin.

Ferrier, D. (1876). *The Functions of the Brain.* Smith, Elder, London.

Flourens, M.-J.-P. (1824). *Recherches expérimentales sur les propriétés et les fonctions du système nerveux, dans les animaux vertébrés.* Crevot, Paris.

Fritsch, G., and Hitzig, E. (1870). Über die elektrische Erregbarkeit des Grosshirns. *Archiv für Anatomie, Physiologie, und wissenschaftliche Medicin.,* 37: 300–332.

Funahashi, S., Bruce, C. J., and Goldman-Rakic, P. S. (1989). Mnemonic coding of visual space in the monkey's dorsolateral prefrontal cortex. *J. Neurophysiol.,* 61: 331–349.

Gross, C. G., Rocha-Miranda, C. E., and Bender, D. B. (1972). Visual properties of neurons in inferotemporal cortex of the macaque. *J. Neurophysiol.,* 35: 96–111.

Haaland, K. Y., Harrington, D. L., and Knight, R. T. (2000). Neural representations of skilled movement. *Brain,* 123: 2306–2313.

Halgren, E., Marinkovic, K., and Chauvel, P. (1998). Generators of the late cognitive potentials in auditory and visual oddball tasks. *Electroencephalogr. Clin. Neurophysiol.,* 106(2): 156–164.

Halgren, E., Squires, N. K., Wilson, C. L., Rohrbaugh, J. W., Babb, T. L., and Crandall, P. H. (1980). Endogenous potentials generated in the human hippocampal formation and amygdala by infrequent events. *Science,* 210(4471): 803–805.

Hariri, A. R., Mattay, V. S., Tessitore, A., Kolachana, B., Fera, F., Goldman, D., Egan, M. F., and Weinberger, D. R. (2002). Serotonin transporter genetic variation and the response of the human amygdala. *Science,* 297: 400–403.

Hubel, D. H., and Wiesel, T. N. (1959). Receptive fields of single neurons in the cat's striate cortex. *J. Physiol.,* 148: 574–591.

Hubel, D. H., and Wiesel, T. N. (1962). Receptive fields, binocular interaction and functional architecture in the cat's visual cortex. *J. Physiol.,* 160: 106–154.

Huettel, S. A., McKeown, M. J., Song, A. W., Hart, S., Spencer, D. D., Allison, T., and McCarthy, G. (2004). Linking hemodynamic and electrophysiological measures of brain activity: Evidence from functional MRI and intracranial field potentials. *Cereb. Cortex,* 14: 165–173.

Keck, M. E., Welt, T., Muller, M. B., Erhardt, A., Ohl, F., Toschi, N., Holsboer, F., and Sillaber, I. (2002). Repetitive transcranial magnetic stimulation increases the release of dopamine in the mesolimbic and mesostriatal system. *Neuropharmacology,* 43(1): 101–109.

Kuffler, S. W. (1953). Discharge patterns and functional organization of mammalian retina. *J. Neurophysiol.,* 16: 37–68.

Liu, A. K., Belliveau, J. W., and Dale, A. M. (1998). Spatiotemporal imaging of human brain activity using functional MRI constrained magnetoencephalography data: Monte Carlo simulations. *Proc. Natl. Acad. Sci. U.S.A.,* 95(15): 8945–8950.

Logothetis, N. K. (2002). The neural basis of the blood-oxygen-level-dependent functional magnetic resonance imaging signal. *Philos. Trans. Royal Soc. London Series B Biol. Sci.,* 357(1424): 1003–1037.

Logothetis, N. K., Pauls, J., Augath, M., Trinath, T., and Oeltermann, A. (2001). Neurophysiological investigation of the basis of the fMRI signal. *Nature,* 412(6843): 128–130.

Luders, H., Lesser, R. P., Hahn, J., Dinner, D. S., Morris, H., Resor, S., and Harrison, M. (1986). Basal temporal language area demonstrated by electrical stimulation. *Neurology,* 36(4): 505–510.

Marshall, W. H., Woolsey, C. N., and Bard, P. (1937). Cortical representation of tactile sensibility as indicated by cortical potentials. *Science,* 85: 388–390.

Mottaghy, F. M., Gangitano, M., Krause, B. J., and Pascual-Leone, A. (2003). Chronometry of parietal and prefrontal activations in verbal working memory revealed by transcranial magnetic stimulation. *NeuroImage,* 18(3): 565–575.

Pascual-Leone, A., Valls-Sole, J., Brasil-Neto, J. P., Cohen, L. G., and Hallett, M. (1992). Seizure induction and transcranial magnetic stimulation. *Lancet,* 339(8799): 997.

Penfield, W. (1950). *The Cerebral Cortex of Man: A Clinical Study of Localization of Function.* Macmillan, New York.

Puce, A., Allison, T., and McCarthy, G. (1999). Electrophysiological studies of human face perception III. Effects of top-down processing on face-specific potentials. *Cereb. Cortex,* 9: 445–458.

Puce, A., Allison, T., Spencer, S. S., Spencer, D. D., and McCarthy, G. (1997). A comparison of cortical activation evoked by faces measured by intracranial field potentials and functional MRI: Two case studies. *Hum. Brain Mapping,* 5: 298–305.

Puce, A., Constable, R. T., Luby, M. L., McCarthy, G., Nobre, A. C., Spencer, D. D., Gore, J. C., and Allison, T. (1995). Functional magnetic resonance imaging of sensory and motor cortex: Comparison with electrophysiological localization. *J. Neurosurg.,* 83(2): 262–270.

Rees, G., Friston, K., and Koch, C. (2000). A direct quantitative relationship between the functional properties of human and macaque V5. *Nat. Neurosci.,* 3: 716–723.

Rossini, P. M., Caltagirone, C., Castriota-Scanderbeg, A., Cicinelli, P., Del Gratta, C., Demartin, M., Pizzella, V., Traversa, R., and Romani, G. L. (1998). Hand motor cortical area reorganization in stroke: A study with fMRI, MEG and TCS maps. *NeuroReport,* 9(9): 2141–2146.

Rushworth, M. F., Hadland, K. A., Paus, T., and Sipila, P. K. (2002). Role of the human medial frontal cortex in task switching: A combined fMRI and TMS study. *J. Neurophysiol.,* 87(5): 2577–2592.

Salzman, C. D., Britten, K. H., and Newsome, W. T. (1990). Cortical microstimulation influences perceptual judgments of motion direction. *Nature,* 346(6280): 174–177.

Schlosser, M. J., Luby, M., Spencer, D. D., Awad, I. A., and McCarthy, G. (1999). Comparative localization of auditory comprehension using functional MRI and cortical stimulation. *J. Neurosurg.,* 91: 626–635.

Schlosser, M. J., McCarthy, G., Fulbright, R. K., Awad, I. A., and Gore, J. C. (1997). Cerebral vascular malformations adjacent to sensorimotor and visual cortex: Functional magnetic resonance imaging studies before and after therapeutic intervention. *Stroke,* 28: 1130–1137.

Staudt, M., Lidzba, K., Grodd, W., Wildgruber, D., Erb, M., and Krageloh-Mann, I. (2002). Right-hemispheric organization of language following early left-sided brain lesions: Functional MRI topography. *NeuroImage,* 16(4): 954–967.

Talairach, J., and Tournoux, P. (1998). *Co-planar Stereotaxic Atlas of the Human Brain.* Thieme Medical Publishers Inc., New York.

Teuber, H. L. (1955). Physiological psychology. *Annu. Rev. Psychol.,* 9: 267–296.

Wernicke, K. (1874). *Der aphasische Symptomencomplex. Eine psychologische Studie auf anatomischer Basis.* Breslau, Germany.

Wood, C. C., Spencer, D. D., Allison, T., McCarthy, G., Williamson, P. D., and Goff, W. R. (1988). Localization of human sensorimotor cortex during surgery by cortical surface recording of somatosensory evoked potentials. *J. Neurosurg.,* 68(1): 99–111.

Woolsey, C. N., Erickson, T. C., and Gilson, W. E. (1979). Localization in somatic sensory and motor areas of human cerebral cortex as determined by direct recording of evoked potentials and electrical stimulation. *J. Neurosurg.,* 51(4): 476–506.

Glossary

Numbers in parentheses refer to the chapters in which the term is introduced.

action potential A wave of depolarization that travels down a neuronal axon. (6, 15)

adaptation A change in the response to a stimulus following its repeated presentation. (8)

adenosine triphosphate (ATP) A nucleotide containing three phosphate groups that is the primary energy source for cells in the human body. (6)

aerobic glycolysis The process, consisting of glycolysis, the TCA cycle, and the electron transport chain, that breaks down glucose in the presence of oxygen, resulting in a gain of 36 ATP. (6)

aliasing The sampling of a signal at a rate insufficient to resolve the highest frequencies that are present. The energy at those frequencies becomes artifactually expressed at lower frequencies, distorting the measured signal. (9)

alpha value An a priori probability (e.g., 0.001) chosen as the threshold for statistical significance. If the probability that the data would be obtained under the null hypothesis is less than the alpha value, the data are considered to be statistically significant. (12)

alternating design A blocked design in which two conditions are presented one after another for the duration of the experimental run. (11)

anaerobic glycolysis The conversion of glucose to lactate in the absence of oxygen. (6)

anatomical ROI Region of interest that is chosen based on anatomical criteria. (12)

angular momentum (J) A quantity given by multiplying the mass of a spinning body by its angular velocity. (3)

anisotropic Having different properties in different directions; often referenced in the context of anisotropic diffusion, where molecules tend to diffuse along one axis but not others. (5, 14)

anode A source of positive charge or ions, and an attractor for free electrons. (15)

antiparallel state The high-energy state in which an atomic spin precesses around an axis that is antiparallel (i.e., opposite) to that of the main magnetic field. (3)

apical dendrites The dendrites that are distant from the neuronal cell body. For typical pyramidal cells in the cortex, the apical dendrites extend to the superficial layers of cortex, while the cell bodies are located in deeper layers. (15)

apparent diffusion coefficient (ADC) The quantification of diffusivity assuming isotropic diffusion. (5, 14)

arachnoid The middle membrane covering the brain; its name comes from its weblike appearance. (6)

arterial spin labeling (ASL) A family of perfusion imaging techniques that measure blood flow by labeling spins with excitation pulses and then waiting for the labeled spins to enter the imaging plane before data acquisition. (5)

arteries Blood vessels that carry oxygenated blood from the heart to the rest of the body. (6)

arterioles Small arteries. (6)

ascending/descending slice acquisition The collection of data in consecutive order, so that slices are acquired from bottom to top or from top to bottom. (10)

astrocyte A type of glial cell that regulates the extracellular environment. (6)

autoradiography An invasive imaging technique that labels molecules using radioactive isotopes and then measures the concentration of those molecules by exposing slices of tissue to photographic emulsions. (7)

averaged epoch The result of averaging a large number of epochs that are time-locked to similar events. (11)

axial A horizontal view of the brain (along the x–y plane in MRI). (6)

axon hillock A region of the cell body located at the emergence of the axon. Changes in its electrical potential lead to the generation of action potentials. (6)

axon A neuronal process that transmits an electrical impulse from the cell body to the synapse, performing a primarily signaling function. (6)

b factor The degree of diffusion weighting applied within a pulse sequence. (5, 14)

B The sum of all magnetic fields experienced by a spin. (4)

B$_0$ The strong static magnetic field generated by an MRI scanner. (3)

B$_1$ The magnetic field caused by the application of an electromagnetic pulse during excitation. (3)

B$_{1eff}$ The effective magnetic field experienced by a spin system during excitation. (3)

balloon model A model of the interaction between changes in blood volume and changes in blood flow associated with neuronal activity. (7)

basal ganglia A set of nuclei in the forebrain that includes the caudate, putamen, and globus pallidus. (6)

base image The image on which a statistical map is displayed, often a high-resolution anatomical image. (12)

between-subjects A manipulation in which different conditions are assigned to different subject groups. (11)

bias field estimation A technique for estimating inhomogeneities in the magnetic field based upon intensity variation in collected images. (10)

binocular rivalry The alternation of images presented independently to each eye. (13)

blindsight A phenomenon in which individuals with cortical damage have no experience of visual stimuli within the damaged part of the visual field, but can nevertheless report the characteristics of those stimuli under particular conditions. (13)

Bloch equation An equation that describes how the net magnetization of a spin system changes over time in the presence of a time-varying magnetic field. (3, 4)

block A time interval that contains trials from one condition. (11)

blocked design The separation of experimental conditions into distinct blocks, so that each condition is presented for an extended period of time. (8, 11)

blood-oxygenation-level dependent (BOLD) contrast The difference in signal on T_2^*-weighted images as a function of the amount of deoxygenated hemoglobin. (6, 7)

bolus A quantity of a substance that is introduced into a system and then progresses through that system over time. (5, 7)

Bonferroni correction A stringent correction for multiple comparisons in which the alpha value is decreased proportionally to the number of independent statistical tests. (12)

brain stem The midbrain, pons, and medulla. (6)

Brodmann areas Divisions of the brain based on the influential cytoarchitectonic criteria of Korbinian Brodmann. (6, 12)

capillaries Small and thin-walled blood vessels. The extraction of oxygen and glucose from the blood and the removal of waste carbon dioxide occur in the capillaries. (6)

capillary recruitment The idea that increased blood flow through the capillary bed results in perfusion of previously unperfused capillaries. (6)

categorical variable A variable that can take one of several discrete values. (11)

cathode An attractor for positive charge or ions, and a source of free electrons. (15)

caudal Toward the back of the brain. (6)

central nervous system (CNS) The brain and spinal cord. (6)

central sulcus A deep fissure that separates the frontal and parietal lobes of the brain. (6)

cerebellum A large cortical structure at the caudal base of the brain that plays an important role in motor function. (6)

cerebrospinal fluid (CSF) A colorless liquid that surrounds the brain and spinal cord and fills the ventricles within the brain. (6)

cerebrum The two hemispheres forming the major part of the brain. (6)

circle of Willis The interconnection between the basilar artery and the carotid arteries at the base of the cranial vault. (6)

clustering A data-driven technique that looks for clusters of voxels with similar time courses. (12)

cluster-size thresholding The adoption of a minimum size, in voxels, for a cluster of active voxels to be labeled as significant. (12)

coactivation The simultaneous activity of two or more brain regions within a single experimental task. Coactivation of brain regions does not imply that the regions are functionally connected. (13)

collinear factors Model factors that are highly correlated with one another. The inclusion of collinear factors reduces the validity of general linear model analyses. (12)

complex cell A neuron in the visual cortex with a larger receptive field than a simple cell and that responds to a stimulus with preferred orientation anywhere within its receptive field. (15)

concentration gradient A difference in the density of a substance across space. Substances diffuse along a concentration gradient from areas of high concentration to areas of low concentration. (6)

conditions (or levels) Different values of the independent variable(s). (11)

confounding factor Any property that covaries with the independent variable within the conducted experiment but could be distinguished from the independent variable using a different experimental design. (11)

conjugate mirroring A partial k-space imaging technique in which data collected from one half of k-space is used to estimate data from the other half. (14)

connectional fingerprint The pattern of anatomical connections to and from a given brain region. The term fingerprint conveys that connectivity patterns are unique to particular brain regions. (13)

connectivity The form of the relations between different brain regions, including whether they are directly or indirectly connected, whether one region influences another, and whether feedback processes exist. (13)

construct An abstract concept that explains behavior but which itself is not directly observable. Attention is an example of a psychological construct. (15)

continuous ASL A type of perfusion imaging that uses a second transmitter coil to label spins within an upstream artery while collecting images. (5)

continuous variable A variable that can take any value within a range. (11)

contrast agent A substance injected into the body to increase image contrast. (7)

contrast The intensity difference between different quantities being measured by an imaging system. It also can refer to the physical quantity being measured (e.g., T_1 contrast). (1, 9)

contrast-to-noise ratio (CNR) The magnitude of the intensity difference between different quantities divided by the variability in their measurements. (1, 9)

control block A time interval that contains trials of the control condition. (11)

control condition A condition that provides a standard to which the experimental condition(s) can be compared. Also called the baseline condition or nontask condition. (11)

converging operations The use of two or more techniques to provide complementary evidence used to test an experimental hypothesis or scientific theory. (15)

coregistration The spatial alignment of two images or image volumes. (10)

coronal A frontal view of the brain (along the x–z plane in MRI). (6)

corpus callosum The large white-matter bundle that is the primary connection between the cerebral hemispheres. The anterior portion is known as the genu and the posterior portion is known as the splenium. (6)

correlation analysis A type of statistical test that evaluates the strength of the relation between two variables. For fMRI studies, correlation analyses typically evaluate the correspondence between a predicted hemodynamic response and the observed data. (12)

correlation coefficient (or r-value) A number between –1 and 1 that expresses the strength of the correlation between two variables. (12)

cortex (neocortex) The thin wrapping of cell bodies around the outer surface of the brain. (6)

cortical mapping The mapping of function to different areas of the cerebral cortex, in order to guide plans for clinical treatment. (12)

cost function A quantity that determines the amount of residual error in a comparison. (10, 12)

counterbalancing A process for removing confounding factors by ensuring that they have equal influence upon the different conditions of the independent variable, usually by matching values across conditions. (11)

covariates Experimental factors that can take any of a continuous range of values. (12)

cross product The vector product of two vectors, its direction is perpendicular to the plane defined by those vectors and its magnitude is given by multiplying their product times the sine of the angle between them. (3)

cryogens Cooling agents used to reduce the temperature of the electromagnetic coils in an MRI scanner. (2)

current dipole A positive and negative point charge separated by an infinitesimal distance. A current dipole is used as a simple and convenient model for the electromagnetic fields produced by an activated neuron. (15)

current sink An attractor of positive ions. A depolarized patch of neuronal membrane is a current sink because positively charged ions will flow toward it. (15)

current source A source of positive ions. (15)

cytoarchitecture The organization of the brain on the basis of cell structure. (6, 10, 12)

data-driven analyses Exploratory techniques that examine the intrinsic structure of the data. (12)

dB/dt The change in magnetic field strength (dB) over time (dt). (2)

deactivations Decreases in BOLD activity during task blocks compared to nontask blocks. (11)

declarative memory Processes that support the conscious encoding and retrieval of information about facts and events. (13)

degrees of freedom (*df*) The number of independent observations within a data set. For many statistical tests, there are $n - 1$ degrees of freedom associated with n data points. (12)

dendrite A neuronal process that receives signals from other cells, performing a primarily integrative function. (6)

deoxygenated hemoglobin (dHb) Hemoglobin without attached oxygen; it is paramagnetic. (7)

dependent variables (DVs) Quantities that are measured by the experimenter in order to evaluate the effects of the independent variables. (11)

descriptive statistics Statistics that summarize the sample data but do not allow inferences about the larger population. (12)

design matrix In fMRI implementations of the general linear model, the specification of how the model factors change over time. (12)

detection Determination of whether or not activity within a given voxel changes in response to the experimental manipulation. (8, 9, 11)

detector coil An electromagnetic coil that measures energy emitted back to the environment after its initial absorption by the sample. (1)

diamagnetic Having the property of a weak repulsion from a magnetic field. (7)

diffusion tensor imaging (DTI) The collection of images that provide information about the magnitude and direction of molecular diffusion. It is often used to create maps of fractional anisotropy. (5, 13, 14)

diffusion weighting The application of magnetic gradients to cause changes in the MR signal that are dependent upon the amplitude and/or direction of diffusion. (5, 8, 14)

diffusion The random motion of molecules through a medium over time. (5)

direct cortical stimulation Applying small currents directly to brain tissue to excite or disrupt neural activity. Direct cortical stimulation is usually conducted in humans to localize critical brain regions in the context of neurosurgery. (15)

disdaqs An abbreviation for "discarded data acquisitions"; it refers to images at the beginning of a functional run that are deleted without examination. This is done because MR signal is greatest in these first images, as the change in net magnetization following excitation has not yet reached a steady state. (8)

distribution The pattern of variation of a variable under some conditions. For example, the normal distribution has a characteristic bell shape. (12)

domain specificity The segregation of functional regions in the brain according to the type of information that they process. (13)

dorsal Toward the top of the brain. (6)

dot product The scalar product of two vectors, it is created by summing the products along each dimension. (3)

double dissociation The demonstration that two experimental manipulations have different effects on two dependent variables. One manipulation affects the first variable but not the second, and the other manipulation affects the second but not the first. (13, 15)

dura The outermost membrane covering the brain; its name comes from its thickness and toughness. (6)

dynamic IVIM imaging A technique for generating images based on changes in IVIM. It can be used to generate images sensitive to hemodynamic changes within capillaries. (14)

easy problem A research question that can be addressed, in principle, using existing experimental methods. (13)

echo-planar imaging (EPI) A technique that allows collection of an entire two-dimensional image by changing spatial gradients rapidly following a single electromagnetic pulse from a transmitter coil. (1, 5)

ecological validity The degree to which the processes studied in an experiment are similar to those produced in the natural environment. (13)

effect size The numerical difference between means divided by the standard deviation. (9)

effective bore size The clearance within the bore of the MRI scanner that limits the maximum size of the sample that can be scanned. (14)

electroencephalogram/electroencephalography (EEG) The measurement of the electrical potential of the brain, usually through electrodes placed on the surface of the scalp. (1, 11, 15)

electrogenesis The explanation for electrophysiological phenomena such as EEG or evoked potentials based upon ionic current flows instigated by synaptic activity. (15)

electromotive force A difference in electrical potential that can be used to drive a current through a circuit. The MR signal is the electromotive force caused by the changing magnetic field across the detector coil. (3)

electron transport chain The third step in aerobic glycolysis; it generates an additional 34 ATP. (6)

encoding The conversion of information, such as stimuli in the sensory environment, into a mental representation suitable for storage in long-term memory. (13)

endogenous contrast Contrast that depends upon an intrinsic property of biological tissue. (5)

epiphenomenal Being of secondary consequence to a causal chain of processes, but playing no causal role in the process of interest. (11)

episodic memory Processes that support the conscious encoding and retrieval of information about occurrences of particular events. (13)

epoch A time segment extracted from a larger series of images, usually corresponding to the period in time surrounding an event of interest. (7, 11)

equipotentiality The concept that a function is so widely distributed within the brain that it depends upon the activity of the brain as a whole. Equipotentiality is the antithesis to localization of function. (15)

equivalent dipole A simplifying model that represents the electromagnetic field produced by a population of neurons as though it were produced by a single dipole. (15)

ERP component A stereotypic feature of an ERP waveform, such as a peak or trough at a particular latency, that has a presumed functional significance. (15)

estimation Measurement of the pattern of change over time within an active voxel in response to the experimental manipulation. (8, 9, 11)

Euler characteristic The number of clusters of significant activity due to chance that can be expected based upon the number of resels and the smoothness. (12)

event A single instance of the experimental manipulation. Also known as a trial. (11)

event-related design The presentation of discrete, short-duration events whose timing and order may be randomized. (8, 11)

event-related potentials (ERPs) Small electrical changes in the brain that are associated with sensory or cognitive events. (11, 15)

evoked magnetic fields (EMFs) A change in the MEG that occurs in response to a particular stimulus. An EMF is the magnetic equivalent of an evoked potential or event-related potential in EEG. (15)

evoked potential A field potential that occurs in response to a sensory stimulus. (15)

excitation The process of sending electromagnetic energy to a sample at its resonant frequency (also called transmission). The application of an excitation pulse to a spin system causes some of the spins to change from a low-energy state to a high-energy state. (2, 3)

excitatory postsynaptic potential (EPSP) A depolarization of the postsynaptic cell membrane. (6, 15)

executive function The top-down control of cognition, based on goals and context. (13)

exogenous contrast Contrast that requires the injection of a foreign substance into the body. (5)

experiment The controlled test of a hypothesis. Experiments manipulate one or more independent variables, measure one or more dependent variables, and evaluate those measurements using tests of statistical significance. (11)

experimental condition A condition that contains the stimuli or task that is most relevant to the research hypothesis. Also called the task condition. (11)

experimental design The organization of an experiment to allow effective testing of the research hypothesis. (11)

experimental factors Model factors that are associated with specific experimental hypotheses. (12)

far field The weak electric field distant from the current source–sink where small changes in distance result in very small changes in field strength. (15)

field map An image of the intensity of the magnetic field across space. (10)

field of view (FOV) The total extent of an image along a spatial dimension. (4)

field potential Change in electrical potential over space associated with postsynaptic neuronal activity. (15)

filling *k*-space The process of collecting samples from throughout *k*-space in order to collect data sufficient for image formation. (4)

filter Within the context of fMRI, an algorithm for removing temporal or spatial frequency components of data. (10)

fixed-effects analysis Intersubject analysis that assumes that the effect of the experimental manipulation is fixed across subjects, with differences between subjects caused by random noise. (12)

flat map An unfolded and flattened representation of the cortical sheet to allow viewing of topographic changes over cortical space. Flat maps are most commonly used in fMRI to illustrate the organization of the visual cortex. (12)

flip angle The change in the precession angle of the net magnetization following excitation. (3)

flux A measure of the strength of a magnetic field over an area of space. (3)

fMRI-adaptation (fMRI-A) A reduction in the BOLD response to the repeated presentation of a set of stimuli that differ along some attribute, indicating that the brain region being studied is insensitive (as measured by fMRI) to the stimulus attribute being varied. (8)

forward solution The direct calculation of the electric and magnetic fields that would occur at an array of sensors based upon a given distribution of dipoles with known orientations and magnitudes. (15)

Fourier transform A mathematical technique for converting a signal (i.e., changes in intensity over time) into its power spectrum. (12)

fractional anisotropy (FA) The preference for molecules to diffuse in an anisotropic manner. An FA value of 1 indicates that diffusion occurs along a single preferred axis, while a value of 0 indicates that diffusion is similar in all directions. (5)

frequency domain The expression of a signal in terms of its power at different frequencies. (12)

frequency-encoding gradient A gradient turned on during the data acquisition period, so that the frequency of spin precession changes over space.

frontal lobe The most anterior lobe of the cerebrum; it is important for executive processing, motor control, memory, and many other functions. (6)

functional connectivity map An image or diagram of the pattern of connectivity between different regions of the brain, independent of activity associated with experimental tasks. (13)

functional contrast A type of contrast that provides information about a physiological correlate of brain function, such as changes in blood oxygenation. (1)

functional magnetic resonance imaging (fMRI) A neuroimaging technique that uses standard MRI scanners to investigate changes in brain function over time. (1)

functional neuroimaging A class of research techniques that create images of the functional organization of the brain. Common functional neuroimaging techniques include fMRI, PET, SPECT (single-photon emission computerized tomography), and optical imaging. (1)

functional resolution The ability to map measured physiological variation to underlying mental processes. (1)

functional ROI Region of interest that is chosen based on functional criteria, such as the output of a voxelwise analysis. (12)

functional signal-to-noise ratio (functional SNR) The ratio between the intensity of a signal associated with changes in brain function and the variability in the data due to all sources of noise. Functional SNR is sometimes called dynamic CNR or functional CNR. (9, 10)

game theory A set of mathematical approaches for studying choices made by individuals in cooperative or competitive social situations. (13)

γ-aminobutyric acid (GABA) One of the most important inhibitory neurotransmitters. (6)

Gaussian random fields A branch of mathematics that deals with the properties of smooth, spatially extended data. Application of random field theory to fMRI data can help ameliorate the multiple comparisons problem. (12)

general linear model A class of statistical tests that assume that the experimental data are composed of the linear combination of different model factors, along with uncorrelated noise. (12)

glass-brain view A two-dimensional projection of fMRI data, as if the brain were made transparent and only the activations were visible. (12)

glial cells (glia) Brain cells that support the activities of neurons but are not primarily involved with information transmission. (6)

glucose A sugar made by the human body whose stored energy is used to form ATP. (6)

glutamate One of the most important excitatory neurotransmitters. (6)

glycolysis The process of breaking down glucose into other compounds to produce ATP. (6)

gradient coils Electromagnetic coils that create controlled spatial variation in the strength of the magnetic field. (2)

gradient-echo (GRE) imaging One of the two primary types of pulse sequences used in MRI; it uses gradients to generate the MR signal changes that are measured at data acquisition. (5)

gyri Rises in the cortical surface. (6)

gyromagnetic ratio (γ) The ratio between the charge and mass of a spin. The gyromagnetic ratio is a constant for a given type of nucleus. (3)

hard problem A research question that cannot be answered, even in principle, by existing experimental methods and scientific principles. (13)

hemifield One half of a visual display, usually referring to the left or right half. (8, 13)

hemodynamic response (HDR) The change in MR signal on T_2^* images following local neuronal activity. The hemodynamic response results from a decrease in the amount of deoxygenated hemoglobin present within a voxel.

hemodynamic Having to do with changes in blood flow or other blood properties. (6)

heteroscedastic Having the property that the distributions of noise are different across experimental conditions. (12)

higher cognition The set of processes that are considered to be more representative of the mental function of humans than of nonhuman animals. Examples include consciousness, executive function, abstract reasoning, and autobiographical memory. (13)

higher-order gradient A magnetic field gradient whose strength changes in a nonlinear fashion, such as in a quadratic manner, across space. (14)

homogeneity Uniformity over space and time. In the context of MRI, a homogeneous magnetic field is one that has the same strength throughout a wide region near the center of the scanner bore. (2)

homoscedastic Having the property that the distributions of noise are similar for all experimental conditions. (12)

homotopic The cortex in one cerebral hemisphere that corresponds to the same region in the other hemisphere. (15)

hypothalamus A brain nucleus that supports homeostatic functions, including the regulation of food and water intake. (6)

hypothesis-driven analyses The evaluation of activity based on testing of the validity of the null hypothesis. (12)

image reconstruction The process by which raw MR signal, as acquired in *k*-space form, is converted into spatially informative images. (4)

image A visual description of how one or more quantities vary over space. (1, 4)

imaging genomics A new field that investigates the effect of genetic variation upon brain structure and function. (15)

imaging plane The plane in which changes in MR signal are recorded during perfusion imaging. (5)

impulse A single input to a system. Impulses are assumed to be of infinitely short duration. (8, 11)

independent components analysis (ICA) An important class of data-driven analysis that identifies spatially stationary sets of voxels whose activity varies together over time and is maximally distinguishable from that of other sets. (12)

independent variables (IVs) Aspects of the experimental design that are intentionally manipulated by the experimenter and that are hypothesized to cause changes in the dependent variables. (11)

indicators Experimental factors that have integral values to indicate a qualitative level. (12)

inferential statistics Statistics that make inferences about the characteristics of a population based upon data obtained from a smaller sample. (12)

inflated brain A transformation of the cortical sheet into a balloonlike structure, removing gyral and sulcal folds so that activation can be more easily viewed. (12)

inhibitory postsynaptic potential (IPSP) A hyperpolarization of the postsynaptic cell membrane. (6, 15)

initial dip The short-term decrease in MR signal immediately following the onset of neuronal activity, before the main positive component of the hemodynamic response. The initial dip may result from initial oxygen extraction before the later overcompensatory response. (7, 14)

insula The "island" cortex hidden inside the anterior part of the Sylvian fissure; it is important for emotional processing and for the chemical senses. (6)

integrative activity The collection of inputs from other neurons through dendritic or somatic connections. (6, 15)

interleaved slice acquisition The collection of data in an alternating order, so that data is first acquired from the odd-numbered slices and then from the even-numbered slices, to minimize the influence of excitation pulses upon adjacent slices. (4, 10)

interleaved stimulus presentation The presentation of events of interest at different points within a TR over trials (e.g., one-quarter, one-half, and three-quarters of TR in addition to TR onset), increasing the effective sampling rate of an experiment at the expense of fewer trials per condition. (8, 14)

interocular trauma test An intuitive test of significance based on highly visible effects of the experimental manipulation. It states that data are significant if, when plotted, they hit you between the eyes. (12)

interstimulus interval (ISI) The separation in time between successive stimuli. Usually refers to the time between the offset of one stimulus and the onset of the next, with the term stimulus-onset asynchrony (SOA) used to define the time between successive onsets. (11)

intersubject variability Variability in fMRI data across a set of subjects; it includes the factors associated with intrasubject variability, along with between-subjects differences in task performance and physiology. (9)

intrasubject variability Variability in the fMRI data from a single subject associated with thermal, system, and physiological noise, as well as with variability in the pattern of brain activity during task performance. (9)

intravoxel incoherent motion (IVIM) The uncorrelated motion of spins within a voxel. (14)

inverse problem The mathematical impossibility of determining the distribution of electrical sources within an object based upon the measurement of electrical or magnetic fields at the surface of the object. (1, 13, 15)

inversion recovery A technique for increasing T_1 contrast by adding a 180° inversion pulse before a standard pulse sequence.

ion channel A pore in the membrane of a cell that allows passage of particular ions under certain conditions. (6)

ion A charged atom. (6, 15)

ionizing radiation Electromagnetic radiation that has sufficient energy to separate electrons from electrically neutral atoms, turning them into ions. (7)

isomorphic Having an identical form. A physiological measurement that is isomorphic with a psychological construct would have the same sign and temporal dynamics as the construct. (15)

isotropic Having similar properties in all directions. (5, 14)

item-related processes Changes in the brain that are assumed to be caused by the properties of individual stimuli, or items. Item-related processes are more easily measured with event-related designs. (11)

jittering Randomizing the intervals between successive stimulus events over some range. (8, 11)

keyhole imaging A partial *k*-space imaging technique in which only the center of *k*-space is collected following each excitation, in order to maximize raw SNR while minimizing acquisition time. (14)

Kolmogorov–Smirnov (K–S) test A test for statistical significance that evaluates whether two samples are drawn from the same distribution. The K–S test is sensitive to differences in variability and skew between distributions, but it is much less sensitive to differences in mean than the *t*-test. (12)

***k*-space trajectory** A path through *k*-space. Different pulse sequences adopt different *k*-space trajectories. (4)

***k*-space** A notation scheme used to describe MRI data. The use of *k*-space provides mathematical and conceptual advantages for describing the acquired MR signal in image form. (4)

labeling plane The plane in which initial excitation pulse(s) are applied during perfusion imaging. (5)

laboratory frame The normal reference frame that is aligned with the magnetic field of the scanner. (3)

large-vessel effects Signal changes in veins that drain a functionally active region but are distant from the neuronal activity of interest. (8)

Larmor frequency The resonant frequency of a spin within a magnetic field of a given strength. It defines the frequency of electromagnetic radiation needed during excitation to make spins change to a high-energy state, as well as the frequency emitted by spins when they return to the low-energy state. (3, 4)

lateral Toward the edge of the brain. (6)

least-squares error A commonly used cost function, the sum of the squared residuals. (12)

linear gradient A magnetic field gradient whose strength varies linearly across space. (14)

linear system A system that obeys the principles of scaling and superposition. (8, 11)

localization of function The idea that the brain may have distinct regions that support particular mental processes. (1, 15)

longitudinal Parallel to the main magnetic field, or *z*-direction, of the scanner (i.e., into the bore). (3, 4)

longitudinal relaxation (or spin–lattice relaxation) The recovery of the net magnetization along the longitudinal direction as spins return to the parallel state. (3)

Lorentz effect imaging (LEI) A potential technique for direct visualization of electrical activity (e.g., of neurons) using MRI. (14)

Lorentz force The force on a moving charge within a magnetic field. Lorentz forces cause spatial displacements in conductors (e.g., wires, neuronal axons) if those conductors are placed in MRI scanners. (14)

magnet diameter The diameter of the electromagnetic coil that generates the strong static field used in MRI. (14)

magnetic field mapping The collection of explicit information about the strength of the magnetic field at different spatial locations. (10)

magnetic moment (μ) The torque (i.e., turning force) exerted on a magnet, moving electrical charge, or current-carrying coil when it is placed in a magnetic field. (3)

magnetic resonance angiography (MRA) The creation of images of the vascular system using MRI. (5)

magnetic resonance The absorption of energy from a magnetic field that oscillates at a particular frequency. (1)

magnetic susceptibility The intensity of magnetization of a substance when placed within a magnetic field. (7)

magnetoencephalogram/magnetoencephalography (MEG) A noninvasive functional neuroimaging technique that measures very small changes in magnetic fields caused by the electrical activity of neurons, with potentially high spatial and temporal resolution. (1, 15)

matched filters The principle that the filter of the same frequency as the signal of interest provides maximal signal-to-noise ratio. (10, 14)

matrix A set of numbers arranged in a grid of rows and columns. (3)

mean The average value of a set of observations. (9)

medial Toward the middle of the brain. (6)

medulla oblongata A continuation of the spinal cord at the base of the brain that is important for the control of basic physiological functions. (6)

meta-analysis The statistical analysis of data collected from multiple experiments. (13)

microstimulation Applying currents through microelectrodes to stimulate activity in a small number of neurons. (15)

midbrain A section of the brain rostral to the pons; it includes a number of important nuclei. (6)

mixed design A design that contains features of both blocked and event-related approaches. (8, 11)

mock scanner A simulated MRI scanner that does not have a magnetic field present, used for training research participants. Some mock scanners simulate scanner noises and measure subject head movement. (10)

model factors A set of hypothesized changes in BOLD activity associated with the manipulations of the independent variables or with other known sources of variability. (12)

morphometric Relating to the measurement of shape. (14)

motion contrasts Contrast mechanisms that are sensitive to the movement of spins through space (e.g., diffusion, perfusion). (5)

MR signal equation A single equation that describes the obtained MR signal as a function of the properties of the object being imaged under a spatially varying magnetic field. (4)

MR signal The current measured in a detector coil following excitation and reception. (2, 4)

multiple comparison problem The increase in the number of false-positive results (i.e., Type I errors) with increasing number of statistical tests. It is of particular consequence for voxelwise fMRI analyses, which may have many thousands of statistical tests. (10, 12)

multiple-channel imaging (or parallel imaging) The use of multiple receiver channels to acquire data following a single excitation pulse. (14)

mutual information In the context of MRI, the amount of information about one image that is provided by knowledge of another image. For example, T_1 and T_2 images have different contrast and thus are very different on measures of squared deviation. However, the intensity of a voxel in a T_1 image can be predicted based on its intensity in a T_2 image, so T_1 and T_2 images of the same brain would have high mutual information. (10)

myelin A fatty substance that forms sheaths surrounding axons that serve to speed the transmission of action potentials. (6)

near field The strong electric field that occurs near the current source–sink where small changes in distance result in large changes in field strength. (15)

net magnetization (M) The sum of the magnetic moments of all spins within a spin system. (3)

network A description of the relations of a set of brain regions, including their connectivity and causal relations. (13)

neural correlates Patterns of brain activity that covary with another phenomenon, such as a mental state or behavior. (1, 13)

neurological convention The practice of displaying images of the brain so that the left and right sides of the image correspond to the same sides of the brain, as if one were behind the subject. (12)

neuron A cell that is the basic information-processing unit of the nervous system. (6)

neurotransmitters Chemicals released by presynaptic neurons that travel across the synaptic cleft to influence receptors on postsynaptic neurons. (6)

noise Nonmeaningful changes in some quantity. There are many sources of noise in fMRI studies, and some changes may be classified as either noises or signals depending upon the goals of the study. (9)

nonlinearity The property whereby the combined response to two or more events is not equivalent to the summation of the responses to the individual events in isolation. (8)

normalization The transformation of MRI data from an individual subject to match the spatial properties of a standardized image, such as an averaged brain derived from a sample of many individuals. (8, 10)

nuclear induction The initial term for nuclear magnetic resonance effects, as labeled by Bloch and colleagues. (1)

nuclear magnetic resonance (NMR) The measurable changes in magnetic properties of atomic nuclei induced by the application of an oscillating magnetic field at the resonant frequency of the nuclei. (1)

nuisance factors Model factors that are associated with known sources of variability that are not related to the experimental hypotheses. (12)

null hypothesis The proposition that the experimental manipulation will have no effect upon the experimental data. Most statistical analyses evaluate the probability that the null hypothesis is true, i.e., that the observed data reflect chance processes. (12)

null-task block A control block in which there are no task requirements for the subject. Also called a baseline block or nontask block. (11, 13)

nutation The spiraling change in the precession angle of the net magnetization during an excitation pulse. (3)

Nyquist frequency The highest frequency that can be identified in a digitally sampled signal; it is defined as one-half of the sampling rate. (10)

occipital lobe The most posterior lobe of the brain; it is primarily associated with visual processing. (6)

ocular dominance The degree to which a given neuron in the visual cortex responds more to stimuli presented to one eye than to stimuli presented to the other eye. (8)

off-resonance excitation The presentation of an excitation pulse at a frequency other than the resonant frequency of the sample, resulting in reduced efficiency. (3)

oligodendrocyte A type of glial cell that constructs the myelin sheaths around axons. (6)

on-resonance excitation The presentation of an excitation pulse at the resonant frequency of the sample, resulting in maximal efficiency. (3)

oscillating magnetic field A magnetic field whose intensity changes over time. Most such fields used in MRI oscillate at the frequency range of radio waves (megahertz, or MHz) and as such they are often called radiofrequency fields. (1)

outer *k*-space (OK) imaging A partial *k*-space imaging technique in which only the periphery of *k*-space is collected following each excitation, in order to ensure that high-spatial-frequency components of the MR signal are present. (14)

oxygen extraction fraction (OEF) The proportion of available oxygen that is removed from the blood. (11)

oxygenated hemoglobin (Hb) Hemoglobin with attached oxygen; it is diamagnetic. (7)

parallel state The low-energy state in which an atomic spin precesses around an axis that is parallel to that of the main magnetic field. (3)

paramagnetic Having the property of being attracted to a magnetic field, though with less concentration of magnetic flux than ferromagnetic objects. (7)

parameter weights For most fMRI analyses, quantities that reflect the relative contribution of the different model factors to the observed data within a given voxel. (12)

parietal lobe The lobe on the posterior and dorsal surfaces of the cerebrum; it is important for spatial processing, cognitive processing, and many other functions. (6)

partial *k*-space imaging A technique for reducing data acquisition time (and thus increasing temporal resolution) by collecting only part of the *k*-space data following each excitation and filling the uncollected portions of *k*-space with estimated data. (14)

partial volume effects The combination, within a single voxel, of signal contributions from two or more distinct tissue types or functional regions. (8)

peak The maximal amplitude of the hemodynamic response, occurring typically about 4 to 6 s following a short-duration event. (7)

perfusion imaging A technique for measuring blood flow through capillaries using MRI. (14)

perfusion Blood flow through capillaries. (5)

periodic event-related design An experimental design in which events of interest occur at regular intervals. (11)

phantom An object used for testing MR systems. Most phantoms are filled with liquids or gels with known properties, so that problems with the scanner system can be readily identified. (10)

phase Accumulated change in angle. (4)

phased array A method for arranging multiple surface detector coils to improve spatial coverage while maintaining high sensitivity. (2, 14)

phase-encoding gradient A gradient turned on before the data acquisition period, so that spins can accumulate differential phase offset over space. (4)

phrenologists Adherents to the belief that bumps and indentations on the skull provided information about the magnitude of some trait supported by the underlying brain region. (1)

physiological noise Fluctuations in MR signal intensity over space and time due to physiological activity of the human body. Sources of physiological noise include motion, respiration, cardiac activity, and metabolic reactions. (9)

pia The innermost membrane covering the brain; it closely adheres to the brain's contours. (6)

pixel A two-dimensional picture element. (1)

plasticity The change in the normal functional properties of brain tissue following injury or experience. (15)

polymorphism A common variation in a gene or segment of DNA. (15)

pons Part of the brain stem; it serves as a relay system for motor and sensory nerves. (6)

positron emission tomography (PET) A functional neuroimaging technique that creates images based upon the movement of injected radioactive material. (1, 7)

power analysis A calculation that estimates the likelihood of detecting an effect of a given size based upon the parameters of the experimental design. (9)

power spectrum A representation of the strength of different frequency components within a signal. The Fourier transform converts a signal (i.e., changes in intensity over time) into its power spectrum. (9)

power The probability of detecting an effect of the experimental manipulation. (9)

precession The gyroscopic motion of a spinning object, in which the axis of spin itself rotates around a central axis, like a spinning top. (3)

prefrontal cortex The parts of the frontal lobe anterior to regions that support motor processes. (13)

preprocessing Computational procedures that are applied to fMRI data following image reconstruction but before statistical analysis. Preprocessing steps are intended to reduce variability in the data that is not associated with the experimental task and to prepare the data for statistical testing. (10)

prestimulus baseline The calculation of a baseline value based on the BOLD signal present before events of interest. (11)

primary current The current flow within a neuron caused by the inflow of ions through ionic channels opened by synaptic activity. (15)

principle of reciprocity The rule stating that the quality of an electromagnetic coil for transmission is equivalent to its quality for reception (i.e., if it can generate a homogeneous magnetic field at excitation, it can also receive signals uniformly). (3)

projectile effect The movement of an untethered ferromagnetic object through the air toward the bore of the MRI scanner. (2)

PSP Any postsynaptic potential, excitatory or inhibitory, that results from synaptic activity. (15)

pulse sequence A series of changing magnetic field gradients and oscillating electromagnetic fields that allows the MRI scanner to create images sensitive to a particular physical property. (1, 2)

pulsed ASL A type of perfusion imaging that uses a single coil both to label spins in one plane and to record MR signal in another plane, separated by a brief delay period. (5)

pump A transport system that moves ions across a cell membrane against their concentration gradient. (6, 15)

quality assurance (QA) A set of procedures designed to identify problems with fMRI data so that they do not compromise experimental analyses. (10)

radiofrequency coils Electromagnetic coils used to generate and receive energy at the sample's resonant frequency, which for field strengths typical to MRI is in the radiofrequency range. (2)

radiological convention The practice of displaying images of the brain so that the left side of the image is the right side of the brain and vice versa, as if one were facing the subject. (12)

random-effects analysis Intersubject analysis that treats the effect of the experimental manipulation as variable across subjects, so that it could have a different effect upon different subjects. (12)

randomization A process for removing confounding factors by ensuring that they vary randomly with respect to the independent variable. (11)

raster A depiction of the firing rate of action potentials by a neuron in which time is represented along the horizontal axis and a dot indicates the occurrence of an action potential. (15)

raw signal-to-noise ratio (raw SNR) The ratio between the MR signal intensity associated with a sample (e.g., the brain) and the thermal noise that is measured outside the sample. (9, 10)

reaction time The time required for someone to make a simple motor response to the presentation of a stimulus. Note that this is distinct from response time, which applies to situations in which someone must choose between two or more possible responses. (8, 9)

real-time analysis A set of computational steps designed for rapid analysis of fMRI data, so that statistical tests are conducted immediately following acquisition of the images. (12)

reception The process of receiving electromagnetic energy emitted by a sample at its resonant frequency (also called detection). As spins return to a low-energy state following the cessation of the excitation pulse, they emit energy that can be measured by a receiver coil. (2, 3)

receptive field The part of the visual field that, when stimulated, will result in an increase in firing of a particular neuron. (15)

recovery of function The improvement in a previously impaired ability over time, due to functional or structural changes within the brain. (15)

reference volume A target image volume to which other image volumes are to be aligned. (10)

refocusing pulse A 180° electromagnetic pulse that compensates for the gradual loss of phase coherence following initial excitation. (5)

refractory effects Changes in the amplitude and timing of a response based on the characteristics of preceding responses. (8)

refractory period A time period following the presentation of a stimulus during which subsequent stimuli evoke a reduced response. For BOLD fMRI, the refractory periods for many types of stimuli last approximately 6 s. (8)

region-of-interest (ROI) analysis Evaluating statistical tests on a predetermined collection of voxels, often chosen to reflect a priori anatomical distinctions within the brain. (12)

registry A patient database. A registry might include information about the locations of brain lesions in a large population of individuals who might then be asked to participate in experimental studies. (15)

relaxation A change in net magnetization over time. (3)

rendered image A display of MRI data in three-dimensional perspective. (12)

repetition time (TR) The time interval between successive excitation pulses, usually expressed in seconds. (5)

repetitive TMS (rTMS) A series of closely spaced TMS stimulation pulses. (15)

research hypothesis A proposition about the nature of the world that makes predictions about the results of an experiment. For a hypothesis to be well formed, it must be falsifiable. (11, 12)

residual The variability in the data that remains unexplained after accounting for the model factors. (12)

resistance vessels Arterioles that control the flow of blood through the capillary bed. (6)

resolution elements (or resels) The number of independent statistical tests within an fMRI volume. (12)

resonant frequency The frequency of oscillation that provides maximum energy transfer to the system. (1)

response time The time required for someone to execute a choice between two or more possible responses. Note that this is distinct from reaction time, which applies to situations when only one possible response is present. (9)

retinotopic mapping A technique for delineating functional regions within the visual cortex based upon their responses to stimuli presented at different retinal locations. (10, 13)

retrieval The accessing of information from long-term memory stores so that it can guide thought or behavior. (13)

right-hand rule A heuristic that can be used to determine the direction of a magnetic moment generated by a moving charge or electrical current. If the fingers of the right hand are curled around the direction of spin, then the magnetic moment will be in the direction indicated by the thumb. (3)

rigid-body transformation A spatial transformation that does not change the size or shape of an object; it has three translational parameters and three rotational parameters. (10)

rostral Toward the front of the brain. (6)

rotating frame A reference frame that rotates at the Larmor frequency of the spin of interest. The rotating frame is adopted to simplify mathematical descriptions of the effects of excitation. (3)

rotation The turning of an object around an axis in space (in the absence of translation). (10)

run An uninterrupted presentation of an experimental task, usually lasting 5 to 10 minutes for fMRI studies. It also refers to the set of functional images collected during that task presentation. (8)

sagittal A side view of the brain (along the y–z plane in MRI). (6)

sample size The number of observations that are made by an experiment. For fMRI data, sample size can refer to the number of trials for a given subject or to the number of subjects within an experiment. (9)

sample (1) A set of observations drawn from a larger population of potential observations. (2) An object to be imaged using magnetic resonance. (12)

sampling rate The frequency in time with which a measurement is made. (1)

scalar A quantity that has magnitude but not direction. Scalars are italicized in this text. (3)

scaling A principle of linear systems that states that the magnitude of the system output must be proportional to the system input. (8)

scanner drift Slow changes in voxel intensity over time. (9, 11)

semantic memory Processes that support the conscious encoding and retrieval of information about facts, independent of particular events. (13)

semirandom design A type of event-related design in which the probability that an event will occur within a given time interval changes systematically over the course of the experiment. (11)

sequence effects Changes in behavior in response to a stimulus based on the context formed by preceding stimuli. (13)

session A single visit to the scanner by a subject. For fMRI studies, each session usually includes both structural and functional scans. (8)

shimming coils Electromagnetic coils that compensate for inhomogeneities in the static magnetic field. (2, 10)

signal averaging The combination of data from multiple instances of the same manipulation in order to improve functional SNR. (9, 11)

signal Meaningful changes in some quantity. For fMRI, an important class of signals includes changes in intensity associated with the BOLD response across a series of T_2^* images. (9)

signaling activity The transmission of the outcome of an integrative process from one neuron to another. (6, 15)

signal-to-noise ratio (SNR) The relative strength of a signal compared to other sources of variability in the data. (9)

significance testing The process of evaluating whether the null hypothesis is true. Also known as hypothesis testing. (12)

simple cell A neuron in the visual cortex that responds with increased firing to a stimulus with a preferred orientation in its receptive field and with decreased firing to a stimulus in the region surrounding its receptive field. (15)

single dissociation The demonstration that an experimental manipulation has an effect upon one variable but not upon a second variable. (15)

single-unit recording Collection of data about the electrophysiological activity (e.g., action potentials) of a single neuron. (15)

sinuses Cavities. The term sinus has two primary meanings in neuroanatomy: (1) long venous channels formed by meningeal coverings that form the primary draining system for the brain, and (2) air-filled cavities in the skull. (6)

slice selection The combined use of a spatial magnetic field gradient and an electromagnetic pulse to excite spins within a slice. (4)

slice A single slab of an imaging volume. A slice has thickness defined by the strength of the gradient and the bandwidth of the electromagnetic pulse used to select it. (4)

smoothness The degree to which the time courses of nearby voxels are temporally correlated. (12)

sodium–potassium pump A transport system that removes three sodium ions from within a cell while bringing two potassium ions into the cell. (6)

soma The body of the cell; it contains cytoplasm, the cell nucleus, and organelles. (6)

spatial extent The number of active voxels within a cluster of activity (i.e., the size of the active region). (9)

spatial frequency The frequency with which some pattern occurs over space. (4)

spatial gradient (G) A magnetic field whose strength varies systematically over space. Note that since a given spatial location only experiences one magnetic field, which represents the sum of all fields present, spatial gradients in MRI act to change the effective strength of the main magnetic field over space. (1, 4)

spatial interpolation The estimation of the intensity of an image at a spatial location that was not originally sampled, using data from nearby locations. (10)

spatial resolution The ability to distinguish changes in an image (or map) across different spatial locations. (1, 8)

specific absorption rate (SAR) A quantity that describes how much electromagnetic energy is absorbed by the body over time. (2)

speed–accuracy trade-off The improvement in the speed of a response at the expense of accuracy, or vice versa, within an experimental task. (9)

spin-echo (SE) imaging One of the two primary types of pulse sequences used in MRI; it uses a second 180° electromagnetic pulse to generate the MR signal changes that are measured at data acquisition. (5, 8)

spins Atomic nuclei that possess the NMR property; that is, they have both a magnetic moment and angular momentum. (3)

spiral imaging A technique for fast image acquisition that uses sinusoidally changing gradients to trace a corkscrew trajectory through *k*-space. (5, 14)

spiral-in trajectory A corkscrew path that begins at the periphery of *k*-space and ends at the center. Spiral-in imaging has the advantage that data acquisition can begin before time TE and thus the total time needed to collect an image is reduced. (14)

spiral-out trajectory A corkscrew path that begins at the center of *k*-space and ends at the periphery. It is the most common form of spiral imaging. (14)

standard error of the mean The uncertainty in the observed mean value, as calculated based upon both the standard deviation of the data and the number of data points. (9)

state-related processes Changes in the brain that are assumed to reflect distinct modes, or states, of function. State-related processes are more easily measured with blocked designs. (11)

static contrasts Contrast mechanisms that are sensitive to the type, number, and relaxation properties of spins (e.g., T_1, T_2, proton density). (5)

static magnetic field The strong magnetic field at the center of the MRI scanner whose strength does not change over time. The strength of the static magnetic field is expressed in Tesla (T). (1)

statistical map (or statistical parameter map) In fMRI, the labeling of all voxels within the image according to the outcome of a statistical test. (12, 13)

stereotaxic space A precise mapping system (e.g., of the brain) using three-dimensional coordinates. (10)

structural equation modeling (SEM) A mathematical technique for elucidating the causal relations between a set of variables. In fMRI studies, SEM can be used to create models of the connectivity between different brain areas. (13)

subject A participant in a research study. (8)

subthreshold stimuli Stimuli presented below the threshold for detection. In psychophysics, the threshold is also known as the limen, and thus subthreshold stimuli are also known as subliminal stimuli. (13)

subtraction In experimental design, the direct comparison of two conditions that are assumed to differ only in one property, the independent variable. (11, 12)

sulci Troughs in the cortical surface. (6)

superconducting electromagnets A set of wires made of metal alloys that have no resistance to electricity at very low temperatures. By cooling the electromagnet to near absolute zero, a strong magnetic field can be generated with minimal electrical power requirements. (2)

superposition A principle of linear systems that states that the total response to a set of inputs is equivalent to the summation of the independent responses to the inputs. (8, 11)

surface coil A radiofrequency coil that is placed on the surface of the head, very near to the location of interest. Surface coils have excellent sensitivity to signal from nearby regions but poor sensitivity to distant regions. (2)

surrogate marker A measurement that provides information about the clinical progression of a disease or condition.

susceptibility artifacts Signal losses on T_2^*-dependent images due to magnetic field inhomogeneities in regions where air and tissue are adjacent. (5, 14)

susceptibility-weighted imaging (SWI) A class of techniques for creating images of the venous system based on microscopic susceptibility effects. (14)

Sylvian fissure The deep sulcus separating the temporal lobe from the frontal and parietal lobes. (6)

synapse A junction between neurons where the presynaptic process of an axon is apposed to the postsynaptic process of a dendrite or cell body. (6)

synaptic cleft A gap between presynaptic and postsynaptic membranes. (6)

system noise Fluctuations in MR signal intensity over space or time that are caused by imperfect functioning of the scanner hardware. (9)

T_1 (recovery) The time constant that describes the recovery of the longitudinal component of net magnetization over time. (3)

T_1-weighted (T_1-dependent) Images that provide information about the relative T_1 values of tissue; also known as T_1 images. (5)

T_2 (decay) The time constant that describes the decay of the transverse component of net magnetization due to accumulated phase differences caused by spin–spin interactions. (3)

T_2^* (decay) The time constant that describes the decay of the transverse component of net magnetization due to both accumulated phase differences and local magnetic field inhomogeneities. T_2^* is always shorter than T_2. BOLD-contrast fMRI relies on T_2^* contrast. (3)

T_2^* blurring Distortions in T_2^* images that result from having a data acquisition window that is sufficiently long that significant T_2^* decay occurs over that interval. (8)

T_2^*-weighted Images that provide information about the relative T_2^* values of tissue. T_2^*-weighted images are commonly used for BOLD-contrast fMRI. (5)

T_2-weighted (T_2-dependent) Images that provide information about the relative T_2 values of tissue; also known simply as T_2 images. (5)

Talairach space The most commonly used space for normalization of fMRI data. (10)

task frequency The rate of presentation of a periodic experimental task. (10)

TCA cycle The second step in aerobic glycolysis; it involves the oxidation of pyruvate. (6)

temporal interpolation The estimation of the value of a signal at a time point that was not originally collected, using data from nearby time points. (10)

temporal lobe The lobe on the ventral surface of the cerebrum; it is important for auditory and visual processing, language, memory, and many other functions. (6)

temporal resolution The ability to distinguish changes in an image (or map) across time. (1, 8)

tensor A collection of vector fields governed by three principal axes. (5)

thalamus A brain nucleus that is important for many aspects of perception and cognition; it is highly interconnected with many regions of the cerebral cortex. (6)

theory An organized set of ideas that guides thinking on a topic and that can be used to generate a variety of experimental hypotheses. (11)

thermal noise Fluctuations in MR signal intensity over space or time that are caused by thermal motion of electrons within the sample or scanner hardware. (9)

time course The change in MR signal over a series of fMRI images. (7)

time domain The expression of a signal in terms of its intensity at different points in time. (12)

time series A large number of fMRI images collected at different points in time. (8)

time-locking Synchronization of analyses to events of interest, usually for the extraction of epochs. (11)

time-of-flight (TOF) MRA A type of MR angiography that generates contrast by suppressing signal from spins within an imaging plane so that voxels with inflowing spins (i.e., those with blood vessels) have high signal. (5)

torque A force that induces rotational motion. (3)

torsion A rotation (twisting) of an object. Even if the motion of objects is restricted so that they cannot translate, a strong magnetic field will still exert a torque that may cause them to rotate so that they become aligned with the magnetic field. (2)

transcranial magnetic stimulation (TMS) A technique for temporarily stimulating a brain region to disrupt its function. TMS uses an electromagnetic coil placed close to the scalp; when current passes through the coil, it generates a magnetic field in the nearby brain tissue, producing localized electric currents. (1, 13, 15)

translation The movement of an object along an axis in space (in the absence of rotation). (2, 10)

translational medicine The practice of modifying clinical practice based on findings from basic science research and of modifying the direction of basic science research based on evidence from clinical studies. (13)

transmitter coil An electromagnetic coil that generates an oscillating magnetic field at the resonant frequency of atomic nuclei within a sample. (1)

transverse Perpendicular to the main magnetic field of the scanner, in the x–y plane. (3)

transverse relaxation The loss of net magnetization within the transverse plane due to the loss of phase coherence of spins. (3)

trial sorting The post hoc assignment of events to conditions, often based on behavioral data. (11, 13)

trial A single instance of the experimental manipulation. (8)

t-test A test for statistical significance based on the Student t-distribution. The t-test typically evaluates whether the mean values of two sets of observations are sufficiently different to preclude their being drawn from the same distribution. (12)

Type I error Rejecting the null hypothesis when it is in fact true. Also known as a false positive. (12)

Type II error Accepting the null hypothesis when it is in fact false. Also known as an incorrect rejection or false negative. (12)

ultrahigh-resolution MRI The acquisition of MR images with voxel sizes on the order of tens of micrometers. Applications of ultrahigh-resolution MRI to animal tissue are known as MR microscopy. (14)

undershoot The decrease in MR signal amplitude below baseline due to the combination of reduced blood flow and increased blood volume. (7)

variable A measured or manipulated quantity that varies within an experiment. (11)

vascular-space-occupancy (VASO) imaging A technique for estimating cerebral blood volume through nulling of intravascular signal and measurement of changes in parenchymal signal. (14)

vasoactive substances Substances that change the caliber of blood vessels. (6)

vector A quantity with both magnitude and direction. Vectors are boldface in this text. (3)

veins Blood vessels that carry blood from the body to the heart. Blood in the veins (except for the pulmonary vein) is deoxygenated. (6)

velocity-encoded phase contrast (VENC-PC) MRA A type of MR angiography that uses gradient fields to induce phase differences associated with vascular flow so that the flow velocity of vessels can be measured. (5)

venogram An image of the venous system. (14)

ventral Toward the bottom of the brain. (6)

ventricles Fluid-filled cavities within the brain. (6)

venules Small veins. (6)

virtual reality Computer simulations of real-world experiences, often presented using immersive visual displays and manipulated using specialized tools. (13)

visual extinction The loss of experience of a visual stimulus due to simultaneous presentation of another stimulus in another part of the visual field. (13)

volume coil A radiofrequency coil that surrounds the entire sample, with roughly similar sensitivity throughout. (2)

volume conductor A continuously conductive medium. The brain, meninges, skull, and scalp constitute a volume conductor throughout which currents created by ionic flow can be measured. (15)

volume current The return current through the extracellular medium that balances the primary current within a neuron. (15)

volume A single image of the brain, itself consisting of multiple slices and voxels. (8)

volumetric Relating to the measurement of volume. (14)

voxel A three-dimensional volume element. (1)

voxelwise analysis The evaluation of statistical tests at the level of individual voxels. (8)

within-subjects A manipulation in which each subject participates in all experimental conditions. (11)

Illustration Credits

Index